Microsoft Flight Simulator
The Official Strategy Guide

SECRETS OF THE GAMES SERIES
COMPUTER GAME BOOKS

SimEarth: The Official Strategy Guide
JetFighter II: The Official Strategy Guide
The Official Lucasfilm Games Air Combat Strategies Book
Wing Commander I and II: The Ultimate Strategy Guide
Chuck Yeager's Air Combat Handbook
Ultima: The Avatar Adventures
Ultima VII and Underworld: More Avatar Adventures
A-Train: The Official Strategy Guide
PowerMonger: The Official Strategy Guide
Dynamix Great War Planes: The Ultimate Strategy Guide
Global Conquest: The Official Strategy Guide
Empire Deluxe: The Official Strategy Guide
Gunship 2000: The Official Strategy Guide
Falcon 3: The Official Combat Strategy Book (with disk)
SimLife: The Official Strategy Guide
Populous: The Official Strategy Guide
Stunt Island: The Official Strategy Guide
Prince of Persia: The Official Strategy Guide
X-Wing: The Official Strategy Guide
Empire Deluxe: The Official Strategy Guide
Lemmings: The Official Companion
Secret of Mana: Official Game Secrets
7th Guest: Official strategy Guide
Myst: The Official Strategy Guide
Strike Commander: The Official Strategy Guide

VIDEO GAME BOOKS

Nintendo Games Secrets, Volumes 1, 2, 3, and 4
Nintendo Game Boy Secrets, Volumes 1 and 2
Sega Genesis Secrets, Volumes 1, 2, 3, 4, and 5
Super NES Games Secrets, Volumes 1, 2, 3, and 4
Nintendo Games Secrets Greatest Tips
Sega Genesis Games Secrets Greatest Tips
Super NES Games Secrets Greatest Tips
Official Sega Genesis Power Tips Book, 2nd Edition (in full color!)
Super Mario World Game Secrets
The Legend of Zelda: A Link to the Past Game Secrets
Super Star Wars Official Games Secrets
Super Empire Strikes Back Official Game Secrets
Battletoads: The Official Battlebook

How to Order:
Quantity discounts are available from the publisher, Prima Publishing, P.O. Box 1260BK, Rocklin, CA 95677; fax (916) 632-4405. On your letterhead include information concerning the intended use of the books and the number of books you wish to purchase. Turn to the back of the book for more information.

Microsoft Flight Simulator
The Official Strategy Guide

Nick Dargahi

Prima Publishing
P.O. Box 1260BK
Rocklin, CA 95677

Library of Congress Catalog Card Number: 93-85785

ISBN: 1-55958-466-1

Executive Editor: Roger Stewart

Managing Editor: Neweleen A. Trebnik

Project Editor: Dan J. Foster

Book Design and Production: Marian Hartsough Associates

Technical Editor: Tom Basham

Copy Editor: Susan Christophersen

Proofreader: Mary Jane Mahoney

Cover Production Coordinator: Kim Bartusch

Cover Illustration: Hugh Syme

Cover Design: The Dunlavey Studio

Special Image Processing: Ocean Quigley

Indexer: Katherine Stimson

Prima Publishing

Rocklin, CA 95677-1260

94 95 96 97   10 9 8 7 6 5 4 3 2

Printed in the United States of America

Table of Contents

Acknowledgments

Much of the research and fact finding that went into this book was made possible by the efforts of many other individuals. I am indebted to them all for the help, advice, and support they rendered in bringing this project to fruition. In particular, I wish to thank all the people on the CompuServe Flight Simulator Forum, including Jim Ross, Mike Barrs, Rick L./Assoc. Sys Op, Richard Cook, Terry Carraway, Tom Canafax, Dan Samuels, Steve Wigginton, Robert MacKay, Rich Noren, Skip Wagner, George Lorsche, and Scott Holtzman. Scott Cutler at Chips & Technologies assisted me with questions about piloting and propeller/pitch/thrust concepts, and Jeff Miller at Learjet, Inc. provided much information on the Learjet. Steve Wigginton let me publish the results of his Frame testing program for comparing the performance of different CPUs and video cards running FS 5.0, while Dan Samuels provided me with a program that enabled me to crack open and list all the VOR/NDBs in *Flight Simulator 5.0*. Robert MacKay of *MicroWings* also assisted in opening doors for me at Microsoft/BAO that ordinarily would have been shut. Cessna Aircraft, Learjet Corporation, and Schweizer Aircraft were most gracious in providing me with photographs, brochures, and other flight performance data for their featured aircraft in FS 5.0. Andy Fisher at Hercules was most helpful in assisting me with the testing of his company's video cards.

The production staff at Prima Publishing also deserve mention for their work. Dan Foster was a great project editor, Diane Pasquetti took care of innumerable miscellaneous details, the inimitable artist Ocean Quigley performed his customary magic on my graphics, Marian Hartsough developed the design for the book, Roger Stewart had his hand in everything, and Ron Resnick pushed, prodded, promoted, and peddled the book everywhere.

All my family, including Xenia Lisanevich, Kira and Milou Ivanovsky, Ali, and Alec, offered unflagging support while I was writing. To Adriene goes my special appreciation for being supportive and understanding when I disappeared without a trace for weeks at a time.

Introduction

The wizards of Microsoft and Bruce Artwick Organization (BAO) have performed miracles again with the release of *Flight Simulator 5.0*. Developers at BAO have teamed up with the marketing, program management, documentation, and support services of Microsoft to produce the most amazing flight simulator yet developed for the personal computer. This fifth-generation *Flight Simulator* has been completely rewritten, incorporating newer flight models, a new graphics engine with vastly improved photorealistic scenery, flight instruments that are also photorealistic, and specially written code to take advantage of the latest hardware and video display technology advancements that are available today.

Make no mistake, *Flight Simulator 5.0* is a sophisticated flight simulation program; it is not just a game. For instance, prior versions of *Flight Simulator* have been used to train U.S. Navy pilots as well as countless other private pilots. Someday, in the near future, it may be possible to use PC-based flight simulators to help you qualify for your instrument flight rating license.

NEW HARDWARE REQUIREMENTS

Since this simulation represents the state of the art in personal computer (PC) simulation technology, the program will tax the full power and resources of your PC. Currently, an 80486 DX-based CPU running at 66 MHz with a Local Bus video card interface and a Local Bus video accelerator card is the best hardware configuration that can take full advantage of *Flight Simulator 5.0*'s capabilities (hereafter referred to as FS 5.0). When Intel's new Pentium microprocessor, previously called the 586, becomes available in quantity in 1994, FS 5.0's performance will improve even more.[1] The

---

[1]By improvement, I mean FS 5.0 will display more picture frames per second with faster processors.

CPU, or Central Processing Unit, is commonly referred to as a "386" or "486," which are abbreviations for the 80386 or 80486 microprocessor, respectively, and the name Local Bus refers to a new kind of expansion slot in the latest PCs, which allow super fast video cards to have faster access to the CPU. The speed at which a PC runs is measured in millions of cycles per second, or *megahertz*. Thus, FS 5.0 will run 50 to 80 percent faster on a 66-MHz 486 than on a 33-MHz 486.[2]

That is not to say that a 386 will not run FS 5.0; rather, you will suffer degraded performance, and the simulated view out of the cockpit will be unacceptably choppy and slow. The faster your computer, the more frequently the individual view "frames" will be drawn, so that the more frames per second your computer can draw, the better sense you have of smooth flight. With fewer frames per second being displayed, as, for example, on a 386 33-MHz microcomputer, you will have a choppy motion that is very irritating to watch and that doesn't allow you enough control to realistically fly your airplane. Furthermore, with slower machines, less scenery detail can be painted on the screen per frame without serious frame speed degradation, thus depriving you of the breathtaking, new photorealistic scenery that gives you the sensation of flying. Although a 386 or 486 SX-based PC will run FS 5.0 with the photorealistic scenery, it is not satisfying because of the slow speed with which the screen frames are updated. Microsoft, however, has made FS 5.0 fully customizable so that you can switch off those features that bog down your machine. This makes it possible for owners of slower 386 and 486 machines to run FS 5.0, minus the scenery enhancements, but fast enough so that your computer can still keep up with frequent screen updates to make possible the illusion of flying.[3]

FLIGHT SIMULATOR CHRONOLOGY

Commercial flight simulators have been with us for more than 50 years, although computerized simulation trainers only became available in the late

---

[2]My benchmark test is based on a test program called Frame.zip, which measures the frames per second a particular computer system achieves while running *Flight Simulator*. Frame.zip is a free shareware program distributed by BAO/Microsoft and is available in the CompuServe Flight Simulator Forum Library. For more information on Frame.zip and to see comparison results for various video and CPU setups, refer to Appendix A.

[3]It is best to avoid 486 SXs because these CPU chips have been effectively rendered brain dead. In the SX chip, the math co-processor has been lobotomized from the chip to make it cheaper to produce. DX-suffixed chips have the math co-processor on board and are well worth the additional cost.

1950s and early 1960s. Early simulators were very crude mechanical devices that could not offer the pilot any view outside of the cockpit. Primarily, these mechanical training devices were used to develop pilot skills in using instruments, especially for flying airplanes under conditions in which the pilot could not rely on outside geographical sources for determining the aircraft's position, speed, altitude, or attitude, because of weather or night flying conditions. The first use of simulators in ground training occurred during the late 1930s when the Army Air Corps decided to purchase Link Trainers to better prepare their pilots. The simulators were very successful in preparing the pilots for situations they might encounter while flying. They also offered two other benefits: they were less costly to operate than actually flying an airplane, and they offered a safe way to subject pilots to all kinds of situations without risking life or limb.

The early Link trainer was an enclosed cockpit that could rotate 360 degrees by means of a vacuum-operated bellows, but offered no view out the windshield, and was used primarily for instrument flight training. The Link simulator was connected to a map plotter on a nearby table, and an instructor would monitor the student's progress as he tried to navigate by instruments alone. The instructor could communicate with the student in the cockpit via a radio headset, and he also had direct control over all the cockpit instruments. Thus, with a twirl of a knob, the instructor could, for example, simulate an instrument failure, or could challenge the student pilot to some unexpected event. After the training session was over, the student would get to look at the paper map on which his airplane's course was plotted, and could then take it home to evaluate his performance. A new paper map would be inserted on the map plotter for the next student.

By the end of the 1970s, simulation technology had become computerized, with computer graphics of outside scenery projected onto the windshield, and cockpit capsules that moved in three dimensions in response to the pilot-trainee's control movements. Unfortunately, these simulators were big, bulky, and expensive, in part because they ran only on huge mainframe computers. With the advent of the cheap microprocessor in the late 1970s, computers became accessible to the average consumer. With this micro-electronic revolution taking place, it was only a matter of time before somebody developed a flight simulator that would run on a PC.

That time arrived in 1978 when Bruce Artwick, an electrical engineer and programmer with a pilot's license, decided to create a three-dimensional flight simulator on the Apple II computer. This simulation met with instant success and became quite popular. Then, in 1981, Artwick was asked by Microsoft to produce a new version of *Flight Simulator* for the newly introduced IBM PC. Microsoft told Artwick that it wanted a simulation to show off the power and graphics capability of the PC. Thus was born version 1.05 of Microsoft's *Flight Simulator* program and it became a smash hit among computer buyers. Because of its ground-breaking foray into new 3-D graphics routines, it pushed the design limits of the original PC to its limits. In fact, for many years, the ultimate test of a computer's ability to clone the IBM PC was the ability to run *Flight Simulator* without causing a system crash. If a clone system could pass muster and run *Flight Simulator*, it proved that the clone was beyond reproach — it could run any PC software without hardware conflicts.

Over the years, newer versions of *Flight Simulator* were released that improved the graphics, introduced color, and provided support for AT-class PCs and 386s. When FS version 3.0 was released in June of 1988, it was substantially rewritten and offered many new features, including dual player mode via modem or direct connection via serial cable, new aircraft, and support for multiple windows so that you could see two different views simultaneously. For example, you could view your plane from a "spot" or "track" plane and have it displayed in one window while watching your cockpit view and instrumentation in another window. FS version 4.0, introduced in September of 1989, offered experimental aircraft, the sail plane, a customizable weather system including random weather patterns, custom 386 software drivers, dynamic scenery such as other aircraft and ground vehicles moving about, runway approach lighting systems for night flying, and air traffic control.

Today's modern flight simulators are marvels to behold. Link, which is now called Singer-Link-Miles, still makes simulators today, but there are many other competitors, including CAE of Canada and Hughes-Rediffusion of England. Simulators must also come with software, or visual scenery that has been digitized, but you can buy a simulator from one company and equip it with scenery from another company. The visuals for many simulators are done by Evans & Sutherland and SPX-Wide (a division of Rediffusion), and represent a significant portion of the overall investment in the simulator system, since digitizing the scenery for airports around the world is quite costly. A commercial simulator can cost between $15 to $20 million, and operational costs for running it can hover around $500 to $800 per hour. Compared to the $250 million cost of a real Boeing 747, and hourly operating costs of $20,000 per hour, simulators are a real bargain.

Are commercial simulators realistic? Richard Cooke, a pilot who works daily with simulators, describes a simulator experience he recently tried:

> After the Schiphol 747 crash, I tried that flight in our 747-400 (simulator), with engine surges, engine fires, and engine separations

happening going up through 3,000 and 4,000 feet after takeoff.[4] Thereafter I was sweating, my leg was in pain from trying to keep the thing (flying) straight, and I was totally locked onto keeping that thing flying, while the fuel-dump took us closer to living. After 10 minutes of real knife-edge stuff, my co-pilot said, "There's the runway," and I looked up and knew where I was for the first time in 10 minutes. I got the thing on the ground (didn't have flap-asymmetry selected, unlike the real thing!), and was then totally unfit for work for 3 hours afterwards due to adrenaline overload! Yes it's realistic, and a load of fun!

The commercial simulator's realism is helped by the use of real cockpit instrumentation, with real switches, lights, gauges, knobs, and levers. Bumps and thumps during taxiing, and the raising and lowering of the landing gear are felt inside the cockpit; routine noises emanating from various aircraft systems add to the illusion of being in a real cockpit. Air-conditioning vents blow air on you, and every motion of the aircraft is implemented through hydraulic jacks, pistons, and control rods that move the cockpit so that you can actually feel the movement of the plane. In addition, highly detailed, digitized scenery is projected onto the cockpit's windshields. The SPX-Wide system used on many commercial airline full-flight simulators uses three projectors, with each projection screen displaying 800,000 pixels (picture elements), thereby giving a panoramic view area of 180 degrees (horizontal) by 40 degrees (vertical) inside the cockpit. Overall, by combining all three screens, the display resolution works out to 3,000 horizontal by 800 vertical pixels.

Compared to this, FS 5.0 still has a long way to go to catch up with the commercial flight simulators. The maximum display resolution of 640 horizontal by 400 vertical pixels at 256 colors with a field of view of only 20 degrees (for a single-view direction) still is inferior to what commercial simulators are capable of doing. Even so, the improvement of FS 5.0 over FS 4.0, which had a maximum resolution of 640 horizontal by 340 vertical pixels with only 16 colors possible, is dramatic. With 240 additional colors and 60 extra lines of vertical resolution, FS 5.0's scenery is 16 times more realistic.

The power of the latest generation of microprocessors has given the flight simulation buff the best opportunity yet of experiencing the miracle of

---

[4]The 747 Schiphol disaster was attributed to an engine pylon separating from the wing. This crash, in Amsterdam, resulted in the loss of many lives on the ground, as the plane crashed into a crowded apartment building. More cracks on engine pylons were discovered on other 747s and as a result, Boeing issued an airworthiness directive for many older 747s to have their original engine pylons inspected and replaced.

flight. Microsoft's latest *Flight Simulator* offering takes advantage of these new capabilities, and through some impressive software engineering brings you closer to what the million-dollar simulators are doing today. With the new super-scalar RISC (Reduced Instruction Set Computing) Power PC, and CISC (Complex Instruction Set Computing) Pentium processor on the horizon, many more exciting developments lie ahead in the world of flight simulation.

FLIGHT SIMULATOR'S NEW FEATURES

To summarize, these are some of the new features and improvements of *Flight Simulator 5.0* over version 4.0:

- *New menus and dialog boxes* that make it easier than before to select commands and customize the simulation.
- *New flying models* for each aircraft. Mathematical description and flight characteristics have been completely upgraded and revamped. Some drawbacks in the model remain, however. There are still no spins, and stalls are not realistically implemented.
- *Enhanced, photo realistic scenery* and instrumentation implemented in Super VGA 640×400 256-color mode using new photorealistic/ray-tracing graphics technology. Includes real, digitized, high-altitude photos of airports and cities around the country, where vegetation, streets, urban areas, parks, rivers, lakes, oceans, and other topography are realistically portrayed. Using new Cyber-Graphics/Synth City graphics technology, buildings, bridges and other three-dimensional objects have realistic features. You can see windows that are lit in buildings, building ornaments and company logos, real roofs, shading and texture of building sides, etc. The city of Chicago has more than 100 such Cyber-Graphic mapped buildings when you set the scenery to its densest setting. The airport around Meigs Field uses new photorealistic scenery for a breathtaking view when landing or departing. Scenery expands with greater detail the closer you get. At night, airports and cities light up in a brilliant and colorful display of street lights, building lights, and airport runway-lighting systems. The sky and clouds are absolutely stunning in the first realistic display of weather on a PC. No longer do you see the puff-ball-like cumulus clouds of FS 4.0, but instead whispy cirrus clouds, layered stratus clouds that mist your windshield, and angry looking, anvil-shaped thunderstorms. There are now vanishing horizons for both

the land and sky, with realistic gradient textures. A new graphics technology called "seeding" is employed, which allows scenery to represent different areas such as suburbs in cities, forests, farm lands, mountains, coastline, swamps, tundra, prairies, and snow. Thus, when a particular area is designated as a suburb, it uses the generic computer-generated seed for suburbs. Gone are the vast, bleak, empty landscapes of FS 4.0. The default scenery areas now include:

- San Francisco
- Los Angeles
- Seattle
- Chicago
- New York
- France-Paris
- West Germany-Munich

- *Future add-on scenery disks* possible for any part of the Earth, including auto-switching scenery when flying between scenery areas. Mallard Software will be releasing photorealistic scenery disks, based on high-altitude aircraft and satellite pictures. Initially they will offer San Francisco, Washington, D.C., and the Las Vegas-Grand Canyon areas, with other cities around the world to follow. Photorealistic effects make ground scenery look three dimensional, with shadows and ground shading revealing the valleys, gulleys, and canyons of the mountains and hills. Gone are the triangular-shaped mountains of FS 4.0.

- *New dynamic scenery:* Good Year blimp, a new hot-air balloon, jet traffic, sailboats, and other new dynamic scenery has been added for your enjoyment.

- *True world-wide spherical coordinate system* in latitude and longitude. Replaces older two-dimensional North and West coordinate system. On-screen display of longitude/latitude coordinates, or older 2-D coordinate system. Alternatively, both coordinate systems can be displayed simultaneously.

- *Automatic scenery transfer* between scenery areas when flying cross country or anywhere on Earth. Ability to fly anywhere around the globe.

- *Map that zooms out to 160,000 miles in space* for a view of the entire planet. In this orbital-like view, all continents, major lakes, rivers, islands, and even polar ice caps are depicted on a spherical earth, with backside of planet shaded darker to represent nightfall.

- *New Learjet.* Aircraft included are the Cessna 182 Skylane RG (same as before), Learjet 35A (the Learjet 35A replaces the Gates-Learjet 25G), Schweizer Skyplane 2-32, and Sopwith Camel (both same as before).

- *New instrument panels and controls for each aircraft.* The Cessna, Learjet, Sopwith Camel, and Schweizer sailplane have more realistic and authentic instrument panels. No longer must you fly different aircraft with the same instrument panels, for each aircraft has its own distinct instrument panels. With the addition of Microsoft's new Aircraft and Scenery Designer 5.0, you will be able to have aircraft with up to four engines and three different instrument panels that you can easily jump between on-screen. Many new engine controls and instruments give you added control and flexibility to monitor your aircraft's performance.

- *Autopilot.* New autopilot capabilities include pitch and bank hold, ILS and glide slope lock, approach hold, and back course hold. The wing leveler, heading lock, altitude lock, and NAV 1 lock remain as they were in FS 4.0.

- *Dynamic crash graphics.* You can enable this feature if you want to see (and hear) your plane break apart when it crashes, thereby determining the cause of the accident. Unlike FS 4.0, in FS 5.0 collisions with dynamic scenery, such as other airplanes and ground vehicles, will result in your aircraft crashing. No longer can you fly blissfully unaware of neighboring air traffic, or get away with flying through imaginary "ghost" aircraft.

- *New shadowing effects.* Building and airplane shadows change with time of day and latitude/longitude position. Advanced new real time ray-tracing code gives photorealistic scenery realistic shadows that match the 3-D folds of the terrain.

- *Accurate portrayal of time and seasons.* At night, stars become visible. Instead of the instant changes between night and day that were present in FS 4.0, FS 5.0 now has richly colored, beautiful reddish-blue sunsets and sunrises that take place gradually.

- *New weather generator.* You can create local weather areas with different weather from the global weather. There is enhanced control over weather, including the ability to create local weather fronts that move, copying and pasting weather to other areas. There are totally customizable wind layers, barometric pressure, temperature layers, and cloud layers. Thunderstorms are visually spectacular, having the distinctive anvil-shaped top of real cumulonimbus clouds, and they look very ill tempered indeed.

- *Dual player mode.* Support for higher-speed modems and user-definable modem strings.

- *More realism and reliability options.* Jet Engine Flameout, instrument failures, etc.

- *Quick practice.* Fast and easy new menu command to walk you through a basic familiarization with your airplane and teach you how to land the plane under varying conditions.

- *Jump to airport feature.* You can choose to be instantly transported to any major airport in the default scenery areas without needing to know the latitude or longitude of the airport. Also, your navigation and communication radios can be automatically set to the new location, without having to look up the frequencies in the airport sectional maps in the manual.

- *Set exact location.* You can precisely position your aircraft anywhere on Earth using the new latitude/longitude coordinate system, or the older FS 5.0 North-East coordinate system. You can even set your altitude and desired heading.

- *New VOR/NDB navigational radio beacons added for North America and Europe.* FS 5.0 contains many, but not all, VOR/NDB navigational radio beacons for North America, the Caribbean basin, the Pacific Ocean region, and Europe. However, don't be too disappointed if you can't find a favorite VOR/NDB station outside the USA.[5] Microsoft only promises that the USA VOR/NDB database is complete. It is now possible to navigate cross country using VOR/NDB stations for guidance, though there may little scenery of any interest when flying between scenery areas. (This should be remedied soon with Mallard's new scenery add-ons.) There are more than 1,225 VOR/NDB radio stations built into FS 5.0's database, and you can bring up a dialog box that lists the call letters, name, and location of any VOR/NDB station that you have tuned in on your NAV radios. Range-to-station, DME (distance measuring equipment), and out-of-range indicators are accurate for each VOR station. Some VOR/NDB stations are not implemented or are incorrectly placed. For example, many Canadian and North Atlantic VOR/NDBs are missing, and not all of Europe is in the database. Curiously enough, many out of the way Mid-Pacific and South-Pacific VOR/NDB stations are implemented.

- *Land Me feature.* You can now have the computer auto-land your Cessna at the nearest airport, in the event that you don't want to manually land your aircraft.

---

[5]In the early version of FS 5.0 that I had, the North Atlantic region had no VOR/NDB stations. But interestingly enough, many out of the way mid-Pacific and South Pacific VOR/NDB stations were implemented, including for example, Darwin, Australia; Wake Island; and Tahiti.

- *International support.* Conversion of units, U.S. to metric for non-U.S. pilots.

- *New digitized aircraft and instrument sounds.* Sound support for many industry standard sound cards. Engine pitch changes with throttle settings. Airplane crashes are heard, and navigational instruments have their own distinctive sounds.

- *Video card support* for many industry-standard video accelerator chips.

- *Improved mini-control.* On-screen moveable indicator box for ailerons, elevator, and rudder now includes airspeed and throttle indication level. Used for when instrument panel is not on-screen, as in full-screen cockpit view.

- *Customizable scenarios.* You can specify the start-up situation, aircraft, weather, location, realism and reliability, etcetera. Use to create a situation you can return to.

- *Flight photographs.* Capture screen shots of your 3-D view windows, map, or instrument panels to a PCX graphic file on disk that you can later print out.

- *Expanded/extended memory support.* Ability to use Extended Memory (XMS) and Expanded Memory (EMS) above DOS's 640K conventional memory limitation. *Flight Simulator* will run with only 530 Kb of conventional RAM, provided that you can allocate 2 Mb or more of expanded memory (if you have 4 Mb of RAM, you can use DOS 6's MEMMAKER to automatically configure this for you—no extra drivers are needed other than HIMEM.SYS and EMM386.EXE). A new Simulator Info dialog box tells you how much memory FS 5.0 is using of each type, and how much disk space is available. Also, you can easily determine which situation you are currently using, along with the situation's file name, the aircraft type you are using (also with its filename), and the type of scenery being used.

- *Backwardly compatible with FS 4.0 scenery files. Flight Simulator 5.0* will be backwardly compatible with FS 4.0 standard scenery files, such as the F1 database and .SCN files, including those from Mallard. Both FS 4.0 .MOD and .VID files will be supported in FS 5.0.

- *Backwardly compatible with Aircraft and Scenery Designer 4.0 files* (often abbreviated as A&SD 4.0). When using A&SD 4.0 files, however, FS 5.0 will return you to the FS 4.0 scenery world when those scenery elements are called up. When the new A&SD 5.0 is released, you will be able to fully convert scenery and aircraft created with A&SD 4.0 into A&SD 5.0 files that FS 5.0 will be able to use with the photorealistic scenery.

ABOUT THE SCENERY

Three types of scenery are used in FS 5.0:

1. *F1 scenery.* Older FS 4.0 type of scenery (VGA 640 × 350, 16 colors)
2. *Cyber-Graphics/Synth City style* (Super VGA 640 × 400, 256 colors)
3. *Photorealistic/ray-traced* (Super VGA 640 × 400, 256 colors)

The older scenery that was used in FS 4.0 is called F1 Scenery. It employed simple polygon vector-draw routines that simulated 3-D buildings and other objects, and filled in the ground terrain with various pattern fills. Although it was an improvement over previous flight simulators, it was 1988 graphics technology that was long overdue for an overhaul. You can still use FS 4.0 scenery in FS 5.0, which is a boon to the many arm-chair pilots who have designed their own add-on scenery using the Aircraft and Scenery Designer 4.0, or who bought add-on scenery packages from Mallard or Sub-Logic. You will not be able to utilize the newer graphics that are available in FS 5.0, however, while using the older scenery. When the new Aircraft and Scenery Designer 5.0 comes out, you will be able to convert your older files so that they can be used with the newer graphics of FS 5.0.)

Cyber-Graphics/Synth City style (for Synthesized City) is a newer technology graphics engine, developed by BAO (Bruce Artwick Organization) that is used in FS 5.0 to simulate city buildings, bridges, and other standard 3-D objects. The city buildings of Chicago, off to the right of Meigs Field, are an example of Cyber-Graphics/Synth City Style. Cyber-Graphics/Synth City style differs from the previous FS 4.0 scenery in that you see many more features and details of individual buildings. For example, you can see lighted windows in skyscrapers, company logos on certain buildings, and building shadows that move according to the time of day. (Try checking out the Prudential building sign in Chicago with scenery density set to high.) As such, this type of scenery is vector drawn; that is, each image's shape is mathematically described and then filled in with a texture and color. Vector-drawn graphics are easily scalable to any size, and form perfectly straight lines, smooth curves, round circles, and symmetrical ellipses. Thus, for example, you can see perfectly round wheels on the landing gear of FS 5.0's four aircraft, as opposed to the triangular shaped wheels of FS 4.0, and the appearance of the airplanes themselves is much more pleasing, with smooth curving fuselages and wings, as opposed to the jagged, polygon-shaped surfaces of FS 4.0.

Cyber-Graphics/Synth City technology also allows highly detailed, complex, 256-color scenery such as sky shading and shadows, urban and suburban sprawl, coastlines, clouds, and oceans to be generated using a minimum of hard disk storage space. Using a new graphics technique called "seeding," a scenery area can be assigned a generic appearance, whether it be forests, suburbs, mountains, coastline, etcetera. An example of seeded scenery are the suburbs and ground terrain of Chicago, on top of which sit the Cyber-Graphics/Synth City style 3-D buildings. Seeded scenery such as this can be generated using just 700 bytes of data!

The photorealistic/ray-traced scenery is derived from actual high-altitude photos of the ground taken by satellite and aircraft. The airport runway at Meigs Field and the immediate airport vicinity, are examples of photorealistic/ray-traced scenery. The satellite photo of Meigs Field has been texture-mapped onto the ground, much like a decal is applied to a surface, but the ray-tracing algorithm goes one step further: The photo or texture map can be wrapped around three dimensional topographical features such as mountains, valleys, or other ground contours. As a result of this contour mapping, the scenery looks three dimensional. What is truly amazing about this, though, is that it is all done in "real" time, rather than the many hours it would take using conventional ray-tracing algorithms.

The term *ray tracing* itself refers to a computer graphics technique used to create complex 3-D images. Every pixel in a ray-traced image is drawn to reflect a light ray from a source of light, and then is traced from the pixel to the viewer's eyes. Unfortunately, conventional ray-tracing techniques can take many days just to produce a single image, even when using a super computer. In FS 5.0, an advanced and speedy new real-time ray tracing algorithm, developed by the Bruce Artwick Organization, breaks new ground with its speedy, ray-traced rendition of surface scenery. It allows simulated sunlight to produce the ground shadows and varying hues and colors of the terrain that produce the illusion of 3-D perspective and depth.

The actual photos of the ground are digitized into bitmaps broken up into many millions of pixels. Bitmaps are simply facsimiles of the original picture; that is, they copy each picture element and assign it a pattern and color, much like a PCX, BMP, GIF or TIFF computer graphic. Unlike vector graphics, a bitmap is not easily scalable, meaning that significantly resizing the bitmap causes it to become deformed and misshapen, much like bitmapped fonts become jagged and unreadable when you print them out in a font size that is much larger or smaller than the original bitmap font. With these new terrain bitmaps, the closer you fly to the ground, the less realistic the scenery will become because the individual pixel elements are expanded larger to the point where they become distorted.

The FS 5.0 scenery is a combination of the photorealistic/ray-traced and Cyber-Graphics technology. The Cyber-Graphics vector-drawn buildings are superimposed on the background bitmaps of the photorealistic ground scenery to arrive at a pleasing synthesis of 3-D ground terrain with 3-D buildings and objects. It is a significant advance in PC-based flight simulation graphics.

SO YOU WANT TO BE A PILOT?

Flight Simulator is already used by many schools as a basic training tool for students to learn the basics of aeronautics. The U.S. Navy, in fact, has used FS 4.0 for emergency situational training, but up until now, the Federal Aviation Administration (FAA) has refused to approve *Flight Simulator* as an official flight-training device. The FAA claimed that PC-based flight simulators did not have sufficient fidelity with an aircraft to ensure the development of the psychomotor skills and sense of coordination necessary to control an aircraft solely by reference to instruments. They also expressed other reservations: a flight simulator was required to have a course plotter; that is, a means of recording flight path. Prior to *Flight Simulator 3.0*, there was no means to record your flight path, but with FS 3.0 this feature was added. Also, prior to flying an aircraft, according to the FAA, you were supposed to perform a control check (verifying that the flaps, elevators, ailerons, and rudder are in working order), which could not be done on Flight Simulator 2.0. With *Flight Simulator 3.0*, this problem was addressed by implementing an on-screen control position indicator (that could be moved around as needed when using your whole screen as a scenery window), and you could now actually see the wing flaps, ailerons, rudder, and elevators move in response to yoke/rudder movements that you made through an external view of your aircraft.[6]

The FAA is now reconsidering its position with regard to PC-based flight simulators. In a test that they are conducting of 90 students, of which 60 are being trained on PC-based simulators and 30 on other simulators, they will compare the two groups of students to see which group learns the most and performs the best. The results of this experiment should be known very soon. There is some talk that Microsoft and BAO may be pushing to have FS 5.0 approved by the FAA as an instrument flight-training device. This could conceivably save millions of dollars for thousands of students across the country who could take a part of their instrument flight training instruction on a PC instead of on an expensive simulator or aircraft! For the moment, though, the FAA is disinclined to approve any PC-based simulator. A final determination will not be made for some time to come.

There are various classes of pilot's licenses. At the bottom of the ladder is the private pilot license. Next is the Instrument rating, which is a requirement for flying in bad weather or at night. To fly non-airline type jobs, such as charters, towing banners, transporting cargo, etc., you will need to obtain the Commercial Pilot's license. If, however, you relish the thought of becoming a

---

[6]You can see the airfoil surfaces move only on the Cessna while in spot view. Unfortunately, even in FS 5.0, this remains the case.

passenger jet pilot, you will need to earn the Airline Transport Pilot (ATP) license, which is the penultimate pilot license. Or, if you prefer, you can become a Certified Flight Instructor (CFI) and teach others how to fly while getting paid for it.

To acquire a private pilot's license, you must be at least 17 years old, log at least 40 hours of flying time (55 is average), have 20 hours of supervised flight instruction, and pass written and oral exams along with a practical check flight. You must also obtain a Third Class medical certificate, attesting that your vision is correctable and that your heart, lungs, and other aspects of your health are in good working order. This certificate must be renewed every 2 years.

If you want to obtain an instrument rating—a requirement if you want to become a commercial pilot or airline transport pilot—you must log at least 125 hours of flight time, which includes 50 hours of cross-country flying in addition to your student pilot time. You must also log 40 hours of instrument flight time, of which 20 hours can be performed in a ground trainer or simulator, and 15 additional hours that must be accompanied by a certified instrument flight instructor. Obviously, if FS 5.0 were certified as a simulator for instrument flying training, it would make this type of license more easily accessible, and at far lower cost than traditional approaches. Additionally, for the instrument rating license, you must pass a written test on aviation regulations and procedures and must perform a certification flight test. Instrument ratings are becoming more and more common among private pilots because this type of rating is necessary for a pilot to fly safely and legally in bad weather, as well as at night. Without the instrument rating, you won't be able to get any legitimate flying job (although some South American drug cartels might be interested).

The certified flight instructor (CFI) license allows you to legally teach others how to fly. This kind of license is often used by former airline pilots and others who like to fly and teach.

To obtain the commercial pilot's license, you must log 250 hours of flying time, including 100 hours as pilot-in-command, along with 50 hours of cross-country flying. In addition, you must undergo 10 hours of instrument instruction or have an instrument rating license with at least 5 hours of night flying logged. You must also pass the Second Class medical check, which is a more stringent physical exam than is the Third Class medical check, and you must renew this medical certificate each year. Finally, you will need to pass the Commercial Pilot Written Exam, which covers the myriad details about FAA rules and regulations.

The airline transport pilot (ATP) license requires that you be at least 23 years old, have the equivalent flying time that is required of the commercial license, and have an instrument rating license. Furthermore, you must obtain a First Class medical certificate, a rigorous physical exam which is even more thorough than the Second Class exam, and you must renew it every 6 months. And then there are the written tests on airline rules, regulations, and the specific kind of plane being flown, including an oral exam and check ride for the aircraft in question. The typical total cost for the training that would qualify you for the ATP license can easily exceed $20,000 over two years. But for most people, it takes three years and more than $30,000 of schooling and training before they are able to qualify for an entry-level airline job. And usually, such beginning jobs would entail flying small commuter planes for regional carriers. After all this, are you still interested?

THE PURPOSE OF THIS BOOK

This book is designed to explain to you some of the finer points of *Flight Simulator 5.0*. As a supplementary companion guide, it is not designed to replace the Microsoft manual, but to offer you insights and practical advice on how to fly the different kinds of airplanes offered in the simulation. In this book you will learn some of the basics of airplanes and engines, flight basics, how to read your instruments and understand how they work, perform some basic flight maneuvers, learn how to navigate using your aircraft's radio navigational equipment, and finally, you'll have an opportunity to try out some of your newly acquired skills in a specially prepared solo adventure.

Action Icons and Sidebar Notes

To aid in understanding the text, special icons and sidebar notes are inserted in the margins. The action icon ✈ tells you that you need to perform some action or task mentioned in the text. The sidebar notes are placed in the margins to draw attention to important points in the text or to summarize the topics of a given text passage.

How This Book Is Organized

This book is divided into three major parts, and concludes with three important reference appendices:

    I. The World of Flight Simulator
    II. Flight Academy: Ground School
    III. Navigation and Aircraft Communication Systems
    IV. Appendices

Part I: The World of *Flight Simulator*

The first four chapters cover how you control and customize the simulator. Chapter 1 is a get-your-feet-wet introduction to *Flight Simulator*, where you will experience your first solo flight and get to know how to use some of the simulator's controls. Chapter 2 amounts to a quick, hands-on tutorial of manipulating the 3-D windows and view systems, while Chapter 3 touches upon customizing the simulator's many options using the pull-down menu system. Chapter 4 describes how the weather generator works and offers you an example of creating and editing your own weather.

If you are already familiar with FS 5.0, or feel that this is material you have already mastered in FS 4.0, you can skip this section and proceed to Part II of the book.

Part II: Flight Academy: Ground School

The second part of the book deals with the actual airplane itself, covering cockpit instrumentation, flight dynamics, and some fundamentals of airplanes and engines. Chapter 5 describes the operating principles of airplanes and engines, and Chapter 6 goes into some of the physics of flight, including a description of aerodynamic forces. Chapter 7 explains the operation and use of the cockpit instrumentation for the Cessna, Learjet, Schweizer sailplane, and Sopwith Camel. All the flight instruments and indicators are covered in detail, along with a brief description of how they work. Chapter 8 instructs you on how to perform some basic flight maneuvers, including takeoff, climb, flying straight and level, the standard turn, descent, and landing. Chapters 9 through 11 focus on the operating characteristics of three of the aircraft that are included in FS 5.0: the Cessna, the Learjet, and the sailplane.

Part III: Navigation and Aircraft Communication Systems

The third part of the book gives you basic information on how to use the navigation and communication systems aboard your aircraft. Specific examples are offered as an aid to helping you learn how to use the different systems.

Chapter 12 teaches you how to use the NAV/VOR/DME and ADF/NDB instruments to successfully navigate. This chapter also touches upon the new EFIS/CFPD, electronic, heads-up navigational display system. Also covered is the operation of the autopilot and use of the Instrument Landing Systems (ILS). The EFIS/CFPD system is mentioned as a useful tool when navigating or making landings. Chapter 13 challenges you with adventure situations, where you have a chance to barnstorm the Golden Gate

Bridge in San Francisco and try your hand at radio navigation by flying the Cessna from Oakland to Los Angeles and the Learjet from Oakland to New York via Chicago.

Part IV: Appendices

Appendix A covers the installation of *Flight Simulator*. Because *Flight Simulator* is so dependent on hardware speed, a brief performance comparison is also given for some popular graphic accelerator cards, along with a benchmark comparison of 386 vs. 486 PCs in 33 MHz, 50 MHz, and 66 MHz clock speeds. Appendix B offers you a quick look-up guide for the various airports and the VOR and NDB stations in FS 5.0. Using the material in this appendix, you can find the VOR/NDB call signs and radio frequencies, state by state, for the continental U.S. and for other surrounding areas. Also included are a few maps to help you navigate some of the scenery areas.

Appendix C provides a keyboard command summary for all the keyboard controls, along with a description of how the mouse works in yoke and slew modes.

The information found in this book will prove invaluable in your quest to master the latest and most sophisticated PC flight simulator on the market today.

P A R T

I

The World of
Flight Simulator

CHAPTER

1

Your First Solo Flight

In this chapter, you will take your Cessna Skylane 182 RG out for its maiden flight. But before taking off, to best take advantage of *Flight Simulator*'s features, you will need to learn how to customize the simulator environment for your particular situation. Don't worry, you needn't understand a thing about flying; all you need are your sunglasses and a desire to sightsee Chicago from the air. Landing will be accomplished via the new Land Me feature, so you can sit back and enjoy the flight. You will take off from Meigs field, along Chicago's Lake Michigan waterfront, then take a leisurely flight over downtown Chicago. Once past Chicago, you will turn back and return to Meigs field, whereupon the simulator's auto pilot will land you safely without any intervention on your part. Along the way you will see the photorealistic scenery around Meigs field, the downtown skyscrapers of Chicago, including the Sears tower and the Prudential Building. While enjoying the picturesque view out the window, you will also learn how to use some of the aircraft's instruments and controls.

Because no two people have the same kind of hardware setup, this chapter will have special portions of the text devoted to people with special considerations, such as those with slower 386 machines, and those people with joysticks or flightsticks (a flightstick is an airplane-like yoke that sits on your desk). By reading this chapter, you should gain some skill in modifying your FS 5.0 software to suit your needs.

If you are eager to fly, or you are already somewhat familiar with Flight Simulator and you want to dispense with some of the formalities of getting to know the simulation, you can skip ahead to the section titled "Takeoff."

STARTING *FLIGHT SIMULATOR*

Assuming that you have installed *Flight Simulator 5.0* (See Appendix A for instructions if you haven't done so) and that you are currently in the *Flight Simulator*

Directory, start up *Flight Simulator* by typing **FS5** from the DOS prompt. If all goes well, you will see the Bruce Artwick Organization opening screen and then, a few moments later, the cockpit view should appear before you.

Using the Keyboard and Mouse to Open Menus and Select Commands

In *Flight Simulator*, you can choose menu commands, menu options or other controls in one of two ways:

1. Using the Mouse: Aim the mouse pointer at the menu command, option or other control and click the left mouse button.

2. Using the Keyboard: Press (Alt) to highlight the pull down menu; to access any individual menu name, command, option, or other control, press the key which matches the underlined letter. In some instances, there is a keyboard shortcut listed next to the command, so that you can directly access the command from the keyboard without opening any menus.

After hearing a squeal of tires on pavement, you should be able to see the menu names that appear on the overhead menu bar. Aim the mouse pointer on the Options menu and click on it using the left mouse button and you should see a pull down menu appear as in Figure 1.1. If you are only using a keyboard, press (Alt) and then (O) to open the Options menu. The underlined letter "O" in the Options menu tells you which key you need to press in order to select that command. To close a menu using the mouse, all you need to do is click anywhere outside the menu, or using a keyboard, press (Esc) or (Spacebar). All other menu commands and options that have a single character underlined in their name, can be accessed from the keyboard by pressing that character from the keyboard (except the top menu bar commands, in which you need to first press (Alt)). Thereafter in this book, when using the terms "select," or "click," we will mean that you select a command, using either the mouse or the keyboard.

Figure 1.1
The Options menu

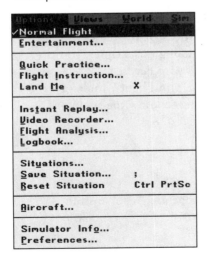

✈ **Tip:** Clicking the right mouse button causes the mouse pointer to disappear, allowing you to use the mouse as the Yoke control for piloting the airplane. To restore the mouse pointer, again click on the right mouse button. The left mouse button is used solely to select menus, commands or aircraft controls by pointing the mouse pointer arrow on the object in question, then clicking.

For Owners of 386 PCs: Minimize Your Display Overhead to Speed up Your Computer (486 users skip ahead to next section)

Due to your 386's limited processing power, it is highly recommended that you minimize your scenery and display complexity options in order to speed up the frame rate for FS 5.0. To do this, you will first need to open the Preferences dialog box under the Options menu and click on the Display button, as is illustrated in Figure 1.2. In this dialog box, you can change the Graphics Mode (SVGA, VGA, or EGA), the Image Quality (High/Slow, Medium/Medium, Low/Fast), Flicker/Speed (No Flicker/Slow, Some Flicker/Med., Much Flicker/Fast), the SVGA Board Maker, and various other scenery options.

For now, click on the Graphics Mode pull down list box (or press the up or down arrow cursor keys) and select the VGA 320x400 256-Color option. This will decrease the number of lines being drawn on your computer, thereby degrading the resolution, but lessening the load on your 386 PC. Next, click on the Image Quality/Speed list box and select the Low/Fast option. This will allow FS 5.0 to draw fewer surface details and building features in an effort to speed the frame display rate. (Remember, just as in film, the more frames per second that are displayed, the better the fluidity of motion, as perceived by the viewer.) Finally, click on the Flicker/Speed list box and highlight the Much Flicker/Fast option. By doing this, you will see more screen flickering, but you will have considerably lightened the workload for your computer in handling FS 5.0's complex graphics.

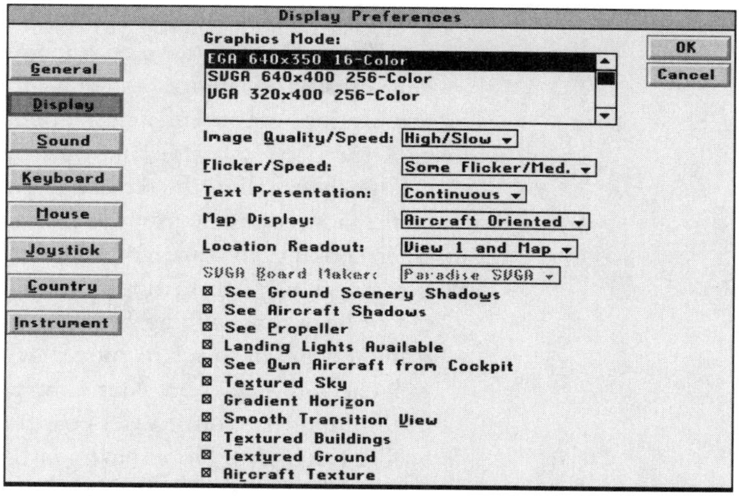

When you are done, click the OK button. A Preferences Alert dialog box will pop up to warn you that you must restart FS 5.0 for the changes to take effect. If you made a mistake and wish to reconsider your selections, click the OK button, else if you are ready to restart FS 5.0, click the Exit Flight Simulator and Restart button, as is depicted in Figure 1.3.

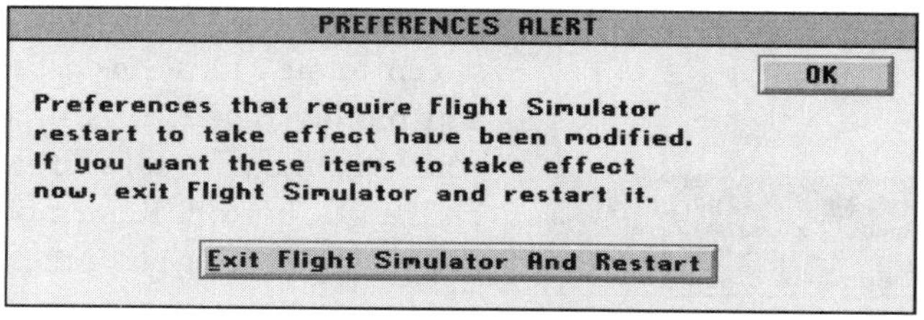

Figure 1.2
The Display Preferences dialog box

Figure 1.3
The Preferences Alert dialog box

For 486 or Pentium Owners: Maximize Your Scenery Display

For those of you fortunate to have a 486 or rich enough to own a Pentium, you are allowed to pull out all the stops out for FS 5.0, and set your scenery complexity to very dense so that you can see some spectacular Chicago scenery. To do this, pull down the Scenery menu, and select Scenery Complexity, as is shown in Figures 1.4 and 1.5. Immediately, you will see the Scenery Complexity dialog box open up with various checkbox selections arranged in two columns, one for the View 1 window, the other for the View 2 window. The View 1 window is your primary view out of your cockpit windshield, and through adjusting the Image Complexity setting, you can elect to have more scenery detail drawn on-screen. The second View 2 window can be opened up to show a second external view of your aircraft, but for now, ignore this side of the dialog box. If you have a screamingly fast 486 DX machine or Pentium, pull down the Image Complexity list box under the View 1 window column, and select Very Dense. When you are done, exit the dialog box by clicking the OK button. Don't, however, press [Esc] or click outside of the menu to exit the dialog box, because your newly modified image complexity settings will not take effect.

If you have a fast video Super VGA accelerator card, you can modify your display preferences and jazz up the quality of your scenery. Pull down the Options menu and select Preferences. In the dialog box that follows, click the Display button and click on all the check box options that appear on the lower half of the screen. You will want to see the ground scenery, aircraft shadows, engine propeller, landing lights, see parts of your own aircraft when looking out different windows, enjoy a textured sky with a gradient horizon along with textured buildings and ground, and observe a smooth transition when jumping from view to view (i.e., when using [S] to switch from cockpit to tower to spot view). While in this window, you might as well check to make sure your Graphics Mode is set for SVGA 640x400 256 Colors, and that your SVGA board maker is correctly set for your particular SVGA video card. If you have a fast 486 DX or Pentium you might want to also set the Image Quality/Speed on High/Slow, and the Flicker/Speed on No Flicker/Slow for maximum visual impact. Later, if you notice that the screen frame rate seems a little slow, you can come back to this dialog box and modify the settings to a lower quality, higher flicker rate to speed up your graphics. For now, exit the Display Preferences dialog box by clicking on the OK button. Remember, if you want to keep any changes you make to this dialog box, or any other, you must select the OK button and not press [Esc], or the Cancel button. (See Figure 1.2 for a view of the Display Preferences dialog box.)

Figure 1.4
The Scenery menu

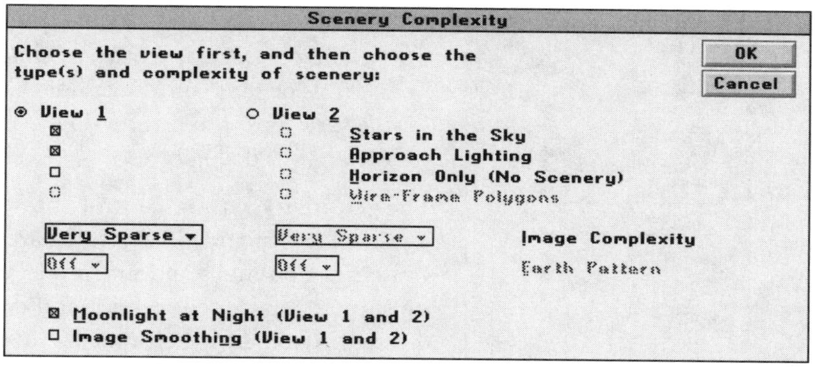

Figure 1.5
The Scenery Complexity dialog box

Calibrating Your Joystick/Flightstick

If you have a joystick or flightstick plugged into the game port of your PC, then you will need to configure and calibrate it before you can fly Flight Simulator. Some people prefer to use two joysticks in combination, one to control the ailerons/rudder and elevator, the second to control the throttle and brakes. (Or when using pedals as your second joystick, you can set the second joystick to control the rudder.) But for now let's assume that you are using a single joystick. Since FS 5.0 has no way of knowing beforehand where your joystick/flightstick is centered, you will need to instruct the program as to its initial settings via a process known as calibration. If you didn't do this, then your joystick might send the wrong signal to the program as to its true position, and you would have to fly a plane that chronically turns, climbs, or dives, even though your stick is apparently centered.

To set and calibrate your joystick/flightstick, follow these steps:

1. Open the Options menu.
2. Select the Preferences command.
3. Click the Joystick button.
4. Click the pull down list box for Joystick 1: and select Aileron & Elevator. (A list box is a text box with several options listed that drops down when you click on it. Notice that the current selection in the list box has a dot on the left hand side.)
5. If you are using a second joystick, pedals, or a flightstick with throttle/brake controls, click the pull down Joystick 2 list box and select Throttle & Brakes (or Throttle & Rudder if using pedals).
6. Center the joystick or flightstick, then click the Calibrate button as shown in Figure 1.6. Your joystick/flightstick is now calibrated!

You can skip this section if you plan to fly your plane using the mouse or keyboard.

You can also calibrate your joystick from the keyboard by pressing ⎡K⎤.

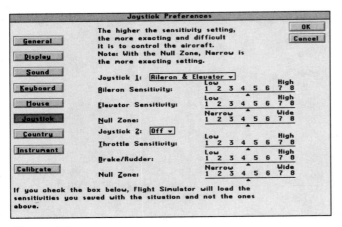

Figure 1.6
Setting up and calibrating your joystick

7. For now, don't bother with adjusting the aileron/elevator sensitivity slide controls or the Null Zone slide. Click the OK button to exit the Joystick Preferences dialog box.

The sensitivity setting controls how much joystick movement will affect the aircraft. If you notice too much movement of the controls, then you can come back and decrease the sensitivity. On the other hand, if you don't get enough movement of the controls, you can increase the sensitivity. The null zone refers to that portion of the center of the joystick where the ailerons are centered. By adjusting the null zone sensitivity, you can find a comfortable zone where you can move your joystick slightly without causing the plane to bank. A wider null zone gives your joystick a looser feel, while a narrower zone gives your joystick a tighter feel. Too narrow a zone can be annoying since every joystick jitter can cause the plane to start turning. Click the Load Sensitivities Saved with Situation check box if you want to load these settings so that you don't have to constantly reset them each time you start the situation again.

✈ **Tip:** To move the Slider Sensitivity controls from the keyboard, press the character key that is the same as the underlined letter on the control's name, then press the right cursor arrow key to increase the setting, or the left cursor arrow key to decrease the setting. When the control has been properly selected, the slide and its marker numbers will turn red, indicating that you can now move the sliding pointer triangle.

PRE-FLIGHT PREPARATION: LEARNING THE SIX BASIC FLIGHT INSTRUMENTS OF THE STANDARD INSTRUMENT CLUSTER

The Three Pitot-Static Instruments

Stepping back into your cockpit, take a moment to glance over your cockpit instruments and controls. It's better to do this now than later, when you are being fished out of Lake Michigan because you didn't know where your controls were located, or you didn't understand one of your flight instrument readings. There are six basic flight instruments of which the first three to be discussed are the so called pitot-static instruments, because their measurements and displayed readings are derived from responses to air pressures in the pitot-static system. The pressure altimeter, the vertical speed indicator, and the airspeed indicator all calculate the amount of air pressure that is being rammed into the pitot tube, a hollow cylindrical pipe which is mounted externally on the leading edge of the wing, nose, or tail of the aircraft. Each of these three instruments then compares the pitot tube pressure to the air pressure in a static chamber, where the air is not being subjected to any motive forces. The pressure difference thus calculated is displayed as the indicated airspeed in knots per hour (nautical miles per hour in the air, not on the ground) on the airspeed indicator, rate of climb or descent in hundreds of feet per minute on the vertical speed indicator, and the altitude in feet over mean sea level on the altimeter. In FS 5.0, you should know that, unlike real airplanes, the airspeed indicator shows true airspeed, not indicated airspeed. We will get into this topic in later chapters.

The Airspeed Indicator

Looking at your airspeed indicator, as shown in Figure 1.7, you can see that presently it registers 0 knots per hour, but that it can measure up to 210 knots per hour.

The Altimeter

Turning to your altimeter, it resembles a clock with 10 divisions, instead of a clock's usual 12. For the large hand of the altimeter's "clock," each number marking represents 100 feet, although the smallest reading is in 50 foot increments. Since the large hand is almost over the 6, this means that the aircraft is at 590 feet or so. Notice that this means that you are approximately

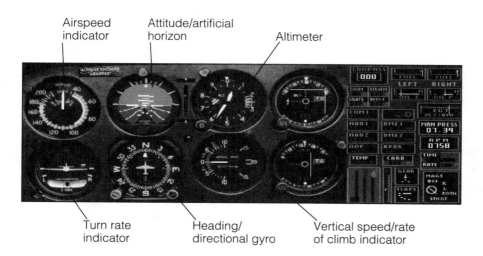

Airspeed indicator

Attitude/artificial horizon

Altimeter

Turn rate indicator

Heading/ directional gyro

Vertical speed/rate of climb indicator

Figure 1.7
The six primary flight instruments of the standard instrument cluster

590 feet above sea level, but *not* 590 feet above ground. Many a pilot has crashed because of forgetting the crucial distinction between above ground level (abbreviated as AGL) and mean sea level (MSL). The smaller hand of the altimeter's "clock" measures the altitude in thousands of feet, but since it has not reached the 1 yet, the altimeter shows that the aircraft is below one thousand feet. If the small hand were to travel past the 1, then you would add to your altitude 1,000 feet for each number that it passes. There is also a smaller triangular dot that you can see over the zero that moves and tells you how many tens of thousands of feet above MSL you are.

The Vertical Speed Indicator

The vertical speed indicator lets you know how many hundreds of feet per minute you are descending or ascending at any given time and at present shows no activity since you are motionless on the ground.

The Three Gyroscopic Instruments

The remaining three flight instruments, the attitude indicator, the turn indicator, and the heading indicator, are known as gyroscopic instruments, since their readings are obtained from the inertial frame of reference of a spinning gyroscope. The gyroscopic instruments provide information about the aircraft's direction and attitude.

The Attitude Indicator

The attitude indicator, also known as the artificial horizon, tells you the airplane's attitude at all times. It shows the actual pitch and roll of the aircraft in relation to the ground, and thus gives the pilot an internal horizon inside the cockpit that serves as a reference point for flying the aircraft in any kind of weather, night or day. The lower colored portion of the attitude indicator's ball represents the ground, or horizon, and the two white horizontal lines in the center of the scope denote the aircraft's wings. If you bank the airplane to the left, for example, the colored half of the horizon ball will rotate to the right, signifying a turn to the left. If you pull up the nose, the colored half of the ball will drop below the level of the wings, as indicated by the two white horizontal lines, thereby showing the aircraft is climbing.

The Turn Indicator

The turn indicator measures the turning rate of the aircraft, and it shows the amount of slip or skid the aircraft is experiencing in a turn. In auto-coordinated flight, you will not need to concern yourself with this instrument, although if you were fly with pedals simulating the rudder controls of a real aircraft, you would watch this gauge in order to make a stable turn.

The Heading Indicator

The last instrument, the heading indicator, or directional gyro, shows the compass heading the aircraft is currently on. It differs from the magnetic compass in that a highly precise gyroscope provides a precise, instantaneous display of the course heading, even when the aircraft experiences pronounced accelerative forces such as when climbing, diving or turning. The principal drawback of the directional gyro is that it tends to drift away from an accurate compass reading over time due to processional errors in the rotating gyroscope. From time to time, therefore, you must recalibrate the directional gyro so that it agrees with the magnetic compass.

PRE-FLIGHT CHECKOUT: VIEWING YOUR AIRCRAFT EXTERNALLY THROUGH SPOT VIEW

While you are parked on the Meigs runway tarmac waiting to takeoff, you might as well try out some of the different viewing options. In FS 5.0, you can have up to two different view screens displayed simultaneously along with a map and your instrument panel. Each view screen can be independently controlled from the keyboard, and you can resize or move them at will using either the mouse or keyboard. Thus, if you are so inclined, you can have your main view screen #1 show your cockpit view, while view screen #2 might show a spot view of your aircraft from behind. The map window might also be concurrently displayed so that you can keep an eye on your bearings.

Using Spot View

Let's inspect your airplane from outside the cockpit. Press [S] on the keyboard and immediately you will see that the scene changes to that of an airport tower view of your airplane sitting at the end of the runway. Press [S] once more to obtain a spot plane view of your plane. Press [S] a third time, and you will return to your cockpit view. In spot view, you can look at your plane as if you were following your plane in a chaser plane at a discrete distance. By holding down [Shift] and pressing [7], [8], [9], [6], [3], [2], [1], [4] on the numeric keypad in succession, you will cycle through all possible angles from which to view your airplane. (You can also do this in cockpit view to get a 360 view around your plane.) If you want to zoom in or out

The more windows you have displayed, the slower the frame rate will be.

Table 1.1 Cycling Through the Three Possible Views in the View Window[1]	
Pressing (S) from Cockpit View	View
First Time	Tower View
Second Time	Spot View
Third Time	Cockpit View

Open the Second
View Window by
pressing ⑴.

Figure 1.8
External Spot View

with this spot view, press (+) or (−) on the main keypad and your spotting position will move farther away or closer in towards your airplane. If you want to return to your normal cockpit view, press (S) once more. Table 1.1 summarizes the cycling of all the possible views by pressing (S) in succession. The different vantage points are depicted in a 360 degree circle around your aircraft in both spot and cockpit views.

Try experimenting to discover which vantage point you prefer in Spot View by using (Shift), (7), (8), (9), (6), (3), (2), (1), (4) combinations on the numeric keypad, and (+) or (−) on the main keypad to zoom in or out. In Figure 1.8, you can see the results of pressing (Shift) + (7) combination, which gives you a left forward view of your Cessna. When you are finished, press (S) once more to return to cockpit view.

You can also call up a second view window that can display another view while simultaneously displaying the first view. Simply press ⑴ once to call the window up, and to close the window, press ⑴ twice quickly in succession. As with the first view window, you can choose which view you want to see from the tower, cockpit, track or spot view options.

Call Up the Map View

To keep an eye on your ground location, you can call up a third window (in addition to the two available view windows),

---

[1]There is one more view, the track view, available only in Dual Player mode. It can only be turned on from the pull down view options menu. This view is really only useful when flying in Dual Player mode, where you can use track view to see your flying companion's plane no matter how far away he or she is.

to display your airplane's position on a map. Opening the map window is accomplished by pressing `Num Lock` once, while to close it you would press `Num Lock` twice quickly. Sometimes the map window will come up behind the main display window. To bring it to the foreground, press `'` (apostrophe key). The map's magnification can be zoomed in or out, depending on your preferences by using `+` or `−` on the main keyboard. Your airplane's position is centered on a red

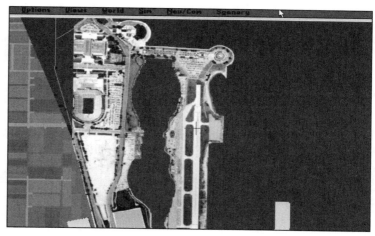

Figure 1.9
The Map window

crosshair in the middle of the map, with the aircraft's nose always pointing towards the top vertical crosshair. As you turn, the map will rotate, showing that your aircraft is now facing a different direction. If you find this discombobulating, you can change the map display through the Display Preferences dialog box under the Options menu, and freeze the map in a north orientation. Then, regardless of your plane's heading, the map would always appear fixed (meaning that it wouldn't rotate), although your airplane's cross hairs would move around as your position changed. Figure 1.9 shows the map in a zoomed-in close-up view of the runway.

Call up the Map window through the following steps:

1. Press `Num Lock` once. (You may have to press `'` to bring the map to the foreground.)
2. Zoom out by pressing `−` on the main keypad.
3. Zoom in by pressing `+` on the main keypad.
4. Close the map window by pressing `Num Lock` twice quickly in succession.

Call up the Map window by pressing `Num Lock`.

YOUR PRIMARY FLIGHT CONTROLS

Whether you are flying your airplane with just a keyboard, mouse, or joystick, your basic flight controls are controlled in the same way. The ailerons in the wings control your bank, or aircraft roll (left or right); the elevators determine the airplane's pitch angle (up and down), and the rudders affect which way the airplane is headed, or yawing (pivoting left or right). For all intents and purposes, the wing surface controls are placed in the same general location on the Learjet, Sailplane, and Sopwith Camel.

Keyboard Yoke Control

On the numeric keypad, ⑧ and ② control the down elevator and up elevator respectively, ④ and ⑤ control the left and right ailerons along with the rudder, when flying in auto-coordinated mode.

Auto-Coordination

In FS 5.0, auto-coordination of your rudder and ailerons is essential if you are to make smooth coordinated turns. In real aircraft, however, pilots must coordinate any turns by using foot pedals, which are connected to the rudder, along with the aileron controls that are manipulated with the pilot's yoke. In the program, you can disable auto-coordination mode and fly your plane using the rudders and ailerons as separate controls. When you do this, ④ and ⑥ on the numeric keypad control only the left and right ailerons, and ⓪ and Enter (also on the numeric keypad) now control left and right rudder movements, respectively. Turning off auto-coordination is a very useful feature if you are using pedals in conjunction with a flightstick to more realistically simulate the actual controls on the Cessna. (The pedals, which are connected to the rudders on a real airplane, are used to yaw the aircraft left or right.) You might also want to switch off auto-coordination in order to perform some tricky aerobatic maneuvers. However, for ease of flying when learning *Flight Simulator*, you will want to keep auto-coordination turned on to lesson the complications of making smooth turns.

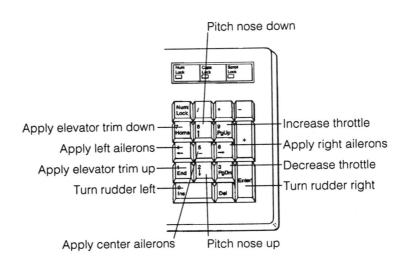

Figure 1.10
Keyboard yoke and throttle controls on the numeric keypad

Mouse Yoke Controls

You can fly your plane using the mouse as well. To control your aircraft's pitch, move the mouse straight forward to lower the elevators (nose down), or straight backwards to raise the elevators (nose up). In auto-coordinated flight, moving the mouse right or left will cause the rudder and ailerons to move in a coordinated fashion that forces the plane to turn right or left respectively. But if you disable auto-coordination, the left/right mouse movements will control only the ailerons, and you will have to use [0] and [Enter] on the numeric keypad to move the rudder left or right.

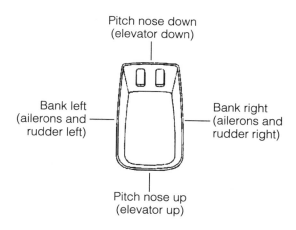

Figure 1.11
Mouse yoke controls

Practice Moving Your Yoke

Let's practice moving the yoke, whether by keyboard, mouse, or joystick. You should note the main control position indicators on your instrument panel, lodged between the artificial horizon/attitude indicator. The vertical indicator in the center shows the current position of your elevators, while the top horizontal indicator shows the ailerons position and the lower horizontal indicator shows the rudder position.

Let's watch what happens outside your airplane when you move your controls. Press [S] two times till you are in Spot view, then press [+] on the main keyboard once, so that you can zoom in on the aircraft close enough to see the airfoil controls move.

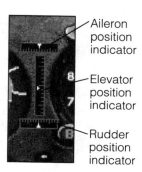

Figure 1.12
The control position indicators

Lower the Elevators and Watch Them Move on Your Plane

Move your yoke all the way forward by repeatedly pressing [8] on the numeric keypad or by moving your mouse or joystick in the forward direction. Observe how the elevators move downwards on your plane and how, simultaneously, the triangular pointer on the elevator control position indicator moves down, signifying that your elevators have been lowered. If you were flying, the nose of the aircraft would drop in response to this action. Return your elevators to the neutral, or center position, by holding down and pressing [2] or by moving your mouse/joystick backwards. This centered position is the most favorable for level flight, although in some cases it may be necessary to trim your elevators at a different position in order to keep the nose of the aircraft level. This is where the elevator trim control comes in handy.

Elevator Trim

The elevator trim control allows you to remove the pressure that you would have to make on the yoke to maintain a desired attitude. For example, if you were flying a real airplane, during flight you might have to pull back the yoke slightly and hold it in that position to maintain a level flight without gaining or losing altitude. After a while, you would get tired of holding the yoke against the pressure which the outside airstream exerts on the elevators. To relieve this pressure and hold the yoke in its current position, you would adjust the elevator trim control until it takes up the slack and you can release the yoke.

In the make-believe world of *Flight Simulator*, the elevator trim control doesn't do you much good, unless you are using a joystick or flightstick. Because these input devices have springs, which cause them to exert a force on the stick which you must counteract, they act more like actual yokes in that there is neutral or centered position where the stick will position itself once you let go. The keyboard has no such feedback, so that if you release the elevators at a certain position, they will remain fixed at that position.

Here is an example of how you might want to use the elevator trim in the event that you are using a joystick/flightstick. To fly with the elevators slightly raised, you need to pull back the joystick/flightstick towards yourself, against the counter-pull of the spring. To release the pressure on the stick without changing the elevator setting, you would raise the elevator trim by pressing 1, or lower it by pressing 7, both of which are on the numeric keypad. Your plane would maintain its current attitude, even though you have now let go of your yoke and it has returned to its neutral or centered position.

Practice pulling the yoke back, which would cause your plane's nose to pitch up in response to raising the elevators. When you are done, return the elevators to the centered position.

Move the Ailerons/Rudder (Auto-Coordinated Mode)

Center the ailerons/rudder by pressing 5. Elevators must be centered manually.

Now move your yoke all the way left by pressing 4 or moving the joystick/flightstick all the way to the left. You should see the ailerons moving in opposite directions on each wing, along with the rudder turning to the left. The rudder and aileron control position indicators should also show this movement. If you were flying, the aircraft would start banking to the left and the plane would be executing a left hand turn. Press 5 to center the rudder and ailerons, then repeat this maneuver for a right-hand turn. Notice that the ailerons again are on opposite sides, one up and one down, but this time the rudder is pointing right.

Before proceeding to the next section, exit spot view and return to your cockpit view by pressing S once more. Also make sure that you have returned the aileron/rudder controls to the centered position by pressing ⑤. (The ⑤ key does not center the elevators. You will still have to manually center the elevator using ⑧ and ②, or your mouse/joystick.)

TAKEOFF

Since this is your first solo flight, you might be bewildered by the array of instrumentation and controls that sits before you. Don't worry, even if you haven't read the preceding warm-up section, you will be walked through a perfect takeoff, relax on a sightseeing tour of Chicago, and return for an exciting but safe dusk landing at Chicago's Meigs field. Your landing will be handled by the computer on this, your first solo flight, but hey — you wouldn't want to risk a $75,000 airplane on its maiden voyage would you?

At the end of this chapter, I have included a summary of all the steps you perform in actually flying the airplane as a mnemonic aid for those of us who don't have elephantine memories.

The first thing you'll need to know before you can start rolling down the tarmac, is what speed you must be traveling before you can rotate the aircraft (meaning pull back on the yoke, joystick/flightstick, or up elevator using ② on the numeric keypad). If you pull back on the yoke too soon, before the aircraft's stall speed, the aircraft will fail to leave the runway, or even more ominously, may lift up briefly, stall and then crash. A stall is a condition whereby the smooth airflow over the wing is interrupted and the aircraft loses its lift. This can happen when the plane is not traveling fast enough for the airflow over the wings to create the forces of lift.

For the Cessna, the stall speed is 54 knots with the flaps up and landing gear retracted. (54 knots, or nautical miles per hour, is the equivalent of 62 miles per hour).[2] Therefore, you must accelerate the aircraft by pushing up

---

[2]A nautical mile is based on the spherical coordinate system of degrees longitude and latitude that allows us to locate our geographical position on Earth. It is defined as the length that one minute of arc would take on a great circle all the way around the Earth. Since there are 60 minutes in each degree of arc, this means that there are 60 nautical miles in every degree of longitude or latitude. 360 degrees of longitude constitutes a great circle around the Earth, and as such, the distance around the Earth, as measured at the equator would be 360 degrees * 60 nautical miles = 21,600 nautical miles. However, because the Earth is not a perfect sphere, the nautical mile varies at certain locations around the planet. By international agreement, the nautical mile has been fixed at 6076.115 feet. The standard English mile, from which we base our ground measurements of speed is founded upon the length of 5,280 feet. A nautical mile, then, is approximately 1.15 (or 15 percent) times longer than a standard mile.

the throttle to maximum, and then wait until the aircraft has gained sufficient speed to pass 54 knots per hour.

Turn On the Axis Indicator on Cockpit Windshield

Figure 1.13
The axis indicator is selected from the View Options dialog box

To help you better see which direction your aircraft's nose is pointed with regard to the horizon, let's turn the Axis Indicator on. This is a little V shaped pointer that you can turn on or off in the center of your cockpit windshield. When you are flying straight and level, the top of V should line up exactly with the horizon to let you know that you are not gaining or losing altitude. This handy little device gives you the same information that the artificial horizon/attitude indicator gives, but since you tend to look out the cockpit window, rather than at your instruments, it's a little bit easier to use (although it does not tell you how steeply your plane is banking).

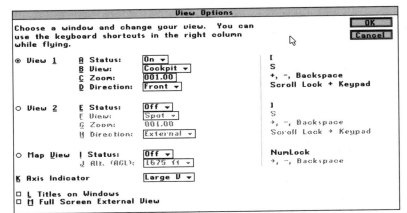

To turn on the Axis Indicator, follow these steps:

1. Pull down the Views menu.
2. Select the View Options command.
3. In the Axis Indicator list box select the Large V option.
4. Exit the View Options dialog box, and return to the simulator by clicking on the OK button.

Release Parking Brakes

Release your parking brakes by pressing ⊡. This will enable the aircraft to start rolling down the runway. You will see the parking brake warning disappear from your lower left view screen.

Increase Throttle

Now that you're ready to go, increase the throttle to maximum by pressing and holding down ⑨ on the numeric keypad. (Or briefly press F4 once on

Figure 1.14
Increasing the throttle

Manifold pressure gauge

RPM

Throttle lever

the top function keypad.) If you prefer using the mouse to increase the throttle, grab the throttle lever, as is illustrated in Figure 1.14, with the mouse and drag it up to the top of its scale. Notice that the pitch of the airplane goes up as the engine revs up to its maximum thrust. Immediately, the airplane should begin to move and the airspeed indicator will show that you are picking up speed. You will also see the RPM (propeller rotations per minute) indicator increase along with a rise in manifold pressure, which is displayed above the RPM indicator. The manifold pressure tells you how much vacuum, or suck, the engine is developing in the intake manifold of the engine, and is a direct indicator of engine power. It measures vacuum in pressure unit of inches of mercury, and the scale goes from 0 inches (0 percent power) all the way up to 29 inches (100 percent power).

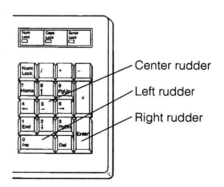

Center rudder

Left rudder

Right rudder

Be sure you keep your plane centered on the runway as it takes off by using [0] for steering left, and [Enter] for steering right, both of which are located on the numeric keypad.

Rotation (Apply Up Elevator)
When Airspeed Reaches 65 Knots

To play it safe, you should rotate the aircraft only when the speed has reached 65 knots per hour. This gives you an added margin of safety, and

Figure 1.15
Steering while on the runway is accomplished by using rudder controls located on the numeric keypad

The Cessna will stall at speeds of less than 54 knots per hour. Therefore, when taking off, be sure you rotate (i.e., apply the joystick/flightstick) when the aircraft has accelerated past this speed.

If you are running FS 5.0 in EGA or VGA modes, you will not see the Manifold Pressure Gauge, or any other engine indicators on-screen, unless you press Tab to bring up the sub panel from the main instrument panel. Press Tab to return your view of the radio stack.

will ensure that the plane does not stall on takeoff. To lift off, gently tap 2 several times or pull back on the mouse/joystick, until the triangle pointer on the elevator control position indicator moves to the first mark above the center line. In a few moments, you should feel the entire plane lift off the runway, and shortly thereafter, the end of the runway should make its appearance.

✈ **Hint:** Move the elevator to the first mark above the center line before you take off, and the Cessna will take off by itself when you apply 100 percent throttle. Just sit back and keep your hands off the keyboard. Try it!

After Takeoff, Move Throttle Back to 22.40 Inches of Manifold Pressure

Soon after you have passed the runway threshold, you will notice that your airplane gets buffeted by some wind. After this little bit of turbulence ceases, this is your cue to ease back on the throttle. Move the throttle down (using 3, or drag throttle indicator via mouse) until the manifold pressure gauge gives a reading of 22.40 inches. (It doesn't have to be exactly 22.40, just reasonably close.) This corresponds to a throttle setting of approximately 75-80 percent. Doing so will ease the burden on the engine, and it will also stabilize your rate of climb to 500 to 1000 feet per minute.

Raise Landing Gear

To further streamline the airflow around the fuselage, thereby reducing drag, and improving fuel economy, let's retract the landing gear. From the keyboard press G, or click on the GEAR Up/Down Indicator on the control panel. You should see the gear indicator slide to the UP position, and if you were so inclined, you could view the gear being raised in spot view.

Climb to 1,500 Feet Altitude

During this phase of the flight, it is important to not put the plane into too steep a climb, else your airspeed will drop below 54 knots and the plane will stall and crash. This is where your six primary flight instruments help you to figure out what is happening. As your airplane continues to ascend, as shown on the vertical speed indicator, try to keep your climb rate between 500 to 1,000 feet per minute by judicious application of the throttle. Watch the altimeter's long hand move around clockwise until it passes the zero. At this point you have reached 1,000 feet above MSL (Mean Sea Level), and you should start thinking about leveling the plane off soon. The airspeed indicator will show you traveling at approximately 100 knots per hour, and your compass heading should be due North at 0 degrees.

Just before the long hand on the altimeter reaches 1,300 feet, begin to level the plane off by reducing throttle. If you have succeeded in leveling the plane, you should see the vertical axis pointer on the windshield line up with the horizon. Although there is a delayed effect, the vertical speed indicator needle should hover around the zero mark, and the artificial horizon should show the wings are now lined up with the horizon semicircle circle.

Bank Left Towards Chicago:
Course Heading West (Between 240–280 degrees)

Glance at your directional gyro and notice that you are headed north. Since Chicago is on your left, to the west, you must begin banking the aircraft left if you are to fly through the downtown district. Gently tap [4] several times, or move the mouse/joystick yoke control to the right until the plane begins

Airspeed
is 80 knots

Artificial horizon shows
the plane is climbing

Axis indicator above horizon
shows plane is climbing

Turn indicator shows the
airplane is not turning

Compass and Directional
Gyro heading in 359°

Altimeter shows
1,200 feet

Warning: Don't let your speed drop below 54 knots per hour, as measured on the airspeed indicator; otherwise the plane will crash.

Airspeed 100 knots, Vertical Speed 500 to 1,000 feet per minute, Engine Throttle set to 22.40 inches on Manifold Pressure Gauge.

Level the airplane at 1,500 feet altitude by reducing throttle only. Do not touch yoke controls. As a general rule, altitude changes should be made using the throttle.

Figure 1.16
The six flight instruments during the climb

The vertical axis "V" marker on the cockpit windshield lets you know where the nose of the airplane is actually pointing. If you are flying straight and level, the top of the V should precisely line up with the horizon edge.

Change Course Heading to between 240-275 degrees. Call up the map, if necessary, by pressing Num Lock.

Pull out of your turn by pressing 6, or applying right joystick/flightstick pressure.

turning. Carefully monitor this turn so that you don't bank the plane too steeply. If you must, apply corrective steering to the right by applying right mouse/joystick movement, or by pressing 6. Watch the progression of the turn on the artificial horizon and the turn indicator. If the wings just line up on the L division marker on the turn indicator, you are performing a standard turn, whereby the airplane, if allowed to continue on its path, will make a complete 360 degree turn in 2 minutes.

When the directional gyro shows that you are headed on a course heading of between 240-275 degrees, and you see the city of Chicago straight ahead, pull out of the turn by applying right aileron/rudder. If you are having trouble finding your bearings, call up the map by pressing Num Lock. Zoom in and out of this view by using + and - on the main keyboard. When you are done, close the map by pressing Num Lock twice quickly.

When you see the skyline of Chicago's skyscrapers line up with your V axis indicator on the cockpit windshield, you should have completed your standard turn. The plane should be flying straight and level, as ascertained by the position of the wings on the artificial horizon, the turn indicator should show your wings are horizontal. If you are on course, you should be headed towards the downtown Chicago metropolis.

Figure 1.17
Banking the airplane to the left

Note Turn Indicator shows wings on L marker, indicating a standard turn

Pointer on Directional Gyro shows current heading of 283°

Map display turned on using Num Lock and - to zoom out

Buzz Downtown Chicago

Try flying through some of the canyons of buildings, taking special care not allow your airplane to hit a building structure. With the scenery density turned up high, you should be able to see the Prudential Building, the Sears Building, and many other building landmarks.

If you are feeling a little adventurous, fly around the downtown area, taking in the sights. Every so often, call up the spot view by pressing ⑤ twice. To return to the cockpit, press ⑤ once again.

Figure 1.18
Full-screen Spot View of your aircraft negotiating the downtown canyons of Chicago (Press ⑤ twice, then Ⓦ)

Change the Time of Day to Dusk, and Pause the Simulation

Before turning home, for a change of pace, let's try flying at Dusk, just before the sun has completely set. With *Flight Simulator*'s awesome new color capabilities, you are in for a real treat when viewing the glorious sunrises and sunsets.

Because you may not want to be distracted while flying, lets pause the simulation so that there is no danger of crashing while you are fiddling with the controls. You can pause the simulation at any time by pressing Ⓟ. On-screen, you will see a pause message indicator informing you that all on-screen activity has been halted. While paused you can pull down menus, change your controls or views, alter the weather, and even change airplanes. To resume flying, press Ⓟ once again.

To quickly change the time of day, all you need to do is set the digital clock that you see on the instrument panel. To increase the hours, you must click the mouse pointer to the right side of the hours display on the digital clock. Conversely, to move the clock back, you must click the mouse pointer to the left side of the hours display. You can hold down the mouse button to advance or retard the time quickly, or you can click each individual number change.

Changing the minutes is also accomplished in the same way. Thus to increase the minutes, click the pointer on the right of the minutes indicator, and to decrease the minutes, click the pointer on the left of the minutes indicator.

Press Ⓦ to summon up a full screen view. To return to the cockpit, press Ⓦ again.

At any time you can pause the simulation by pressing Ⓟ. To resume flying, press Ⓟ again.

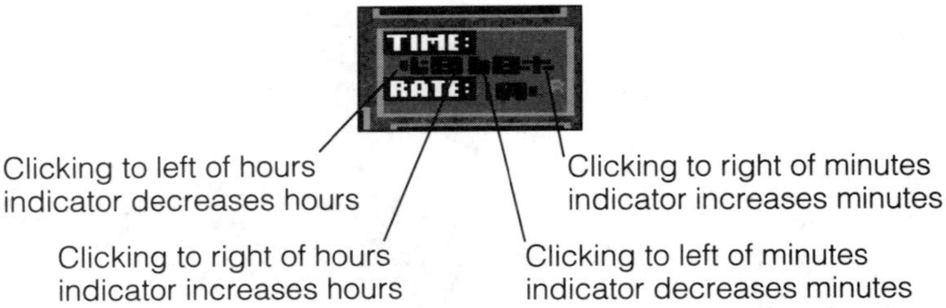
TIME:
RATE:
Clicking to left of hours indicator decreases hours
Clicking to right of hours indicator increases hours
Clicking to right of minutes indicator increases minutes
Clicking to left of minutes indicator decreases minutes

Figure 1.19
The 24-hour format digital clock controls the time of day or night

Change the time to dusk.

Let's change the time to dusk at 17:40 (or in 12-hour format 5:40 P.M.) by performing the following steps[3]:

1. First pause the simulator by pressing [P].
2. Click on the right of the hours indicator till it reads 17: (in 24 hour time this is 5:00 P.M.).
3. Click on the right of the minutes indicator till it reads 40. Note the gradual darkening of the sky as you do so. If you were to click once more to 41 minutes past 17:00, the sky would darken even more as the sun sets, and the instrument panels would light up red.
4. Click on the left of the minutes indicator, to reverse the time, and watch as the sky lightens as daylight returns. Adjust the minutes indicator back to 40 when you are done.
5. Press [P] to cancel pause and resume flying the plane.

I hope you are as impressed as I am by the amazing colors that appear in the horizon during the gradual change from dusk to nightfall. It is fascinating to watch the darkening blue sky turn red, and the city lights slowly switch on as the sunset approaches. In the distance you can see the blue glow of the Meigs runway lighting system.

Come to a course heading of 120 degrees for the return home.

NIGHT FLIGHT HOME

Now let's swing back to a course heading of 120 degrees for the return leg home. Again, if you are lost and need to find your location, call up the map.

[3]Time is recorded in a 24-hour format, so that 1:00 P.M. becomes 13:00 and 1:00 A.M. becomes 1:00.

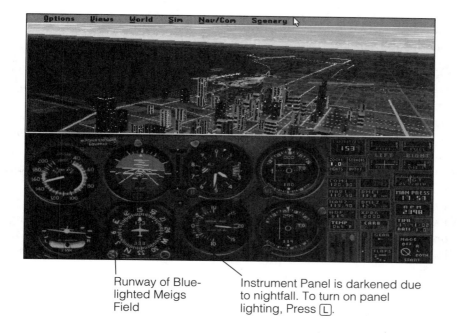

Figure 1.20
Dusk in Chicago,
after changing the
digital clock (simulator
paused using [Pause])

Runway of Blue-
lighted Meigs
Field

Instrument Panel is darkened due
to nightfall. To turn on panel
lighting, Press [L].

Turn On Aircraft Lights

Flight Simulator has four types of night flying lights: instrument panel lights, navigational lights, strobe lights, and landing lights. You can turn them all on or off by pressing [L] or clicking the LIGHTS indicator. For individual manipulation, the instrument panel lights can be turned off and on by pressing [Shift] + [L]; the navigation lights are only controlled by the LIGHTS indicator, the strobe is controlled by the letter O, and the landing lights by pressing [Ctrl] + [L]. The navigation lights are located on your wings, and serve to identify your position to other aircraft while flying at night. The strobe is a tail-mounted flashing light that acts as a beacon to other aircraft in your vicinity. The landing lights, which are like head lamps on an automobile, are used to illuminate the runway while taking off or landing at night.

Perform these steps in order to get acquainted with your lighting systems.

1. Turn on the landing lights by pressing [Ctrl] + [L]. When you are on or over the runway, you will notice a spotlight beam of light that illuminates the ground in front of your airplane.

2. Make sure all lights are on by looking at the LIGHTS indicator. It should say on. If you look at a spot view of your aircraft, you will see a green light under one wing, and a red light under the opposite wing.

3. Turn on the strobe by pressing [O]. (Or click on STROBES control.) You should see a bright flashing strobe light on the tail.

Press [X] to engage
Land Me. To disen-
gage Land Me, press
[X] again.

Using the New Land Me Command for a Safe Touchdown at Meigs Field

Let's now have *Flight Simulator* land our plane for us automatically. This will take some of the frustration out of not being able to bring the airplane back in one piece. Land Me is a new feature of FS 5.0 that allows you to have an instructor take over the control of your airplane (only with the Cessna), and then land you at the nearest airport, wherever that might be. *Flight Simulator* will automatically pick the proper airport for landing.

Press [X] from the keyboard to engage Land Me. In a few seconds, you will see a message on-screen from your flight instructor informing you of what flight maneuvers are being performed. Sit back and relax now while the Land Me instructor takes over. If you are interested in seeing what is going on outside your cockpit, press [S] twice to bring up Spot view. The Land Me instructor will return your plane to Meigs field and execute a flawless text-book landing.

✈ **Tip:** Watching the instructor's actions using the Land Me feature is very useful in learning how to properly land your airplane. To disengage Land Me at any time, press [X] again.

SUMMARY

Steps Performed for Your Solo Flight:

1. Turn on the Axis Indicator on Cockpit Windshield, and release parking brakes by pressing [.].

2. Increase throttle to maximum (press and hold down [9] on numeric keypad, or drag throttle control to top).

3. Keep airplane centered on runway by using [4] to steer left and [6] to steer right (yoke mouse/joystick left or right).

4. When aircraft passes 65 knots per hour airspeed, rotate (apply up elevator) aircraft by gently tapping [2] on the numeric keypad (or pull back on yoke mouse/joystick), until the triangle pointer on the elevator control indicator moves to the first mark above the center line.

5. After lifting off and passing the runway threshold (the airplane will be buffeted by a pocket of air turbulence), move throttle back to 22 inches of manifold pressure by pressing [3], or dragging down the throttle control.

6. Climb rate should be 500 to 1,000 feet per minute on vertical speed

indicator. Airspeed should be approximately 80 to 100 knots per hour. Use throttle to adjust climb rate (⑨ increases, ③ decreases).

7. Raise landing gear by pressing Ⓖ (or click on GEAR indicator).

8. Climb to 1,500 feet altitude MSL then level off by reducing throttle.

9. Bank left towards Chicago by applying left ailerons (press ④): Course Heading West (Between 240-280 degrees on directional gyro). To straighten out a banking turn that is too steep, apply right ailerons (press ⑥). Move joystick/mouse left for banking turn to left. Move joystick/mouse right to return to level flight.

10. When Chicago city skyline is lined up on "V" Axis indicator on cockpit windshield, fly straight and level. If you are lost, call up the map by pressing Num Lock. Zoom the map's magnification in and out by pressing ➕ and ➖ on the main keyboard.

11. Fly by downtown Chicago.

12. Pause simulator by pressing Ⓟ.

13. Change time to dusk by clicking right side of hours on digital display until 17: is displayed. Click right side of minutes until 40 is displayed. Note change of color in sky as it darkens gradually because of sunset.

14. Resume simulation play by pressing Ⓟ once again.

15. Swing back to a course heading of 120 degrees for the return leg home. Use map if necessary.

16. Turn on Aircraft Navigation Lights: Press Ⓛ or click on LIGHTS control. (The instrument panel may be already on, due to changes you made in the clock. Therefore, to make sure everything is on, check the LIGHTS indicator to see if is ON.)

17. Turn on Landing Lights: Press Ctrl + Ⓛ.

18. Turn on Strobe lights: Press Ⓞ.

19. Press Ⓧ to engage the Land Me auto land function.

20. Watch plane land by switching back and forth between spot and cockpit view (press Ⓢ twice for spot view, then once more to return to cockpit view).

21. Pat yourself on the back.

Congratulations, you have completed your first solo flight! In this chapter, in addition to flying, you have learned how to use some of the simulator's most powerful features. I hope you are as excited as I am about the incredible new graphics technology that went into FS 5.0.

CHAPTER
2
Windows on Your World

This chapter introduces you to the different kinds of views that are possible in *Flight Simulator's* windowing environment and the various viewing options that are available under the Views menu. *Flight Simulator 5.0* offers not only a standard view from the cockpit, but also several external views outside the cockpit. The external views, otherwise known as tower, spot, and track view, and the internal cockpit view can be displayed on two separate, three-dimensional windows. Each 3-D window's size attributes, direction of view, zoom or magnification factor, and placement on-screen are controlled by you. Along with the two 3-D windows, there is a map window, which charts the airplane's movement on a terrain map, and an instrument panel window, which can be moved but not resized. Both view windows and the map view can be displayed simultaneously, if you so wish, but only at the expense of slower CPU processor speed. Only one instrument panel may be displayed at a given time, but you can quickly jump between the available instrument panels by pressing Tab.

Under the Views menu, you can also choose to disable or cover any instrument, instrument panel, or aircraft system for training purposes. If you need more visual cues as to your plane's attitude, you can include axis pointers on the cockpit windshield and also display the name or title of your current view in each window. Using the Flight Photograph command, you can screen capture PCX-formatted graphics of the entire screen, or of individual windows and instrument panels, and then save them to a disk for later printing. Figure 2.1 shows the View menu, where all windowing menu options and commands are found.

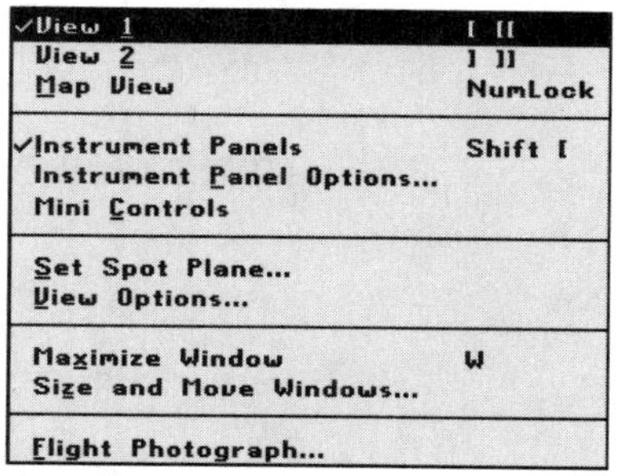

Figure 2.1 The Views menu

47

ACTIVATING A WINDOW

With up to three different windows on-screen, not including the instrument panel, you need to activate a window in order to let the simulator know which window you wish to move, resize, or zoom in. To activate a window you can:

1. Click inside the window using the mouse.
2. Under the Views menu, select View 1, View 2, or Map View.
3. From the keyboard, press ⟦[⟧ to bring up the View 1 window, press ⟦]⟧ to bring up the View 2 window, or press ⟦Num Lock⟧ to bring up the Map window.

When the window has been activated, you will see a thin white border gilding its edges.

To bring to the foreground a view or map window that is covered or concealed in the background, press ⟦'⟧. After you activate the window by clicking it, a thin white border will appear around its edges.

RESIZING AND MOVING A WINDOW

Resizing or moving a window can be accomplished with either the mouse or the keyboard, although using the mouse is the preferred method due to its simplicity and ease of use. This simple procedure is often necessary if you are trying to expand your window to show more detail. Note that while it is possible to move an instrument panel, or mini-control, it is not possible to resize it.

Resizing the Window Via the Mouse

Resizing the window using the mouse is the simplest and easiest way to manipulate the size of your window. To size the window click and drag the lower right corner of the window. As you do this, the window will stretch and look distorted as it adjusts to its new size, as pictured in Figure 2.2. If the window you wish to move is covered up by another window, press ⟦'⟧ to bring it to the foreground.

Figure 2.2
Resizing the window via the mouse

Resizing the Window Via the Keyboard

Using the keyboard:

1. Pull down the Views menu and select Size and Move Windows.

2. In the Size and Move Windows dialog box (illustrated in Figure 2.3), click the button of the window that you wish to resize.

3. When the window is displayed, press (Shift) in combination with the arrow cursor keys to resize it.

4. After finishing, press (Esc) to return to the Size and Move Windows dialog box, then click the OK button to return to the cockpit, or the Cancel button to cancel your resizing modification.

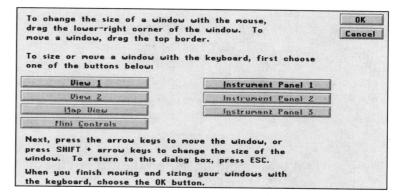

Figure 2.3
The Size and Move Windows dialog box

Moving a Window, Instrument Panel, or Mini-Control Via the Mouse

When moving on-screen objects, you can move any window, instrument panel, or mini-control using the mouse by clicking and dragging the top edge of the window, instrument panel, or mini-control to move it to a new location. If the window you wish to move is covered up by another window, press the ['] key to bring it to the foreground.

Figure 2.4
Moving a window via the mouse

Moving a Window, Instrument Panel, or Mini-Control Via the Keyboard

With the keyboard, to move a window, instrument panel, or mini-control, you must:

1. Pull down the Views menu and select Size and Move Windows (See Figure 2.3).
2. In the Size and Move Windows dialog box, click the button of the window that you wish to move.
3. When the window is displayed, press one of the arrow cursor keys to move it.
4. After finishing, press (Esc) to return to the Size and Move Windows dialog box, then click the OK button to return to the cockpit, or the Cancel button to cancel the object's new placement.

Enlarging a Window to Full Screen View

Figure 2.5 Enlarging a window to full screen

The View 1, View 2, and Map windows can be enlarged to full screen by pressing (W), or by choosing Maximize Window from the View menu, as demonstrated in Figure 2.5. These three windows can be quickly returned to their former size by once again pressing (W). If you select the Full Screen External View option in the View Options Dialog Box, you can have the simulator always switch to a full screen display for the spot and tower views.

ZOOMING THE MAGNIFICATION FACTOR OF A WINDOW

You use the zoom control to better view objects in your view and map windows. For example, you would use the zoom control to magnify and bring into close view a plane that is flying far away. Or, for another example, in map view you might want to zoom in close to the ground so that you can see local surface features, and then later zoom to a higher altitude to see a broader view of your position in relation to the rest of the country.

The two view windows and the map view can be zoomed in or out to various magnification factors by selecting and activating a window, then pressing ⊞ on the main keypad to zoom in, or ⊟ on the main keypad to zoom out. You can quickly restore normal 1x magnification by pressing ⌊Backspace⌋. There are various other ways to zoom an activated window, which we shall summarize here:

- Using the Mouse:
    1. Select the window you wish to zoom. When it is activated, you should see a thin white border circumscribing it.
    2. On the instrument panel, click the zoom indicator. To increase zoom, click to the right side of the numbers; to decrease zoom, click to the left side of the numbers.

- Using the Keyboard:
    1. Select the window you wish to zoom. When it is activated, you should see a thin white border circumscribing it.
    2. Press ⊞ on the main keypad to zoom in, or ⊟ on the main keypad to zoom out.

- Using the View Options menu command:
    1. Pull down the View menu.
    2. Select the View Options command.
    3. In the View Options Dialog Box, select the window you wish to zoom.
    4. In the list box for zoom, type in the amount of zoom you want. (You must type in numbers from the main keypad, not from the numeric keypad.) If you want to zoom the map view, select the Alt list box, and pull it down to display a list of altitudes from which you can pick.
    5. Click the OK button.

The view windows zoom factor ranges from 0.25 to 511, while the map zoom, which is measured in terms of altitude, ranges from 200 feet to a whole earth view at 160,000 miles (257,440 kilometers).

Learjet Zoom Indicator

Cessna Zoom Indicator

Figure 2.6
The Zoom Indicator zooms the active view or map window

```
 C  Zoom:        001.00
```

Figure 2.7
Type in the zoom factor for the 3-D view windows

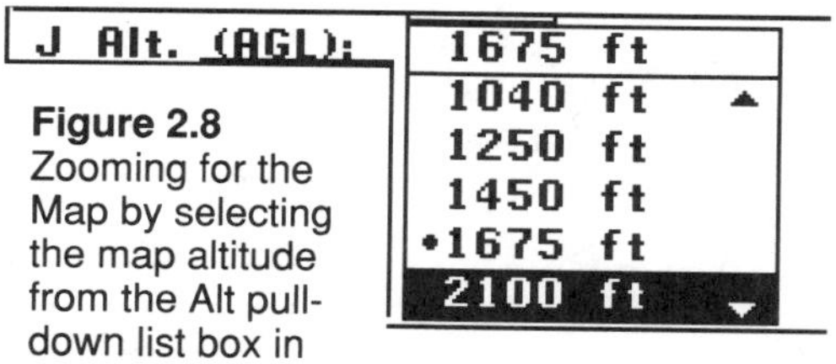

```
 J  Alt. (AGL):    1675 ft
                   1040 ft  ▲
                   1250 ft
                   1450 ft
                  •1675 ft
                   2100 ft  ▼
```

Figure 2.8
Zooming for the Map by selecting the map altitude from the Alt pull-down list box in the View Option dialog box

To zoom any window, activate the window, then press + to zoom in or − to zoom out. Alternatively, you can click to the right or left of the zoom indicator numbers to increase or decrease zoom.

Whenever you type numbers into list boxes or other option text fields in Flight Simulator, you must use the number keys on the main keypad, not the numeric keypad. This is because the numeric keypad is used to control the plane, and using these keys could affect the way your plane flies when you return to the simulation.

Zooming with Finer Resolution

You can control the zoom rate so that you have a finer and narrower resolution change by using [Shift] in combination with the + and − keys. Table 2.1 summarizes the zoom keyboard controls.

THE 3-D VIEW WINDOWS

The two three-dimensional view windows (hereafter called 3-D windows) can be switched on from the keyboard using [for the first 3-D window, and] for the second 3-D window. To close the first 3-D window, you would press [twice quickly; and to close the second 3-D window, you would press] twice quickly. Table 2.2 summarizes these keyboard commands. Alternatively, you can pull down the Views menu and select View 1 or View 2 to turn on or off these two view windows. The selection of these two menu options is a toggle; that is, when you first select them, you enable them, or turn them on, and a check mark appears to the immediate left of the menu option, as illustrated in Figure 2.1. When you again select the menu option, you disable or turn off the menu command, and the check mark disappears.

Cycling Between Cockpit, Tower, Track, and Spot Views

There are four possible views out of each of your two 3-D windows: cockpit, tower, track, and spot views. Cockpit view is just that: a view from inside your airplane looking outside through one of nine possible view angles. Tower view gives you a fixed-point perspective of your aircraft from inside the control tower of your scenario's startup airport, but you cannot change

Table 2.1 Zooming Keys	
Zoom	**Key**
Zoom In	+
Zoom In with Fine Resolution	Shift +
Zoom Out	−
Zoom Out with Fine Resolution	Shift −
Restore Normal Magnification	Backspace

Table 2.2   Turning Your Windows Off/On from the Keyboard

Window	Description	Opening Window from the Keyboard	Closing Window from the Keyboard
View 1	The first 3-D window	[I]	[I] [I]
View 2	The second 3-D window	[I]	[I] [I]
Map View	Navigational map	[Num Lock]	[Num Lock] [Num Lock]
Instrument Panels	Aircraft cockpit instrumentation	[Tab][1]	Not applicable

To quickly restore normal magnification, press [Backspace].

the view direction since it is automatically set to track your airplane. In this view, you can watch the runways and airspace around the airport while keeping an eye on your airplane. Track view lets you view your friend's plane while directly connected via modem or serial cable in dual-player mode, whereas spot view gives you an external view of your airplane as seen from the vantage point of a chase aircraft that is following your airplane.

To switch between cockpit, tower, and spot views from the keyboard, simply press [S]. The 3-D view that is currently active, as indicated by a white border around its periphery, will cycle from cockpit to tower view on the first press of [S], then will cycle from tower to spot view, upon a second press of [S]. Pressing [S] again will cause you to return to the cockpit view. Track view, which allows you to watch another player's airplane while in dual-player mode, is not accessible in the 3-D windows from the keyboard unless you are in dual-player mode.

You can also switch views, using the keyboard or mouse, by selecting View Options from the View menu and pulling down the View list box to then choose from the available options. While in this dialog

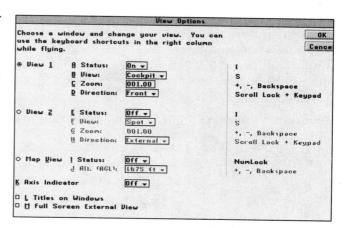

Figure 2.9
The View Options dialog box allows you to modify your view and map window options

---

[1]This key brings up an instrument subpanel. To return to the previous instrument subpanel, press [Tab] once again.

3-D View	Description	Keyboard Command (Press S to Cycle Forward, Shift S to Cycle in Reverse Order)	Zoom Command	View Directions	Pan View
Table 2.3	**The Four Possible Views Looking Out of the Two 3-D View Windows**				
Cockpit	View out of aircraft's windshield	S	+ Zoom in magnification — Zoom out magnification	Shift Key plus 7 8 9 / 4 5 6 / 1 2 3	Up: Shift plus Backspace Down: Shift plus Enter Right: Ctrl Shift Enter Left: Ctrl Shift Backspace Return to no pan view (straight and level): Scroll Lock (or *) plus keypad 8
Tower	Control tower observation of your plane	S	+ Zoom in — Zoom out	View changes automatically	No panning possible
Spot	View of your plane, as seen from a chasing spot plane	S	+ Zoom in — Zoom out	Shift Key plus 7 8 9 / 4 5 6 / 1 2 3	Up: Shift plus Backspace Down: Shift plus Enter Right: Ctrl Shift Enter Left: Ctrl Shift Backspace Return to no pan view (straight and level): Scroll Lock (or *) plus keypad 8
Track (only available in dual player mode)	Track the other player's plane in dual player mode	S[2]	+ Zoom in — Zoom out	View changes automatically	No panning possible

Press S to quickly cycle between Cockpit, Tower, Track, and Spot views. (Track view is available only in dual-player mode).

box, you can also set the zoom magnification factor and direction for each view window.

Changing the Viewing Direction (Keyboard Method)

In both spot and cockpit views, you can choose one of nine different directions by pressing Shift in combination with the number keys 1, 2, 3, 4, 5, 6, 7, 8, and 9 from the numeric keypad, as seen in Figures 2.10 and

---

[2]Pressing S to switch to track view is only possible while in Dual Player Flight mode.

2.11. Along with choosing a directional view, you can also pan the view up by pressing [Shift] together with [Backspace], or down by pressing [Shift] together with [Enter]. To pan the view left, press [Ctrl] + [Shift] + [Backspace]; to pan the view right, press [Ctrl] + [Shift] + [Enter]. Table 2.3 displays the different view options that are available for the two 3-D view windows.

To change view directions in the Cockpit and Spot View windows, press [Shift] in combination with [1], [2], [3], [4], [5], [6], [7], [8], or [9] from the numeric keypad. To pan your view window up, press [Shift] + [Backspace]. To pan your view down, press [Shift] + [Enter]. To pan the view left, press [Ctrl] + [Shift] + [Backspace]; to pan the view right, press [Ctrl] + [Shift] + [Enter]. To return to straight and level view, with no panning, press [Scroll Lock] (or [*] from the numeric keypad) + [8].

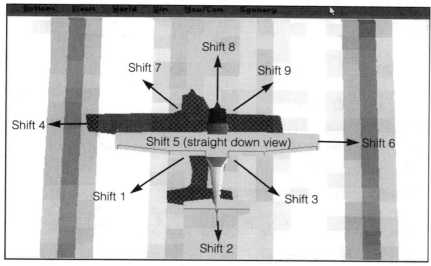

Figure 2.10 Cockpit view directions

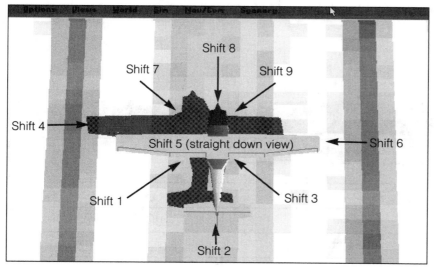

Figure 2.11 Spot view directions

Changing the Viewing Direction (View Options Dialog Box)

A second method of changing your view direction in both the spot and cockpit views is to set the view using the View Options command. Here is how to do this:

1. Open the Views menu.
2. Select the View Options command.
3. In the View Options dialog box, click open the Direction list box and select a particular direction you want.

Panning the 3-D View

In cockpit view only, you can pan the 3-D view window up and down, or left and right by using the keyboard. To pan up or down using the keyboard:

1. Press [Shift] + [Backspace] to pan your cockpit view up.
2. Press [Shift] + [Enter] to pan your cockpit view down.

You can also smoothly pan your view left or right in a 360-degree sweep around your aircraft by using the keyboard. To pan left or right:

1. Press [Ctrl] + [Shift] + [Backspace] to pan left.
2. Press [Ctrl] + [Shift] + [Enter] to pan right.

In all panning or view modes, press [Scroll Lock], or [*], then [8] (on the numeric keypad) to bring back a straight-ahead, level view.

Table 2.4 Panning Keys	
Pan Direction	**Key Combination**
Up	[Shift] [Backspace]
Down	[Shift] [Enter]
Left	[Ctrl] [Shift] [Backspace]
Right	[Ctrl] [Shift] [Enter]
Return to Normal Level View	[Scroll Lock], or [*], [8] (on numeric keypad)

Axis Indicator

If you have trouble determining exactly where your aircraft's nose is pointing, you can switch on the axis indicator, which displays either 4 dots, a
small v, or a large V in the center of the cockpit windshield. The axis indicator is useful for establishing your plane's current pitch. To turn on the axis
indicator:

1. Select the View Options command from the Views menu.
2. From the Axis Indicator list box, select one of the following options:
   4-Dots, Small V, Large V, or Off if you want to turn off the axis indicator.

Figure 2.12
Selecting the Axis
Indicator in the View
Options dialog box

Although the axis indicator shows the direction the
nose is pointing and its pitch in relation to the
ground, it does not tell you what direction the airplane is flying. This is because crosswinds, and using
certain yoke positions for your flight control scan
cause you to fly in a slightly skewed direction.

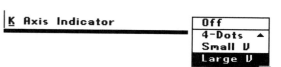

Titles on Windows

If you have trouble identifying which view you are currently looking at in
your windows, you can have the simulation display the title of each view for
all open windows. This is especially helpful when you are displaying more
than one window. To turn on titles:

1. Select View Options from the Views menu.
2. Toggle on the Titles on Windows check box.

Customizing Spot Plane View
Using the Set Spot Plane Command

Although you can easily switch view directions for the spot
plane view from the keyboard using [Shift], [1], [2], [3], [4],
[5], [6], [7], [8], or [9] numeric keypad combinations, and
zoom in or out, you can customize viewing parameters with
greater precision using the Set Spot Plane command and
control aerobatic viewing preferences. Using this menu command, you can precisely set the spot plane's position, set its
exact altitude, and set its distance from your plane. What's
more, for aerobatic maneuvers, you can select whether your
spot plane view is optimized for loops or for rolls, so you can
better keep your airplane in view.

For more precise positioning control
of your spot plane view, use the Set
Spot Plane command under the
Views menu to set altitude, precise
viewing angle, and aerobatic viewing
preferences. When you use the view
dot slider in the Set Spot Plane dialog box, you are not limited to 15-
degree view angle increments that
the keyboard method constrains you
to. Rather, you can specify any viewing angle from 0 to 360 degrees
around your plane.

Precision Placement of Spot Plane Viewing Angle

To precisely specify which direction you want to view your aircraft from, perform the following steps:

1. Select the Set Spot Plane command under the Views menu.

2. In the View Direction box of the Set Spot Plane dialog box, pictured in Figure 2.13, click the mouse on the dot next to the aircraft and drag it to the new viewing position. The dot, which turns red when selected, represents your spot plane and the direction it will view your plane, as depicted by the aircraft in the center.

3. If you are using the keyboard, the dot can be moved using the cursor arrow keys.

4. Click the OK button when you are finished.

Figure 2.13
Setting your spot
view angle for
viewing your plane

```
                    Set Spot Plane
Choose the window you want for Spot view.        ┌──────┐
View: [View 1 ▾]                                 │  OK  │
                                                 └──────┘
Choose how far away the spot plane is:           ┌────────┐
Distance (ft): [+000123]                         │ Cancel │
                                                 └────────┘
Altitude (ft): [+000016]

Preference:        Transition:        View Direction
◉ Roll             ◉ Slow           ┌──────────────────┐
○ Loop             ○ Fast           │                  │
                                    │       ╈        ● │
Use the mouse or the arrow keys to  │       ┬          │
move the spot plane position in the │                  │
View Direction box.                 └──────────────────┘

Once you've set the spot plane position, choose the OK
button and then press the S key to cycle to Spot view.
```

Click and drag this dot to set your spot plane's viewing position. Using this control, you are *not* limited to the standard 15° viewing angles that are possible from the keyboard.

Setting the Spot Plane's Distance and Altitude

The spot plane's distance and altitude are set in the Distance and Altitude text entry boxes of the Set Spot Plane dialog box. Distance is the span that separates the spot plane from your plane, whereas altitude is the difference in altitude between the spot plane and your plane. Positive altitudes put the spot plane above your plane, and negative altitudes put the spot plane below your plane. Altitude can never be set such that your spot plane would be below ground level.

✈ **Tip:** For an undocumented and interesting spot view from straight above looking down at your plane below, press Shift + 5 and then set the distance (in this case, distance is the same as altitude) in the Set Spot Plane dialog box.

Rolling or Looping Preferences

These viewing preferences are used exclusively to optimize your spot view of aerobatic rolls and loops that you perform in your plane.

Selecting Roll causes the spot plane to fly on the same heading on one side of your plane while it completes a full barrel roll. Selecting Loop causes the spot plane to fly relative to one side of your wing in a horizontal plane. When your plane starts to loop, the spot plane flies on in a horizontal direction, tracking one wing side of your aircraft. This allows you to stay on one side of your looping plane so that you can watch the entire maneuver.

Transition Slow/Fast

If you prefer to instantly jump between views while in spot view, select the Fast transition option in the Set Spot Plane dialog box. I prefer the Slow transition because I like to view the gradual panning between different viewing angles, and I think it has a much more thrilling 3-D effect.

MAP VIEW

The Map view, which is brought up in a separate window from the two 3-D windows, gives you a scrolling terrain map that you can use for navigation purposes. The map can be zoomed from 200 feet all the way to a whole earth view at 160,000 miles (257,440 kilometers) by using the zoom indicator on-screen or by activating the map, and then pressing ⊞ to zoom in, or ⊟ to zoom out. (Both keys are on the main keyboard, not the numeric keypad.) The center of the map has two red crosshairs, which define the location of the aircraft. The top vertical line of the crosshairs represents the aircraft's nose and the current direction the plane is traveling. You will notice that the map is aircraft oriented; that is, the map will rotate in response to changes in the aircraft's heading. If you find this confusing, you can always change the map display through the Display Preferences dialog box under the Options menu, and freeze the map in a north orientation. Then, regardless of your plane's heading, the map would always appear fixed (meaning that it wouldn't rotate), although your airplane's crosshairs would move around as your position changed. Figures 2.14 and 2.15 show the map in two different magnification factors: the first is a zoomed-in, close-up view of the runway, and the second is a zoomed-out, far-away view of the Earth.

To change the map orientation, follow these steps:

1. Under the Views menu, select Preferences.
2. Click the Display button.
3. Pull down the Map Display list box.
4. Select either North Oriented for a non-rotating map fixed in a north direction, Aircraft Oriented for a rotating map that has the aircraft's heading always pointing toward the top red crosshair, or North at High Altitude for a north-oriented, non-rotating map at zoomed out to a high altitude.

The map can be viewed in aircraft orientation (the map rotates when the aircraft turns), or north orientation (the map moves, but does not rotate when the aircraft turns. Also, north is always pointing straight up). A third map orientation, North at High Altitude, causes the map to display a north orientation but at high altitude for navigating long distances. All of these map-viewing options are found under the Display Preferences command of the Options menu.

Figure 2.14
Map zoomed in to 200
feet altitude

Map is zoomed
to 200 ft above
ground level

Runway numbers show runway
heading. 36 signifies runway
faces 360° or 0° due north

This marker
represents
your plane

You can also zoom
the map by clicking
the zoom indicator

Orbital view of Earth,
160,000 miles in space

Figure 2.15
Map zoomed out to
160,000 miles

Map Display:	Aircraft Oriented
	North Oriented
	•Aircraft Oriented
	North at High Alt.

Figure 2.16 The Map
Display list box

MINI-CONTROLS

Enabling this option under the Views menu causes a separate control position indicator window to be displayed on-screen. This indicator shows the position of your plane's elevators, ailerons, rudders, and throttle controls, as well as displaying the current airspeed, and is useful for when you cannot see your instrument panel, such as when flying with full screen view for a 3-D window.

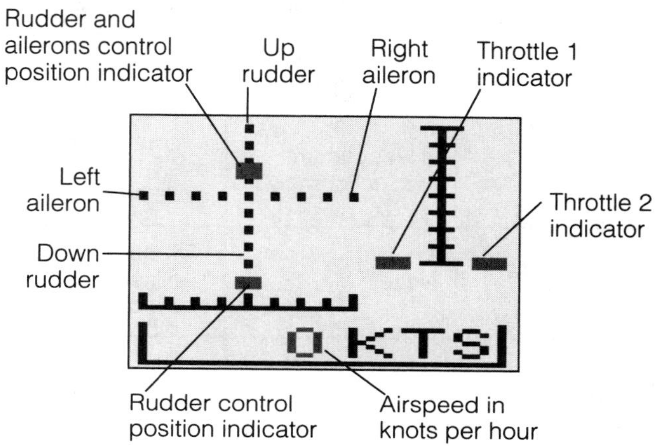

The mini-control window can be moved to any point on the screen by clicking and dragging the mouse pointer on the top of the window, or from the keyboard by using the Size and Move Windows command from the Views menu. (See earlier section on moving windows using the keyboard in this chapter.) It cannot be resized.

Figure 2.17
The mini-control window

INSTRUMENT PANELS

Flight Simulator 5.0 allows up to three different instrument panels, although at present only the Learjet is able to use more than one panel.[3] As mentioned earlier, the instrument panel can be moved on-screen by dragging the top border of the panel with the mouse, or by using the Size and Move Windows command via the keyboard, but it cannot be resized. Moving the instrument panel down is useful for when you want to make room to display a larger 3-D window or map on-screen.

Instrument Subsections

Flight Simulator 5.0 has a new feature that allows some aircraft to have additional instrument subsections displayed. Don't confuse instrument subsections with the three instrument panels, for they are separate. Table 2.5 shows that only the Learjet has instrument subsections and additional instrument panels available.

---

[3]The Learjet's second instrument panel is the digital magnetic compass that you see displayed on the right cockpit windshield. There are no other instruments associated with this panel.

Table 2.5 Instrument Panels and Subsections that are Available for the Flight Simulator Aircraft				
	Cessna Skylane 182 RG	**Learjet 35A**	**Schweizer 2-32 Sailplane**	**Sopwith Camel**
Instrument Panel 1	No instrument subsections[4]	Instrument subsections available (Use Tab to cycle between)	No instrument subsections	No instrument subsections
Instrument Panel 2	None	Compass Center Post (No instrument subsections available)	None	None
Instrument Panel 3	None	None	None	None

Press Tab to cycle among the instrument subsections on each instrument panel.

To access the instrument subsections, simply press Tab, and to return to the normal instrument panel display, press Tab again. The Learjet's instrument subsection displays engine monitoring devices, such as turbine speed gauges, engine switches, oil pressure and temperature gauges, as well as fuel-flow and fuel-capacity meters.

Switching Among the Three Instrument Panels

Switching among the three instrument panels is accomplished by first enabling the TAB On/Off option under the three Instrument Panel list boxes. At present, you cannot switch among other instrument panels using Tab, because none of the four basic aircraft have multiple panels that you can fully use. (The Learjet's second instrument panel consists of only one instrument: the compass center post.)

Switching the Three Instrument Panels On or Off

Why would you want to turn any of these instruments, controls, or aircraft systems off, you may wonder? Well, for training purposes, you might want

---

[4]The Cessna has an instrument subsection only while in VGA or EGA modes, but not in Super VGA. This is because, at the lower resolutions, not all the instruments can be displayed simultaneously like they are in Super VGA. While using FS 5.0 at these lower resolution, use the Tab to bring up the instrument subsections.

to simulate the failure of some part of the aircraft and learn how to keep the aircraft under control. While instrument flying at night, you might lose your gyroscope, pitot-static, or vacuum system, thereby disabling most of your crucial altitude/attitude instruments. Or, you might experience a complete radio failure, or lose an entire instrument panel due to an electrical short circuit, and be unable to navigate. What would you do under such circumstances? *Flight Simulator 5.0* gives you the tools to learn and test how you would react under emergency situations, all without risking your life.

Through the Instrument Panel Options command under the Views menu, you can:

- Switch any of the three instrument panels on or off.
- Turn on or off any primary instrument from among the standard instrument cluster.
- Turn on or off any NAV/COM instrument.
- Disable or enable any aircraft subsystem, including the pitot-static, vacuum, fuel, engine, and electrical systems.

To switch off or switch on any one of your three instrument panels, perform one of the following steps:

- Open the Instrument Panel Options dialog box from the Views menu and click the Instrument Panels option. This option is a toggle; that is, you can turn it off or on by selecting it again. A check mark will appear beside the option name when the panel is on. No check mark will appear when the panel is off.

- To switch off or on all instrument panels, toggle the Master Switch (All Panels) check box switch, as illustrated in Figure 2.18. Alternatively, while you are in the cockpit, from the keyboard simply press (Shift) + ([). A check mark appears beside the option name when the switch is on. No check mark appears when the switch is off.

- To switch off or on any individual panel, select the appropriate panel from one of the three Instrument Panel list boxes, and select Off or On. If your aircraft does not have multiple panels, the Instrument Panel 2 and Instrument Panel 3 list boxes will be dimmed out.

The (Shift) + ([) combination is a toggle, which will quickly turn on or off all instrument panels.

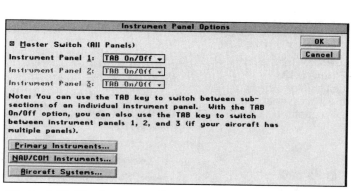

Figure 2.18 The Instrument Panel Options dialog box

How to Turn Off the Learjet's Compass Center Post (Instrument Panel 2)

To turn off the Learjet's compass center post, which is sometimes annoying because it blocks your cockpit view, follow these steps:

1. While the Learjet's instrument panel is displayed on-screen, select the Instrument Panels Options from the Views menu.
2. Select the Instrument Panel 2 list box, and highlight the Off option.
3. Click the OK button. When you return to the cockpit, the compass center post will be gone.

Covering or Disabling Instruments and Aircraft Systems

To cripple, or cover, any aircraft instrument or system, follow these steps:

1. Select the Instrument Panel Options command from the Views menu.
2. Choose the type of instrument or system you wish to cover or cause a malfunction to. In the Instrument Panel Options dialog box, shown in the previous figure, click on one of the following:

   - Primary Instruments button if you want to disable the airspeed indicator, attitude indicator, turn rate indicator, altimeter, vertical speed indicator, or heading indicator.
   - NAV/COM Instruments button if you want to disable the COM, NAV, Transponder, ADF, or magnetic compass.
   - Aircraft Systems button if you want to disable the entire pitot-static, vacuum, fuel, engine, or electrical systems.

3. Select the instrument or system you wish to incapacitate by clicking the list box and selecting from among:

   - Operative,
   - Inoperative, or
   - Covered

Figure 2.19
Options for disabling
the instruments and
subsystems

Figure 2.20
The Primary
Instrument list boxes

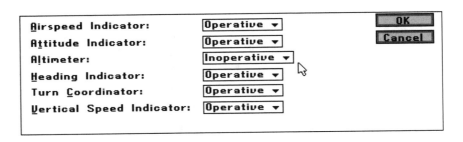

Table 2.6   Aircraft Instruments and Systems

	Cessna Skylane 182 RG	Learjet 35A	Schweizer 2-32 Sailplane	Sopwith Camel
Primary Instruments				
Airspeed Indicator	X	X	X	X
Attitude Indicator	X	X		
Altimeter	X	X	X	X
Heading Indicator	X	X		
Turn Coordinator	X	X		
Vertical Speed Indicator	X	X	X	
NAV/COM Instruments				
COM	X	X	X	
NAV	X	X		
Transponder	X	X		
ADF	X	X		
Magnetic Compass	X	X	X	X
Aircraft Systems				
Pitot /Static	X	X	X	X
Vacuum	X	X		
Fuel	X	X		X
Engine	X	X		X
Electrical	X	X	X	

(See Figure 2.20 for an example of how to disable the altimeter. In this figure, the altimeter has been made inoperable, and will not appear on the standard instrument cluster when you return to the cockpit.)

4. When you are finished, click OK to return to the Instrument Panel Options dialog box, then click OK again to return to the cockpit.

The instruments or aircraft systems will now be inoperative or covered.

Note that for some aircraft, not all the instruments and systems are available. Table 2.6 illustrates which instruments and systems are present on the four default FS 5.0 aircraft.

PRINTING YOUR FLIGHT PHOTOGRAPHS

Flight Simulator includes a great new feature for snapping pictures of your screens. Through the Flight Photograph command under the View menu, you can screen capture the whole screen, an individual 3-D window, the map view, or any individual instrument panel into a .PCX graphic file that you name on your hard disk.

Let's try capturing and printing a full-screen spot plane view of your plane as it is flying towards Chicago. We will be using Windows Paintbrush and assume that you have a good graphics-capable printer. Here's how to do this:

1. Take off from Meigs Field and head towards downtown Chicago, flying at a level of 1,500 feet or so.
2. Press ⟨S⟩ twice to bring up spot view.
3. Select your viewing angle. For this example, I have used the right rear view, or from the keyboard, ⟨Shift⟩ + ⟨3⟩.
4. Press ⟨W⟩ to maximize the 3-D window to full screen.
5. Pull down the Views menu and select Flight Photograph.
6. In the Flight Photograph dialog box, pictured in Figure 2.21, click the Window list box and select Whole Screen.
7. Type a file name, such as **Chicapic**, in the Filename text entry box. This is the name that the .PCX graphic will be given.
8. Click the OK button and quickly move your mouse to the top of the screen (or click the right mouse button to make the pointer disappear) to avoid having it mar your picture.
9. In a few seconds the screen will freeze and remain frozen until the screen capture is complete.
10. Exit Flight Simulator.
11. Start up Windows and open Paintbrush, in the accessories group.

Figure 2.21
The Flight Photograph
dialog box

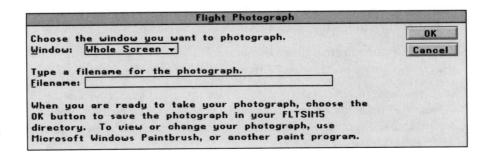

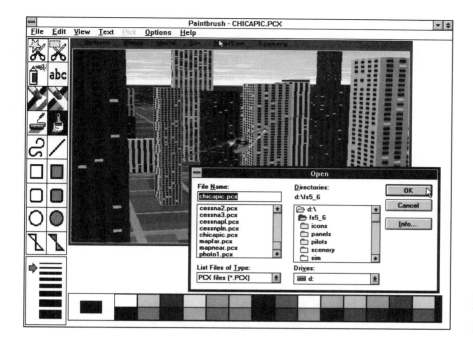

Figure 2.22
The Open File dialog
box in Paintbrush

12. In Paintbrush, pull down the File menu, select Open, and move to the Flight Simulator directory.

13. Select the List Files of Type list box and highlight PCX. Your window should look like Figure 2.22.

14. Click on the Chicapic.pcx file; in a few moments the picture will open up on-screen.

15. Open the File menu and select Print.

16. Click OK and your picture will commence printing.

C H A P T E R

3

Simulation Controls

Flight Simulator has many menu options and commands that affect how the simulator operates. This chapter introduces you to some of the main controls that you access through the pull-down menus. Each person has a unique set of preferences, and through the simulator's ability to customize itself to your liking, you can modify the "off the shelf" default characteristics of the program until you are happy with how the program runs.

SETTING YOUR PREFERENCES

Through the Preferences option under the Options menu, you can choose *Flight Simulator*'s default drivers as well as choose which startup features the program will include when you first boot the program up. Within the Preferences dialog box (Figure 3.1) you will find buttons for:

- General Preferences
- Display Preferences
- Sound Preferences
- Keyboard Preferences
- Mouse Preferences
- Joystick Preferences
- Country Preferences
- Instrument Preferences

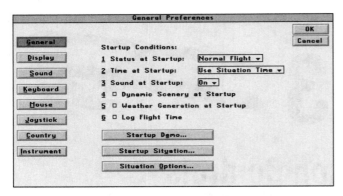

Figure 3.1
The General
Preferences dialog box

To bring up each Preference dialog box, click the button's name. When you are finished with a particular preference box, but need to modify another preference, click on the Preference button you wish to activate; it will open up the dialog box you wish. After completing all your selections, click the OK button.

Rebooting *Flight Simulator* When New Software Drivers Are Selected

Software drivers are special modules of computer code that are written so that a particular device can work properly. For example, in Windows 3.1, most printers and super VGA cards have their own drivers, which must be installed before they can work. Windows, or any program that uses a driver, must be told about the choice of drivers, and then must be restarted before the drivers can be used. This is what must also happen in *Flight Simulator*; if you have modified any of the startup software drivers, you will be presented with a dialog box that tells you that you must exit *Flight Simulator* and restart it for the changes to take effect. In this instance, click the Exit Flight Simulator and Restart button if you want *Flight Simulator* to exit and then restart the program automatically with the new drivers; or click the OK button if you are not yet prepared to do this.

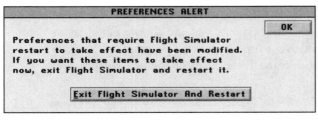

Figure 3.2
Reboot dialog box

General Preferences

Under the General Preferences dialog box, shown in Figure 3.1, you can select your startup situation, startup demo, or various other startup aspects, including what options are saved or are loaded each time you restart the program or situation.

Figure 3.3
Status at startup

Status at Startup

Using this list box, you can choose whether *Flight Simulator* starts up in Normal Flight mode, Demo Flight mode with Sound, or Demo Flight mode without Sound. You will probably always want to leave this selected on Normal Flight Mode, since this mode is the only one you can fly the simulator in. In Normal Mode, the situation that you have chosen in the Startup Situation button becomes the default opening situation. (If you haven't selected a situation, FS 5.0 will default to Chicago's Meigs Field.)

Use demo mode if you want an instant, walk-through tour of Flight Simulator's capabilities. If you were a retailer selling *Flight Simulator*, for example, and you wanted to show what the program could do, you might want to leave the program perpetually on in demo mode, perhaps with the sound off so as not to deafen your customers while you give the sales pitch.

Time at Startup

This list box offers you the choice of using your computer's clock as the basis for setting *Flight Simulator*'s clock, or the time that you saved in a particular situation. If you want the program at startup to always match the time of day with your computer's clock, select Use System Time. If, on the other hand, you always like to fly at night, and you want the situation time you have saved on disk to override the system clock, choose Use Situation Time.

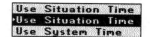

Figure 3.4
Time at startup

Sound at Startup

There are three options for enabling sound at startup:

- **Off:** Sound always off
- **On:** Sound always on
- **See Situation File:** Sound off or on depending on whether you had it turned on or off at the time of saving the situation file

Figure 3.5
Sound at startup

Dynamic Scenery at Startup

This checkbox toggle switches on or off the dynamic scenery at startup. Dynamic scenery consists of all moving objects, such as other airplanes, airport traffic, ground traffic, boats, hot air balloons, etcetera.

4 ☐ Dynamic Scenery at Startup

Figure 3.6
Scenery at Startup

Weather Generation at Startup

Toggling on Weather Generation at Startup enables the automatic weather generator to function. Toggling it off shuts off any random weather fluctuations.

5 ☐ Weather Generation at Startup

Figure 3.7
Weather Generation
at Startup

Log Flight Time

The Log Flight Time checkbox allows you to decide whether to keep track of all your flights in a special pilot log. If toggled on, at the end of every flight a pilot log will be displayed in which you can record the number of hours flown at night, day, or under IFR rules, the type of aircraft, the date, and the aircraft flown. Even if you toggle this feature off at startup, you can always turn it on manually from inside the program.

Figure 3.8
Log Flight Time

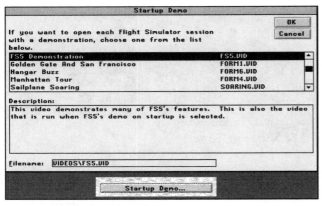

Figure 3.9
Startup Demo

Startup Demo

Press this button in the General Preferences dialog box to select which startup demo *Flight Simulator* will show. The demo options appear as shown in Figure 3.7. You can record your own demo and then use this command to run it, instead of using the default FS 5.0 demo.

Startup Situation

This button command allows you to select the default startup situation. Use this button to bring up a favorite situation that you have previously created and saved as your default startup situation.

Figure 3.10
Startup Situation

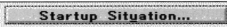

Situation Options

This button brings up a dialog box with many different situation options that you can save or not save each time you start up a situation. You can save Instrument Panel and View Window positions, aircraft, scenery, dynamic scenery, and the weather. You can also choose whether you want to load specific aircraft, scenery, keyboard sensitivities, mouse sensitivities, and joystick sensitivities.

Figure 3.11
Situation Options

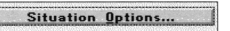

Display Preferences

The Display Preferences dialog box presents you with many options that affect your display. It is in this dialog box that you can choose a different graphics driver, select your graphics mode, and set various options that make the scenery more interesting. You can also choose to degrade your image quality, and increase your flicker rate in order to increase the frame rate for a smoother, less choppy image. To really speed up your frame rate, however, you should also open the Scenery Complexity and

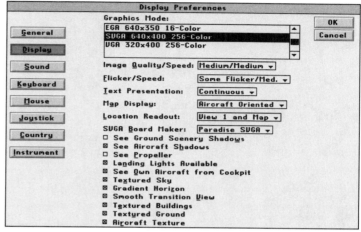

Figure 3.12
The Display
Preferences dialog box

Dynamic Scenery menu items under the Scenery Menu, and choose Very Sparse for the Image Frequency and Scenery Frequency options. Figure 3.12 illustrates the Display Preferences dialog box.

Graphics Mode

With the Graphics Mode list box, you can choose what display resolution Flight Simulator will display. There are three options: EGA 640 horizontal lines by 350 vertical lines with 16 colors; VGA 320 horizontal lines by 400 vertical lines with

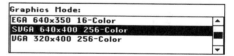

Figure 3.13
Graphics Mode list box

256 colors; and Super VGA or SVGA 640 horizontal lines by 400 vertical lines with 256 colors. For some 386 users, it may be advisable to use VGA instead of SVGA, for faster speed despite the fact that you have an SVGA card.

Image Quality/Speed

Figure 3.14
Image Quality/Speed
list box

Because there is always a tradeoff between image quality and speed, you must decide whether you prefer lower quality images and a faster display, medium-quality images and a medium-fast display, or high-quality images and a slow display. I prefer the High quality/Slow display option, but since I am running FS 5.0 on a 486 66 MHz PC with an extremely fast video accelerator card, this does not present a problem to me. If you are experiencing choppy frame rates, then choose Low/Fast. The Image Quality/Speed tradeoff is dependent on the area you are in; the more complex the scenery area, the slower the speed will be.

Figure 3.15
Flicker/Speed list box

Flicker/Speed

Flicker rate determines the rate at which multiple windows are repainted. If there is no flicker, each 3-D scenery window that is open gets repainted more often. (The lower the flicker rate, the more frequent the view windows are refreshed; whereas the higher the flicker rate, the less frequent the view windows are refreshed.) The tradeoff is that, with a low or nonexistent flicker rate, the speed at which scenery can be drawn slows down. (There are more frames per second to complete because of the low flicker rate.) In essence, like image quality/speed, you must make a call as to which tradeoff you prefer. With faster machines, this isn't a problem, and you can select No Flicker/Slow.

Figure 3.16
Text Presentation list box

Text Presentation

This list box allows you to choose between having air traffic control messages horizontally scrolled across your screen in a continuous stream, or having your messages displayed a single line at a time.

Figure 3.17
Map Display list box

Map Display

Your on-screen map can be displayed in three forms:

- North Oriented—The map does not rotate and north is always facing towards the top of the display
- North at High Altitude—This is like North Oriented, except that the aircraft is zoomed out to a high altitude so that more landscape is covered
- Aircraft Oriented—The map rotates and the aircraft, which is represented by the center crosshair, is always pointed toward the top of the display.

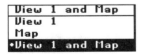

Figure 3.18
Location Readout list box

Location Readout

Your geographical coordinates can be displayed at the top of the screen using one of the following configurations:

- View 1 window (displayed only in the 3-D View 1 window)
- View 1 and Map (displayed in both 3-D View 1 window and Map window)
- Map (displayed only in the Map window)

To toggle on your on-screen coordinates, press (Shift) (Z).

SVGA Board Maker

You should already have installed the correct display driver for *Flight Simulator*, but in case you want to change drivers, you can call up the SVGA Board Maker list box to summon a list of the graphic accelerator chips and boards that are supported. If you don't know what board you have, try selecting VESA 1.2 Compatible, since many board makers try to conform to this standard.[1]

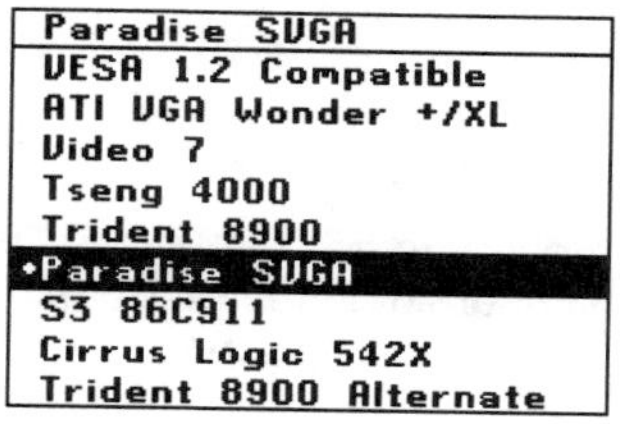

Figure 3.19
SVGA Board Maker list box

Other Visual Effects

At the bottom of the Display Preferences dialog box, you can see a series of check boxes, which allow you to add special effects to the scenery. With a 486 or faster, you should toggle on all of the check boxes to take advantage of aircraft shadows, propeller motion, ground scenery, sky texture for gradient hues that change for the time of day, textured buildings, textured aircraft, textured ground, landing lights, smooth transition when panning or switching different views, and seeing your own aircraft when looking out your cockpit windows.

Sound Preferences

Although you don't need a sound card to play *Flight Simulator* (you can use the PC's built-in speaker with less than desirable results), for best sound fidelity you should consider using a sound card. The Sound Preferences dialog box, shown in Figure 3.22, allows you to choose which sound card driver you want to use, the driver's hardware settings, and what kinds of sounds you want played back. There are three check boxes for Engine Sounds, Cockpit Sounds, and Navigation Sounds. If you get easily tired by monotonous sounds, you might want to toggle off the Engine Sounds control, or you might consider sliding the Volume control to a lower setting. To move the Volume slide, click and drag it with the mouse, or with the keyboard press [V], then the right cursor key to increase, or the left cursor key to decrease. You cannot, however, set the volume on your PC's built-in speaker. On some cards, the Volume slide will be dimmed out, which tells you that the sound card's volume cannot be adjusted while in *Flight Simulator*. All is not lost in such a situation, though, for most cards have a dial on the back of

Figure 3.20
Engine Sounds list box

---

[1]At present, the Hercules Graphite does not work with FS 5.0. There is a work around available that will enable you to use the card. Call Hercules or Microsoft for an updated driver.

Figure 3.21
Sound Boards
supported under the
Sound Board list box

the card, which allows you to manually set the volume.

The Cockpit Sounds check box, when switched on, allows you to hear warning klaxons when your aircraft is about to stall. It also enables crash sound effects, and beeps to alert you to messages from your friend while in dual-player flight.

The Navigation Sounds check box, when switched on, allows you to hear the marker beacons while using the ILS landing system.

If you have problems with your sound card, more likely than not, it is because your hardware defaults are incorrectly set. You may have to reset the Base Address, Interrupt, or DMA Channel list box settings to match the configuration of your card. There is nothing to fear about doing this. Just check your documentation and setup on your PC to see if you can figure out what the correct settings are. For my Sound Blaster 16, for example, I had to reset the Interrupt from 7 to 5, and presto—the card worked.

If you are the proud owner of a Sound Blaster 16ASP (Advanced Signal Processing) with Wave Blaster, and you experience fade-out problems or any other glitches, try using the plain Sound Blaster driver, and not the Sound Blaster Pro driver. Otherwise, if it works under the Sound Blaster Pro driver, leave well enough alone.

Note that the Adlib card does not support digitized sounds, so most sounds are shunted through the PC's crummy little speaker.

For those cards that support XMS memory (extended memory above your conventional 640K), you can allow this memory to be used by selecting

Figure 3.22
Sound Preferences
dialog box

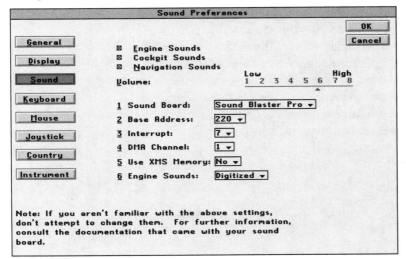

Yes from the Use XMS Memory button. If you can us EMS memory with your sound card, do so. It will considerably speed up your frame rate.

The Engine Sounds list box is best set to Digitized for more authentic-sounding noises. The Synthesized option sounds much worse because it uses FM (Frequency Modulated) synthesized tones to approximate the engine sounds. Digitized uses real wave forms, and sounds much more realistic.

Keyboard Preferences

The three slider preference controls in the Keyboard Preferences dialog box, pictured in Figure 3.23, allow you to set the sensitivity for the keyboard yoke controls. The higher the sensitivity is set, the faster the controls react to your touch, but at the expense of controlling your aircraft as well. Too low a sensitivity, on the other hand, tends to make the keyboard controls too sluggish and unresponsive.

To save your favorite sensitivity setting, so that you don't have to keep re-entering it every time you start up *Flight Simulator*, toggle on the Load Sensitivities Saved with Situation check box.

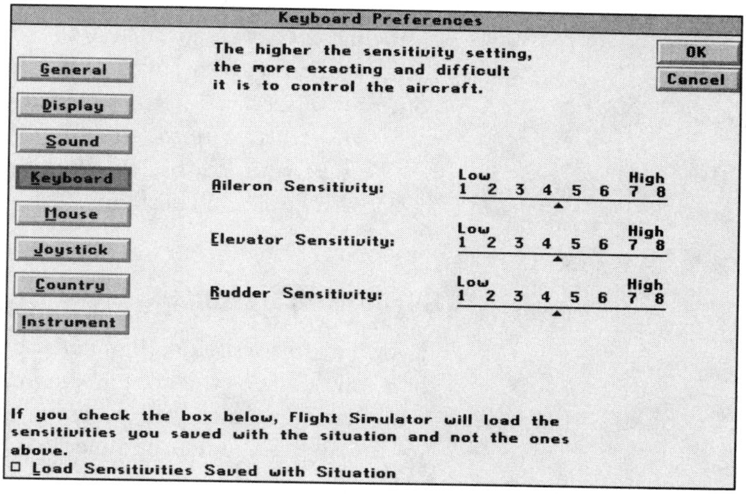

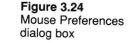

Figure 3.23
Keyboard Preferences
dialog box

Mouse Preferences

There are four slider preference controls in the Mouse Preferences dialog box, illustrated in Figure 3.24 that allow you to set the sensitivity for the mouse yoke. Only the aileron and elevator yoke controls are listed because the mouse is usually flown in auto-coordinated mode, and the rudder is automatically turned when you move the ailerons. In uncoordinated flight, the mouse would control only the ailerons and elevators, and you would use the keyboard to move the rudder. In such a situation, the sensitivity level for the rudder would be set in the Keyboard Preferences dialog box.

Figure 3.24
Mouse Preferences
dialog box

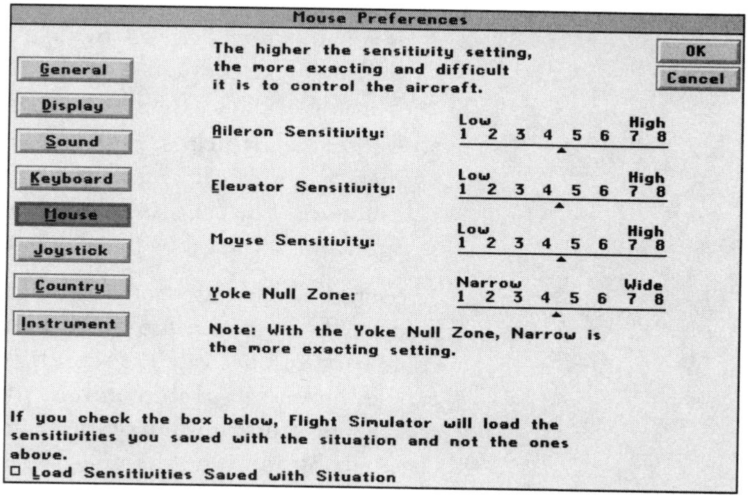

By adjusting the Yoke Null Zone width, you can find a comfortable zone where you can move your joystick slightly without causing the plane to bank, climb, or descend. The null zone refers to that portion of the center of the joystick where the ailerons remain centered. A wider null zone gives your joystick a looser feel, whereas a narrower zone gives your joystick a tighter feel. Too narrow a zone can be annoying since every joystick jitter can cause the plane to start turning. Click the Load Sensitivities Saved with Situation check box if you want to load your previously saved settings so that you don't have to constantly reset them each time you start up the situation.

To save your favorite sensitivity setting, toggle on the Load Sensitivities Saved with Situation check box.

Joystick Preferences

If you have a joystick or flightstick plugged into the game port of your PC, then you will need to configure and calibrate it before you can fly *Flight Simulator*. Some people prefer to use two joysticks in combination, one to control the ailerons/rudder and elevator, the second to control the throttle and brakes. (Or when using pedals as your second joystick, you can set the second joystick to control the rudder.) But for now, let's assume that you are using a single joystick. Since FS 5.0 has no way of knowing beforehand where your joystick/flightstick is centered, you will need to instruct the program as to its initial settings via a process known as calibration. If you don't do this, then your joystick might send the wrong signal to the program as to its true position, and you will have to fly a plane that chronically turns, climbs, or dives, even though your stick is apparently centered.

To set and calibrate your joystick/flightstick, follow these steps:

1. Click the pull-down list box for joystick 1: and select Aileron & Elevator. (A list box is a text box with several options listed that drops down when you click on it. Notice that the current selection in the list box has a dot on the left side.)

2. If you are using a second joystick, pedals, or a flightstick with throttle/brake controls, click the pull-down Joystick 2 list box and select Throttle & Brakes (or Throttle & Rudder if using pedals).

3. Center the joystick, or both joysticks (or flightstick and rudder pedals), then click the Calibrate button. Your joystick/flightstick is now calibrated! You can also calibrate your joysticks directly from the simulator keyboard by pressing K.

The sensitivity setting controls how much joystick movement will affect the aircraft. If you notice too much movement of the controls, then you can come back and decrease the sensitivity. On the other hand, if you don't get enough movement of the controls, you can increase the sensitivity. The null zone refers to that portion of the center of the joystick where the ailerons are centered. By adjusting the null zone sensitivity, you can find a comfortable zone where you can move your joystick slightly without causing the plane to bank, climb, or descend. A wider null zone gives your joystick a looser feel, whereas a narrower zone gives your joystick a tighter feel. Too narrow a zone can be annoying since every joystick jitter can cause the plane to start turning. Click the Load Sensitivities Saved with Situation check box if you want to load these settings so that you don't have to constantly reset them each time you start up the situation.

Country Preferences

Because *Flight Simulator* has now developed a huge international following, BAO/Microsoft decided to include worldwide support in the form of metric units of measurement and a spherical, latitude-longitude coordinate system to replace the older FS 4.0 "flat world," North-East coordinate system. In the Country Preferences dialog box, shown in Figure 3.25, you can select the units of measurement that you prefer from among the following:

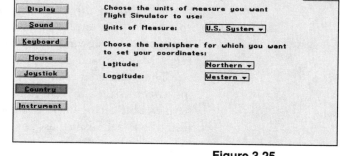

Figure 3.25
Country Preferences dialog box

- U.S. System: Distances measured in miles, altitude in feet, weight in pounds.

- Metric (Alt feet): Altimeter is measured in feet, but distances and speed in mks or SI units (mks-meters, kilograms, seconds, otherwise called the Systeme Internationale for the worldwide agreement on the adaptation of the metric system for standard measurements of time, mass, and length).

Metric (Alt meters): SI or mks units, but altimeter is now measured in meters instead of feet.[2]

Latitude is measured from 0 to 90 degrees from the equator to the poles in both the Northern and Southern Hemispheres of the Earth. Longitude is measured from 0 to 180 degrees from the Prime Meridian in England in both the Western and Eastern Hemispheres. Knowing your latitude and longitude is not enough to locate you if you don't specify which hemisphere you are in. For example, if you say that you are at 30 degrees latitude, 90 degrees longitude, another person trying to locate you would not know if you are at 30 latitude degrees South of the equator, or 30 degrees latitude North of the

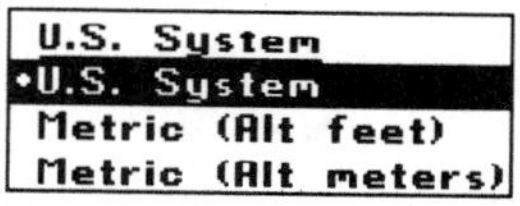

Figure 3.26
Units of measure

---

[2]In the world of International Aviation, altitude is always measured in feet. Also, interestingly enough, the lingua franca of Air Traffic Contol (ATC) communication is English.

equator. To prevent confusion as to your correct latitude, or longitude, in *Flight Simulator*, you must specify the proper hemisphere in the Country Preferences dialog box.

Thus, for example, to fly in the Northern and Western Hemispheres, select the Northern option from the Latitude list box and the Western option from the Longitude box.

Instrument Preferences

Through this dialog box, illustrated in Figure 3.27, you can change your instrument gauges, update rate to make them more realistic, make your panel display more legible, display indicated airspeed instead of true airspeed, and modify the number of frequencies your radios can receive.

Maximizing the gauge update rate causes your instruments to display changes in your airplane's attitude, speed, or position more quickly, but at the expense of slowing down the scenery display. You can choose between High, Medium, and Low update rates.

The numbered readings on the dials and gauges of the photo realistic instrument panel are not easily readable because of their small size. If you have trouble seeing these instruments, you can select Enhanced Readability from the Panel Display list box, and the photo-realistic panel will be replaced by a new panel with more legible numbers. It's not as pretty, but it is easier to make out the dial markings.

If you are interested in super-realism, then you should toggle on the Display Indicated Airspeed check box to have your airspeed indicator show indicated airspeed instead of true airspeed. True airspeed is defined as the speed of an aircraft in undisturbed air, corrected for air-density variations from the standard value at sea level. Indicated airspeed is the value read on the airspeed indicator, without regard to altitude or outside air density. In the imaginary world of *Flight Simulator*, your airspeed indicator tells you the true airspeed at which you are traveling, despite the fact that your airspeed indicator can only give you accurate readings at sea level. In the real world, however, the higher you go, the less the air density is, and the less reliable the air pressure readings are in the pitot-static pressure system, from which the airspeed indicator derives its speed measurements.

The correction factor for true airspeed when you are flying at higher altitudes can be summarized by the following rule:

> Add two percent to your indicated airspeed per
> thousand feet of altitude gained.

Thus, if you are showing an indicated airspeed of 100 knots at sea level, your true airspeed will also be 100 knots. But if you are at 5,000 feet, your true airspeed will be 110 knots (i.e., 5 × 2 percent = 10 percent, add 10 percent to 100 knots = 110 knots).

Additionally, in the Instrument Preferences dialog box, you can increase the number of radio channels to 725 by choosing to have a narrower 25 KHz COM Radio frequency channel separation. (For the same bandwidth, the narrower the channel width, the more channels can be squeezed in the band.) You can also modify the tuning parameters of the ADF Radio so that it too has a narrower 500 Hz channel separation.

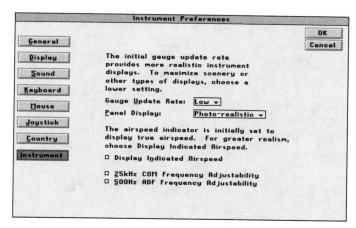

Figure 3.27
Instrument Preferences dialog box

SOUND OFF/ON

Under the Sim menu, you can toggle all sound on or off by selecting the Sound command. Pressing Q accomplishes the same task. If you prefer, you can selectively turn off engine sounds, cockpit sounds, and navigation sounds under the Sound Preferences dialog box under the Options menu.

PAUSE

To completely pause the simulation, select the Pause command under the Sim menu. When you do this, you will see the word "Pause" displayed on-screen. During this time, when all simulation events are frozen, you can still access all the menus and controls that you could normally access while flying. You can also activate the pause function by pressing P. To resume play, press P again.

Figure 3.28
The Crash Detection dialog box

CRASH DETECTION

By disabling crash detection, you can practice flying your plane without fear of crashing. Any accidents or collisions are ignored. There are various other crash options, which are self explanatory, as illustrated in Figure 3.28.

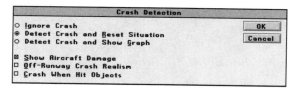

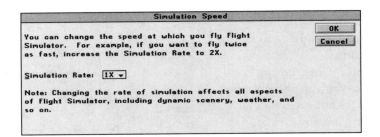

Figure 3.29
The Simulation
Speed dialog box

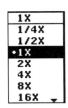

Figure 3.30
The Simulation
Rate list box

SIMULATION SPEED

You can also affect the time rate at which *Flight Simulator* runs through the Simulation Speed command. This command can be activated by selecting the Simulation Speed option from the Sim menu, then choosing a rate from the Simulation Rate list box, shown in Figure 3.29 and Figure 3.30. You can choose to slow down the simulation to as much as ¼ times normal time, or increase the time rate to as much as 128 times normal time. This function is useful for long cross-country or cross-oceanic trips in which you want to speed up the simulation so that you can quickly skip over the dull, monotonous portions of the flight. Note that increasing or decreasing the simulation speed control does not affect the frame rate or the speed of your CPU. The only thing that changes is your time, as measured on the digital clock, which speeds up or slows down.

Normal simulator speed is 1x. Choosing a higher speed will change not only the speed of your aircraft, but will increase the activity of the world around you. Clouds and weather will whip by, and every minute motion that you make using the yoke controls becomes amplified. At high simulator speeds, it is very easy to slam into the ground in a fraction of a second, so exercise caution when using this feature.

Learjet and Cessna Simulation Speed Can Be Set On-Screen

On both the Learjet and Cessna, you can adjust the simulation speed by clicking on the RATE indicator, just below the digital clock. To increase the rate, click to the right of the number, and to decrease the rate, click to the left of the number.

Unfortunately, the Sailplane and Sopwith Camel Simulation Speed must be set from the menu because there is no Simulation Rate control/indicator on their respective instrument panels.

SMOKE SYSTEM

To create contrails, or puffs of smoke emanating from the tail of the aircraft, press ☐ or select the Smoke System option from the Sim menu. These smoke streams are visible from all views and help you track your plane's movement.

REALISM AND RELIABILITY

To create a more realistic flight, you can choose to have certain aircraft systems behave more as they would in the real world. You can also increase the degree of difficulty from easy to realistic, and the aircraft reliability from unreliable to reliable using a sliding pointer. The more realistic a setting you choose for the flight controls, the harder it is to fly your plane. The more unreliable your aircraft, the greater the probability that instruments and aircraft systems will catastrophically fail during flight. To set the slide pointer using the mouse, click and drag the triangular-shaped pointer to the difficulty level you want. From the keyboard, select the slider so that the scale indicator turns red. Then, either press the setting number from the main keyboard, or slide it by pressing the left or right cursor keys. Figure 3.31 shows the Realism and Reliability dialog box.

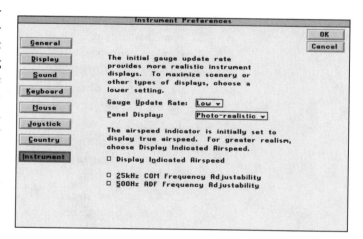

Figure 3.31
Realism and Reliability dialog box

The most realistic setting for flight control realism would be to move the slides to the middle of the scale. Other realism options you can change are as follows:

- *Elevator Trim:* The elevator trim is a small control surface on the elevators that relieves the pilot of continually applying pressure on the yoke to maintain the desired flight path. With this feature toggled off, the program automatically trims the elevators when you are flying with the keyboard or mouse, but not with spring-back joysticks/flightsticks. (The spring causes the joystick to return to the "null zone," which should be where the controls are centered at the neutral position.) Enabling this feature will cause the elevators to drift (the airflow over the elevators tends to move the elevators back to their centered position), and you will have to constantly compensate using the elevator trim control, or apply more yoke pressure to correct the drift.

- *Gyro Drift:* With Gyro Drift enabled, your HeadingIndicator/Directional Gyro will tend to drift from the correct course heading, due to friction and precessional effects of the gyroscope. You will need to recalibrate the Gyro by pressing ⒟.

- *Airframe Damage from Stress:* Choosing this option will make your aircraft more sensitive to hard landings or aerobatic maneuvers with high G (gravity) forces. When the aircraft exceeds the manufacturer's performance specifications, the plane will suffer airframe damage that could cause a fatal crash.

- *Engine Stops When Out of Fuel:* With this option toggled on, you must pay attention to your fuel tank gauges, or else you may find yourself hitching a ride back to town.

- *Instrument Lights:* If you select this option, you must manually switch on your instrument lights at dusk in order to see your instrument panel. To turn on your instrument lights, you must press ⓈⓗⒾⓕⓉ Ⓛ.

- *Lights Burn Out:* Lights may randomly burn out on your instrument panel, thereby obscuring vital data from your view. Leaving your lights on during the day increases the probability of failure.

- *Fuel Tank Selector:* With this option enabled, you must manually switch fuel tanks when they become empty. To display remaining fuel levels in multiple fuel tanks, including auxiliary tanks, bring up the Engine and Fuel dialog box.

- *Prop Propulsion Realism:* This realism option is available only for the Cessna, although this option may be available for other future propeller aircraft that will be available with Microsoft's Aircraft and Scenery Designer 5.0. You have two options:

  1. *Fast Throttle:* Increasing the throttle too fast can cause the engine to quit suddenly.

  2. *Prop Advance:* The Prop Advance list box controls how your propeller's pitch is governed by the simulation under different conditions. The basic idea is that there is a speed governor that tries to keep your propeller spinning at a constant speed under varying speed and altitude conditions. There are three options under the Prop Advance list box:

     - *Fixed Pitch:* The propeller's pitch is fixed and you cannot alter the prop pitch control. This setting is the least realistic to use.

- *Automatic:* The default setting is automatic. FS 5.0 adjusts the prop pitch for you automatically as you set the throttle, thereby allowing you to maintain a constant RPM for different altitudes. This setting is the easiest to use, but is the least realistic.

- *Manual:* With this option, you can manually override the speed governor, and advance or decrease the prop pitch control independently of the throttle. This option is for advanced users who understand the relationship between prop pitch, RPM, airspeed, and Power settings for different altitudes. This setting is the most realistic for flying the Cessna.

- *Jet Propulsion Realism: Flameout:* Only available for the Learjet or other future jet aircraft. Jet aircraft can lose their engine thrust when combustion inside the engine falters. Volcanic ash that is deposited into the upper atmosphere by volcanoes, for example, can clog the jet engine's intake ports, causing a catastrophic engine failure. Enabling this option will allow jet flameout failures to occur. When this happens, you must attempt to restart your engines by using the Starter Engine control (Press J 1 and J 2 followed by the +) to re-light your burners and spool up the compressor turbine blades.

Figure 3.32
Prop Advance list box

Figure 3.33
The Prop Pitch and Throttle controls for the Cessna

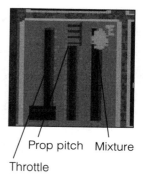

Prop pitch   Mixture

Throttle

CHOOSING YOUR AIRCRAFT

To select a different aircraft to fly:

1. Open the Options menu and select Aircraft.

2. In the Aircraft Selection dialog box, click on the name of the aircraft you wish to fly. In the description text box, you will see some text describing the type of plane you have chosen, and in the Display window, you will see an image of the selected plane rotating in three dimensions, as is illustrated in Figure 3.34.

3. Click OK to return to the simulation.

Figure 3.34
The Aircraft Selection dialog box

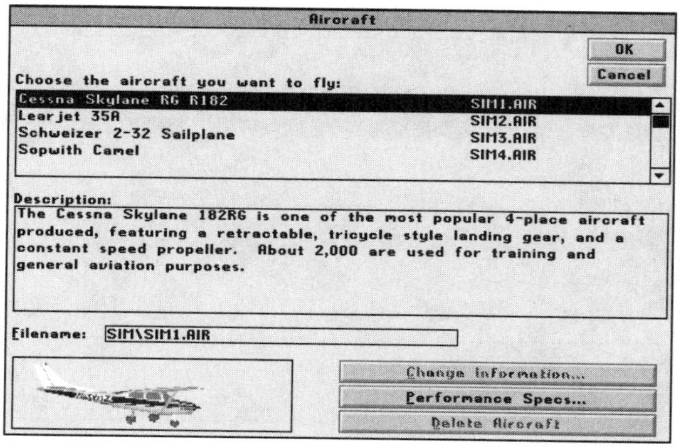

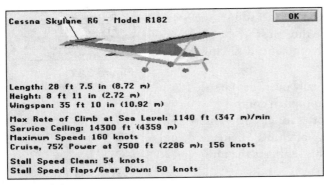

Figure 3.35
Aircraft Performance
Specifications dialog
box

You can also call up the performance specifications for any aircraft by doing the following:

1. Select the aircraft's name.
2. Click on the Performance Specs button (See Figure 3.35).
3. Click OK to return to the Aircraft Selection dialog box, and OK again to return to the simulation.

SELECTING YOUR SITUATION

Situations are files that store ready-made scenarios which are instantly available to fly. You can create your own situations, or use pre-existing situations, to practice a difficult landing, or test your flying skills under a variety of self-imposed flying conditions. All your settings including plane type, yoke position settings, speed, altitude, location, weather, time of day, and season are stored in the situation file. You can also save the instrument panel, view windows position, and size on the screen, and save any scenery or dynamic scenery and their density levels, along with keyboard, mouse, and joystick sensitivity levels.

To Open a Situation

To recall a situation:

1. Under the Options menu, select Situations.

2. In the list of situations that are displayed in the Situations dialog box, pictured in Figure 3.36, select the situation you want to load.

3. Click OK.

Table 3.1 lists all the packaged situations found in *Flight Simulator 5.0.*

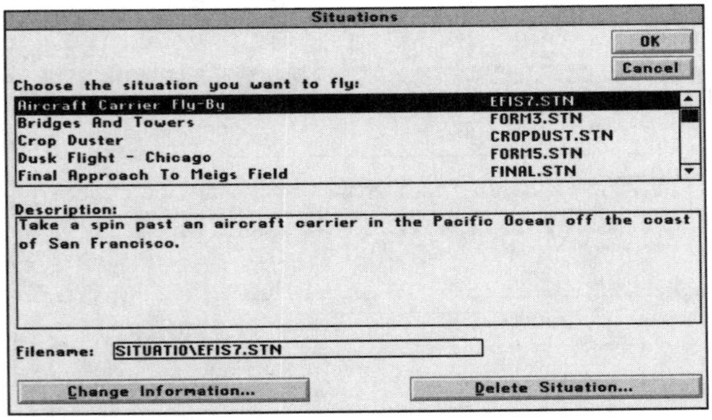

Figure 3.36 Situations dialog box

Table 3.1 Situation Descriptions and Listings

Situation	Description	Filename
Aircraft Carrier Fly-By	Take a spin past an aircraft carrier in the Pacific Ocean off the coast of San Francisco.	EFIS7.STN
Bridges and Towers	Fly under the bridges and around the towers.	FORM3.STN
Crop Duster	This is a special flight area reserved for the crop duster game	CROPDUST.STN
Dusk Flight—Chicago	Take a sightseeing tour of Chicago at dusk. If you fly for about half an hour, it will become totally dark.	FORM5.STN
Final Approach to Meigs Field	This situation illustrates that when landing, proper setup is most important. You are lined up and trimmed out for a straight-in approach to Meigs Field. The plane will land itself on the numbers, hands off. You may want to flare.	FINAL.STN
Find the Hot Air Balloon	Out on a morning flight north of Seattle heading southeast. Keep your eyes open and you will see a hot air balloon.	EFIS5.STN
Golden Gate Fly-by	Fly by (not under!) the Golden Gate Bridge and head for the Oakland Bay Bridge.	FORM1.STN
Hanger Buzz	Buzz the hangar at this small airport.	FORM6.STN
Learjet Cruise to O'Hare Intl.	Just cruising southeast toward O'Hare.	EFIS3.STN
Manhatten Tour	Take this aerial tour of New York City.	FORM4.STN
Meigs Takeoff Runway 36	You are at Chicago's Merrill C. Meigs Field, cleared for takeoff.	FS5.STN
Munich	Fly over Munich, Germany.	MUNICH.STN
New York City Tour	Fly ENE towards New York City.	EFIS6.STN
Nimitz	Fly over the aircraft carrier and head for the soaring ridge near San Francisco.	FORM7.STN
Oakland 27R Landing Approach	Setup on approach to Runway 27R at Oakland International. Cleared to land.	MODE4.STN
Oakland 27R Take off	Cleared for takeoff on Oakland runway 27R.	MODE2.STN
Paris	Fly over Paris, France.	PARIS.STN

Table 3.1   Situation Descriptions and Listings (continued)

Situation	Description	File Name
Sailplane—Ridge Soaring	Catch the updrafts (caused by wind blowing in from the ocean) on the soaring ridge near San Francisco.	SAIL1.STN
Sailplane—Thermal Soaring	Warm air is rising from the sunheated farm fields. Catch the thermal lift as you soar between fields. Use the map view to see your position.	SAIL2.STN
San Francisco 28ILS Approach	On approach to San Francisco International Airport at dusk. The approach is 28L just before the outer marker.	EFIS1.STN
Storms at Champaign ILS	Approaching Willard Airport in a driving rainstorm.	EFIS2.STN
Stormy ILS approach to Oakland	Approaching Oakland runway 11, in a driving rainstorm.	EFIS4.STN
Synthberg	Fly over an imaginary city created with FS's scenery synthesizer.	SYNTH.STN

To Save a Situation

To save a situation:

1. Press the ⌐;⌐ key, or select Save Situation from the Options menu.

2. In the dialog box that follows, type in a descriptive title name of up to 30 characters and then press ⌐Enter⌐.

3. The first 8 characters of your title will then be displayed in the Filename text box as the proposed DOS file name for the situation. If this is OK, click the OK button; otherwise, select the text box and give the situation a new filename of up to 8 characters. (Do not add a file extension, and you must use only characters that DOS will recognize for filenames.) Figure 3.37 shows the Save Situation dialog box.

4. In the Description text box, type in any comments that will help you describe what the situation does.

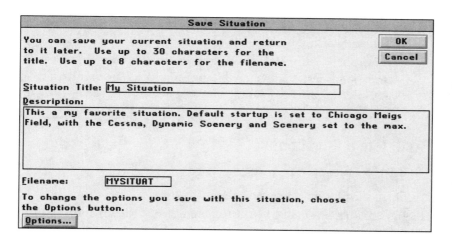

Figure 3.37
Save Situation dialog
box

To store keyboard,
mouse, and joystick
sensitivities in a sit-
uation, you must
first toggle on these
check box items in
the Situation
Options dialog box,
found under the Sit-
uations Option but-
ton in the General
Preferences dialog
box. Any changes
made in this dialog
box will affect all
your situations, but
any changes made in
the Situation
Options dialog box
found under the
Save Situation menu
command, with the
Options button, will
affect only the cur-
rent situation.

Changing the Options Stored in a Situation

To change the types of options stored with your situation:

1. In the Save Situations dialog box, shown in Figure 3.38, click the
   Options button. Select from the following list of options:

   • *Instrument Panel and View Windows Positions:* Saves the size and
     location of all instrument panels, 3-D view windows, and maps. Next
     time the situation is opened, all windows will open to their last saved
     position.
   • *Aircraft:* The aircraft type is saved so that when the situation is
     restarted, it will default to the last saved aircraft used in the situation.
   • *Scenery:* The scenery density and scenery file(s) used are saved so that
     when the situation is restarted, the scenery will look the same as when
     you last saved the situation.
   • *Dynamic Scenery:* The Dynamic scenery that is currently active, along
     with the dynamic scenery density, are saved in the situation file.

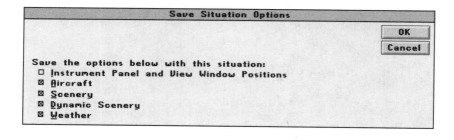

Figure 3.38
Situation Options
dialog box (under the
Save Situations menu
command)

Upon restarting the situation, the dynamic scenery is restored to the state in which it was last left when the situation file was saved.

- *Weather:* Weather data is saved in the situation file. When the situation is restarted, you will experience the same weather that occurred when the situation was last saved.

To Delete a Situation

To delete a situation:

1. Open the Options menu and select Situations.
2. In the Situations dialog box, select the name of the situation you wish to delete.
3. Click the Delete Situation button. The situation will then be erased from your hard drive.

Resetting a Situation

To restart a situation from its initial conditions:

1. Press Ctrl Print Screen, or select Reset Situation from the Options menu.
2. The simulator will reset itself to the beginning conditions of the currently active situation.

Changing the Information About a Situation

To change the description, filename, or title of a situation:

1. Choose Situations from the Options menu.
2. Select the Situation you want to change.
3. Click the Change Information button.
4. Change any listed information.
5. Click OK to return to the Situations dialog box. Click OK once again to return to the simulator.

Selecting Startup Situation

To have *Flight Simulator* always load a particular situation upon startup:

1. Open the Options menu and select the Preferences menu item.

2. In the Preferences dialog box, click the Startup Situation button. The Startup dialog box will open, as pictured in Figure 3.39.

3. Select the startup situation.

4. Click OK to return to the Preferences dialog box.

5. Click OK to return to the simulator.

The next time the simulator starts up, it will load the situation you specified in the Startup Situations dialog box.

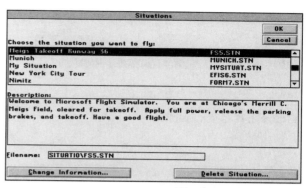

Figure 3.39
The Startup Situation dialog box

Selecting Situation Save/Load Options for All Situations

You can have various situation options saved or loaded for all your situations by customizing the Situation Options dialog box, activated by clicking on the Situation Options button in the General Preferences dialog box. Do not confuse this dialog box with the Situation Options dialog box that is activated under the Save Situation command. When you toggle on the options in this dialog box, pictured in Figure 3.40, they apply to ALL situations.

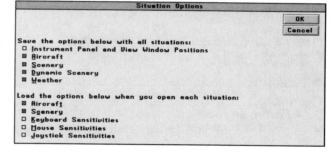

Figure 3.40
Situation Options for the General Preferences dialog box

Reset All Joystick/Flightstick Controls, Including Trim Controls, Before Resetting Situation

Before resetting a situation, be sure to center all your joystick(s) and trim controls, or else you must recalibrate them under Joystick Preferences (or by pressing K) when the situation restarts.

QUICK PRACTICE AND FLIGHT INSTRUCTION

As a learning aid, FS 5.0 includes a computer-aided tutorial on flying. The Quick Practice feature under the Options menu, illustrated in Figure 3.41, picks four of the lessons from among the basic lessons found under Flight Instruction for a quick overview of taking off and landing.

If you want to make a copy of a favorite situation, and then modify it slightly without changing the original setup, give the situation a new filename, description, and title by using the Change Information option in the Situations dialog box.

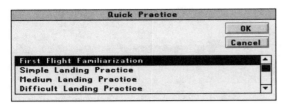

Figure 3.41 Quick Practice

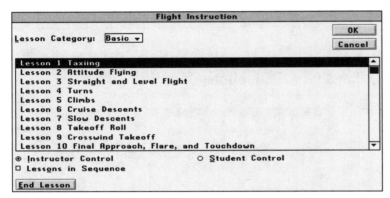

Figure 3.42
Basic lessons available
under Flight Instruction

While in Instructor
Control mode during
Flight Instruction,
you can return
control of the
aircraft to yourself
by pressing Esc.

The Flight Instruction command, also located under the Options menu, offers a more comprehensive tutorial package. There are three lesson categories: Basic, Advanced, and Aerobatic. Each category has seven to ten individual lessons that emphasize a particular flight maneuver. Figure 3.42 shows the lessons that are available for the Basic lesson category. If you prefer to watch a particular lesson before trying it yourself, have the flight instructor take command of the plane by toggling on Instructor Control. You can take charge of the plane at anytime, while in Instructor Control, by pressing Esc. Otherwise, select Student Control if you want to fly the lesson yourself. The lessons can be executed in strict sequence if you click on the Lessons in Sequence button. To exit the lessons, click the End Lesson button.

During Instructor Control mode, the instructor flies the plane and makes comments and suggestions in the message box. After the instructor finishes with the demonstration lesson, control is switched back to the student mode so that you can try out what you've just learned. Later, you will get feedback on your performance.

USING THE LAND ME COMMAND TO AUTOLAND YOUR PLANE

The most difficult task in *Flight Simulator* is to safely land your airplane in one piece. Because most people cannot do this easily, FS 5.0 has included a new feature for auto-landing the plane at the airports in the default scenery areas. Land Me is activated by pressing X from the keyboard, or by selecting Land Me from the Options menu. When you do this, an instructor takes over control of the plane and tells you what actions he is performing in a message box on-screen. By following along, and watching the controls, you can actually learn a great deal about how to properly land the airplane. You can disengage Land Me at any time by pressing X once again, or by selecting Land Me from the Options menu.

SETTING THE TIME AND SEASON

To set the time in *Flight Simulator*, you can adjust the digital clock on-screen, or call up the Set Time and Season dialog box using the Set Time and Season command from the World menu. Besides setting the exact time with this command, you can also set the season, or choose the time of day you wish to fly, whether it be dawn, day, dusk, or night.

The Set Time of Day feature is especially handy if you want to jump right into a sunset or night flight without having to endlessly fiddle with the clock.

Upon booting up *Flight Simulator*, flight conditions are set to correspond to the exact time, day, and month that your computer's clock is currently showing, unless, of course, you have chosen not to use your system clock. The startup preference for whether to use your system's time or situation time is found under General Preferences from the Options menu. If you do choose to base the simulator's clock on your system time, transition times for dawn, day, dusk, and night will be altered according to the latitude and longitude of your airplane and the Earth's inclination toward the sun.

When you change the season, you will experience new difficulties: icy runways in winter or reduced lift in summer, for example. Under visual flying rules, you must finish your flight before sundown and so must know when the sun sets for each season.

To change the season:

1. Select Set Time and Season from the World menu.
2. Open the Set Season list box and select one of the following options:
   - Winter
   - Spring
   - Summer
   - Autumn
3. Click the OK button to return to the simulator.

The season you have selected will now be in effect. The outside temperature will be adjusted to reflect the season, and the exact time of transition for dawn, day, dusk, and night will also be varied according to season.

To select the time of day you wish to fly:

1. Select the Set Time and Season command from the World menu.
2. Click the Set Time of Day radio button.
3. Open the Time of Day list box and choose from among the following:

To set the time from the cockpit:

- To increase the hours, you must click the mouse pointer to the right side of the hours display on the digital clock. Conversely, to move the clock back, you must click the mouse pointer to the left side of the hours display. You can hold down the mouse button to advance or retard the time quickly, or you can click each individual number change.

- Changing the minutes is also accomplished in the same way. Thus, to increase the minutes, click the pointer on the right of the minutes indicator; to decrease the minutes, click the pointer on the left of the minutes indicator.

Figure 3.43
Time of day options

To set the time using the menu:

1. Select the Set Time and Season command from the World menu.
2. When the Set Time and Season dialog box opens, as shown in Figure 3.44, click the Set Exact Time radio button.
3. Enter the hour of day in 24-hour format (must be from 0 to 23).

4. Enter the minutes (must be from 0 to 60).
5. Click the Reset Seconds to Zero if you want to reset the seconds portion of the clock.
6. Click the OK button to return to the simulator.

```
┌──────────────────────────────────────────────────┐
│              Set Time and Season                  │
│ Current Time:   09:18:21                  ┌──────┐ │
│                                           │  OK  │ │
│ Set Season:  [Spring ▾]                   └──────┘ │
│                                         ┌────────┐ │
│ ⦿ Set Time of Day      Time of Day:  [Dawn ▾]│    │
│                                         └────────┘ │
│ ○ Set Exact Time:      Hours:        09            │
│                        Minutes:      18            │
│                        ☐ Reset Seconds to Zero     │
└──────────────────────────────────────────────────┘
```

Figure 3.44
The Set Time and
Season dialog box

A CHANGE OF SCENERY

Using *Flight Simulator*'s Scenery Library command under the Scenery menu, you can run older FS 4.0 version scenery or new scenery made especially for FS 5.0. *Flight Simulator* automatically switches between scenery areas for any version of 5.0 scenery you might have, including add-on scenery disks. To auto-switch between version 4.0 scenery areas, however, you must toggle on the Automatic Scenery Area Switching command in the Scenery Library dialog box.

With the Scenery Complexity command, you can choose how much scenery is to be displayed, and make various other scenery modifications. The Dynamic Scenery command allows you to reduce or increase the frequency with which moving scenery, such as other airplanes, boats, etcetera appear in your field of view.

Choosing Scenery Areas from Your Scenery Library

To choose a different scenery file for your flight, perform the following steps:

1. Select the Scenery Library command from the Scenery menu.

2. In the Scenery Library dialog box, shown in Figure 3.45, choose the scenery file from the list that is displayed.

   - Select FS5World scenery to use all FS 5.0 version scenery areas. Choosing this option makes all version 5 scenery areas available automatically, without having to individually select the files. (Version 5 Scenery is called F5 WORLD.VIS scenery.)

   - Select any FS 4.0 scenery. (Version 4 scenery is called F1 scenery.).

Figure 3.45
The Scenery Library dialog box

3. If you want to auto-switch between version 4 scenery areas, be sure to toggle on the Automatic Scenery Area Switching check box. *Flight Simulator 5.0* automatically auto-switches all version 5.0 scenery areas.

4. Click the OK button to load the scenery and return to the simulator.

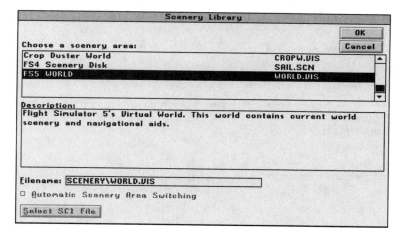

Adjusting Scenery Complexity

The scenery in FS 5.0 can be increased or decreased in display complexity by using the options found in the Scenery Complexity dialog box, pictured in Figure 3.47. Generally, the more complex the scenery, the slower your display frame rate will be. Each 3-D view window can have its scenery individually adjusted, so you can have one window display a high degree of detail, while a second window might just show bare-bones, wire-frame outlines.

To increase or decrease the number of buildings and other types of scenery:

1. Select Scenery Complexity from the Scenery menu.

2. Choose whichever 3-D View window you wish to apply the scenery modifications.

If you select Very Dense for the Image Complexity for Chicago, you will see more than 60 buildings crowded into the downtown area!

Figure 3.46
Image Complexity
options

3. Open the Image Complexity list box and select one of the choices as shown in Figure 3.46.

4. Click OK to return to the simulator.

Other options you can control include having stars in the sky, displaying runway-approach lighting at airports, displaying no scenery at all (Horizon Only), and having buildings and other objects displayed as wire-frame polygons. The Earth Pattern list box, which only works for FS 4.0 scenery, allows you to choose the texture pattern you want for the Earth's landmass. Image smoothing gives your screen image a smoother looking display.

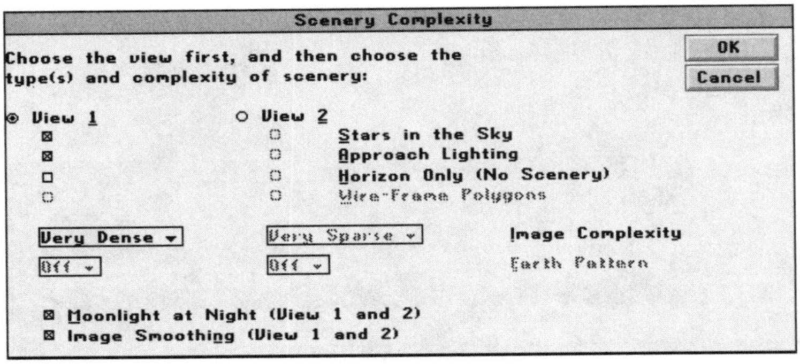

Figure 3.47
Scenery Complexity
dialog box

The Wire Frame Polygons option affects only certain kinds of scenery, and may or may not be visible, depending on what scenery you are using.

Controlling the Density of Dynamic Scenery

Dynamic scenery refers to all scenery that moves, whether in the air, on the ground, or on the water. *Flight Simulator* has ground traffic, other aircraft, blimps, hot air balloons, and sailboats, to enhance your enjoyment of the scenery. You might want to reduce the density of dynamic scenery, however, if you have a slow 386, and you want to increase your display frame rate so that it is a bit smoother. If, on the other hand, you like to see lots of dynamic scenery and you have a fast 486 system, you can choose to increase the density of dynamic scenery. Dynamic scenery customization options are located in the Dynamic Scenery dialog box, which is activated by selecting Dynamic Scenery from the Scenery menu. The various options, illustrated in Figure 3.48, can be applied selectively to each 3-D view window.

To modify the dynamic scenery frequency settings:

1. Select the View 1 or View 2 window, depending on which view window you want to customize.

2. Open the Scenery Frequency list box and select one of the choices as shown in Figure 3.48:

3. Click the OK button.

Figure 3.48
Dynamic Scenery
Frequency options

You can also choose what kinds of dynamic scenery you wish to have displayed. Available options are as follows:

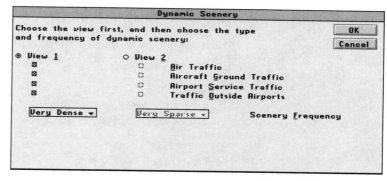

- Air Traffic
- Aircraft Ground Traffic
- Airport Service Traffic
- Traffic Outside Airports

To activate or deactivate each dynamic scenery option, click on the check box under the appropriate 3-D view window.

Figure 3.49
The Dynamic Scenery dialog box

SETTING YOUR EXACT START LOCATION

You can specify your exact location by using the Set Exact Location command under the World menu. But before you do this, you need to understand how latitude and longitude coordinate systems work.

World Latitude/Longitude Maps

Because *Flight Simulator* relies in large measure upon the terrestrial latitude and longitude coordinate system, you will need to know where these lines fall on a map so that you can accurately locate yourself. The equator is defined as 0 degrees latitude, whereas the Prime Meridian, which passes through Greenwich, England, is defined as 0 degrees longitude. The latitude of a position is the angular distance measured from the equator northward or southward through 90 degrees, and the direction of measurement is indicated by placing a suffix N (north) or S(south) after the angular measure. Longitude is the angular distance measured from the prime meridian eastward or westward through 180 degrees. The direction of movement is indicated by placing a suffix E (east) or W (west) after the angular measure.

Each degree of latitude or longitude is subdivided into 60 minutes, and each minute is further subdivided into 60 seconds. For navigational purposes, every great circle that girdles the earth subtends 60 nautical miles for every degree of arc. A minute of arc therefore subtends one nautical mile. Thus, the distance between 90W and 91W is exactly 60 nautical miles. By the same token, the distance between 37N and 40N is 180 nautical miles (3 degrees of arc times 60 nautical miles/per degree).

How to Move Your Plane

Moving your plane to any location on Earth is now possible using the Set Exact Location command. Here is how to do this:

1. Open the World menu and select Set Exact Location.
2. In the Set Exact Location dialog box, shown in Figure 3.50, activate the Set Location of list box and choose Aircraft.

Now you must choose which coordinate system you plan to use to precisely place the plane.

3. If you are using FS 4.0 North and East Coordinates, select the Set Location with X/Z coordinates. Otherwise, if you are using FS 5.0 latitude/longitude coordinates, select Set Location with Latitude/Longitude.
4. Enter the coordinates by typing in the appropriate text boxes. For longitude/latitude, preface North coordinates with an "N," South coordinates with an "S," East coordinates with an "E," and West coordinates with a "W." Thus, for example, to enter 45 degrees 55 minutes 35 seconds North Latitude, 35 degrees 28 minutes 45 seconds West Longitude, type (with or without spaces between numbers)[3]:

    N45 55 35 in the North/South text box
    W35 28 45 in the East/West text box

5. Enter the altitude you wish your plane to be in the Altitude text box.
6. Enter the course heading you want your airplane to be facing. If you are trying to place your airplane on a runway, you should remember that runway numbers refer to compass headings. For example, Runway 32 faces 320 degrees, runway 9 faces 90 degrees, and so forth.
7. Click OK when you are satisfied with your position entries.

```
╔══════════════ Set Exact Location ══════════════╗
 Set Location of:  [Aircraft ▼]              ┌────────┐
                                             │   OK   │
 ⊙ Set Location with Latitude/Longitude      ├────────┤
   North/South Lat.:  [N045° 55' 34.9999"]   │ Cancel │
                                  N045° 55' 34.9999"
   East/West Lon.:    [W035° 28' 44.9999"]
                                  W035° 28' 44.9999"
 ○ Set Location with X/Z coordinates
   North:             19719.9708    19719.9708
   East:              32312.9450    32312.9450
   Region:            [USA ▼]
 Altitude (ft):       [+000594]      +000594
 Heading (deg magnetic): [000.83]    000.83
 Note: To cancel changes and reset to the original
 latitude/longitude or X/Z coordinates, choose the Cancel
 button.
 ┌─────────────────────────────────────────────┐
 │ Set Tower View (from Aircraft Location)      │
 └─────────────────────────────────────────────┘
```

Figure 3.50
The Set Exact
Location dialog box

[3]Longitude and Latitude are usually expressed in degrees, minutes, and seconds. There are 360 degrees in a great circle of the Earth, 60 minutes in a degree, and 60 arc seconds in a minute.

Displaying Latitude/Longitude Coordinates or Alternate FS 4.0 North and East Coordinates

You can display your current position using FS 4.0's North and East coordinate system, and/or FS 5.0's new latitude/longitude coordinate system. To activate the display in your 3-D view windows and map window, press [Shift] [Z]. You can press [Shift] [Z] again to toggle between displaying the two coordinate systems separately or simultaneously. To shut off the display, keep pressing [Shift] [Z] until the display is turned off.

HOW TO JUMP TO ANY AIRPORT

Included in FS 5.0 is a new feature that enables you to jump to any major airport in the default scenery areas. You can also choose to have your radios automatically tuned to local air traffic control. You should use this command only while your plane is on the ground. This is because, when you change locations, you may crash at the new airport location because of differences in altitude and airspeed.

The Airports command is available only with FS 5.0 scenery. It will not work with FS 4.0 scenery.

To jump to any airport, perform the following steps:

1. Open the World menu, and choose Airports.
2. In the Airports dialog box, shown in Figure 3.52, select the scenery area where the airport you wish to go to is located.
3. Select the airport and click the OK button.

Your plane will now appear on the tarmac of the selected airport.

Table 3.2 lists all the airports that are available for the seven scenery areas of New York, San Francisco, Los Angeles, Chicago, Seattle, Paris, and Munich.

Figure 3.51
Scenery areas available for the Airports command

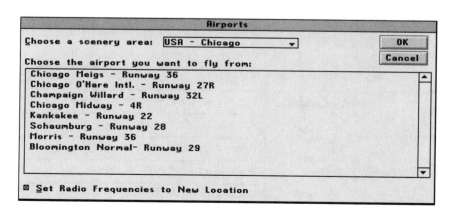

Figure 3.52
The Airports dialog box

Table 3.2	Available Airports for the Jump to Airport Command

Scenery Area	Airports
New York	New York Kennedy Intl. — Runway 31L
	New York Kennedy Intl. — Runway 4L
	Boston Logan Intl. — Runway 22R
	Boston Logan Intl. — Runway 33L
	Bridgeport Sikorsky — Runway 33L
	Martha's Vinyard — Runway 24
	Hartford–Brainard — Runway 20
	New York LaGuardia — Runway 13
	New York LaGuardia — Runway 22
	New Haven-Tweed — Runway 14
	Willimantic Windham — Runway 9
	Block Island State — Runway 28
San Francisco	San Francisco Intl. — Runway 28R
	Oakland Intl. — Runway 29
	San Jose Intl. — Runway 12R
	Concord Buchanan — Runway 32R
	Salinas Muni. — Runway 26
	Marysville–Yuba County — Runway 5
	Sacramento Executive — Runway 2
	Sacramento Metro — Runway 34R
	Fresco Air Terminal — Runway 29R
	Santa Rosa–Sonoma County — Runway 32
Los Angeles	Los Angeles Intl. — Runway 25R
	Avalon–Cataline — Runway 4
	Santa Ana–John Wayne — Runway 19R
	San Diego–Lindbergh — Runway 27
	Santa Monica — Runway 21
	Van Nuys — Runway 16R

Table 3.2   Available Airports for the Jump to Airport Command (*continued*)

Scenery Area	Airports
Seattle	Seattle Tacoma Intl. — Runway 34R
	Boeing Field — Runway 31L
	Everett–Paine Field — Runway 34L
	Olympia — Runway 26
	Port Angeles–Fairchild Intl. — Runway 8
	Bremerton Natl. — Runway 1
Chicago	Chicago Meigs — Runway 36
	Chicago O'Hare Intl. — Runway 27R
	Champaign Willard — Runway 32L
	Chicago Midway — Runway 4R
	Kankakee — Runway 22
	Schaumburg — Runway 28
	Morris — Runway 36
	Bloomington Normal — Runway 29
Paris, France	Paris–Charles de Gaulle — Runway 10
	Paris–P. Orly — Runway 26
	Pontoise-Cormailles–en–Vexin — Runway 5
	Reims–Prunay — Runway 25
	Toussus–le–Noble — Runway 7L
	LeHavre–Octeville — Runway 5
Munich, Germany	Augsburg — Runway 25
	Eggenfelden — Runway 27
	Munich — Runway 26R
	Oberpfaffenhofen — Runway 22
	Donauworth–Genderkingen — Runway 9
	Gunzenhausen–Reutberg — Runway 24

CHAPTER
4

Weathering the Weather

Using *Flight Simulator*'s powerful weather editor, you can micro manage local weather fronts or macro manage global weather. The automatic weather generator allows you to have your weather randomly determined, or you can control individual aspects of weather such as wind, clouds, temperature, and barometric pressure. You can create local weather areas with specific kinds of weather, then copy and paste them into other areas, thereby creating a library of different weather scenarios. Or you can copy and paste individual weather elements between weather areas, such as a favorite thunderstorm, or a pleasant wind shear.

CHOOSING WEATHER CONDITIONS

Weather is defined as the state of the atmosphere, and includes the temperature, precipitation, humidity, cloudiness, visibility, pressure, and winds. Five factors determine the weather for a given area. They are, in order, as follows:

- *The amount of solar energy* received because of the area's latitude. Higher latitudes near the North Pole, for instance, receive less solar energy than lower latitudes at the equator, which receive the most solar energy.
- *The elevation* of the area. Higher altitudes have lower temperatures, and vice-versa.
- *Proximity to large bodies of water.* This moderates temperature fluctuations and provides a more temperate climate. Coastal regions, for example, have milder winters and cooler summers than inland areas.
- *The number of storm systems* such as cyclones, hurricanes, and thunderstorms that result from air-mass differences. The Earth's rotation causes air flow to be

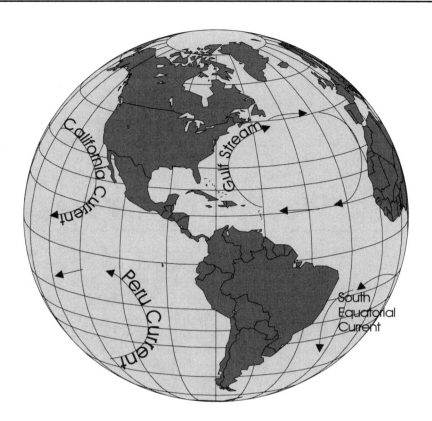

Figure 4.1
The Coriolis effect

deflected to the right of its direction in the Northern Hemisphere, and to the left in the Southern Hemisphere. Figure 4.1 illustrates this effect, known as the Coriolis effect, named after the 19th Century French mathematician G. Coriolis.

- *The distribution of barometric air pressure* over the land and nearest oceans. This produces varying wind and air-mass patterns.

All your weather modifications are performed by using the Weather command under the World menu. But if you are used to using the metric system, you can switch measurement systems in the Country Preferences dialog box.

Selecting Metric/U.S. Measurement System

To change your units of measurements from metric to U.S., or vice-versa:
Select the Preferences command under the Options menu. Click the Country button.

In the Units of Measure list box, choose:

- *U.S. System* if you want temperature measured in Fahrenheit, distances measured in feet and miles, and weight measured in pounds.
- *Metric (Alt feet)* if you want temperature measured in Fahrenheit and distances measured in meters and kilometers, except for the altimeter, which measures altitude in feet. Mass is measured in kilograms.
- *Metric (Alt meters)* if you want all instruments and readings, including the altimeter, to measure metric units.

Creating Clouds/Thunderstorms

Clouds in the atmosphere form whenever the relative humidity, or moisture content, of an air mass exceeds 100 percent. Water vapor, always present in the atmosphere, is produced from the evaporation of water due to the sun's heating effect on the oceans and other bodies of water. Intermolecular dipole-dipole and London forces cause the water vapor molecules to bind together; eventually, cloud formation occurs.

Clouds can be hazardous to flying because they can obstruct your visibility for navigating, and if cold enough, they can freeze on impact with your airplane, causing ice to build up on the fuselage and wings. Warm clouds with temperatures greater than 32 degrees F (0 degrees Celsius), are generally safe, but cold clouds with temperatures below 32 degrees F (0 degrees Celsius) are to be avoided.

Types of Clouds

There are two classifications of clouds:
- *Stratiform* (from *stratus*, which means spread out) are flat, layered clouds that form when upward air currents are relatively uniform over a wide area. Because of the smoother air currents, flying near stratiform clouds causes less turbulence than cumuliform clouds.
- *Cumuliform* (which means *heap* in Latin) are cottony, billowing, puffball clouds that form when upward and downward air currents are closely interspersed. Thunderstorms are cumuliform and generally the air is turbulent around them.

Clouds that form at ground level are called fog. Clouds that form in the upper troposphere are referred to as *cirrus* clouds (also sometimes called *cirrocumulus* and *cirrostratus*), whereas clouds that form in the middle troposphere are called *altostratus* and *altocumulus.* Clouds that form in the lower troposphere are given the names *stratus* and *cumulus.* When precipitation falls from lower

Figure 4.2
Cumuliform clouds

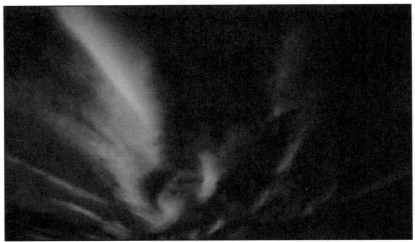

Figure 4.3
Stratiform clouds

troposphere clouds, the clouds are called *nimbostratus* and *cumulonimbus*. Nimbostratus clouds are often produced by cyclones, whereas cumulonimbus clouds are associated with thunderstorms in which rainfall is brief but heavy. The term *nimbus*, first coined by the Romans, describes dark gray rain clouds, so a cumulous cloud with rain is called *cumulonimbus*. Figure 4.4 shows the different cloud types and their relationships to each other.

Under visual flying rules (VFR), you are allowed to fly your plane only when the visibility is more than three statute miles. Also, when flying near clouds, you must maintain a separation distance of at least 500 feet below, 1,000 feet above, or 2,000 feet horizontal distance from the cloud. If you

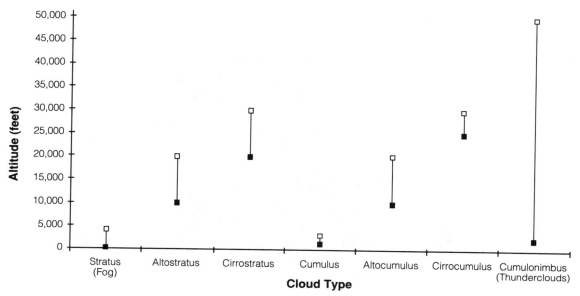

Figure 4.4
Troposphere cloud types

have an instrument rating, these rules do not apply to you, since you will have acquired the skills necessary to navigate under all conditions, including night and bad weather with zero visibility.

Thunderstorms

Thunderstorms form when the atmosphere is thermally unstable and large warm air currents, laden with moisture, rise upward in the form of a towering cumulus cloud. When many such cumulous clouds merge, a cumulonimbus, or thunderstorm cloud appears, with its distinctive anvil-shaped top. Thunderstorms play an important role in the Earth's hydrological cycle in that they transport large portions of surface heat and water vapor to the upper regions of the atmosphere. In fact, in many areas of the world, especially those

Table 4.01 Visual Flight Rules	
Minimum Flight Visibility for VFR	**Minimum Distance from Clouds for VFR**
3 statute miles	500 feet below cloud
	1,000 feet above cloud
	2,000 feet horizontal separation distance from cloud

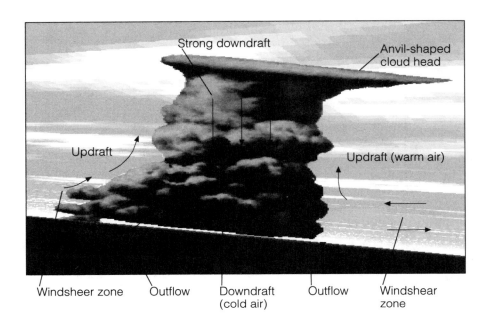

Figure 4.5
Elements of a
thunderstorm

If you are running in
EGA graphics mode,
you cannot create
thunderstorms.

agricultural regions in the United States, Canada, and the Ukraine where corn and wheat are grown, most rainfall is produced by thunderstorms.

When a thunderstorm is brewing, katabatic wind downbursts (often called *microbursts*) from the cirrus anvil can produce downdrafts as strong as 6,000 feet per minute. Horizontal surface winds can be as strong as 45 knots. (Resultant horizontal shear is 90 knots per hour because of the headwind-to-tailwind change for a traversing aircraft.) Moderate to heavy rainfall occurs over broad regions below the base of the clouds, but frequently small hail and snowflakes will emanate from the interior of the cloud. Thunderstorms can produce violent windstorms, windshear, tornadoes, large hailstones, heavy rainfall, and intense lightning. Because of this destructive potential, thunderstorms are extremely hazardous to aircraft, especially those landing or departing from airports. Many aircraft accidents, in fact, have been attributed to the windshear associated with thunderstorms. Figure 4.5 shows some of the principal elements of a thunderstorm generated in *Flight Simulator 5.0*.

Windshear

What is windshear? It is basically a change in wind direction or velocity that occurs with a change in altitude. When an airplane experiences a sudden reversal in wind direction, the airspeed of the airplane changes dramatically and at low speeds, such as during approaches and landings, you can stall the airplane because there is insufficient airflow over the wings. When this happens, there isn't enough lift and the airplane crashes.

How does windshear occur around thunderstorms? Let's use an example of an airplane that is flying toward a thunderstorm to describe what happens. In a thunderstorm, rain is pouring down the center and air is rushing downward and fanning out at the surface. At the same time, a large amount of warm air is being sucked into the storm around the edges. The warm air is shearing past the cold air (*shearing* is a term used to describe the action of two bodies that move in opposite directions in planes parallel to each other) and is moving above the cooler air that is coming out of the storm. If you stand on the ground facing the storm, you feel a strong cool breeze in your face. This is the cold air that is being pushed out of the storm; the air hits the ground and then is shunted outwards. But if you were to move vertically several hundred feet above where you stand, you would feel the wind in the opposite direction because it is the warm and humid air that is being drawn into the storm.

Suppose, then, that your airplane is flying toward the storm, which is between it and the airport. Your airspeed is 130 knots and the wind is nominally calm. When your plane approaches the storm, a warm air current updraft is encountered. This is no problem, for this is the air being sucked into the storm. The real trouble starts when you enter the interior of the storm. Here you run into the downdraft of the cold air and rain from the center. This translates into a 30-knot headwind, not to mention the loss of lift from the downdraft, since this airflow is rushing outward toward the edge, or perimeter, of the cloud. Your airplane's speed across the ground is equal to its true airspeed minus any headwind component or plus any tailwind component, so your ground speed is reduced to 100 knots because of the 30-knot headwind. But before you have time to increase your engine thrust to get your ground speed up to 130 knots, you cross the center of the storm and the 30-knot headwind now turns instantly into a 30-knot tailwind. This means that you will now have to increase your speed not by 30 knots, but by 60 knots to achieve a ground speed of 130 knots (your ground speed of 100 knots plus the 30 knots tailwind, plus the loss of the 30 knot headwind). The acceleration and power that you need, in addition to the power needed to counter the effect of the downdraft, is often greater than your engines can provide, and the result can be a disastrous stall, loss of airspeed, or worse, a crash.

Many airports around the country are now equipped with ground-based windshear detecting devices. But these warning instruments have not been totally reliable. Therefore a new, highly advanced Doppler radar system is being installed that can detect shifting wind patterns. Airborne windshear radars that can be carried aboard an airplane are also being developed, so in

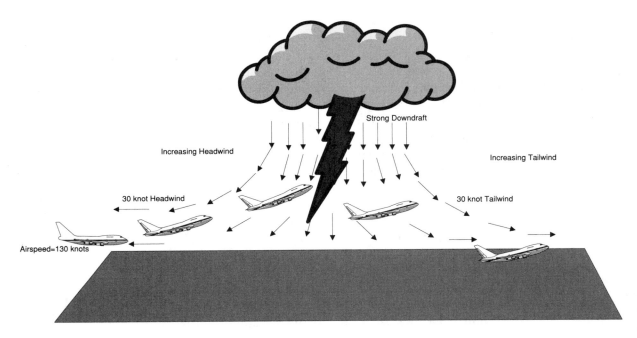

Strong Downdraft

Increasing Headwind

Increasing Tailwind

30 knot Headwind

30 knot Tailwind

Airspeed=130 knots

Figure 4.6
Thunderstorm
windshear

the not-too-distant future, the probability of encountering unexpected wind-shear will be reduced to nearly zero.

The general rule for all pilots is to avoid thunderclouds, skirting around them by at least 20 miles to avoid turbulence. If you see lightning or spot large anvil-shaped clouds, it indicates the probability of a severe thunderstorm. Never land or take off in the face of an approaching thunderstorm, and never attempt to fly under a thunderstorm, even if you can see clear to the other side. Turbulence and windshear under the storm, invisible to your eye, could be disastrous. If you must pass by a thunderstorm, it is preferable to fly on the upwind side of the storm's directional movement because it is less turbulent than the downwind side. Also, if you have to cross a thunderstorm's path, clear the top of the anvil cloud top by at least 1,000 feet altitude for each 10 knots of wind speed for the storm. If a thunderstorm is near the airport, airport operations will be suspended until the thunderstorm activity has passed. Many flight delays can be attributed to this phenomena, especially at the busy Dallas-Fort. Worth airport in Texas, which is a central hub for many airline travelers in the United States.

To create a cloud layer or thunderstorm in *Flight Simulator*, you must decide whether the clouds will appear locally or globally, what kind of clouds you want, the base and ceiling altitudes, the coverage area, and the deviation factor, which governs the randomness with which the clouds appear.

Creating a Cloud Layer

Perform the following steps to create a Cloud Layer:

1. Select the Weather menu option from the World menu.
2. Select the Weather Area list box and choose either Global or the name of a local area that you have previously created.
3. Click the Clouds button. You should see a list of cloud layers appear in the Weather dialog box, seen in Figure 4.7.
4. Click the Create button to add a new cloud layer. Keep in mind that you are allowed to create only two cloud layers and one thunderstorm layer per weather area.
5. In the Create Cloud Layer dialog box, you must choose the type of cloud, base or bottom elevation of the cloud, top or ceiling of the cloud, coverage, and deviation, as shown in Figure 4.8.

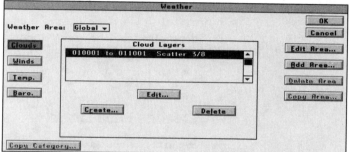

Figure 4.7
The Weather dialog box, showing the cloud layers currently available

Type

Choose Clouds if you want a cloud layer or Thunderstorm if you want a thunderstorm. Note that in EGA graphics mode, thunderstorms are not available.

Base

The base refers to the bottom of the cloud and how far it is above mean sea level (MSL). If you are starting at Meigs Field, which is at an altitude of 593 feet, and you want your clouds to appear 1,000 feet above the ground, you would enter 1,593 feet.

You can create only two cloud layers and one thunderstorm layer per weather area.

Tops

This is the ceiling, or top, of the cloud. This can be any altitude above the base, or bottom of the cloud. For a cloud that is 3,000 feet tall, with a base altitude of 1,593 feet, you would enter 4,593 feet.

Coverage

In the Coverage list box, you can decide how extensively your clouds will blanket the sky. For clouds, the coverage options are clear, scattered, broken,

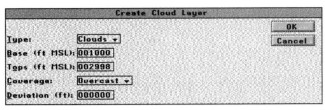

Figure 4.8
Create Cloud
Layer dialog box

or overcast. The fractional numbers appearing after the scattered and broken cloud layers indicate the fraction of sky that is covered by clouds.

The coverage options for thunderstorms are scattered or dense.

Deviation

This list box controls the amount of randomness that *Flight Simulator* throws in when creating your cloud layers. The randomness factor you enter determines the size of the cloud plus or minus the number of feet you specify in this box. Primarily, this option allows you to create more realistic clouds that are not all monotonously identical.

Creating Wind Layers

Wind is defined as air that is in motion relative to the rotating surface of the Earth. Wind possesses both vertical and horizontal speed components, although typically the horizontal speed component is much larger than the vertical. Horizontal wind speeds usually average 31.25 mph (50 km/hr), though in the jet streams high up in the atmosphere, speeds in excess of 180 mph (300 km/h) are not uncommon. Vertical wind speeds, on the other hand, typically are measured in only tenths of a kilometer per hour. When we talk about wind speed, it is almost always horizontal speed that is being referred to. The location from which a wind blows is used to indicate the wind's direction. For example, a northeasterly wind blows from the northeast to the southwest. In *Flight Simulator*, wind directions are measured in terms of compass headings: a wind with a heading of 0 degrees is a north wind, a wind with a heading of 90 degrees is an east wind, and so on.

Figure 4.9
Wind direction is based on compass heading

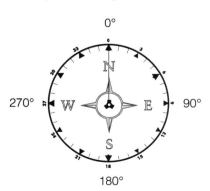

The movement of air around the planet is largely the result of force imbalances due to large temperature variations, the Coriolis effect, and varied air-pressure gradients around the Earth. Whenever there is a warm mass of air, it tends to move in the direction of the cooler air masses, and the wind flow that results is an attempt to restore the atmosphere to an equilibrium temperature state. The equatorial and polar regions have the largest temperature difference, and this causes the winds to carry heat from the equator toward the poles. As described before, the Coriolis effect, which is caused by the Earth's rotation, produces zero wind forces at the equator and maximum wind forces at higher latitudes near the poles.

Winds are classified into three types:

- *Planetary Winds:* These include the trade winds and middle latitude westerlies.
- *Secondary Winds:* Sea breezes, monsoon winds, and cyclonic winds are included in this type.
- *Regional Anabatic and Katabatic Winds:* Anabatic winds ascend vertically and are usually associated with geographic features such as mountain ranges. Katabatic winds descend vertically. An example is the microburst, an intense localized downdraft that spreads along the ground, causing windshear. These winds are often the result of thunderstorm activity.

Winds at different altitudes can have varying speeds and directions. At the boundaries or junctions of these wind layers, turbulence occurs. The wind that comes into frictional contact with the rotating earth, for example, causes the most turbulence at altitudes of less than 3,225 feet. Above this altitude, winds are generally smooth except for wind layers that come into contact with the jet stream. The jet stream is a fast-moving current of air in the upper atmosphere.

Clear air turbulence, or CAT, is a serious concern for all flights since it can create passenger discomfort and even cause injuries in severe instances. Turbulence is rated by four intensity levels, as described in Table 4.2.

You can create only three wind layers and one surface wind layer per weather area.

Table 4.2	Clear Air Turbulence Rating Criteria	
Intensity	**Aircraft Reaction**	**Reaction Inside Aitcraft**
Light	Slight erratic changes in altitude and attitude (pitch, yaw, roll). Slight bumps.	Passengers feel slight strain against seatbelts. Unsecured objects may move.
Moderate	Changes in altitude and attitude occur. Causes rapid bumps or jolts.	Passengers feel definite strains against seatbelts. Unsecured objects will move, and walking and food service are difficult.
Severe	Large, abrupt changes in altitude and attitude. Aircraft may be momentarily out of control.	Passengers are forced violently against seatbelts. Unsecured objects are thrown about. Walking and food service are all but impossible to perform.
Extreme	The aircraft is violently tossed about and is difficult to control. May cause structural damage to aircraft.	You don't want to know.

How to Create a Wind Layer

To create a wind, follow this procedure:

1. From the World menu, select the Weather command.
2. Select the Weather Area list box and choose either Global or the name of a local area that you have previously created.
3. Click the Winds button and you should see a list of wind layers in the Weather dialog box, seen in Figure 4.10.
4. Click the Create button to add a new wind layer. (You can create only three wind layers and one surface wind layer per weather area.)

Figure 4.10
Available wind layers in the Weather dialog box

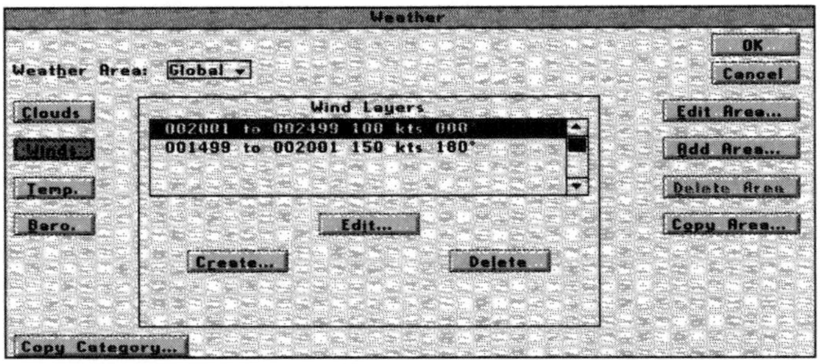

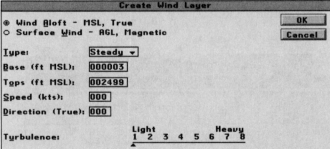

Figure 4.11
The Create Wind Layer dialog box

5. In the Create Wind Layer dialog box, you must choose whether you want a surface wind or a wind aloft, and then you must select the type of wind, add the base or bottom elevation of the wind, enter the top or ceiling altitude of the wind, enter the speed and direction of the wind, and enter the turbulence factor, as shown in Figure 4.11.

Wind Aloft vs. Surface Winds

When you choose Surface Winds, the Base text box disappears and the Tops text box is replaced by the Depth text box. By definition, surface winds have no base or bottom, so all you need to do is enter the height above ground in the Depth text box. Winds Aloft are those wind layers that are above ground level.

Type

Select between Steady and Gusty winds.

Base

The base refers to the bottom of the wind layer and how far it is above mean sea level (MSL). If you are starting at Meigs Field, which is at an altitude of 593 feet, and you want your wind to appear 1,000 feet above the ground, you would enter 1,593 feet.

Tops

The ceiling, or top, of the wind layer. This can be any altitude above the base, or bottom of the wind layer. For a wind layer that is 3,000 feet tall, with a base altitude of 1,593 feet, you would enter 4,593 feet.

Speed

Enter the speed, in knots (nautical miles per hour) for the wind layer.

Direction

Enter the wind direction in degrees from the compass heading. Winds blowing north would be 0 degrees; east would be 270 degrees.

Setting the Turbulence Factor

For a bumpier ride, slide the turbulence control to the Heavy side. Otherwise, if you get airsick easily, leave it on Light.

Adding Temperature Layers

The effect of increasing temperature causes the atmosphere to decrease in density (density is defined as the mass per unit volume), for a constant air pressure. Conversely, lowering the temperature increases air density, also for a fixed air pressure. Thus, the density of air varies inversely with the air temperature.

$$Temperature \propto \frac{1}{Density}$$

Increasing air pressure, on the other hand, increases air density, whereas decreasing air pressure decreases density. Thus, the density of air is directly proportional to pressure.

$$Pressure \propto Density$$

In the atmosphere, both temperature and pressure decrease with altitude. Air pressure drops more rapidly than temperature, however, as altitude is increased; therefore, air density decreases with altitude, despite the air density rise due to the temperature increase.

Air Density Affects Airplane's Performance Characteristics

The density of the air, which is affected by altitude, barometric pressure, and temperature, has a significant influence over the airplane's handling characteristics. As air becomes less dense, it does three things:

1. *Engine power is reduced* because the engine takes in less air.
2. *Propeller thrust is reduced* because the propeller is less efficient in thin air.
3. *Lift is reduced* because thinner air exerts less force on the wings.

The Effect of Temperature on the Airplane's Lift

You can create up to four temperature layers per weather area and create diurnal day/night temperature variations.

Should the temperature drop appreciably, the air density increases and, as a result, lift increases. If the temperature increases, air density decreases, and lift decreases. This means that if you are taking off on a very hot day, you won't be able to lift off as quickly as you would on a day that was cold. As a consequence, you must plan for using a longer length of runway. Furthermore, on hot days, your airplane must be flown at a greater true airspeed than on a cool day, if it is to maintain the same amount of lift. Table 4.3 summarizes these relationships.

Temperature Variations with Altitude

Temperature drops by 3.5 degrees Fahrenheit (2 degrees Celsius) per 1,000 feet of increased altitude. In fact, this relationship helps to create stability in the atmosphere. Greater temperature variations than this can cause destructive atmospheric disturbances such as thunderstorms, cyclones, tornadoes, typhoons, and hurricanes. (See Table 4.4 for a list of temperatures vs. different altitudes.)

You can experience the temperature drop with increased altitude in *Flight Simulator* by entering slew mode (press Y), then increase your altitude by pressing F4 . Notice that your temperature changes as your altitude increases.

Day/Night Temperature Variations

The diurnal temperature variation between night and day exists everywhere, but varies by region and season. During the day, when the sun's heating

Table 4.3 Temperature's Effect on Aircraft Lift	
Temperature	**Aircraft Lift**
Increases	Decreases
Decreases	Increases

effect on the atmosphere is at a maximum, temperatures can vary from their nighttime lows by as much as 36 degrees Fahrenheit (12.8 Celsius degrees). By toggling on the Day/Night Variation Range check box, and entering a temperature differential in the text box, you can realistically simulate this diurnal temperature fluctuation. The variance must be between 0 and 36 degrees F (0 to 20 degrees C).

How to Create a Temperature Layer

To create a temperature layer, follow these steps:

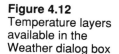

Figure 4.12
Temperature layers available in the Weather dialog box

1. From the World menu, select the Weather command.
2. Select the Weather Area list box and choose either Global or the name of a local area that you have previously created.
3. Click the Temperature button and you will see a list of temperature layers appear in the Weather dialog box, as seen in Figure 4.12.

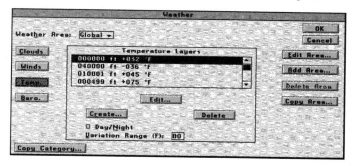

4. Click the Create button to add a new temperature layer. You are allowed to create only four temperature layers per weather area.
5. In the Create Temperature Layer dialog box, enter the altitude above sea level that you want the temperature layer to appear, and the daytime temperature, as shown in Figure 4.13.

Temperature Altitude MSL

Enter the altitude above mean sea level (MSL) for the temperature layer. If you wanted to enter an altitude of 3,000 feet above Chicago's Meigs Field, for example, you would enter 3,593 feet.

Daytime Temperature

Type in the daytime temperature of the temperature layer. If you have toggled on the Day/Night Variation Range, the temperature will drop at night by the number of degrees you have entered in the Variation Range text box. To enter a negative temperature, press ⊟ on the main keyboard before typing in the temperature.

When entering weather altitudes, be sure you add to the altitude your ground level. For example, to enter an altitude of 3,000 feet above Meigs Field, you would add the 593 feet surface level altitude to 3,000 to obtain 3,593 feet.

Figure 4.13
The Create Temperature Layer dialog box

Fiddling with the Barometric Pressure

Pressure, which is defined in physics as force applied per unit area, is measured in inches of mercury, Pascals (Newtons/meter squared), and Millibars (1/100 of a Pascal). The mercury barometer, invented by Evangelista Torricelli in 1643, measures the height of a column of mercury due to the pressure the atmosphere exerts on it. The greater the air pressure, the greater the height of the mercury column, which is measured in inches, or inches of Hg. (Hg represents the element Mercury on the Periodic Table of Elements.) Atmospheric pressure can be calculated by multiplying the height of the mercury column by the mercury density and the acceleration due to gravity. (This would give you the pressure in pounds per square inch.) But meteorologists often use the term "inches of Hg" to express the atmosphere's pressure, rather than pounds per square inch, and it is just as valid. At sea level, one atmospheric pressure equals 15 lb. per sq. inch, or equivalently, 29.9 inches of Hg. Expressed in metric units, one atmosphere of pressure at sea level equals 101.3 kilopascals, or 1,013 millibars.

The Standard Atmosphere (International Standard Atmosphere, or ISA) has been defined as an atmospheric pressure of 29.92 inches of Mercury (29.92" Hg), or 1,013.2 millibars, at 15 degrees Celsius (59 degrees Fahrenheit). An inch of mercury is equivalent to 34 millibars of pressure.

Atmospheric Pressure Decreases with Altitude

The standard decrease in pressure with increasing altitude is approximately 1" Hg per 1,000 feet, along with a 3.5 degree F drop in temperature per 1,000 feet. Table 4.4 lists the pressures of the standard atmosphere according to different altitudes, temperatures, and air densities.

The Effect of Pressure Changes on Aircraft Performance

When air pressure increases, air density increases, and so does aircraft lift. Conversely, if air pressure decreases, air density decreases, and so does lift. Looking at the table, you can see that the density of air at 18,000 feet is almost one half the density of air at sea level. Therefore, an airplane must fly at a greater true airspeed at a higher altitude in order to maintain the same lift than it would at a lower altitude.

When the pressure changes, not only do your airplane's performance characteristics change, but your pitot-static flight instruments are adversely affected. Thus, your measurements of altitude, airspeed, and rate of climb become inaccurate and must be corrected according to special charts and tables that are available. Table 4.5 summarizes these results.

Table 4.4	Properties of Standard Atmosphere			
Standard Atmosphere				
Altitude (Feet)	Pressure (Inches Hg.)	Temperature (Celsius)	Temperature (Fahrenheit)	Density (slugs per cubic foot)
0	29.92	15.0	59.0	0.002378
1,000	28.86	13.0	55.4	0.002309
2,000	27.82	11.0	51.9	0.002242
3,000	26.82	9.1	48.3	0.002176
4,000	25.84	7.1	44.7	0.002112
5,000	24.89	5.1	41.2	0.002049
6,000	23.98	3.1	37.6	0.001988
7,000	23.09	1.1	34.0	0.001928
8,000	22.22	-0.9	30.5	0.001869
9,000	21.38	-2.8	26.9	0.001812
10,000	20.57	-4.8	23.3	0.001756
11,000	19.97	-6.8	19.8	0.001701
12,000	19.02	-8.8	16.2	0.001648
13,000	18.29	-10.8	12.6	0.001596
14,000	17.57	-12.7	9.1	0.001545
15,000	16.88	-14.7	5.5	0.001496
16,000	16.21	-16.7	1.9	0.001448
17,000	15.56	-18.7	-1.6	0.001401
18,000	14.94	-20.7	-5.2	0.001355
19,000	14.33	-22.6	-8.8	0.001310
20,000	13.74	-24.6	-12.3	0.001267

While on the ground at Meigs Field, you can change the barometric pressure and then observe how this affects your altimeter. Decrease the barometric pressure from 29.12 inches of Hg to 25.00 inches of Hg. Return to

Table 4.5   The Effects of Pressure on Aircraft Performance

Barometric Pressure	Aircraft Lift	Pitot-Static System
Increases for lower altitudes	Increases	Altimeter shows you at a lower altitude than you really are; you are really traveling slower than your Airspeed Indicator shows.
Decreases for higher altitudes	Decreases	Altimeter shows you at a higher altitude than you really are; you are really traveling faster than your Airspeed Indicator shows.

To quickly calibrate your altimeter, press [B].

the simulator and observe how your altimeter shows that you are at a higher altitude than you really are.

Your altimeter is set to show the correct altitude based on a Standard Atmosphere of 29.12" Hg. Thus, if the local barometric pressure differs from this pressure, your altimeter will give you an incorrect reading, showing you to be at a higher altitude than you really are. You must, from time to time, calibrate your altimeter for local barometric conditions if you are to avoid becoming one of the fatality statistics classified as "pilot error."

How to Alter the Barometric Pressure

To change the barometric pressure, perform these steps:

1. Select the Weather command from the World menu.
2. Click the Barometer button.
3. In the Barometric Pressure section of the Weather dialog box, enter the new barometric pressure either in the Pressure (Hg) text box or the Pressure (Millibars) text box.
4. If you want some random variation in pressure thrown in, select Drift.

Inches of Mercury

Enter the barometric pressure in inches of mercury. Allowed values are from 25.00 inches to 35.00 inches. 29.12 inches is standard pressure at sea level.

Millibars

Enter the barometric pressure in Millibars. Allowed values are from 847 Millibars to 1,185 Millibars. 1,103 Millibars is standard pressure at sea level.

Drift

Check this box to have *Flight Simulator* add some randomness to your barometric pressure.

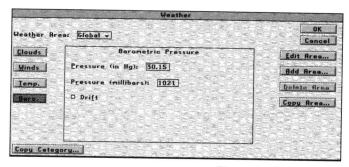

Figure 4.14
The Barometric Pressure section of the Weather dialog box

GLOBAL WEATHER AREAS

There are two types of weather areas in *Flight Simulator:* global and local. There is only one global weather area for a situation, and it affects the weather over the entire planet. Global weather does not preempt local weather, and you can have up to two local weather fronts in addition to the global weather. Since global weather applies to all regions of the Earth, you cannot edit a global area's coordinates, speed, course, width, or transition distance between other weather areas. You can only add specific weather such as winds, clouds, thunderstorms, temperature layers, and make changes in barometric pressure. There is also an option for having the weather automatically generated in global weather areas, and you can specify whether you want clouds and/or winds to be randomly created. When automatic weather is enabled, though, any other weather that you have created will not function until you toggle off this feature.

Adding Weather to the Global Weather Area

To add clouds, wind layers, temperature gradients, and barometric pressure changes to the global weather area, first select the Weather command from the World menu. Then choose Global from the Weather Area list box under the Weather dialog box. Finally, add each weather element as described earlier in this chapter.

Automatic Global Weather Generation

With automatic weather generation, you can have all weather randomly created for you, although this will disable other weather that you may have created. The steps for switching on automatic weather generation globally are as follows:

When automatic weather is enabled in the Global Edit Weather Area dialog box, all other weather options are temporarily disabled.

1. Choose the Weather command from the World menu.

2. In the Weather Area list box, select Global.

3. Click the Edit Area button, as pictured in Figure 4.14.

4. Toggle on the Automatic Weather Generation check box in the Edit Weather Area dialog box. Notice that all other options are dimmed out. This is as it should be, for you cannot edit the global weather area's coordinates, direction, or speed.

5. If you want to have clouds randomly generated, click on the Clouds check box. If you want to have wind layers automatically produced, click on the Winds check box.

CREATING AND EDITING LOCAL WEATHER AREAS

Local weather is that weather which applies to a specific area of the Earth that you determine. You can have only two local weather areas, in addition to your global weather, but the local weather preempts the global weather, except when automatic weather generation is turned on. For each area, you must define the coordinates, width, speed, course heading, and transition distance between other weather areas. Figure 4.15 shows the elements of a local weather area front that is moving from east to west, and which is 10 miles long with a width of 15 miles.

Creating a Chicago Area Weather Front with Thunderstorms

Let's create a 10-nautical-mile-long thunderstorm weather front, with a width of 15 nautical miles that approaches Chicago from the East, heading in a westerly direction at 12 knots per hour.

1. Select Weather from the World menu.

2. In the Weather dialog box, click the Add Area button.

3. In the Add Weather Area dialog box, type **Chicago Area Weather** in the Area Name text box.

4. Click on the Beginning Latitude text box, and type

N42 00 00

(*Flight Simulator* will round this number down to N41 59' 59.9999".)

5. Click on the Beginning Longitude text box, and type

W88 00 00

(*Flight Simulator* will round this number down to W87 59' 59.9999".)
Looking at your map in Figure 4.15, you can see that 42 degrees 00' 00"
N, 88 degrees 00' 00" W is on the upper-west side of Chicago.

6. Since you want to make the length of the weather front exactly 10 miles
long, in a vertical north-south line from the beginning coordinates, you
will need to set your lower coordinate 10' (minutes = nautical miles)
lower than the 42 degrees 00' 00" latitude previously given. In the
Ending Latitude text box, type

Figure 4.15
The latitude/longitude
coordinate lines that
you need to locate the
geographical area for
your local weather
area

N41 50 00

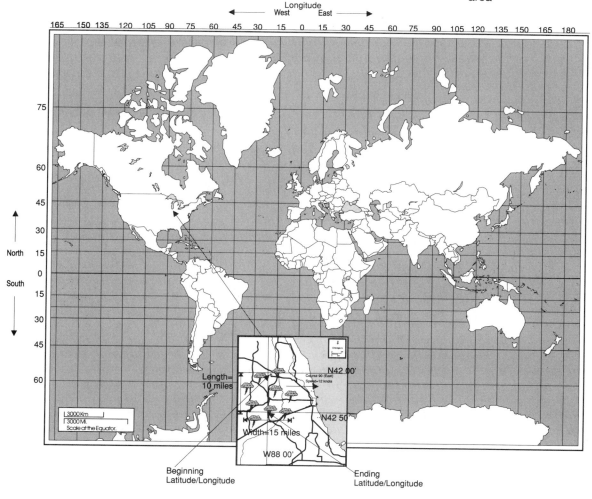

(*Flight Simulator* will round this down to N41 49' 59.9999".)

This latitude was calculated by subtracting ten minutes of arc from 42 degrees (or 41 degrees 60 minutes, which is equivalent to 42 degrees).

7. Because the length of the front is in a north-south orientation along a meridian, there is no change in longitude and you type in the same longitude coordinate of

W88 00 00

in the Ending Longitude text box.(*Flight Simulator* will round this down to W87 59' 59.9999".)

8. Enter a width of **15** miles in the Width text box.

9. For the transition text box, which controls the distance between adjacent weather areas, type in **5** miles.

10. Because your weather area is headed due east, enter a course heading of **90** degrees in the Course text box.

11. Type a speed of **12** knots for the weather area in the Speed text box. See Figure 4.16 for a view of what your dialog box should look like.

12. Click OK to exit the Add Weather Area dialog box. You will return to the Weather dialog box.

13. In the Weather Dialog box, select the Chicago Area Weather in the Weather Area list box.

14. Click the Clouds button.

15. Click the Create button, and the Create Cloud Layer dialog box will open.

16. In the Type list box, select Thunderstorms.

17. Enter a base of **1,000** feet and a tops of **10,000** feet. *Flight Simulator* will round off some altitudes by plus or minus a foot, so don't be alarmed if your entry has been slightly changed.

18. Choose Dense in the Coverage text box. See Figure 4.17 for a view of what your Create Cloud Layer dialog box should look like.

19. Click OK to exit the Cloud Layer dialog box.

20. Click OK once more to return to the simulation.

Now if you look west, you should see thunderstorms approaching Chicago.

The next section describes the various options available in the Add Weather dialog box, as seen in Figure 4.16. Note that most of these features are dimmed out and unavailable when you select the global weather area; they are used only with creating local weather fronts.

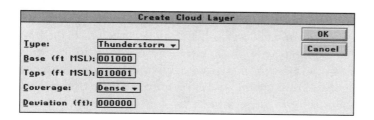

Add Weather Area

		OK
Area Name:	Chicago Area Weather	Cancel

Beginning Lat: N041° 59' 59.9999"   N041° 59' 59.9999"
Beginning Lon: W087° 59' 59.9999"   W087° 59' 59.9999"
Ending Lat: N041° 49' 59.9999"   N041° 49' 59.9999"
Ending Lon: W087° 59' 59.9999"   W087° 59' 59.9999"
Width (mi): 0015
Transition (mi): 05
Course (deg): 090
Speed (kts): 12
☐ **Automatic Weather Generation**
  ☐ Clouds
  ☐ Winds

Figure 4.16
Completed entries for the Add Weather Area dialog box

Beginning Latitude/Longitude

The Beginning Latitude/Longitude coordinates defines one vertex of the weather front's line.

Prefix your latitude entry with an N if you are entering a northern latitude, or an S if you are entering a southern latitude. For example, typing **N42 35 16** in the Beginning Latitude text box will result in a latitude coordinate of 42 degrees 35' 16" N being entered. Longitude entries must be prefixed with an E if you are in the Eastern Hemisphere, or a W if you are in the Western Hemisphere.

Ending Latitude/Longitude

The Ending Latitude/Longitude defines the second set of coordinates needed to draw the weather front's line.

Width

The width of the weather front determines how far across the weather area is. Widths must fall between the range of 0 to 2,000 miles.

Create Cloud Layer

		OK
		Cancel

Type: Thunderstorm ▾
Base (ft MSL): 001000
Tops (ft MSL): 010001
Coverage: Dense ▾
Deviation (ft): 000000

Figure 4.17
Completing the Thunderstorm in the Create Cloud Layer dialog box

Transition

In this box, enter the transition distance you want between weather areas. If you want to fly from one weather system to another in a relatively short time, pick a low distance such as five miles. Valid transition distances range from 0 miles to 99 miles.

Course

Type in the course heading in which the weather area is moving. This direction corresponds to the direction of the compass; that is, if the weather front is moving east, it is traveling on a course of 90 degrees. If it is moving south west, the course heading is 225 degrees. Valid entries are from 0 to 359 degrees.

Speed

Enter the speed, in knots per hour, with which the weather front is moving. Speeds can vary from 0 knots per hour to 99 knots per hour.

Automatic Weather Generation

This feature enables automatic weather generation of clouds or winds. It disables any other weather you may have created for this area.

Copying a Weather Area or Category

Flight Simulator 5.0 allows you only two local weather areas and one global weather area. Unfortunately, because each weather area can store only a limited number of weather categories, your repertoire of weather conditions is finite. For example, even though you have three weather areas (one global, two local), you can have a maximum of only nine different kinds of cloud layers, since only three cloud layers per weather area are allowed.

You can copy an entire category of weather from one weather area to another, but the destination weather area will have its own similar category erased when you do this. For example, if you have three wind layers that you like in one part of the country, and you want to copy them to another area, you would use the copy command to do this. When the three wind layers are copied, however, they will overwrite the three previous wind layers that you might have in the second area.

Here is how to copy a weather category:

1. Choose Weather from the World menu.
2. In the Weather dialog box, select the Weather Area where the weather you wish copied is found.
3. Select the category of weather you wish copied, whether it be clouds, winds, temperatures, or barometric pressure.
4. Click the Copy Category button. You will be prompted to select the weather area where the weather is to be pasted, as shown in Figure 4.18.

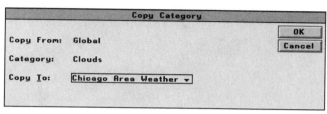

Figure 4.18
Choosing the weather area to which the copied weather category is to be sent

If you would like to copy an entire region's weather, including all wind, temperature, barometric pressures, and clouds, to another region, you would copy a weather area. Again, the second area's own weather will be overwritten when you do this.

To copy a weather area, follow these steps:

1. Choose Weather from the World menu.
2. In the Weather dialog box, select the Weather Area from which you wish to copy.
3. Click the Copy Area button.

In the Copy Weather dialog box, select the Weather Area which is to be overwritten by the copied area, as illustrated in Figure 4.19

Click OK once to return to the Weather dialog box, and once more to return to the simulator.

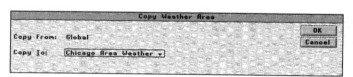

Figure 4.19
The Copy Weather Area dialog box

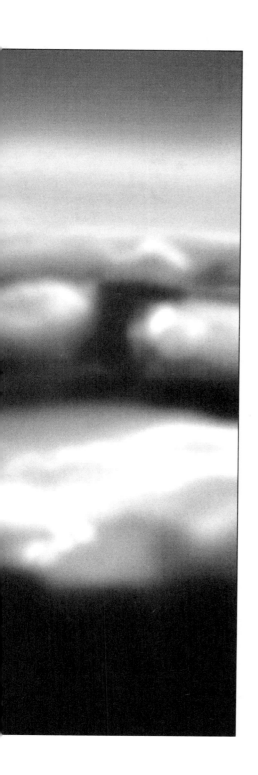

II

Flight Academy: Ground School

C H A P T E R

5

Introduction to
Airplanes and Engines

This chapter introduces you to the basic airplane, its engine, and its associated equipment. It is important to have a basic knowledge of the airplane so that you can understand how your airplane is affected by what you do. The main structural components of any airplane are as follows:

- Fuselage
- Wings
- Empennage
- Flight Controls and Airfoil Control Surfaces
- Landing Gear
- Engine

Figure 5.1 identifies these principal structural elements, as well as some other airplane components.

FUSELAGE, WINGS, EMPENNAGE

The fuselage houses the passenger cockpit, cargo, engine compartment, instruments, retractable landing gear, and other essential equipment. The engine is attached to the front of the fuselage in the engine compartment, but is separated from the passenger compartment by a heat resistant steel firewall.

The wings produce the lift necessary for flight to occur and are considered an airfoil. Airfoils are surfaces on the airplane that produce some desired action when in motion. Besides wings, other examples of airfoils include propeller blades, elevators,

131

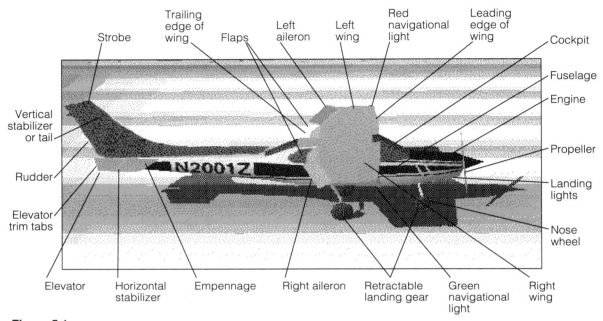

Figure 5.1
Basic structural components of the airplane

Figure 5.2
Cantilevered wing of the Learjet

flaps, ailerons, rudders, trim tabs, spoilers, horizontal and vertical stabilizers, and slats. Attached to the trailing edge of the wing are the flaps, spoilers, ailerons, and trim tabs. On modern, swept-wing, commercial aircraft, such as the Boeing 707, 727, 737, 747, 757, 767, and 777, there are lift devices on the front of the wings called leading-edge slats, which extend in conjunction with the flaps to further increase the lift of the wings.

There are two types of wings: semicantilever and cantilever. The semicantilevered wing is braced both externally by means of wing struts attached to the fuselage, and internally by spars and ribs. In the cantilever type wing, there is no external bracing; the stress is carried by internal wing spars, ribs, and stringers. Figure 5.1 shows the semi-cantilevered wing of the Cessna 182RG, and Figure 5.2 shows the Learjet's cantilevered wing. The fuel tanks in most modern aircraft today are integrated within the wing's structure.

The tail section, or empennage, of the airplane contains the airfoil surfaces necessary for pitch (up and down) and yaw (left and right) movements. It includes the fixed surfaces of the horizontal and vertical stabilizers, and includes all movable surfaces such as the vertical and horizontal stabilizers, rudder, elevator, and trim tabs.

FLIGHT CONTROLS AND SURFACES

When you fly your airplane, you control its movement via a control stick, or wheel (also called the yoke), which moves the ailerons and elevator, and pedals, which steer the rudder. In addition, there are other moveable wing surfaces such as the flaps, trim tabs, and spoilers, which allow finer control over various aspects of flight. Small aircraft, such as the Cessna Skylane 182RG, the Schweizer 2-32 sailplane, and the Sopwith Camel, have their flight control surfaces (otherwise known as "airfoil surfaces") controlled by means of cables, pulleys, and rods. For larger high-speed jet aircraft, the airfoil surfaces are moved by hydraulic pistons. Such power-assisted systems are needed because of the vastly increased forces needed to move the wing surfaces when traveling at high speeds. Usually there is some auxiliary power plant that is run off of the engine, and which provides hydraulic fluid throughout the plane at very high pressure. When the pilot moves a flight control, the movement is amplified and transmitted to the proper wing surface by means of high pressure hydraulic fluid through an elaborate network of hoses and pipes. Once the fluid reaches its destination, it moves a piston, and the piston in turn moves the wing surface.

Figure 5.3
Ailerons control aircraft roll (or bank) and are linked to the yoke by cables

Ailerons

Ailerons, which means "little wings" in French, are two moveable wing surfaces located on the trailing edges of each wing near the outer tips. When they are deflected up or down, they change the wing's lift\drag characteristics and so enable the aircraft to roll about its longitudinal axis. Both ailerons are interconnected so that they move in opposite directions of each other.

In *Flight Simulator*, the ailerons are usually moved together with the rudder

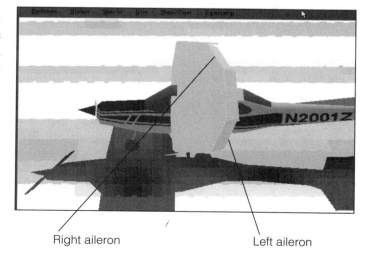

Right aileron

Left aileron

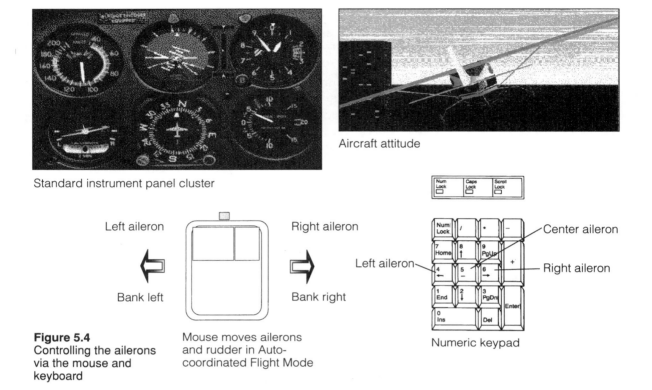

Standard instrument panel cluster

Aircraft attitude

Figure 5.4
Controlling the ailerons via the mouse and keyboard

Mouse moves ailerons and rudder in Auto-coordinated Flight Mode

Numeric keypad

in what is known as auto-coordinated mode. This mode enables you to make smooth turns without moving the rudder and ailerons separately. Thus when you move the yoke, stick, mouse, or keyboard controls to the right, the plane will make a right turn using the proper amount of rudder and aileron in concert.

Wing Flaps

Extendible flaps on the inside trailing edges of the wings allow the wing to produce more lift, thereby permitting slower landing speeds as well as decreasing the required landing strip distance. In some cases, they are used to shorten takeoff distance. The flaps can be extended in 10-degree increments, to a maximum of 40 degrees. Each flap extension, however, increases both lift and drag.

The flaps must never be extended beyond the airplane's maximum flap extended speed (V_{fe}); to do so may result in damage to the flaps.

In *Flight Simulator*, you can adjust the flaps from the keyboard or by using the mouse, as described in Figure 5.6.

Wing flaps
deployed

Figure 5.5
Wing flaps permit
slower landing speeds
and thus decrease
required landing
distances

Rudder

Attached to the vertical stabilizer of the empennage, the rudder is used to control the airplane's yaw (nose left or right). Contrary to popular belief, the rudder by itself does not make the airplane turn. It is only when it is used in coordination with the ailerons that it is possible for the airplane to make a smooth turn.

In auto-coordinated mode, moving the yoke left forces the rudder to the left, whereas moving the yoke to the right causes the rudder to move right. In auto-coordinated mode, moving the mouse left or right will also cause the ailerons to move the proper amount so that there is no slippage when making a turn. But in uncoordinated flight (if you have rudder pedals or are

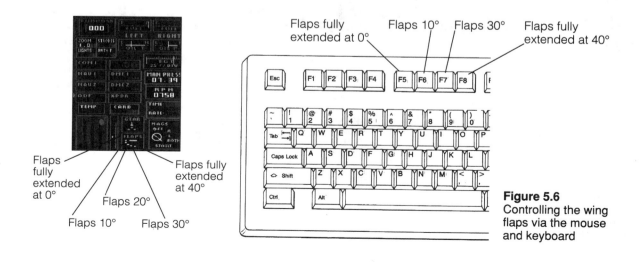

Flaps fully
extended at 0°

Flaps 10°   Flaps 30°

Flaps fully
extended at 40°

Flaps
fully
extended
at 0°

Flaps 20°

Flaps fully
extended
at 40°

Flaps 10°   Flaps 30°

Figure 5.6
Controlling the wing
flaps via the mouse
and keyboard

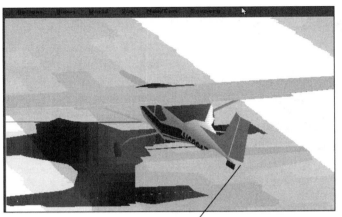

flying in uncoordinated mode via the keyboard), you must set the rudder position independently of the ailerons when making turns. Figure 5.8 shows the keyboard and mouse controls for the rudder.

Figure 5.7
The rudder controls aircraft yaw (nose left or right movement) and is linked to foot pedals beneath the dashboard via cables

Right rudder applied

Standard instrument cluster

Rudder   Aircraft yaws left or right when rudder is moved left or right

Left aileron and rudder   Right aileron and rudder

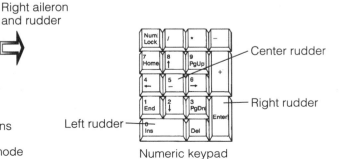

Center rudder

Right rudder

Left rudder

Numeric keypad

Figure 5.8
Controlling the rudder via the mouse and keyboard

Mouse moves ailerons and rudder in Auto-coordinated Flight mode

Elevator

The elevators are attached to the trailing edge of the horizontal stabilizer of the empennage. They act as airfoils to deflect the airflow up or down, thereby causing the nose of the aircraft to be pitched up or down. When you pull back on your yoke stick, the elevators go up, and the nose of your plane pitches upwards. When you push the yoke stick forward, the elevators go down and the nose pitches down. Up elevator reduces lift behind the center of gravity of the plane, causing the tail to drop and the nose to go up. Down elevator increases lift behind the center of gravity, and the tail rises, forcing the nose down.

Figure 5.10 illustrates the proper keyboard

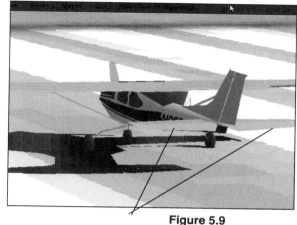

Elevators

Figure 5.9
The elevators control aircraft pitch (nose up or down movement) and are linked to the yoke by cables

Elevator position indicator

Standard instrument panel cluster

Aircraft climbing (Up elevator pitches nose up)

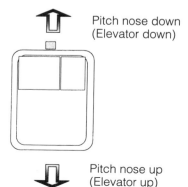

Pitch nose down
(Elevator down)

Pitch nose up
(Elevator up)

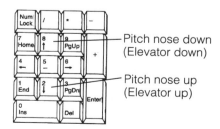

Pitch nose down
(Elevator down)

Pitch nose up
(Elevator up)

Figure 5.10
Controlling the elevator via the mouse and keyboard

Figure 5.11
The elevator trim tabs aid the pilot in maintaining level flight and are linked to a lever via cables

Elevator Trim Tabs

and mouse yoke movements for manipulating the elevator.

Trim Tabs

In addition to the primary flight control surfaces, there are secondary airfoils called trim tabs, which help to maintain the aircraft's attitude while correcting for unbalanced aerodynamic forces on the plane. For example, if the pilot needs to pull the yoke back in order to keep the plane flying straight and level, he or she would quickly tire of keeping the pressure on the yoke indefinitely. The aerodynamic forces tend to force the elevator back to its neutral position, so to prevent this, and relieve the pilot of constantly applying yoke pressure, the trim tab can be set to take up the slack.

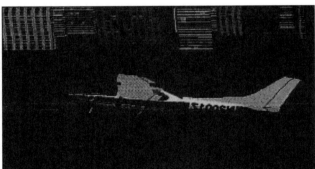

Use elevator trim to make minor adjustments to nose pitch

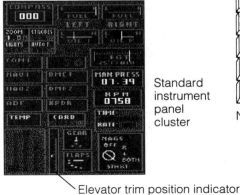

Standard instrument panel cluster

Elevator trim position indicator

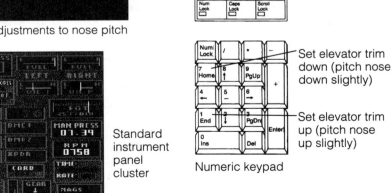

Set elevator trim down (pitch nose down slightly)

Set elevator trim up (pitch nose up slightly)

Numeric keypad

Figure 5.12
Controlling the elevator trim tabs from the keyboard

Spoilers

The spoilers, found on most jets and gliders, are hinged wing panels mounted on the upper surface of each wing. Their purpose is to spoil or disrupt the flow of air over the wings, thereby reducing the lifting force of the wings. This allows the pilot to increase the rate of descent without increasing the airplane's speed. Spoilers are also used as a form of air braking, and if you have ever traveled on a commercial airliner and watched the wings during the descent phase of a flight, you may have noticed these panels deploying on top of the wing to slow the jet down.

On the Schweizer 2-32 Sailplane, the spoilers are called "dive brakes."

Figure 5.13
The Sailplane and the Learjet both have spoilers, which act as air brakes

LANDING GEAR

The landing gear of the aircraft serves as its principal means of support whether on land or water. For amphibious water landings, special pontoons are mounted on each wheel, allowing the plane to hydroplane while landing or taking off, and to float while stationary. Special ski landing gear can be mounted for snow-bound areas, allowing operations in Arctic areas on unimproved ice runways. Both pontoons and skis can have retractable wheels built into each wheel and strut assembly so that the plane can operate on land, water, or ice without changing landing gear.

Airplanes can have either a tailwheel or nosewheel, which not only help support the airplane on the ground, but also allow steering. Today, most modern airplanes are designed with a nosewheel and two main wheels mounted on the wings or fuselage. This landing gear arrangement is often called a "tricycle gear" since there are three wheels arranged in a triangular shape.

In Flight Simulator, the Cessna and Learjet have a tricycle landing gear, while the Sopwith Camel has a tailwheel type landing gear. The Schweizer 2-32 Sailplane has an unusual landing gear setup; there is a tailwheel and one center wheel mounted in the center of the fuselage along with a "tip wheel" on each wing tip. When the aircraft is at rest, you will notice that one wing

Figure 5.14
The spoiler on/off indicator

tips onto the ground, and the wing tip wheel prevents it from rubbing or dragging on the runway.[1]

Retractable Landing Gear

Retractable landing gear, as found on the Cessna and Learjet, allow the plane to fly with reduced air drag. By retracting the landing gear into the wings and fuselage, the aircraft becomes more streamlined and offers less air resistance. This improves performance and fuel economy.

Because of the tremendous airflow pressures outside of the aircraft, the retraction and extension of the landing gear cannot be performed by hand. Instead, hydraulic- or electrical-activated mechanisms force the landing gear up or down, and a locking device ensures that the gear is in place. A warning indicator informs the pilot when the wheels are down or stowed. In the event of a failure, a backup system is always provided to allow manual deployment of the landing gear. In the actual Cessna Skylane 182RG, there is an emergency, hand-operated hydraulic pump that allows you to manually extend the landing gear in the event of a hydraulic system failure. But the landing gear cannot be retracted with the hand pump. The Learjet provides a manually controlled pneumatic system that blows the landing gear down with compressed air.

Nosewheel Steering

In both the Cessna and Learjet, the nosewheel can be steered by means of the rudder pedals. The linkage to the wheels can be via cables, push-pull rods, or hydraulic fluid, depending on the amount of force needed to turn the wheels. Large, heavy aircraft utilize hydraulically assisted power steering because of the enormous forces needed to turn the wheel. The Learjet uses such power-assisted steering via the rudder pedals.

Differential Wheel Brakes

When taxiing or landing, the wheel brakes are used for slowing, stopping, or steering the airplane. Differential brakes, found on the Cessna and Learjet, are wheel brakes installed on each main landing wheel that can be actuated

The brakes for any aircraft in FS 5.0 can be activated by pressing [.] on the main keyboard. For differential braking, [F11] applies the left brake, and [F12] applies the right brake. To set the parking brake, press [Ctrl] [.]; to release the parking brake, press [.]. For more realistic controls, you can buy rudder pedals that you hook up to your joystick port. These pedals have special toe fittings that allow you to individually control the left or right differential brake.

---

[1]Notice that when you are on the ground and looking at the sailplane in spot view, out of airplane view, the wings are tilted. This is because one of your wings is resting its tip wheel on the ground.

independently of each other by the pilot. The right-hand brake is controlled by applying pressure to the top of the right rudder pedal, whereas the left-hand brake is controlled by pressure applied to the top of the left rudder pedal. By judicious use of the right or left brake pedal, you can steer the aircraft while on the ground during landing or taxiing. To apply both brakes, simply press on both toe pedals together.

Most small airplanes, such as the Cessna Skylane, have what is known as an "independent" brake system, because each brake has its own hydraulic fluid reservoir and is entirely independent of the airplane's main hydraulic system. The system operates much like conventional automobile brake systems, with master cylinders, brake fluid reservoirs, fluid lines, and drum or disc brakes on each wheel comprising the main components. When the pilot applies toe pressure to a rudder pedal, the master cylinder builds up pressure through the movement of a piston inside a fluid-filled cylinder. The brake fluid is then transmitted at high pressure through fluid lines to each brake assembly, where pistons force brake pads on the wheel's drum or disk surfaces. When parking, the brakes can be left on by employing a ratchet type locking device that maintains brake fluid pressure on the wheels.

AIRCRAFT ENGINES

The engine develops the power that gives the airplane forward motion, thereby generating the lift that enables it to fly. Engines are also commonly referred to as "powerplants," since not only do they provide propulsion, but also produce electrical power for the operation of electric motors, pumps, controls, lights, air conditioning, radios, and navigational instruments. In addition, they provide hydraulic power necessary to pressurize the hydraulic system for the movement of the airfoil surfaces and landing gear. Furthermore, the engine furnishes heat for the crew members' and passengers' comfort, and for de-icing of the wings in cold weather, and it provides compressed air for pressurizing the cabin when flying above 8,000 feet.

The two most common types of internal combustion powerplants in use today are the reciprocating piston engine and the turbine jet engine.

Piston

The reciprocating engine is so called because pressures from burning and expanding gases cause a piston in an enclosed cylinder to move up and down. The reciprocating motion of the piston is transferred into rotary motion by a crankshaft that is connected to the propeller.

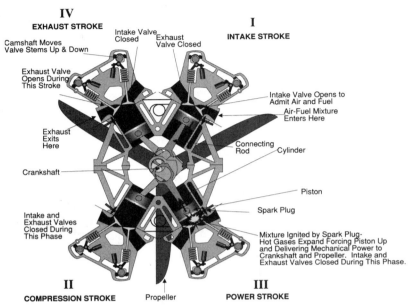

IV
EXHAUST STROKE

Camshaft Moves
Valve Stems Up & Down

Intake Valve
Closed

Exhaust
Valve Closed

I
INTAKE STROKE

Exhaust Valve
Opens During
This Stroke

Intake Valve Opens to
Admit Air and Fuel

Air-Fuel Mixture
Enters Here

Exhaust
Exits
Here

Connecting
Rod

Cylinder

Crankshaft

Piston

Intake and
Exhaust Valves
Closed During
This Phase

Spark Plug

Mixture Ignited by Spark Plug.
Hot Gases Expand Forcing Piston Up
and Delivering Mechanical Power to
Crankshaft and Propeller. Intake and
Exhaust Valves Closed During This Phase.

II
COMPRESSION STROKE

Propeller

III
POWER STROKE

Figure 5.15
The four-stroke cycle
of the reciprocating
piston engine

There are two principal means by which fuel is mixed with air into the cylinder of a reciprocating piston engine. The most common method of fuel mixing is called *carburetion*, whereby the fuel is atomized, vaporized, and mixed with air in a mechanical device called the carburetor. Air and fuel are drawn into the cylinder by the suction of the piston moving down in the cylinder, where it is then ignited by spark plugs. The other method of fuel mixing is called *fuel injection*, because the fuel is injected under pressure by an electrical pump directly into the cylinders, where it vaporizes and mixes with air. The fuel is precisely metered and controlled by a computer, along with the timing of the ignition by the spark plugs so that greater power, fuel economy, engine efficiency, and reliability can be achieved.

The reciprocating piston engine must go through four stages in order for complete combustion of the fuel to occur. This cycle is known as the "Four-Stroke Cycle" and is illustrated in Figure 5.15. When the piston moves downward, sucking in air and atomized fuel through the intake valve, it is in the *intake stroke*. After the piston reaches the bottom of its downward stroke, the intake valve closes and the piston begins to move upward compressing the gaseous mixture of fuel and air. This is called the *compression stroke*. Just before the piston reaches the top of the cylinder on its way up, a spark plug over the cylinder head ignites the fuel mixture and an explosion of rapidly expanding hot gases ensues. The piston reaches the top of the cylinder head and, at the peak of the detonation, is forced downward in what is called the *power stroke*. Both intake and exhaust valves are closed during this phase. The piston, which is moving downward under great force, imparts momentum to the crankshaft, which in turn rotates the propeller. After this, when the piston reaches the bottom of the cylinder, the exhaust valve opens, and as the piston returns to the top of the cylinder, the gases are ejected into the atmosphere. This last stage is called the *exhaust stroke*.

With the Cessna's six-cylinder (and six-piston), Lycoming Model O-540-L3C5D engine, each individual cylinder has its own four-stroke cycle, but staggered at even intervals so as to create a balanced power stroke. Two complete revolutions of the crankshaft are required for all the pistons to accomplish their four-stroke cycle.

Carburation, Air/Fuel Mixture Controls, and Ignition Systems

Liquid fuel in all internal combustion engines must be first vaporized into small particles and then mixed with air in precise quantities before combustion can occur. This process is called carburetion. The carburetor must sense the temperature, altitude, and other data to calculate how much fuel to mix at any given time. Because altitude affects the air/fuel ratio, a mixture control is provided for the pilot to manually control the carburetor's mixture ratios. The purpose of the mixture control is to prevent the mixture from becoming too rich (excess fuel) at high altitudes due to the decreasing density (weight) of the air. Using the mixture control in conjunction with the EGT (Exhaust Gas Temperature) gauge, you can also *lean* the mixture (decrease the amount of fuel mixed per mass of air) to conserve fuel and provide maximum fuel efficiency.

Air/Fuel ratios are described by a ratio expression such as "12:1." This means that 12 pounds of air are being mixed with each 1 pound of fuel. Richer mixtures have lower ratios, for example 8:1, in which more fuel is being burned per mass of air. Leaner mixtures have higher ratios, for example, 16:1, because less fuel is being mixed per quantity of air.

As altitude increases, the air fuel ratio decreases and the mixture becomes richer. At 18,000 feet, for example, the air is only half as dense as at sea level, and a cubic foot of space contains only half as many molecules of air. Likewise, the engine cylinder drawing in air will contain only half as much air as the same cylinder at sea level; consequently, if you use the same amount of fuel at sea level that you use at 18,000 feet, the mixture will be much too rich and the engine will lose power and/or run roughly. Climbing higher and higher at the same throttle setting, the mixture becomes progressively richer and richer, since less oxygen is available the higher you go. Table 5.1 and Figure 5.16 summarize these results.

Using the mixture control, you can counteract over-riching the mixture by leaning the engine as you climb. How do

Figure 5.16
Air/fuel mixture gets richer with increasing altitude due to thinning atmosphere (fewer molecules of oxygen are available)

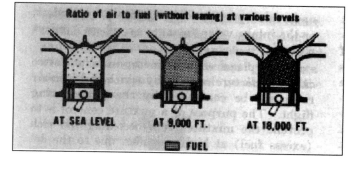

Ratio of air to fuel (without leaning) at various levels

AT SEA LEVEL   AT 9,000 FT.   AT 18,000 FT.

☐ FUEL

Table 5.1   Air–Fuel Mixture and Relationship with Altitude and EGT Temperature

Air–Fuel Mixture	EGT (Exhause Gas Temperature)	Effect of Altitude
Lean (less fuel per mass of air)	Temperature rises, engine gets hotter	Mixture leans with lower altitudes
Rich (more fuel per mass of air)	Temperature falls, engine gets cooler	Mixture is enriched with higher altitudes

you do this? By watching the EGT gauge (sometimes called the "EGT Bug Needle"), you can observe how hot the engine's exhaust is running. The exhaust gets hotter as you lean the engine, and cooler as you enrich it. The best fuel economy/power setting is found when you enrich the mixture 50 degrees less than peak lean temperature. With aviation gas costing $2.50 a gallon, you should pay close attention to this fact! Here are the steps you should follow to properly lean your engine:

1. Lean the Mixture Control until you establish what the peak EGT temperature is.

2. When the EGT needle reaches its highest temperature, enrich the Mixture Control until the temperature has declined 50 degrees below the peak EGT temperature. This is the recommended lean mixture setting, although the leanest (but hottest) setting offers the best fuel economy.

Remember, be very careful not to overlean your engine, since too lean a mixture can damage the engine due to overheating. The following basic rules regarding changes to mixture settings should be followed at all times:

1. Always enrich the mixture before increasing the throttle.

2. Reset the mixture after any change in power/throttle settings or altitude.

3. Use full, rich mixture for takeoff and climb, unless the manufacturer recommends leaning at high altitudes to eliminate roughness and loss of power.

 In *Flight Simulator*, the Mixture Control is automatically adjusted for you, although you can switch this feature off under the Realism and Reliability menu command. To manually set the mixture perform these steps:

1. Select the Sim menu, and click on Realism and Reliability.

2. In the Realism and Reliability dialog box, locate the Prop Propulsion Realism area and toggle on the Mixture Control checkbox.

Table 5.2 Mixture and Exhaust Gas Temperature	
Mixture Description	**Exhause Gas Temperature**
Recommended Lean	50 Degrees Rich of Peak EGT (50 degrees cooler than peak lean temperature)
Best Fuel Economy	Peak EGT (hottest or peak lean temperature)

3. Click OK to return to the simulation. You can now manually adjust the Mixture Control.

You can richen the mixture by dragging the Mixture Control to the top, or lean it by dragging the control to the bottom.

The ignition system provides the spark that ignites the air/fuel mixture in the cylinders. On reciprocating piston engines, a magneto type ignition system is used in which self-contained magneto generators, driven by the engine, supply electrical power to fire the spark plugs. Since the ignition system is so vital to the proper operation of the engine, the Federal Aviation Administration requires that modern airplane engines have dual ignition systems, and that they be completely separate from the rest of the plane's electrical system. Each ignition system has separate magnetos, cables, and spark plugs so that, in the event of one system failing, the engine may be operated until a safe landing is made. There is an ignition switch located on the instrument panel, which allows you to select the Left or Right Magneto system, shut off the magnetos entirely, or operate the starter motor when starting the engine up.

Turbochargers

Many newer airplanes come equipped with turbocharging systems to increase the power of the engine as well as allow high-altitude operations. These superchargers are powered by the energy of the exhaust gas spinning a turbine blade and driving an air compressor, which packs in more oxygen to each cylinder of the engine. This allows more air/fuel to be compressed into the cylinder for combustion, thereby increasing the maximum power the engine can produce. At high altitudes this is a very important feature, since the density of the air is much less and engine power decreases because of the lack of oxygen (despite leaning).

Richer mixture

Leaner mixture

Figure 5.17
Mixture control

Figure 5.18
The EGT (Exhaust Gas Temperature Gauge). Each tick mark represents 25 degrees Fahrenheit

Figure 5.19
Starter/magneto controls

Fixed-Pitch Propellers vs. Constant-Speed Propellers

The propeller transforms the rotary motion of the engine into forward thrust for the airplane. Each blade of the propeller is a moving airfoil surface, and is thus essentially a rotating wing.

There are two kinds of propellers:

- Fixed-Pitch
- Constant-Speed

The fixed-pitch propeller has the blade pitch (blade angle) set to a constant angle that cannot be changed. These propellers are designed for operating best at one rotational and forward speed. The constant-speed propeller, on the other hand, has a speed governor that regulates the blade pitch in order to maintain a constant engine RPM. In *Flight Simulator*, the Sopwith Camel comes equipped with a fixed-pitch propeller, whereas the Cessna Skylane 182RG has a constant-speed propeller.

As mentioned previously, the constant-speed propeller is an automatically controlled pitch propeller with a governor that regulates the blade angle for a given engine RPM, altitude, and power setting. The purpose of having the blade's pitch adjusted is to maintain a constant propeller speed under varying engine loads. For example, if the engine RPM increases due to thinning air at higher altitudes, the speed governor increases the propeller's blade angle (increasing the air load) until the RPM has returned to a preset speed. The speed governor will respond automatically to small variations in RPM so that a constant propeller speed is maintained at all times.

The propeller's blade angle affects the motion of the propeller through the airstream. When the blade angle is at a low pitch, as illustrated in Figure 5.20, the propeller slices through the air more easily and a high RPM is maintained. A low propeller pitch is thus useful for obtaining maximum power on takeoff. When the blade angle is increased so that it bites into the air more forcefully, the RPM is lowered. This is useful for flying at higher altitudes or at higher speeds, at which the approaching windstream tends to cause the propeller to windmill faster than you would like. By increasing the blade angle, the propeller's RPM will decrease and you can maintain a comfortable engine load. Changing the pitch angle may be compared to changing gears in an automobile. When you start a car from a standstill, you shift into low gear; this corresponds to setting a high pitch on the propeller. Next, to prevent overstraining your engine after you have reached cruising speed, you shift the automobile's transmission into high gear; this corresponds to setting a low pitch angle on the propeller.

The Prop Advance Control is initially set in *Flight Simulator* to

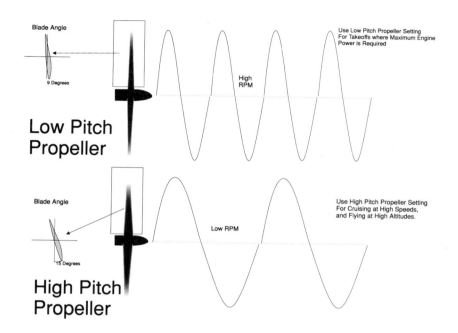

Figure 5.20
Propeller blade angle vs. engine RPM

automatic.[2] This means that you need not pay any attention to the lever when you make changes in your throttle settings, altitude, or speed. If you want to manually advance or decrease the propeller's pitch, however, you must select Manual from the Prop Advance Control list box found in the Realism and Reliability dialog box. Here is how to do this:

1. Select the Sim menu and click on Realism and Reliability.

2. In the Realism and Reliability dialog box, locate the Prop Propulsion Realism area and click open the Prop Advance list box.

3. Select Manual from among the three options of Automatic, Fixed Pitch, and Manual.

4. Click OK to return to the simulation. You can now manually adjust the Propeller's pitch angle by sliding the Propeller Control lever up or down.

Low pitch
angle/high RPM

Low pitch
low/high RPM

Figure 5.21
Prop pitch control

---

[2] The FS 5.0 manual uses the term Propeller Control, although this is factually incorrect. The Prop Advance control is really a knob that sets the speed governor's maximum propeller speed. The speed governor actually takes care of the dirty business of deciding the proper blade angle. Essentially, the setting you choose determines the maximum speed for the propeller; the governor won't let the prop pitch advance to allow a propeller speed faster than your setting.

Table 5.3 Propeller Blade Angle and Engine RPM Relationship		
Pitch	**Effect on Engine RPM**	**Useful For**
Low blade angle	Higher RPM	Takeoffs, where maximum power is needed
High blade angle	Lower RPM	Cruising at high speed, or flying at high altitudes

When you slide the Propeller Control lever up, you decrease the propeller's pitch and increase the engine's RPM. If you slide the Propeller Control down, you increase the propeller's pitch and decrease the engine's RPM.

Manifold Pressure Gauge and Tachometer

The two instruments that give you a measure of your engine's power output are the Manifold Pressure Gauge and the Tachometer (RPM or Engine Rotations Per Minute). The Manifold Pressure Gauge measures the amount of engine vacuum, or suction, that the pistons are exerting on the incoming air/fuel mixture. It is measured in inches of Mercury (Hg) *below atmospheric pressure*, and ranges from 0° all the way to 30° or more. On turbocharged engines, the Manifold Pressure readings can go as high as 40°. For most aircraft, there is a never-exceed manifold pressure limit for any given RPM; this limit, if exceeded, can cause severe stress on the engine cylinders to the point at which structural failure could occur. For the Cessna, the Manifold Pressure averages around 29° to 31° Hg for most conditions.

The tachometer simply measures how many times the engine's crankshaft revolves per minute. It can range from 0 RPM all the way up to 3,000 RPM or more for piston-powered engines. This instrument tells you whether your engine is rotating excessively fast, just right, or too slow. On the Cessna, typical cruising RPM is about 2,100 to 2,400 RPM.

Maximum

Minimum

Figure 5.22
Throttle control

Relationship Between Manifold Pressure and Engine RPM

As the throttle is increased, the power output of the engine increases and is indicated by an increase in manifold pressure. The Propeller Control, or Prop Advance, changes the pitch of the propeller blades and governs the RPMs of the engine, as indicated on the tachometer. Increasing the throttle further causes the manifold pressure to rise, and the pitch angle of the propeller blades is then automatically increased through the action of the speed governor to hold down the speed of the propellers. (As the blade angle increases to a higher pitch angle, the air load on the propeller increases; this increases the load on the engine and causes the RPMs to be held down to a constant level.) Conversely, when the throttle is reduced, the manifold pressure falls and the pitch angle of the propeller blades is automatically decreased. This decrease in propeller pitch lightens the load on the engine, which is developing less power because of the reduced throttle setting, and the RPM thus remains constant.

Figure 5.23
Manifold pressure gauge and tachometer

Turbine (Turbojet)

Turbine jet engines use a different principle to produce thrust. A turbine inside the turbojet is driven by high speed exhaust gases; in turn, this turbine spins a compressor turbine to compress the incoming air. After the incoming air is compressed, it becomes very hot and is forced into a combustion chamber, where fuel is mixed and ignited by special burners. The resulting explosion of hot gas exits the rear of the engine, passing through the turbine that spins the compressors. The hot gas rushes out the rear of the engine at high velocity, thus creating great thrust for the aircraft.

Turbofan Jet

The favored type of engine for commercial jet aviation is the turbofan jet engine. This engine is a variation of the turbojet, and has a distinctively large, oversized low pressure compressor in the front of the engine, which creates a relatively cool and slow propulsive jet exhaust. Its advantages over the turbojet include reduced fuel consumption, better propulsive efficiency, and dramatically lower noise levels. This is an important consideration for airports that have restricted night flying because of neighborhood noise complaints. Jet aircraft equipped with turbofan engines can then enjoy less restrictive flying schedules. In fact, to reduce noise and extend their useful life spans, many older aircraft, such as the McDonnell Douglas DC-9 (now called the MD-80 or Super 80) and Boeing 737, have had their turbojet engines replaced by the newer technology high-bypass turbofan engines. Some aircraft, notably the Boeing 727, cannot be re-engined with these newer engines, and so have become obsolete. Due to these considerations, production of the turbojet engined Boeing 727 was discontinued in September 1984.

Figure 5.24
Operating principles of the Turbojet engine

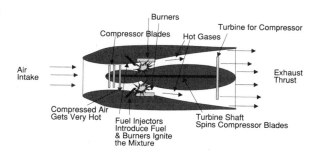

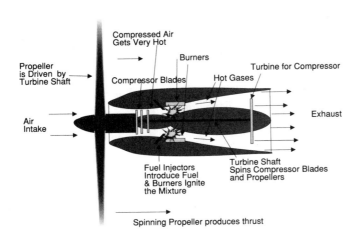

Figure 5.25
Operating principles of
the Turboprop engine

The two Garrett AiResearch TFE731-2-2B turbofan engines used on the Learjet 35A are rated at 3,500 lbs of thrust each. Present-day turbofan engines, such as the GE CF6-80C2, used on the Boeing 747, 767, and Airbus A310 and A330, produce thrust in the range of 50,000 to 60,000 lbs. Powerful new turbofan engines under development for the new twin engine Boeing 777, expected to enter service in the mid 1990s, will generate thrust of nearly 100,000 lbs!

Modern turbofan jet engines are one of the most compact sources of power known to mankind, other than one-shot devices (meaning they can be used only once) such as explosives. These engines can be found in other diverse roles, such as driving air-cushion vehicles, powering warships, producing electrical power in power plants, driving pumps, and in general being used wherever high-sustained power is required with the utmost reliability. Because there are fewer moving parts in a jet engine than in the reciprocating piston engine, the turbojet/turbofan powerplant is inherently more reliable than its piston-powered counterpart. For example, the mean time between overhaul (TBO) can range from 1,400 hours for the Garrettt turbofan jet engines, to 3,000 hours for the General Electric CFE 738 turbofan engine. The TBO applies only to the hot section of the engine core, and the TBO for the other parts of the engine can be as much as 6,000 hours before an engine rebuild is necessary! Compared to this, the 1,000 to 2,000 hours TBO for a piston-powered, reciprocating engine is not very appealing.

Turboprop

In another variant of the turbine jet engine, the turbo-prop (turbo-propeller) engine has a turbine that also drives a propeller in addition to the compressor blades. The propeller in the turbo-prop engine supplies most of the engine's thrust, although some of the exhaust gas vented out the back of the engine contributes a portion of the overall thrust. Although the turbo-prop has a theoretical fuel efficiency advantage over most jet engines, and some airplane manufacturers are at present investigating their use in large commercial jet-liners, problems remain with unacceptably high noise levels, particularly inside the cabin.

CHAPTER
6

Mastering Flight Basics

This chapter discusses the basic principles of flight. Although the actual physics and mathematical description of flight dynamics is a complex topic that goes far beyond the scope of this book, a limited discussion on fluid dynamics, Bournelli's Equation, and the fundamental aerodynamic forces is provided to demystify the principles of flying. The chapter concludes with a brief overview of stalls and how to avoid them.

THE PHYSICS OF FLIGHT

For any discussion of aerodynamics, you must have a firm understanding of the nature of forces. The next section covers the application of Newton's laws to the physics of flight.

Newton's Laws

Sir Isaac Newton, the brilliant 17th-century English physicist and mathematician, formulated the basic concepts of mechanics (the laws of motion, action, and reaction) in 1687. Not only did he codify the principles of mechanics in three famous laws, but he also discovered the law of universal gravitation, and invented calculus.

Newton's first law of motion was formalized by the following definition:

An object at rest will remain at rest and an object in motion will continue in motion with a constant velocity until it experiences a net external force.

His second law of motion defined force as follows:

The acceleration of an object is directly proportional to the resultant force acting on it and inversely proportional to its mass.

Force is thus defined as

$$F = ma$$

where F is defined in Newtons (or $\dfrac{Kilogram - meters}{Second^2}$) or pounds (English unit of force is the pound, which has units or $\dfrac{Slug - Feet}{Second^2}$), m is defined as mass in kilograms or slugs (English unit of mass is the slug), and a is the acceleration of the object in $\dfrac{meters}{second^2}$ or in English units ($\dfrac{feet}{second^2}$).

Acceleration is defined as the change in velocity per unit time of an object, and it has the following derivation:

$$a = \frac{v_{final} - v_{initial}}{t_{final} - t_{initial}} = \frac{\Delta v}{\Delta t}$$

Δv is the difference between the final velocity and the initial velocity. Δt is the change in time from the initial time to the final time.

For an airplane to fly at a constant speed, according to Newton's first law of motion, the four forces of lift, weight, drag, and thrust must all cancel each other out. If the airplane is to climb, the force of lift must be greater than the force of weight. Conversely, if the airplane is to descend, the force of lift must be less than the force of weight.

Likewise, to increase the airplane's speed, the thrusting force of the engines must be greater than the drag forces on the airplane. And to decrease the airplane's speed, the drag force must be greater than the thrust force.

Figure 6.1
The four forces acting on the airplane

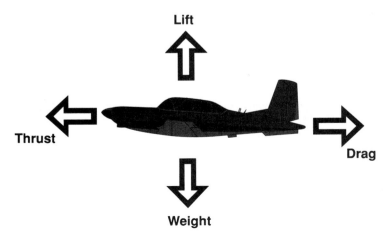

Lift

Thrust

Drag

Weight

The Four Basic Forces of Aerodynamics

There are four forces that affect your aircraft and that must be balanced for stable flight to occur (see Figure 6.1). These forces are lift, weight, thrust, and drag.

Lift

Lift is an upward force on the wings that counteracts the opposing force of weight caused by the Earth's gravitational field on the mass of the airplane. Lift acts perpendicular to the relative wind to oppose the force of gravity. Two forces create lift: the Bournelli pressure differential on the upper and lower surfaces of the wing, and air deflection caused by the wing's angle of attack(see Figure 6.2). A discussion of Bournelli's Law for fluids (or airflow, since air is considered a compressible fluid) follows later in this chapter. The lift must exactly counteract the opposite force of weight if the aircraft is to fly straight and level. Lift must be greater than the aircraft's weight in order to gain altitude, and less than the aircraft's weight in order to descend.

Greater lift is achieved if the wing travels faster through the air or if its angle of attack is increased. The angle between the wing and the relative wind is called the angle of attack. Increasing the angle of attack increases lift, but also deflects more air and increases induced drag. This induced drag at high angles of attack occurs because violent vortices form over the wing, creating more turbulence and disrupting the smooth flow of air over the wing.

As shown in Figure 6.3, lift is proportional to the square of the airplane's velocity. An airplane traveling at 200 knots,

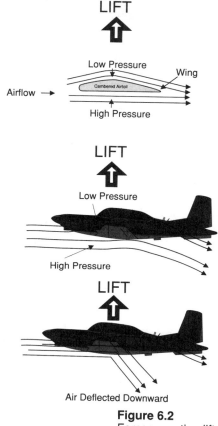

Figure 6.2
Forces creating lift

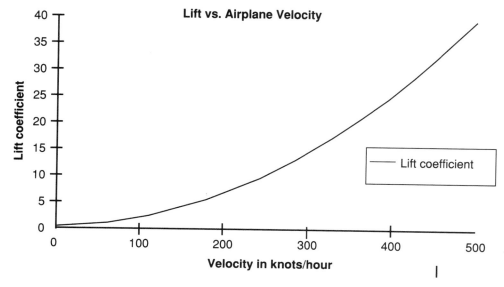

Figure 6.3
Lift is proportional to the square of the airplane's velocity

Table 6.1 Takeoff Distance vs. Temperature					
Temperature (Fahrenheit)	60	70	80	90	100
Takeoff distance for the Learjet (feet). Flaps set at 20 degrees	5020	5150	5560	6130	7370
Takeoff distance for the Cessna Skylane 182RG (Feet), Flaps set at 20 degrees	790	855	925	975	1000

for example, has four times the lift of an airplane traveling at 100 knots, if the angle of attack and other factors remain constant.

You can also increase lift by extending the flaps. Any extension of the flaps, however, also increases parasitic drag and unless you apply more thrust, the aircraft will lose airspeed.

Lift also varies directly with the density of the air; the denser the atmosphere, the greater the lift. At an altitude of 18,000 feet, the density of air is one-half the density of air at sea level. Thus, to maintain its lift at a higher altitude, the airplane must fly at a greater airspeed. Also, on warm days, the air is less dense than on cold days. This means that on a hot day, the airplane must travel at a greater speed than on a cold day if it is to maintain the same amount of lift. Furthermore, landings and takeoffs require longer runways on hot days than on cold days because of the decreased lift caused by the less dense hot air (see Table 6.1). Similarly, a takeoff from Denver's Stapleton International Airport at an altitude of 5,871 feet will take a longer runway distance than from San Francisco International at an altitude of 11 feet.

Weight

Weight is the attractive force that the Earth's gravitational field exerts on the mass of the airplane and on its passengers, cargo, and fuel. It is diametrically opposed to lift and is mathematically described as

$$F = mg$$

where F is the Force of gravity, m is the mass of the airplane and its occupants, and g is the acceleration of gravity

$$9.8 \; \frac{meters}{second^2} \quad \text{or} \quad 32 \; \frac{feet}{second^2}.$$

The Cessna, which has a weight of 3,122 lbs, according to the above formula, has a mass of 97.56 slugs.

$$m = \frac{F}{g} = \frac{33{,}122 \; lbs}{32 \; \frac{feet}{second^2}} = 97.56 \; slugs.$$

In metric terms, the Cessna has a weight of 13,887 Newtons, and dividing out the acceleration of gravity, ($9.8 \frac{meters}{second^2}$), we get a mass of 1,417 kilograms as follows:

$$m = \frac{F}{g} = \frac{13{,}887 \; Newtons}{9.8 \; \frac{meters}{second^2}} = 1{,}417 \; kilograms$$

An aircraft has a center of gravity that is usually determined by the center of mass of the airplane. If an aircraft is loaded in an unbalanced way so that too much weight is distributed in one place, the center of gravity (center of mass) can change and drastically affect the airplane's stability. This can cause an airplane to crash, and in fact, years ago a jetliner carrying a cargo of steer crashed because the cattle shifted around inside the plane and caused its center of gravity to be shifted too far forward. As a result, the jet lost its lateral stability and it nose-dived into the ground.

Thrust

Thrust is the force applied by the engines that causes forward motion of the airplane through the air. When applied, thrust causes the airplane to accelerate forwards, gaining speed until the counteracting force of drag equals that of thrust. In order for a constant speed to be maintained, thrust and drag must be equal, just as lift and weight must be equal to maintain a constant altitude.

To increase thrust, the throttle is pushed forward (or up on the FS 5.0 control panel), whereas to decrease thrust the throttle is pulled back (or down on the FS 5.0 control panel). Contrary to what you might think, increasing thrust does not translate into a direct increase in horizontal airspeed. Due to the airflow over the wings and tail, increasing the thrust tends to force the nose up causing the aircraft to ascend, as illustrated in Figure 6.4. Similarly, decreased power causes the nose to lower and the aircraft to enter a descent. This explains why you use the engine throttle settings to control your vertical speed (up and down ascending and descending velocity) in what is known as the Power/Pitch Rule:

> *Use the Throttle power settings to make changes in vertical airspeed;*
> *use the Elevator pitch controls to make changes in airspeed.*

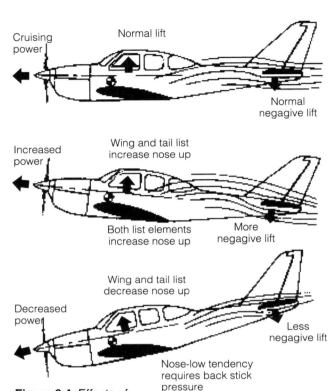

Figure 6.4 Effects of power/airspeed changes

Figure 6.5
Drag vs. speed chart

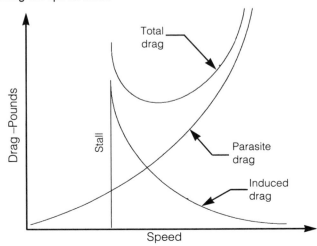

Drag

Drag is the force that retards forward motion of the aircraft. There are two types of drag: *parasitic*, and *induced*. Parasitic drag comes from the disruption and friction of the airflow over the surface of the airplane, whereas induced drag comes from the turbulent vortices of air currents that are created whenever a wing moves through the airstream. With careful design of an aircraft, parasitic drag can be reduced, but induced drag is an inherent penalty of the wing's producing lift and it is always present in some form.

As illustrated in Figure 6.5, total drag is equal to the sum of parasitic drag and induced drag:

Total Drag = Parasitic drag + Induced drag

Furthermore, as can be seen in the figure, the faster the airplane travels, the greater the parasitic drag. Induced drag, on the other hand, decreases for greater aircraft speeds. Because parasitic drag increases much more rapidly than induced drag decreases for greater aircraft speeds, you can see that total drag on the aircraft increases overall for greater airspeeds.

Bournelli's Law for Pressure, Kinetic Energy, and Potential Energy

The study of fluids in motion is called fluid dynamics. A fluid is defined as having particles that easily move and change position. The particles can be compressible, as in a gas, or incompressible, as in a liquid, but in both cases the particles are capable of flowing easily. The airflow over a wing and the flow of water through a pipe are examples of fluid dynamics.

To understand the physics of flight, one must understand Bournelli's Equation and how it relates to the motion of a particle on a streamline. We first will use the example of fluid moving through a pipe to explain the general principles involved, and then turn to the direct case of the streamlined flow of air around an airplane wing.

As fluid moves through a pipe of varying cross section and elevation, the pressure will change along the pipe. The Swiss physicist Daniel Bournelli (1700-1782) discovered an expression that relates the pressure to fluid speed and elevation. The equation he developed was derived from the laws of conservation of energy, as applied to an ideal fluid. Bournelli discovered that if the velocity of a fluid (air) is increased at a particular point, the pressure of the fluid (air) at that point is decreased. He derived a law for this observation, which is now called the Bournelli equation.

As applied to a wing, Bournelli's equation explains how lift occurs. Quite simply, the airplane's wing is designed to increase the velocity of the air flowing over the top of the wing. To do this, the top of the wing is curved, whereas the bottom is relatively flat. The air flowing over the top, curved portion of the wing travels a farther distance than the air flowing over the flat bottom, hence it must flow faster (see Figure 6.6). According to Bournelli's law, the airflow over the top of the wing, since it is faster, must have less pressure than the slower airflow underneath the wing. The higher pressure underneath the wing (associated with the slower speed airstream below the wing) pushes or lifts the wing up toward the lower pressure area above the wing (associated with the higher speed airstream above the wing). This is how lift occurs.

To understand how the Bournelli equation works, consider the flow of water through a pipe with different widths at each end, as illustrated in Figure 6.7. The force on the lower end of fluid is P_1A_1, where P_1 is the pressure in

Figure 6.6
Bournelli forces creating lift

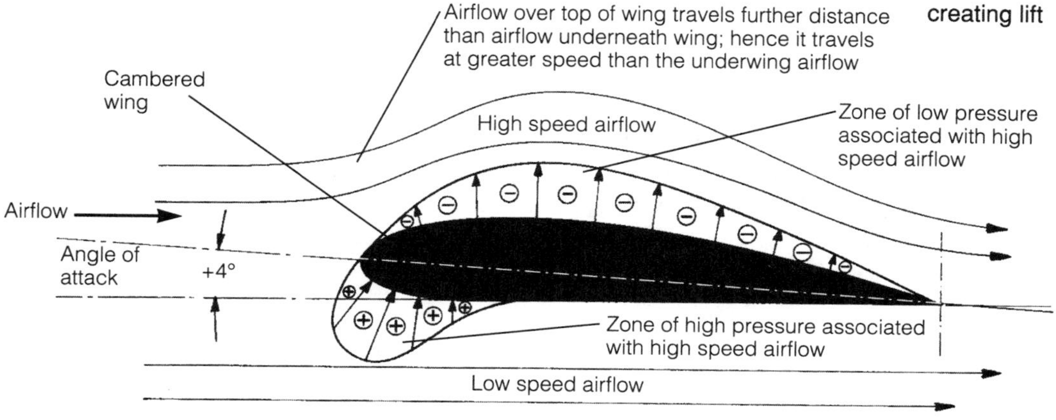

Airflow over top of wing travels further distance than airflow underneath wing; hence it travels at greater speed than the underwing airflow

Cambered wing

High speed airflow

Zone of low pressure associated with high speed airflow

Airflow

Angle of attack

+4°

Zone of high pressure associated with high speed airflow

Low speed airflow

Figure 6.7
Incompressible fluid flowing through a pipe of varying cross-section.

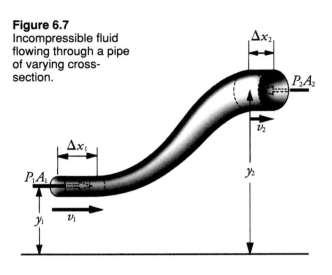

Pascals (Newtons/Meter²) and A_1 is the Area in Meters² of the lower pipe end.

$$Force = F_1 \Delta x_1 = P_1 A_1 \Delta x_1$$

The force on the upper end of the fluid is $P_2 A_2$, where P_2 is the pressure and A_2 is the cross-sectional area of the upper pipe end.

$$Force = F_2 \Delta x_2 = P_2 A_2 \Delta x_2$$

The Volume of both shaded regions of fluid is the same, e.g.:

$$\Delta x_1 A_1 = \text{Volume 1} = \Delta V$$
$$\Delta x_2 A_2 = \text{Volume 2} = \Delta V$$

The work done by the force acting on the lower section of water Δx_1 is (work is equal to Force*Distance and is expressed in Joules or Newton-meters):

$$W_1 = F_1 \Delta x_1 = P_1 A_1 \Delta x_1 = P_1 \Delta V$$

By the same token, the work done by the force acting on the upper section of water Δx_2 is:

$$W_2 = F_2 \Delta x_2 = P_2 A_2 \Delta x_2 = P_2 \Delta V$$

Since the two sections of fluid are trying to move in directions against each other, the net work done is:

$$Net\,Work = W_1 - W_2 = P_1 \Delta V - P_2 \Delta V = (P_1 - P_2)\,\Delta V$$

Kinetic Energy is defined as ½ × Mass × Velocity² or $KE = \frac{1}{2} mv^2$. The change in kinetic energy for the water in this system is

$$\Delta KE = \frac{1}{2} \Delta mv_2^2 - \frac{1}{2} \Delta mv_1^2$$

The potential energy of the system, which is defined as $\Delta U = Mass \times acceleration\ of\ gravity \times height\ above\ ground$, must take into account the two sections of water Δx_1 and Δx_2 and their respective distances above the ground. Since both volumes of water contain the same amount of mass, and the acceleration of gravity

$$(g = 9.8\ \frac{Meters}{Second^2})$$

is a constant, this becomes:

$$\Delta U = \Delta mgy_2 - \Delta mgy_1$$

By applying the work energy theorem in the form of

$$Work = Kinetic\ Energy + Potential\ Energy$$

or

$$Net\ Work = \Delta K + \Delta U$$

and plugging in the expressions for Net Work, Kinetic Energy, and Potential Energy from the previously listed equations, we get:

$$Net\ Work = \Delta K + \Delta U$$

which becomes

$$(P_1 - P_2)\Delta V = \frac{1}{2}\Delta mv_2^2 - \frac{1}{2}\Delta mv_1^2 + \Delta mgy_2 - \Delta mgy_1$$

If we then divide the above equation by ΔV, we get:

$$(P_1 - P_2) = \frac{1}{2}\frac{\Delta m}{\Delta V}v_2^2 - \frac{1}{2}\frac{\Delta m}{\Delta V}v_1^2 + \frac{\Delta m}{\Delta V}gy_2 - \frac{\Delta m}{\Delta V}gy_1$$

Realizing that density is equal to mass divided by volume or

$$Density = p = \frac{mass}{Volume} = \frac{\Delta m}{\Delta V}$$

the equation then becomes:

$$(P_1 - P_2) = \frac{1}{2}pv_2^2 - \frac{1}{2}pv_1^2 + pgy_2 - pgy_1$$

Finally, rearranging the terms of the above equation, we get:

$$P_1 + \frac{1}{2}pv_1^2 + pgy_1 = P_2 + \frac{1}{2}pv_2^2 + pgy_2$$

This is Bournelli's equation as applied to a non-viscous, incompressible fluid in a steady flow. It is often expressed as

$$P + \frac{1}{2}pv^2 + pgy = constant$$

Bournelli's Equation

Bournelli's euation states that the sum of the Pressure (P) plus the energy per unit volume ($\frac{1}{2}$pv^2) plus the potential energy per unit volume (*pgy*) has

the same constant value at all points along the stream line. This means that, in Figure 6.8, the volume of fluid at the bottom of the pipe (Δx_1) has the same value of

$$P + \frac{1}{2}pv^2 + pgy =$$

as the volume of water at the top of the pipe (Δx_2)! This has important applications for the dynamics of flight, as we shall soon see.

Consider the wing and the flow of air around it that is illustrated in Figure 6.8. The shape of the airplane's wing is designed so that the upper surface is more curved than the lower surface. Air flowing over the upper surface follows a more curved path than the air flowing over the lower surface. According to the Bournelli principle of equivalence for all particles in a stream flow, the air flowing over the top of the wing must have the same Bournelli constant as the air flowing over the bottom of the wing. This means that for both the top air flow and the bottom air flow

$$P_1 + \frac{1}{2}pv_1^2 + pgy_1 = P_2 + \frac{1}{2}pv_2^2 + pgy_2$$

where P_1, v_1, and y_1 are the pressure, speed, and distance above ground for the air flow underneath the wing, and P_2, v_2, and y_2 are the pressure, speed, and distance above ground for the air flow above the wing. Since the top air flow needs to travel a more lengthy and circuitous route per unit time over the curved cambered portion of the wing than does the bottom air flow (they both arrive at the same time and at the same location on the trailing edge of the wing), the speed of the top air flow v_2 is greater than the speed v_1 of the airflow beneath the wing:

$$v_1 = \textit{speed of airflow "underwing"}$$
$$v_2 = \textit{speed of airflow over top of wing}$$
$$v_2 > v_1$$

Assuming for the sake of this argument that the distances above the ground y_1 y_2 have a negligible effect on the Bournelli equation, you can see that in order for the two equations to balance, the pressure P_1 of the airflow underneath the wing MUST BE GREATER than the pressure P_2 of the airflow above the wing. The pressure being greater below the wing than above causes a net upward force F on the wing, which is called *dynamic lift*. The faster the air flows over the wing, all things being equal, the greater the

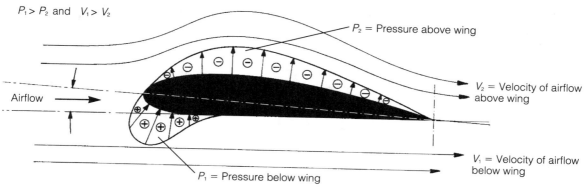

$P_1 > P_2$ and $V_1 > V_2$

P_2 = Pressure above wing

V_2 = Velocity of airflow above wing

V_1 = Velocity of airflow below wing

Airflow

P_1 = Pressure below wing

Figure 6.8
Bournelli Equation
applied to the wing

dynamic lift since the speed differential between $v_2 > v_1$ becomes much greater, causing P_1 to be much greater than P_2.

It is a well-known phenomenon that if you place a piece of paper on a table and blow across its top surface, the paper rises. This is because the faster air moving over the top surface causes a reduction in pressure above the paper and thus a net upward force. This is a simple example of the Bournelli principles. By the same token, the roofs of buildings are often blown off by strong winds, hurricanes, or tornadoes because of the Bournelli forces at work. This is because the rushing air over the outside surface of the roof causes a drop in outside pressure, and if the building is not well vented, the air pressure inside the building can build up and literally blow the roof off!

THE DANGER OF STALLS

A stall occurs when the smooth airflow over the airplane's wing is disrupted and the lift degenerates. It is important to realize that a stall can occur *at any airspeed, in any aircraft attitude, or with any engine power setting.* Without prompt corrective action, the airplane will crash into the ground. Fortunately, as an aid for armchair pilots, *Flight Simulator* has a visual stall warning indicator that appears on screen, warning you of an imminent stall situation. Figure 6.9

Figure 6.9
In the stall, smooth
airflow is disrupted
over the wing, causing
loss of lift

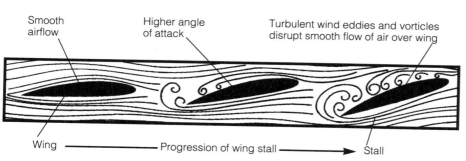

Smooth airflow

Higher angle of attack

Turbulent wind eddies and vorticles disrupt smooth flow of air over wing

Wing ——————— Progression of wing stall ——————→ Stall

Table 6.2   Stall Speeds for the Cessna, Learjet, Sailplane, and Sopwith Camel

Aircraft	V_{S0} Stall Speed with Landing Gear & Flaps Extended	V_{S1} Stall Speed with Flaps Retracted, Landing Gear Retracted
Cessna Skylane 182RG	54 Knots	50 Knots
Learjet 35A	97 Knots	No published info
Schweizer 2-32 Sailplane	Not applicable (no landing gear or flaps)	48 Knots
Sopwith Camel	Not applicable	50 Knots

shows what a typical stall looks like, along with an illustration of the turbulent airflow over the wings that robs the airplane of its lift.

Stall Recovery

Here are the fundamental steps to follow in any stall recovery:

1. *Lower the pitch of the aircraft* so that the wing's angle of attack is decreased. Since the basic cause of the stall is always an excessive angle of attack for a given airspeed, lowering the airplane's nose by using the elevators (press 8 on the numeric keypad, roll the mouse forward, or push the joystick forward) will remedy this problem.

2. *Increase throttle to maximum* (press F4). This will increase the wing's speed and generate more lift.

3. *Resume straight and level flight* using ailerons, rudders, and elevators as necessary.

All aircraft manufacturers publish stall airspeed charts for different flight conditions. These charts tell you the minimum speed you can fly the aircraft before a stall will occur. You *must never fly below these stall speeds*, or else your plane will lose all its lift and crash. Two stall speeds are defined:

V_{S0}: The stall speed or minimum flight speed at which the aircraft is controllable with the landing gear down, flaps extended to the 20° or 40° setting.

V_{S1}: The stall speed with or minimum flight speed at which the aircraft is controllable when the landing gear is up and the flaps are retracted to the 0° setting.

CHAPTER
7

Exploring the Cockpit

The cockpit of an airplane contains many instruments, displays, controls, and navigational equipment. This chapter discusses the cockpit instrumentation found on the Cessna, Learjet, Sailplane, and Sopwith Camel. Because many of the controls and instruments are similar on the four planes, I have omitted the complete discussion on those instruments where the text would merely duplicate what is found in the Cessna section. Therefore, if you are skipping ahead and reading the sections about the Learjet, Sailplane, and Sopwith Camel, and want a better explanation about a particular instrument or control, you should check the Cessna section in the first part of this chapter for more information. The Learjet and Sailplane are discussed (in detail) in Chapters 10 and 11. After reading this chapter, you should have a basic understanding of each control and instrument as it pertains to the operation of your aircraft.

UNDERSTANDING YOUR INSTRUMENTS AND CONTROLS ON THE CESSNA

The new photorealistic Cessna instrument panel offers many new features over the previous Flight Simulator 4.0 version. In addition to the throttle control, there is a carburetor mixture control, a propeller pitch control (speed governor), an EGT (Exhaust Gas Temperature) gauge, a manifold pressure indicator, and an outside digital temperature gauge. In the radio stack, there is a new DME indicator for the NAV 2 radio, and the autopilot has been enhanced. There are new landing lights, and you can now set the simulator's speed directly from the Rate control underneath the digital clock.

All the instruments can be displayed without the photorealism for easier readability, or to speed up the simulation. If you find your flight instruments hard to read in

Figure 7.1
The Cessna's instrument control panel

the photorealism mode, you can open the Instrument Preferences dialog box from the Options menu, and select the Panel Display list box to choose the Enhanced Readability option. In the same dialog box, you can also choose to have your instruments updated more frequently for added realism, but doing so slows down the simulation slightly. Figure 7.1 shows the Cessna's instrument panel.

Standard Instrument Cluster

Six primary flight instruments comprise what is known as the standard instrument cluster. Based on their *modus operandi*, these instruments can be further divided into two categories: pressure instruments (also called *pitot-static*), and gyroscopic instruments. The pitot-static instruments include the following:

- Airspeed Indicator
- Altimeter
- Vertical Speed/Rate of Climb Indicator

The gyroscopic instruments include the following:

- Artificial Horizon/Attitude Indicator
- Heading Indicator/Directional Gyro
- Turn Coordinator

Figure 7.2
The standard instrument cluster on the Cessna

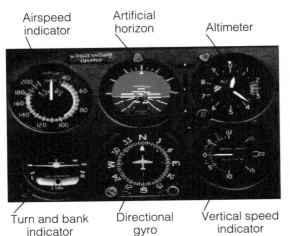

Airspeed indicator   Artificial horizon   Altimeter

Turn and bank indicator   Directional gyro   Vertical speed indicator

Pitot-Static Instruments

The pitot-static system takes impacted air pressure from a pitot tube, which is mounted face forward to the aircraft's direction of movement. This dynamic pressure is ducted through the pitot line to the altimeter, airspeed indicator, and the vertical speed indicator. These instruments operate by measuring differences in air pressure to obtain their readings.

Airspeed Indicator

The airspeed indicator shows the aircraft's indicated airspeed (IAS), and is calibrated in nautical miles per hour, or knots. The airspeed readings are obtained by measuring differences between ram air pressure from the pitot head and atmospheric pressure from the static vents. When the aircraft is parked on the ground, the pressure difference in the pitot-static system is zero, but when the aircraft is moving, pressure builds up and there will be a pressure difference that increases with speed. Note that the IAS is *not the same* as your ground speed, since the airspeed readings are dependent on a hypothetical, standard atmospheric air pressure at sea level. Air pressure depends on temperature, altitude, and weather, and thus when these conditions change, the airspeed indicator will no longer show the aircraft's true airspeed (TAS).

At higher altitudes, since the air pressure is less than at sea level, the airspeed indicator gives you a slower reading for your speed than is actually the case.

As shown in Figure 7.3, the airspeed indicator in FS 5.0 is calibrated to show 5-knot-per-hour increments. It reads from 40 knots all the way up to 220 knots, although for the Cessna, you are not supposed to exceed 178 knots per hour, as shown by the red-lined zone on the dial. Traveling faster than this speed, called the V_{NE} (Never Exceed V speed), will cause structural damage to the airplane and possibly result in a crash.

There are several types of airspeed defined for aviation purposes:

Figure 7.3
The Airspeed indicator

- *Indicated Airspeed (IAS)* is the value read on the face of your airspeed indicator, uncorrected for changes in standard atmospheric conditions at sea level.

- *True Airspeed (TAS)* is the airspeed of the aircraft relative to undisturbed air, corrected for altitude, temperature, and barometric pressure conditions. True airspeed increases with altitude because of the effects of the thinning atmospheric pressure. Thus, at higher altitudes, TAS is always greater than IAS, which means that you will always travel faster than your airspeed indicator shows you to be traveling.[1] To calculate true airspeed from indicated airspeed, multiply the IAS by 1 plus 1.5 percent for every thousand feet of altitude. For example, if you are flying at 12,000 feet at an IAS of 200 knots, your true airspeed (TAS) will be 200 Knots/Hour $\times$ {1 + [12 (thousand feet) $\times$ 0.015]} = 236 knots/hour.

In *Flight Simulator*, the airspeed indicator is initially set to show true air speed (TAS), but you can change the altimeter's readings to show indicated

Flight Simulator's airspeed indicator shows True Airspeed (TAS), not Indicated Airspeed (IAS). You can change the airspeed indicator to show IAS by opening the Instrument Preferences dialog box under the Options menu and toggling on the Display Indicated Airspeed checkbox.

---

[1]Exception: In FS 5.0, True Airspeed (TAS) is initially shown on the airspeed indicator. Also, this assumes that you are not flying into a strong head wind.

airspeed (IAS) corrected for altitude, temperature, and barometric pressure. To do this, toggle on the Display Indicated Airspeed checkbox in the Instrument Preferences dialog box, found under the Options menu.

Federal Aviation Rules (FAR) also prohibit flying your aircraft at high speeds below certain minimum prescribed altitudes. For the controlled airspace below 10,000 feet, you must limit your speed to less than 250 knots (288 mph). Around airports, and around terminal control areas, the speed limit drops to less than 200 knots (230 mph).

Each aircraft also comes with its own set of restrictions for flying at certain speeds (called "V" speeds). The operating manuals for Cessna and Learjet, for example, show that there are maximum speeds for flying with the landing gear extended which, when exceeded, will cause damage to the aircraft. Table 7.1 lists some of the airplane performance speeds and their descriptions.

Altimeter

The altimeter measures your altitude above mean sea level (MSL) by means of sampling the air pressure. At higher elevations, the air density and pressure is lower; whereas at lower elevations, the density and pressure are higher. Unfortunately, due to variations in air temperature and barometric pressure, the air pressure can vary with a given altitude, so the altimeter can give

Table 7.1 Description of Airspeed Limitation Speeds	
V speed	**Description**
V_{S0}	Stalling speed with the landing gear down
V_{S1}	Stalling speed with the landing gear up
V_{LE}	Maximum landing gear extended speed
V_{LO}	Maximum landing gear operating speed
V_{FE}	Maximum flap extended speed
V_{NO}	Maximum structural cruising speed
V_{NE}	Never exceed speed; doing so will cause loss of airplane due to structural failure
V_{A}	Design maneuvering speed; do not make full or abrupt movements with your controls at this speed

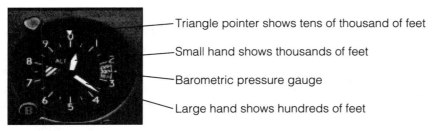

Triangle pointer shows tens of thousand of feet

Small hand shows thousands of feet

Barometric pressure gauge

Large hand shows hundreds of feet

Figure 7.4 The Altimeter

erroneous readings. These nonstandard conditions can result in altimeter differences as much as 2,000 feet between true altitude and indicated altitude! This is why, from time to time, you must calibrate your altimeter for the local barometric pressure in order to obtain accurate altitude measurements.

In *Flight Simulator*, the altimeter is read like a clock, with the large hand showing hundreds of feet MSL, and the small hand showing thousands of feet MSL. Barometric pressure is shown in a small gauge on the outer-right rim of the altimeter. The smallest increment on the altimeter is scaled at 50 feet for each tick mark.

Several terms are used to define altitude, as follows:

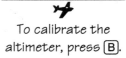

To calibrate the altimeter, press B.

- *AGL*: Altitude in feet above the ground.
- *MSL*: Altitude in feet above mean sea level. All pressure operated altimeters show MSL. Sea level is not the same as ground level. At Meigs Field, your altitude is 592 feet MSL, but your AGL is 0 feet.
- *Indicated altitude*: The altitude read on your altimeter. It tells you the altitude of your aircraft above mean sea level (MSL), but does not take into account nonstandard atmospheric conditions that cause the altimeter to show false readings.
- *True altitude*: True height above sea level (MSL), corrected for standard atmospheric conditions.[2]
- *Absolute altitude*: The height above ground level (AGL). It is usually found on radio/radar type altimeters, which measure the time interval of a vertical signal bounced from the aircraft to the ground and back.

Most large terminal areas around the United States now require the installation of encoding altimeters. These special altimeters work in conjunction

---

[2]See Chapter 4 for a table listing the Standard Atmospheric Conditions for different altitudes, temperatures, and pressures.

with the aircraft's transponder to send your altitude to air traffic control (ATC), along with your identification or squawk code. This enables the ATC to monitor your position and altitude on special computers to prevent any mid-air collisions.

Under Visual Flying Rules (VFR), the Federal Aviation Rules (FAR) require that you fly at certain altitude levels when flying a particular course heading. These highways in the sky are called Victor airways, and for altitudes less than 18,000 feet and more than 3,000 feet you must travel at odd thousand-foot increments plus 500 feet (e.g., 13,500, 5,500, 7,500 feet) for course headings of 0–179 degrees. For course headings of 180-359 degrees, you must fly at even thousand-foot increments plus 500 hundred feet (e.g., 2,500, 4,500, 6,500 feet).

Under instrument flying rules (IFR), FAR regulations require that for altitudes below 29,000 feet, you fly slightly different altitude levels. Below 29,000 feet, for course headings of 0–179 degrees, you can fly at any odd-thousand-foot increments (e.g., 1,000, 3,000, etc.). For course headings of 180–359 degrees, you can fly any even-thousand-foot increments (e.g., 2,000, 4,000, etcetera).

Vertical Speed/Rate of Climb Indicator

The vertical speed indicator tells you the rate at which the aircraft is climbing or descending. The display is calibrated in units of hundreds of feet per minute (FPM). The dial shows a reading of 0 to 10, up or down, signifying a climb or descent of 0 to 2,000 feet per minute. Thus, when the needle of the indicator is on the number 5 on the upper scale, you are climbing at the rate of 500 feet per minute. Because of delays in registering air pressure changes, this instrument should not be relied on for instantaneous readouts of vertical speed.

Gyroscopic Instruments

The three gyroscopic instruments are so called because they are controlled by gyroscopes. Gyroscopes are rotating platforms that can detect changes in motion, whether by changes in velocity or attitude. The basic gyroscopic

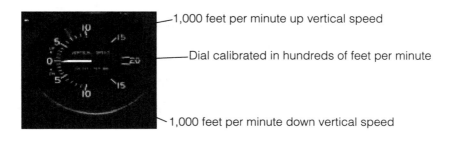

Figure 7.5
The Cessna's vertical speed/rate of climb indicator

principle allows gyroscopes to retain their position in space regardless of changes in velocity or position made by outside forces on the aircraft. Thus, by measuring the position of the gyroscope in relation to the aircraft, the gyroscopic instruments can make determinations as to the true aircraft orientation without any external visual references. Without the gyroscope, inertial navigation and all-weather precision flying would be all but impossible. Generally, the platter of the gyroscope is spun by engine vacuum, which sucks air past rotating vanes on the platter. Newer gyroscopes today, however, can be electrically operated for greater precision and accuracy.

Artificial Horizon/Attitude Indicator

The artificial horizon/attitude indicator shows the airplane's attitude at all times. It shows the actual pitch and roll of the aircraft in relation to the ground, and provides a view of the natural horizon that may not be visible to the pilot otherwise.

A gimbal-mounted gyroscope inside the artificial horizon retains its position in space regardless of the aircraft's attitude. By watching a colored ball that depicts the horizon, the pilot can determine whether the plane is pitching to the right or left, or is climbing or descending. The bank index on the gauge shows markers for 10°, 20°, 30°, 60°, and 90°, telling you the aircraft's angle of bank. When the center horizontal bar, which represents your wings, is aligned with the top of the horizon (the horizon is represented by the lower, colored half of the sphere), you are flying straight and level. Executing a 30° right turn causes the horizon to pivot to the left and the arrow pointer to rotate toward the 30° marker. When climbing, the wings will move above the horizon bar, and when descending the wings will move below the horizon bar.

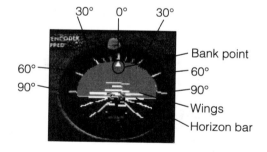

Figure 7.6
The artificial horizon/attitude indicator

Heading Indicator/Directional Gyro

The heading indicator, or directional gyro, is a compass that shows the aircraft's nose direction with much greater accuracy than the ordinary magnetic compass. Because it is driven by a gyroscope, the heading indicator can quickly show changes in course, even while executing turns and other maneuvers that would ordinarily throw a magnetic compass off due to pronounced accelerative forces or vibrations. The disadvantage of the directional gyro is that it tends to drift from the true course heading over time, due to the deviation caused by gyroscopic precession. The chief cause of precession in the gyroscope is friction from the bearings, so many sophisticated inertial

Click here on the knob to manually calibrate the directional gyro.

Figure 7.7
Heading indicator/
directional gyro

navigational systems go to great lengths to dampen the frictional effects so as to minimize errors. Because of this tendency to drift, you must periodically calibrate the heading indicator to match the magnetic compass. In FS 5.0, you do this by pressing D. You can also manually calibrate the directional gyro by clicking on the left knob at the bottom of the indicator. This has the effect of rotating the directional gyro's heading indicator left or right to match the magnetic compass heading.

In the directional gyro, the aircraft's nose always points toward the course heading. To ascertain your current course, all you need to do is examine what course number the nose of the airplane is currently pointing at. The numbers on the dial must be multiplied by ten to obtain the correct reading. Thus, a 3 represents 30°, while 33 represents a course heading of 330°. The dial is calibrated so that each tick on the scale represents 5°.

Turn Coordinator

The Turn Coordinator is often called the Turn and Bank Indicator. This instrument has two functions; it measures turn rate, and it measures the amount of slip or skid the aircraft has in making a turn. The aircraft wings on the turn indicator will bank whenever you make a turn. The "L" and "R" markers on the indicator show you where the wings must align if you are to make what is called a standard turn. A *standard turn* means that the aircraft will complete a 360° turn in two minutes, coming back to its original course heading in that space of time. Thus, for example, if you want to make a standard left turn with a turn rate of 3° per second (thereby completing a 360° turn in 2 minutes), you would bank the aircraft left until the wing tips on the dial match up with the "L" mark. If you had started at a course heading of 90°, after two minutes you would find that your aircraft has made a complete 360° turn and would be again headed on a course of 90°.

The ball rolling in the inclinometer at the bottom of the dial tells you whether your turn is coordinated or not. In an uncoordinated turn, the plane will slip or skid because of unbalanced centrifugal and horizontal lift forces, as illustrated in Figure 7.9. If the ball stays in the center position during a turn, then all the forces are in balance. Fortunately, in FS 5.0's auto-coordinated mode (which is the default setup), you don't need to worry about coordinating your turns, since the ailerons and rudder are moved together whenever you make a turn.

Left standard turn indicator

Inclinometer

Right standard turn indicator

Ball should stay centered here for coordinated turns

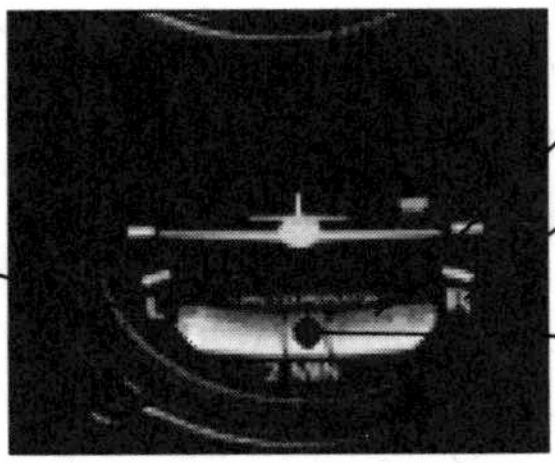

Figure 7.8
Turn coordinator

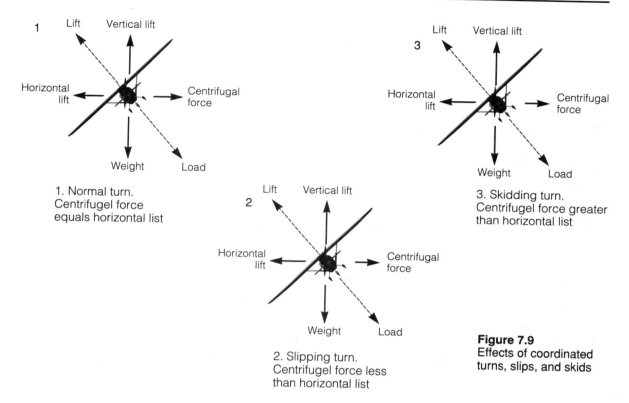

1. Normal turn.
Centrifugel force
equals horizontal list

2. Slipping turn.
Centrifugel force less
than horizontal list

3. Skidding turn.
Centrifugel force greater
than horizontal list

Figure 7.9
Effects of coordinated
turns, slips, and skids

Radio Stack

The radio stack contains all your communication and radio navigational aids. It consists of one COM 1 radio, two NAV radios, two DME indicators, an ADF radio, and a transponder (XPDR). Each radio can be set from the keyboard, via the mouse, or even from the Nav/Com menu.

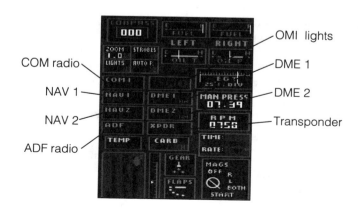

Figure 7.10
Radio stack

Changing the Frequency of the NAV, COM, and ADF Radios and XPDR Squawk Code Using the Mouse

To change the frequency settings for any of the radios using the mouse, follow these steps:

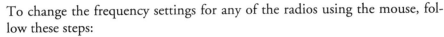

Figure 7.11
Changing radio
frequency

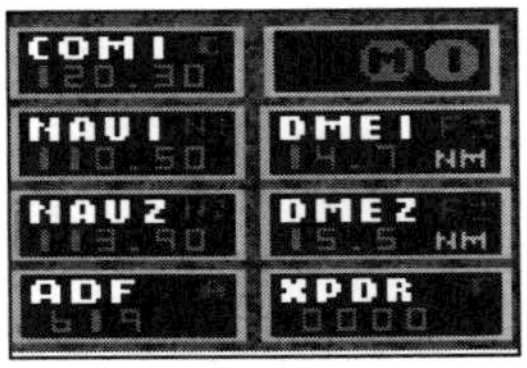

1. To increase a frequency setting, first click on the part of the frequency you wish to change. The color of the numerals will change from red to yellow, indicating that you can now tune in a different frequency. Note that you can't change individual digits for the NAV 1 and NAV 2 radios; you can change the fractional part of the frequency to the right of the decimal or change the integer part of the frequency to the left of the decimal point. For the ADF radio, you can select each digit separately but you cannot decrease the number. (See Figure 7.11.)

2. Click to the right of the numbers to increase the frequency, or click to the left of the numbers to decrease the frequency, except for the ADF radio and XPDR (Transponder), in which you can only increase the digit and cycle it from 0 to 9.(See Figure 7.12.)

Figure 7.12
Increasing digits to
change frequency

Changing the Frequency of the NAV, COM, and ADF Radios and XPDR Squawk Code Using the Keyboard

Table 7.2 summarizes the keystrokes necessary to change the radio frequencies for the ADF, COM, NAV 1, NAV 2, and Transponder radios. Using this table, for example, to increase the ADF radio frequency, you would press [A] [+] (plus key on the main keypad) to change the hundreds digit. For the tens (or middle) digit, press [A] [A] [+]. For the ones digit, press [A] [A] [A] [+]. To decrease the ADF radio frequency, you would, for the hundreds digit, press [A] [−] (minus key on the main keypad). For the tens (or middle) digit, press [A] [A] [−]. For the ones digit, press [A] [A] [A] [−].

Changing the Frequency of the NAV, COM, ADF, Radios and Squawk Code for the XPDR Using the Nav/Com Menu

You can change the frequency for any of the radios by calling up the appropriate dialog box from the Nav/Com menu and entering the frequency in the listed entry text box.

To change the COM radio frequency using the menus, for example, perform these steps:

1. Select Communication Radio from the Nav/Com menu.

2. In the Communication Radio dialog box, enter the new radio frequency you wish to tune into.

Table 7.2   Changing the Radio Frequency and XPDR Squawk Code via the Keyboard

Radio	Keyboard Procedure
ADF	First digit: Press Ⓐ followed by ⊞ to increase or ⊟ to decrease. Second digit: Press Ⓐ Ⓐ followed by ⊞ or ⊟ Third digit: Press Ⓐ Ⓐ Ⓐ followed by ⊞ or ⊟
COM	For integer part of frequency to left of decimal point: Press Ⓒ followed by ⊞ to increase or ⊟ to decrease For fractional part of frequency to right of decimal point: Press Ⓒ Ⓒ followed by ⊞ or ⊟
NAV1	For integer part of frequency to left of decimal point: Press Ⓝ ① followed by ⊞ to increase, or ⊟ to decrease For fractional part of frequency to right of decimal point: Press Ⓝ Ⓝ ① followed by ⊞ or ⊟
NAV2	For integer part of frequency to left of decimal point: Press Ⓝ ② followed by ⊞ to increase or ⊟ to decrease For fractional part of frequency to right of decimal point: Press Ⓝ Ⓝ ② followed by ⊞ or ⊟
XPDR (Transponder)	For first digit (thousands digit): Press Ⓣ followed by ⊞ to increase, or ⊟ to decrease For the second digit (hundreds digit): Press Ⓣ Ⓣ followed by ⊞ or ⊟ For the third digit (tens digit): Press Ⓣ Ⓣ Ⓣ followed by ⊞ or ⊟ For the fourth digit (ones digit): Press Ⓣ Ⓣ Ⓣ Ⓣ followed by ⊞ or ⊟

To change the NAV 1 or NAV 2 radio frequencies using the menus, follow this procedure:

1. Select Navigation Radios from the Nav/Com menu.
2. In the Navigation Radios dialog box, enter the new radio frequency you wish to tune into. There are two frequency boxes, one for each NAV radio.

Similarly, you can change the ADF frequency and XPDR squawk code in the ADF dialog box, or the Transponder dialog box, both of which can be opened up from the Nav/Com menu.

COM Radio

This communication radio transmits and receives voice signals between 118.00 and 135.95 MHz. The COM radio is used to communicate with Air Traffic Control and to tune in the automatic terminal information service (ATIS) for current weather information. The 360 available channels each occupy a bandwidth of 50 kHz, although you can double channel capacity to 720 channels by toggling on the 25 kHz COM Frequency Adjustability check box found in the Instrument Preferences dialog box under the Options menu. By doing this, you halve the bandwidth of each channel from 50 kHz to 25 kHz, thus enabling your radio to squeeze in twice as many channels in the available bandwidth.

For many of the situations in FS 5.0, the COM radio is tuned to a frequency that is one digit less than the frequency of the ATIS for the nearest airport. Thus, to hear the weather report in any of the these situations, all you need to do is to increase the integer part of the frequency by one digit to see the ATIS message scroll across your screen. In the Chicago Meigs Field situation, for example, to tune in the ATIS message, just increase your COM frequency by one digit from 120.30 MHz to 121.30 MHz.

NAV 1/NAV 2 Radio

The NAV 1 and NAV 2 radio receivers are used for navigation, and tune in either VOR (Very High Frequency Omni-Directional Range) or ILS (Instrument Landing Systems) radio stations. They both receive up to 200 channels between the frequencies of 108.00 and 117.95 MHz, with a channel separation of 50 kHz. VOR's transmit an omnidirectional signal, followed by a circular sweeping signal which your NAV radios receive and decode. The information is forwarded to the OBI indicators on your instrument panel, and you can then see which radius angle you are from the station. Each VOR station pulses out a radial signal for each of the 360° of arc around it. Using special navigational maps, you can then plot where you are in relation to the VOR station. If you also are receiving DME signals through your NAV radios, your DME indicator will show you how far away the VOR station is from your current position, and it will tell you your ground speed in relation to the station. The NAV 1 radio is used in conjunction with the OBI 1 display and the DME 1 indicator, whereas the NAV 2 receiver is used with the OBI 2 display and the DME 2 indicator. Using both NAV 1 and NAV 2 radios tuned to two different VOR stations, it is possible to triangulate your position and obtain a precise "fix."

Unlike OBI 1, the OBI 2 does not have a provision for an ILS glide slope. Thus, if you plan to tune in an ILS runway, do so on the NAV 1 radio.

Besides tuning in VOR and ILS stations, the NAV 1 radio is also used for the EFIS/CFPD advanced navigational graphics display system.

DME 1 and 2

Both DME 1 (Distance Measuring Equipment) and DME 2 indicators can be toggled back and forth between displaying speed or distance to the VOR station. To do this, merely click on the DME indicator with the mouse, or from the keyboard, press F1 + for DME 1 or F2 + for DME 2. You will see "KT" displayed in the upper-right corner of the DME when the aircraft speed in relation to the VOR station is being measured in knots per hour. On the other hand, when the DME is displaying distance information, you will see "NM" signifying nautical miles to the VOR station and distance to the VOR station.

ADF

The Automatic Direction Finder, or ADF, is a navigational radio that tunes in low-frequency AM signals from 0 kHz to 999 kHz from AM commercial stations as well as special non-directional beacon radio stations (called "NDB"). Essentially, the ADF calculates the relative bearing to the station and displays it on the ADF bearing indicator. The bearing to the NDB or AM broadcast station is relative to the nose of your aircraft, so to point your aircraft at the radio station you are currently tuning in, just turn the airplane so that the needle on the ADF bearing indicator is pointing straight up at the number 0.

In FS 5.0, the ADF bearing indicator is not normally displayed on the instrument panel. To call it up, you must press Shift Tab, and it will take the place of the OBI 2 display. If you prefer to use the menu system, you can also switch on the ADF display by clicking on the Activate ADF gauge in the ADF dialog box, which is opened by selecting ADF under the Nav/Com menu.

Normally, the ADF radio can tune only stations that are 1 kHz apart. But if you toggle on the 500 Hz ADF Frequency Adjustability check box found in the Instrument Preferences dialog box under the Options menu, the ADF receiver will be able to tune in stations that are only 500 Hz apart (500 Hz is exactly half of 1 kHz). This effectively doubles the number of channels available. Figure 7.14 shows what the display looks like with the addition of the extra digit to the right of the decimal point for setting the increments of 500 Hz.

Figure 7.13
The ADF relative bearing indicator and radio receiver

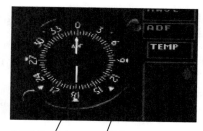

ADF Relative   ADF Receiver
bearing
indicator

Figure 7.14
The ADF radio showing 500 Hz channel separation

Transponder

Figure 7.15
Transponder

Whenever you fly into a terminal control area (TCA), Air Traffic Control will assign you a four-digit, special transponder squawk code that will identify your aircraft to their computers. You must enter this code into your transponder and then you can forget about it. Many transponders today are required to have Mode C capability, meaning that they can take information from an encoding altimeter, and when questioned by the ATC computer, will broadcast this information. When coupled with radar, this gives the ATC computers a three-dimensional fix on your aircraft for collision avoidance purposes. In an emergency, there are special squawk codes that can be used to alert the ATC to hijackings and mayday distress calls.

Navigational Instruments

Five additional navigational instruments that display important aircraft position information are as follows:

- Magnetic Compass
- OMI Marker Lights
- Omnibearing Indicator 1 (OBI 1) with Glide Slope for ILS System
- Omnibearing Indicator 2 (OBI 2)
- Automatic Direction Finder (ADF)

Figure 7.16
Magnetic compass

Magnetic Compass

This is a standard magnetic compass that shows your current heading in digital form.

OMI Marker Lights

Figure 7.17
OMI marker lights

The Outer (O), Middle (M), and Inner (I) marker lights are used in the instrument landing system (ILS) to give you a visual and audio cue as to the distance remaining to the runway. At approximately 5 miles from the runway, the blue outer marker light comes on and a 400-Hz audio signal sounds (two long beeps per second). At a distance of 0.6 miles or so, the yellow middle marker lamp comes on, and a 1300-Hz audio signal sounds (a long beep followed by a short beep). The inner marker, which may not be supported on some FS 5.0 runways, alerts you to the fact that you are crossing the threshold of the runway.

Omnibearing Indicator with Glide Slope (OBI 1)

The omnibearing indicator 1, or OMB 1, is a navigational instrument used with the NAV 1 radio to tune in VOR and ILS stations. It also contains a glideslope indicator with moving crosshairs that is used with instrument landing systems to ascertain whether or not your aircraft is on the proper glideslope to the runway.

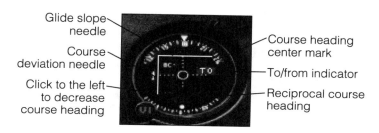

Glide slope needle

Course deviation needle

Click to the left to decrease course heading

Course heading center mark

To/from indicator

Reciprocal course heading

Figure 7.18
Omnibearing Indicator with Glide Slope (NAV 1). Click to the right to increase course heading.

If you have tuned the NAV radio to a VOR station, and the DME indicator shows that it is in range, you can figure out which VOR radial you are on by clicking on the course heading on the OBI until the course deviation needle is centered. With the TO/FROM indicator showing TO, the top reading on the course heading displays the direction to the VOR station. To head toward the VOR station, just fly your plane on the OBI course heading, making sure all the while that the CDI needle is centered. When you pass directly over the VOR station, the needle will abruptly jump, and the TO/FROM indicator will change to FROM.

To set the OBI 1 heading using the mouse, click to the right of the course heading to increase the reading, and to the left of the course heading to decrease the reading. Using the keyboard, to change the OBI 1 heading, press [V] [1] followed by [+] to increase the readout, or [−] to decrease the readout. You can also change the OBI 1 heading by directly entering it in the OBI Heading text box, found in the Navigation Radio dialog box, which is accessed under the Nav/Com menu.

Omnibearing Indicator 2 (OBI 2)/Automatic Direction Finder (ADF)

Like the OBI 1, the OBI 2 tunes in VOR stations and allows you to see what radial direction the VOR station is in relation to your aircraft. The OBI 2 is used with the NAV 2 radio, but unlike the OBI 1, the OBI 2 does not contain a glide slope and so cannot be used with ILS-equipped runways.

OBI 2 used with
NAV 2 radio

ADF indicator used
with ADR radio

Figure 7.19
Omnibearing Indicator
(NAV 2)/ADF. Press
Shift Tab to replace the
OBI 2 with the
Automatic Directions
Finder (ADF).

If you press Shift Tab simultaneously, you will disengage the OBI 2 indicator and replace it with the Automatic Direction Finder (ADF) gauge, which tells you the relative bearing to an NDB or AM broadcast station in relation to the nose of your aircraft.

To set the OBI 2 heading using the mouse, click to the right of the course heading to increase the reading, and to the left of the course heading to decrease the reading. Using the keyboard, to change the OBI 2 heading, press V 2 followed by + to increase the readout, or the - key to decrease the readout. You can also change the OBI 2 heading by directly entering it in the OBI Heading text box, found in the Navigation Radio dialog box, accessed under the Nav/Com menu.

Flight Instruments/Indicators

The remaining flight instruments and indicators supply information about the status of the aircraft.

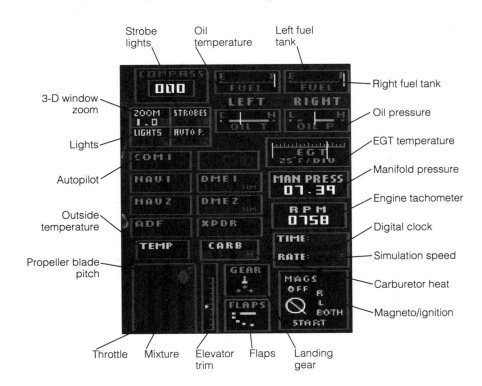

Figure 7.20
Flight instruments/
indicators

Zoom indicator

The zoom indicator shows the current magnification or zoom factor of the selected 3-D view window. To increase magnification, press 〔+〕. To decrease magnification, press 〔-〕. You can also click to the right of the zoom number to increase the zoom, or alternatively, click to the left to decrease the zoom. Note that the zoom indicator does not work with the Map window, although when the Map window is currently active, 〔+〕 and 〔-〕 will zoom the map in and out.

Lights

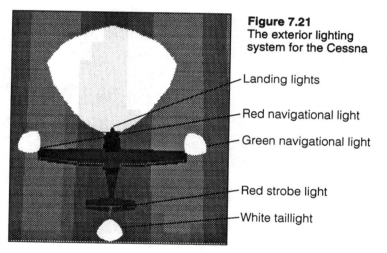

Figure 7.21
The exterior lighting system for the Cessna

Landing lights

Red navigational light

Green navigational light

Red strobe light

White taillight

The lights switch, which turns on the instrument panel lighting and exterior navigational lighting for night flying, can be toggled off and on by clicking on it. Or, from the keyboard, press 〔L〕. You can separately turn on or off the instrument lights by pressing 〔Shift〕〔L〕. To turn on only the landing lights for illuminating the runway, press 〔Ctrl〕〔L〕.

Strobe

This indicator tells you whether the red flashing strobe is on or off. To turn the strobe on or off, merely click on the control, or press 〔O〕.

Autopilot

Using the autopilot, you can have the plane automatically level its wings or attitude, maintain a constant altitude, line up with a particular glide slope of an ILS runway or NAV 1/VOR radial, or you can choose a particular heading, approach, or back course. To engage or disengage the autopilot, click on it. From the keyboard, you can turn it off or on by pressing 〔Z〕. Alternatively, you can engage or disengage the autopilot by selecting Autopilot from the Nav/Com menu, and then selecting Connect in the Autopilot Switch list box.

Temp

Temp measures the outside temperature. If you have selected U.S. units of measurement in the Country Preferences dialog box, the reading will be in degrees Fahrenheit. Otherwise, the Temp gauge will show degrees Celsius.

Clock

The clock is used not only to tell time, but also to modify the time of day in FS 5.0. To set the time using the mouse, you must first click on the hours, minutes, or seconds portion of the display separately, then click to the right to increase the time, or to the left to decrease the time. Alternatively, you can adjust the time in the Set Time and Season dialog box from the World menu.

Rate of Simulation

This indicator shows the current simulation speed. By clicking to the right of this number, you can increase the passage of time, or if you click to the left, slow down time. You can also modify the simulation's speed by entering it directly into the Simulation Speed dialog box from the Sim menu. This feature is very helpful for long, boring transcontinental or transoceanic trips when you don't want to wait six hours to complete a trip. But be careful, since speeding up the simulation makes your aircraft very difficult to control, and very subtle movements of the controls can cause you to come careening down to the ground. Note that this control affects only the passage of time on your clock; it does not cause your computer to "speed up" *Flight Simulator*.

Landing Gear Indicator

This indicator tells you the current position of your landing gear. When the wheels are down, the three wheel lights below the gear icon glow green. When the gear is being retracted, the wheel lights will briefly turn red before flickering out. The gear can be retracted or extended by clicking on the gear indicator, or by pressing $\boxed{G}$.

Don't extend the landing gear when traveling faster than the V_{LO} (maximum airspeed when operating the landing gear). For the Cessna, this is 140 knots IAS.

Flaps Position Indicator

The flaps are used to create extra lift when landing or taking off. The flaps position indicator shows the current extension angle for the flaps. They can be deployed incrementally by 10° from a fully retracted position of 0°, all the way to 40°. You deploy the flaps by clicking on the individual angle settings on the flaps position indicator. Or, from the keyboard, you can use $\boxed{F5}$ through $\boxed{F8}$. When the arm of the flaps position indicator points to the bottom dot, a flap position of 40° has been set; whereas if the arm points to the upper dot, the flaps are fully retracted at 0°.

You must not fly faster than the V_{FE} (Flap Extension Speed) or else damage to the flaps will occur. For the flaps set to 30° or 40°, the V_{FE} is 95 knots IAS; for the flaps set to 20°, the V_{FE} is 120 knots IAS; for the flaps set to 10°, the V_{FE} is 140 knots IAS.

Left Wing/Right Wing Fuel Tank Gauge

These fuel gauges tell you the current fuel supply left in your gas tanks. The left gauge is for the left wing fuel tank, and the right gauge is for the right wing fuel tank.

Oil Temperature Gauge

This gauge tells you the oil temperature of the engine. Normal operating temperature is 100° Fahrenheit to 245° Fahrenheit (38° to 118° Celsius).

Oil Pressure Gauge

This gauge alerts you to the oil pressure inside the engine. Normal operating pressure is 60 to 90 pounds per square inch (PSI).

Exhaust Gas Temperature (EGT Gauge)

The EGT gauge measures the temperature of the engine exhaust gas exiting your engine cylinders. This temperature ranges up to 1,750° Fahrenheit. The EGT is used in conjunction with the manifold pressure gauge and the mixture control to fine tune the engine's cruise performance. When the engine runs hotter, usually it means that you are running a very lean fuel mixture, in which case you should enrich the carburetor by moving up the mixture control. Watch the gauge to make sure that you don't overheat your engine. Temperature is measured in twenty-five-degree increments on the scale.

Manifold Pressure Gauge

The manifold pressure gauge tells you the amount of power your engine is developing. It measures the pressure difference between the atmosphere and the inside of the manifold chamber of the engine. The usual measurements are made in terms of inches of Hg (Mercury). The normal operating range is 17 to 25 inches Hg, with a maximum of 31 inches Hg.

Tachometer

The engine speed is measured by the tachometer in rotations or revolutions per minute (RPM). Normal operating range is from 2,100 to 2,400 RPM.

Throttle, Propeller Control, and Mixture Control

The throttle sets the amount of power the engine develops. You can increase the power, and hence the speed, of the engine by dragging the throttle control up or down with the mouse. From the keyboard, you can also adjust the throttle by pressing the function keys [F1], [F2], [F3], and [F4]. The [F1] key cuts engine power to idle, [F2] decreases the engine power gradually, [F3] increases engine power gradually, and [F4] opens the throttle to its maximum setting.

The propeller control sets the propeller's blade angle so that you can maintain an optimum RPM for the engine. The propeller control is optional. You can change the settings by choosing the Realism & Reliability command from the Sim menu. At higher altitudes or at high speeds, the prop blade angle should be increased to avoid having the engine RPM exceed engine tolerances. For takeoffs and landings, or when flying at slow speeds, decrease the prop blade angle so that the propeller will spin faster and develop more thrusting action.

Remember this simple rule:

Increasing the Prop Blade Angle *decreases* RPM.
Decreasing the Prop Blade Angle *increases* RPM.

With the mouse, to reduce RPM and increase the prop blade angle (decrease RPM), drag the propeller control down; to increase RPM and decrease the blade angle (increase RPM), drag the lever down. From the keyboard, press [Ctrl] [F1] to decrease Propeller RPM to its minimum setting, or [Ctrl] [F2] to gradually decrease it. To increase propeller RPM gradually, press [Ctrl] [F3], or [Ctrl] [F4] to increase it to its maximum setting (maximum RPM).

Because the atmospheric pressure declines as you go higher, the engine's air/fuel ratio tends to get too rich as less air is burned per unit of fuel. The mixture control allows you to manually adjust the air/fuel ratio, not only to compensate for altitude differences, but also to optimize fuel economy and engine performance. Using the mouse, to enrich the air/fuel ratio, drag the mixture lever up; to lean the engine, drag the mixture lever down. From the keyboard, press [Ctrl] [Shift] [F1] to lean the engine to its highest air/fuel ratio, or press [Ctrl] [Shift] [F2] to gradually lean the engine. To gradually enrich the mixture, press [Ctrl] [Shift] [F3], or [Ctrl] [Shift] [F4] to enrich it to its lowest air/fuel ratio. Generally, when taking off, you will want to set the mixture to rich so that you don't encounter any sudden power drops or engine stalls. By default, in FS 5.0 the mixture control is automatically controlled and synchronized with the movement of the throttle. If you want to manually set the mixture, you must toggle on the Mixture Control check box in the Realism and Reliability dialog box under the Sim menu.

Carburetor Heat

The carburetor heat switch turns the carburetor heat on or off. You use the carburetor heat to prevent icing, or clear ice that has formed inside the engine, thus preventing ice-caused engine failure in cold weather. To toggle this control on or off, click on it with the mouse, or press $\boxed{H}$.

Magnetos Switch

The magnetos switch specifies whether you have switched on the left, the right, or both magnetos for the engine's ignition system. As a precautionary back up, there are two separate magneto systems, each of which is able to supply electrical current to enable the spark plugs to fire. To change the magneto switch setting, click on the indicator, or press $\boxed{M}$, plus $\boxed{+}$ or $\boxed{-}$, to cycle among Off, Right, Left, or Both. For added realism, you can choose to start your engines yourself by setting the magnetos to the START position, but you must first toggle on the Magnetos check box in the Realism and Reliability dialog box, found under the Sim menu.

Control Position Indicators

The control position indicators tell you the current position of the ailerons, elevators, rudder, and elevator trim.

Aileron Position Indicator

The ailerons are moveable, hinged surfaces on the outside trailing edges of your wings. They control the rotational movement of banking or roll.

Elevator Position Indicator

The elevators are moveable, hinged control surfaces on the horizontal stabilizer (the tail wing). They control the up and down pitch of the aircraft's nose.

Rudder Position Indicator

The rudder is a hinged, vertical control surface mounted on the trailing edge of the vertical stabilizer (the tail). It controls the rotational movement of yaw (left or right pivoting motion).

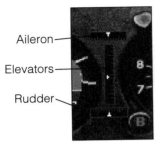

Aileron

Elevators

Rudder

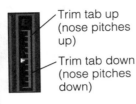

Trim tab up
(nose pitches
up)

Trim tab down
(nose pitches
down)

Figure 7.22
Yoke control position
indicators and the
elevator trim control
position indicator

Press Tab to switch
between the Lear-
jet's subpanels.

Elevator Trim Position Indicator

The elevator trim allows fine adjustment of the elevators, and relieves the pilot of continually applying pressure on the yoke in order to maintain level flight. This hinged, horizontal control surface is located on the elevator and looks like a miniaturized version of the elevator.

The elevator trim is activated from the keyboard by pressing 7 for nose-down pitch movements, and by pressing 1 for nose-up pitch movements (both 7 and 1 are found on the numeric keypad).

When you press 7 to pitch the nose down, the pitch trim indicator moves down, and when you press 1 to pitch the nose up, the pitch trim indicator moves up.

UNDERSTANDING YOUR INSTRUMENTS AND CONTROLS ON THE LEARJET

The Learjet comes equipped with a much more elaborate set of avionics than any of the other FS 5.0 aircraft. The six flight instruments of the standard instrument cluster are classified as EFIS (Electronic Flight Information Systems) avionics because they are microprocessor controlled. There are two instrument subpanels associated with the FS 5.0 Learjet; the first default display shows the radio stack, while the second instrument subpanel shows the engine monitoring gauges. Figure 7.23 illustrates both the Learjet's instrument subpanels. To switch between each panel display, press Tab.

Standard Instrument Cluster

The standard instrument cluster for the Learjet is similar to the Cessna's. Because of the Learjet's far superior thrust and agility, however, the instruments are specially tailored to measure different performance parameters.

Airspeed Indicator

The airspeed indicator is calibrated to read true airspeeds, despite the fact that the display shows IAS, or indicated airspeed.[3] The analog dial displays

[3]For added realism, you can have the airspeed gauge display indicated airspeed (IAS), not true airspeed (TAS). To do this, go to the Instrument Preferences dialog box under the Options menu, and click on the Display Indicated Airspeed checkbox.

Learjet radio stack subpanel 1

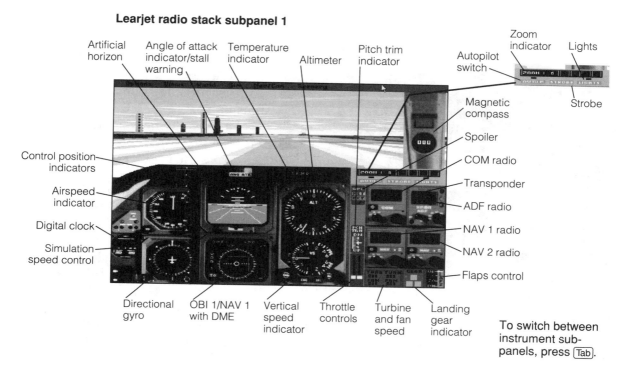

To switch between instrument sub-panels, press [Tab].

Learjet radio stack subpanel 2

speeds only up to 450 knots, but the digital readout below can display speeds past this point.

The Learjet has a maximum cruise speed of 471 knots true airspeed (542 miles per hour, 872 kilometers per hour), although typical cruise speeds will vary for different altitudes. At 45,000 feet, for example, the Learjet cruises at 423 knots TAS (487 mph, 783 km/hr), while at 25,000 feet the Learjet cruises at 471 knots TAS.

Typical landing approach speeds are 128 knots IAS, and the V_{so} stall speed with the landing gear down is 97 knots IAS.

Figure 7.23
The Learjet's two instrument panels

Altimeter

The altimeter shows the aircraft's height above sea level (MSL). The display has a digital readout for an accurate count of your altitude, but it also shows an analog display of your altitude in hundreds of feet. For example, when the digital display reads 4,500 feet, the analog hand on the altimeter covers the number 5 to tell you that you are at 500 feet above 4,000 feet.

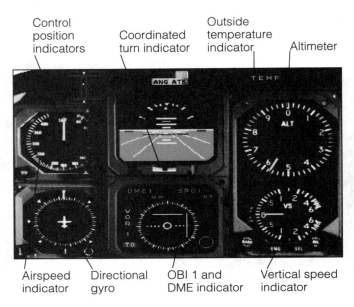

Control position indicators   Coordinated turn indicator   Outside temperature indicator   Altimeter

Airspeed indicator   Directional gyro   OBI 1 and DME indicator   Vertical speed indicator

Figure 7.24
The standard instrument cluster for the Learjet

Figure 7.25
The airspeed indicator for the Learjet

Figure 7.26
The altimeter for the Learjet

Just below the altimeter, the barometric pressure is displayed in digital form. Since your altimeter readings may be off due to nonstandard atmospheric conditions, you should calibrate the altimeter from time to time by pressing B.

Since the Learjet routinely cruises at altitudes of over 45,000 feet, under FAR regulations you must fly IFR in one of the jet airways or "J" routes. These are special routes created above 18,000 feet for the purposes of creating safe aircraft separation distances that are monitored by air traffic control centers.

When you enter the airspace above 18,000 feet, the FAR regulations require that you fly at odd thousand-foot increments (e.g., 21,000, 23,000, 25,000 feet) for course headings 0–179 degrees; for course headings 180–359, you must fly at even thousand-foot increments (e.g., 18,000, 20,000, 22,000 feet). Above 29,000 feet different rules apply: for course headings 0–179, fly at 4,000-foot intervals beginning with 29,000 feet (e.g., 29,000, 33,000); for course headings 179–359, fly at 4,000-foot intervals beginning with 31,000 feet (e.g., 31,000, 35,000).

With only one engine operational, the Learjet has a service ceiling altitude of 25,000 feet (7,260 meters). This means that the airplane cannot climb higher than this altitude on only one engine.

Vertical Speed/Rate of Climb Indicator

The vertical speed indicator is calibrated to show vertical speeds in units of thousands of feet per minute. The scale registers speeds from 0 to 6, meaning that speeds of 0 to 6,000 feet per minute up or down can be displayed.

On one engine, the Learjet can climb at a rate of 1,290 feet per minute. With two engines running, the Learjet can climb at a

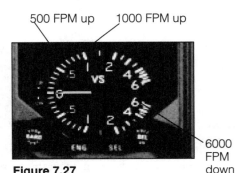

500 FPM up   1000 FPM up

6000 FPM down

Figure 7.27
The vertical speed/rate of climb indicator for the Learjet, calibrated in thousands of feet per minute

rate of 4,340 feet per minute, assuming maximum takeoff/landing weight at sea level, standard ISA atmospheric day conditions. With less fuel on board, the airplane is lighter and can climb faster.

Artificial Horizon/Attitude Indicator

The artificial horizon/attitude indicator shows the airplane's pitch, bank, and roll in relation to the horizon or ground. It provides a view of the natural horizon that may not be visible to the pilot otherwise.

By watching the lower half of the display that depicts the horizon, the pilot can determine whether the plane is pitching to the right or left, or is climbing or descending. The bank index on the display shows markers for 10°, 20°, 30°, 60°, and 90°, telling you the aircraft's angle of bank. When the center horizontal bar, which represents your wings, is aligned with the top of the horizon (the horizon is represented by the lower half of the display with the perspective lines vanishing into the distance), you are flying straight and level. Executing a 30° turn right causes the horizon to pivot to the left and the arrow pointer to rotate toward the 30° marker. When climbing, the wings will move above the horizon bar, and when descending, the wings will move below the horizon bar. There are pitch indexes on the display that indicate 5°, 10°, 15°, and 20° angles for the nose of the airplane in relation to the ground. When the horizon just touches the uppermost horizontal line, for example, the airplane is climbing with the nose pitched up in a 20° ascent. Likewise, if the horizon touches the lowermost horizontal line, the nose is pitched down in a 20° descent.

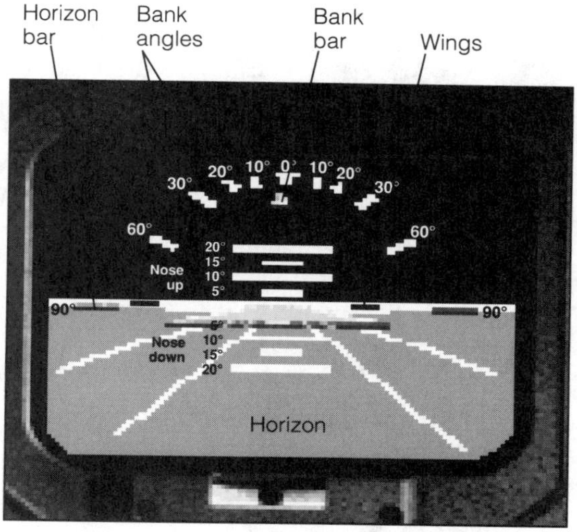

Figure 7.28
The artificial horizon/ attitude indicator for the Learjet

Turn Indicator

The turn indicator is located just below the artificial horizon. When the ball is centered in the inclinometer during a turn, the aircraft is executing a coordinated turn in which all the lateral forces are in balance. If the ball moves to the left or right, however, the turn is uncoordinated and the airplane is skidding or slipping through the air. Since FS 5.0, by default, has your rudder and ailerons synchronized in auto-coordinated mode, you need not worry about making coordinated turns. But if you are flying in uncoordinated mode (which is switched on/off under the Sim menu), for example, using pedals for your rudder and a yoke for your ailerons, you need to try to keep the ball centered when making a turn.

Figure 7.29
The heading indicator/
directional gyro for the
Learjet

Heading Indicator/Directional Gyro

With the Learjet, the heading indicator is output in digital form. The nose of your plane on the dial points to your current heading. At the bottom of the display, the reciprocal course heading (180° apart) is shown.

Because of the directional gyro's tendency to drift, you must periodically calibrate the heading indicator to match the magnetic compass. In FS 5.0, you do this by pressing Ⓓ.

Radio Stack and Navigational Instruments

Located on the first instrument subpanel, the radio stack contains all your VOR/ILS/DME/ADF navigation radios as well as the COM communication radio used to call air traffic control. You set the frequencies in much the same way as you do for the Cessna radios: to increase the frequency, click to the right of the numbers; to decrease the frequency, click to the left of the numbers. As mentioned earlier in this chapter, you can also use the keyboard and menu equivalents to change the frequencies.

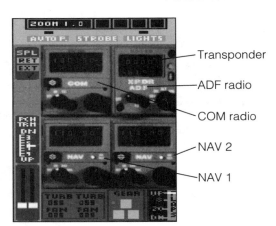

— Transponder

— ADF radio

— COM radio

— NAV 2

— NAV 1

Figure 7.30
The Radio Stack for
the Learjet

COM Radio

Use the COM radio to call up air traffic control, or display the ATIS (Automatic Terminal Information Service) weather report.

NAV 1 Radio/Omnibearing VOR 1 Display and the NAV 2 Radio/Omnibearing VOR 2 Display

The NAV 1 radio is used with the omnibearing indicator 1 display, or OBI 1, to tune in VOR and ILS stations and display navigational information. The NAV 1 radio tunes in a VOR or ILS station for the OBI 1 display, while the NAV 2 radio tunes in a VOR/ILS station for the OBI 2 display.

In addition to displaying the VOR course radial your aircraft is currently on, the OBI 1 also contains a glideslope indicator with moving crosshairs that when used with instrument landing systems, tells you whether your aircraft is on the proper glideslope to the runway. A DME (Distance Measuring Equipment) indicator on the display shows the aircraft's current speed and distance to the VOR/ILS station.

A second OBI 2 display is provided so that you can tune in a second VOR station, using the NAV 2 radio, and thus precisely fix your coordinates

Figure 7.31
The COM radio

on a map. It, too, is equipped with a DME indicator for measuring speed and distance to the VOR station tuned on the NAV 2 radio. The intersection of the two VOR radials from both the OBI displays when plotted on a map tells you the aircraft's exact position. Unlike OBI 1, the OBI 2 does not have a provision for an ILS glide slope. Thus, if you plan to tune in an ILS runway, do so on the NAV 1 radio.

The omnibearing VOR 1 display is found on the first instrument subpanel, while the second omnibearing VOR 2 display is found on the second instrument subpanel along with the engine monitoring gauges. To switch between subpanel displays to view the VOR 1 and VOR 2, press [Tab]. Alternatively, if you want the same instrument panel to remain on-screen, you can press [Shift] + [Tab] to cycle among VOR 1, VOR 2, and the ADF gauge.

The Learjet's computerized OBI display is a little easier to use than is the OBI for the Cessna because all the readouts for the DME, including both range and speed, are included on the same display as the OBI.

Besides tuning in VOR and ILS stations, the NAV 1 radio is also used for the EFIS/CFPD (Electronic Flight Instrument Systems/Command Flight Path Display) advanced navigational graphics display system. Using EFIS/CFPD, you can project special symbols onto the cockpit windshield that tell you where you should fly your aircraft. This display, which is called a "Heads Up Display," or HUD, is used on many military and commercial jet aircraft today.

To turn on the CFPD and display red rectangles in the sky that point towards a particular VOR station, follow these steps:

1. First tune in a VOR or ILS station on your NAV 1 radio.

2. Select EFIS/CFPD Display from the Nav/Com menu.

3. In the dialog box that next opens up, click on the EFIS Master Switch.

4. Click on the Lock to VOR and Altitude check box.

5. Click on the Plot Intercepting Path check box.

6. Click OK, and exit the dialog box.

When you return to the cockpit, if you don't see the red rectangles at first, change your view angle, sweeping around in a 360° arc until they come into sight.

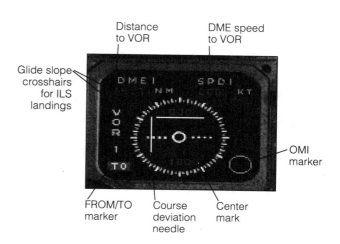

Figure 7.32
The NAV 1/VOR 1 display

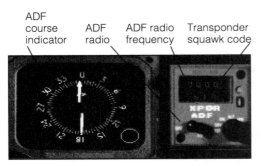

ADF course indicator   ADF radio   ADF radio frequency   Transponder squawk code

Figure 7.33
The Transponder (XPDR), ADF radio, and ADF course indicator

Click here and drag with mouse to move the compass to a different part of the screen.

Figure 7.34
The magnetic compass on theLearjet

You can easily move the magnetic compass using the mouse by clicking and dragging the top part of the compass.

ADF/Transponder

The Automatic Direction Finder, or ADF, is a navigational radio that tunes in low-frequency AM signals from 0 kHz to 999 kHz from AM commercial stations as well as special non-directional beacon radio stations (called "NDB"). Essentially, the ADF calculates the relative bearing to the station and displays it on the ADF bearing indicator. The bearing to the NDB or AM broadcast station is relative to the nose of your aircraft, so to point your aircraft at the radio station you are currently tuning in, just turn the airplane so that the needle on the ADF bearing indicator is pointing straight up at the number 0.

The ADF Course Indicator is not normally displayed on the Learjet's instrument panel. To summon it on-screen, press (Shift) + (Tab) to cycle among the VOR 1, VOR 2, and ADF course indicator.

The four-digit transponder squawk code is entered in above the ADF frequency, as shown in Figure 7.33. The transponder sends out this radio code to the air traffic control computers, which allows them to get a three-dimensional fix on your aircraft for collision avoidance purposes. In an emergency, there are special squawk codes that can be used to alert the ATC to hijackings and mayday distress calls.

Magnetic Compass

As with the Cessna, the magnetic compass reports your plane's current course heading. The magnetic compass for the Learjet is located on a separate instrument panel mounted on a center post above the instrument panel. If you object to having this panel partly obscure your view out the window, you can turn it off by turning off Instrument Panel 2 in the Instrument Panel Options dialog box found under the Views menu. You can also drag it to a different part of the screen by clicking and dragging the top portion of the compass.

Engine Monitoring Instruments/Controls

All the Learjet's engine monitoring equipment is located on an instrument subpanel. To display this subpanel, press (Tab).

Turbine and Fan Speed Gauges

In FS 5.0, there are two sets of turbine speed gauges — one digital, the other analog — for measuring the fan and turbine rotational speeds. None of the

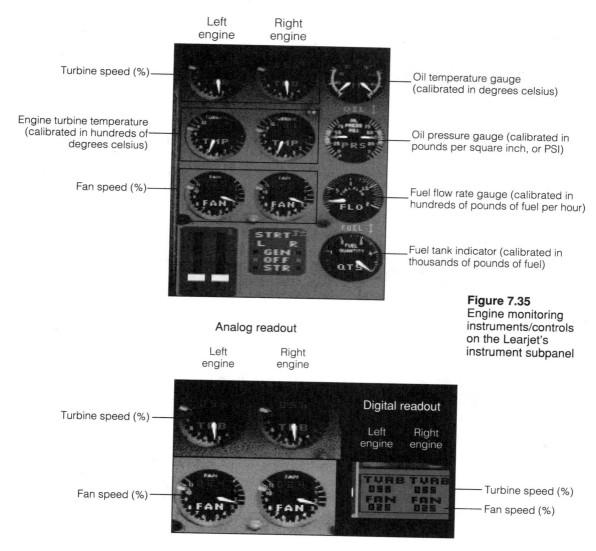

Left engine
Right engine

Turbine speed (%)

Engine turbine temperature (calibrated in hundreds of degrees celsius)

Fan speed (%)

Oil temperature gauge (calibrated in degrees celsius)

Oil pressure gauge (calibrated in pounds per square inch, or PSI)

Fuel flow rate gauge (calibrated in hundreds of pounds of fuel per hour)

Fuel tank indicator (calibrated in thousands of pounds of fuel)

Figure 7.35
Engine monitoring instruments/controls on the Learjet's instrument subpanel

Analog readout

Left engine
Right engine

Turbine speed (%)

Fan speed (%)

Digital readout

Left engine
Right engine

Turbine speed (%)
Fan speed (%)

Figure 7.36
Learjet's Fanjet engine speed gauges

Learjet's engines display the precise RPM; rather, they display the RPM as a percentage of maximum engine speed. Since the two Garrett AiResearch TFE731-2-2B engines are turbofan engines, there are separate instruments to monitor the speed of the low-pressure frontal fan assembly and the turbine core section. Note that the speeds for the turbine and fan are expressed as a percentage of maximum fan/turbine speed because they rotate at different speeds. The rotational speed for the turbine core of the engine runs around 30,000 RPM, while the fan runs at approximately 11,000 RPM. A reading of 56 on the turbine dial, for example, tells you that the engine is spinning at

Left engine   Right engine

Figure 7.37
Turbine temperature gauge dials are calibrated in hundreds of degrees celsius

56 percent of 30,000 RPMs, or 16,800 RPMs. On the other hand, a reading of 56 on the fan speed indicator tells you that the fan is spinning at 56 percent of 11,000 RPMs, or 6,160 RPMs.

Turbine Temperature Gauge

You will want to periodically monitor your engine core's temperature by observing this gauge. At average cruising speed, the temperature should hover around 799° Celsius. The dial indicates hundreds of degrees Centigrade, so if the needle points to the number 6, the engine's turbine core has a temperature of 600° Celsius.

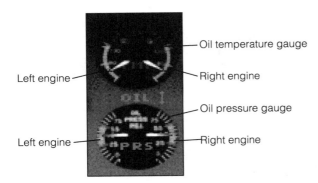

Oil temperature gauge

Left engine — Right engine

Oil pressure gauge

Left engine — Right engine

Oil Temperature and Pressure

The current temperature of the engine oil is displayed on the oil temperature gauge in degrees Centigrade. There are two gauges, one for each engine. Normal operating temperature is 90° to 100° Celsius. Oil pressure is shown on the oil pressure gauges below. Each engine has a separate gauge with normal operating presure in the range of 38 to 91 pounds per square inch (PSI).

Figure 7.38
Oil temperature and pressure gauges on the Learjet. Pressure dial is calibrated in pounds per square inch, or PSI.

Fuel Flow

Your current fuel consumption, measured in hundreds of pounds per hour, is displayed on the fuel flow meter. This gauge has two pointers, one for each engine, and each number on the scale represents 100 pounds. Thus, if the needle pointer is aiming at the number 0.5, it means that one engine is burning 50 lbs of fuel per hour. Average fuel consumption runs 400 to 600 lbs per hour for each engine, which, when combined, equals a total fuel burn of 800 to 1,200 pounds of fuel per hour. Since each pound of fuel weighs 6.7 pounds per gallon, this translates to a fuel burn of between 119 to 179 gallons per hour.

Fuel Quantity

The current fuel remaining in the fuel tanks is displayed on the fuel quantity gauge. The dial is measured in thousands of pounds, so if the needle rests on the number 4, it means that 4,000 pounds of fuel remain in the tanks. The Learjet 35A can carry 6,198 pounds of fuel (925 U.S. gallons, or 3,501 liters, or 2,811 kgs), which gives it a range of about 2,200 miles (2,528 statute miles or 4,066 kilometers), or a flying time of about 5 hours, 35 minutes under optimum flying conditions (economy cruise at 394 knots per hour).

Figure 7.39
Fuel quantity gauge (measured in thousands of pounds)

Engine Start/Generator Switch

Because the Learjet is powered by twin fanjets that don't use sparkplugs, the engine start/generator switch replaces the magneto ignition system as found on the Cessna. This switch tells you whether the left, right, or both fanjets are turned on. By clicking the STR switch, you can start the engines, and by clicking on the OFF switch, you can turn them off. From the keyboard, you can press J, then press + or − to cycle among OFF, STR, GEN. The GEN, or generator setting, is used to power the Learjet's electrical system from generators attached to the engines.

Throttle Controls/Thrust Diverters(Reverse Thrust)

Since the Learjet is powered by twin Garrett AiResearch TFE731-2-2B turbofan engines, there are separate throttle controls for each engine. Each engine is rated at 3,500 pounds of thrust, and is equipped with electrically controlled and hydraulically operated thrust reversers (sometimes called *thrust diverters*) for slowing the aircraft on landings. The thrust diverters, which are pictured in Figure 7.42, shunt engine exhaust gases away from the rear of the engine, thereby enabling much of the engine's thrust to be converted into a braking action.

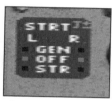

Figure 7.40
Engine start/generator switch on the Learjet

The throttle controls can be moved in tandem or individually. To choose the left engine throttle, press E 1, then drag the left throttle control up or down. To choose the right engine throttle, press E 2, then drag the right throttle control up or down. To move both throttles together, press E 1 2, then drag the throttle levers up or down. The throttle levers can be moved via the mouse, the function keys F1, F2, F3, and F4, or by pressing 9 on the numeric keypad to increase the throttle, or 3 on the numeric keypad to decrease the throttle.

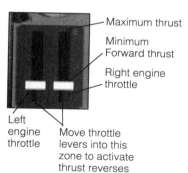

Maximum thrust

Minimum Forward thrust

Right engine throttle

Left engine throttle

Move throttle levers into this zone to activate thrust reverses

Figure 7.41
Throttle controls/thrust diverters for the Learjet

From the keyboard, you can also adjust the throttle by pressing the function keys F1, F2, F3, and F4. The F1 key cuts engine power to idle, F2 decreases the engine power gradually, F3 increases engine power gradually, and F4 opens the throttle to its maximum setting.

To apply the thrust reversers on landing, drag both throttle controls downward into the red zones. Full reverse thrust is achieved when the throttles are pushed down to the lowest possible setting. From the keyboard, you can activate the thrust reversers by pressing Ctrl F1.

 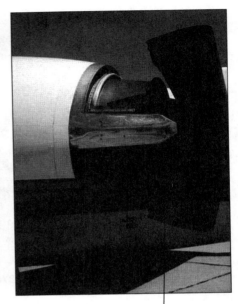

Figure 7.42
Thrust diverters for the Learjet (*Courtesy of Learjet*)

Thrust reverse disengaged   Thrust reverse engaged

Other Instruments/Indicators

There are various other instruments and indicators used on the Learjet. They are listed as follows in this section.

Spoilers (SPL)

The spoilers are special flaps on the top surface of the Learjet's wings that act as air brakes. They can be used to slow the aircraft, or prevent it from gaining too much speed when descending. After touchdown, you can extend the spoilers and flaps together, along with activating the thrust reversers, to quickly slow the aircraft. To deploy the flaps, click on the EXT button. To retract the flaps, click on the RET button. From the keyboard, press [/] to extend or retract the spoilers.

Flaps

The flaps are used to create extra lift when landing or taking off. The flaps position indicator shows the current extension angle for the flaps. They can be deployed incrementally from 0° to 8°, and from 20° to 40°. You deploy the flaps by clicking on the individual angle settings on the flaps position indicator. Or, from the keyboard, you can use [F5] through [F8]. When the

Retract spoiler here

Extend spoiler here

Figure 7.43
The spoilers control on the Learjet

arm of the flaps position indicator points to the DN marker, the flaps are fully extended at 40°. If the arm points to the UP marker, the flaps are fully retracted at 0°.

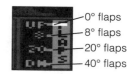

Figure 7.44
The flaps indicator/
control on the Learjet

The Learjet's flaps have only four settings as opposed to the Cessna's five flap settings:

UP: Flaps fully retracted up to 0°

8°: Flaps set to 8°

20°: Flaps set to 20°

DN: Flaps fully extended down to 40°

You must not fly faster than the V_{FE} (Flap Extension Speeds), or else damage to the flaps will occur. For the flaps fully down, the V_{FE} is 150 knots IAS, and for the flaps set to 20°, the V_{FE} is 185 knots IAS.

Control Position Indicators

The position of the ailerons, rudder, and elevator are depicted on the control position indicators.

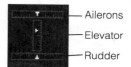

Figure 7.45
Control position
indicators on the
Learjet

Pitch Trim Indicator

The pitch trim is the Learjet's counterpart to the Cessna's elevator trim, and is used to fine tune the aircraft's pitch (nose-up or nose-down angle). It also relieves the pilot of constantly applying pressure to the yoke to maintain level flight.

In FS 5.0, you will find this control most helpful when you are using a joystick/flightstick yoke because it enables you to fly at a level attitude without constantly pushing the stick forward or backward.

The pitch trim is activated from the keyboard by pressing 7 for nose down pitch movements, and by pressing 1 for nose up pitch movements. (Both 7 and 1 are found on the numeric keypad.)

Note that the direction of movement of the Learjet's pitch trim indicator is the reverse of the Cessna's elevator trim indicator. When you press 7 to pitch the nose down, the pitch trim indicator moves up (on the Cessna it moves down); and when you press 1 to pitch the nose up, the pitch trim indicator moves down. (On the Cessna it moves up.)

Figure 7.46
Pitch trim indicator
on the Learjet

Angle of Attack/Stall Warning Proximity Indicator

The angle-of-attack indicator (ANG ATK) is a rectangular, horizontal gauge that tells you how close you are to stalling the aircraft. A stall occurs when smooth airflow over the wings is disrupted, causing a loss of lift. The farther

Keep needle in this zone while flying | Needle in this zone indicates a stall

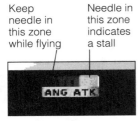

Figure 7.47
Angle of attack/stall warning proximity indicator on the Learjet

Figure 7.48
Outside temperature gauge on the Learjet

Figure 7.49
Landing gear indicator on the Learjet

the needle moves to the right, the closer you are to a stall condition. When the needle enters the light-colored zone on the right of the gauge, you are in danger of stalling and must take immediate action to prevent the airplane from crashing. Lower the nose and increase thrust.

Although there is some relationship between a stall and the wing's angle of attack, a stall can occur at any speed, angle of attack, or engine setting; therefore, this instrument would more aptly be called the stall proximity warning indicator.

Outside Temperature Gauge

Measures the temperature outside the aircraft in degrees Fahrenheit. At higher elevations the temperature will drop.

Landing Gear

This indicator tells you the current position of your landing gear. When the wheels are down, the three wheel lights below the gear icon glow green. When the gear is being retracted, the wheel lights will briefly turn red before flickering out. The gear can be retracted or extended by clicking on the gear indicator, or by pressing G.

Don't extend the landing gear when traveling faster than the V_{LO} (maximum airspeed when operating the landing gear). For the Learjet, this is 200 knots IAS.

Autopilot/Strobe/Lights/Zoom/Clock/Simulation Speed Rate

The autopilot, strobe, lights, zoom, clock, and simulation speed rate controls are all similar to the Cessna's, with the exception of the landing lights. The Learjet has twin landing lights, one on each main landing gear. To turn on the autopilot, strobe, or lights, simply click on the indicator and it will light up. To turn off any control, click again and the light will blink out.

Simulation speed control — Digital clock

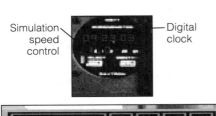

Figure 7.50
Autopilot, strobe, lights, zoom, clock, simulation speed rate

The zoom indicator allows you to change the magnification of the currently active 3-D view window, but it does not work with the Map view. To increase magnification, press +. To decrease magnification, press −. You can also click to the right of the zoom number to increase the zoom; alternatively, click to the left to decrease the zoom.

For a more complete description of each indicator and control, see the earlier section on the Cessna's instrumentation.

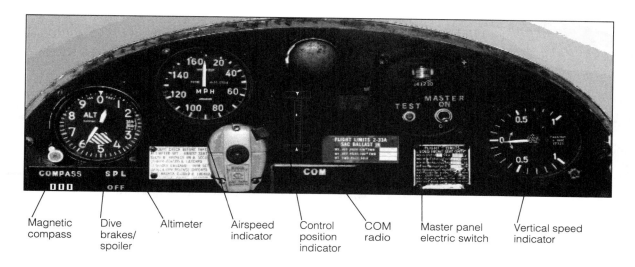

Magnetic compass   Dive brakes/ spoiler   Altimeter   Airspeed indicator   Control position indicator   COM radio   Master panel electric switch   Vertical speed indicator

Figure 7.51
Schweizer 2-32 sailplane's instrument panel

UNDERSTANDING YOUR INSTRUMENTS AND CONTROLS ON THE SCHWEIZER 2-32 SAILPLANE

Because the Schweizer 2-32 sailplane is used primarily for recreation, the cockpit instrumentation is kept simple. There are no engine controls or navigational aids other than a simple magnetic compass. Only a radio, altimeter, airspeed indicator, vertical speed indicator, and dive brake control comprise the instrumentation package for the sailplane.

Airspeed Indicator

The airspeed indicator measures the aircraft's indicated airspeed, although in FS 5.0, the true airspeed is actually displayed. The sailplane's maximum speed is about 158 miles per hour, so the dial is calibrated to read speeds of 20 mph to 160 mph.

Altimeter

Like the altimeter on the Cessna, this altimeter is read like a clock. The large hand shows hundreds of feet MSL, and the small hand shows thousands of feet MSL.

Vertical Rate of Climb Indicator

The vertical rate of climb indicator, which is calibrated in units of hundreds of feet per minute, tells you how fast up or down you are traveling. Thus, when the needle rests on the upper number 0.5, you know that the sailplane is climbing at the rate of 50 feet per minute.

Spoilers/Dive Brakes

The dive brakes, like the Learjet's spoilers, act to slow down the aircraft's rate of descent. To deploy these air brakes, click on the SPL indicator, or press [/].

Master/Test Switch

This switch activates the aircraft's electrical system, which is totally dependent on battery power. In the early version of FS 5.0, this switch is not implemented.

COM Radio

The COM Radio is used to contact Air Traffic Control or to display the ATIS weather information. To change the frequency, see the instructions found earlier for the Cessna.

Magnetic Compass

The magnetic compass shows your aircraft's current heading.

Control Position Indicators

The position of the ailerons, rudder, and elevator are depicted on the control position indicators.

UNDERSTANDING YOUR INSTRUMENTS AND CONTROLS ON THE SOPWITH CAMEL

The walnut-faced control panel found on the Sopwith Camel is simple but practical. There are no sophisticated controls or instruments; nevertheless,

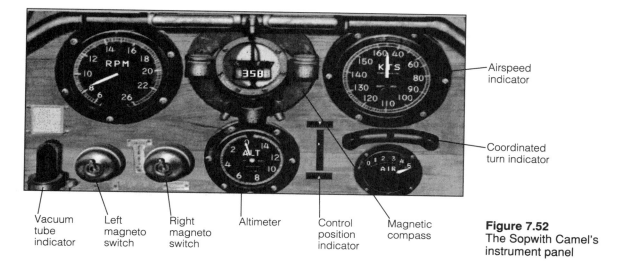

Vacuum tube indicator · Left magneto switch · Right magneto switch · Altimeter · Control position indicator · Magnetic compass

Airspeed indicator

Coordinated turn indicator

Figure 7.52
The Sopwith Camel's instrument panel

you still have much the same flight information displayed to help you fly the plane.

Airspeed Indicator

The Sopwith Camel's airspeed indicator shows the plane's true airspeed in knots per hour. Your aircraft speed will register if it falls within the range of 40 knots per hour to 160 knots per hour.

Altimeter

The altimeter measures the plane's altitude in feet, and is scaled in units of thousands of feet. For an altitude of 4,000 feet, the needle covers the number 4 on the dial. The highest altitude the instrument can measure is slightly over 14,000 feet, although practically speaking, the Sopwith Camel would never fly that high.

Turn Indicator

The turn indicator is used to determine whether you are making a coordinated turn or not. Like the Cessna, unbalanced forces in a turn can cause uncoordinated turns, meaning that the airplane slips and skids through the air. When this happens, the ball rolls to one side or the other, but if the turn is coordinated, the ball stays centered. By default, FS 5.0 starts you out with your rudders and ailerons synchronized in auto-coordination mode. If you want more selective control over your turns, deselect the Auto-Coordination option under the Sim menu.

RPM Indicator

The engine's RPM (rotations per minute) indicator tells you how fast your engine is running, and is calibrated in hundreds of revolutions per minute. A reading of 16 on the scale thus shows an engine RPM of 1,600. For average cruising, the needle on the dial should hover around 2200 RPMs.

Magnetic Compass

The magnetic compass tells you your plane's current compass heading.

Magneto Switches/Vacuum Tube

The two metal throw switches are used to turn on and off the right and left magnetos. Each magneto system generates electrical power for the spark plugs, and is independently redundant in case one should fail. To shut them off, click below each magneto switch; to turn them back on, click above the switch. When you shut off both magnetos, the vacuum tube ceases to glow, telling you that your ignition system is without power.

Control Position Indicators

The position of the ailerons, rudder, and elevator are depicted on the control position indicators.

C H A P T E R
8
Basic Flight Maneuvers

This chapter introduces you to the basic ground and flight maneuvers of taxiing, taking off, climbing, flying straight and level, making turns, and landing. But because flight planning is such an important part of flying, you will also be introduced to ATIS (Automatic Terminal Information Service) for weather information, air traffic control, and the checklists.

Make sure, before starting this chapter, that *Flight Simulator* is properly configured to work with your computer, display card, keyboard, sound card, and mouse or joystick. Then start *Flight Simulator* by typing **FS5** at the DOS prompt. In a moment, you should see the tarmac of Chicago's Meigs Field runway 36 out of the cockpit window of your Cessna Skylane 182RG airplane. In the background, you should hear the steady drone of your engines idling.

If you want to take off right away, you can skip the next section on taxiing and go directly to the takeoff.

TAXIING

Before practicing how to taxi around the runway, you will want to first be familiar with your flight controls and how they operate. It's best if you have already studied the keyboard layout for the numeric keypad so that you know which keys move the ailerons, elevators, rudder, and throttle setting. If you don't already know how to operate your controls, take a moment now to review this material. A quick reference for the keyboard commands can be found on the inside back cover of this book and in Appendix C. To use the mouse as your control yoke, you must click the right mouse button so that the cursor disappears from the screen. At this point, any movement of the mouse will be translated into movements of the rudder, ailerons, and elevator. To

Mouse users can switch back and forth between mouse yoke control and normal mouse control by clicking on the right mouse button.

disengage the mouse/yoke, simply press the right mouse button once again, and the mouse pointer will reappear.

Panoramic View

Next, spend a few moments practicing how to use your 360° field of view out the windows. Your initial view out the window is the front view. Press Shift and 9 on the numeric keypad to see out your right front window. Holding down Shift, press the numeric keypad keys 6, 3, 2, 1, 4, 7, and 8 to cycle through all the eight possible views that make up your field of vision. Press Shift 8 to return to the front cockpit view.

The Map Window

To better orient yourself while on the ground, bring up the map window by pressing Num Lock. Zoom in and out of the map view by pressing + and - on the main keyboard until you get a good view of your immediate surroundings. The center cross in the map window represents your airplane, and when you move, the map will scroll accordingly. To remove the map, press Num Lock twice in succession. (But for now, keep it open.)

Enlarge any view or map window by pressing W.

Flight Simulator also has a new feature that allows you to view any of your view or map windows full screen. Simply press W once to enlarge the window to full screen, and press W again to reduce it to its normal size. Try this by pressing W, then press - several times until you have the entire Meigs Field runway environs in view.

For this exercise in taxiing, you should follow the path illustrated in Figure 8.1, and then return to your starting position on runway 36. Notice that you will make a left turn off the main runway onto a small turnoff runway, then make another left turn and taxi straight until you see the turnoff for the main runway where you started. When you reach this turnoff, turn left and you will be back again on runway 36. All you need to do at this point is make a 90° left turn and you will be back to your original starting position.

Figure 8.1
The map window open to full screen, showing the taxi path you should take

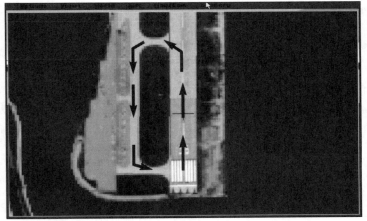

Flight Simulator 5.0 now has painted runway guides off the main runways, which helps you keep your plane from running off the pavement, or worse-crashing into some ground object. All you need to do to stay out of trouble is make sure that your plane follows the runway guide. Don't veer to the left or right of the guide; just stay right on top and you will be fine.

Whenever taxiing off the main runway, follow the painted runway guides!

Practice Turning, Starting, and Stopping While Taxiing

Before taxiing, see if your parking brakes are on by looking at the lower-left corner of your cockpit window. If it says "Parking Brake" then you must release the parking brake by pressing ⌶. To begin taxiing, press ⑨ on the numeric keypad seven times. The airplane will begin to roll down the runway as the tachometer shows the engine speed increasing to between 1,055 and 1,155 RPMs. You steer the aircraft by pressing ⓪ on the numeric keypad to steer left, and by pressing Enter on the numeric keypad to steer right. Avoid the unfortunate practice of steering using ④ and ⑥ aileron/rudder; this will only get you into trouble later on when you try to break the habit. Practice steering left and right now using the ⓪ and the Enter keys. Stopping the airplane is accomplished by pressing ⌶ on the main keyboard to engage the wheel brakes. You should also cut the throttle by pressing ③ on the numeric keypad until the engine is again idling at 645 RPM. Press ⌶ and hold down ③ to stop the plane now. After the airplane has come to a complete halt, press ⌶ again to release the brakes and then press ⑨ seven times to allow the airplane to start rolling again.

How to Pivot Your Airplane 360° While on the Ground

You can pivot your airplane 360° while on the ground by using *Flight Simulator*'s new differential brakes. (You might need to pivot your plane, for example, when looking for traffic at an uncontrolled airport.) A differential brake system allows you to apply different braking pressures on each wheel. This allows you to lock one wheel in place, for example, while allowing the other to rotate freely.

To perform a 360° pivot left, follow these steps:

1. Press the F11 function key to apply the left differential brake.
2. Increase the throttle by pressing ⑨ on the numeric until you start moving (engine RPM 1,055–1,100 RPM). You may have to repeatedly press F11 to re-engage the differential brake while you do this, since it has a tendency to release itself every few moments. Your airplane will begin to rotate left while staying in place.

To use the differential brakes, press F11 for the left differential brake, and F12 for the right differential brake.

To perform a 360° pivot right, follow these steps:

1. Press F12 to apply the right differential brake.
2. Increase the throttle by pressing 9 on the numeric keypad until you start moving (engine RPM 1055-1100 RPM). You may have to repeatedly press F12 to re-engage the differential brake while you do this, since it has a tendency to release itself every few moments. Your airplane will begin to rotate right while staying in place.

Taxi Around Meigs Field and Return to the Takeoff Position on Runway 36

Now that you have had some practical experience stopping and turning the aircraft while on the ground, let's try taxiing back to the beginning of runway 36. Allow the aircraft to roll forward and look for the runway turnoff to the left, all the while making sure that your speed does not become excessive. When you see the turnoff, press [.] to slow the aircraft then press 0 on the numeric keypad to pivot left. If you pass the runway turnoff, don't worry: simply stop the airplane, and apply the left differential brake (F11) to rotate the aircraft left and head back. (See the previous section on pivoting the airplane 360°.) Look for the painted runway guides, as illustrated in Figure 8.2, and follow the line veering off to the left.

Follow the runway guide until you reach the turnoff for runway 36. Make a left turn, applying the brake ([.]) and left rudder (0) to precisely maneuver your plane. Don't be afraid to come to a complete stop and reconnoiter your position via the map window. You can always pivot the aircraft in place, using the differential brakes, and point it in the right direction.

Don't fret if you at first have trouble taxiing around the airport. These movements take much practice. If you get stuck, or too frustrated, simply press Ctrl Print Screen, and the simulator will reset itself.

Figure 8.2
Follow the painted runway guides and stay right on top of them, or your plane may crash or get mired in the mud. In this figure, you will want to stay with the left guide.

Painted runway guides

ATIS AND AIR TRAFFIC CONTROL

Before taking off, you should obtain weather information for your area by tuning in the local ATIS (Automatic Terminal Information Service) radio station on your COM radio. You will also need to request takeoff clearance from Air Traffic Control. The next two sections discuss how the ATIS and Air Traffic Control work.

To see the ATIS message scroll across your screen while at Chicago's Meigs Field, tune your COM radio to a frequency of 121.30 MHz by clicking on frequency digits (left to increase the digits, right to decrease the digits). This will tune in the ATIS station for Meigs Field.

The following information appears on your screen:

Scrolling ATIS Message On-Screen	Explanation
Meigs Field Information Alpha 15:00 Zulu	ATIS station identification 1500 (3:00 P.M.). Coordinated Universal Time: Note that this time is not local time, but GMT, or Greenwich Mean Time in England, and it is expressed in 24-hour format.
Weather:	Weather Conditions
Measured Ceiling 10,000	Clouds are found at up to 10,000 feet
Visibility 10	Visibility is 10 miles
Temperature 74 F	Temperature is 74°Fahrenheit
Winds 90 at 10	Wind direction 90° (due east) at 10 knots per hour
Altimeter 30.15	Air pressure is 30.15 inches of Hg
Landing and Departing Runway 36	Landing and departing on runway 36: Runway numbers are always described by the direction the runway is facing. For example, runway 36 means that the runway faces due north at 360°. Likewise, if ATIS tells you that you are "Landing and Departing Runway 18," it means that you must go to the opposite end of the runway to take off or land on a compass heading of 180°, or due south.
Advise Controller on initial contact you have Alpha	Contact Air Traffic Control for permission to land or take off. Tune your COM radio to the airport's control tower frequency for clearance.

You must request take-off or landing clearance from Air Traffic Control whenever you take off or land.

To request Air Traffic Control Clearance:

1. Select the Air Traffic Control option from the Nav/Com menu. This command is a toggle; that is, each time you select it, it either turns on or

off. If it is on, you will see a check mark next the menu name.

2. From the Nav/Com menu, select Communications Radio.

3. In the Communications Radio dialog box, click the Send Message button. The Air Traffic Control dialog box should open.

4. If you are taking off, click Request to Takeoff button. Alternatively, if you are landing, click Request to Land button.

5. Follow the instructions from the tower, and set your 4-digit transponder squawk code to the code that the ATC specifies.

6. Go through your takeoff checklist.

BEFORE TAKEOFF, PERFORM THE TAKEOFF CHECKLIST

Before taking off, you should go through the takeoff checklist to make sure all is in order. Very briefly, move all your controls, checking that the elevators, rudder, and ailerons all move, as is displayed on the control position indicator. Examine your other instruments, being sure to check the items as shown in Table 8.1. After going through this checklist, you will be ready for takeoff.

TAKING OFF

For this section of the chapter, you will need to have your Cessna aircraft poised for takeoff at the very beginning of runway 36. If your aircraft is not in takeoff position, simply press Ctrl + Print Screen, and the simulation will reset itself.

Next, read the Takeoff Checklist for the Cessna, as outlined in Table 8.2. This table is a handy reference guide for taking off. When you are sure you understand what needs to be done, proceed to the next section.

Performing the Checklist

Make sure that the wing flaps are fully retracted and the carburetor heat is turned off. Increase the throttle to just shy of its maximum setting. Watch now as the aircraft begins to move slowly down the runway. Align the Cessna on the center of the runway using 0 on the numeric keypad to steer left, and Enter on the numeric keypad to steer right These keys control the

Table 8.1   Before Takeoff Checklist

Item	Indicator/Control	Action
1	Parking Brake	Set (press ⌈Ctrl⌉ ⌈.⌉)
2	Ailerons, rudder, elevator, elevator trim	Check operation, then center as indicated on control position indicators
3	Mixture	Set to rich (move lever up)
4	Fuel quantity	Check left and right tanks are full
5	Throttle	1700 RPM
6	Magnetos	Perform magneto check: Set engine to 1700 RPM with parking brake engaged. Move ignition switch first to R position and note RPM. Next move switch back to BOTH position to clear the other set of spark plugs. Then move switch to the L position, note RPM, and return the switch to the BOTH position. RPM drop should not exceed 175 RPM on either magneto or show greater than 50 RPM differential between magnetos.
7	Carburetor heat	Off
8	Propeller	Cycle from high to low pitch (meaning low RPM to high RPM). Return pitch to low setting for maximum RPM (i.e., move Prop Pitch Lever to top).
9	Oil pressure and temperature	Gauge Indicators Centered
10	Throttle	800–1000 RPM
11	Strobe lights	Set by pressing ⌈O⌉
12	COM radio	Set to local ATIS frequency
13	Directional gyro	Press ⌈D⌉ to Calibrate
14	Altimeter	Press ⌈B⌉ to Calibrate
15	Autopilot	Off
16	Wing flaps	Set to 0°
17	Parking brakes	Release by pressing ⌈.⌉ on main keyboard

Table 8.2 Takeoff Checklist

Item	Indicator/Control	Action
1	Wing flaps	0° for normal runway 20° for soft runways or short field takeoff (flaps settings greater than 20° not allowed for takeoff)
2	Carburetor heat	Cold (off)
3	Throttle	Set to 29" to 31" Hg (maximum) and 2400 RPM
4	Prop pitch control	Move to highest RPM setting (slide prop pitch control lever UP) for lowest propeller pitch angle
5	Mixture	Full rich (move mixture level to top)
6	Elevator control	Lift Nose Wheel at 55 knots IAS (Press ② or pull back on yoke)
7	Airspeed indicator	Climb airspeed should be 80 knots IAS (Flaps at 0°) or 70 knots IAS (Flaps at 20°)
8	Wheel brakes	Apply momentarily when airborne and prior to retracting landing gear. This will stop wheel from rotating and prevent any rubbing as it is retracted into the wheel well. Press ⨀.
9	Landing gear	Retract landing gear. Press Ⓖ.
10	Wing flaps	For short field takeoff/soft runways where flaps are set to 20°, retract slowly once airborne and after reaching 70 knots IAS.

To quickly center the steering wheel, press ⑤ on the numeric keypad.

right and left movement of your steering wheel on the ground. In auto-coordination mode (the default mode in this case), the ailerons are linked with the rudders, so you also steer with ④ and ⑥, or the mouse. To quickly center the rudders, ailerons, or steering wheel, press ⑤ on the numeric keypad.

With your throttle set to maximum, your speed will increase very rapidly, as shown on the airspeed indicator. Strong crosswinds often make a controlled takeoff difficult, so you may have to counteract this drift by carefully moving the rudder and ailerons (press ④ and ⑥). Try not to zigzag down the runway by moving the rudder ailerons excessively, and do not hesitate to abort the takeoff if you run into trouble. To abort the takeoff, decrease the throttle by pressing ③ on the numeric keypad, and then apply the brakes repeatedly by pressing ⨀ on the main keypad.

The normal takeoff ground roll distance is about 1,215 feet for the Cessna. But to gain sufficient altitude to clear a 50-foot obstacle at the end of the runway, you need at least 2,310 feet of horizontal distance. Meigs Field, with its 3,948-foot runway, gives you ample room to take off and land.

Rotation: At a speed of 55 knots per hour, press ⓶ once or twice (or pull back on your joystick/mouse slightly) to pull your nose up. This act is called "rotation," and each aircraft has a different rotation speed.

Retract the Landing Gear

As soon as you have lifted off (you will know this because your wings will start to rock if you make any slight motions left or right), apply the wheel brake momentarily by pressing ⌷, then retract the landing gear by pressing Ⓖ. Since the wheels are still spinning furiously from the takeoff, you will want to slow them before stowing them in the wheel well. Try to keep your airspeed around 70 to 80 knots during the climb away from the runway by applying a light touch to the elevators (⑧ and ② on the numeric keypad).

In general, it is always best to lift off into the wind, if possible, because the headwind adds to your takeoff speed and so reduces your takeoff distance. Figure 8.3 shows the screen as the plane takes off.

Figure 8.3
Taking off (spot view)

Taking Off with a Crosswind

Crosswinds are winds that cross the runway in a semi-perpendicular angle. To successfully take off with a crosswind, *you must switch off auto-coordination* and then use your ailerons to correct the aircraft's tendency to yaw to the left or right. Auto-coordination, you will remember, links your rudder and ailerons together, and if you leave this option on when trying to correct a crosswind force, your rudder will interfere. Figure 8.4 shows what happens to your airplane when a crosswind blows across the runway.

Here is how to take off with a crosswind present:

1. Switch off auto-coordination under the Sim menu.
2. Create a surface crosswind blowing 90° with a speed of 15 knots. To do this, pull down the World menu and select Weather. In the Weather dialog box, click the Winds button, and then click the Create button. In the Create Wind dialog box that next opens, click the Surface Winds radio button, and then enter a speed of 15 knots and a course heading of

Switch off auto-coordination while taking off with a crosswind.

Effects of the Crosswind on Takeoff

No Correction
Plane Blown Off Runway

Proper Correction
Ailerons Applied Into Wind
& Plane Stays on Course

Figure 8.4
On takeoff with a
crosswind present,
airplane skips to the
left with no correction;
by applying ailerons
into the direction of the
wind, you can have
better control during
takeoff

90. Click OK to exit all the dialog boxes and return to the simulator.

3.   Tune in the ATIS frequency to listen for the weather report. The wind direction should be given, which tells you where the wind is blowing. If the report says "Wind 90 at 15," you will know that a wind is blow-ing at 15 knots with a direction of 90° (or due east).

4.   Apply FULL ailerons into the direction of the wind. Thus, since you are facing 00° due north, and the wind is blowing 90° due east, you will turn your ailerons all the way left (press ④ on the numeric keypad until the control position indicator shows the aileron at the far left). Figure 8.4 shows the proper procedure for taking off in a crosswind.

5. Use the rudder to steer left and right. Before taking off, however, move the rudder in the direction of the wind. This will prepare the airplane for what is yet to come. For this example, apply left rudder by pressing ⓪.

6. Increase the throttle to maximum.

7. Steer down the center of the runway, correcting any zigzag movements with the rudder (⓪ and Enter on the numeric keypad).

8. At an airspeed of 50 knots (just before rotation), center the ailerons and rudder with ⑤. This will prevent your plane from tipping over once it leaves the ground.

9. After passing 55 knots, raise the nose (apply the up elevator by pressing ②).

Your plane may soar in an awkward direction just after it leaves the ground. But you should now be able to stabilize the airplane into a level climb.

Later in this chapter you will find information on how to land with a crosswind.

CLIMBING

Climbing is often defined as the transition between takeoff and flying straight and level at cruising altitude. The Cessna performs normal climbs at 610 feet per minute, while climbs that require quick ascents, such as when clearing mountains or obstacles rapidly, can be performed at a maximum rate of 1,040 feet per minute (at sea level).

| Table 8.3 Normal and Maximum Climb Rates for the Cessna |||
Climb Type	Feet per Minute	Airspeed
Normal climb	610	90 to 100 knots/AS
Maximum climb	1,040	90 knots/AS

Both the normal rate of climb and the maximum rate of climb numbers are affected by altitude, aircraft speed, and weather. Due to thinner air at high altitudes, the rate of climb decreases. At 16,000 feet, for example, the normal rate of climb falls to 495 feet per minute, while the maximum rate of climb falls to 755 feet per minute.

To achieve a normal climb, you should increase the throttle and apply the up elevator. Use the elevator sparingly; the engine should take over most of this responsibility.

To climb, follow these steps:

1. Increase the throttle and apply up elevator (press ②) or pull back on the mouse/yoke) to initiate the climb. Watch as the vertical speed indicator creeps upwards. You can fine tune your climb rate by moving the throttle (use ⑨ and ③ on the numeric keypad), and by making minute adjustments to the elevator trim (use ⑦ and ① on the numeric keypad).

2. For a normal climb, adjust throttle and propeller control until airspeed is 90 to 100 knots, 25 inches of Hg (manifold pressure), with 2,400 RPM, and the vertical speed indicator shows approximately 600 feet per minute rate of ascent. For a maximum rate of climb, increase throttle and propeller control until 31 inches of Hg manifold pressure is developed at 2,400 RPM. Use full rich mixture and watch that your airspeed stays around 87 to 90 knots, with a vertical rate of climb of 1,040 feet per minute at sea level, or 755 feet per minute at 16,000 feet.

Figure 8.5
The Normal climb

Figure 8.5 shows the screen during a normal climb. Note that the vertical speed indicator shows a vertical speed of around 600 feet per minute and the airspeed is hovering around 90 knots.

Table 8.4	Minimum Climb Checklist for the Cessna	
Item	**Indicator/Control**	**Action**
1	Airspeed indicator	90 to 100 knots IAS
2	Vertical speed indicator	At sea level, temperature 60° F, normal rate of climb is 610 feet per minute.
3	Throttle and propeller controls	Set engine power to 25 inches Hg and 2400 RPM using prop control and throttle. Adjust both controls as necessary. (Sliding the prop pitch control down slightly often increases engine power.)
4	Mixture	Full rich (move mixture lever to top)

Table 8.5	Maximum Climb Checklist for the Cessna	
Item	**Indicator/Control**	**Action**
1	Airspeed indicator	90 knots IAS at sea level to 87 knots at 20,000 feet
2	Vertical speed indicator	Degrees F, maximum rate of climb is 1,040 feet per minute. At 16,000 feet, maximum rate of climb is 755 feet per minute
3	Throttle and propeller control	Set engine power to 29–31 inches Hg and 2400 RPM using prop control and throttle. Adjust both controls as necessary. (Sliding the prop pitch control down slightly often increases engine power.)
4	Mixture	Full rich (move mixture lever to top)
5	Propeller	Lowest pitch angle (move lever up)

✈

Use the throttle to effect changes in your climb rate. Don't use the elevators to climb.

Tables 8.4 and 8.5 detail the climbing procedures for both the normal and maximum climb.

Your plane will enter a stall if your airspeed is too low (below 55 knots at sea level), or if your rate of climb is too high (see Figure 8.6). *Flight Simulator* reacts to this condition by sounding an audible warning klaxon and displaying a stall indication message on the right side of the cockpit windshield. (On the Learjet, the stall warning message is hidden from view by the magnetic compass.) The best way to recover from this situation is to lower the nose to regain flying speed and lift.

If you continue to climb, eventually the atmosphere will thin to the point where there is not enough lift to support your plane. This also constitutes a stall situation, and you must descend to a lower altitude to regain lift.

Furthermore, at higher altitudes, the manifold pressure gauge will indicate a loss of power. This is because the total air pressure in the manifold is decreased, due to the less dense air. The manifold pressure decreases at the rate of approximately 1 inch of Hg for each 1,000-foot gain in altitude. Thus, during prolonged climbs, the throttle must be continually advanced if constant power is to be maintained.

Figure 8.6
External view of a stall

CRUISING STRAIGHT AND LEVEL

After your climb has been completed, you will want to enter the cruise phase of your flight. To make the transition to straight and level flight, reduce the throttle and lower the elevators as necessary. Be sure to start the leveling-off process well before your desired cruising altitude, because it takes time to stabilize the aircraft.

Leveling Off from the Climb

To level off the aircraft and exit the climb, reduce your throttle. Use the elevator trim to make any last-minute adjustments to nose pitch. The general rule of thumb is to start the level off approximately 50 feet below the desired altitude for each 500 feet per minute rate of climb.

Level-Off Distance = 50 Feet per 500 FPM Climb Rate

Thus, for example, if you were climbing at a rate of 1,000 feet per minute, you would start your level off at 100 feet below the altitude you wish to establish.

Normal Cruise

Normal cruising does not require full throttle. In fact, flying straight and level usually is performed using only 55 percent to 75 percent of the engine's

At higher altitudes, the Cessna's engine will lose power, as indicated on the manifold pressure gauge.

rated horsepower. The throttle, propeller pitch control, and mixture control all influence the amount of power the engine produces. In addition, altitude and temperature affect the power setting needed for a level cruise. Therefore, you must adjust your throttle, mixture, and propeller pitch settings for different altitudes in order to achieve straight and level flight. Table 8.7 tabulates the cruise airspeeds versus altitude for a power setting of 75 percent. Thus, if you set your engine to 23 to 25 inches of Hg (75 percent), you will see that in order to cruise straight and level at an altitude of 5,000 feet, your airspeed will need to be 151 knots. Notice that the higher you travel, the faster your cruise speed must be. This fits in with aerodynamic theory, which predicts that as the atmosphere thins at higher elevations, less lift is generated by the wings of an airplane. To maintain level flight and generate the same amount of lift, therefore, the plane must have a higher forward velocity.

Flight Simulator 5.0 Hot Cruise Tip

A good power setting for cruising at 5,000 feet and below can be found when the engine is set to 2,300 RPM with 23.0 inches Hg of manifold pressure. To achieve this:

1. Reduce the RPM through the propeller control by pressing Ctrl + F2 until you get 2,300 RPM.

2. Next, reduce the throttle by pressing F2 until you get 23 inches Hg of manifold pressure.

3. Adjust elevator trim as necessary for level flight by pressing 7 and 1 on the numeric keypad.

For a summary of the steps to be performed for cruising straight and level, see Table 8.6.

Figure 8.7
Cruising straight and level in the Cessna

EXECUTING TURNS

The turn is a basic flight maneuver used to change the aircraft's heading. You make turns by banking the wings of the aircraft, using the ailerons and rudder in combination. It is often necessary to apply the elevators to maintain altitude.

The artificial horizon and the turn indicator are used to obtain information about the turn. The artificial horizon

Table 8.6 Cruise Checklist for the Cessna

Item	Indicator/Control	Action
1	Throttle	17 to 25 inches Hg, 2100 to 2400 RPM
2	Mixture	Lean to hottest EGT temperature, then enrich by 50° (slide mixture control down to lean, up to enrich)
3	Propeller pitch	Set RPM to 2400 by adjusting propeller pitch up or down as needed.
4	Vertical speed indicator	0 feet per minute
5	Elevator trim	Adjust up or down as necessary (Press 7 or 1 on the numeric keypad)
7	Artificial horizon	Horizontal flight is displayed when the shaded horizon is centered on the gull wing marker in center of dial. Roll pointer should also be centered on 0° roll marker.

Table 8.7 Cruise Airspeed Varies by Altitude for the Cessna

Altitude	Airspeed in Knots TAS
5,000	151
10,000	158
15,000	165
20,000	173

Engine Power at 75 percent (Engine power varies with altitude, temperature, RPM, and airspeed. 75 percent power is developed at 4,000 Feet, 2,400 RPM, 45° F, 150 knots TAS)

tells you how much of a bank angle your wings are making with the ground, while the turn indicator tells you whether you are making a standard coordinated turn. The standard turn is defined as a turn that takes the aircraft two minutes to pivot 360° in a circle. If you ever get lost in a cloud with zero visibility, for example, you could use the turn indicator to help you make a standard turn and head out of the cloud from whence you came. This precision instrument helps you to make very tightly controlled turns.

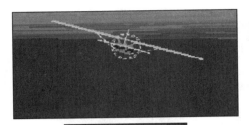

20°
marker

Artificial horizon
bank angle shows 20°.
Triangular pointer is
lined up with 20° marker.

Shallow turn (20°)

30°
marker

Artificial horizon
Bank angle shows 30°.
Triangular pointer is
lined up with 30° marker.

Medium turn (30°)

60°
marker

Artificial horizon
bank angle shows 60°.
Triangular pointer is
lined up with 60° marker.

Steep turn (60°)

Figure 8.8
The shallow, medium,
and steep turns

Turns are divided into three classes:

- *Shallow turns* have a bank angle of less than 20°. With no action on your part, the aircraft's wings will tend to level themselves unless some force is used to maintain the bank.

- *Medium turns* have a bank angle of 20° to 45°. The plane continues to turn without any additional application of the ailerons.

- *Steep turns* have a bank angle of more than 45°. At this angle, the plane continues to bank ever more steeply unless some counteracting aileron pressure is applied.

The Standard Turn

In all turns in which you plan to maintain your altitude, you will have to apply a little up elevator ([2] on the numeric keypad, or pull back on mouse/yoke). If you are flying in auto-coordinated mode, turning is made easier since the simulation takes over the responsibility of synchronizing the ailerons and rudder. On the other hand, if you are flying in non-coordinated mode with rudder pedals and a flightstick (or just from the keyboard), you must use the turn indicator to make coordinated turns. When the wings of the plane symbol in the turn indicator align with the L (left) or the R (right) markers, the plane will make what is known as a standard turn. This means that in two minutes, the plane will complete a 360° turn and be headed once again in the same direction. In a standard turn, the plane will turn at a rate of 3° per second.

To make a standard turn, follow these steps:

1. In auto-coordinated mode, apply the right aileron to turn right (press ⑥ on the numeric keypad or move the mouse/yoke right), or the left aileron to turn left (press ④ on the numeric keypad or move the mouse/yoke left). If you are flying in non-coordinated mode, to make a right turn, apply the right aileron with the right rudder (⑥ with Enter on the numeric keypad), or to make a left turn, apply the left aileron with left rudder (④ with ⓪ on the numeric keypad).

Figure 8.9 Executing a standard right turn while maintaining altitude

2. As you move your controls, watch your turn indicator to see that the airplane wings symbol stays lined up with either the L or R marker. In uncoordinated mode, you must move your ailerons and rudder in concert together so that the moving ball in the turn indicator's inclinometer stays centered.

3. For level flight, apply a little up elevator (② or pull back on the mouse/yoke). See that your plane is flying horizontally with respect to the horizon by checking the artificial horizon.

Figure 8.10 Executing a right turn while climbing

4. Observe your heading and the time on the clock. In exactly two minutes, the plane should have completed the turn and be back on its original heading.

Figures 8.9 through 8.11 illustrate what your instrument panel would look like executing various turns.

Figure 8.11 Executing a left turn while descending

Coming Out of the Turn

Follow these steps to come out of the turn:

To Exit Medium or Steep Turns of 20° or Greater:

1. Apply reverse aileron pressure to counteract the turn. Thus, if you are turning left, you must apply the right aileron (⑥ on the numeric keypad or right mouse/yoke movement). If you are turning right, then you would apply the left aileron (④ on the numeric keypad or left mouse/yoke movement).
2. When the plane is level, press ⑤ on the numeric keypad to center the ailerons.

To Exit Shallow Turns of Less than 20°:

Center the ailerons by pressing ⑤ on the numeric keypad.

After you finish your turn, make sure that the artificial horizon is level with the gull wings symbol at the center of the dial, and that the vertical speed indicator is at 0 FPM. This will ensure that the aircraft is flying straight and level.

To exit the shallow turn, neutralize the ailerons by pressing ⑤ on the numeric keypad. To exit medium or steep turns, apply reverse aileron pressure, then center the ailerons when the plane is level by pressing ⑤.

How to Come out of a Turn to a Predetermined Heading

To come to a desired heading, you must roll out of the turn at the right time. The standard rule of thumb for doing this is as follows:

$$Rollout\ Angle° = \frac{Bank\ Angle°}{2}$$

For example, suppose you are turning right with a bank angle of 20° and you want to come to a course heading of 90°. Using the above formula, you can figure that your rollout angle will be:

$$\frac{20°}{2} = 10°$$

Thus, you begin the rollout from the turn when you reach 80°, and by the time the rollout has been completed, you will be on a course of 90°.

DESCENDING AND LANDING

Landing the plane is the most difficult aspect of flying. Even in the simulated world of *Flight Simulator*, learning how to land is not simple. This section will teach you the essential principles and steps you need to perform to land, but do not expect to master them the first time around. You will need to practice descending and landing many times, as the procedures and skills needed are involved and tricky.

Fortunately, FS 5.0 includes two new features to help teach you how to land properly:

- *Land Me:* A *Flight Simulator* instructor will take over the operation of your plane and land it for you. You can then watch and learn how to land the plane. Press X to activate. At any time, you can disengage Land Me by pressing X once again.

- *Final Approach to Meigs Field:* This built-in situation illustrates the proper setup for a hands-off, perfect landing at Meigs Field. With no intervention on your part, the Cessna will land by itself on the runway. When you think you can land the plane yourself, simply take the controls and fly. This is an excellent training scenario for learning how to land. Load this situation from the Options menu by clicking the Situations command. Then, when the Situations dialog box opens, select Final Approach to Meigs Field and click OK.

The Final Approach to Meigs Field situation is a good scenario for learning how to make your final approach. It does not place you far enough away from the runway, however, to let you plan your descent properly. To better learn how to perform the complete descent and landing operation, *Flight Simulator* includes another excellent flying mode, called Oakland 27R Landing Approach.

Oakland 27R Landing Approach

After starting up *Flight Simulator,* select the Options menu and then click on the Situations command. In the Situations dialog box, click on the lower scroll bar button arrow until you see the Oakland 27R Landing Approach situation in the list box. Once Oakland 27R-Landing Approach is selected, you are ready to start the simulator by clicking on the OK button.

Planning Your Landing

Before leaving cruising altitude, you will need to make preparations for the descent and landing. Pause the *Flight Simulator* program by pressing P. This will freeze the simulation until you have time to plan your approach.

Check Weather and Runway Condition Information

Tune in the ATIS weather and runway information service on your COM radio by clicking on the frequency selector to a frequency of 128.50 MHz. The ATIS message will soon scroll across your windshield, giving you helpful information in planning your approach and landing.

To quickly land your plane using FS 5.0's new Land Me feature, press X. An instructor will take over your plane and land it at the nearest airport. You can take over at any time by again pressing X.

Press P to pause Flight Simulator in order to plan your landing.

Cross-Check Your Instruments

While the simulator is still paused, take a few moments to scan your instruments.

- Start with the altimeter. Your altitude is 1,490 feet above mean sea level (MSL), which means that you are actually 1,477 feet above ground level (AGL), since Oakland Airport is 13 feet above sea level. Do not confuse AGL with MSL, as the results could be fatal! For example, at higher-elevation airports, your altimeter MSL readings may tempt you to think that you have plenty of altitude above the ground, while in reality you may be plummeting toward the ground.

- Next, check your airspeed indicator reading of 100 knots along with your engine speed of 2,390 RPM developing 22.66 inches Hg on the manifold pressure gauge.

- Observe the turn and bank indicator, artificial horizon, and vertical speed indicator. These instruments confirm that you are flying straight and level.

- Your directional gyro shows that you are on a course of 276°. Since Oakland 27R is oriented on a course of 270° (remember, you multiply the runway number by ten to obtain the proper course heading), you will have to correct your heading by 1°.

- Looking at your other miscellaneous controls and instruments, note that your flaps are set to 10°, the landing gear is extended, the temperature is 64°, your COM radio is tuned to 127.5 MHz, and the DME (Distance Measuring Equipment) shows that the distance to the runway is 3.6 miles.

Calculating the Rate of Descent

In order to touchdown precisely on the runway, you need to calculate your rate of descent, or vertical speed, that you need to maintain. First, calculate how much time you have before reaching the runway, using the following formula:

$$Time\ to\ Runway\ in\ Minutes = \frac{Distance\ to\ Runway}{Airspeed}$$

Since the DME indicator shows you to be 3.6 miles from the runway, and your airspeed is 100 knots (1.66 nautical miles per minute), you will cross the threshold of the runway in 2.16 minutes

$$2.16\ Minutes = \frac{3.6\ Nautical\ Miles}{1.66\ \frac{Knots}{Minute}}$$

This means you must decrease your altitude from 1,490 feet MSL within 2.16 minutes, which requires a rate of descent of 687 feet per minute, as is illustrated by the following formula:

$$Vertical\ Speed = \frac{Altitude}{Time\ to\ Runway\ in\ Minutes}$$

Due to inaccuracies in the simulation, however, we will use a steeper glide angle of 800–1,000 feet per minute to help position the plane a little in front of the runway.

Use a vertical speed of 800–1,000 feet per minute as your rate of descent for the Oakland 27R landing.

Starting the Descent

Before resuming the simulation, perform these preliminary steps:

1. Turn the Axis Indicator on. Under the Views menu, select View Options, and in the dialog box that follows, turn on option K Axis Indicator Large V. When you are done, click the OK button to return to the simulation. This V-shaped marker on your cockpit windshield helps you point your aircraft in the right direction. It also tells you whether your nose is pointed into the ground or above the ground, by the relationship of its gull wing with the horizon.

2. Make sure the landing gear is down (gear indicator light should glow green).

3. Set flaps to 30° by pressing F7. This helps the airplane maintain lift at very slow approach speeds.

4. Turn carburetor heat on.

5. Reduce the throttle to about 1/4 of the full setting. (Press 3 on the numeric keypad to lower throttle.)

6. Lower the elevators a notch by pressing 8 on the numeric keypad a few times.

Now you are ready to continue with the descent. Your screen should look like Figure 8.12.

7. Press P to resume the simulation.

8. Immediately reduce engine speed to 1,889 RPM with a manifold pressure of about 12.45 inches Hg. (Press 3 on the numeric keypad to lower throttle, or 9 to increase throttle.)

Figure 8.12
Pause the simulation so that you can take your time completing the landing preparations

9. Use the elevator to lower your pitch until your vertical speed indicator shows a downward movement. (Press ⑧.) When the vertical indicator settles on 800 to 1,000 feet per minute, you must again readjust your elevators upward with ②. This stabilizes your descent and prevents it from becoming steeper.

10. Use the elevator trim to fine tune your nose pitch (press ⑦ to lower the nose, and 1 to raise the nose).

11. Apply ailerons, if needed, to line up your nose with the runway. (Press ④ to turn left, or ⑥ to turn right.) The axis indicator should be lined up with the beginning of the runway.

Figure 8.13
The terminal descent

Table 8.8 shows the general descent checklist for the Cessna. This checklist should not be followed verbatim for the Oakland 27R Landing, but can be used for all other descents.

Final Approach and Landing

At a distance of 1.6 miles from the runway, your altitude should be 300 to 500 feet, and the middle marker alarm will sound. When this happens, you will see an amber-colored M appear on the OMI marker indicator and a beeping sound will ensue. Figure 8.13 illustrates what your screen should look like.

Table 8.8	Descent Checklist for the Cessna	
Item	**Indicator/Control**	**Action**
1	Throttle	Decrease engine RPM as necessary to obtain 500 feet per minute rate of descent. Use throttle to control vertical speed, not horizontal speed.
2	Vertical speed indicator	500 feet per minute
3	Airspeed indicator	Hold speed to 133 Knots IAS
4	Mixture	Lean for smoothness (move mixture control down)
5	Carburetor heat	On to prevent carburetor icing
6	Wing flaps	Set flaps at 0 to 10° below 140 knots IAS

Final Approach

- At a distance of ½ mile from the runway (monitor the DME indicator for closing distance), your altitude should be 100 to 200 feet MSL.
- Increase throttle (press 9) to decrease vertical speed to between 200 and 500 feet per minute. Do not use your elevators to adjust your descent rate, because increasing or decreasing engine thrust accomplishes the same thing.
- Your airspeed should be around 60 to 75 knots.
- If the landing approach is going according to plan, you should be on the correct glide path to the runway. Check that your vertical speed is between 200 and 500 FPM again. If your rate of descent is too high, increase the throttle by pressing 9. If you start climbing, decrease the throttle by pressing 3.
- Make sure the axis indicator on your cockpit windshield is aimed at the head of the runway. Adjust your pitch angle if it is too low by pressing 2, or if it is too high by pressing 8. Left and right course corrections can be made by applying the left and right ailerons (press 4 to turn left, or 6 to turn right).

Figure 8.14
Final approach to Oakland

Figure 8.14 shows what your screen should look like on the final approach to Oakland.

Landing

- After crossing the runway threshold, pick your touchdown point just beyond the runway numbers.
- At 20 to 30 feet above the ground, flare the plane. (i.e., pull back on the yoke by gently applying the up elevator. Gently tap 2 once or twice.) By performing the flare maneuver, you will be trying to create a controlled stall onto the runway.
- Reduce throttle to idle.
- As the airplane descends in the final moments, gently keep the nose up so that the main wheels hit first. Then, when touchdown occurs, gently lower the nose (press 8) and cut the engines (press 3 repeatedly or press F1).
- Apply the brakes (repeatedly press .) until the airplane rolls to a halt.

Figure 8.15
Performing a flare
while landing at
Oakland

Figure 8.15 shows a spot view of the airplane performing the flare maneuver while landing at Oakland.

Don't be discouraged if, at first, you don't succeed and you crack up your plane. Reset the simulation by pressing Ctrl Print Screen, and you can practice some more.

Table 8.9 shows the general landing checklist for the Cessna. This checklist should not be followed verbatim for the Oakland 27R-Landing, but can be used for all other landings.

Landing with a Crosswind

Winds that cross the runway in a perpendicular direction present some difficulties when landing. These crosswinds, as they are called, can be successfully dealt with when landing by using one of two landing techniques:

- *Crabbing Method:* The airplane is slightly turned to face the direction of the wind when landing. Although easier for the pilot to maintain during final approach, it requires a high degree of skill to remove the crab prior to landing, when the wheels of the plane must be quickly aligned with the runway to avoid sideways skidding.
- *Wing-Low Method:* The airplane faces the runway when landing, but lowers one wing in the face of the oncoming crosswind. This method is recommended in most cases.

In both the crabbing and wing-low methods, auto-coordination must be turned off. Therefore, to successfully land with a crosswind, *you must switch off auto-coordination* so that you can independently work the rudder and ailerons. Auto-coordination, you will remember, links your rudder and ailerons together, and if you leave this option on when trying to correct a crosswind force, your rudder will interfere.

Switch off auto-
coordination while
trying to land with a
crosswind.

Crabbing Method

The crab method is executed by establishing a heading, called a crab, toward the crosswind. The airplane's direction of movement, even though the nose direction is slightly askance to the runway heading, is in a straight line towards the runway. The crab angle is maintained until just prior to touchdown, when the pilot must quickly realign the nose of the plane with the

Table 8.9 Landing Checklist for the Cessna

Item	Indicator/ControlEvent	Action
1	Seat backs, seatbelts	Most upright position, seatbelts secure
2	Throttle	Reduce throttle (press ③ on numeric keypad) to 1836 RPM with 13 to 16 inches of Hg manifold pressure
3	Airspeed indicator	Below 140 knots
4	Landing gear	Gear down, press Ⓖ. Check to see that green indicator light is illuminated.
5	Mixture	Full rich (move mixture lever up)
6	Propeller	Pitch set to low blade angle, highest RPM setting (move propeller control up)
7	Carburetor heat	On
8	Airspeed indicator	Reduce airspeed to 70–80 knots IAS (with flaps UP or at 10°), or 66 knots IAS (with flaps full down)
9	Flaps	Set flaps to 30° (press F7), or as desired.
10	Airspeed indicator	Reduce airspeed to between 65 and 75 knots IAS
11	Elevator trim	Adjust nose pitch angle (press ⑦ and ① on numeric keypad)
12	Vertical speed indicator	Reduce vertical speed to 200–500 feet per minute by increasing the throttle with ⑨
13	Altimeter	Watch that you maintain on altitude reading of 120 to 250 feet AGL (above ground level). For example, when landing at Meigs Field, make your landing approach to the runway at about 800 to 850 feet MLS (which is 200 to 250 feet above ground level).
14	Pick touchdown point just beyond runway numbers	Aim nose of aircraft for touchdown just past the runway numbers
15	Flare	Flatten out your approach at 20 to 30 feet above AGL
16	Touchdown	Main wheels first, then gently lower nose wheel to the ground
17	Throttle	Reduce to idle (press F1)
18	Brakes	Apply brakes (press [.] on main keyboard). For maximum braking power, retract the flaps (press F5), and apply full up elevator (press ⑧ on numeric keypad)
19	Taxi off runway	Use differential braking (F11 left brake, F12 right brake) with steering control (⓪ - right, Enter - left) to navigate and make turns on runways. Increase throttle to 1055-1100 RPMs to begin taxiing.
20	After landing checklist	Retract flaps, switch off carburetor heat, turn off lights, turn magnetos to OFF position, set parking brake (press Ctrl[.])

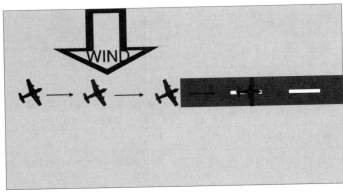

Crosswind Landing using the Crabbing Method

Figure 8.16
Crosswind landing using the crabbing method

runway to avoid sideways skidding of the wheels. Figure 8.16 illustrates the crosswind landing using the crabbing method.

To fly using the crab approach, keep your wings level using the aileron controls, but apply rudder to aim your nose slightly in the direction of the oncoming crosswind. Your plane will be blown slightly off from its nose direction, but this should put you on a precise heading for the runway.

Wing Low Method

This preferred method for landing the plane in a crosswind has the pilot bank the wings of the airplane in the direction of the crosswind. To use this method, you must align the airplane's nose with the runway heading, and then lower the wing that faces the crosswind. The amount of lowering depends on the force of the crosswind, but generally, the stronger the wind, the lower you will want the wing to be. When one wing is lowered, however, the airplane will want to turn in the lowered wing's direction. To counteract this, you must also simultaneously apply opposite rudder pressure to prevent turning into the wind and drifting off course from the runway heading.

Figure 8.17
Crosswind landing using the wing low method.

Crosswind Landing Using the Wing Low Method

For example, if the crosswind has a direction of 90° and you are on a heading of 0°, you must apply left ailerons (press ④ on the numeric keypad) while simultaneously applying right rudder (press Enter on the numeric keypad) to counteract the tendency of the aircraft to turn left. This will allow you to maintain your course heading of 0° while landing with the crosswind.

CHAPTER
9

Flying the Cessna

This chapter contains a short history of the Cessna Skylane and also includes actual performance data that will aid you in planning your flights.

CESSNA SKYLANE HISTORY

Cessna Aircraft Company, now a subsidiary of General Dynamics Corporation, was started by the late Clyde V. Cessna in 1911. Incorporated in 1927, the company has designed and built more than 177,553 aircraft at its Wichita, Kansas, factory, including 7,500 Model 152s, 35,773 Model 172 Skyhawks, 1,159 Cutlass RGs, 19,812 Model 182 Skylanes, 2,102 Model 182 Skylane RGs, 2,400 Citation Jets, and various other models.

The Cessna Skylane 182 RG II (Figure 9.2) had its design origins in the 1949 Cessna Model 170A, which was an all metal, 145-hp, four-seat taildragger. In 1952 the Cessna 180, a derivative of the 170A, was introduced, and it sported a larger 225-hp engine, although the same airframe was used. Tricycle landing gear replaced the taildragger wheel in 1956, when the Cessna 182 was introduced. The name "Skylane" was added to the 182 when a new deluxe version was offered in 1958 that included full instrumentation and radio equipment as standard equipment.

The 1958 Skylanes continued to retain the basic airframe of the 170 and 172. In 1962, however, the airplane was redesigned with a sportier body that included a new rear window and a larger cabin. The new airframe for the 182 enjoyed much success and was retained over the years. In fact, today's Skylane is much the same as that of the 1962 model, except for internal structural and equipment changes.

227

Figure 9.1
The 1984 Cessna
Skylane 182 RG II
(*Photo courtesy of
the Cessna Aircraft
Company*)

Production of the Cessna Skylane RG series of aircraft was suspended on December 31st, 1987. In all, there were 2,102 Skylane RG aircraft produced, although this number was surpassed by its fixed-gear brother, the Cessna Skylane, which had a production run of over 19,812. Cessna has found it more economical to produce larger cargo and commercial aircraft, such as the Caravan Model 208 and the Cessna Citation business jets, and has closed a chapter on one of aviation's most popular personal aircraft.

CESSNA PERFORMANCE

This section includes performance tables, specifications, and charts that will prove useful to you in flying the Cessna. Please note that these tables, charts, and figures are to be used *only* with Microsoft's *Flight Simulator 5.0*, and are *not to be used for real flying purposes*. In many cases, the numbers will not jibe with FS 5.0's flight data due to inaccuracies in the flight model. For example, the actual cruise speeds at 20,000 feet are much slower than is the case with the real Cessna Skylane. The FS 5.0 Skylane RG achieves around 120 knots

Figure 9.2
Cessna Skylane 182
RG II (*Photo courtesy
of the Cessna Aircraft
Company*)

true air speed (TAS), while the real Skylane RG should be able to reach 173 knots (TAS).

In Flight Simulator, true air speed, or TAS, is what is shown on your airspeed indicator. On real aircraft, however, indicated air speed, or IAS, is shown on the airspeed indicator. Since the airspeed indicator bases its readings on static and dynamic air pressure, IAS does not tell you your true ground speed, due to varying air pressure differences at different altitudes and temperatures. At sea level, IAS and TAS are approximately the same, but at high altitudes IAS is *always less* than TAS. For example, in the FS 5.0 Skylane, if you had changed your airspeed indicator to show IAS instead of TAS[1], and you were traveling at 14,000 feet with an IAS of 70 knots, your TAS (or groundspeed) would be more like 110-120 knots. Most performance charts show TAS, so you need a special aviation calculator to calculate your TAS from the IAS shown on your airspeed indicator. For a rough

---

[1]Exception: In FS 5.0, True Airspeed (TAS) is initially shown on the airspeed indicator. Also, this assumes that you are not flying into a strong head wind.

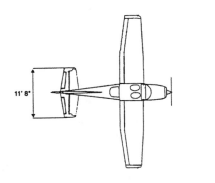

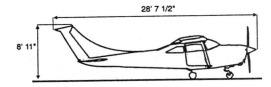

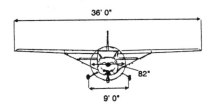

Figure 9.3
Aircraft dimensions

approximation, the correction factor for true airspeed when flying at higher altitudes can be summarized by the following rule: Add two percent to your indicated airspeed per thousand feet of altitude.

Setting the Optimum Air/Fuel Mixture

The Exhaust Gas Temperature (EGT) gauge is used to determine how the throttle mixture is affecting engine performance. At higher altitudes, the air/fuel mixture gets richer due to the rarefied atmosphere. Therefore, you must lean the engine, or reduce the air/fuel ratio, by using the mixture control. To determine the optimum mixture setting, slide the mixture control up and down until you see the EGT needle move as far to the right as possible. When this happens, the engine is running at its hottest temperature and leanest mixture setting. For better engine performance, you should enrich the mixture (slide the mixture control down) by about 50° cooler as measured by the EGT gauge. This means that the needle should move about two notches to the left.

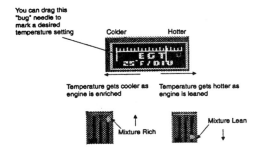

The Effect of Air/Fuel Mixture Ratio on EGT Gauge Temperature

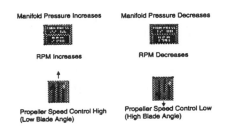

Propeller Speed Control (Propeller Blade Pitch) and Its Effect on Manifold Pressure and RPM

Figure 9.4 Effects of air/fuel mixture and propeller speed control

Table 9.1 Cessna Performance Specifications

Speed		
Maximum at 20,000 ft.		187 knots
Cruise 75% power at 20,000 ft.		173 knots
Cruise 75% power at 10,000 ft.		158 knots
Cruise Range and Time		
75% power at 20,000 ft.	Range:	825 nm
88 gallons usable fuel	Time:	5.0 hours
75% power at 10,000 ft.	Range:	800 nm
88 gallons usable fuel	Time:	5.1 hours
Minimum range at 20,000 ft.	Range:	1,010 nm
88 gallons usable fuel	Time:	8.1 hours
Minimum range at 10,000 ft.	Range:	1,030 nm
88 gallons usable fuel	Time:	8.5 hours
Rate of Climb		
At sea level		1,040 FPM
10,000 feet		890 FPM
18,000 feet		710 FPM
Certificated Maximum Operating Altitude		
Maximum ceiling altitude		20,000 feet
Takeoff Performance		
Ground roll		820 feet
Total distance over 50-ft obstacle		1,570 feet
Landing Performance		
Ground roll		600 feet
Total distance over 50-ft obstacle		1,320 feet
Stall Speed (Knots True Airspeed)		
Flaps up, power off		54 knots
Flaps down, power off		50 knots
Maximum Weight		
Ramp		3,112 lbs.
Takeoff or landing		3,100 lbs.
Standard Empty Weight		
		1,824 lbs.
Maximum Useful Load		
		1,288 lbs.
Baggage Allowance		
		200 lbs.
Fuel Capacity		
		92 gallons
Oil Capacity		
		9 quarts
Engine: Turbocharged Avco Lycoming		
235 British horsepower at 2400 RPM		

Table 9.2   Cessna Airspeed Limitations

V speed	Speed	Knots TAS	Knots IAS	Explanation
V_{NE}	Never exceed speed	175	178	Do not exceed this speed under any circumstance.
V_{NO}	Maximum safe structural cruising speed	155	157	Do not exceed this speed except in smooth air, but only with caution.
V_{A}	Maneuvering speed	111	112	Do not make full or abrupt movements of the rudder, ailerons, or elevator.

Table 9.3   Mixture and Exhaust Gas Temperature

Mixture Description	Exhaust Gas Temperature
Recommended lean	50° rich of peak EGT (50° cooler than peak lean temperature)
Best fuel economy	EGT (hottest or peak lean temperature)

Note that you must first activate the propeller control and mixture control in *Flight Simulator* by clicking on the Propeller Control Manual setting, and the Mixture Control check box, under the Realism and Reliability dialog box, found under the Sim menu.

Propeller Speed Control and Mixture Relationship to Engine Power

The propeller speed control adjusts the pitch of the propeller's blade angle. When the blade angle is high, the RPM of the propeller decreases because the propeller is "biting" larger slices of air. When the blade angle is low, the RPM of the propeller increases because the propeller is slicing through the air more easily. At higher altitudes, the air is thinner and the propeller can spin faster than is good for the engine. This is because the air offers less resistance to the propeller, allowing the engine to turn it more easily. The RPM can then exceed engine tolerances and cause damage to the engine. You can use the propeller control to slow down the propeller by sliding the control down to reduce RPM. Note that engine power, as shown on the manifold pressure gauge, changes when you make alterations to the propeller's blade angle. Engine power generally decreases as you slow down the RPM (slide the prop lever down), and increases as you speed up the RPM (slide the prop lever up). See Figure 9.4 for an illustration of this principle.

The mixture control also affects engine power. If you slide the lever up, thereby enriching the air/fuel ratio, you will notice that the engine's power, as shown on the manifold pressure gauge, goes up. On the other hand, if you slide the lever down, thereby leaning the air/fuel ratio, you will notice that manifold pressure goes down.

Thus, to set the engine's power setting you will need to combine movements of the mixture control and propeller speed control and observe their results on the manifold pressure gauge.

Generally, to set engine power, follow these steps:

1. Set the mixture control to Recommended Lean, as shown on the EGT gauge.

2. Adjust the propeller speed control until you achieve the RPM and manifold pressure you want.

3. Set engine throttle.

Refueling and Range

The Cessna Skylane RG II has a maximum range of 1,040 nautical miles (1,197 statute miles) when flying at a cruise speed of 122 knots, 45 percent

Table 9.4	Cessna Cruise Performance					
	75% POWER (Engine power varies with altitude, temperature, RPM, and airspeed. 75% power is developed at 4,000 feet, 2,400 RPM, 45° F, 150 knots TAS)		**65% POWER** (Engine power varies with altitude, temperature, RPM, and airspeed. 75% power is developed at 4,000 feet, 2,400 RPM, 45° F, 140 knots TAS)		**55% POWER** (Engine power varies with altitude, temperature, RPM, and airspeed. 75% power is developed at 4,000 feet, 2,400 RPM, 45° F, 131 knots TAS)	
Altitude	Airspeed in Knots TAS	Nautical Miles per Gallon	Airspeed in Knots TAS	Nautical Miles per Gallon	Airspeed in Knots TAS	Nautical Miles per Gallon
5,000	151	10.6	142	11.5	132	12.5
10,000	158	11.1	148	12	137	12.9
15,000	165	11.6	155	12.5	142	13.4
20,000	173	12.1	162	13.1	147	13.9

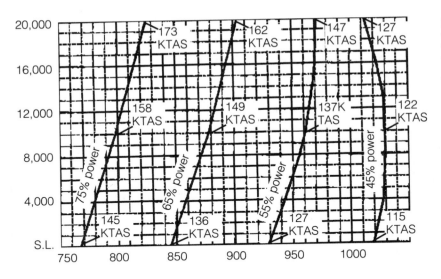

Figure 9.5
Range profile chart for
the Cessna Skylane

power. At this speed and power setting, the 88-gallon fuel tank can keep the plane aloft for over 8.5 hours, not including a 45-minute reserve. When flying at higher power settings, range is considerably reduced, as Figure 9.5 illustrates. Looking at the chart, you can see that average range at 10,000 feet, 75 percent power, traveling at 158 knots is about 810 miles.

In *Flight Simulator* you can have your aircraft serviced and refueled by landing at an airport that has a refueling facility, as indicated in the airport directory. To refuel and have the aircraft serviced, locate the fuel rectangle, displayed as a yellow border with the letter "F" inside it, and then taxi your airplane inside the rectangle. Almost immediately, your aircraft will be refueled and serviced, and you can resume flying. You can also add fuel to your tanks manually by adjusting the fuel quantity in the Engines and Fuel dialog box under the Sim menu. You don't, however, have to refuel unless you choose Engine Stops When Out of Fuel from the Realism and Reliability command under the Sim menu.

Engine Failure

If an engine failure occurs during takeoff, the most important thing to be done is to abort the takeoff and stop the airplane on the remaining length of runway. If the engine fails after takeoff, promptly lower the nose to maintain airspeed. Airspeed above 55 knots TAS means your airplane can still generate enough lift to fly, and if you allow the speed to fall below this minimum, the plane will crash. The best glide speed, if you are trying to prolong your time in the air, is 83 knots IAS. If you have enough altitude to make a 180° turn back to the airport, do so. Otherwise, look for the nearest flat field or highway to land on.

If you have enough altitude, follow these steps to restart the engine:

1. Maintain airspeed of 80 knots IAS

2. Carburetor heat ON

3. Mixture rich

4. Restart the engine by turning the master magneto switch OFF, then to BOTH (or START position, if the propeller has stopped)

  Figure 9.6 shows the maximum glide at the optimum glide airspeed of 83 knots IAS. Note that if you are at 10,000 feet, you have approximately 17 miles ground distance in which to find an airport where you can land.

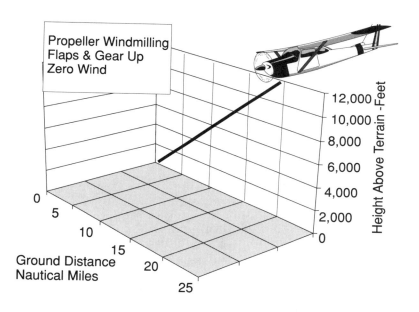

Maximum Glide Distance at 83 Knots IAS

Figure 9.6
Maximum glide chart for the Cessna

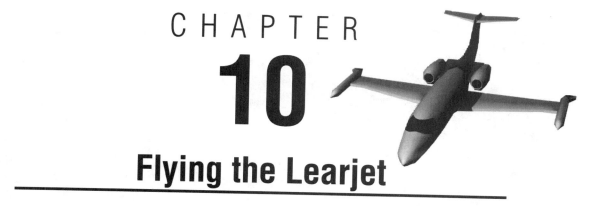

CHAPTER
10

Flying the Learjet

In this chapter you will learn more about the Learjet 35A and its performance characteristics. Information is also provided on how to turn the Learjet while on the ground, and how to fly with an inoperable engine. With the knowledge you obtain from the material herein, you can go about making realistic mission planning profiles for trips around the world.

Regardless of what aircraft you are currently flying, whether on the ground or in the air, you can fly the Learjet at any time by following these steps:

1. Select the Options menu and click on the Aircraft command.
2. Next, in the Aircraft dialog box, highlight Learjet 35A and then click the OK button. The Learjet instrument panel will then be displayed.

LEARJET HISTORY

Learjet, Inc., was originally founded in 1960 by Bill Lear, Sr., as the Swiss American Aircraft Company (SAAC). In 1962, the company was transferred to Kansas and renamed the Lear Jet Corporation. Gates Rubber Company bought out a 60 percent majority stake in the company in 1967 and the company was subsequently renamed Gates Learjet Corporation. Following a 1987 acquisition by Integrated Acquisition Inc., the company was renamed Learjet Corporation, and all manufacturing was moved from Tucson, Arizona, to Wichita, Kansas. The most recent change in company ownership was completed in 1990, when Canada's Bombardier group took over Learjet's line of credit.

Figure 10.1
The Learjet 35A
(*Courtesy of Learjet*)

The first Learjet produced was the Lear 23, and it was one of the world's first light, twin-turbojet-powered business jets. Next came the Learjet 25G which, as most *Flight Simulator* buffs will tell you, was the original Learjet for Microsoft *Flight Simulator* (first introduced with FS 3.0 in 1988). With the introduction of newer turbofan technology in the late 1960s, Learjet embarked on a new research and development program to design a more technologically advanced business jet. This was to be the Learjet 35A, with a variant of much greater range—the Learjet 36A produced later. The first flight of the turbofan Learjet 35A, using Garrett TFE731-2 powerplants, occurred on January 4, 1973. The $3 million Learjet 35A, with its distinctive fuel tank pods on the wing tips, soon became a resounding success, with more than 720 sold over the years. Learjet now makes four newer jets: the Lear 31A, the 55B and 55C, and the Lear 60.

Today there are more than 1,700 Learjets of all types in operation around the world. They are flown by the U.S. Air Force, the U.S. government, 20 countries around the world, multinational corporations, and countless other private companies.

The Learjet 35A is an all-metal, pressurized, low-wing monoplane. It can

Figure 10.2
The Learjet 35A
(*Courtesy of Learjet*)

fly at a maximum altitude of 45,000 feet at a speed of 471 knots (542 mph, or approximately 9 miles a minute) and climb at nearly a mile a minute. The cabin has room for eight passengers and two crewmembers with a maximum height of 52 inches and a maximum width of 59 inches. At the rear of the cabin is the baggage compartment, which has approximately 40 cubic feet of space and a 500-pound storage capacity. Inside, the cabin has many amenities, including swivel seats, a three-place divan, folding tables, a refreshment cabinet with ice chest, hot and cold beverage service, running water, a warming oven, an audio-visual entertainment center, and a private toilet.

The Learjet 35A has also been engineered for superior reliability and strength. The fail-safe fuselage exceeds most operational requirements and has been tested for metal fatigue by pressurizing and depressurizing the cabin through 50,000 continuous cycles from sea level to 50,000 feet and back again without a single problem. This is the equivalent of 100 years of normal flying. The windshield is also fail-safe tested for bird strikes, and with its one-inch thickness, is designed for an unlimited life. Each main landing gear puts two tires on the pavement, adding an extra measure of safety during takeoff and landing.

Figure 10.3
Learjet interior
(Courtesy of Learjet)

PERFORMANCE AND MISSION PLANNING

This section includes performance tables, specifications, and diagrams that will prove useful to you in flying the Learjet. Please note that this information is to be used *only* with Microsoft's *Flight Simulator 5.0* and *should not be used for real flying purposes*. In many cases, the numbers will not match the FS 5.0 Learjet's flight model. But even if some of the data is off, you will still gain some useful insights into the aircraft.

Operating Speeds

As noted in previous chapters, true airspeed, or TAS, is different from the indicated airspeed, or IAS, that is ordinarily shown on your airspeed indicator. Your airspeed indicator relies upon outside static and dynamic ram air pressures in the pitot-static system to determine airspeed. At higher elevations, the airspeed indicator shows you to be traveling *slower* than you actually are because of the more rarefied atmospheric pressure. True airspeed is

Figure 10.4
Learjet 35A cockpit

defined to mean your airspeed, corrected for this altitude error, and is approximately equivalent to ground speed, in the absence of any wind.

On the real Learjet, airspeed is displayed as Indicated Air Speed (IAS). Airspeed on the FS 5.0 airspeed indicator, on the other hand, is displayed as True Air Speed (TAS). You can change the FS 5.0 display to show IAS, for more realism, by toggling on the Indicated Airspeed checkbox in the Instrument Preferences dialog box, found under the Options menu.

You may wonder what difference IAS and TAS makes to you. On the real Learjet, your IAS airspeed, as measured on the airspeed indicator, *will never show more than 350 knots or so even though you may actually be traveling at 459 knots (542 MPH) TAS!* This is why the airspeed indicator shows only speeds up to 400 knots. In the FS 5.0 Learjet, because the analog portion of the dial only shows speeds up to 400 knots, a special digital readout has been added to show the TAS airspeeds above 400 knots. Naturally, if you choose to display IAS airspeed on your dial, you won't need the digital display.

Maximum operating speed from sea level to 8,000 feet is 300 knots IAS. Above 8,000 feet, your speed should not exceed 350 knots IAS (471 knots

Table 10.1   Performance Specifications*

Weight Limits	
Maximum Ramp Weight	18,500 lbs.
Maximum Takeoff Weight	18,300 lbs.
Maximum Landing Weight	15,300 lbs.
Approximate Standard Empty Weight	10,022 lbs.
Useful Load	7,981 lbs.
Approximate Fuel Capacity	6,198 lbs.
Takeoff Field Length	4,972 feet
Landing Distance	3,075 feet
Landing Approach Speed	128 knots IAS (147 mph, 237 km/hr)
Stall Speed (Landing Configuration)	97 knots IAS (112 mph, 180 km/hr)
Rate of Climb	
Two Engine	4,340 feet per minute
Single Engine	1,290 feet per minute
Single Engine Service Ceiling	25,000 feet
Maximum Cruise Speed	
39,000 Feet	471 knots TAS (542 mph, 850 km/hr)
41,000 Feet	453 knots TAS (521 mph, 839 km/hr)
43,000 Feet	441 knots TAS (508 mph, 817 km/hr)
Range	2,196 Nautical miles (2,525 miles, 4,670 km)
Maximum Operating Altitude	45,000 feet
Passenger Seating Capacity	Up to ten
Power Plant	
Type	Garrett TFE 731-2-2B
Number	2
Takeoff Thrust (Sea Level)	7,000 lbs. (#,500 lbs./engine)
Exterior Dimensions	
Length	48 feet 8"
Height	12 feet 3"
Wing Span	39 feet 6"
Wing Area	253.3 square feet
Wing Sweep	13°
Wheel Base	20 feet 2"
Range	2,196 Nautical miles (2,525 miles, 4,670 km)

*This data not for flight planning purposes; use only with Microsoft *Flight Simulator*

TAS). Note that while flying in regulated airspace, Federal Aviation Regulations prohibit flight speeds of more than 250 knots IAS (288 mph) below 10,000 feet MSL, or 200 knots IAS (230 mph) below 2,500 MSL.

Cost of Operating the Learjet

Well, it ain't cheap, but the Learjet is pretty reasonable when the cost of operating it is compared to other business jets in its class. The most costly item in the equation is fuel, which runs you around $400 an hour. Then you must consider the expense of maintenance and scheduled inspections, whose costs rise steeply the longer you own the jet. Assuming an average of 400 hours a year utilization, for the first year, the maintenance and repair budget will come to about $68 per hour of flight, rising to $400 per hour in the fourth year. Of course, when you throw in insurance, and the salaries of the pilot and co-pilot, it becomes quickly apparent that the Learjet is an expensive investment for getting around. But when money is no object, the Learjet will get you there no matter what. And it will land you on short, unimproved airstrips that no commercial jetliner could possibly attempt.

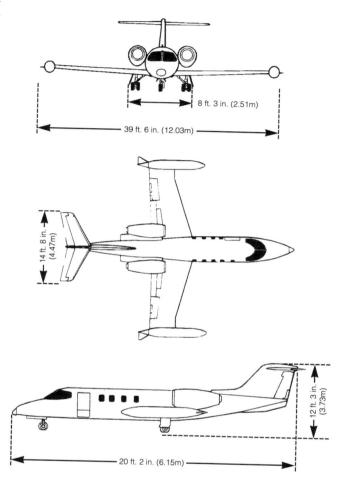

Figure 10.5
Aircraft dimensions

Turning the Learjet on the Ground

Turning the Learjet while on the ground is slightly more complicated than with the Cessna. When making a turn, you must apply the differential brake on the wheel that is on the same side of the turn direction, *and* apply engine throttle on the *opposite* engine side from which the turn is being made on. To illustrate this technique, observe Figure 10.6 to see how the Learjet is pivoted to the left. Notice that to turn left, the *right* engine throttle is increased and the *left* differential brake is applied. Turning to the right would be the exact opposite of this: you would increase the *left* engine and apply the *right* differential brake.

Table 10.2 Airspeed Limitations*

Maximum Operating Speeds	Speed
Sea Level to 8,000 Feet	300 knots IAS
8,000 Feet to 24,000 Feet	350 knots IAS
Above 24,000 Feet	0.81 Mach
Flap Extension Speeds	
Flaps 8 Degrees	200 knots IAS
Flaps 20 Degrees	185 knots IAS
Flaps 40 Degrees	150 knots IAS
Landing Gear Operating and Extending Speed	
Maximum Speed Extending Gear	200 knots IAS
Maximum Speed Retracting Gear	200 knots IAS
Maximum Speed Operating Gear	260 knots IAS

Table 10.3 Hourly Cost of Operation

Fuel	$349.00
Maintenance	$69.00
Miscellaneous	$40.00
Total Per Hour	$458.00
Total Per Nautical Mile	$1.21

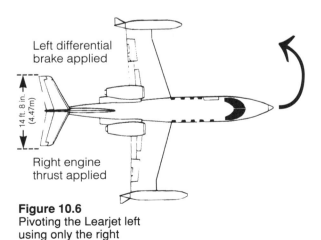

Left differential brake applied

14 ft. 8 in. (4.47m)

Right engine thrust applied

Figure 10.6
Pivoting the Learjet left using only the right engine and the left differential brake

Here is a summary of the actions to take when turning left or right for the Learjet while on the ground:

To pivot left:

1. Press [F11] to apply the left differential brake.

2. Increase the *right* engine throttle by pressing [E] [2] (on the main keyboard), then [9] (on the numeric keypad) until

*This data not for flight planning purposes; use only with Microsoft *Flight Simulator*

you start moving. (Or you can simply drag the right throttle up using the mouse.) You may have to repeatedly press [F11] to re-engage the differential brake while you do this, since it has a tendency to release itself every few moments. (You will see the word "BRAKE" on the lower-left corner of the cockpit window when the brake is on.) Your airplane will begin to rotate right while staying in place.

3. To stop the plane, press [.] and reduce the left engine throttle. (Simply press [3] on the numeric keypad; you don't need to press [E] [2] this time.)

To pivot right:

1. Press [F12] to apply the right differential brake.

2. Increase the *left* engine throttle by pressing [E] [1] (on the main keyboard) then [9] (on the numeric keypad) until you start moving. (Or you can simply drag the right throttle up using the mouse.) You may have to repeatedly press [F12] to re-engage the differential brake while you do this, since it has a tendency to release itself every few moments. (You will see the word "BRAKE" on the lower-left corner of the cockpit window when the brake is on.) Your airplane will begin to rotate right while staying in place.

3. To stop the plane, press [.] and reduce the left engine throttle. (Simply press [3] on the numeric keypad; you don't need to press [E] [1] this time.)

Takeoff Performance

Tables 10.4 and 10.5 show some of the Learjet's takeoff performance statistics. Using Table 10.4, you can estimate the length of runway needed for a takeoff under various conditions. For a takeoff at a temperature of 70° F at sea level, the 14,000-pound Learjet needs a runway of at least 2,950 feet. But a fully loaded, 18,000-pound Learjet would need at least 5,150 feet under the same conditions. When taking off at Meigs Field with a runway length of 3,948 feet, the 14,000-pound Learjet barely clears the end of the runway. Obviously, you shouldn't even take off from Meigs with a fully loaded, 18,000-pound Learjet. Although the FS 5.0 flight model should theoretically assume a weight of 18,000 pounds, for the purposes of simplifying the program, I think the Learjet's characteristics were slightly tweaked to allow it to take off with an implied weight of 15,000 to 16,000 pounds.

Table 10.5 gives you the safe takeoff speeds for the Learjet with different flap settings. For a shorter takeoff distance, and slower takeoff speed, you can set the flaps to 20°, although you can also take off with the flaps set to 8°.

Flaps should be set to 8° or 20° on takeoff.

Table 10.4 Takeoff Performance

	60° F (16° C)	70° F (21° C)	80° F (27° C)	100° F (38° C)
18,300 lb. Learjet	Takeoff Distance (Feet)	Takeoff Distance (Feet)	Takeoff Distance (Feet)	Takeoff Distance (Feet)
Runway Altitude				
Sea Level	5,020	5,150	5,560	7,370
2,000 Feet	5,630	5,960	7,110	Not possible
4,000 Feet	6,700	7,120	9,350	Not possible
6,000 Feet	8,785	10,100	5,370	Not possible
8,000 Feet	Better not try it	Better not try it	Better not try it	Not possible
17,000 lb. Learjet	Takeoff Distance (Feet)	Takeoff Distance (Feet)	Takeoff Distance (Feet)	Takeoff Distance (Feet)
Runway Altitude				
Sea Level	4,340	4,350	4,760	7,090
2,000 Feet	4,810	5,020	5,690	7,930
4,000 Feet	5,575	5,950	7,560	Not possible
6,000 Feet	6,750	8,080	10,580	Not possible
8,000 Feet	9,880	8,800	Not possible	Not possible
16,000 lb. Learjet	Takeoff Distance (Feet)	Takeoff Distance (Feet)	Takeoff Distance (Feet)	Takeoff Distance (Feet)
Runway Altitude				
Sea Level	3,800	3,800	4,160	5,085
2,000 Feet	4,205	4,400	4,900	6,590
4,000 Feet	4,810	5,120	5,895	9,070
6,000 Feet	5,810	6,400	8,385	Not possible
8,000 Feet	7,870	8,800	11,245	Not possible
15,000 lb. Learjet	Takeoff Distance (Feet)	Takeoff Distance (Feet)	Takeoff Distance (Feet)	Takeoff Distance (Feet)
Runway Altitude				
Sea Level	3,325	3,340	3,640	4,410
2,000 Feet	3,680	3,850	4,265	5,255
4,000 Feet	4,190	4,420	4,995	6,965
6,000 Feet	4,940	5,330	6,565	8,835
8,000 Feet	6,000	6,880	8,190	Better not try it.
14,000 lb. Learjet	Takeoff Distance (Feet)	Takeoff Distance (Feet)	Takeoff Distance (Feet)	Takeoff Distance (Feet)
Runway Altitude				
Sea Level	2,910	2,950	3,175	3,825
2,000 Feet	3,210	3,350	3,700	4,540
4,000 Feet	3,640	3,900	4,325	5,660
6,000 Feet	4,275	4,620	5,370	6,680
6,000 Feet	5,060	5,600	6,340	Better not try it.

Plate 1 Cessna instrument panel

Plate 2 Learjet instrument panel

Plate 3 Sailplane instrument panel

Plate 4 Sopwith Camel instrument panel

Plate 5 Learjet instrument panel illuminated for night flying. New landing lights illuminate the runway. The downtown Chicago skyline is seen in the distance.

Plate 6 Default startup

Plate 7 The Cessna over Chicago

Plate 8 Learjet at dusk flying over
Chicago's O'Hare International Airport

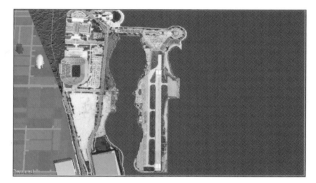

Plate 9 Photorealistic scenery of Meigs field

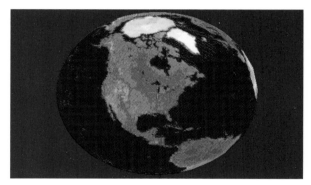

Plate 10 The FS 5.0 Map view of the Earth

Plate 11 Sailplane over San Francisco

Plate 12 Photorealistic satellite view of New York area (*Microsoft New York scenery add-on*)

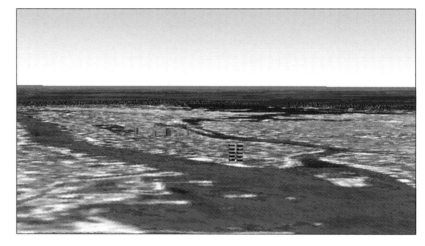

Plate 13 Photorealistic view of Manhattan (*Microsoft New York scenery add-on*)

Plate 14 Statue of Liberty fly-by (*Microsoft New York scenery add-on*)

Plate 15 World Trade Towers fly-by in Manhattan (*Microsoft New York scenery add-on*)

Plate 16 The bridges and skyline of New York City at dusk (*Microsoft New York scenery add-on*)

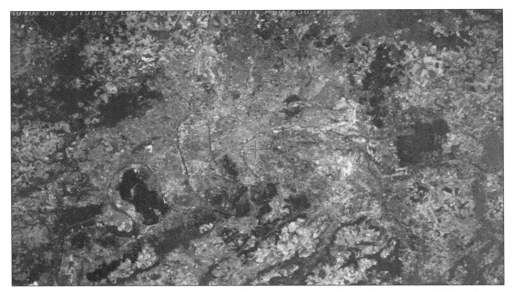

Plate 17 Photorealistic satellite view of Paris (*Microsoft Paris scenery add-on*)

Plate 18 View of the Seine river in Paris at dusk (*Microsoft Paris scenery add-on*)

Plate 19 Nighttime downtown view of Paris, with the Eiffel Tower in the distance (*Microsoft Paris scenery add-on*)

Plate 20 The Eiffel Tower in Paris (*Microsoft Paris scenery add-on*)

Plate 21 The Louvre museum in Paris with Notre Dame in the distance (*Microsoft Paris scenery add-on*)

Plate 22 A view of Paris from the Arc de Triomphe to the Grande Arche (*Microsoft Paris scenery add-on*)

Table 10.5 Takeoff Speeds (Knots IAS)		
Weight (Lbs.)	20° Flaps	8° Flaps
	Takeoff Speed (Knots)	Takeoff Speed (Knots)
18,300	137	142
14,000	127	125
13,000	125	125

Climb Performance

Under full thrust with a maximum rate of climb of 4,340 feet per minute, the climb from sea level to a 45,000-foot cruise altitude for the 14,000-pound Learjet takes about 19 minutes and covers 121 nautical miles. Using Table 10.6, you can see how much fuel is burned and the distance covered to achieve this climb, and climbs to other intermediate altitudes.

Cruise Performance

After the Learjet has achieved straight and level cruising speed, you may want to know its true airspeed and fuel flow for various altitudes. For example, if you wanted to know what the true airspeed would be for a cruising Learjet at an altitude of 45,000 feet, you would look up the row for 45,000 feet in Table 10.7 and see that the Learjet travels at 423 knots TAS (487 statute miles per hour TAS), and burns 954 pounds of fuel per hour (142 gallons per hour). The indicated airspeed, or IAS, on your airspeed indicator would be around 250 knots.

Descent Performance

The Learjet can safely descend at speeds of 3,000 to 4,000 feet per minute. Even with this high rate of vertical speed, however, the Learjet will still take about 14 to 16 minutes to descend from 45,000 feet to sea level. Furthermore, if you are planning to land, you must begin your descent no later than 109 nautical miles from the airport!

For a landing approach descent from 45,000 feet to sea level, you should start your descent no later than 109 nautical miles from the airport.

Table 10.6 Time, Fuel, and Distance to Climb*	
Sea Level To:	**Aircraft Weighs 14,000 Lbs.**
25,000 Feet	
Time (Minutes)	5.4
Fuel (Lbs.)	235
Distance (Nautical Miles)	27
30,000 Feet	
Time (Minutes)	7.1
Fuel (Lbs.)	289
Distance (Nautical Miles)	39
35,000 Feet	
Time (Minutes)	9.2
Fuel (Lbs.)	348
Distance (Nautical Miles)	53
37,000 Feet	
Time (Minutes)	10.2
Fuel (Lbs.)	370
Distance (Nautical Miles)	59
39,000 Feet	
Time (Minutes)	11.3
Fuel (Lbs.)	369
Distance (Nautical Miles)	67
41,000 Feet	
Time (Minutes)	12.9
Fuel (Lbs.)	426
Distance (Nautical Miles)	77
43,000 Feet	
Time (Minutes)	15.2
Fuel (Lbs.)	467
Distance (Nautical Miles)	92
45,000 Feet	
Time (Minutes)	19.4
Fuel (Lbs.)	545
Distance (Nautical Miles)	120

*This data not for flight planning purposes; use only with Microsoft *Flight Simulator*

Table 10.7   Cruise Performance*

Cruise Altitude		Aircraft Weights 14,000 Lbs.
25,000 Feet		
	Knots TAS	471
	Fuel flow (lbs./hr.)	2007
30,000 Feet		
	Knots TAS	469
	Fuel flow (lbs./hr.)	1759
35,000 Feet		
	Knots TAS	463
	Fuel flow (lbs./hr.)	1487
37,000 Feet		
	Knots TAS	462
	Fuel flow (lbs./hr.)	1425
39,000 Feet		
	Knots TAS	459
	Fuel flow (lbs./hr.)	1320
41,000 Feet		
	Knots TAS	453
	Fuel flow (lbs./hr.)	1204
43,000 Feet		
	Knots TAS	441
	Fuel flow (lbs./hr.)	1085
45,000 Feet		
	Knots TAS	423
	Fuel flow (lbs./hr.)	954

Landing Performance

The normal landing distance for a 14,000-pound Learjet landing at sea level, with an outside air temperature of 70° F, is 2,900 feet. Thus, in the FS 5.0 Learjet, you should be able to just *barely* land at Chicago's Meigs Field (3,948 feet length). You have only 1,000 feet of spare runway to land on, so don't squander precious real estate by overshooting on your approach.

---

*This data not for flight planning purposes; use only with Microsoft *Flight Simulator*

Table 10.8   Normal Descent

| Descending at 3,000 Feet Per Minute @ 350 Knots IAS Down to 10,000 Feet | | | |
| Descending at 3,000 Feet Per Minute @ 250 Knots IAS from 10,000 Feet to Sea Level | | | |
From Altitude to Sea Level (Feet)	Time (Minutes)	Fuel (Lbs.)	Distance (Nautical Miles)
45,000	16.4	285	109
43,000	15.7	278	104
41,000	15.0	271	99
39,000	14.4	262	94
37,000	13.7	252	88
35,000	13.0	241	83
33,000	12.4	228	78
30,000	11.3	205	70
25,000	9.7	158	57

For more realism when landing, you can toggle on the Airframe Damage From Stress checkbox in the Realism and Reliability dialog box.

Table 10.9 shows some of the different landing distance requirements for the Learjet at different altitudes and air temperatures. Notice that as the temperature gets colder, the landing distance gets shorter; as the temperature gets hotter, the landing distance gets longer. Likewise, as the altitude increases, the landing distance requirement also increases. This is in accordance with aerodynamic theory, which predicts that as the air density gets lower (i.e., higher altitude, hotter temperatures), the lifting forces on the airplane decrease. The airplane must make up for this loss of lift by flying faster and taking a longer distance to land.

For the landing approach, the flaps should be set to 8° or 20°. Be sure not to extend the flaps when traveling at speeds in excess of 200 knots. Also, the gear should be lowered only when the indicated airspeed is below 200 knots. Your vertical speed should be under 500 feet per minute when landing. If you land at a little over 500 FPM, you will probably loosen a few fillings in your teeth and give your passengers something to think about. For realistic airframe stress damage when landing, or even during flight, you can toggle on the Airframe Damage From Stress checkbox in the Realism and Reliability dialog box, found under the Sim menu. (Currently, in the present release of FS 5.0, there is a bug in the Airframe Damage From Stress feature. If you turn it on, even if you so much as lower your flaps, the airplane will be damaged. Damage occurs much more easily than is the case in real life.)

When you get close to the airport, lower the flaps all the way and check to see that your landing gear is fully extended (the green landing gear light

Table 10.9 Landing Distance

14,000 lbs. Learjet	60° F (16° C)	70 ° F (21° C)	80° F (27° C)	100° F (38° C)
Runway Altitude	Landing Distance (Feet)	Landing Distance (Feet)	Landing Distance (Feet)	Landing Distance (Feet)
Sea Level	2,870	2,900	2,930	2,995
2,000 Feet	3,005	3,035	3,065	3,130
4,000 Feet	3,115	3,145	3,180	3,250
6,000 Feet	3,265	3,300	3,335	Have life insurance?

Table 10.10 Landing Speeds (Full Flaps)

Aircraft Weight (Lbs.)	Landing Speed (Knots)
13,000	119
14,000	123
15,000	127

should be lit). Under no circumstances should you allow your airspeed to fall below 128 knots IAS (147 mph). Remember, the aircraft's stall speed in the landing configuration is 97 knots IAS (112 mph).

Coping with Engine Failure

Before dealing with any engine failure, you *must immediately* switch off Auto Coordination under the Sim menu. With only one engine operative, the aircraft is experiencing a torque force that creates aerodynamic instability. To counteract this torque imbalance, you will need to fly the plane with the rudder and ailerons independently applied. When auto-coordination is on, you cannot do this, since the rudder and ailerons are synchronized to move together.

Many pilots erroneously believe that if an aircraft has two engines, it will continue to operate at least half as well with only one engine working. This is not so. In any multi-engine aircraft, the loss of an engine causes a 70 percent to 90 percent reduction in performance. When one engine fails, not only does the remaining engine have to carry the full burden of the aircraft's forward thrust, but drag is increased because of asymmetric thrust. For example,

To deal with an engine failure on the Learjet, you must switch off auto-coordination. The rudder and ailerons must each be used independently to achieve stable flight, and this can only be done if you are flying in uncoordinated flight mode (under the Sim menu, toggle off Auto Coordination).

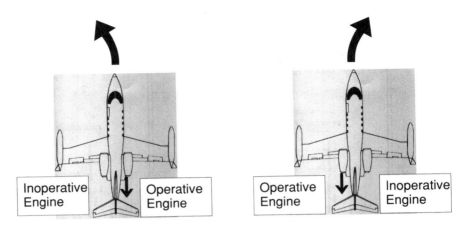

Figure 10.7
Unbalanced forces
created during single-
engine operation

Unbalanced Forces Created
During Single-Engine Operation

in the Learjet, the maximum rate of climb with both engines operating is 4,340 feet per minute (FPM). With only one engine functioning, *the rate of climb drops to 1,290 FPM*. This is a performance loss of over 70 percent!

Figure 10.7 illustrates the asymmetric and unbalanced engine thrust forces at work when either the right or left engine fails.

The correct way to deal with the loss of an engine is to turn your rudder in the direction of the still-operative engine, and bank the wings of the aircraft at least 5° onto the good engine. The amount of rudder and aileron pressure needed will vary, but you should first apply rudder to counteract the yawing tendency of the jet to turn left or right. After stabilizing the yaw, apply the ailerons. Figure 10.8 illustrates the proper V_{MC} technique for flying the Learjet on one engine.[1] In this example, to counteract this, apply right rudder and trim aircraft to bank at least 5° right with right ailerons. In general, always apply rudder in the direction of the still-operative engine, and bank aircraft 5° toward the operative engine with the ailerons.

The in-cockpit view is illustrated in Figure 10.09, where you will notice from the position of the throttle levers that the left engine is not operating. To counteract the yawing forces to the left, right rudder was applied, as

---

[1]The V_{MC} is defined as the minimum airspeed, with the critical engine inoperative, at which the airplane is controllable. It does not assume that the aircraft can climb or hold its present altitude. It means only that a particular course heading can be maintained, using the rudder and ailerons to overcome the asymmetrical yawing forces caused by the still-operable engine.

shown by the lower control position indicator. Also, a 5° bank angle to the right (toward the still-operative right engine) was achieved by applying right ailerons, as indicated by the upper control position indicator and by the artificial horizon (note that the bank angle pointer is less than 10°).

The next section summarizes the procedure to follow when flying with only one engine operating.

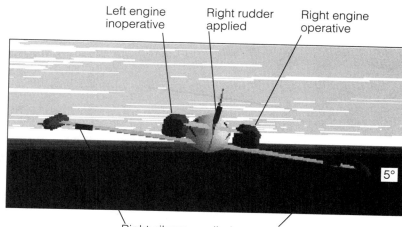

Left engine inoperative

Right rudder applied

Right engine operative

Right aileron applied causes right wing to bank down 5°

5°

Figure 10.8
With the loss of left engine power, the operative right engine causes the aircraft to veer left

Aileron control position indicator shows right aileron applied

Rudder control position indicator shows right rudder applied

Artificial horizon shows 5° bank angle towards the still operating engine

Left engine inoperative (throttled down)

Right engine operative (throttled up)

Figure 10.9
In the cockpit of the Learjet with the left engine inoperative

To stabilize the Learjet when an engine failure occurs, follow these steps:

1. Switch off auto-coordination under the Sim menu.
2. Determine which engine has failed by looking at your engine turbine and fan speed indicators. If necessary, call up your engine instruments by pressing Tab.
3. Turn the rudder (⓪ –Yaw Right, Enter –Yaw Left) toward the direction of the still-operative engine until the aircraft's yawing (left-right turning motion) is stopped.
4. Apply the ailerons (④ –Left Aileron, ⑥ – Right Aileron) in the direction of the still-operative engine to trim and stabilize the aircraft.
5. Using the ailerons (④ –Bank Left Wing Down, ⑥ – Bank Right Wing Down), bank the wings *down* by 5° in the direction of the still-operative engine. Note the bank angle on the artificial horizon indicator. The arrow pointer should hover between the 0° and 10° pitch markers.

You can practice flying with one engine by merely reducing the thrust on one of the engines.

Range and Refueling Requirements

The Learjet's fuel tank capacity of 6,198 pounds (2,811 kg or 925 gallons) of fuel allows the aircraft to have a maximum range of 2,196 nautical miles (2,525 statute miles or 4,062 km). When flying nonstop at this range, however, the Learjet can carry only four passengers and two crew members (normal passenger load is 8). Figure 10.10 shows some of the mission capabilities for the Learjet around the world. Note that the missions indicated with an arrow are flights that may be accomplished by the Learjet in the opposite direction to the arrow only with favorable wind conditions. If there is a strong headwind, then the range of the aircraft is diminished, and the mission will have to be scrubbed until weather conditions permit.

For a typical 575-statute-mile trip, the Learjet 35A can complete the voyage in 1½ hours on about 200 gallons of fuel. Since aviation fuel has a density of about 6.7 pounds per gallon, this translates to 1,340 pounds of fuel. Fuel flow and quantity are measured in pounds, and the Learjet burns around 938 to 1,252 pounds of fuel per hour (140 to 187 gallons per hour). As you can see from these figures, fuel costs can be enormous. With fuel averaging about $2.25 per gallon, the cost of operating the jet per hour is $400. For long-range trips, Table 10.11 gives you the Learjet's fuel burn, airspeed, and altitude performance data that are useful for planning a mission.

The Learjet 35A's high fuel efficiency, when compared to other business jets, comes in part from the higher cruise altitude from which it can operate.

Table 10.11 Long-Range Cruise Performance

Distance (Nautical Miles)	Cruise Altitude (Feet)	Time to Travel (Hrs:Min)	Fuel Burned (Lbs.)	Speed (Knots TAS)
200	35,000	0:45	744	266
400	41,000	1:14	1,182	324
600	43,000	1:41	1,620	356
800	43,000	2:10	2,063	369
1,000	43,000	2:39	2,528	377
1,200	43,000	3:07	3,009	385
1,400	43,000	3:35	3,509	390
1,600	45,000	4:05	4,020	391
1,800	45,000	4:34	4,549	394
2,000	45,000	5:02	5,089	397
2,200	45,000	5:30	5,648	400
2,400	45,000	5:58	6,207	402

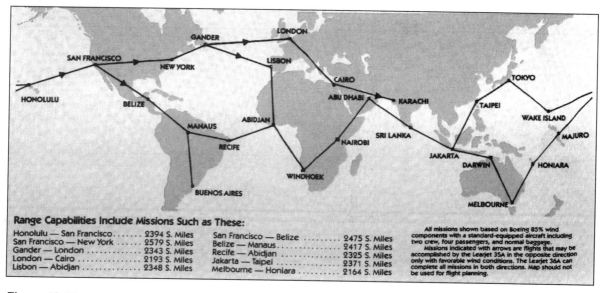

Range Capabilities Include Missions Such as These:

Honolulu — San Francisco...... 2394 S. Miles
San Francisco — New York ..... 2579 S. Miles
Gander — London .... 2343 S. Miles
London — Cairo .... 2193 S. Miles
Lisbon — Abidjan .... 2348 S. Miles

San Francisco — Belize .... 2475 S. Miles
Belize — Manaus.............. 2417 S. Miles
Recife — Abidjan .... 2325 S. Miles
Jakarta — Taipei .... 2371 S. Miles
Melbourne — Honiara .... 2164 S. Miles

All missions shown based on Boeing 85% wind components with a standard-equipped aircraft including two crew, four passengers, and normal baggage.
Missions indicated with arrows are flights that may be accomplished by the Learjet 35A in the opposite direction only with favorable wind conditions. The Learjet 36A can complete all missions in both directions. Map should not be used for flight planning.

Figure 10.10
Range capability for the Learjet 35A carrying four passengers and two crew members.
(This data *not* for flight planning purposes; use only with Microsoft *Flight Simulator*)
(*Courtesy of Learjet*)

The 35A is certified to cruise at 45,000 feet, more than a *mile* above most commercial passenger jets and above the 100 mph jet stream head-winds. Butting into such wind for lower-flying jets causes ground speed to drop from 500 mph to 400 mph, and this causes lower fuel efficiency. Flying at this higher altitude, due to the thinner air, the Learjet can fly faster and with lower drag and air resistance friction.

Fuel Realism on the *Flight Simulator* Learjet

If you want the engines to stop when they run out of fuel, toggle on Engine Stops When Out of Fuel in the Realism and Reliability dialog box.

By default, *Flight Simulator* allows you to fly the Learjet with unlimited fuel. For greater simulation realism, you can choose to have your engines stop when they are out of fuel. To do this:

1. Select the Sim menu.
2. Click on the Realism and Reliability menu option.
3. Toggle on Engine Stops When Out of Fuel.
4. Click OK to return to the simulation

Press [;] to save the Learjet situation with the limited fuel option. (First toggle on Engine Stops When Out of Fuel.) Then, each time you reset the situation, limited fuel will be enabled.

If you don't want to keep resetting the Engine Stops When Out of Fuel checkbox each time you fly the Learjet, remember to save the situation and give it a name so that you can reload it from disk. Then, each time that the simulation resets itself, either by your crashing the plane or by your pressing [Ctrl] [Print Screen], the Learjet situation will start up with limited fuel enabled.

C H A P T E R

11

Flying the Sailplane

This chapter discusses the history, performance characteristics, and gliding techniques of the Schweizer 2-32 sailplane. You will also learn how to best take advantage of thermals and ridge currents to gain altitude. Please note that all of the tables, charts, and information are for use with Microsoft's *Flight Simulator* only; they are *not to be used for real flight planning purposes.*

SCHWEIZER SAILPLANE HISTORY

Since 1930, the Schweizer Aircraft Corporation has produced over 2,000 sailplanes. The first glider, constructed by the Schweizer brothers in 1929, was the model SGP 1-1, of which only one was completed. During the war years, Schweizer was asked to produce metal training gliders for the U.S. Air Corps training program, and they created the model TG 2 and the TG 3, of which 171 sailplanes were produced. In the postwar period, Schweizer began to market a new series of sailplanes that culminated in the popular 2-22 (1945), the 1-26 (1954), the 2-32 (1962), and the 2-33 (1967). The first digit in the serial number identifier for each Schweizer sailplane tells you the number of seats, and the second number tells you the chronology of the firm's design sequence.

The SGS 2-32 is an all-metal, two-seat-high performance sailplane that has won world and national records in glider competitions. It has a large, roomy cockpit and, in the two-seat version, has dual flight controls.

Figure 11.1
Schweizer 2-32
Sailplane *(Courtesy
of Schweizer Aircraft
Corporation,
copyright 1993)*

FUNDAMENTALS OF THERMAL SOARING

A thermal is a rising air current caused by the sun's heating of the surface. As the air expands from the heat radiated by the Earth, it becomes lighter than the surrounding atmosphere. It then rises like a hot-air balloon, which, by itself, is nothing but an enclosed thermal.

Different kinds of surfaces absorb heat at different rates. Dark surfaces, in general, get hotter than light ones, while smooth surfaces get hotter than rough ones. Blacktop highways, runways, and parking lots are both smooth and dark and thus generate vigorous thermals. Sandy beaches, dry river beds, and smooth deserts are also good sources of thermals. On the other hand, vegetation, forests, and green fields do not get as hot because they exude moisture and their large surface area dissipates much heat. Thus, flying over forests and green fields usually means the sailplane will sink, whereas flying over bare brown fields means that the sailplane will experience lift.

Thermals cannot be seen by the naked eye; however, studies have shown them to be bubble shaped. The air is warmed by the ground, swells, breaks free of the ground, and then rises like bubbles in boiling water. Cooler air then moves in from the sides to replace the warm air, and there is a delay while a new bubble forms.

If the surface is hot enough, the air bubbles will be produced more rapidly. The net result is the formation of a roughly cylindrical column of warm air that extends from the surface and that occasionally penetrates the stratosphere at 60,000 feet. Most soaring, however, is done in the range of 8,000 feet to ground level.

The basic idea for thermaling is that you try to find thermals and ride them up to higher altitudes. You can circle up them, or perform figure eights, but in all cases you want to remain inside the thermal. Knowing that brown, or darker, land masses absorb more heat than lighter-colored land, you can head for those areas that have a high probability of generating thermals.

Brown field causes thermal updrafts

Figure 11.2
Thermal soaring. The brown fields are where the thermaals are. In thermal soaring, circle upwaards to take advantage of rising hot air.

FUNDAMENTALS OF RIDGE SOARING

Ridge soaring is another sailplane technique used for gaining altitude. Winds are deflected upward by mountains, cliffs, and hills. In ridge soaring, you fly the sailplane *parallel* to the upwind slope, crabbing into the wind as necessary. The wind, which is shoved upward by the contour of the mountain, provides an upward lift for the sailplane. When you notice that the glider is no longer gaining altitude, you simply reverse direction and retrace your path parallel to the slope. Make sure that when you turn, you *always turn away from the ridge* (*into the wind*), and that you do not fly over the ridge. Essentially, you will be performing figure eights on one side of the ridge.

Figure 11.3
Ridge soaring

Note that with the ridge lift technique, you can never fly more than a few hundred feet over the ridge. With thermal soaring there is no such limit. Another gliding technique used, called *wave soaring,* offers tremendous amounts of lift, but it is a complex topic that goes

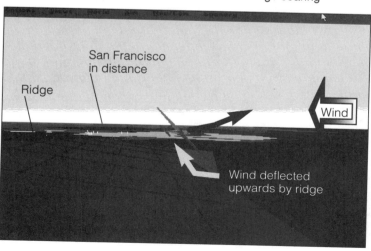

San Francisco in distance

Ridge

Wind

Wind deflected upwards by ridge

beyond the scope of this book. All the current soaring altitude records were accomplished using the wave soaring method.

SCHWEIZER 2-32 SAILPLANE PERFORMANCE

Figure 11.4 shows the 2-32 sailplane's overall dimensions, while Table 11.1 gives its physical specifications.

Figure 11.4
Schweizer 2-32
sailplane dimensions

CONTROLS

The Schweizer sailplane has an altimeter, airspeed indicator, magnetic compass, dive brakes (called spoilers or SPL), a COM radio, master electrical switch, control position indicators, and a vertical speed indicator. The airspeed indicator shows speeds in statute miles per hour, unlike most other airspeed indicators, which are calibrated to display knots. The dive brakes, like the spoilers on the Learjet, are moveable airfoils located on the top of the wing. When deployed, they act to slow the aircraft's rate of descent, and they can be used to slow the aircraft's horizontal velocity as well.

OPERATIONAL PLACARD

Every glider carries an *operations limitation placard*. It is there to inform the pilot of the glider's minimum safe operating characteristics. The placard states the safe maximum glide speed, maximum aero tow and ground launch speeds, maximum gross weight permissible, maximum maneuvering speed (operating your controls past this speed is deemed dangerous to the aircraft), wind gust limit, and balance and load factors. On the FS 5.0 sailplane, you can barely discern the placard below the master electrical switch (above and to the side of the COM radio).

TAKEOFF

Normally, the 2-32 must be towed, or winched up to an altitude that can enable it to glide. In *Flight Simulator*, you can start one of the built-in soaring situations or you can create your own. To create your own soaring situation, simply fly the Cessna to any location where you want to soar, then select the 2-32 sailplane as your aircraft under the Options menu. Alternatively, you can also move your sailplane to whatever location you choose by entering slew mode. To enter slew mode, press [Y], then press [F4] to gain altitude or [F1] to descend. (If your function keys are on the left, press [F2] to ascend and [F10] to descend.) To freeze all slewing motion, press [5] on the numeric keypad.

IMPORTANT SPEEDS

The sailplane's stall speed when fully loaded is 48 mph. In level flight, the sailplane has a minimum sink rate of 2.1 feet at 50 mph. Do not fly the sailplane at less than the minimum stall speeds. When spiraling in thermals,

Table 11.1   Schweizer 2-32 Sailplane Specifications

Length	26 feet, 9 inches
Wingspan	57 feet
Height	9 feet
Wing Area	180 square feet
Aspect Ratio	18.05
Gross Weight	1,340 lbs
Standard Empty Weight	830 lbs
Maximum Useful Load	490 lbs
Wing Loading	7.44 lb/square feet
Maximum Operating Speed	150 mph
Stall Speed (Single Seater)	48 mph
Maximum L/D	34 at 59 mph
Minimum Sink (Single Seater)	2.1 feet per second at 50 mph
Landing Gear	Non-retracting wheels in underbelly. Hydraulic brakes included.

Table 11.2   Maximum Stall Speed When Banking or Spiralling in Thermals

Bank Angle	Speed in Miles Per Hour
30°	55
45°	57

Table 11.3   Maximum Speeds for the Schweizer Sailplane

Description	Speed in Miles Per Hour
Maximum Glide Speed, Dive Brakes Off	150
Maximum Glide Speed, Dive Brakes On	158

be careful not to fly at less than 55 mph for a 30° bank, or 57 mph for a 45° bank. If you do so, you run the danger of stalling the craft. Also, be sure not to exceed 150 mph when descending, because this is the maximum speed that is safe for the airframe.

Best Glide Is at 55 Mph

Table 11.4 reveals the sailplane's sink rate for various speeds. The sink rate is the number of feet the glider falls per second at a given speed in the absence of a thermal. In the table, the sink rate has been calculated per mile from various performance charts, and you can see that the slowest, or best, sink rate is to be found when the glider is traveling at 55 mph. From this information you can figure out how many miles you can glide before having to land. Use the following formula:

$$Distance\ in\ Miles = \frac{Altitude}{Feet\ of\ Altitude\ Lost\ per\ Mile}$$

At a speed of 55 mph, and an altitude of 5,000 feet, therefore, you would look at the table and find your rate of sink. For 55 mph, this is 344 feet of altitude lost per mile. Plugging all this information into the formula, we arrive at:

$$14.53\ miles = \frac{5,000\ Feet\ Altitude}{344\ \frac{feet}{mile}}$$

So, at 5,000 feet, you have 14.53 miles to find an airstrip to land on, otherwise you might end up in some cow pasture. If you must land in a field, be sure to look for one without a bull penned inside.

Table 11.4	Glide Performance: Altitude Lost vs. Distance and Speed											
Speed (mph)	35	40	45	50	55	60	65	70	75	80	85	90
Minutes Required to Fly One Mile	1.71	1.50	1.33	1.20	1.09	1.00	0.92	0.86	0.80	0.75	0.71	0.67
Feet of Altitude Lost Per Mile	448	393	365	351	344*	346	353	366	382	401	422	446

*With flattest glide angle, the best sink rate is achieved at 55 mph. At an altitude of 5,000 feet, you could glide more than 14.5 miles down to seal level!

Navigaton and Aircraft Communication Systems

12

Radio Navigation

This chapter discusses how to use your navigation and communication radio equipment. You must understand how radio navigation works in order to travel from one point to another in the *Flight Simulator* world. *Flight Simulator 5.0* now includes *all* the VOR/NDB radio beacon stations for the continental U.S.; in all, over 1,200 stations. In addition, there are VOR/NDBs included for many other parts of the world. For example, VOR/NDBs for the entire Pacific Ocean region from the South Pacific to the North Pacific, extending west to the Far East, are now included. The Caribbean basin, including many parts of Mexico and South America, is now included. Using these beacons you can now navigate transoceanic flights if you so wish. Unfortunately, at least in the *initial* release of FS 5.0, *no* VOR/NDB stations for the North Atlantic are available. For the moment, this means that transatlantic navigation is impossible. Hopefully, some company or clever individual will provide a way to update the navigational file list so that at last we can circumnavigate the globe. (As this book went to press, a way has been found to edit the FS 5.0 navigational files. For more information, see the CompuServe Flight Simulator Forum Library 2.)

AIR TRAFFIC CONTROL

Radio communication with air traffic control (ATC) is vital to establishing safe operating conditions in the air and on the ground. When talking on the radio, concise phrasing and clarity of expression are crucial to getting messages across accurately. To prevent miscommunication, special radio communication procedures and phrases have been uniformly adopted.

Voice Contact Procedure

To contact a given FAA facility, control tower, or other airplane, communicate following this format:

1. Name of contact facility, tower, or plane you are calling.
2. Your full aircraft identification, using the phonetic alphabet to identify single letters and numbers (see Table 2.1).
3. Your message. For example:

> "NEW YORK RADIO, CESSNA THREE ONE SIX ZERO FOXTROT, REQUEST TRAFFIC ADVISORY."

Table 12.1   Phonetic Alphabet

Character	Pronounced	Character	Pronounced
A	Alpha	S	Sierra
B	Bravo	T	Tango
C	Charlie	U	Uniform
D	Delta	V	Victor
E	Echo	W	Whiskey
F	Foxtrot	X	X-Ray
G	Golf	Y	Yankee
H	Hotel	Z	Zulu
I	India	0	Zero
J	Juliett	1	Wun
K	Kilo	2	Too
L	Lima	3	Tree
M	Mike	4	Fo-wer
N	November	5	Fife
O	Oscar	6	Six
P	Papa	7	Seven
Q	Quebec	8	Ait
R	Romeo	9	Niner

In *Flight Simulator*, you don't need to send messages to ATC using this terminology. You can request clearance to land or take off by summoning up the Air Traffic Control dialog box and clicking on the Request to Take off or the Request to Land buttons. The simulator will then take care of sending the message for you. To send a message to ATC, follow these steps:

1. Click on the Air Traffic Control option under the Nav/Com menu.
2. Select the Communication Radio menu command.
3. In the Communication Radio dialog box, click on the Send Message button.
4. In the Air Traffic Control dialog box, click on the Request to Land or Request to Take off radio buttons.

Figure 12.1 shows the Air Traffic Control dialog box.

Air Traffic Control

OK

Cancel

○ **Request to Take Off**
○ **Request to Land**

(Choose the OK button to transmit)

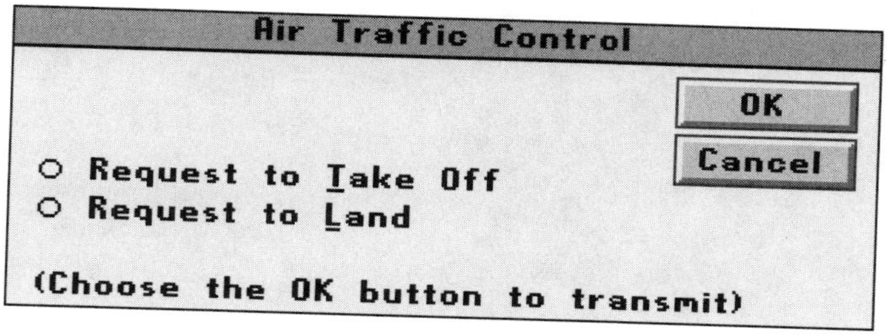

Figure 12.1
The Air Traffic Control dialog box

Use of Numbers

Normally, numbers are spoken by speaking each number separately. There are exceptions to the above rule, however. Figures indicating hundreds and thousands are spoken like this:

9,000	"Niner-thousand"
500	"Fife-hundred"
14,500	"Wun-fo-wer-thousand-fife-hundred"

Course headings are always spoken with three digits of bearing.

Course Heading 005°   "Zero-Zero-Fife"

Also, time is stated in 24-hour format with four digits.

06:45   "Zero-six-fo-wer-fife"

COM RADIOS

The COM radio is used to tune in ATIS weather reports and the Air Traffic Control. It has 360 channels on frequencies between 118.00 and 135.95 MHz, with 50 kHz channel separation. You can make the radio capable of receiving more than 720 channels by selecting the 25 kHz COM Frequency Adjustability check box in the Instrument Preferences dialog box under the Options menu. For a list of airport control tower and ATIS frequencies, see Appendix B.

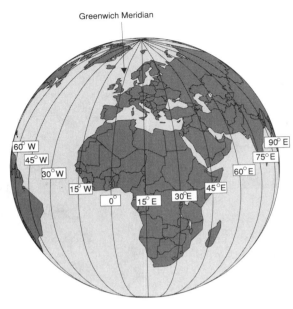

Figure 12.2
Lines of longitude

LATITUDE/LONGITUDE

Any discussion of navigation must include the topic of coordinate systems. The principal means of determining your position on the spherical earth is to use the latitude/longitude coordinate system. This coordinate system is the foundation for all navigational methods, including the VOR/NDB, Loran C, Omega, Global Positioning Satellite system (hereafter called GPS), and celestial navigation.

Lines of longitude, also known as meridians, run north and south, connecting the North Pole and the South Pole. They are numbered in angular degrees from 0° to 180° east and west of the prime meridian, which runs through Greenwich, England. Each longitude line forms what is known as a great circle; that is, it outlines a plane that cuts through the center of the earth. All great circles circumscribe the earth, and are approximately the same length.

Lines of latitude, also called parallels, run east and west, parallel to each other. They, too, are numbered in angular degrees from 0° to 90° north and south of the equator. However, only the equator latitude line forms a great circle; the other latitude lines get smaller as they get closer to the poles.

If you fly mostly on the North American continent, an easy way to remember which way the latitude/longitude coordinates change along your flight route is to memorize these two expressions:

East is Least and West is Best
North is Up, South is Down

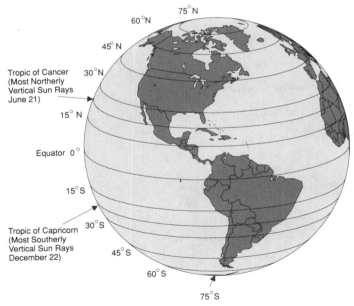

Figure 12.3
Lines of latitude

Thus as you go east, the longitude decreases. As you go west, the longitude increases. As you go north, the latitude increases. As you go south, the latitude decreases. (This rule only applies to the Western Hemisphere above the equator.)

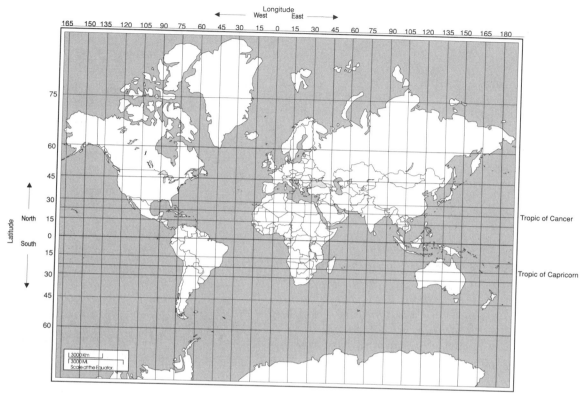

Figure 12.4
Mercator projection of the Earth showing latitude/longitude lines

As mentioned in earlier chapters, each degree of arc is divided into 60 minutes of arc, and each minute of arc is in turn divided into 60 arc seconds. Since a degree of arc is equivalent to 60 nautical miles on a great circle around the earth, each minute of arc is equal to 1 nautical mile, and each second of arc is equal to 1/60 nautical mile. But this distance relationship only applies to lines of latitude or longitude on a great circle. As you get closer to the poles, the lines of longitude converge, and thus you cannot use the distance ratio of 60 miles/degree of arc anymore. To accurately determine distances, you would therefore need to know some spherical geometry. Rather than plunge into a discussion on this complex topic, let's skip straight to the mathematical formula that is used to calculate the distance between any two locations on earth.

Calculating Distances between Two Locations

If the longitude and latitude of two locations are known, the distance between them can be calculated by the following equation:

$$Distance = 69.094 \times \cos^{-1}\{[\sin(A) \times \sin(T)] + [\cos(A) \times \cos(T) \times \cos(L)] - G\}$$

where

Distance =	The distance between the two places in statute miles (multiply by 1.15 to obtain nautical miles).
A =	The latitude of the first place (must be entered in decimal degrees). Enter south latitudes (Southern Hemisphere) as a negative number.
L =	The longitude of the first place (must be entered in decimal degrees). Enter east latitudes as a negative number.
T =	The latitude of the second place (must be entered in decimal degrees). Enter south latitudes (Southern Hemisphere) as a negative number.
G =	The longitude of the second place (must be entered in decimal degrees). Enter east latitudes as a negative number.
$\cos^{-1}$ =	Arc cosine function (inverse cosine)

You must have a scientific calculator that has trigonometric functions and inverse trigonometric functions. Also, you must make sure that the calculator is being run in degree display mode, not radian display mode. Radians are arc measurements made in units of PI and cannot be used in this formula.

Note that the variables *A, L, T,* and *G* must be entered in decimal degree form; you cannot enter them as a normal latitude/longitude coordinate. To convert latitude/longitude to decimal format, follow this formula:

When performing any of the calculations listed here, make sure your calculator is displaying results in degree form, not radians.

$$Convert\ Latitude\ /\ Longitude\ to\ Decimal\ Degree = HHH + \frac{MM}{60} + \frac{SS}{3600}$$

where

HHH	=	Degrees of latitude/longitude
MM	=	Minutes of latitude/longitude
SS	=	Seconds of latitude/longitude

For example, to convert a starting longitude coordinate of W132° 55' 15" to decimal degree format, add

$$132° + \frac{55'}{60} + \frac{15"}{3600} = 132.92083°$$

You would then use 132.92083° as your input for the variable L in the above-listed distance equation.

This conversion of the latitude/longitude coordinates is greatly simplified if you have a scientific calculator that converts degrees in the hour-minutes-seconds format to the decimal-hours format. On a Hewlett Packard Scientific Calculator 22S, for example, you would use the H-HMS function by entering the latitude or longitude as HHH.MMSS, where the HHH represents the hours, the MM represents the minutes, and the SS represents the seconds. Thus, to convert W132° 55' 15", you would enter 132.5515 in the calculator, and then press the H-HMS button and on the menu display select HM, to convert the longitude to decimal-hour format.

> EXAMPLE: Calculate the distance between San Francisco International Airport (N37° 37' 00" latitude, W122° 22' 00" longitude) and Paris' Orly Airport (N48° 44' 00" latitude, E02° 23' 00" longitude).

> SOLUTION: After performing the decimal degree conversions, San Francisco has a decimal degree coordinate of N37.61666° latitude, W122.36666° longitude. Paris has a decimal degree coordinate of N48.73333° latitude, and E2.38333° longitude. Plugging these numbers into the equation:

VARIABLE	VALUE	DESCRIPTION
$A =$	37.61666	Decimal Latitude SF
$T =$	48.73333	Decimal Latitude Paris
$L =$	122.366664	Decimal Longitude SF
$G =$	-2.38333	Decimal Longitude Paris (Notice that a negative sign was added because Paris has an Eastern Longitude)
Distance =	5,578 statute miles	Total Air Miles between SF and Paris

Flight Simulator 4.0 North/South Coordinate System

Flight Simulator 4.0's coordinate system has been rendered obsolete with the introduction of FS 5.0's spherical latitude and longitude coordinate system. *Flight Simulator 4.0*'s older coordinate system assumed a flat, square earth with two coordinate identifiers; north and east. When this older coordinate system was designed, the programmers never thought to include parts of the world outside of the North American continent. So as a result, it was unable to include Europe, Asia, and Australia, along with other exotic locales. Several kludges where developed to overcome this deficiency; but overall, like the DOS operating system, the flat-earth geodetic map was ill-conceived from the start. In the meantime many people developed scenery and other add-ons to FS 4.0 that depended on the older north/east coordinates. *Flight Simulator 5.0* leapfrogs the coordinate switch problem by allowing you to display both coordinate systems at once by pressing [Shift] [Z] twice. Also, you can set your aircraft's position using the Set Location command under the World menu using either coordinate system.

NAVIGATION

Air navigation is the science of flying the airplane from one place to another place and determining its position along the way. In FS 5.0, to navigate using radio beacons, you will need to have charts that show the locations and frequencies of VOR/NDB stations on your intended path. *Flight Simulator* provides you with a few sectional maps, but they don't really help you if you want fly cross-country. You can easily purchase sectionals, as they are called, for all parts of the country by going to your local airport's pilot shop. Or, if you prefer, you can buy each aeronautical chart directly from the U.S. Department of Commerce's National Oceanic and Atmospheric Administration (NOAA) for $6 plus shipping and handling. To see the coverage area for some of the sectionals in the U.S., look at Figure 12.8 later in this chapter. There are also enroute low-altitude charts and IFR high-altitude charts for cross-country navigation, and these charts can be ordered for $9 plus shipping and handling. In addition, if you want maps of other parts of the world, the Department of Defense Mapping Agency publishes aeronautical charts through the NOAA that are also available. Particularly interesting are the NOA North Pacific Route Charts and the North Atlantic Route Charts, which show all the navigational beacons for transoceanic flights.

How to order maps and aeronautical sectionals from the NOAA in Maryland
To order the NOAA map catalog or to place an order, contact the NOAA at:
NOAA Distribution Branch, N/CG33
National Ocean Service
Riverdale, Maryland 20737-1199
Telephone and Fax orders are also accepted by the NOAA Distribution Branch.
General information and individual orders: 301-436-6990
Fax orders: 301-436-6829

In general, aeronautical navigation can be categorized into the following methods:

- *Pilotage:* Navigation by following visual landmarks; limited to daytime flight with good visibility.
- *Dead Reckoning:* Deduced or "dead" reckoning based on computations of speed limited to daytime flight with good visibility.
- *VOR:* Very High-Frequency Omnirange Radio Beacons; maximum range of 69 miles in FS 5.0. (In reality, high-powered VOR stations can be received as far as 130 nautical miles away.)
- *NDB:* Low-Frequency, Non-Directional Radio Beacons; maximum 75-mile day range, 200-mile night range.
- *ILS:* Instrument Landing System Radio Beacons; 18-mile range extending from runway.
- *Loran C:* Long-Range Low-Frequency Radio Navigation; semi-global coverage; 1,200-mile range by day, 2,300-mile range by night.
- *Omega:* Very Low-Frequency Radio Navigation; global coverage.
- *GPS:* High-Frequency Radio Navigation. Using the Global Positioning System's Navstar satellites, a GPS receiver can determine its position, speed, and altitude worldwide.
- *Inertial Navigation:* Using gyroscopes, accelerometers, and computers, inertial navigation equipment can internally determine the airplane's position without input from outside sources.
- *Celestial Navigation:* Tracking the stars using optical methods. This method has been abandoned in favor of more reliable electronic navigational aids.

In *Flight Simulator,* there are only three radio navigation methods available to you.[1] They are as follows:

- VOR
- NDB
- ILS

Pilotage

The most basic method of navigation is called *pilotage.* In this method you navigate using only a chart and fly from one visible landmark to another.

---

[1] You can simulate the GPS satellite radio system by displaying your latitude/longitude coordinates on screen.

Use visible land-
marks to navigate
using the pilotage
method.

Figure 12.5
Airspeed vs.
groundspeed

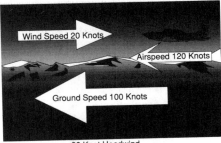

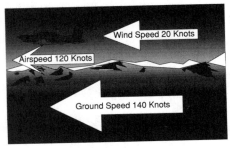

The flight must be conducted during the day at comparatively low altitudes so that landmarks can be seen easily. Because pilotage relies upon line-of-sight recognition of landmarks, bad-weather and/or night flying are ruled out. The main advantage of pilotage is that it is easy and requires no special skills or equipment. The pilotage method's main drawback is that you often cannot fly a direct course and must follow a zigzag route from landmark to landmark. For example, if you fly from San Francisco to Los Angles using the coastline to orient yourself, your route will not be the most direct or shortest because of the curvature of the coast.

When flying under the pilotage method, use highways, railways, coastlines, major power-transmission lines, aqueducts, rivers, and lakes as visual references to be checked against your chart. Be very careful when flying over large stretches of water or land which have no reference points to check. You can easily become disoriented and get lost. For this reason, pilotage should not be relied upon exclusively to navigate the aircraft.

Dead Reckoning

Dead reckoning refers to the technique of navigation by computations based on airspeed, course heading, wind direction and speed, ground speed, and elapsed time. Most VFR (visual flying rules) flying is based on a combination of dead reckoning and pilotage. During the course of a flight, the airplane's position is calculated by dead reckoning and then corrected for errors by visually checking for nearby landmarks.

To effectively use dead reckoning, you must know what the wind speed and direction are. Knowing your aircraft speed and course heading, you can then plot your aircraft's motion on a map using vectors to correct for the amount of deviation caused by the wind.

Let's see how dead reckoning works. In Figure 12.5 you can see that an airplane flying at an airspeed of 120 knots in calm air will have a groundspeed of exactly 120 knots. At the end of one hour, your aircraft will have covered 120 nautical miles. But if there is a tailwind of 20 knots in the direction of the aircraft's heading, the speed of the aircraft over the ground will jump to 140 knots, even though the airspeed indicator may still show only 120 knots. This happens because the wind carries the airplane along with it, boosting its speed by 20 knots. Likewise, if there is an opposing headwind of 20 knots, the aircraft's groundspeed will fall to 110 knots, even though the airspeed indicator may still show an airspeed of 120 knots.

Armed with this information, if you were planning a flight with an airspeed of 120 knots and knew that there was a tailwind of 20 knots, you would know that by the end of 1 hour you would have traveled not 120 nautical miles, but 140 nautical miles. This is because the aircraft's true groundspeed was boosted by the 20-knot windspeed.

If the wind is blowing perpendicular to the aircraft's heading (called a crosswind), then not only will the aircraft speed change but its heading will deviate from your intended path. Figure 12.6 shows the effect of a 20-knot crosswind on the aircraft after one hour. As you can see, the plane is blown off course by 20 miles from its intended destination.

To correct this drift, you can yaw the aircraft's nose in the direction of the wind, as illustrated in Figure 12.7. If the crosswind is from the right, the airplane will drift to the left; and you must therefore head the airplane sufficiently to the right to counteract the wind. If the wind is from the left, you must turn the airplane to the left, or slightly into the wind.

Using the dead-reckoning method, you can compute your position by deducing where it should be after a given amount of time, based on the aircraft's speed and direction, corrected for wind drift.

Radio Navigation Using VOR/NDB Stations

The next section discusses how the VOR and NDB radio beacons work and how they are used to navigate in *Flight Simulator*.

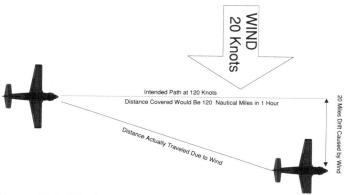

Figure 12.6 Effect of wind in one hour

VOR (Very High-Frequency Omnirange Radio Beacons)

More than 1,200 VOR radio beacons in the United States form the backbone of aeronautical radio navigation today. Transmitting signals in the VHF band between 108 MHz and 118 MHz, these ground-based stations provide reference points from which aircraft

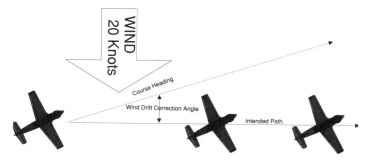

Figure 12.7 Correcting wind drift by turning into the wind

equipped with special VOR radios can situate themselves. Some of the advantages of VOR radios are:

- Static-free reception in all kinds of weather
- Precise heading information for navigation provided by course radials
- When receiving two or more VORs, a quickly determined coordinate fix, or line of position

VORs do have some drawbacks. They are strictly line-of-sight, meaning that their signal can be blocked by the curvature of the Earth or by mountains. Because of this, VORs do not provide worldwide coverage and are therefore useless for transoceanic voyages.

There are three classes of VORs. The T (Terminal) VOR has a normal usable range of 25 nautical miles at altitudes of 12,000 feet and below. It is used for short-range purposes adjacent to airports or in terminal areas for instrument approaches. The *L* (Low-Altitude) VOR sends out signals for 40 nautical miles at altitudes of 18,000 feet and below. The *H* (High-Altitude) VOR transmits for 100 nautical miles between 14,500 and 17,999 feet and 130 nautical miles between 18,000 and 45,000 feet. In *Flight Simulator*, the VOR range is limited to 80 miles, although in the real world VOR nighttime coverage can extend as far as 200 miles. Appendix B classifies all the VOR stations by type for the United States and surrounding areas. Figure 12.8 shows a map of the VOR installations for the United States.

The VOR range in FS 5.0 is limited to 80 nautical miles.

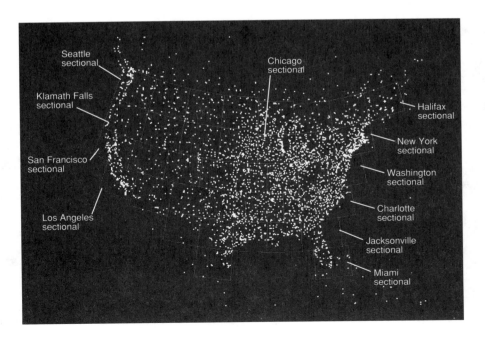

Figure 12.8
VOR stations for the United States
(Courtesy of Terry Carraway and Tom Canafax)

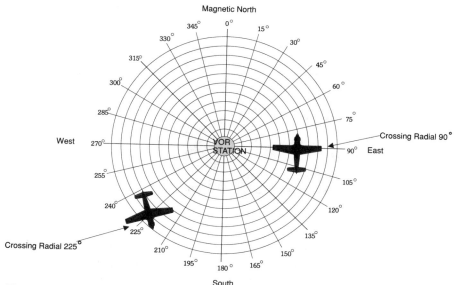

Figure 12.9 VOR radials

How VOR Navigation Works

Each VOR station sends out a signal that can be segmented into radials in all 360 degrees of the compass. The signal is rotated electronically at 1800 RPM, and its beam flashes out in a circular pattern, much like a lighthouse. There are two components to the signal; one which is in phase with magnetic north, the other which is out of phase to a varying degree in all other directions. The VOR receiver measures the phase difference of the two signals and then calculates the correct radial direction to display on the OBI (Omni-Bearing Indicator).

Setting the NAV Radios

The NAV 1 radio is used in conjunction with the OBI 1 display, while the NAV 2 radio is used with the OBI 2 display. Note that the NAV 1/OBI 1 radio can be used to tune in VOR or ILS stations, but that the NAV 2/OBI 2 radio can be used only with VOR stations.

To tune in a VOR station, first look up the VOR frequency on your chart for the VOR station you wish to use. Then click on the integer portion of the NAV radio frequency indicator to adjust the frequency. Click on the right-hand side above the decimal to increase the frequency, or click on the left of the numbers to decrease the frequency. For the fractional part of the frequency,

Only the NAV 1/OBI 1 radio can be used with both VOR and ILS radio beacons. The NAV 2/OBI 2 can only be used with VOR stations.

VOR stations between 108 MHz and 112 MHz are tuned to even tenths on the frequency dial, while ILS stations on this band are tuned to odd tenths on the frequency dial. Above 112.0 MHz, VOR stations can have even or odd tenth decimals.

Figure 12.10
The OBI azimuth display

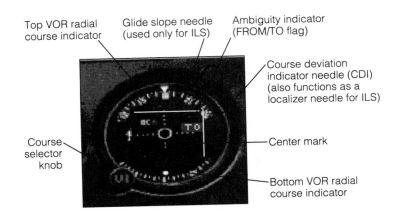

Top VOR radial course indicator

Glide slope needle (used only for ILS)

Ambiguity indicator (FROM/TO flag)

Course deviation indicator needle (CDI) (also functions as a localizer needle for ILS)

Course selector knob

Center mark

Bottom VOR radial course indicator

To select OBI 1, press V 1; to select OBI 2, press V 2. Follow this by pressing + or − to increase or decrease the course heading. To adjust the OBI course indicator in tens of degrees from the keyboard, hold down Shift and press + or − to increase or decrease the course heading.

click on the right to increase the frequency, and to the left, above the decimal point, to decrease. If you prefer to use the keyboard, see Appendix C for a list of the keyboard strokes necessary to adjust the radio frequency.

VOR stations broadcast their signals with a power output of 200 watts. In the frequencies between 108.0 MHz to 112.0 MHz, they have their frequency assignments set to even tenth decimals to avoid conflict with ILS stations. Thus, for example, VOR stations can have frequencies of 109.0, 109.2, 109.4, etcetera, while ILS stations are assigned odd tenth decimals, such as 109.1, 109.3, 109.5, etcetera. Above 112.0 MHz, the frequency assignment may be either even or odd tenth decimals, as for example Chicago's O'Hare International VOR which is set to 113.9 MHz.

Using the OBI Azimuth Display

The OBI azimuth display is used to project the VOR radial the aircraft is currently on. It also displays the deviation from the radial on a CDI (Course Deviation Indicator Needle) so that you can determine whether you are to the right or left of the specified VOR radial.

To determine the VOR radial you are currently on, follow these steps:

1. Using the NAV radio, tune in the VOR station by entering the proper frequency. (From the keyboard press N 1 followed by + or −.)
2. Click the course indicator or click on V to adjust the course until the CDI needle is centered. (From the keyboard, press V 1 followed by + or −. To increment by tens of degrees, press Shift followed by + or −.)
3. If the TO/FROM indicator shows TO, then you are on the radial shown by the bottom course indicator. If the TO/FROM indicator shows FROM, you are on the radial shown by the top course indicator. Note that this does not mean you are headed toward or away from the VOR station!

In the above procedure for determining the VOR radial, if you are using the NAV 2/OBI 2, simply replace [N] [1] with [N] [2], and [V] [1] with [V] [2].

In the following example, you will learn how to tune in a VOR radial and see it displayed on your OBI indicator.

1. Start up FS 5.0 so that you are on the ground at Chicago's Meigs Field.
2. Select Chicago's O'Hare VOR by tuning in 113.9 MHz on the NAV 1 radio. Use the mouse to click on the frequency selector; or from the keyboard, press [N] followed by [+] or [−] to increase or decrease the integer portion of the frequency. Next, press [N] [N] followed by [+] or [−] to increase or decrease the fractional portion of the frequency.

3. With the mouse, click the OBI display's course indicator until you see the CDI needle centered and the TOP flag is lit. With the keyboard, press [V] followed by [+] or [−] to increase or decrease the course indicator.
4. When the CDI needle is centered and the TOP flag is lit, your VOR radial is displayed on the lower course indicator as 120°. This is the direction from the VOR station to your plane as measured from 0° magnetic north. The top course indicator showing a compass direction of 300° tells you the heading you would need to take if you wanted to fly directly to the O'Hare VOR station. If the FROM flag is lit, then simply reverse the course headings shown on the top and lower indicators so that the top reading is your direction from the VOR station and the lower reading is your direction to the VOR station.
5. The DME 1 indicator shows that the Chicago O'Hare VOR station is exactly 15.5 nautical miles from your present location.

The TO/FROM Indicator

Also called the ambiguity indicator, the TO/FROM flags on the OBI tell you whether the displayed heading on the top course indicator will take the aircraft TO or FROM the station. It does *not* tell you whether the aircraft is heading to or from the station, as Figure 12.11 illustrates. When TO is displayed, the top course indicator shows the heading you would need to take to travel straight to the VOR station. When FROM is displayed, the top course indicator tells you the radial from the VOR station to your aircraft you are currently on.

The Course Deviation Indicator (CDI)

The CDI, or course deviation indicator, is a needle that moves left and right on the OBI to tell you whether you are within 10° of a selected radial. When the needle deflects right, it tells you that you are to the left of the selected course radial. (You need to turn right to get back on the radial.) When the

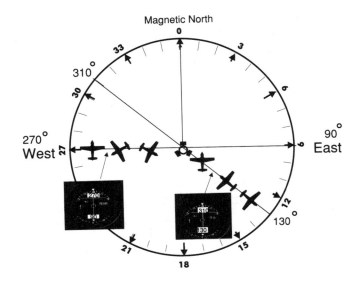

Figure 12.11
TO/FROM indicator
and the relationship to
the VOR station

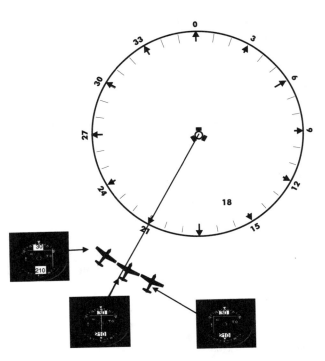

Figure 12.12
CDI needle deflection
and relationship to
course radial

needle deflects left, it means you are to the right of the selected course radial. (You need to turn left to get back on the radial.) Full-needle deflection to the right or left tells you that you are off from the displayed course indicator

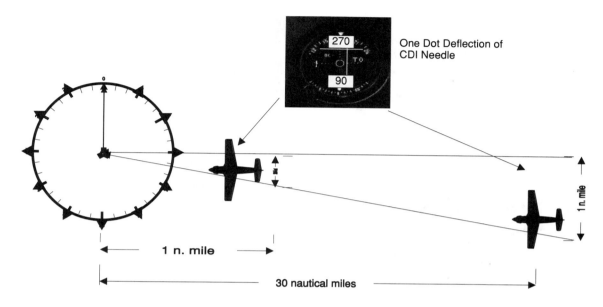

One Dot Deflection of
CDI Needle

1 n. mile

1 n. mile

30 nautical miles

radial by more than 10°, in which case you need to adjust the course indicator setting until the needle is again centered.

There are four horizontal dots on either side of the center mark on the OBI. Each dot indicates a horizontal displacement from course of 200 feet per nautical mile. For example, at 30 nautical miles from the VOR station, one dot deflection means that the aircraft is approximately one nautical mile off the side of the displayed course radial. Figure 12.13 shows how this works.

As you pass directly over a VOR station, the needle will fluctuate from side to side, and the TO/FROM indicators will change flags.

Understanding the DME Indicator

The DME, or Distance Measuring Equipment, tells you the distance to the VOR station from your present location. It can also tell you your speed in relation to the VOR station. Note that the distance to the VOR station is measured in slant range form; that is, the distance from your plane directly to the VOR station. This distance is not the same as your horizontal distance to the VOR station. For example, when flying directly over a VOR station at 6,000 feet, your DME distance is approximately one nautical mile even though you are passing right over it.

By the same token, the DME speed is not the same as your ground-speed. If you are traveling parallel to a VOR station, for example, your speed is measured in terms of how fast you are moving towards or away from the VOR station.

Figure 12.13
When the CDI needle deflects by one dot on the scale, the aircraft is off the VOR radial centerline by 200 feet for each mile from the VOR station

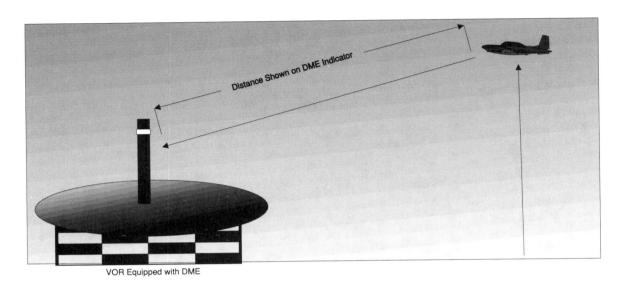

Distance Shown on DME Indicator

VOR Equipped with DME

Horizontal Ground Distance to VOR Station

Figure 12.14
The DME indicator shows the diagonal distance to the VOR station, not the ground distance

When combined with the VOR radial information, the DME makes it possible for you to know the exact geographic position of your aircraft.

To toggle between speed and range displays on the Cessna DME, press F followed by +.

Setting the Autopilot VOR Lock

The autopilot can be used to lock-in a particular VOR station and fly the airplane toward it. This allows you to devote your attention to other important activities, such as looking out your window at the pretty scenery.

To set your autopilot to lock onto a VOR station, follow these steps:

1. Tune in the VOR station you want on the NAV 1 radio. (This only works on the NAV 1 radio.)

2. Select Autopilot from the Nav/Com menu.

3. In the Autopilot dialog box, click on the NAV 1 (Heading Hold) checkbox.

4. Select the Autopilot Switch listbox and highlight Connected.

5. Click OK to return to the simulation.

6. Keep the CDI needle centered by clicking on the course indicator. From the keyboard you can press V followed by + to increase the course, or - to decrease the course.

Press F followed by + to toggle the Cessna DME indicator between speed and range displays.

7. If you want to shut off the autopilot at any time, press Z, or click on the autopilot indicator.

Your airplane will now automatically follow a direct course for the VOR station you selected (as long as the CDI needle is centered).

While in the Autopilot dialog box, you can also set the autopilot to lock in a particular altitude lock and automatically level the wings for you. Just click on the autopilot checkbox options you want to engage.

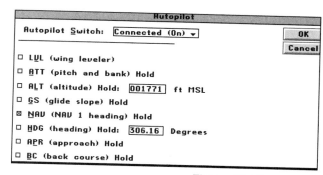

Figure 12.15
Using the autopilot to lock onto a VOR radial

Using EFIS/CFPD for VOR and Altitude Tracking

Using the EFIS (Electronic Flight Information System)/CFPD (Command Flight Path Display), you can project the path to the VOR station on your cockpit windshield. To do this follow these steps:

1. Select EFIS/CFPD Display from the Nav/Com menu.
2. Click on the EFIS Master Switch.
3. Toggle on the Lock to VOR 1 and Altitude Tracking radio button.
4. Select the Altitude (Feet Above Ground Level) textbox and type in **5000**. This will be the altitude in feet at which the CFPD display will appear.
5. Toggle on the Plot Intersecting Path checkbox.
6. Choose Rectangles for the Type listbox, although you can also choose telephone poles or a yellow brick road.
7. Click the OK button.

How to use the EFIS/CFPD heads-up display to show VOR radials.

When you return to the simulation, you will see bright red rectangles showing you the way to the VOR station. All you need to do is fly through them, one by one, until you reach the VOR station.

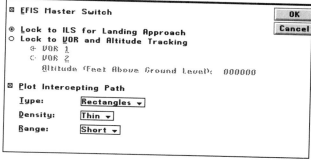

Figure 12.16
EFIS/CFPD dialog box

Using the VOR Tracking Method

VOR tracking is a technique used to navigate toward a VOR station, correcting for unknown wind drift-forces. To track inbound toward a VOR station, follow these steps:

1. On the NAV 1 radio, tune in the VOR station on which you want to home in.

CFPD rectangles

Figure 12.17
Fly through the CFPD red rectangles to get to the VOR station

The VOR Tracking Method

2. Click on the OBI course indicator until the CDI needle is centered and the TO flag is lit.

3. Turn the aircraft until its course heading, as indicated on the directional gyro, is the same as is displayed on the OBI course indicator.

4. As you fly toward the VOR station, observe the CDI for deflection to the left or right. If the CDI deflects left, it means there is a crosswind from the right. If the CDI deflects right, it means there is a crosswind from the left.

5. Turn 20° toward the CDI needle. If the needle is on the left, turn your plane to a course heading 20° left of its present heading. If the needle is on the right, turn your plane to a course heading 20° right of its present heading.

6. When the CDI needle centers, reduce the drift correction by 10° and note whether this drift correction keeps the CDI needle centered. If not, reduce or increase the drift correction as necessary.

7. Keep the CDI needle centered, and soon you will fly over the VOR station, which will be indicated when the needle makes a full deflection from side to side and the TO/FROM flag changes.

Figure 12.18 illustrates the technique of VOR tracking.

Using Two VORs to Get a Position Fix

Because *Flight Simulator* provides two NAV radios and corresponding OBIs, you can tune in two different VOR stations and obtain a position fix. By plotting on a navigational map the intersection of the two VOR radials on which you are currently, you can accurately determine your coordinates. The procedure is quite simple and is illustrated in Figure 12.19. Note that in order to

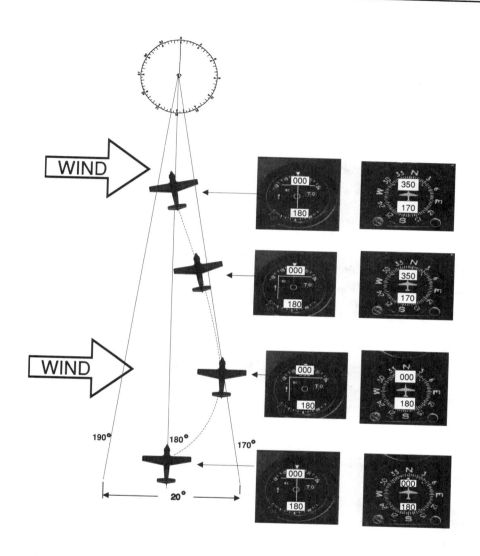

Figure 12.18
VOR tracking

Use both NAV 1/OBI 1 and NAV 2/OBI 2 navigational radios to get a position fix from two separate VOR stations.

use this method, you should have both FROM indicators lit, and you should obtain your course radials from the top of each OBI course indicator.

Let's try to fix our position on the runway at Meigs Field. Follow these steps and then examine Figure 12.19 to check out your results:

1. Tune in your VOR 1 radio to DuPage VOR on a frequency of 108.4 MHz. Set with the mouse or press N followed by + or − for the integer part of the frequency, and N N followed by + or − for the fractional part of the frequency.

2. Adjust the course indicator on OBI 1 until the CDI needle is centered

and the FROM flag is lit. Click to the right or left of the course indicator with the mouse, or press [V] followed by [+] or [-]. (To adjust the course in increments of 10°, press [Shift] and [+] or [-].) If you have done this correctly, your top course indicator should read 90°.

3. Tune in VOR 2 to Joliet VOR on a frequency of 112.3 MHz. Use the mouse to set the frequency; or, from the keyboard, press [N] [2] followed by [+] or [-] for the integer part of the frequency and [N] [N] followed by [+] or [-] for the fractional part of the frequency.

4. Set the OBI 2 course heading so that the CDI needle is centered and the FROM flag is lit. Click the OBI 2 course indicator with the mouse, or press [V] [2] followed by [+] or [-]. (Use [Shift] and [+] or [-] to increment by 10°.) If you have done this correctly, your top course indicator on OBI 2 should read 58°.

5. Now, using the map shown in Figure 12.19, plot a line from DuPage VOR on radial 90° and then plot a second line from Joliet on radial 58°. Where the two lines intersect is where your plane is located.

Figure 12.19
Using two VORs to fix your position

This is the basic method of fixing your position using two VOR stations.

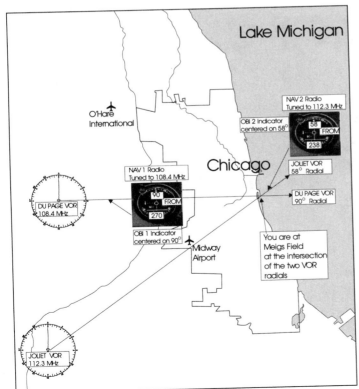

Non-Directional Beacon Navigation (NDB)

The NDB, or Non-Directional Beacon station, is an older navigational system that can be used as a backup for the VOR/OBI instruments. It consists of many low-frequency transmitters operating on a frequency of 200–415 kHz with a maximum power of 2,000 Watts. With a maximum range of 75 nautical miles by day and up to 200 miles by night the NDB station still has not outgrown its usefulness. Its primary disadvantages are that it is susceptible to storm interference and it is not as accurate as the VOR system. In *Flight Simulator* you tune in an NDB station by using the ADF radio and then consult the ADF indicator to see which direction the NDB station is in relation to your aircraft.

How NDB Works

How does it work? The NDB sends out an omnidirectional signal that radiates out in all directions. The NDB's electromagnetic waves consist of two components: fluctuating magnetic fields and fluctuating electric fields that are always oriented 90° with respect to each other. The magnetic field propagates outwards from the transmitter as concentric circles, while the electric field propagates outwards in radials. When the signal is received by your ADF radio, it rotates a loop antenna to determine which direction improves the signal's strength. According to Lenz's law of physics, the maximum signal strength in the loop will occur when a magnetic force field enters perpendicular to the plane of the loop. This occurs when the antenna is rotated so that the plane of the loop points in the direction of the electromagnetic wave emanating from the transmitter tower. As the loop is rotated, it rotates the needle on the ADF gauge, thereby showing the direction of the NDB station. If you want to head directly for the NDB station, all you do is reorient the aircraft so that the arrow points to the 0° mark.

In *Flight Simulator*, the ADF gauge is not normally displayed. In order to use it, you must replace the OBI 2 indicator with the ADF dial. To do this, simply press [Shift] [Tab].

How non-directional beacon navigation works

Setting the ADF Frequency

Flight Simulator 5.0 now includes an option for allowing your ADF radio to tune in increments of 500 Hz and to tune in frequencies higher than 999 kHz. (Theoretically, you can now tune in AM broadcast stations on 540 to 1610 kHz!) Normally, each NDB is separated by a frequency of at least 1 kHz so by allowing a 500 Hz separation, the number of receivable stations is increased.

To have your ADF radio tune in NDB stations with 500 Hz selectivity, follow these steps:

1. Open the Instrument Preferences dialog box under the Options menu.
2. In the Instrument Preferences dialog box, toggle on the 500 Hz ADF Frequency Adjustment checkbox.
3. Click the OK button to return to the simulator.

Your ADF radio will now have four integer digits and one fractional digit for the frequency selection.

Tuning in ADF frequencies with 500 Hz separation is a little bit different from the method used for the ordinary ADF radio. With the mouse, you select the first two digits, then click to increase. If you want to decrease the digits, you must use the keyboard's [–]; you cannot use the mouse alone. The third digit of the frequency can be set individually by clicking on it, followed

Tuning in frequencies with 500 Hz separation on the ADF radio

by ⊞ or ⊟. The fourth and fractional fifth digit are set together. Click on these last two digits, followed by ⊞ or ⊟.

To tune in a frequency using the keyboard alone, follow these steps:

1. Press Ⓐ followed by ⊞ or ⊟ to adjust the first two digits.
2. Press Ⓐ Ⓐ followed by ⊞ or ⊟ to adjust the third digit.
3. Press Ⓐ Ⓐ Ⓐ followed by ⊞ or ⊟ to adjust the fourth and fractional fifth digits.

ADF (Automatic Direction Finder)

The ADF, or Automatic Direction Finder, gauge shows you the bearing, relative to the nose of the aircraft, to the NDB station. The ADF display has a 360° scale and a needle pointer. The compass scale is read just like that of the directional gyro, with each number multiplied by 10 to obtain the bearing. For example, a reading of 9 on the scale means 90°, and a reading of 27 means 270°.

To navigate using an NDB station, you must first look up the station's frequency and enter it on the ADF radio. If you are in range of the NDB, your ADF gauge will then show the direction towards the station. Don't confuse the ADF gauge's course markings with your aircraft's current heading, for they are not the same. The needle pointer only points to the relative bearing of the NDB station in relation to your aircraft's nose. Thus, if your airplane is heading south on a course of 180° and your ADF pointer is aimed at 9, it means that the NDB station is off to the right by 90° from your present heading.

Note that when the pointer tracks 0°, the airplane is homed in on the station. If you keep flying with the needle pointing at 0°, eventually you will pass over the station.

Don't confuse the ADF gauge's course markings with your aircraft's current heading.

Using the ADF Homing Method

ADF homing is a navigational technique used to fly the aircraft towards an NDB station. Follow these steps to use the ADF homing method:

1. Tune in a desired NDB station on your ADF radio.
2. Bring up the ADF gauge by pressing Shift Tab.
3. Turn the aircraft until the azimuth needle moves to the 0° position on the ADF gauge.
4. If crosswinds start blowing you off course, turn the airplane until you again have the needle centered on 0°.

When the needle suddenly jumps to 180°, you will have crossed over the NDB station below and be headed on an outbound path. If you want to

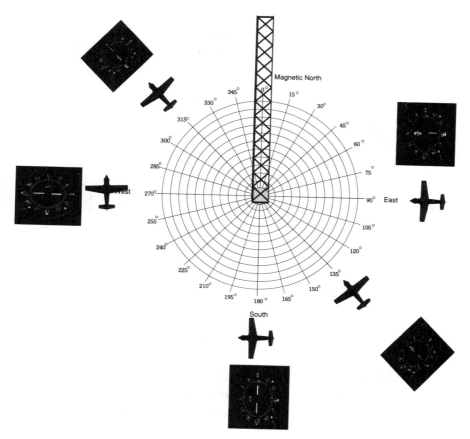

Figure 12.20
When the ADF pointer
tracks 0°, the airplane
is headed directly for
the NDB station.

continue traveling straight away from the NDB station, keep the azimuth needle pointed on 180°. However, with the NDB station behind you, be aware that turning the aircraft left and right will make the azimuth needle move in the opposite direction.

The disadvantage of the ADF homing method is that in the presence of a crosswind your path to the NDB station will not be the most direct or straight. In essence you will be flying a curved route, as is illustrated in Figure 12.21

The ADF Homing Method

The Instrument Landing System

The ILS, or Instrument Landing System, offers a means of safely landing your aircraft in conditions of poor visibility. Each ILS ground station is situated next to major runways and can be tuned in by your NAV radios. The

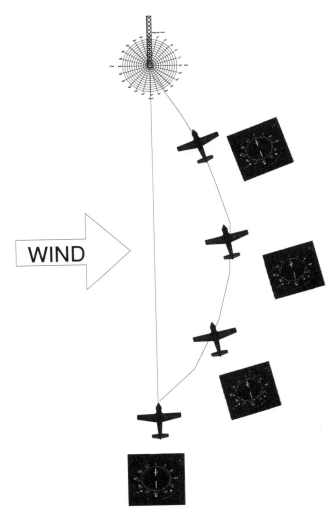

CDI needle on the OBI indicator is joined by a second needle, the glide slope needle, to offer both vertical and horizontal range indications for the proper glide slope to the runway.

The ILS has four main components:

- Localizer radio course
- Glide slope radio course
- VHF marker beacons
- Approach lights for the runway

The localizer and glide slope transmitters together provide a radio beam that the aircraft rides down to the runway. Using crosshair needles on the OBI indicator, the pilot can follow the precise glide angle necessary to reach the runway. Three additional VHF radio marker beacons, located at precise distances from the runway threshold, give the pilot range information. The outer marker warning comes on about four to seven miles from the runway, while the middle marker warning comes on about 3,250 feet from the runway. There is an additional inner marker warning that some ILS runways come equipped with that comes on when the runway is 1,000 feet off.

In addition, many ILS stations have DME equipment so that your DME indicator can tell you how far away the runway is.

Figure 12.21
ADF homing method

✈
The ILS system consists of marker beacons, approach lights, and the localizer/glide slope radio course.

Using the Localizer and Glide Slope for Your Landing

Each runway that is equipped with an ILS has a localizer transmitter, a glide slope transmitter, and at least two OMI radio marker beacons. The localizer transmitter furnishes horizontal guidance information to the OBI localizer needle (same as the CDI needle for the VOR), causing it to move left or right when the aircraft is off the runway centerline. For vertical guidance information, the glide slope transmitter sends out a signal that allows a special glide slope needle on the OBI to move up and down, thereby indicating the aircraft's vertical position with respect to the proper glide slope. When both needles converge in the center of the OBI indicator, the aircraft is on the proper course for the runway.

Localizer

Located off the runway on a centerline, the localizer radiates a fan-shaped radio field with an angular width of 3° to 6°, as seen in Figure 12.22. The localizer beam extends out for about 18 miles from the runway threshold and

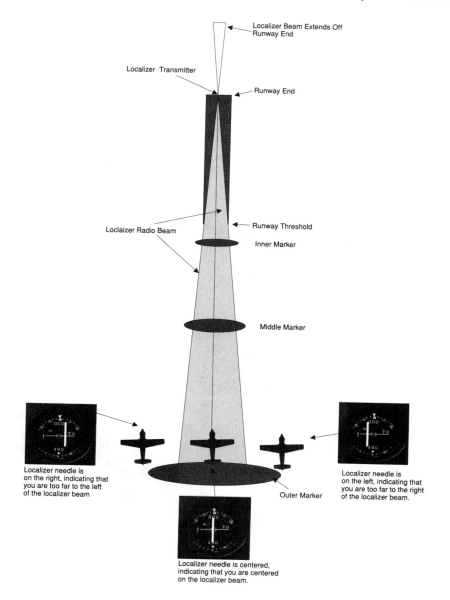

Figure 12.22
Localizer and glideslope on the OBI indicator

The localizer gives
horizontal guidance.

is transmitted on frequencies between 108.10 MHz to 111.95 MHz with a power of about 100 watts. All ILS localizer frequencies are assigned odd tenth decimals, so that an ILS station could use, for example, 108.10, 108.30, 108.50 MHz, etcetera, frequencies.

Notice that the localizer needle on the OBI is the same as the CDI needle, and it serves the same function of showing horizontal deviation. In Figure 12.22, you can see that if the needle is deflected to the right, your plane is too far to the left of the runway. Likewise, if the needle is deflected to the left, your plane is too far to the right of the runway.

Glide Slope

The glide slope gives
vertical guidance.

The glide slope UHF (Ultra High Frequency) transmitter sends out a radio beam that radiates diagonally upward from the ground. The angle which the glide slope makes with the ground is about 3°, which gives it a very gradual slope. In fact, at the middle marker distance of 3,250 feet to the runway, the glide slope is only 200 feet above the ground. At the outer marker distance of four to seven miles from the runway, the glide slope is only 475 feet above the ground. The beam itself is transmitted on a frequency between 329.15 MHz and 335 MHz with a power of only 5 watts. Don't worry, though. In *Flight Simulator*, the NAV radio automatically tunes in the proper glide slope frequencies for you when you tune in an ILS station.

On the OBI, the glide slope needle moves up and down to show whether the plane is deviating from the glide slope. If the needle is above the centerline, your airplane is too low, and you must regain some altitude. If the

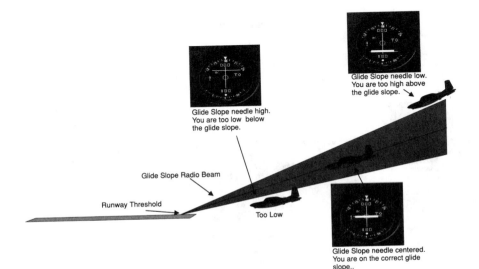

Glide Slope needle low.
You are too high above
the glide slope.

Glide Slope needle high.
You are too low below
the glide slope.

Glide Slope Radio Beam

Runway Threshold

Too Low

Glide Slope needle centered.
You are on the correct glide
slope..

Figure 12.23
Glide slope OBI
indicator for various
glide slopes

needle is below the centerline, your aircraft is too high and you will therefore need to shed some altitude. Of course, if the glide slope needle is smack in the middle of the center mark, your airplane is right on the money.

What the OMI Marker Beacons Tell You

In an ILS approach, the VHF OMI marker beacons provide the pilot with distance information to the runway. There are three markers: the outer, middle, and inner. Each VHF marker sends out a cone-shaped radio beam straight up into the air on the approach to the runway. When the airplane passes over the cone, it causes the OMI indicator in the cockpit to sound off with a distinctive signal and colored light. Table 12.2 lists the standard distance designation, sound signal, and light color for each marker.

All OMI beacons operate on a frequency of 75 MHz, with a power output of 3 watts.

Getting Guidance from the Approach Lighting Systems

When landing at an ILS-equipped runway, there are approach lighting systems to help the pilot discern the runway orientation, distance to the end of the runway, and the correct glide path. There are three separate approach lighting systems in common use with ILS equipped runways:

- *REIL:* Runway End Identifier Lights
- *VASI:* Visual Approach Slope Indicator
- *MALSR:* Medium Approach Lighting System with Runway Alignment Indicator Lights

Rotation of the course indicators on the OBI has no effect on the operation of the localizer needle.

The OMI marker beacons warn you how far you are from the runway.

Table 12.2	Aircraft Marker Beacons		
Marker Designation	**Typical Distance to Runway Threshold**	**Audible Signal in Cockpit**	**OMI Light Indicator Color**
Outer	4 to 7 nautical miles	Continuous dashes (400 Hz)	Blue
Middle	3,250 to 3,750 feet	Continuous alternating dot-dash (1300 Hz)	Amber
Inner	1,000 feet	Continuous (6/second)	White

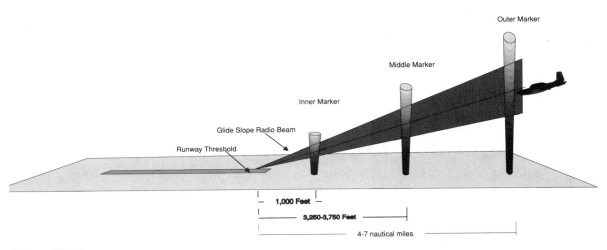

Outer Marker

Middle Marker

Inner Marker

Glide Slope Radio Beam

Runway Threshold

1,000 Feet

3,250-3,750 Feet

4-7 nautical miles

Figure 12.24
ILS marker beacons
and glidepath

In addition, there are airport beacon lights, which help you spot the airport from among the bright lights of the city.

The flashing REIL lights are installed at the end of the runway.

REIL (Runway End Identifier Lights)

The REIL, or Runway End Identifier Lights, are mounted on each side of the runway's end. These flashing strobe lights warn the pilot of the end of the runway, giving a visual cue as to how much runway length is left.

VASI (Visual Approach Slope Indicator)

The Visual Approach Slope Indicator (VASI) lights give the pilot descent guidance information during the approach to the runway. The FS 5.0 VASI configuration consists of rows of colored lights on each side of the runway. The lighted bar colors of the lights tell you if your approach is too high, just right, or too low. When the upper and lower lights are both white, you are too high. If the upper row is white and the lower row is red, you are on the correct glide slope. If you are too low, however, both lights are red.

VASI lights tell you if you are on the correct glide path to runway.

Not all the FS 5.0 airports have VASI lights installed. Some airports where you will find VASI lights include (this list is not all-inclusive; many other airports have VASI):

- Los Angeles International
- Chicago's Midway Airport
- Champaign, Illinois
- Chicago's Meigs Field

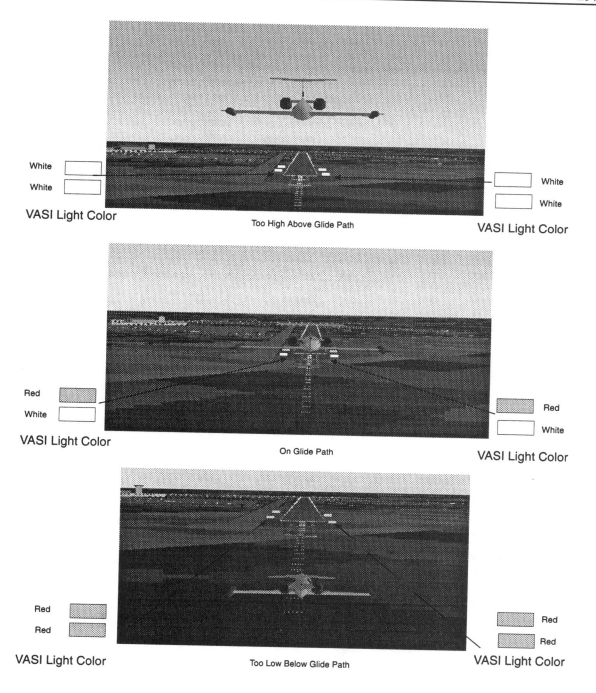

White

White

VASI Light Color

White

White

Too High Above Glide Path

VASI Light Color

Red

White

VASI Light Color

Red

White

On Glide Path

VASI Light Color

Red

Red

VASI Light Color

Red

Red

Too Low Below Glide Path

VASI Light Color

Figure 12.25
VASI approaches

MALSR (Medium Intensity Approach Lighting System with Runway Alignment Indicator Lights)

MALSR consists of a row of flashing strobe lights that resemble tracer shells being fired at the runway, along with steadily burning horizontal roll guidance lights just before the runway.

MALSR, or the Medium Intensity Approach Lighting System, are runway lights that resemble tracer shells being fired at the runway. You will see these strobe lights at most major airports.

MALSR lights are included for the following airports in *Flight Simulator*:

- San Francisco International
- Los Angeles International
- John F. Kennedy International
- Champaign, Illinois
- Chicago's O'Hare International

Airport Beacons

Airport beacons are marked as star-shaped symbols on the airport maps and sectionals that come with the FS 5.0 manual.

Flight Simulator 5.0 now includes flashing beacon lights which help you locate the airport at night from among the many bright lights of the city. Airport beacons, which operate from dusk until dawn, flash a bright light which alternates between green and white. They are clearly marked on the sectionals and airport maps as a star-shaped symbol.

Using EFIS/CFPD for Landings

Using EFIS/CFPD's heads-up display for landings

The EFIS/CFPD display can be used to project a path to the runway on your cockpit windshield. Using the NAV 1 radio, tune in the ILS station

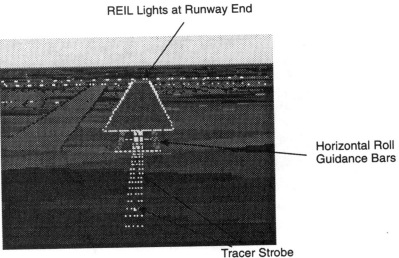

Figure 12.26
MALSR lights

REIL Lights at Runway End

Horizontal Roll Guidance Bars

Tracer Strobe

MALSR Lights

where you wish to land, then activate the CFPD display. You can have rectangles, telephone poles, or a yellow-brick road show you the exact glide path to the runway in zero visibility.

To set up EFIS/CFPD for ILS landings, follow this procedure:

1. First, tune in the ILS station on your NAV 1 radio.

2. Next, select the EFIS/CFPD Display command from the Nav/Com menu.

3. In the EFIS/CFPD dialog box, click on the EFIS Master Switch checkbox.

4. In the same dialog box, click on the Lock to ILS for Landing Approach radio button.

5. Click the Plot Intercepting Path checkbox and choose the type of graphic you wish. You can pick from rectangles, telephone poles, and a yellow-brick road.

6. Click the OK button.

When you return to the simulation, you will see a computer-generated glide slope path to the runway, as is pictured in Figure 12.27.

OTHER NAVIGATIONAL AIDS IN THE REAL WORLD

Today, there are various other navigational systems in use around the world. The Omega, Loran C, GPS (Global Positioning System), and inertial navigation systems are used for long-range navigation. Ultimately, however, the satellite-based GPS navigation system will replace all other navigational methods. In fact, the Department of Transportation foresees the day when

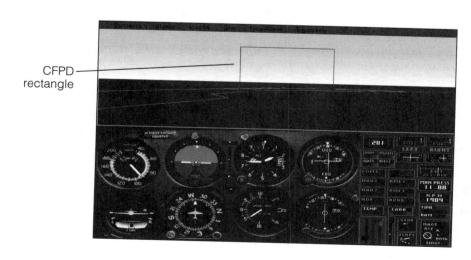

CFPD rectangle

Figure 12.27
EFIS rectangles displayed on cockpit windshield showing glide slope to ILS runway

GPS will replace the entire VOR/NDB radio beacon network. With the advent of the high-accuracy differential correction-GPS, the ILS and MLS (Microwave Landing System that is proposed to replace the ILS in the late 1990s) may well be rendered obsolete. A brief description of each system is given in the next section.

LORAN

Loran C (for Long-Range Navigation) is a long-range hyperbolic navigation system that has a coverage area of 1,200 miles by day and 2,300 miles by night. Expanded and improved over the years since its first introduction in 1957, Loran C now covers most regions of the northern Atlantic and Pacific Oceans, along with the Mediterranean. Nighttime skywaves are receivable over most of the northern hemisphere (except the Indian Ocean). The system operates by having a master station transmit a pulse at a frequency of 100 kHz, which then triggers the slave stations to emit a radio pulse. By recording the unique time differences between the master pulse and the slave pulse, a Loran C receiver can plot a line of position and thus fix its coordinates. Loran C is still used in much of the world; but with the advent of GPS, its usefulness may soon be outlived.

OMEGA

One of the major disadvantages of terrestrial-based navigation systems such as VOR/NDB and Loran C is that they do not truly offer worldwide coverage. For most of the world, in fact, there is no coverage at all. The Loran C range falls off after about 1,200 miles by day (2,300 miles by night), and the range for VOR/NDB stations is at most 200 miles. Because of this, in 1947 the U.S. Navy began a research and development program to develop a low-frequency radio navigation system that could achieve worldwide coverage. By 1960, the last technical hurdles were overcome and the Omega system, as it is called, was put into operation.

The Omega system consists of eight stations located 5,000 to 6,000 miles apart, transmitting on the VLF (very low frequencies) band on a frequency of 10 to 14 kHz. The low frequency radio waves are propagated very long distances with very little loss of signal or distortion. These frequencies can also penetrate the surface layers of ocean water, enabling submerged submarines to receive the signal.

By comparing phase differences in signals from four or more Omega stations, an Omega-equipped aircraft can plot its position within one nautical mile by day and two nautical miles by night anywhere in the world.

GPS (GLOBAL POSITIONING SYSTEM)

The GPS, or Navstar Global Positioning System, is a satellite-based navigation system that is operated by the Department of Defense. The system, when finally completed, will consist of 24 satellites distributed in three orbits containing eight satellites each. Each satellite will orbit the earth at an altitude of 10,900 nautical miles, with a period of 12 hours. For precise latitude and longitude determination, at least 3 satellites' signals must be received by the GPS receiver. For precise altitude determination, a fourth satellite signal is needed. At present, there are 17 satellites in orbit, so there are lapses in coverage for altitude determination.

When fully operational, the GPS system will be capable of achieving worldwide accuracy of less than 18 meters (60 feet) in latitude and longitude and less than 28 meters (92 feet) in altitude. But because the system was designed for the U.S. military, the best accuracy will be reserved for the armed forces. Commercial services will have to subscribe to a degraded GPS signal that provides accuracy of about 100 meters (330 feet) for latitude and longitude and 156 meters (514 feet) in altitude.

In *Flight Simulator 5.0*, you can simulate having a GPS receiver by activating your latitude/longitude display. To do this, press Shift Z.

Press Shift Z to display your GPS latitude/longitude coordinates.

GPS—The Wave of the Future

GPS, as presently envisioned, is the most accurate and reliable navigational system ever invented by humankind. To see why this is so, compare the benefits of GPS over all other systems.

- *GPS provides worldwide coverage.* Loran C does not, VOR/NDB stations do not, and Omega is only accurate to one nautical mile.

- *GPS is more accurate* than Loran, VOR/NDB, or Omega.

- *GPS signals are not affected by bad weather.* Rain, electrical thunderstorms, and other weather can wipe out Loran C and interfere with the VOR/NDB signal.

- *Differential correction GPS can be used in place of ILS.*[2] In the future, with differential correction of the GPS signal a pilot could land at virtually any airport in the world.

---

[2] Differential GPS Correction is a land based way of improving the basic accuracy of the GPS fix. A ground station broadcasts a "differential" coordinate correction to the GPS receiver, thereby allowing it to narrow the accuracy of its position fix down to a few meters or less. Eventually, this system may replace the instrument landing systems currently in use.

GPS—How Does It Work?

GPS works by having each satellite transmit a signal on a frequency of 1575.42 MHz and 1227.6 MHz and then having a ground or airborne receiver compare the time differences of the transmissions of at least three of the satellites to determine its position. If a fourth satellite is in a line of sight with the receiver, then an additional position fix can be obtained that tells you your altitude. In order to be as precise as possible, all the satellites and the GPS receiver must have their internal clocks synchronized. There are four atomic clocks on board each satellite which keep time accurate to one second in every 70,000 years! Each clock measures time in nanoseconds (a nanosecond is one-billionth of a second or 10^{-9} seconds); and if a clock should stray by one-thousandth of a second, the resulting position fix could be off by 186 miles! Due to relativistic time dilation effects, the clocks also must be corrected to account for time differences caused by the motion of the satellites. As Einstein explained in his theory of relativity, a clock in a fast-moving vehicle will count time more slowly than a clock in a stationary frame of reference.

So how exactly does the GPS receiver know how to fix its position? Well, if you know when the signal left the satellite and you calculate how long the signal takes to reach the receiver, you can calculate the distance by using the formula

$$distance = time \times c$$

where c is the speed of light, or 186,000 miles per second.[3] The satellite sends out a special code that tells the receiver when the signal was first sent so all the receiver needs to do is calculate the distance from the above formula.

In addition, each receiver has a special almanac database that predicts where each satellite is scheduled to be at any given time. Since the motion of orbital bodies is *very* precise, the receiver knows the exact coordinates of every satellite.

But now that the GPS receiver knows the distance to one satellite, how does it figure out where on earth it is? To understand how this is done, let's see step by step what the GPS receiver does.

First, the GPS receiver tunes in the *first* satellite that it needs for the position fix. This satellite is approximately 11,000 miles out in space; and if you were to tie one end of a string to the satellite and pull it in every possible direction, the free end of the string would trace an imaginary sphere of radius 11,000 miles.

---

[3]All electromagnetic waves propagate through a vacuum at the speed of light.

This, of course, covers quite a bit of area, so the GPS receiver must narrow its position down by locating a second satellite. Using the same distance determination, a line of position, or LOP, is drawn on the intersection of the two imaginary spheres for each satellite. As any geometry student will tell you, the intersection of two spheres is a circle. Therefore, the GPS receiver has narrowed down its position to somewhere on a circle, which is the precise intersection for the two imaginary spheres.

Next, a *third* satellite is tuned in by the GPS receiver to draw a third imaginary sphere. With the intersection of all three spheres, there remain only two points which the GPS receiver can be. But which point is correct? The GPS computer makes a determination based upon what is logically possible, and this result is then displayed in latitude/longitude form on its display.

With the addition of a fourth satellite, the GPS receiver can now make a third-dimensional fix and thus obtain its altitude. Furthermore, from this additional information, the GPS receiver can also calculate its speed in relation to the ground.

Inertial Navigation Systems

All the electronic navigation systems discussed so far, including the GPS, are dependent on electromagnetic waves transmitted by external transmitters. The inertial navigation system was developed during the 1950s by the U.S. Navy to offer an independent means of position determination that was not subject to external disruption or interference during wartime. First deployed on ballistic-missile submarines, inertial navigation systems have decreased in size and cost to the point that today most commercial jetliners have them installed as standard equipment.

Inertial navigation works by calculating movements of the aircraft based on sensed accelerations in known spatial directions. Two accelerometers are stabilized by a system of three gyroscopes so that they are constantly maintained on a plane tangential to the earth's surface. One accelerometer measures movements in a north–south direction, while the other accelerometer measures movements in a east–west direction. Both accelerometers are only sensitive to horizontal movements of the aircraft; they do not care about altitude changes. By using Newton's laws of motion,

$$Distance = \frac{1}{2} \, at^2 = \int_0^t ax \, dx$$

where a = acceleration in

$$\frac{feet}{second^2} \ (\text{or} \ \frac{meters}{second^2})$$

and $t =$ time in seconds, the accelerometers detect the amount of acceleration in each direction and then add and subtract the distance that is traveled
to the plane's known starting location. This process is known as integration
($\int_0^t ax\, dx$ where $t =$ time in seconds, $a =$ acceleration, and x is a dummy
variable), and it occurs second by second.

    Due to gyroscopic precession and other errors, inertial navigation sys-
tems do not offer 100 percent accuracy. On long transoceanic flights, they
can be off by 20 miles or more.

C H A P T E R

13

Solo Adventures

This chapter tests your ability to fly both the Cessna and Learjet. You will first barn-storm the Golden Gate Bridge by flying underneath the deck of the bridge, then try your hand at flying Oakland to Los Angeles in the Cessna. After you have completed this, you can move on to flying the Learjet cross-country from Oakland to Chicago, stopping over to refuel, then going on to JFK International Airport in New York. A complete VOR flight plan is provided for you so that you can jump right away into flying each adventure.

IT'S MORE FUN TO FLY WITH LIMITED FUEL

To make your flights more exciting, you should fly using limited fuel. You make the limited fuel selection in the Realism and Reliability dialog box (under the Sim menu) by toggling on the Engine Runs out of Fuel checkbox. By doing this, your airplane will actually burn fuel in the engine during flight, getting lighter as the fuel is consumed. Limiting your fuel also forces you to think about the range of your aircraft, the amount of fuel consumption per hour, and how your flight is affecting fuel economy. This is a good thing. You will learn much more about flying with this feature enabled than with it off. For example, when you fly the Learjet higher, your fuel consumption falls as measured on the fuel flow meter. But when you fly it at a lower altitude, fuel consumption rises and the fuel flow gauge shows more fuel being burned with a consequent drop in fuel quantity.

You must also factor in the aircraft's weight and runway length requirements when planning a mission. If, for example, you wanted to fly the Learjet from Oakland to Hawaii, a distance of over 2,400 miles, the fuel tanks would need to be filled with

For more realistic flight, turn off unlimited fuel by toggling on Engine Runs out of Fuel, in the Realism and Reliability dialog box.

6,198 lbs of fuel.[1] The aircraft's weight would then tip in at over 18,000 lbs, which means that the needed takeoff distance from Oakland would be 5,150 feet.[2] Consulting the Airport Maps in your Microsoft manual, you can see that Oakland's 27R runway is exactly 5,453 feet, allowing you just barely enough room to take off. If the outside temperature was 90°F or 100°F, you cannot take off because the needed runway length exceeds Oakland's 27R runway!

BARNSTORMING THE GOLDEN GATE BRIDGE

Now that you've acquired some skills in flying the Cessna, let's try your hand at barnstorming the Golden Gate Bridge in San Francisco. You should know beforehand, though, that flying under bridges (or bungee jumping for that matter) in the real world is strictly against the law. If caught, you will be fined and have your pilot's license revoked.

You will begin the flight at Oakland's Metropolitan Airport on runway 27R (not Oakland International, which uses runway 11/29) and then fly across the Bay Bridge and Alcatraz Island on a course heading of 288°. After reaching Alcatraz Island, you will turn left to a heading of 240° and then fly under the Golden Gate Bridge. On the return, you will double back towards San Francisco on a course heading of 83° and acquire the Oakland VOR radial on your NAV 1/OBI radio. Using the VOR radial, you can guide your aircraft back to Oakland where you will land on runway 11 at Oakland International Airport.

First Things First

Start up Flight Simulator and from the Options menu, select the Oakland 27R Takeoff situation from the Situation menu command. Click the OK button to return to the cockpit, and you should have a clear view down Oak-

---

[1] Using Hawaii's coordinates of N21° 18.5' latitude and W157° 55.8' longitude, and knowing that Oakland is located at N37° 43' latitude and W122° 13' longitude, you can use the distance formula given in Chapter 12 to calculate a distance of 2,407 statute miles (not nautical miles). With favorable winds, the Learjet 35A has a maximum range of 2,528 statute miles (2,196 nautical miles), which would allow it to fly to Hawaii.

[2] The 18,000 pound Learjet assumes that an "empty" Learjet with two crewmembers weighs 10,519 pounds, that a full tank of gas adds 6,198 pounds, and that a maximum payload of 1,783 pounds of passengers and baggage is included. Table 10.4 in chapter 10 shows that for an ambient air temperature of 70°F, the needed takeoff runway length for an 18,000 pound Learjet with flaps set to 20° is 5,150 feet.

land's 27R runway. If it is dark, adjust your clock on the instrument panel to a daytime hour.

Flight Preparation

Before you begin any flight, you should establish a flight plan. For long flights, your pre-flight preparation would include the flight routes to be taken, the weather forecast, altitude, projected speed, and transmitter frequencies of VOR stations along the way. You won't need to do such extensive preparation for this short flight since you will rely mainly on visual landmarks and your directional gyro for navigation.

During the barnstorming leg of the trip, keep below 250 feet MSL; otherwise, you may slam into the deck or the cabling of the Golden Gate Bridge. The optimum altitude is 200 feet MSL to allow for minor fluctuations in altitude.

Takeoff

Tune in your NAV 1 radio to the Oakland VOR station on a frequency of 116.8 MHz. Go through the takeoff checklist. You don't need to set your flaps. Increase throttle to maximum and at a speed of 75 knots, lift off. Once clear of the runway, immediately retract your landing gear and reduce your throttle to 2398 RPM, 20.98" of Hg.

Level Off at 200 Feet

Adjust your elevators to bring the plane out of its climb and then fine-tune your vertical speed to 0 FPM by using the elevator trim control. At the end of this phase, you should be at an altitude of 200 feet on a course heading of 275°.

At Two Miles, Turn Right to a Course Heading of 288°

When your DME 1 indicator shows that you are 3.7 miles from the Oakland VOR station, turn right to a course heading of 288°.

Figure 13.1
At approximately 3.7 miles from Oakland, turn right to 288°

Alcatraz Island

Figure 13.2
Passing Alcatraz Island

Pass Alcatraz Island, Then Turn Left to 240°

After passing over the Bay Bridge (the Bay Bridge is not really implemented in FS 5.0; but if it was, you would fly below the deck of the bridge), look ahead to see if you can spot Alcatraz Island, location of the infamous Alcatraz prison. Fly directly towards the island. Then after passing directly over it, turn left to course heading of 240°.

Barnstorm Golden Gate Bridge

You should now see the Golden Gate Bridge directly in front of you. If you look out your left window (press Shift 4 or Shift 7), you can see Fisherman's Wharf and the downtown district. At all times, keep your altitude below 250 feet to enable you to clear the deck of the bridge. Use elevator trim to make small adjustments to nose pitch.

Figure 13.3
Golden Gate Bridge fly-by

Return Home: Turn Left to 83°, Level Off at 800 Feet

With the bridge portion of the flight now completed, turn left to a course heading of 83°. Slightly raise the nose as you do this until you reach an altitude of 800 feet. In the distance, you should see San Francisco and the East Bay hills (scene of the 1991 Oakland Hills firestorm).

Find Oakland VOR Heading on OBI

You will use your OBI 1 to find your way back to Oakland. Since the NAV 1 radio is still tuned to the Oakland VOR, all you need to do is find the VOR radial on your OBI course indicator. To do this, press [V] followed by [+] or [-] to adjust the course indicator until the vertical CDI needle is centered and the TO flag is lit. The course you see displayed on the top course indicator is the heading you should turn to. For example, if the TO flag is on and the CDI needle is centered and you see the top course indicator displaying 95°, then turn your aircraft to a heading of 95° as shown on the directional gyro.

Follow the VOR radial until you see the flashing MALSR strobe lights of Oakland's runway 11.

Begin Landing Approach Three Miles to Runway 29

At three miles to the VOR station, as indicated on your DME 1 indicator, begin the landing checklist. Reduce throttle and adjust your elevators to bring your altitude down to 300 to 500 feet. Next, lower your flaps to 30° and then lower your landing gear.

Landing

Try to line up the aircraft's nose with the tracer strobe lights so that the lights seem to be firing away from you vertically into the runway. If you are on the correct glidepath, your heading will show 110 degrees and your vertical speed will be less than 500 FPM. Follow the landing procedure as outlined in Chapter 8.

Figure 13.4
Landing on Oakland's
Runway 11

USING INBOUND AND OUTBOUND VOR NAVIGATION FOR CROSS-COUNTRY FLIGHTS

Using your NAV/OBI radios and *Flight Simulator*'s new continental U.S. database of Navaids, you can now navigate anywhere in the U.S.[3] You will need to use both NAV/OBI radios to tune in the station behind you as well as the station ahead of you in a radio navigational technique known as Inbound and Outbound VOR tracking. Here's how to do this:

1. Turn to the course you want your aircraft to go.

2. Tune in the VOR station *behind* you on the frequency selector for the NAV 1 radio. Adjust the OBI 1 course indicator until the FROM flag is lit and the CDI needle is centered. The top course indicator tells you the VOR radial you are on *from* the VOR station *behind* you. Watch your DME 1 indicator show the separation distance between you and the VOR station increase. (At 80 miles, you will lose contact with the VOR station.)

3. Tune in the VOR station *ahead* of you on the frequency selector for the NAV 2 radio, although it may not yet be in range. When you are in range, the OBI's CDI needle will flicker, and the FROM/TO flag will appear. Adjust the OBI course indicator until the FROM flag is lit and the CDI needle is centered. The top course indicator tells you the VOR radial you are on *from* the VOR station *ahead* of you.

4. Turn your aircraft to the heading indicated on the *lower* course indicator of the NAV 2/OBI 2 course indicator. You are now headed directly for the next VOR station that is currently tuned in.

5. When you pass over the VOR station, the CDI needle will fluctuate, and the TO/FROM flags will alternate.

6. Turn your aircraft to the new heading you need to take to get you to the *next* VOR station.

7. Repeat steps 2 through 5 as needed for the rest of the trip.

Flight Simulator's VOR stations have a maximum range of 80 miles. This means that from time to time you will be flying out of range of a VOR station along your path. Using the Inbound and Outbound VOR tracking method, if VOR stations are farther than 160 miles apart you will lose contact midway between the two VOR stations. When this happens, simply continue on your present course as indicated on your directional gyro until

---

[3]Although not documented, VOR/NDB's are available for Canada, Mexico, the Bahamas, parts of Europe, and large regions of the Pacific Ocean.

the next VOR station comes into range. In the Learjet flying at cruise speeds, this can take anywhere from 10 to 50 minutes or more of flying time before you regain the next VOR signal.

FLY FROM OAKLAND TO LOS ANGELES IN THE CESSNA

This next trip takes you on a flight from Oakland to Los Angeles, using VOR stations along the way to navigate. We will be using a common air route called Victor 107 on most of the trip and upon reaching the L.A. basin turn to air route Victor 299 to complete the journey. The Victor air route, or "V" ways as they are called, are designated *roads in the sky* for flights below 18,000 feet. Commercial jetliners use the "J" ways, which are air routes above 18,000 feet. The Cessna uses only the Victor air routes since its maximum altitude ceiling is 20,000 feet. Note that your flight will never take you above 9,500 feet MSL.[4]

You will need to use both NAV/OBI radios to tune in two VOR stations simultaneously. The basic technique is to use inbound and outbound VOR tracking as outlined previously.

Because some of the stations are farther apart than 80 miles, you will lose all contact on your NAV radio receivers for both VOR stations. When this happens, don't panic; just fly straight ahead on the course that is shown on your directional gyro. Don't make any turns. In a short time, the next VOR station will come into range. The whole trip takes about three hours and uses about a half a tank of gas.

Figure 13.5 on page 313 shows the navigational chart for the trip.

FLY THE LEARJET FROM OAKLAND TO CHICAGO

Start up the Oakland 27R Takeoff situation using the Situation menu command under the Options menu. Once the runway appears in front of you, make the switch to the Learjet by accessing the Aircraft menu command under the Options menu.

---

[4] Note that since you are flying on a course between 0° and 179°, you are only allowed to fly at odd thousands of feet, plus 500 feet. Thus, since you are on a course of 114°, your altitude can be 7,500, 9,500, 11,500, etcetera. Flying back from L.A., you would need to fly at even thousands of feet, plus 500 feet. Thus, allowable altitudes would be 6,500, 8,500, 10,500, etcetera.

Table 13.1   Oakland to Los Angeles Low Altitude VOR Flight Plan

VOR Station	Name	Frequency	OBI Reading	After Passing VOT Station, Take This Action
Oakland	OAK	116.8	114 FROM	After reaching an altitude of 9,500 feet, turn aircraft to course 114.
Panocche	PXN	112.6	296 FROM	Turn aircraft to course 133.
Avena	AVE	117.1	313 FROM	Turn aircraft to course 129.
Fillmore	FIM	112.5	310 FROM	Turn aircraft to course 148. Tune in LAX VOR, then set OBI on 276 course radial with FROM flag lit. When CDI needle centers on 276 radial, turn aircraft to course 93.
Los Angeles	LAX	113.6	276 FROM	Follow course 93 until LAX is visible.

Stop the Learjet from rolling by engaging the parking brakes ([Ctrl]).

Because you will be flying with limited fuel, you need to make some flight preparations. First, using the distance presented earlier, enter the coordinates for Oakland and Chicago to calculate the number of miles. The Oakland-Chicago distance turns out to be 1,831 statute miles, which means that you will need 4,549 lbs of fuel when cruising at 45,000 feet.[5] Check your fuel gauge now to see that you have enough fuel. The needle should rest in between the four and five on the dial (indicating 4,000 and 5,000 pounds respectively). If you need more fuel, go to the Engine and Fuel dialog box under the Sim menu to add more, *or* taxi over to the fuel quadrangle.

Your Learjet will appear and immediately start rolling. To engage the parking brakes and stop creeping roll, press [Ctrl] + [.].

Next, tune in the Oakland VOR station on your NAV 1 radio to a frequency of 116.8 MHz. Set the OBI course indicator to 53° with the FROM flag lit. On the NAV 2 Radio, tune in the next VOR station along your route, Mina or MVA, at a frequency of 115.1 MHz. Mina is too far to be in range right now, but you may tune it in now in preparation for navigating toward it.

---

[5] For the "J" way air routes above 19,000 feet, you must fly at 4,000-foot intervals beginning at 29,000 feet for course headings 0° to 179° (i.e., 33,000, 37,000, 41,000, 45,000, etcetera.) For course headings 180° to 359°, fly at intervals of 4,000 feet beginning at 31,000 feet (i.e., 35,000 feet, 39,000 feet, 43,000 feet, 47,000 feet).

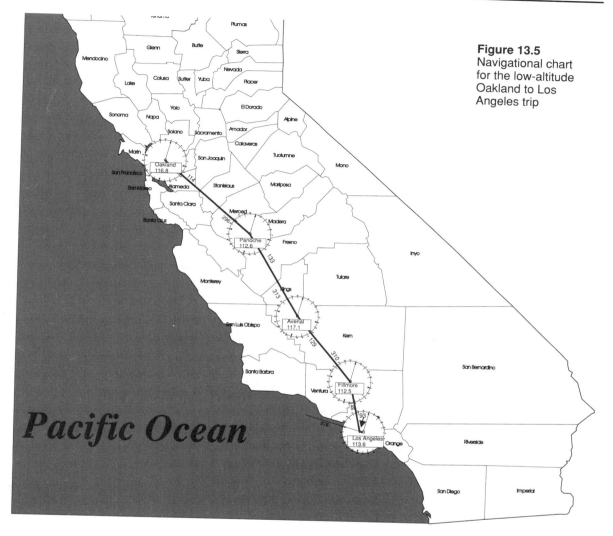

Figure 13.5
Navigational chart for the low-altitude Oakland to Los Angeles trip

Set the flaps to 20° and increase your throttle to maximum. At a speed of 127 knots, execute the takeoff roll and climb. As soon as you clear the runway, retract the landing gear and turn right to a course heading of 53°. When you have gained sufficient altitude and speed, retract the flaps and move the throttle back slightly.

To navigate to Chicago, you will use the Inbound and Outbound VOR Tracking method that was used for the Cessna earlier. The only difference in the procedure is that you must constantly toggle between displaying the OBI 1 and OBI 2 displays. This is because the Learjet's instrument panel

To alternate between OBI 1, OBI 2, and the ADF indicators, press Shift Tab.

Use the autopilot to maintain course heading.

You must turn the autopilot off to make any course corrections.

To have time go by quickly on long flights, click on the simulation speed indicator. (Only 4X speed is possible when autopilot is engaged.)

Be careful when using high-speed rates for the simulation rate control.

only shows one OBI indicator at a time. To bring up OBI 2, *or* to return to OBI 1, you must press the [Shift] [Tab].

For this trip, you will be flying on the J84 air route at an altitude of 45,000 feet. Simply follow the instructions shown in Table 13.2 to navigate to Chicago. Note that some VOR stations are farther than 160 miles apart, and you will lose contact on both VOR radios. Not to worry, though. Just maintain your current course heading, and the next VOR station will soon pop into view on your OBI indicator. The time interval can be as short as 10 minutes or as long as 30 minutes.

Turn on the Autopilot

Once you have reached 45,000 feet and are on the right heading, you can use your autopilot to keep you on course. To do this, select the Autopilot command from the Nav/Com menu and toggle on the Heading lock. Once this is done, you can easily turn the autopilot on and off by clicking on the autopilot indicator on the instrument panel. You must turn off the autopilot to make future course changes.

Use the Simulation Speed Control to Avoid Boredom

If you get too bored passing the time while flying, you can speed up the rate of time by clicking on the simulation rate indicator below the digital clock. Time can be sped up by as much as 128 times normal speed, but all other factors in the program, including fuel consumption, are also sped up. So if 3 hours of simulator time elapse at an accelerated rate and only 3 or 4 minutes of your time pass by, you will have still used up 3 hours of fuel and flown 3 hours, distance. When the autopilot is engaged, your simulation speed rate is limited to 4× normal speed.

Be forewarned that when the simulation speed is increased, all the movements of the aircraft become extremely exaggerated. If you move the controls, the airplane may react violently and crash. It is best to accelerate time only when in level flight. Nonetheless, always be ready to hit the pause key (press [P]) if something goes awry. After pausing the simulation, you can return the speed to 1× normal, then unpause the simulation to restore the aircraft to level flight.

Table 13.2 shows the list of VOR stations you will encounter on your trip from Oakland to Chicago on route J84.

Figure 13.6 on page 317 shows the flight route for the trip from Oakland to Chicago, and from Chicago to New York.

Table 13.2 Oakland to Chicago High Altitude VOR Flight Plan				
VOR Station	**Name**	**Frequency**	**OBI Reading**	**After Passing VOT Station, Take This Action**
Oakland, California	OAK	116.8	53 FROM	Turn to course 53, then climb to 45,000 feet.
Mina, Nevada	MVA	115.1	242 FROM (Inbound) 62 FROM (Outbound)	Turn aircraft to course 62.
Delta, Utah	DTA	116.1	246 FROM (Inbound) 60 FROM (Outbound)	Turn aircraft to course 60.
Meeker, Colorado	EKR	115.2	244 FROM (Inbound) 58 FROM (Outbound)	Turn aircraft to course 58.
Sidney, Nebraska	SNY	115.9	243 FROM (Inbound) 71 FROM (Outbound)	Turn aircraft to course 71.
Wolbach, Nebraska	OBH	114.8	257 FROM (Inbound) 67 FROM (Outbound)	Turn aircraft to course 67.
Dubuque, Iowa	DBQ	115.8	258 FROM (Inbound) 90 FROM (Outbound)	Turn aircraft to course 90.
Northbrook, Illinois	OBK	113.0	274 FROM (Inbound)	Land at Chicago's O'Hare International Airport.

Refueling the Aircraft

After landing, you will want to refuel the aircraft before proceeding on to New York. Head for the yellow fuel rectangle off of runway 32L. Once inside the rectangle, your aircraft will be completely refueled.

FLY THE LEARJET FROM CHICAGO TO NEW YORK

Once refueled, you are ready to continue on your trip to New York. Follow the flight plan listed in Table 13.3 and consult the navigational chart shown in Figure 13.6 for the route to be flown. Again, use the simulation speed control to avoid the monotony of long flights.

This leg of the flight is 738 miles, and you will fly on jet route J584 to J146. From there you will fly to John F. Kennedy International Airport.

Table 13.3   Chicago to New York High Altitude VOR Flight Plan

VOR Station	Name	Frequency	OBI Reading	After Passing VOT Station, Take This Action
Northbrook, Illinois	OBK	113.0	92 FROM (Outbound)	Take off from Chicago O'Hare International, then turn aircraft to course 92
Carleton, Michigan	CRL	115.7	273 FROM (Inbound) 99 FROM (Outbound)	Turn aircraft to course 99
Slate Run, Pennsylvania	SLT	113.9	287 FROM (Inbound) 109 FROM (Outbound)	Turn aircraft to course 109
Williamsport, Pennsylvania	IPT	114.4	290 FROM (Inbound) 118 FROM (Outbound)	Turn aircraft to course 118
Broadway	BWZ	114.2	302 FROM (Inbound) 106 FROM (Outbound)	Turn aircraft to course 106
John F. Kennedy, New York	JFK	115.9	287 FROM (Inbound)	Land at JFK International Airport

Expected fuel burn will be 2,500 pounds. Here is a chronology of a sample flight:

Time	Event
9:25 A.M.	Leave Chicago's O'Hare International on J584 air route using Northbrook VOR (113.0 MHz) radial 92°
9:45 A.M.	Lost Northbrook VOR signal-Out of Range
9:53 A.M.	Acquired Carleton VOR (115.7 MHz)
10:28 A.M.	Lost Carleton VOR signal—Out of Range
10:49 A.M.	Acquired Slate Run VOR (113.9 MHz)
11:34 A.M.	Lost Slate Run VOR—Out of Range
11:40 A.M.	Acquired Williamsport VOR (114.4 MHz)
	Begin Descent to JFK
11:50 A.M.	Acquired Broadway VOR (114.2 MHz)
	Acquired JFK VOR (115.9 MHz). Transfer to air route J146
12:08 A.M.	Final Approach to JFK
12:14 A.M.	Land at JFK

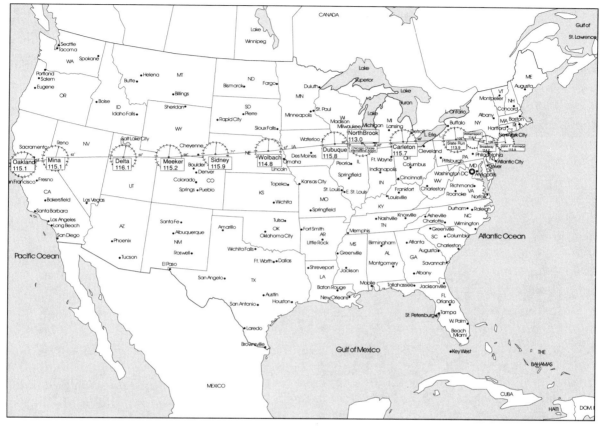

Figure 13.6
Navigational chart for the high-altitude flight from Oakland to Chicago and from Chicago to New York

By the way, don't try landing with Land Me at JFK using the Learjet; you almost certainly will crash. You can only use Land Me with the Cessna.

Figure 13.6 shows the navigational chart for both legs of the Oakland to New York flight with the stopover in Chicago.

FLY YOUR OWN MISSION

You can plan your own flight mission for the Cessna or Learjet if you have some good navigational maps to plot VOR/NDB stations along your route.[6] To simplify matters, in this book the weight calculations are not needed for

Don't use Land Me in the Learjet at JFK.

---

[6]See Chapter 12 for instructions on how to order enroute high-altitude and low-altitude maps from the NOAA.

the Cessna; however, they are necessary for the Learjet. Here is a step-by-step procedure on how to do this.

1. Find the latitude/longitude coordinates of your departure airport and write them down. You can find the airport coordinates in Appendix B for most major airports in the following areas:

   - San Francisco
   - Seattle
   - Los Angeles
   - Chicago
   - New York/Boston
   - Paris, France
   - Munich, Germany

2. Find the latitude/longitude coordinates of your destination airport and write them down. See Appendix B for an airport listing.

3. Use the formula

$$Distance = 69.094 \times \cos^{-1}\{[\sin(A) \times \sin(T)] + [\cos(A) \times \cos(T) \times \cos(L)] - G\}$$

to obtain the distance between the two airports in statute miles. The variables are defined as follows:

A = decimal latitude of first airport[7]
T = decimal latitude of second airport
L = decimal longitude of first airport
G = decimal longitude of second airport

After performing the calculation, write the distance down.

4. Look up your airplane's range capability in the Table 13.4:

Table 13.4 Aircraft Range	
Aircraft	**Range When Fully Fueled**
Cessna	920 statute miles (800 nautical miles)[8]
Learjet	2,528 statute miles (2,196 nautical miles)

[7]See Chapter 12 for a complete description of how to calculate decimal latitude/longitude.
[8]Assumes 75 percent power at 10,000 feet, 88 gallons usable fuel.

If your flight distance is longer than your aircraft's range, you must stop over and refuel at an airport located on your route. Airports that have refueling facilities are listed in Appendix B.

5. Gas up the plane by going to the Engine and Fuel dialog box under the Sim menu. Enter the amount of fuel that you need either as a percentage of a full tank in gallons or in pounds. Note that you must balance the fuel in each tank so that the airplane's center of gravity remains centered. Don't forget to add fuel to the Learjet's auxiliary tanks if needed.

6. For the Learjet, the empty weight of the aircraft is 10,500 pounds. Add to this weight the number of pounds of fuel you will be taking on. Use the relationship 6.6 pounds of fuel per gallon to figure out how many pounds of gas per gallon this adds to the weight of the aircraft. The figure you arrive at is your takeoff weight. Write this number down.

7. For the Learjet, look at your air temperature gauge to ascertain what the ambient temperature is outside. Write the temperature down.

8. For the Learjet, look up the takeoff performance Table 10.4 in Chapter 12. Using the outside air temperature and the takeoff weight of the aircraft, determine how long a runway length is needed.

9. For the Learjet, look up the runway length for the departure airport in the Microsoft manual and see if it is longer or shorter than the needed runway length. If the runway is longer than what you actually need, then it is OK to take off. If the runway is shorter than your takeoff requirements, you cannot take off.

10. On your navigational maps, plot your route and the location of VOR/NDB stations along the way. You will want to fly directly from one VOR/NDB to another VOR/NDB, crossing directly over each one. You will know when you have crossed over a VOR station because the CDI needle will jump from one extreme to the other and the TO/FROM flag will change. (Also the DME indicator tells you your range to the station.) When you cross over an NDB station, the ADF needle will gyrate 180° around. Write down the names, frequencies, and VOR radials for each station in a list. You will use this list to tune in each station as it comes into range and to set the correct OBI VOR radial on the course indicator.

11. The VOR/NDB stations must be no further than 80 miles from your flight route in order for you to use them. However, you can double the VOR range by using a technique called outbound tracking, where you use a VOR station behind you to track a particular radial heading. You then fly on this outbound radial until you come in range of the next VOR station. Using the outbound tracking technique, VOR stations

can be as far as 160 miles apart. Outbound tracking works like this: when you pass over a VOR station, turn to the course you want to take to the next VOR station, *then* retune the OBI's course indicator so that the CDI needle is centered and the FROM flag is lit. Continue flying with the CDI needle centered, and watch as the DME indicator shows the VOR station receding away from you. Tune in the second VOR station on the VOR 2. Hopefully, when you are in range the OBI 2 will come to life. You can still fly on towards the second VOR station even if you have lost the first VOR station and have no VOR signals at all. Just keep to your present course, and in time the second VOR station will come into range.

12. To simplify navigational matters, always plot radials away from the VOR station and then tune in the VOR station so that the FROM flag is lit. When you adjust the course indicator on the OBI so that the CDI needle is centered, the *top* course indicator tells you the radial *from* the VOR station to your plane while the *lower* course indicator tells you the heading you must maintain to stay on this radial and eventually meet up with the VOR station.

C H A P T E R

14

Special Features

This chapter guides you through the many special features that are available under the Entertainment and Flight Analysis menus. You will also learn how to move the aircraft quickly from place to place using a special non-flight mode called slewing and learn how to use the Logbook. Under the Entertainment option for the Options menu, you can fly in dual-player mode with a friend via modem or direct link serial cable, or you can try your hand at formation flying, crop dusting, or EFIS/CFPD navigation. The flight-review tools allow you to analyze your flight maneuvers and landings, record and play back videos of your flights, get instant video replays of the last 50 seconds of flight, and plot your course trajectory for later perusal. Using the special slewing controls, you can quickly move the airplane from place to place or rotate it in three dimensions.

ENTERTAINMENT

There are four options available under the Entertainment menu which you access from the Options menu. They are:

- Dual Player
- Formation Flying
- Crop Duster
- EFIS Navigational Challenges

Inside the Formation Flying and EFIS Navigational Challenges dialog boxes, there are multiple selections that you can choose from. In the next section we will touch upon some of these and learn how to use the Dual Player Mode.

Dual Player Mode via Modem or Direct Link

Flight Simulator can link another player into the simulation using a second computer hooked up to your computer via a serial cable or by modem and a telephone line. If you are hooking up the computers directly via serial cable, *you must use a null-modem cable.* This cable is a special type of serial cable that crosses the internal wires a certain way. It differs from other serial cables, so don't expect a normal serial cable to allow you to communicate directly. You can buy a null-modem serial cable from almost any computer store for $10 to $15. If you have a 25-pin serial port, just ask for a DB25 null-modem serial cable. The DB25 refers to a rectangular connector that has 25 pins; both ends of the null-modem cable should have female connectors; that is, empty sockets that you can connect to the male prongs on the computer's serial COM port. If you have a nine-pin serial port, ask for a DB9 null-modem serial cable, which is a smaller rectangular connector than that of the DB25. Make sure that both ends of the serial cable will fit each serial port on each computer.

When hooking up two computers, use only a null-modem serial cable.

Specifying Dual Player Preferences

When you select the Dual Player command from the Entertainment dialog box, a communications dialog box will open up. In this dialog box you can:

- Select the other plane's color. This is the color that your computer will give to your flying companion's plane on your computer. It is not the color that your flying companion will see for his/her plane. Available colors are:

  - Dark gray
  - Gray
  - Light gray
  - White
  - Red
  - Green
  - Blue
  - Orange
  - Yellow
  - Brown
  - Tan
  - Brick

- Set the autopilot to lock onto the other plane (Autopilot Lock to Other Plane).
- Have your ADF gauge always track the other plane (ADF Track Other Plane, ADF Tracking checkboxes), or have the ADF and DME track the other plane (ADF Track Other Plane, ADF and DME Tracking). You must set the ADF radio to 000 for the ADF needle to point to the other plane or to 001 for the DME indicator to show the distance to the other plane.

- For more realism, allow the other plane to crash into you, or you to crash into it (Other Plane Collision checkbox).
- Set your modem's communications parameters (Communications Preferences button).
- Send a message to the other player if you are already connected (Send Message button).
- Send information about your aircraft to your flying companion's computer (Send Aircraft button).

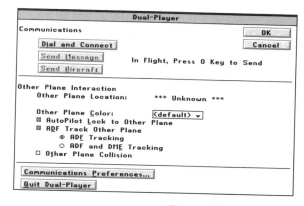

Figure 14.1 shows the Dual Player dialog box options.

Figure 14.1
Dual Player dialog box

Setting the Communications Parameters

Click on the Communications Preferences button to bring up the Dual-Player Communications Preferences dialog box, pictured in Figure 14.2. In this window, you must select the COM port to which your modem or serial cable is hooked up (COM 1 through COM 4 are available)—the baud rate. (The use of the term "baud rate" is really a misnomer here; it should be called bits per second, and it refers to the speed with which your computer is allowed to communicate.) You must also enter the telephone number of the person you wish to call. If you are expecting someone to call you to link up via modem, then you would click the Wait for Ring checkbox, and you would leave the Telephone Number to Dial text box empty.

When linking up two computers, make sure that you set the data transmission rate (baud rate) to the same number for both computers. Use the maximum transmission speed you can for the available hardware. For direct null-modem serial cable hookup (computer to computer, no telephone line), you can use a baud rate of 57,600 bps (bits per second). For high-speed 14,400 bps modems (called V.32bis modems), you can try using 9600 or, if those higher speeds don't work, 4800 or 1200.[1] If you have a slower speed,

Flight Simulator runs most efficiently at modem speeds lower than 9600 bps.

---

[1]Some 14,400 modems are able to use the 19200, 38400, or 57600 bps baud rates even though they can physically transmit at only 14,400 bps. Thus you might try these higher speeds to see if they work with your V.32bis 14.4 modem. The reason you can use a higher speed than your modem can physically transmit is that the modem has a buffer that allows it to absorb data from the computer. When the buffer is full, the modem tells the computer to wait before sending the next chunk of data. The modem will continue to send the data over the telephone at 14,400 bps, its maximum transmission speed; but with the buffer always filled with data, the modem is never left waiting for the computer to send data.

2,400 bps modem, use the 2,400 bps setting. If you have a 9,600 bps modem, try using the 9,600 bps setting. (Your 9,600 bps modem might have a data buffer; if so try using speeds higher than 9,600 bps.)

The rest of the options in the Dual Player Communications Preferences dialog box allow you to customize your modem's operation. If you have an error-correcting, data-compression capable high-speed modem, *you must have these features turned off.* Flight Simulator *will not work with data compression or error correction turned on in your modem.* To turn off data compression and error correction, type in the following characters after the modem initialization string[2]:

&Q0

You must turn off data compression and error correction in your modem for Dual-Player mode.

Note that some modems use a different command to shut off compression and error correction. If you are not sure, consult your modem's operation manual.

Your modem initialization string would thus look like this:

AT&F&C1&D2X4Q0V1S0=0&Q0

Table 14.1 lists what the individual modem commands do in the above-listed modem initialization string.

Establishing the Modem Connection

Using modems, you can fly *Flight Simulator* with friends no matter how far away they live. You can see their plane fly and they can see your plane fly. You can even send each other messages that will appear on screen.

If you are placing the call, here are the steps to follow when connecting via modem:

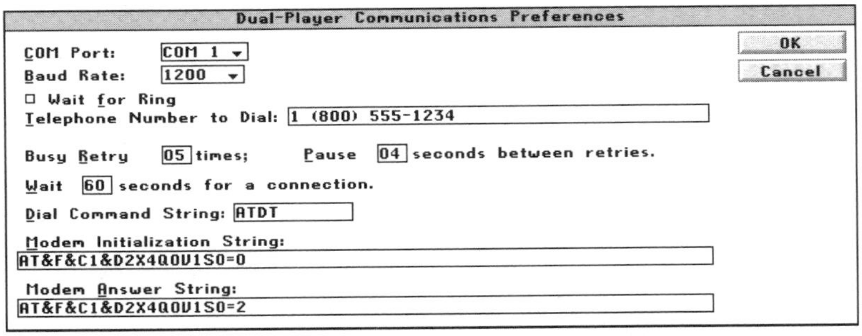

Dual-Player Communications Preferences

COM Port: COM 1 ▾
Baud Rate: 1200 ▾
☐ Wait for Ring
Telephone Number to Dial: 1 (800) 555-1234

Busy Retry 05 times; Pause 04 seconds between retries.
Wait 60 seconds for a connection.
Dial Command String: ATDT
Modem Initialization String:
AT&F&C1&D2X4Q0V1S0=0
Modem Answer String:
AT&F&C1&D2X4Q0V1S0=2

OK
Cancel

1. Under the Options menu, select Entertainment.
2. In the Entertainment dialog box, choose Dual Player and then click OK.
3. In the Dual Player dialog box that next opens, click on the Communications Preferences button.

Figure 14.2
Dual Player Communications Preferences

[2]A "string" is a term used with computers to describe a series of characters or numbers.

Table 14.1 Modem Command Summary	
Hayes Command	**Function Description**
AT	Attention modem, listen for commands to follow
&F	Load Hayes-compatible factory default modem settings
&C1	Track data carrier of external modem to see if it is on. Report the results back.
&D2	Monitor DTR (Data Terminal Ready Line) and if off, hang up the telephone
X4	Modem sends a message to *Flight Similator* if a proper connection has been made (i.e., "connect 9600")
Q0	Modem sends a message to *Flight Simulator* such as "OK," "Busy," or "Ring"
V1	Makes messages appear as words rather than as number codes
S0=0	Disable auto-answer mode for your modem. (Your AA light on an external modem should be snuffed out.)
S0=2	Turn auto-answer mode on for your modem. You can now receive modem calls. (Your AA light on an external modem should be lit.)
&Q0	Turn off Error Correction, Data Buffering, and Data Compression
L2	Medium modem speaker volume
M1	Modem speaker on until other modem answers
ATDT	Tone dial a telephone number (eg., ATDT 8437060).

4. Pull down the COM Port listbox and select the COM port your modem is currently using.

5. Pull down the Baud Rate listbox and choose your modem's maximum baud rate. If you have a 14,400 bps modem, try using 9,600. Make sure your friend is also using the same baud rate.

6. Your friend must now click the Wait for Ring checkbox.

7. Since you are placing the call, type in the telephone number of your friend. If the call is long distance, be sure to type in a 1 before the area code.

Flight Simulator works best with external modems that have hardware "handshaking" serial cables. If you have an internal modem, you don't have any serial cables and don't need to worry about this.

8. Click the OK button to return to the Dual Player dialog box.

9. Click the Dial and Connect button to have the modem connect you to your friend's computer.

You should now hear a dial tone as your modem dials your friend's computer. If all goes well, your friend's computer will pick up the line and answer with a harsh screech. Your computer will retort with an even harsher static-like sound, and you should soon be connected. If something goes wrong, you need to adjust the baud rate, disconnect error correction or data compression on your modem, or perhaps send a different modem string to properly initialize your modem. You might have to enter Q0 after the modem initialization string to disable your modem's error correction and data compression before the connection can be made to work.

When the connection is complete, you will see the message, "Connected!" on your screen. At this point, your computer will exchange latitude/longitude aircraft position coordinates, and you will soon be able to send messages to your friend.

To quit Dual Player mode and hang up the modem, go to the Dual Player dialog box and click on the Quit Dual Player button. (Select the Entertainment command under the Options menu, then click the Dual Player option.)

How to quit Dual
Player mode

Direct Connect Using a Serial Null-Modem Cable

The link-up procedure for a serial cable direct connection, computer to computer, is slightly different than the modem setup.

Follow these steps:

1. Under the Options menu, select Entertainment.

2. In the Entertainment dialog box, choose Dual Player, and then click OK.

3. In the Dual Player dialog box that next opens, click on the Communications Preferences button.

4. Pull down the COM Port listbox and select the COM port the null-modem serial cable is currently using on the first computer. On the second computer, select the COM port that the second computer is using.

5. Pull down the Baud Rate listbox and choose your computer's baud rate. You can choose the fastest speed of 57,600 bps, but be forewarned: speeds less than 9600 are best for *Flight Simulator*. Make sure the second computer is also using the same baud rate.

6. Check to make sure that the Wait for Ring checkbox is toggled off for both computers.

7. Erase all the text in the Modem Initialization String textbox for both computers. To do this, select the textbox and press [Backspace] until the box is cleared of all text; then press [Enter]. (You *must* do this: otherwise, the Direct Connect button will not appear in the Dual Player dialog box.)

8. Click the OK button to return to the Dual Player dialog box.

9. Click the Direct Connect button, and the program will begin the connection procedure. (The Direct Connect button will replace the Dial and Connect button.)

When the connection is complete, you will see the message "Connected!" on your screen. At this point, your computer will exchange latitude/longitude aircraft position coordinates, and you will soon be able to send messages to your friend.

To quit Dual Player mode for directly connected computers, go to the Dual Player dialog box and click on the Quit Dual-Player button. (Select the Entertainment command under the Options menu, then click the Dual Player option.)

How to quit Dual Player mode

How to Send and Receive Messages in Dual Player Mode

You can send text messages to your friend that will appear on his screen. To do this, follow this procedure:

1. Under the Options menu, select Entertainment.

2. In the Entertainment dialog box, choose Dual Player and then click OK.

3. Click the Send Message button. At the bottom of the screen, a text box will appear, and you can type in your message.

4. When you are finished with the message (it can be only as long as the text box is wide), press [Enter]. You can then resume flight.

Once you have sent your first message using the Send Message button, you can send all subsequent messages directly from the keyboard by pressing [0] (zero key on the main keyboard, not the numeric keypad). Type in the message in the message textbox that pops open and then press [Enter] to send the message.

Messages sent to you by your friend will appear at the bottom of the screen. If you have sound turned on, you will hear an audible beep each time you receive a new message.

Your first message must be sent using the Send Message button in the Dual-Player dialog box. Each subsequent message can be sent directly from the keyboard by pressing [0] (the zero key on the main keyboard, not the numeric keypad).

How to Find Your Friend's Plane in Dual Player Mode

It is often difficult to locate your friend's plane while in Dual Player mode. To remedy this, *Flight Simulator 5.0* includes the following multi-player utilities:

New messages are accompanied by an audible beep if your sound is turned on.

- *Send Aircraft*: Before choosing any of the other multi-player utilities, you should click this button in the Dual Player dialog box. *Flight Simulator* will send information about your aircraft to your friend's computer so that both aircraft can be displayed accurately.
- *Track View*: Track View displays your friend's aircraft on your cockpit windshield no matter where he is. Press S to cycle between Cockpit, Tower, Track, and Spot Views. This view is only available in Dual Player mode. Using your second 3-D view window, you can have both your cockpit view and the track view of the other aircraft on screen simultaneously.
- *Other Plane Color*: Change your friend's aircraft color as it is displayed on your screen. Go to the Dual Player dialog box and pull down the Other Plane Color listbox. Choose a distinctive color that you can readily identify.
- *Airports*: Place both aircraft at the same airport using the Airports command under the World menu.
- *Other Plane Location*: In the Dual Player dialog box, you can see the latitude/longitude coordinates of your friend's current aircraft position. Use the Set Exact Location command under the World menu to match these latitude/longitude coordinates for your plane. You don't need to use this option if you use the Airports command listed previously.
- *Quick Catch Up*: Press Ctrl Spacebar to catch up quickly to the other plane. Make sure that both of you are on the ground or in the air simultaneously: otherwise, you will crash.
- *Smoke System*: Press I to activate the smoke emitters on your aircraft or have your friend activate his smoke emitters. At great distances, this will make it easier to see where the aircraft are.
- *ADF Track Other Plane*: Clicking on this option checkbox in the Dual Player dialog box allows you to track your friend's aircraft on your ADF gauge as if the other plane were an NDB radio beacon. However, to use this feature you must also click on the check box and tune in your ADF receiver to 000. To also have your DME indicator show the distance to your friend's plane, click the ADF and DME Tracking checkbox and tune in your ADF receiver to 001. Make sure that your ADF gauge is displayed on your instrument panel. If it is not, press Shift Tab to switch between the OBI 2 and ADF gauge. With this feature enabled, the ADF needle will show you the direction of the other airplane in relation to your aircraft's nose. If the needle points to the 9, for example, then your friend's plane is directly to your right. To aim your aircraft towards your friend's plane, turn the aircraft until the needle is centered on 0.

- *Autopilot Lock to Other Plane:* Both you and your friend should each click on this checkbox in the Dual Player dialog box to have the autopilot fly towards the other plane. Make sure that you are both flying at approximately the same altitude and that the ALT (Altitude Lock) checkbox in the Autopilot dialog box is toggled on.

Formation Flying

The Formation Flying option allows you to follow a second computer generated airplane in one of several different modes that you can select. The second airplane often performs rather reckless flight maneuvers that are aerobatic in nature, so you will need some experience and practice to keep up. Just follow the smoke puff contrails of the plane in front of you and try to keep up. The available modes are available:

- San Francisco Obstacle Course
- Walls in the Sky
- Bridges and Towers
- Manhattan Tour
- Night Flight-Chicago
- WW 1 Hanger Buzz
- NAS North Island Carrier

✈ **Tip:** Use (Spacebar) to instantly catch up with the lead plane in formation flying.

Crop Duster

The Crop Duster Entertainment option gives you the opportunity to try your hand at spraying a field with insecticides. You are scored by how many blocks, or acres, of land you can spray within a given time frame. The entire field is broken up into 64 acres; each acre that you successfully cover with spray turns black. You can see how you are doing by looking at your score card that is displayed on the right side of

Figure 14.3
Crop dusting

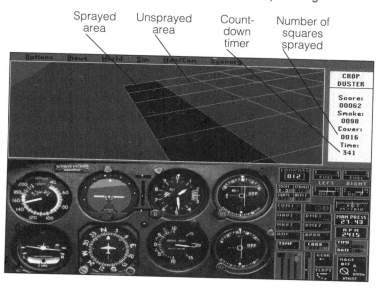

Sprayed area   Unsprayed area   Count-down timer   Number of squares sprayed

the cockpit window, or you can call up the map and see how many squares are black. The remaining green squares need to be sprayed before your time is up. To start spraying, press ⬚. Press ⬚ again to stop spraying.

EFIS Navigational Situations

The EFIS Entertainment option allows you to fly your aircraft in four different ILS landing scenarios using the advanced EFIS (Electronic Flight Information System) cockpit display. Each scenario begins with a landing approach with the EFIS/CFPD (Command Flight Path Display) projecting rectangles on your cockpit windshield leading to the airport. To follow the correct glidepath or course, you must keep your plane flying through each rectangle. Note that in the Chicago Learjet Cruise to O'Hare scenario, the CFPD rectangles do not lead you directly to the runway. Once you have the airport in sight, you need to veer to the right or left to land on one of the parallel runways.

The following EFIS navigational situations are available:

- San Francisco 28L ILS Approach
- Thunderstorms at Champaign
- Learjet Cruise to O'Hare
- Stormy Approach to Oakland

FLIGHT REVIEW

Flight Simulator includes special tools to give you feedback on your maneuvers, landings, and crashes. Using a course plotter, FS 5.0 allows you to track your aircraft's course and see how close to a particular path you were flying. There is also a video recorder for taping flight, and an instant replay camera for recording the last 50 seconds of flight. By using these tools, you can improve your flying abilities by analyzing the flight maneuvers afterward.

To see all your flight review options, select the Flight Analysis command from the Options menu. You will see the Flight Analysis dialog box open up, as pictured in Figure 14.4.

Figure 14.4
Flight Analysis
dialog box

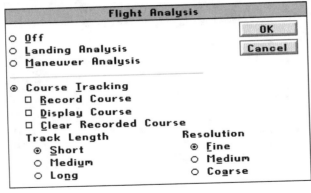

Landing Analysis

Landing Analysis reports your landing speed and flight path to the runway. It is only activated when your airplane comes within 100 feet above the runway.

To activate Landing Analysis, perform these steps:

1. Select the Flight Analysis command from the Options menu. The Flight Analysis dialog box will open.

2. Toggle on the Landing Analysis radio button.

3. Click the OK button to return to the simulation.

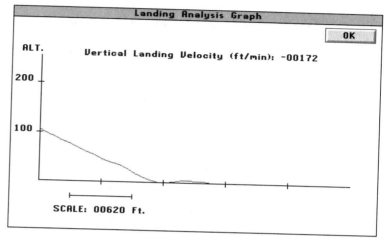

Figure 14.5
Landing analysis

Maneuver Analysis

To display a two-dimensional path of your airplane's flight maneuvers, select Maneuver Analysis in the Flight Analysis dialog box. Maneuver Analysis differs from Landing Analysis in that course recording begins the moment you leave the Flight Analysis dialog box. To end the Maneuver Analysis and bring up the report, press ⟨\⟩. The graph is then displayed, showing your flight path over the ground.

To activate Maneuver Analysis, perform these steps:

1. Select the Flight Analysis command from the Options menu. The Flight Analysis dialog box will open.

2. Toggle on the Maneuver Analysis radio button.

3. Click the OK button to return to the simulation.

You can turn off Maneuver or Landing Analysis by toggling on the appropriate radio button in the Flight Analysis dialog box.

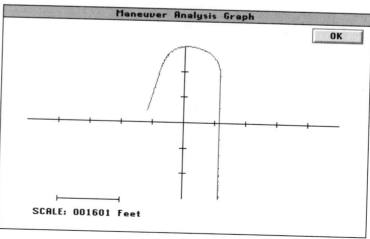

Figure 14.6
Maneuver analysis

Recording and Playing Back Videos of Your Flights

You can record and play back videos of your flights, or of other flights by using Flight Simulator's built-in Video Recorder.

To play a video, follow these steps:

1. Select Video Recorder from the Options menu.
2. In the Video Recorder dialog box, highlight the name of the video you want to play.
3. Click the Play Selected Video button.
4. Click the OK button to start the video.

To end video playback, press (Esc).

To record a video, follow these steps:

1. Select Video Recorder from the Options menu.
2. Click the Record New Video button.
3. In the Record New Video dialog box, choose the recording interval you want. You can choose between 1 second or 5 second intervals. Choosing 1 second intervals gives you a smoother and more accurate video because you are recording 1 frame every second; while the 5 second recording interval will be jerkier, but will offer a longer video recording time.
4. Click the OK button. The Video Recorder is now on, and you can see a status report on the lower left corner of the screen.
5. To stop recording, press (\). You will see a Stop Video Recording dialog box.

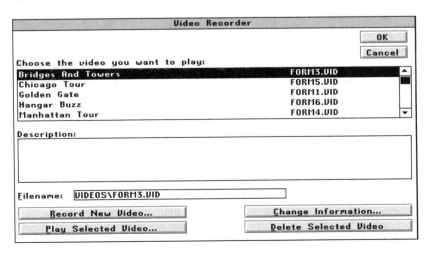

Figure 14.7
The Video Recorder
dialog box

6. Type a title for your video, then click one of the following buttons:

- *Save Video*: Saves your video with the title you gave.
- *Cancel*: Returns to the simulator and resumes video recording.
- *Review*: Reviews your video.
- *Discard Video*: Returns to *Flight Simulator* without saving the video.

Course Tracking

Using the Course Tracking option, you can record the course you flew and display it in your 3-D view window 1 and Map window (but not the 3-D view window 2). The length of the plotted track can be displayed in Short (5 line segments), Medium (15-line segments), or Long (30 line-segments), and the resolution can be set to Fine, Medium, or Coarse. For short flights, use Fine resolution, while for longer flights use Medium or Coarse. Since memory for course tracking is limited, when you run out of memory the oldest part of your course is erased.

You can simultaneously record and view your course as it is being tracked. To do this, simply click on both the Record Course checkbox and the Display Course checkbox. To clear a previously recorded course, click the Clear Recorded Course checkbox. You can see the various Course Tracking options in Figure 14.4.

Instant Replay

Using Instant Replay, you can play back the last 50 seconds of flight at any time. To do this, follow these steps:

1. Select Instant Replay from the Options menu.
2. In the Replay Final Seconds dialog box, type in the number of seconds you want to have replayed in the Replay Final Seconds text box. You can enter from 1 to 50 seconds.
3. Choose the Replay Speed. Enter a percentage of normal speed. (100 percent is normal speed, 200 percent is twice normal speed, and 50 percent is half normal speed.)
4. Click the Repeat Replay check box if you want to have the instant replay repeated indefinitely in a loop. Press [Esc] to stop the instant replay loop.
5. Click the OK button to start the replay of the last few seconds of your flight.

6. After the replay has finished (if it hasn't, you can press [Esc] to stop it), click the OK button in the Instant Replay dialog box, then press [P] to resume flight.

USING THE LOGBOOK

To keep track of your flight time, the aircraft you flew, and the type of flying involved, you can use *Flight Simulator*'s logbook. To create a new logbook for the first time, follow these steps:

1. Select the Logbook command from the Options menu.

2. In the Standard Pilot Logbook dialog box, click the Create Logbook button.

3. In the Create Logbook dialog box that next opens, click OK to accept the proposed name for the new logbook. If you want to change the name, simply type a new name in the textbox. After clicking OK, you will be returned to the Standard Pilot Logbook dialog box.

Any flight that is less than six minutes will not be recorded in the logbook.

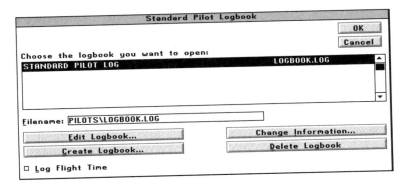

Figure 14.8
Creating your first logbook

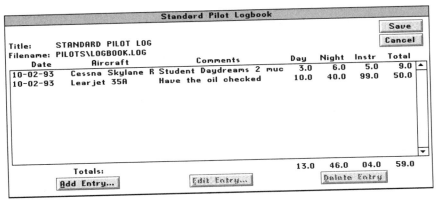

Figure 14.9
Editing the Standard Pilot Logbook

4. Select the logbook you wish to use and then toggle on the Log Flight Time checkbox.

Your logbook is now open and will record your current flight. If you prefer to have the logbook always on, go to the General Preferences dialog box under the Options menu and click on the Log Flight Time check box. Then, whenever you start up *Flight Simulator*, the Logbook will always be on.

Other options in the Standard Pilot Logbook allow you to add new entries, review and edit the logbook, delete entries, change the name of a logbook, delete a logbook, or create other new logbooks. In fact, you can create a logbook for each person in your family, or you can create a separate logbook for each airplane.

SLEWING AROUND THE *FLIGHT SIMULATOR* WORLD

Slewing is a special non-flight mode that allows you to move quickly from point to point in the *Flight Simulator* world. In addition to moving the aircraft in three dimensions (called translation), you can also reorient the plane to any attitude (called rotation). This mode is extremely useful for repositioning your aircraft anywhere in the *Flight Simulator* world. In addition, you can easily view scenery out of your cockpit window and move the aircraft to vantage points that you could not attain in ordinary flight.

The slewing controls will only work when you enter slew mode. To enter and exit slew mode, press [Y].

There are two types of slewing motion: translation and rotation. These are described in the next section along with a list of keyboard and mouse slewing controls.

Translation

Translation is the movement that occurs when you move your plane from one location to another. You can translate the aircraft up and down, left and right, or backwards and forwards using the translation slew keys. With the mouse, you can only translate forward or backward by rolling the mouse forwards or backwards.

Rotation

Rotation is the revolving or turning motion that occurs around one of the plane's axes. Unlike translation, during rotation the plane's position in space does not change. There are three axes of rotation:

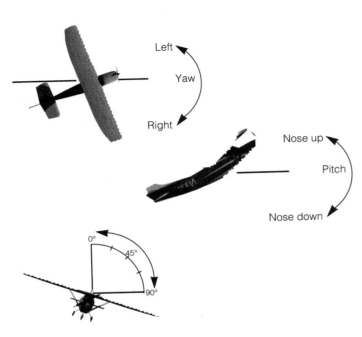

- *Yaw* refers to the rotation about the aircraft's vertical axis. When you change the course heading left or right, you are yawing.

- *Roll* refers to the rotation about the aircraft's longitudinal axis. For example, when the wings bank left or right, this is considered a roll movement.

- *Pitch* refers to the rotation about the aircraft's lateral axis. Pitching causes the plane's nose to go up or down.

Figure 14.10 shows the three rotational movements possible in slew mode.

Using the keyboard, you can effect all the rotational slew movements. With the mouse, however, you can only yaw the aircraft left or right by moving the mouse left or right.

Figure 14.10
Slewing rotation about the airplane's three axes of revolution: yaw, roll, and pitch

Slewing Translation Using the Keyboard

The following keys allow you to translate the aircraft while in slew mode:

SLEW TRANSLATION	KEY (FUNCTION KEYS ON TOP)	KEY (FUNCTION KEYS ON LEFT)
Up or Down in Altitude		
Up Slowly	Q	Q
Up Quickly	F4	F2
Down Slowly	A	A
Down Quickly	F1	F10
Freeze	5	5
Forward and Backward		
Forward	8	8
Backward	2	2
Freeze	5	5
Sideways		
Left	4	4
Right	6	6
Freeze	5	5

Slewing Rotation Using the Keyboard

The following keys allow you to reorient the aircraft's pitch, bank (roll), and heading (yaw) while in slew mode:

SLEW TRANSLATION	KEY (FUNCTION KEYS ON TOP)	KEY (FUNCTION KEYS ON LEFT)
Pitch		
Nose up slowly	9 (on main keyboard)	9 (on main keyboard)
Nose up fast	F5	F1
Freeze	F6	F5
Nose down fast	F8	F9
Nose down slowly	0 (on main keyboard)	F7
Bank (Roll)		
Left	7	7
Right	9	9
Freeze	5	5
Heading (Yaw)		
Left	1	1
Right	3	3
Freeze	5	5

Other keyboard slewing functions include the following:

Z   Toggle position display between On/Off/Latitude Longitude/North–East Coordinate Systems

Spacebar   Reset Aircraft Orientation so that it is level:

Heading: North
Pitch: 0°
Bank: 0°

Using the Mouse to Slew

While in slew mode, the mouse can also be used to move the plane. First enter slew mode by pressing Y. Then to activate the mouse, press the right mouse button so that the mouse pointer disappears. To move forward, move the mouse forward; to move backward, move the mouse backward. To rotate the plane left or right, roll the mouse left or right. Notice that the plane is merely rotating in place and not moving from its present position. To stop all motion, click the left mouse button. To make the mouse pointer reappear, click the right mouse button.

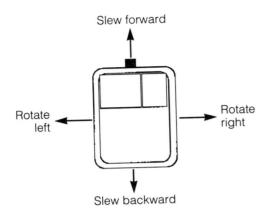

Figure 14.11
Using the mouse
to slew

SIMULATOR INFORMATION

The Simulator Information dialog box is a new feature of *Flight Simulator* that gives you vital memory management information about your computer. In this dialog box, you can learn how much conventional and expanded (EMS) memory is being allocated to *Flight Simulator* and what simulator files are being used.

EASTER EGGS

Some interesting tidbits for you to discover on your own. I won't give away the surprise, but try finding them:

- While in Champaign, Illinois, if you turn on Scenery Density to Dense and then slew your aircraft around into the BAO Headquarters building, I think you will be surprised by what you see.
- If you look into one of the hangars at Chicago's O'Hare International (again, with Scenery Density set to Dense), you will see something unusual.
- Check out the backside of the Statue of Liberty in the default scenery for New York.

Figure 14.12
Simulator information
dialog box

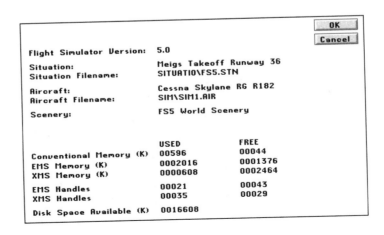

CHAPTER
15

Scenery Enhancements
and Add-Ons

In this chapter you will learn about some of the amazing add-on products and accessories that are available for *Flight Simulator 5.0*. The list presented here is by no means complete; only a representative sample is presented. Prices are shown as suggested retail. Don't be discouraged by some of the prices you see; in most cases, the street price is much lower. If you shop around and compare prices, especially for hardware, you can find terrific deals.

PURCHASING ADD-ON SCENERY DISKS

Probably the most interesting aspect of *Flight Simulator 5.0* is its new photorealistic scenery. You can now buy special scenery disks that fall into two categories. Microsoft's scenery enhancements for FS 5.0 blend detailed hand-drawn landscapes (for close-up viewing) and satellite images (for aerial views). These products fit on one floppy disk and use only 2–3 megabytes of disk space. Mallard's scenery is all satellite and is most effective for farther range viewing. These products ship with several disks and can consume upwards of 17 megabytes of hard disk space! In the future, it is hoped that new scenery will be available on CD-ROM disks which have capacities of 580 megabytes of data. Perhaps not too long from now, you will be able to order the entire world's scenery database on CD-ROM at relatively low cost.

There are several add-on photorealistic scenery packages available right now:

- *Microsoft's New York Scenery*
- *Microsoft's Paris Scenery*
- *Mallard's San Francisco Scenery*
- *Mallard's Washington, D.C., Scenery*

In addition, Mallard will soon be releasing the following photorealistic scenery packages:

- *Las Vegas/Grand Canyon*
- *Seattle*
- *Los Angeles*
- *San Diego*

Microsoft's New Scenery Software

The Microsoft Paris and New York scenery offer photorealistic satellite imagery combined with the revolutionary new FS 5.0 cybergraphics/ray-tracing technology. It also takes up less disk space and memory and offers

Figure 15.1
Microsoft's New York scenery

breathtaking renditions of city buildings and bridges. This combination does not slow the display frame rate as much as the Mallard package. The Microsoft Paris and New York scenery is so stunning it will knock your socks off! Pilots can fly right into downtown and outlying areas of each city and buzz the famous buildings or gain some altitude and see things from a satellite view. Check out Notre Dame in Paris at night for the lit-up stained glass windows. Or fly right into the heart of Wall Street for the full flavor of New York.

The cybergraphic buildings and infrastructure are modeled after the real thing and will give you a real sensation of flying around both cities. The photorealistic satellite imagery of the New York landscape becomes visible while flying at altitudes of 4,500 feet or higher. Below 4,500 feet, you will see detailed ground scenery. For the Paris scenery add-on, the photorealistic satellite imagery of the ground becomes visible only at altitudes of 9,000 feet or higher. Below 9,000 feet, you will see buildings and synthesized ground scenery similar to the technique for New York scenery add-ons. The closer you fly, the more detail you see!

Microsoft's Paris and New York sell for a suggested retail price of $39.95.

Contact:

Microsoft Corporation
One Microsoft Way
Redmond, Washington
Telephone: 206-882-8080
USA Toll Free: 800-426-9400

Mallard's New Photorealistic Scenery

Mallard's new photorealistic scenery for Microsoft's *Flight Simulator 5.0* combines real-time, ray-traced images and high-resolution cybergraphics to take you over the prominent buildings of the metropolitan areas (and even the city lights at night) and all of the major bridges like the Golden Gate, San Mateo and Oakland Bay Bridges. You'll takeoff and land at San Francisco International, Oakland, Alameda Naval Air Station, and other airports complete with runways, taxiways, main buildings, lighting and NAVAIDS. You can fly over photorealistic scenery from Napa in the North Bay all the way to San Jose in the South Bay. Other points of interest include Marin, Southern Napa Valley, San Francisco, Oakland/Berkeley East Bay Hills (Tour the devastating 1991 Oakland Hills Firestorm Zone), Concord/Walnut Creek, and the Santa Cruz mountains. For best viewing of the photorealistic imagery, you should fly at an altitude of 2,000 feet.

Figure 15.2 Mallard's
San Francisco
photorealistic scenery

Soon to be released, Mallard's Washington, D.C., scenery for *Flight Simulator 5.0* will offer the same photorealism that the San Francisco scenery has.

The San Francisco and Washington, D.C., scenery is available from Mallard for a suggested retail price of $49.95.

Contact:
    Mallard Software, Inc.
    3207 Justin Road
    Flower Mound, Texas 75028
    Telephone: 214-539-2575

Figure 15.3 Mallard's Washington, D.C., photorealistic scenery

SubLOGIC's USA East and USA West

Although SubLOGIC's new USA East and USA West scenery do not use photorealistic scenery, they still can be used with *Flight Simulator 5.0*. USA East and USA West are based on the older FS 4.0 graphics technology, which is based on 16-color scenery with a maximum resolution of 640 horizontal by 340 vertical lines.

Figure 15.4 SubLOGIC's USA East

USA East gives all important scenery, airports, and navigational aids east of the Mississippi River, while USA West gives you everything west of the Mississippi. Together, USA East and USA West give you a comprehensive visual package of the entire U.S., plus every paved public access airport (over 7,500 in all!) and all VOR/NDB and ILS radio beacons. A continuous flow of glittering cities, airports, rivers, highways, and railroads (the entire national infrastructure) makes flying cross-country more fun than ever before.

Both USA East and USA West provide instant in-flight information about any airport; elevation, runway dimensions and orientations, as well as ILS approaches. Huge floating traffic patterns and runway approach arrows guide you down to a safe landing at the destination airport. The flight assignment system allows you to print out detailed flight logs of your trips, helping you to develop your flying and navigational skills.

Put yourself at the controls of a Boeing 737, 747, 767, Airbus 320, or a Shorts 360 twin-engine turboprop in Flight Assignment: ATP (Airline Transport Pilot). ATP is a stand-alone program that does not require *Flight Simulator 5.0*. In ATP you can select departure and destination airports, take

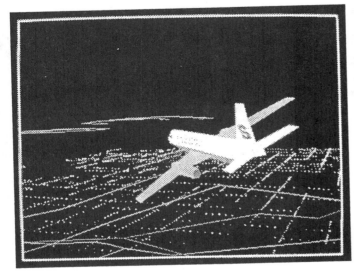

Figure 15.5 Air transport pilot running USA East

on fuel and passengers, then perform the takeoff checklist. Air Traffic Control keeps you in constant radar contact and will speak to you (if you have a SoundBlaster sound card) if you deviate from the assigned heading. Modern full-color weather radar lets you navigate safely through any type of weather. ATP provides multiple instrument panels for each of the four different commercial transport jets you can fly. Separate flight equations and power/engine parameters are used for each aircraft. The program contains over 350 U.S. cities at the proper latitude and longitude coordinates, with textured ground patterns and terrain features. Available aircraft avionics include NAV, ILS, DME, ADF, IRS, RMI indicator, and radio altimeter. In addition, you get a heavy aircraft flight manual, four maps covering the entire continental U.S., and 75 approach charts.

SubLOGIC also makes scenery, other flight simulations, and many other useful add-on products for FS 4.0. Their well-regarded scenery collections for Hawaii, California, Japan, and Great Britain are indispensable for the globe-trotting *Flight Simulator* pilot.

Suggested retail prices are as follows:

USA East..$69.95
USA West...$69.95
Flight Assignment: ATP (Airline Transport Pilot)..........$59.95
California Scenery Collection..$59.95
Great Britain Scenery Collection......................................$59.95
Hawaiian Odyssey Scenery Collection.............................$29.95
Western European Tour Scenery.......................................$29.95

Contact:

SubLOGIC
501 Kenyon Road
Champaign, IL 61820
Telephone: 217-359-8482
USA Toll Free 800-637-4983

Figure 15.6
Maps and plotters
come with SubLOGIC's
scenery software

SCENERY SHAREWARE

Many *Flight Simulator* enthusiasts all over the world have created their own scenery using the older FS 4.0 Aircraft and Scenery Designer. Much of this scenery is available free as "shareware" and can be downloaded easily from bulletin boards and on-line services all over the world. The Flight Simulator Forum on CompuServe has an extensive library of scenery which covers many parts of the world. For a description of the Flight Simulator Forum, see the section entitled "Flight Simulator Forum."

OTHER SHAREWARE SOFTWARE

Along with shareware scenery software, there are many shareware programs and utilities that allow you to get the most out of *Flight Simulator*. Again, these programs can be found on many on-line services, such as CompuServe's Flight Simulator Forum and on many BBS (Bulletin Board Systems).

Two interesting shareware programs that are highly recommended are:

- *Final Approach 2.2 for Windows*: A utility for creating, printing, and viewing instrument approach plates for use with PC-based flight simulators
- *Frame Counter for Flight Simulator 5.0*: This unique utility from Microsoft enables you to display your frame rate on your transponder. It allows you to determine exactly how well your PC is running FS 5.0.

Final Approach 2.2 for Windows

Most modern flight simulators have reached a level of realism that makes the use of real-world Instrument Approach Plates (IAPs) almost a necessity. Unfortunately, only a few charts generally are included with these programs, and the same is true for most of the currently available scenery disks. On the other hand, countless ASD-Sceneries and AAF-Adventures are waiting to be downloaded from bulletin board systems all around the world. This shareware scenery would be more usable if their designers had found a way to include digitized Instrument Approach Plates with their files. This is where Final Approach comes in handy.

With Final Approach you can display and design your own Instrument Approach Plates right on screen. You may also generate vectorized hard copies in the highest resolution available on your printer. Unlike scanned IAPs, the plates you design with Final Approach use little disk space (only around 1K each) and thus can be distributed easily. For obvious reasons, the IAPs you generate are not to be used for real-world navigation.

Final Approach 2.2 is available on CompuServe's Flight Simulator Forum, Library 2.

Features

Because the resolution of current-generation monitors does not allow a complete chart to remain easily readable on screen, Final Approach displays the plan and the profile view in two separate windows. The printing routines, however, will generate a single, realistic IAP with plan and profile view combined.

Plan View: Available Elements

- 1 runway
- 1 approach line with optional procedure turn, localizer, and Middle Marker
- 1 teardrop course reversal symbol
- 1 Outer Marker
- 3 VOR facilities
- 3 NDB facilities
- 5 intersections, placed on the approach track automatically on request
- 15 straight lines
- 16 formatted text strings of up to 256 characters and 1 to 3 lines each
- 6 NAVAID boxes to label VORs and NDBs, automatic Morse code included
- 1 rounded box to label ILS approaches, automatic Morse code included

Profile View: Available Elements

- 1 glidepath with nine user-definable segments
- 1 glide slope symbol for ILS approaches
- 2 symbols for Outer and Middle Marker
- 1 VOR symbol
- 1 NDB symbol
- 5 intersection symbols
- 12 formatted text strings of up to 256 characters and 1 to 3 lines each
- 6 intersection labels, automatically formatted
- 4 altitude labels with automatic calculation and placement of altitude above ground level
- Complete Missed Approach instructions, automatically formatted

- Decision height, circle-to-land altitudes for categories A, B, C, and D
- Timing table automatically calculated and formatted

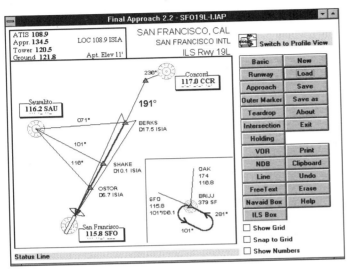

Figure 15.7
Final Approach 2.2 for Windows

Final Approach is distributed as an evaluation version. It is fully functional in its capabilities to design and save realistic Instrument Approach Plates (IAPs). One single limitation applies: whenever you load an IAP from disk (apart from the default plates that come with the program), only the map view of that IAP will be displayed. The profile view will always show the same, standard approach profile. Upon registration ($30), users will receive a special license key by mail, fax, or E-mail. Entering this license key will instantaneously provide complete functionality to the program.

Contacting the Author:
Georges Lorsche
5, rue des Violettes
L-3447 Dudelange
Luxembourg/Europe
Via E-Mail: CompuServe: Georges Lorsche 100041,211
Internet:100041.211@compuserve.com

Frame Counter for *Flight Simulator 5.0* (Filename FC.FSO)

Frame counter for Microsoft *Flight Simulator 5.0.* helps optimize your performance by telling you how fast your screen is updating. Copy it to your root FS5 directory and include the line "DEVICE=FC.FSO" in your FS5.INI file. This will replace your transponder code with a number indicating how many video frames are drawn each second. You can turn display options on or off in the Options/Preferences/Display menu and the Scenery/Scenery Complexity menu and see how they affect performance. This program has been officially released to the public by Microsoft and is free on CompuServe's Flight Simulator Forum Library 2. (You still have to pay for online time while on CompuServe, however.)

Where to Find Free Scenery and Airplanes

There are many scenery shareware files and aircraft that are available for free on CompuServe's Flight Simulator Forum. Just check the library on scenery and aircraft. There are so many kinds of aircraft and so much scenery that have been contributed over the years that it is impossible to list them all here. Be forewarned though. *Flight Simulator 5.0* will not allow you to import aircraft created with the Aircraft and Scenery Designer 1.0 (called A&SD 1.0). You will have to wait until the Aircraft and Scenery Designer 5.0 comes out before you can import such aircraft into FS 5.0. Also, older scenery created with A&SD 1.0 cannot take advantage of the photorealistic 256-color capabilities of FS 5.0.

ADD-ON FS 5.0 PRODUCTS

This section lists some of the hardware add-ons you can purchase separately for *Flight Simulator 5.0*.

CH Products

CH Products is a leading U.S. manufacturer of precision analog joysticks for the home and industry.

The CH Virtual Pilot is a true, professional flight yoke that mounts easily to your desk via clamps. You plug it directly into your joystick port and, *voila*, you are ready to go. The yoke features aileron and elevator control via the yoke, elevator and aileron trim tabs, fire buttons mounted on the wheel, and a throttle lever. You can use the Virtual Pilot in place of a joystick for Microsoft's *Flight Simulator 5.0*, but be fore-warned, you have to have a table that you can clamp it to, and your keyboard will have to be placed to the side. If your throttle control does not work, you may have to upgrade your game card controller to one that can handle dual joysticks. With its built-in springs, the yoke has a realistic amount of travel and tension to that of a real yoke.

The Virtual Pilot Pro is an extended version of the Virtual Pilot. It comes with all the features of the Virtual Pilot, but also offers four-way, 3-D view controls, along with flap and landing gear controls.

Figure 15.8
CH Virtual Pilot

Figure 15.9
CH Flightstick Pro

An IBM compatible joystick, the Flightstick Pro works with all standard analog joystick ports and lets the *Flight Simulator 5.0* pilot choose 3-D views, activate flaps, landing gear, brakes, and trim controls.

Suggested Retail Prices are as follows:

CH Virtual Pilot $109.95
CH Virtual Pilot Pro...$149.95
CH Flightstick Pro ....$ 89.95

Contact:
    CH Products
    970 Park Center Dr.
    Vista, CA 92083
    Telephone: 619-598-2518

Colorado Spectrum

Colorado Spectrum produces the innovative Mouse Yoke, which uses your existing mouse and transforms it into a realistic aircraft-style yoke. Priced less than leading analog joysticks, the Mouse Yoke provides precision movements, a realistic yoke feel, and user-friendly installation. To install it, you simply clamp the Mouse Yoke to a table and slip the mouse under an elastic "seat belt" on top of the device. The yoke's shaft then drives the mouse ball, translating yoke movements into corresponding mouse signals. Pushing forward on the yoke is equivalent to moving the mouse forward on the desk, and turning the yoke right is the same as moving the mouse to the right. The Mouse Yoke is the first product to receive Microsoft *Flight Simulator*'s new "Seal of Approval," and it works on both MS-DOS and Macintosh systems.

Figure 15.10
Colorado Spectrum's
Mouse Yoke

Notebook owners the world over will rejoice now that Colorado Spectrum's Notebook Gameport is out. For the first time, you can hook up your joystick to your notebook and fly your flight simulation programs while on the road or traveling on an airliner. The Notebook Gameport connects to your notebook's 9-pin serial port. You then hook up your joystick directly to the Gameport and, if you have a mouse too, you can hook it up to the pass through the serial mouse port. The Four-Axis Gameport also supports joystick and rudder pedals simultaneously.

The Mouse Yoke sells for a suggested retail price of $34.95, while the Notebook Gameport sells for a suggested retail price of $54.95

Contact:
> Colorado Spectrum
> 748 Whalers Way E-201
> Fort Collins, CO 80525
> Telephone: 303-225-1687
> USA Toll Free 800-238-5983

Figure 15.11
Colorado Spectrum's
Notebook Gameport

R&R Electronics EPIC Controller

EPIC (Extended Programmable Input Controller) is a microprocessor-controlled joystick controller card that replaces your current analog joystick controller card. The controller card is responsible for interpreting the analog signals from the joystick and sending the proper digital signal to your computer. The EPIC controller offers several advantages over conventional controller cards:

- *Support for up to 4 joysticks and 128 buttons.* Up to eight analog channels are supported.

- *Customizable joystick and button mapping.* Any analog channel can be mapped to any joystick axis; any button can be mapped to any joystick button or keyboard key.

- *Extensive button programming.* Any button can be mapped to any function consisting of key presses, delays, joystick button presses, and/or flag changes.

How does it work? The EPIC controller card plugs into a slot of your PC, just like a standard joystick card, but it also plugs into your PC's keyboard port. Your keyboard, joystick, flightstick, yoke, throttle, rudder pedals, view buttons, brakes, and all other controls can be plugged into a "breakout box" which is connected to the EPIC controller via a ribbon cable.

So far as your computer is concerned, nothing has changed; there's still a keyboard and joystick, and they will still work normally. All that has happened is that *Flight Simulator* (or any simulation program) now recognizes the EPIC controller as the official Game Card Joystick Controller.

EPIC's special features come into play when you load into memory a special file (before running your simulator) that remaps your joysticks and buttons. Now any button on your joystick, or any control, can be assigned a specific function in *Flight Simulator*. For example, if you had four buttons on your joystick, one could increase the throttle, a second button could decrease the throttle, a third button could set the brakes, while the fourth

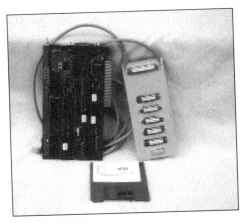

could turn your map window off and on. Or, perhaps you would prefer to have each button control one of your side views in your 3-D view window. The choice is yours. You could even build an entire cockpit, using your own controls, and have the EPIC interface with your simulation program.

R&R Electronics provides several files that enable your EPIC controller to work with many popular joysticks, such as the CH Flightstick Pro.

EPIC, which includes the controller card and breakout box for 40 buttons and software, is available for a suggested retail price of $387.45

Figure 15.12
R&R Electronics EPIC
Controller

Contact:
R&R Electronics
4009 Parkwood St.
Brentwood, MD 20722-1640
Telephone: 301-699-5277

Figure 15.13
ThrustMaster Rudder
Control System
(pedals)

ThrustMaster

ThrustMaster specializes in making flight controls for air combat simulations. However, their unique Mark I and Mark II flight control systems can be used with *Flight Simulator*. They also make rudder pedals, a specialized game card controller, and a basic F-16 cockpit with a fiberglass shell.

The Rudder Control System is constructed out of anodized aluminum and ABS plastic, and works with software supporting external rudder pedal input.

The Mark I Flight Control System is a four-button, four-way hat switch joystick that allows you to switch views, weapons, and other vital simulator functions.

The Mark II Weapons Control System is a fully programmable HOTOS (Hands On Throttle and Stick) version of the Mark I Flight Control System. With six buttons and a three-way switch, the Mark II can be programmed for a total of 21 independent functions. You

Figure 15.14
ThrustMaster Mark II
Weapons Control
System

can reprogram the buttons on the Mark II for any current or future flight simulator.

The ACM Game Controller Card virtually eliminates joystick drift in all simulations. Speed adjustability allows the user to dial in the card to exactly match the computer's speed. You can adjust the card to any speed from 4.77 MHz to 66 MHz.

ThrustMaster's F-16c Cockpit allows you to experience the thrill of flying in a mockup of an F-16c cockpit. Using your computer in conjunction with the ThrustMaster control panels, you can fly your simulations with extra realism.

Figure 15.15
ThrustMaster ACM
game card

Suggested List Prices are as follows:
Rudder Control System...$149.95
ACM Game Card...$ 39.95
Mark II Weapons Control System..............................$149.95
Mark I Flight Control System ....$ 99.95
F 16c Cockpit
Basic Unit $695.00
Switch Control Module..$ 99.00
Switch Kit $350.00
External Fiberglass Skin..$975.00
Seat Pads $199.00
Shoulder Harness ....$ 99.00

Contact:
    ThrustMaster, Inc.
    10150 S.W. Nimbus Ave.
    Suite E7
    Portland, Oregon 97223
    Telephone: 503-639-3200

Figure 15.16
ThrustMaster Cockpit

ThunderSeat Technologies

ThunderSeat Technologies makes various flight simulation products, including a virtual reality chair, yokes, and other cockpit controls and instrumentation. They are also developing virtual reality, full-cockpit simulators that should be available in 1994.

The ThunderSeat Pro Virtual Reality Chair is a seat that contains a special subwoofer type of sonic transducer built into its base. This sonic transducer generates an omnidirectional low frequency sound that rumbles throughout the air chamber hidden inside. The ensuing resonance amplifies the sound waves until the entire chair becomes a radiating speaker. With the resultant air and bone conduction, the user not only hears the sound but feels it as well. In essence, all the vibratory sensations of flight, including engine noise and landing and takeoffs are felt by the person in the chair. The same type of tactile feedback system is used in real F-16 flight simulators. Due to its unique design, an ordinary stereo amplifier can power the ThunderSeat; all you need to do is hook up your PC's sound card to the stereo.

The YM-2 Yoke Module includes not only a yoke, but also switches and buttons that enable you to control up to 39 separate aircraft functions. Aircraft controls on the right side of the panel include a four-position flap switch, landing gear, parking brake, and rotary trim switch. The left side has a total of 23 other aircraft function controls, including a four-position magneto/ignition switch and an assortment of appropriate rocker and push-button type aircraft switches. The function of all the switches on the front panel can be changed easily by software so you can customize the controls to your program. A special batch file is provided for FS 5.0 that is loaded into the program. From that point on, every time FS 5.0 is started, the correct function of all switches is loaded automatically. The YM-2 connects to your PC by means of the parallel port and features a full-travel, aluminum yoke with baked enamel finish. An optional yoke shaker system to give the user full motion feedback will be available in early 1994 and will be designed to work with FS 5.0 stalls, hard landings, and other maneuvers generating appropriate yoke movement.

The YM-1 features the same precision yoke mechanism as the YM-2, but without any of the front panel switches. The YM-1 can be upgraded to the YM-2. Both the YM-1 and YM-2 are housed in a heavy duty steel case

Here's what some people have to say about the ThunderSeat:

"The perfect computer pilot enhancement— realistic sensation of flight has never been this comfortable or this inexpensive."

—Hugo Fuegen, CEO, Bruce Artwick Organization,

"A must have item for your cockpit...ThunderSeat will raise your level of realism to a new dimension!"

—Jon Solon, Program Manager, Aerospace Simulation Software, Microsoft Corporation

designed to hold any monitor. An integrated steel tray puts your keyboard at your fingertips.

The King Air Style Yoke is molded from an actual King Air Yoke, and features a two-way rocker switch on the left stalk for up and down trim control. There is also a built-in trackball on the right stalk that allows you to tune the radios and perform all other mouse controlled actions without taking your hands off the controls. An actual Beechcraft quartz chronometer is also available.

The Three-Lever Power Quadrant for single engine aircraft mates to the YM-2 Yoke Module and offers controls for throttle, propeller speed, mixture, cowl flaps, carburetor heat, and fuel tank selection. Other power quadrants available include a Two-Lever Learjet with Reverse Thrust and Spoiler Extend/Retract controls, and a Six-Lever 310R-type Light Twin Piston powered engine.

The ThunderFlight rudders are all-steel rudders perfect for flying tricky crosswind landings in uncoordinated mode in FS 5.0. Designed to duplicate control forces found in actual aircraft, the ThunderFlight rudders are the only ones on the market with a "progressive loading" resistance feature. Progressive loading refers to the increased force that is required to press the rudder pedal to its full extreme, thus simulating the progressive movement of the aircraft's rudder into the slipstream.

Figure 15.17 ThunderSeat

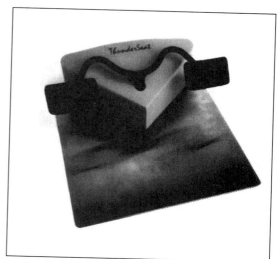

Figure 15.18 ThunderPedals

Figure 15.19
YM-2 with Three-Lever Power Quadrant

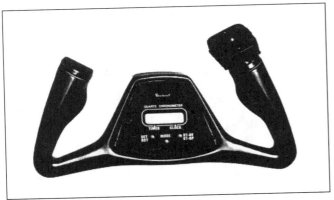

Figure 15.20
King Air Style Yoke

The View Control Module allows you to quickly adjust your cockpit view by flipping an eight-position rotary switch. Push-button control of zoom in and zoom out is also included.

Suggested Retail Prices are listed below:

ThunderSeat Pro $299.95
Side Consoles $179.95
ThunderFlight Rudders..$349.95
Monitor Cowling Shell with custom template $349.95
Retractable-Tactical Keyboard Holder..........................$ 79.95
YM-1 Yoke Module $349.95
YM-2 Yoke Module $995.95
3-Lever, High Performance Power Quadrant $395.95
View Control Module $299.95
Beechcraft King Air Yoke with Trackball.......................$595.00

Contact:
    ThunderSeat Technologies
    6330 Arizona Circle
    Los Angeles, CA 90045
    Telephone: 310-410-0022
    USA Toll Free 800-884-8633

Flightmaster Computer Flight Simulator Control

The Flightmaster control consists of a yoke, throttle, trim control, rudder pedals, and brakes under the toes of the rudder pedals. Some of its features include:

- Ability to put your keyboard on top of the unit for easy access to keyboard commands
- Yoke rotates 90° on roll axis, and travels 3 inches on pitch axis

- Yoke is spring loaded on both axes
- Elevator trim relieves yoke pressure
- Trim pointer assures perfect calibration
- Fire button under left thumb
- Rudder pedals travel 3 inches and are spring loaded
- Brakes under toes of rudder pedals
- Unit plugs directly into your game card
- Lifetime warranty on parts and labor
- 30-day money back guarantee

Flightmaster sells for a suggested retail price of $199.95, while the heavy-duty aluminum-base FlightMaster IV sells for $749.95. (The Flightmaster IV rudder and pedal assembly are also made of aluminum.) In addition, you can order a Hobbs clock and key for an additional $99.95.

Contact:
Flightmaster
421 W.Jefferson, Suite 22
Dallas, Texas 75208
Telephone: 214-264-3652

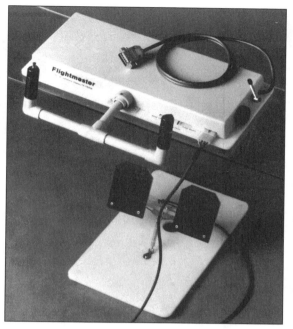

Figure 15.21
Flightmaster Yoke and
Pedals

Wagner Computer Products' Microflight Simulator

For the serious *Flight Simulator* enthusiast, Wagner Computer Products provides the Microflight Simulator, allowing precision flight control responsiveness and realism. This microprocessor controlled device includes an aluminum yoke, rudder pedals with toe brakes, and a console that serves as the control device for Microsoft's *Flight Simulator*. The Microflight simulator is connected to your PC via one of your COM serial ports. Trim and other flight control commands are automatically dispatched from the console to the computer via the serial port. All nine of your available 3-D view angles can be instantly selected by means of a rotary switch. There are also individual controls for your NAV/COM radios, flaps, mixture control, throttle, carburetor heat, landing gear, lights, OBI indicators, transponder, and magnetos.

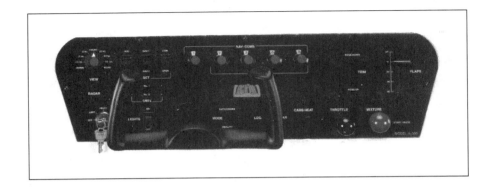

Figure 15.23
Wagner Computer Products' Microflight Simulator

The Microflight simulator has a suggested retail price of $3,995.00

Contact:
Wagner Computer Products, Inc.
Oswego Road
Pleasant Valley, New York 12569
Telephone: 914-677-3794

OTHER RESOURCES:

For Flight Simulation buffs, there are two really excellent sources of information: the CompuServe Flight Simulator Forum, and *MicroWings Magazine*. The next section briefly describes each.

CompuServe Flight Simulator Forum

If you have a modem hooked up to your computer, you can call up the CompuServe on-line information service and obtain up-to-date information on *Flight Simulator*. The CompuServe on-line information service offers hundreds of forums on every conceivable topic. In each forum, you can correspond with other CompuServe members, post messages on the electronic bulletin board, or read other messages that interest you. Today, CompuServe serves over one million members worldwide, and includes over 1,700 databases. You can upload and download files, send and receive E-mail, send faxes, play games, shop, check airline schedules or order airline tickets, conduct research using a vast reference library, obtain the latest financial reports, see the latest Associated Press On-line Hourly News summaries, download satellite weather maps, get weather reports, and just about anything else you can think of. There are also computer hardware and software support forums that offer you instantaneous access to over 30,000 drivers, patches, utilities, templates, clipart, GIF pictures, and demonstration versions of commercial software.

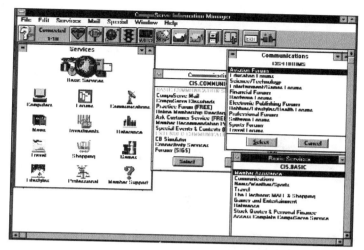

The Flight Simulator Forum is a terrific source of information on the latest developments in flight simulation. There are topics on air combat, scenery design, aircraft design, general aviation, air traffic control, hardware, and space simulations; and there are software libraries from which you can download files. If you have some scenery or aircraft, or some important message that you would like to share with other *Flight Simulator* enthusiasts, you can easily post your files to the forum's message center or library.

Figure 15.24
CompuServe
Information Manager
for Windows

To best use the CompuServe network, you really need to use the CompuServe Information Manager (also called CIM). This program greatly simplifies the task of navigating the labyrinthine passages of the network and removes the burden of having to remember what commands to type each time you log on. If you are running Windows, I strongly recommend the CIM for Windows, which allows you to paste, cut, and copy text back and forth from CompuServe to any of your Windows applications. For example, you could create a message in your favorite word processor, then copy it into CIM for Windows and paste it into an E-mail message you wish to send.

CompuServe is available internationally in many countries and can be accessed elsewhere using special telephone networks. The customer service contact telephone numbers for CompuServe worldwide are as follows:

- Argentina Direct (+54)1-372-7883
- Australia Toll-Free 008-023-158 (Direct +61 2-410-4260)
- Canada Direct (+1)614-457-8650
- Chile Direct (+56)2-696-8807
- Germany Toll-Free 0130-86 46 43 (Direct +49 +89 66 55 0-222)
- Hong Kong Direct (+852)867-0102
- Israel Direct (+972)3-290466
- Japan Toll-Free 0120-22-1200 (Direct +81 3-5471-5806)
- New Zealand Toll-Free 0800-441-082 (Direct +61 2-410-4260)

- South Korea Toll-Free 080-222-4700 (Direct +82 2-569-5400)
- Switzerland Toll-Free 155 31 79 (Direct +49 +89 66 55 0-222)
- Taiwan Direct (+8666)2-515-7035
- United Kingdom Toll-Free 0800 289 458 (Direct +44 +272 760680)
- United States Toll-Free 800-848-8990 (Direct +1 614-457-8650)
- Venezuela Direct (+58)2-793-2984

CompuServe's U.S. monthly service fee is $8.95. For the basic services (including news, weather, E-mail messaging, Electronic Encyclopedia, and shopping) there is no connect time charge; but for the forums (including the Flight Simulator Forum), there is an hourly connect time fee of $16/hr for 9600/14400 bps service, and $8/hr for 1200/2400 bps service.

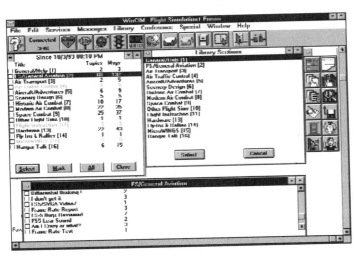

Connect time is billed in one minute increments, with a minimum of one minute per session. Connect time rates do not include communications (network) charges or premium surcharges, which are billed in addition to hourly connect time charges. If you are a resident of the U.S. or Canada, there are special local access telephone numbers that you can call to avoid the network charges. If you live outside the U.S., CompuServe is installing local access telephone nodes in many countries around the world, so call and check to see if there is one near you.

Figure 15.25
CompuServe Flight Simulator Forum

MicroWINGS Magazine

If you want to join an organization devoted to aerospace simulation, then MicroWINGS is the place to be. MicroWINGS bills itself as the International Association for Aerospace Simulations and they have members from all over the world. Once you join, you receive six issues of *MicroWINGS Magazine* a year and you are entitled to the following benefits:

Magazine   A magazine devoted to aviation simulations that is published every two months. The magazine features reviews, how-to's, tutorials, help columns, coverage of aviation simulation product releases and conferences, tips and tricks, interviews, and columns written by prominent authors in the industry.

Free Software
For the first 2,000 members to join, you will get a free copy of one of Mallard's scenery upgrades for the Macintosh or other software. (Valid only for memberships from the USA, Canada, and Mexico.)

CompuServe
A sign-up kit for the CompuServe Information Service (with a $15 usage credit and free first month of basic service).

Bulletin Board System
Access to a computer BBS with a section devoted to MicroWINGS members.

Multi-Player Database
International database of fellow MicroWINGS members who are interested in using the multi-player/modem link features of their aviation simulation products.

Annual Conference
See user presentations, vendor demonstrations, new product/upgrade announcements, hands-on exhibits, user/vender get togethers, and get door prizes.

Mallard Discounts
Members get an exclusive 25% discount off any Mallard Software title, and an anytime discount of 5% off of any Mallard Direct catalog item.

Shareware
Acquire freeware/shareware aviation-related utilities and files.

SubLOGIC Discounts
Exclusive discounts of 30% off on SubLOGIC products through DataWings

Give-Aways
Periodic give-aways of free aviation simulation-related software/hardware products.

Earn Money
MicroWINGS pays up to $100 for any submitted article that gets published in the magazine.

The Membership fee per year is $49. Canada and Mexico add $6 postage surcharge. All other countries add $18 postage surcharge.

Figure 15.26 MicroWINGS Magazine

Contact:
Robert M. MacKay
President
MicroWINGS, Inc.
381 Casa Linda Plaza #154
Dallas, Texas 75218
Telephone 214-324-1406
CompuServe E-Mail ID: 71641,2321

OTHER FLIGHT SIMULATOR PROGRAMS

There are various other flight simulator programs out on the market that offer specialized features not found in *Flight Simulator 5.0*. Two popular flight simulation programs that are used for training purposes are Azuresoft's Elite line of simulators, and MDM Systems' FS-100 Desktop Cockpit. The next section briefly describes some of the features of each program.

Tower from Mallard/BAO

Tower is a new control tower simulation program developed by Aviation Simulations, Inc., a joint venture of the Bruce Artwick Organization and Wesson International. It is a stand-alone simulation that does not need *Flight Simulator* to run.

From atop the control tower of major metropolitan and international airports, you can simulate being an air-traffic controller. You can issue verbal commands (providing you have a voice-recognition-capable sound card), pan your photorealistic view 360° around the tower, and use local and ground con-

Figure 15.22
Tower air traffic control simulation

trol radar to help you guide aircraft traffic in and out of the airport. You can simulate all kinds of conditions, weather, and levels of traffic at any time of the day. Watch as airplanes (superimposed on the photorealistic scenery) take off, taxi, land, fly patterns, and abort takeoffs all under your voice control. Simulated pilots speak back to you using digitized sound files. Tower is expected to include a special communication mode with FS 5.0, using the Dual Player feature, so that you can give Air Traffic Control instructions to FS 5.0 pilots.

"Tower is not all that different from our professional training version of this product," says Hugo Feugen, President of ASI and CEO of BAO. In fact, a variant of Tower is now being used to train air traffic controllers.

Tower will be available for Windows at a suggested retail price of $69.95.

Contact:
    Mallard Software, Inc.
    3207 Justin Road
    Flower Mound, Texas 75028
    Telephone: 214-539-2575

Azuresoft's ELITE/High Performance, ELITE/Advanced, and ELITE/Jet Flight Simulators

Azuresoft actually makes three separate flight simulation programs: ELITE/High Performance, ELITE/Advanced, and the ELITE/Jet. The unique three-microprocessor design of the simulation allows unprecedented realism in desktop simulation. ELITE uses three microprocessors in the following way:

Figure 15.27
Azuresoft's ELITE/
Advanced Flight
Simulator

- The microprocessor in your PC runs the ELITE program
- The math coprocessor in your PC allows the use of floating point arithmetic required for realistic flight dynamics.
- The unique Universal Controls Interface (UCI) uses a high-speed analog-to-digital converter to digitize control inputs to a much finer resolution than ordinary game card controllers. This allows much smoother, more realistic flight control. The UCI connects the flight controls to the serial port of your computer, and is included with each ELITE Personal Simulator.

ELITE/High Performance simulates a Mooney 201, Bonanza, or Cessna 210 class aircraft. The program features include:

- Constant-speed propeller control, mixture and throttle
- EGT, RPM gauges
- Retractable landing gear
- NAV 1/NAV 2/ADF radios with DME
- Digital timer
- Airspeed indicator
- Magnetic compass accurately simulates turning and acceleration errors
- Altimeter
- Vertical speed indicator
- Bendix/King KG 258 attitude indicator
- Bendix/King KI229 RMI or KI 227 ADF Indicator
- Bendix/King KI 525A HSI (horizontal situation indicator) with KCS 55A remote compass system. (or simple directional gyro)
- Trim, flap, controls
- Accurate depiction of VASI, approach, and runway lights
- Customizable weather
- Simulate instrument/control failures
- Detailed, on-screen navigational maps
- Flight recorder for recording your flights.

The ELITE/Advanced simulates a Cessna 172-class aircraft's envelope and instrument panel. For jet flying, the ELITE/JET is an accurate simulator of

Figure 15.28
ELITE/High Performance Flight Simulator

Figure 15.29
ELITE/Jet Flight Simulator

the MD-81 jetliner and it includes the sophisticated MD-81 Advanced Digital Flight Guidance systems.

ELITE Navigation Libraries are computer-created from the official FAA NAVAID and Facility master database. A total of 29 libraries are available, covering the entire continental U.S. Each library includes thousands of square miles, hundreds of real airports, instrument approaches, fixes and NAVAIDS. You can update the ELITE Navigation Libraries yourself with the latest frequency or NAVAID change, or even add your own airport to the database.

The suggested retail prices are as follows:
ELITE/Advanced $499.00
ELITE/High Performance $699.00
ELITE/Jet $849.00
ELITE Navigation Libraries.............................$ 69.95 Each

Contact:
Azuresoft
1250 Aviation Avenue
San Jose, CA 95110
Telephone: 408-947-2070
USA Toll Free 800 282-6675

MDM Systems' FS-100 Desktop Cockpit

The FS-100 Desktop Cockpit is a complete flight system consisting of state-of-the-art software that simulates very accurately the flight characteristics of a single engine high-performance aircraft. Unlike other programs, the FS-100 does not use a keyboard or mouse to control the airplane; instead, there is a unique control console that allows you to make all of the critical flight adjustments using real knobs, switches, and levers, just like you do in a real airplane. The sharp 16-color VGA display shows the aircraft instrumentation in great detail and includes:

- Digital timer
- Attitude indicator
- Runway view with accurate depiction of all VASI, approach, and runway lights
- Magnetic compass accurately simulates northerly turning error and acceleration/deceleration error
- Barometric altimeter
- NAV 1/NAV 2/ADF radios/DME indicator
- Manifold pressure gauge

- RPM gauge
- Vertical speed indicator
- EGT gauge
- NAV 2 VOR/Localizer indicator
- Flaps, elevator trim, and landing gear indicators
- Directional gyro or HSI (horizontal situation indicator)
- RMI (Radio Magnetic Indicator): combined VOR and NDB
- Turn coordinator
- Airspeed indicator
- Marker beacon indicators
- Autopilot annunciator

FS-100 also allows you to graphically replay your flights, display navigational maps all over the world (you have to buy each continental database separately), simulate instrument failures, and set weather conditions.

You can even try out the program before buying by ordering the free FS-100 Demo Diskette. All of the nonflying functions are available for you to explore. The demo also includes two prerecorded flights which demonstrate the performance of this system on your computer.

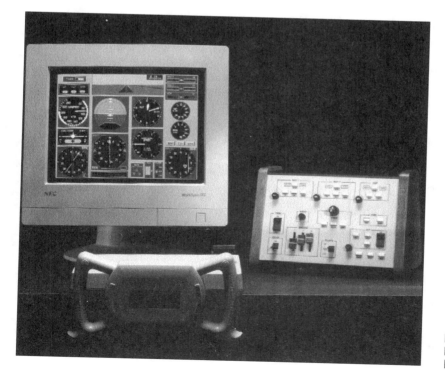

Figure 15.30
MDM Systems' FS-100
Desktop Cockpit

The FS-100 Desktop Cockpit comes in five configurations:

The Basic Package:	Includes the FS-100 Desktop Cockpit and one custom database covering a 125 mile radius around the airport of your choice.	Suggested Retail Price: $634.95
The Starter Package:	Includes the FS-100 Desktop Cockpit and one Continental Database of your choice.	Suggested Retail Price: $744.95
The Intermediate Package:	Includes the FS-100 Desktop Cockpit, one Continental Database of your choice, and the CH Virtual Pilot Control Yoke.	Suggested Retail Price: $854.90
The Advanced Package:	Includes the FS-100 Desktop Cockpit, one Continental Database of your choice, CH Virtual Pilot Control Yoke, and ThrustMaster Rudder Control System	Suggested Retail Price: $1,004.85
The Ultimate Package:	Includes the FS-100 Desktop Cockpit, all seven Continental Databases, CH Virtual Pilot Control Yoke, and the Thrust-Master Rudder Control System	Suggested Retail Price: $1,904.55

Available continental databases have a suggested retail price of $149.95 each and are listed as follows:

- North America
- South America
- Europe
- Africa
- Middle East
- Asia
- Pacific

Figure 15.31
Advanced mapping
features of the FS-100
Desktop Cockpit

Contact:
    MDM Systems
    756 Tyvola Road, Suite 105
    Charlotte, NC 28217
    Telephone: 704-523-7400
    USA Toll Free 800-732-2800

VIDEO AND SOUND HARDWARE

To get the maximum performance out of your *Flight Simulator 5.0* setup, you will want a fast video card and a decent sound card. Although the peripheral cards listed in this section are recommended, they are by no means the only ones available that offer superior performance. It would not be possible to list all the other manufacturers that produce sound and video cards, so only three cards were selected as a representative sample.

Creative Labs SoundBlaster 16ASP with WaveBlaster

The Creative Labs line of SoundBlaster cards is the recognized standard in the PC sound card industry. The new SoundBlaster 16ASP (ASP stands for

Figure 15.32
SoundBlaster 16ASP
and WaveBlaster

Advanced Signal Processing) is a true 16-bit stereo sound card that records and plays back sounds with CD quality. There is a 4-Operator, 20-Voice Stereo FM synthesis chip to create special effects, a CD-ROM interface, high fidelity microphone, and advanced signal processor that can perform specialized sound functions. Using the ASP, the SoundBlaster 16ASP can download complex mathematical sound algorithms, handle compression and decompression of sound on the fly, do highly compact speech data compression, and perform voice recognition. There is also a MIDI (Musical Instrument Digital Interface), a joystick port, and an included library of useful sound programs for Windows. The card is compatible with Windows 3.1, OS 2, and all previous SoundBlaster cards. You will need to buy some speakers to go with the SoundBlaster, but be sure to buy magnetically shielded speakers because unshielded speakers can interfere with your monitor.

The voice recognition capabilities of the SoundBlaster 16ASP allow it to recognize simple spoken words. Using a special Windows program called VoiceAssist, you can issue verbal commands for any Windows program, menu or command. There is also a speech synthesizer that will read-back text for you from any Windows application. When Mallard's Tower is released, you should be able to use the SoundBlaster 16ASP to issue verbal commands to the simulation.

The WaveBlaster MIDI daughterboard (meaning it attaches itself to the SoundBlaster 16ASP) is an add-on accessory for the SoundBlaster 16ASP that allows you to play back real sampled sound effects and musical instruments. It comes bundled with Cakewalk Apprentice for Windows software that allows you to record and play back 256-track MIDI music files. With its 16 MIDI channels and 32-note polyphony, the WaveBlaster comes with 128 instrument presets, 18 drum kits, and 50 sound effects. For playing back realistic orchestral sounds, the WaveBlaster is a good investment; although, for *Flight Simulator 5.0*, you don't really need it. Many simulation games are now including General MIDI sound effects, so if you have the WaveBlaster, you will be able to synthesize these sounds with very high quality.

The SoundBlaster 16ASP sells for a suggested retail price of $349.00, while the WaveBlaster add-on MIDI subsystem sells for a suggested retail price of $249.00.

Contact:

Creative Labs
1901 McCarthy Boulevard,
Milpitas, CA 95035
Telephone: 408-428-6600
USA Toll Free 800-998-5227

Diamond Stealth Pro VESA Local Bus Video Card Accelerator

Diamond Computer Systems is a company well known for its video graphics accelerator cards. The new Stealth Pro VRAM Local Bus Graphic Accelerator card uses the S386C928 graphics processor chip. It achieves high speed in Windows because it offloads graphics functions like line drawing, hardware cursor and BitBLT operations from the CPU.

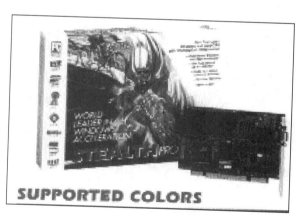

Figure 15.33
Diamond Stealth Pro VESA Local Bus Video Card Accelerator with 2 MB of VRAM

The 2-MB ISA and Local Bus versions of the Stealth Pro display many more colors and have higher refresh rates than standard SVGA cards. Maximum resolution and color combinations include 1280×1024 in 256 colors, 1024×768 in 65,536 colors and up to 800×600 in 16.7 million colors. Maximum refresh rates for modes up to 1024×768 is 72 Hz, with 1280×1024 supporting 74 Hz. For a comparison of video card performances in DOS, see Appendix A.

The suggested retail price is $499 for both the ISA and Local Bus versions of the 2-MB Stealth Pro. A 1-MB version of the Stealth Pro, with fewer colors, sells for $349.

Contact:
> Diamand Computer Systems, Inc.
> 1130 East Arques Avenue
> Sunnyvale, CA 94086
> Telephone: 408-736-2000

Hercules Dynamite VL/Pro Local Bus Video Card Accelerator

The speedy and economical Hercules Dynamite VL/Pro Local Bus Video Accelerator card excels in zipping you through DOS applications. Although it is not as fast when running Windows as the Hercules Graphite and the Diamond Stealth Pro, for the money the Hercules Dynamite can't be beat in running *Flight Simulator 5.0*. It performs on par with the best cards in running DOS applications, and at less than half the price, too.

The Hercules Dynamite VL/Pro uses a powerful Tseng ET-4000/W32i accelerator chip and comes equipped in both VESA Local Bus and ISA versions. It gives you super stable, high screen refresh rates of up to 90 Hz and offers special drivers to get you going quickly in Windows 3.1. Maximum resolution and color combinations include 1280 × 1024 with 16 colors, 1024 × 768 with 256 colors, 800 × 600 with 65,536 colors, 640 × 480 with 16.7 million colors. For a comparison of video card performances in DOS, see Appendix A.

The Hercules Dynamite VL/Pro sells for a suggested retail price of $249.

Figure 15.34
Hercules Dynamite
VESA Local Bus Video
Card Accelerator

Contact:
> Hercules Computer Technology, Inc.
> 3839 Spinnaker Court
> Fremont, CA 94538
> Telephone: 510-623-6030
> USA Toll Free 800-532-0600

Hercules Graphite VESA Local Bus Video Card Accelerator

If you need to have a good Windows video accelerator and a good DOS application accelerator, then the Hercules Graphite VESA Local Bus Accelerator card is a good bet. This card uses a special 32-bit graphics chip called the IIT AGX014, and it draws faster than many other video accelerators on the market, including the Orchid Fahrenheit 1280VA/VESA Local Bus card, the new ATI VESA Local Bus Mach 32 card, and the Weitek P9000-based Diamond Viper VESA Local Bus video card. In fact, PC Magazine and Windows Magazine both reviewed this card and gave it a recommended seal of approval.

Figure 15.35
Hercules Graphite
VRAM Local Bus
Video Accelerator

With a super stable refresh rate of up to 120 Hz, the Graphite offers the following maximum resolution and color combinations: 1280 × 1024 at 256 colors, 1152 × 900 at 256 colors, 1024 × 768 at 65,536 colors, 800x800 at 16.7 million colors, and 640 × 480 at 16.7 million colors.

The Hercules Graphite VESA Local Bus with 2 MB of VRAM sells for a suggested retail price of $549. The less expensive Graphite VESA Local Bus with only 1 MB of VRAM sells for a suggested retail price of $399.

Contact:

Hercules Computer Technology, Inc.
3839 Spinnaker Court
Fremont, CA 94538
Telephone: 510-623-6030
USA Toll Free 800-532-0600

P A R T

IV

Appendices

APPENDIX

A

Installation and Hardware Comparison Guide

This chapter goes over the installation procedure for *Flight Simulator 5.0* and concludes with a hardware comparison guide for 386/486 PCs and related video cards. Because optimum performance for *Flight Simulator 5.0* depends heavily on having a fast CPU and video card, it is important to know what kind of equipment you should have if you are going to get the most out of the program. A side by side comparison of the frame rates for different hardware combinations for running *Flight Simulator 5.0* will help you make this decision. Armed with the information found in the latter half of this appendix, you can then decide which hardware you should purchase or upgrade to.

As this book went to press, Microsoft had released an update for *Flight Simulator 5.0* which corrects sound dropout problems with Sound Blaster cards and joystick bugs. You can download the bug fix file, called FS5fix.exe, from CompuServe's Flight Simulator Forus Library 2, or you can contact Microsoft for an upgrade patch disk.

INSTALLATION IS A SNAP

The installation itself is simple, with self-explanatory instruction screens to help guide you through every step. Before you begin, however, you must know the answers to these questions about your hardware setup:

- Do you have enough hard disk space free for the installation of *Flight Simulator*? You will need at least 14 Mb of free space for just the program itself (not including extra space needed for the optional add-on scenery from Mallard and Microsoft).

Believe it or not, this is how much data is squeezed or compressed onto your two floppy installation disks! If you don't have enough room, it is time to do some hard disk housekeeping. To free up some space on your hard disk, delete only those files and/or directories that you don't need. Run the Chkdsk (type **CHKDSK C:** or **CHKDSK D:**) program on the hard drive to see if you have created enough free space.

- What kind of video card do you have? Super VGA, VGA, or EGA?
- If you have a Super VGA card, do you know the name of your card's manufacturer and the type of video accelerator chip used inside?
- Does your keyboard come equipped with function keys on the top or on the side?
- Do you have a Microsoft-compatible mouse installed?
- What kind of sound card, if any, do you have installed?
- Do you have a joystick installed?
- Do you have at least 530 Kb of free RAM and 256 Kb of extended memory? *Flight Simulator* requires 530 Kb of conventional memory, and you will need to load DOS into high memory above 640 Kb. (This is known as 256 Kb of extended, or "high," memory.)

- Do you have at least 2 Mb of expanded or extended memory? *Flight Simulator* requires you to configure at least 2 Mb of expanded memory in order to use all features of the program. You can run DOS 6 MemMaker program to automatically configure your memory requirements.

If you already know the answers to these questions, then proceed with the installation as outlined in the next section.

To get started with the installation, first make sure you are running the computer from the DOS prompt and are not running DOS from inside Windows 3.1. If you're not sure, reboot your machine by pressing Ctrl + Alt + Del simultaneously and wait until you see the C:> DOS prompt on screen. Follow the next few instructions to complete the installation:

1. Insert your FS 5.0 installation disk #1 into your floppy drive and type **A:** (or **B:** if you are installing from a second floppy drive) and press Enter.
2. Just to be safe, type **dir** (or **DIR**, it makes no difference) and then press Enter.
3. Type **SETUP** and press Enter; the program will start the installation.
4. Since you should already know what kind of video display card you have, select the DISPLAY system configuration item so that it is highlighted and then press Enter.
5. In the Display Mode Setup dialog box, select the kind of display you

have: EGA, VGA, or SVGA. When you have positioned the cursor over the item, press [Enter]. If you have a Super VGA card, choose SVGA.

6. If you don't know the manufacturer or video accelerator chip used for your SVGA card, select VESA 1.2 Compatible. Most SVGA card manufacturers have agreed to adopt this graphics standard and your card should work under this driver. However, for optimum speed you should try to identify which manufacturer/video chip is used for your display card and then select it from the list that appears on-screen. Highlight the card or chip name, then press [Enter] to continue.

7. Returning to the main setup screen, make sure that all the remaining choices for your keyboard and mouse are correct for your system. If they are not, select the item in question and press [Enter] to change it. Otherwise, highlight Install Flight Simulator and press [Enter] to continue.

8. The setup program next asks you whether you agree to install Flight Simulator in the target drive/directory it has chosen for you. If you don't like this drive/directory choice, then select Change Target Directory, and you can edit the directory text.

9. When you're finished making your drive/directory choice, select Install Flight Simulator and press [Enter]. The next few screens you see show the setup program decompressing the files from the floppy disk and storing them on your hard disk.

10. After the setup program has finished with the first diskette, it will prompt you to remove disk #1 and insert disk #2. Be sure to press [Enter], after you have put in disk #2.

11. Again, the program will continue with the process of decompressing files.

12. If all goes well and the program has successfully copied all its files to your hard disk, you will see the initial setup screen information dialog box.

13. Now choose the sound board option for your computer. Select the Sound Board list box, and choose the sound board you currently have installed on your PC from the available list of options. Click OK to proceed.

14. Many sound cards conflict with other cards such as scanner cards, modem cards, and SCSI cards. They don't work unless they are configured differently than their default setting that is programmed in at the factory. Because the FS 5.0 program has no way of checking how your sound board is configured on your PC, you must give it some vital

information to make it work properly. Don't worry if you don't know the answers to these questions, you can continue with the installation and figure this out later. If after installing the program and finding out your sound card doesn't work, just select the Sound button from the Preferences dialog box found under the Options menu and tinker with the settings until you get it right. Of course it would be better if you knew what the proper settings are before doing this, but, have no fear, you aren't going to destroy your computer or sound card. For example, with the SoundBlaster 16ASP, I had to change the default FS 5.0 Interrupt from 5 to 7 to get the board to work. This was because another card I had installed was already using Interrupt 5. By the way, choose Digitized Engine Sounds if you can because it sounds much better than the synthesized version. Click OK to proceed.

15. The next setup screen asks you whether you want to have Dynamic Scenery and Automatic Weather Generation start up by default each time FS 5.0 starts. Dynamic scenery includes other planes, blimps, hot air balloons, ground traffic, boats, and other moving objects. If you have a 486SX- or 386-based PC, you probably won't want to toggle these features on, since it will slow down the simulation too much. If you want to switch Dynamic Scenery on later, you can do so inside the program by toggling on the options as found in the Dynamic Scenery dialog box under the Scenery menu. Likewise, you can turn Automatic Weather Generation on by bringing up the Weather dialog box under the World menu, and toggling on the Automatic Weather Generation list box found in the Edit Weather Area dialog box. Click OK to proceed.

16. The next setup screen prompts you to choose the startup situation that FS 5.0 defaults to when initially booting up. For now choose Normal Flight mode. Click OK to proceed.

17. If you want to have FS 5.0 automatically record your flight hours in a logbook, click the Log Flight Time check box. Click OK to proceed.

18. You can use one or two joysticks with FS 5.0. If you have such a setup, you can customize the second joystick to control the throttle only, the throttle and brakes, the rudder only, or the throttle and rudder. Click OK to proceed. If you have two separate joysticks, you must purchase a special Y adapter plug for the two joysticks to be connected to the same game port.

19. In the next dialog box, press the Run Flight Simulator button if you wish to fly the simulator now. You can also press the Exit to MS-DOS button if you want to come back to the program later, or, if you plan on

installing add-on scenery or other add-on software, you can press the Install Add-On button.

20. If you are installing add-on scenery software, insert the floppy disk containing the add-on scenery or software into your floppy drive. In the Setup Add-On dialog box, select the floppy drive and press [Enter] to begin the installation process. If you have a CD-ROM add-on scenery disk, insert the CD-ROM disk and select the drive letter which corresponds to your CD-ROM, then press [Enter].

RECONFIGURING YOUR SETUP OPTIONS IF YOU DECIDE TO LATER ADD A NEW SYSTEM COMPONENT

If you buy a new sound card, video card, joystick, or flightstick/rudder combination, you can always go back into the setup to change *Flight Simulator 5.0*'s settings. You can do this without reinstalling the entire program from your floppy disk. There are two ways to do this; one from inside the program, the other from outside the program at the DOS prompt.

To reconfigure your setup options while inside the *Flight Simulator* program:

1. Pull down the Options menu and select Preferences.

2. Click on the Display button, the Joystick button, the Sound button, or the Mouse button to make changes in any of these settings. Follow the instructions inside each dialog box, then click the OK button to exit Preferences.

3. The program will need to reboot itself, and will prompt you with the Preferences Alert dialog box. Click the Exit Flight Simulator and Restart button. When the program restarts your new setup options will take effect.

To reconfigure your setup options while outside the *Flight Simulator* program at the DOS prompt:

1. While in the FLTSIM5 Directory, type **Setup**.

2. You will see a setup dialog box asking you to accept the system configuration choices as currently displayed. If you want to make a change in the current Display, Keyboard, or Mouse settings, highlight the selection and press [Enter].

3. After you are satisfied with your choices for the display, keyboard, and mouse, select the Install Flight Simulator item and press [Enter].

4. *Flight Simulator* will prompt you next with the first of the setup screens. Follow the instructions that are displayed on-screen, then press the OK button for each dialog box. Press the Run Flight Simulator button if you wish to fly the simulator now. Otherwise, press Exit to MS-DOS, if you want to come back to the program later.

HARDWARE COMPARISON GUIDE

Unfortunately, due to the design limitations of the DOS operating system, current video accelerator cards can excel in displaying either windows or DOS, but not both very well. So, if you are looking to run a DOS application such as *Flight Simulator 5.0* as fast as possible, you will be looking for a video card that works fast with DOS programs. On the other hand, if you are primarily interested in running Windows programs, then you will want a video accelerator that is designed for Windows acceleration. You should be aware that just because a video card is being trumpeted in advertisements as "Executes 60 Million WinMarks!" it does not mean that the card will run faster in DOS than an ordinary SVGA card! So to get the most bang for your buck, read this next section very carefully. Then, when you are ready to buy, you will be a more savvy consumer.

The two principal hardware components that affect speed are the CPU (Central Processing Unit-sometimes called "386" or "486") and the video card. The best way to gauge the speed of hardware for use with *Flight Simulator 5.0* is to compare the frames per second (FPS) each CPU or video card can produce. An individual frame is comprised of 256,000 pixels, or picture elements (i.e., a SVGA screen puts out 640 pixels horizontally by 400 pixels vertically, giving a total pixel count of 256,000 pixels), although not all of these pixels need to be updated as frequently as others. For example, half the screen in FS 5.0 is devoted to the instrument panel, while the other half comprises the 3-D view window. Since the 3-D scenery window is where most of the complex bit-mapping and vector draw operations occur, this window needs to be updated more frequently than does the instrument panel. This explains why your computer takes longer to draw each frame-when you make the 3-D scenery window larger.

In order to obtain a common reference point by which equipment can be judged equally, a program called "fc.fso" was developed by Microsoft to test the frame rate of computers running *Flight Simulator*. The program is available on CompuServe and, if you are a member, you can easily download it to test your own computer/video card setup. "Frame.zip" is another very useful *Flight Simulator* comparison test program on CompuServe, contributed by member Steve Wigginton. This program greatly simplifies the testing procedure by automating the battery of tests to come up with a uniform comparison number that can be compared fairly to other computer/video card setups. In fact, the hardware/video card comparison charts seen in this chapter are a compilation of Wigginton's program results by many CompuServe members. Frame.zip includes fc.fso, some batch files, and an instruction text file. To use the program, you decompress it using PKUNZIP in your Flight Simulator directory, then type in Framerep followed by your video card's name (a list of names is provided in the text file). Framerep then conducts a series of tests and you record the results. In all cases, the faster the frame rate, the faster the computer is at running *Flight Simulator.*

Fc.fso uses your transponder on the aircraft's instrument panel to display the current video frames per second count. When run on different computers, or by substituting video cards on the same computer, you can get an accurate count of how fast your computer is when running FS 5.0. The next two charts in this appendix graphically illustrate the results of running framerat.bat (which uses Fc.fso to display the frame rate on your transponder) on different CPU platforms and with different video cards. In each chart, the longer the bar, the faster the frames per second, and hence the better FS 5.0 will run.

In the two charts you will see two bars for each card/computer. This is because two measurements are needed; one for drawing complex objects such as the cybergraphics buildings, the other for drawing simple objects such as the synthesized ground terrain. By averaging the frame rates for drawing simple scenery versus complex scenery, you can see what your frame rate is likely to be like when flying FS 5.0. The top bar measures the frame rate in SVGA mode looking out the *rear* of your airplane when sitting on the runway at Chicago's Meigs Field (in other words-simple scenery with no cybergraphic buildings to slow things down). The bottom bar measures the frame rate in SVGA mode looking *forward* toward Chicago while sitting on the runway at Meigs Field (cybergraphic buildings and other complex scenery). Both upper and lower frame rates assume that the scenery is set to the Very Dense setting in the Scenery Complexity dialog box. Since more detail needs to be drawn for the downtown Chicago view, the bottom bar shows fewer frames per second than the top bar. Your actual frame rate will be somewhere between the higher frame count of the upper bar, and the lower frame count of the lower bar.

Chart A.1 shows the results of running Framerep on various CPUs.

Chart A.2 compares various SVGA video card's performance when running Framerep.

CPU Frame Rate Comparison

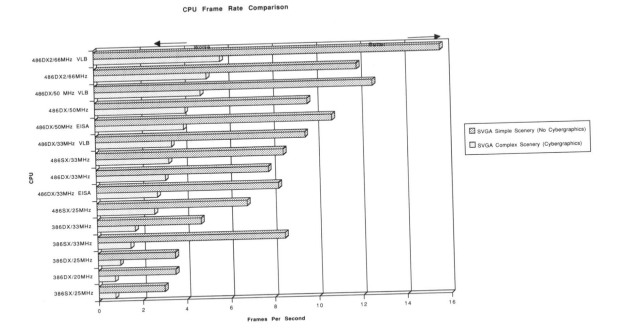

Chart A.1
Flight Simulator frame
rate results for various
CPUs

As you can see in the charts, the best performance was found on VESA Local Bus 486s (66 Mhz clock speed) with Local Bus video cards installed. When you see "VLB" on the chart, it means a VESA Local Bus was used; if you see EISA, then an EISA bus was used; otherwise the bus is assumed to be ISA. If you are on the runway at Meigs looking at Chicago and you get a frame rate of about 5 FPS or better in SVGA mode with the scenery set to Very Dense, then you will get acceptable results in Flight Simulator 5.0. Anything less than this speed will cause choppy screens and other visual annoyances. If you are on the runway at Meigs looking out your rear-view window (i.e., no cybergraphics buildings are displayed) and you get a frame rate of 14 FPS or better in SVGA mode with scenery set to Very Dense, then you will also get good results.

RUNNING *FLIGHT SIMULATOR* UNDER WINDOWS 3.1

Although you can run *Flight Simulator* as a DOS application in Windows 3.1, it is not recommended. You will lose some video performance because

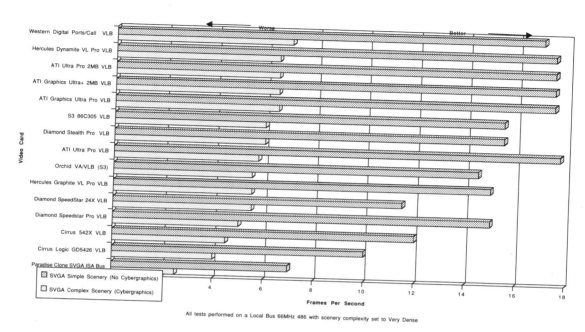

Chart A.2
Video card shootout

Windows will slow down *Flight Simulator* by creating more demands on your CPU. Figure on at least a 25 percent loss in your frame rate.

Also, for some Super VGA accelerator cards you can't switch back to *Flight Simulator* from within Windows without getting a scrambled screen. What happens is that the high video memory that stores the SVGA FS 5.0 screen image is lost when you switch to Windows; when you return, the image is corrupted because the video card doesn't retain the video image in RAM. You must exit *Flight Simulator* and then restart the program.

APPENDIX
B

VOR/NDB Station List, Airports Directory, and Navigational Maps

Appendix B contains various maps and tables useful for navigating in the Flight Simulator world. You will find a complete listing of all the VOR/NDBs found in Flight Simulator, as well as separate listings broken up into various regions of the world. The VOR/NDB regions listed include Europe, Mexico/Southern U.S. and the Caribbean Region, the North Atlantic Ocean, the Western Pacific, and the Eastern Pacific.

  WARNING: ALL INFORMATION IN THIS CHAPTER IS TO BE USED ONLY WITH FLIGHT SIMULATOR. DO NOT USE FOR REAL NAVIGATION PURPOSES.

HOW TO READ THE VOR/NDB STATION LIST

Each VOR/NDB station is listed alphabetically by name. Under each listing, you will find the station's three to four letter identifier, the station type (VOR or NDB), frequency, and latitude/longitude coordinates. This listing of VOR/NDBs was made possible due to the efforts of CompuServe member Dan Samual, who created a program called Listvor.exe which allows you to decipher and list all the VOR/NDBs found in the World3.GBL file in the *Flight Simulator 5.0* Scenery Directory. Listvor is available free for downloading in the CompuServe Flight Simulator Forum, Library 2. The program also allows you to sort by latitude/longitude a list of VOR/NDBs for a particular region of the earth and then export it as a CSV (comma delimited) text file that you can import into a spreadsheet program such as Excel. Once you have imported the VOR/NDB list into Excel, you can re-sort the entire list, print it out, or even search and extract only those stations that interest you. For example, you might only be interested in VOR/NDBs for the state of California. Knowing the latitude and longitude of the state's borders, you could compile a list of only those stations that fall within the state's borders.

Using the information in this file, you can plot a flight path using stations that you know exist along your route. For example, if you wanted to fly form Seattle to San Francisco, you would consult a map or atlas and write down the names of important cities along your route. Then you look up the VOR/NDB stations in the table that match your intended path and write down the frequencies. You can even check to see if the VOR/NDB stations are along your flight path by comparing the latitude/longitude coordinates with your route on the map. Of course, if you have the real aeronautical charts, you don't really need the table since you can consult the listings directly on the map.

For the regional VOR/NDB listings, you can quickly look up interesting navigational waypoints for transoceanic trips. For example, in the East Pacific and West Pacific listings, you could conceivably chart a course for San Francisco–Hawaii–Johnston Atoll (Apollo NDB)–Gaum (Nimitz VOR)–Iwo Jima–Okinawa, and thence onward to the main Japanese Island of Honshu. You could also chart a course to Darwin or Rockhampton, Australia, from Guam.

Unfortunately, FS 5.0 has no refueling facilities in the Western or Eastern Pacific, so you cannot fly the Learjet there on a realistic mission.

Complete VOR/NDB Station List for Flight Simulator 5.0

Name	Ident.	Type	Freq.	Latitude	Longitude
ABATE (LOM)	ABAT	NDB	356.0	45 37.83N	123 2.75W
ABBOTSFORD	XX	NDB	344.0	49 0.93N	122 29.28W
ABERDEEN	ABR	VOR	113.0	45 25.05N	98 22.12W
ABERDEEN	APG	NDB	349.0	39 32.11N	76 6.38W
ABERN (LOM)	ABER	NDB	414.0	46 59.27N	123 47.86W
ABETA (LMM)	ABET	NDB	233.0	40 57.89N	124 5.92W
ABILENE	ABI	VOR	113.7	32 28.89N	99 51.81W
ABRAHAM	AAA	NDB	329.0	40 9.62N	89 20.27W
ABSAM	AB	NDB	313.0	47 17.41N	11 30.10E
ACADI (LOM/NDB)	ACAD	NDB	269.0	29 57.38N	91 51.80W
ACTIVE PASS	AP	NDB	378.0	48 52.45N	123 17.40W
ACTON	AQN	VOR	110.6	32 26.08N	97 39.83W
ADA	ADH	VOR	117.8	34 48.16N	96 40.22W
ADA	AMR	NDB	302.0	34 48.35N	96 40.62W
ADAK	NUD	NDB	347.0	51 55.03N	176 34.01W
ADAMS	BGI	VOR	112.7	13 4.35N	59 29.13W
ADAMS	BGI	NDB	345.0	13 4.12N	59 29.53W
ADDMO (LOM)	ADDM	NDB	400.0	34 13.95N	96 55.99W
ADDYS (LOM)	ADDY	NDB	351.0	39 7.51N	84 40.16W
ADRIAN	ADG	NDB	278.0	41 52.20N	84 4.51W
AHOSKIE	ASJ	NDB	415.0	36 17.97N	77 10.53W
AIKEN	AIK	NDB	347.0	33 39.12N	81 40.62W
AINSWORTH	ANW	VOR	112.7	42 34.16N	99 59.38W
AIRBE (LOM/NDB)	AIRB	NDB	293.0	36 44.23N	87 24.83W
AIRBO (LOM/NDB)	AIRB	NDB	407.0	39 29.59N	83 44.29W
AIRLI (LOM)	AIRL	NDB	281.0	34 11.49N	77 51.98W
AIRPA (LOM)	AIRP	NDB	209.0	39 55.53N	86 14.31W
AITKIN	AIT	NDB	397.0	46 32.86N	93 40.51W
AITUTAKI	AI	NDB	320.0	18 49.40S	159 46.60W
AKLAVIK	YKD	NDB	0.0	68 13.64N	135 0.59W
AKRON	ACO	VOR	114.4	41 6.48N	81 12.09W
AKRON	AKO	VOR	114.4	40 9.34N	103 10.79W
AKRON (LOM/NDB)	AKRO	NDB	362.0	41 4.20N	81 23.25W
ALABY	BVN	NDB	332.0	41 43.78N	98 3.16W
ALAMO (LOM/NDB)	ALAM	NDB	368.0	29 36.46N	98 34.43W
ALAMOGORDO	ALM	NDB	341.0	32 51.03N	105 58.88W
ALAMOSA	ALS	VOR	113.9	37 20.96N	105 48.93W
ALBANY	ALB	VOR	115.3	42 44.85N	73 48.19W
ALBERT LEA	AEL	VOR	109.8	43 41.01N	93 22.15W
ALBUQUERQUE	ABQ	VOR	113.2	35 2.64N	106 48.98W
ALCOT (LOM)	ALCO	NDB	335.0	34 10.45N	79 51.15W
ALEGRE	UPA	NDB	382.0	22 22.42N	78 46.38W
ALENCON	AL	NDB	380.0	48 27.01N	0 6.80E
ALEXANDER CITY	DER	NDB	382.0	32 52.76N	85 57.68W
ALEXANDRIA	AEX	VOR	116.1	31 15.41N	92 30.04W
ALEXANDRIA	AXN	VOR	112.8	45 57.51N	95 13.96W
ALGONA	AXA	NDB	403.0	43 4.89N	94 16.35W
ALIBI (LOM/NDB)	ALIB	NDB	281.0	30 25.93N	95 28.58W
ALICE	ALI	VOR	114.5	27 44.39N	98 1.28W
ALLEGHENY	AGC	VOR	110.0	40 16.73N	80 2.45W
ALLEN (LOM)	ALLE	NDB	365.0	40 24.45N	90 7.17W
ALLEN COUNTY	AOH	VOR	108.4	40 42.44N	83 58.09W
ALLENDALE	ALD	VOR	116.7	33 0.76N	81 17.53W
ALLENTOWN	ABE	VOR	117.5	40 43.61N	75 27.28W
ALLENTOWN (NAVY)	NVK	NDB	368.0	30 46.13N	87 4.36W
ALLIANCE	AIA	VOR	111.8	42 3.35N	102 48.27W
ALMA	AMG	VOR	115.1	31 32.20N	82 30.48W
ALMA	AMN	NDB	329.0	43 19.41N	84 47.12W
ALPENA	APN	VOR	108.8	45 4.98N	83 33.42W
ALPHA	A	NDB	201.0	44 41.43N	63 34.13W
ALPINE	ALP	NDB	245.0	42 14.33N	76 45.84W
ALPINE	ALV	NDB	375.0	45 0.88N	84 48.48W
ALPOS (LOM)	ALPO	NDB	218.0	38 51.32N	89 56.29W
ALTOONA	AOO	VOR	108.8	40 19.54N	78 18.22W
ALTUR (LOM)	ALTU	NDB	362.0	39 45.32N	104 44.51W

Name	Ident.	Type	Freq.	Latitude	Longitude
ALTURAS	ARU	NDB	215.0	41 28.27N	120 33.48W
ALVA	AVK	NDB	203.0	36 46.76N	98 40.27W
ALWOOD	AQE	NDB	230.0	35 42.42N	77 22.31W
AMARILLO	AMA	VOR	117.2	35 17.26N	101 38.36W
AMASON	CZJ	NDB	341.0	31 50.18N	94 8.99W
AMAZON	AZN	NDB	233.0	39 53.05N	94 54.49W
AMBASSADOR	ABG	NDB	404.0	32 35.13N	95 6.78W
AMBLER	AMF	NDB	403.0	67 6.42N	157 51.48W
AMBLER	ING	NDB	275.0	40 7.57N	75 17.11W
AMCHITKA	NIA	VOR	113.2	51 22.54N	179 16.45E
AMEDEE	AHC	VOR	109.0	40 16.08N	120 9.12W
AMERON	AHH	NDB	278.0	45 16.89N	92 22.28W
AMES	AMW	NDB	275.0	41 59.71N	93 37.61W
AMESON	YAN	VOR	112.4	49 46.81N	84 35.49W
AMIENS	GI	NDB	339.0	49 50.51N	2 29.00E
AMOS	9Q	NDB	291.0	48 33.57N	78 14.74W
ANADYR	KB	NDB	790.0	64 44.01N	177 45.00W
ANAHIM LAKE	UAB	NDB	200.0	52 22.79N	125 10.86W
ANAHUAC	CBC	NDB	413.0	29 46.40N	94 39.79W
ANCHORAGE	ANC	VOR	114.3	61 9.06N	150 12.39W
ANDALUSIA	UIA	VOR	110.2	31 18.58N	86 23.53W
ANDERSON COUNTY	AND	NDB	230.0	34 29.89N	82 42.51W
ANDRA (LOM)	ANDR	NDB	223.0	31 23.53N	92 10.92W
ANDRAU	AAP	NDB	269.0	29 44.15N	95 35.41W
ANDREW	AEW	NDB	20.4	25 44.13N	80 9.80W
ANDREWS	ADW	VOR	113.1	38 48.44N	76 51.98W
ANDREWS	ANR	NDB	245.0	32 20.95N	102 32.19W
ANDRI	AJW	NDB	281.0	45 47.51N	95 18.33W
ANGER (LOM)	ANGE	NDB	212.0	30 36.39N	90 25.27W
ANGOLA	ANQ	NDB	347.0	41 38.40N	85 5.22W
ANIAK	ANI	NDB	359.0	61 35.42N	159 35.87W
ANNETTE ISLAND	ANN	VOR	117.1	55 3.64N	131 34.70W
ANOKE (LOM)	ANOK	NDB	272.0	40 37.58N	99 1.54W
ANSON COUNTY	AFP	NDB	283.0	35 1.45N	80 4.99W
ANTELOPE	AOP	NDB	290.0	41 36.26N	109 0.10W
ANTHONY	ANY	VOR	112.9	37 9.54N	98 10.24W
ANTIGO	AIG	NDB	347.0	45 9.51N	89 6.81W
ANTIOCH	AOQ	NDB	287.0	42 0.84N	102 46.09W
ANTLERS	AEE	NDB	391.0	34 11.51N	95 39.11W
ANTON CHICO	ACH	VOR	117.8	35 6.71N	105 2.40W
ANVIK	ANV	NDB	365.0	62 38.50N	160 11.40W
APOLLO	APO	NDB	388.0	16 43.60N	169 32.80W
APPLETON	APE	VOR	116.7	40 9.07N	82 35.30W
ARBOR VITAE	ARV	NDB	221.0	45 55.57N	89 43.73W
ARBUCKLE	AUV	NDB	284.0	34 9.05N	97 7.48W
ARCATA	ACV	VOR	110.2	40 58.90N	124 6.50W
ARDMORE	ADM	VOR	116.7	34 12.70N	97 10.10W
ARKADELPHIA	ADF	NDB	275.0	34 3.33N	93 6.29W
ARMEL	AML	VOR	113.5	38 56.08N	77 28.00W
ARMIN (LOM)	ARMI	NDB	356.0	41 48.63N	71 21.22W
ARMSTRONG	YYW	NDB	223.0	50 18.47N	89 1.33W
ARNOLD AFS	AYX	VOR	112.5	35 23.13N	86 5.22W
ARTDA (LOM)	ARTD	NDB	206.0	42 46.66N	84 29.86W
ARTESIA	ATS	NDB	414.0	32 51.16N	104 27.70W
ARUBA	PJH	VOR	112.5	12 30.54N	69 56.47W
ARUBA (LOM/NDB)	ARUB	NDB	373.0	38 17.46N	104 21.30W
ASH FLAT	AJX	NDB	344.0	36 10.84N	91 36.39W
ASHEE (LOM/NDB)	ASHE	NDB	410.0	36 26.04N	81 19.31W
ASHEY	LJK	NDB	280.0	37 46.40N	77 28.78W
ASHLAND	AAU	NDB	329.0	40 57.81N	82 15.20W
ASHLAND	ASX	VOR	110.2	46 32.97N	90 55.04W
ASHLY (LOM/NDB)	ASHL	NDB	329.0	32 58.58N	80 5.86W
ASTORIA	AST	VOR	114.0	46 9.71N	123 52.82W
ATHENS	AHN	VOR	109.6	33 56.86N	83 19.49W
ATHENS	AHX	NDB	269.0	32 9.57N	95 49.81W
ATIKOKAN	IB	NDB	209.0	48 49.52N	91 34.66W
ATLANTA	ATA	NDB	347.0	33 6.23N	94 11.43W
ATLANTA	ATL	VOR	116.9	33 37.75N	84 26.10W
ATLANTIC	AIO	NDB	365.0	41 24.25N	95 2.78W
ATLANTIC CITY	ACY	VOR	108.6	39 27.36N	74 34.58W

Name	Ident.	Type	Freq.	Latitude	Longitude
ATLIN	YSQ	NDB	260.0	59 37.85N	133 40.52W
ATTU	ATU	NDB	375.0	52 49.75N	173 10.82E
ATWOOD	ADT	NDB	365.0	39 50.34N	101 2.69W
AU SABLE	ASP	VOR	116.1	44 26.83N	83 24.08W
AUDUBON	ADU	NDB	266.0	41 41.43N	94 54.60W
AUGSBURG	AGB	NDB	318.0	48 25.51N	10 56.00E
AUGUSTA	AUG	VOR	111.4	44 19.21N	69 47.79W
AULON (LOM/NDB)	AULO	NDB	287.0	35 3.71N	90 4.30W
AUNEY (LOM)	AUNE	NDB	353.0	41 41.70N	90 39.35W
AURORA	AUH	NDB	278.0	40 53.56N	97 59.83W
AUSTI (LOM/NDB)	AUST	NDB	353.0	30 14.15N	97 37.54W
AUSTIN	AUS	VOR	117.1	30 17.86N	97 42.20W
AUSTIN	JAY	VOR	108.2	43 34.59N	92 55.18W
AUSTN (LOM)	AUST	NDB	371.0	42 7.88N	85 31.79W
AVENAL	AVE	VOR	117.1	35 38.83N	119 58.72W
AVON	AVN	NDB	344.0	43 0.61N	77 46.15W
AYLESFORD	GF	NDB	341.0	45 1.45N	64 48.61W
AYLMER	YQO	VOR	114.2	42 42.41N	80 53.27W
AYR HILL	AYR	VOR	115.5	18 13.49N	77 30.50W
AZALEA PARK	AZS	NDB	336.0	38 0.62N	78 31.09W
BABCO (LOM)	BABC	NDB	385.0	44 51.41N	92 59.07W
BABSY (LOM)	BABS	NDB	419.0	38 15.11N	98 51.35W
BABYLON	BBN	NDB	275.0	40 40.36N	73 23.06W
BAD AXE	BAX	VOR	108.2	43 46.98N	82 59.03W
BADGER	BAE	VOR	116.4	43 7.02N	88 17.06W
BAGOTVILLE	YBG	NDB	356.0	48 20.05N	71 8.75W
BAIE-COMEAU	BC	NDB	414.0	49 7.08N	68 19.57W
BAIE-COMEAU	YBC	VOR	117.7	49 8.05N	68 13.32W
BAKER	BKE	VOR	115.3	44 50.44N	117 48.47W
BAKER LAKE	YBK	VOR	114.5	64 19.30N	96 6.28W
BAKKY (LOM)	BAKK	NDB	278.0	36 11.47N	93 9.61W
BALES (LOM/NDB)	BALE	NDB	396.0	36 35.40N	79 55.04W
BALESIN	BAL	VOR	116.9	14 26.70N	122 2.50E
BALLINGER	UBC	NDB	239.0	31 40.83N	99 58.49W
BALLL (LOM)	BALL	NDB	365.0	40 10.86N	85 19.24W
BALTIMORE	BAL	VOR	115.1	39 10.27N	76 39.67W
BANGOR	BGR	VOR	114.8	44 50.52N	68 52.44W
BARD	BZA	VOR	116.8	32 46.10N	114 36.17W
BARDSTOWN	BRY	NDB	248.0	37 50.88N	85 29.00W
BARNES	BAF	VOR	113.0	42 9.73N	72 42.97W
BARNWELL	BNL	NDB	260.0	33 15.55N	81 22.71W
BARRANQUILLA	BA	NDB	244.0	10 48.00N	74 52.00W
BARRANQUILLA	BAQ	VOR	113.7	10 48.04N	74 51.75W
BARRETTS MOUNTAIN	BZM	VOR	110.8	35 52.14N	81 14.43W
BARRO (LOM)	BARR	NDB	341.0	42 30.88N	94 18.34W
BARROW	BRW	VOR	116.2	71 16.42N	156 47.28W
BARROW COUNTY	BMW	NDB	404.0	33 56.13N	83 35.37W
BARTER ISLAND	BTI	NDB	308.0	70 7.86N	143 38.63W
BARTLESVILLE	BVO	VOR	117.9	36 50.06N	96 1.10W
BARTY (LOM)	BART	NDB	257.0	41 16.62N	75 46.54W
BASTROP	BQP	NDB	329.0	32 45.31N	91 53.01W
BATESVILLE	HLB	NDB	254.0	39 20.99N	85 15.46W
BATHURST	2F	NDB	382.0	47 35.63N	65 50.68W
BATOL (LOM/NDB)	BATO	NDB	272.0	42 21.72N	85 11.07W
BATON ROUGE	BTR	VOR	116.5	30 29.11N	91 17.65W
BATTEN	BAJ	NDB	392.0	40 31.94N	103 13.78W
BATTLE CREEK	BTL	VOR	109.4	42 18.60N	85 15.14W
BATTLE MOUNTAIN	BAM	VOR	112.2	40 34.16N	116 55.34W
BATTLEGROUND	BTG	VOR	116.6	45 44.88N	122 35.49W
BAUDETTE	BDE	VOR	111.6	48 43.38N	94 36.44W
BAY CITY	BYY	NDB	344.0	28 58.35N	95 51.60W
BAY CREEK	BEP	NDB	350.0	32 27.82N	83 45.95W
BAYOU (LOM)	BAYO	NDB	360.0	30 29.13N	89 9.72W
BEADY (LOM)	BEAD	NDB	302.0	44 26.64N	98 20.21W
BEAR CREEK	BCC	NDB	212.0	65 10.45N	152 12.36W
BEAR CREEK	JHN	NDB	341.0	37 38.14N	101 44.08W
BEAR LAKE	BBH	NDB	233.0	42 15.15N	111 20.03W
BEATRICE	BIE	VOR	110.6	40 18.09N	96 45.28W
BEATTY	BTY	VOR	114.7	36 48.04N	116 44.86W
BEAUCE	VLV	VOR	117.2	45 55.51N	70 50.75W
BEAUMONT	BPT	VOR	114.5	29 56.77N	94 0.97W
BEAUVAIS	BV	NDB	391.0	49 29.51N	2 1.80E
BEAUVAIS	BVS	VOR	115.9	49 26.31N	2 9.30E
BEAVER CREEK	BVQ	NDB	260.0	37 1.06N	86 0.55W
BEAVER CREEK	YXQ	NDB	239.0	62 24.54N	140 51.70W
BECCA (LOM)	BECC	NDB	233.0	33 45.40N	118 4.64W
BECKLEY	BKW	VOR	117.7	37 46.83N	81 7.41W
BEDDS (LOM)	BEDD	NDB	332.0	42 28.80N	71 23.32W
BEDFORD	BFR	NDB	344.0	38 50.37N	86 26.21W
BEECHY	BY	NDB	266.0	50 50.53N	107 27.59W
BEEVILLE	BEA	NDB	284.0	28 22.07N	97 47.67W
BEKLOF	FMZ	NDB	392.0	40 35.41N	97 34.08W
BELFAST	BST	NDB	278.0	44 24.67N	69 0.64W
BELIZE	BZE	NDB	392.0	17 32.00N	88 18.00W
BELKNAP	BLO	NDB	328.0	43 32.21N	71 32.22W
BELLA BELLA	YJQ	NDB	325.0	52 11.12N	128 6.82W
BELLAIRE	AIR	VOR	117.1	40 1.03N	80 49.04W
BELLE FOURCHE	EFC	NDB	269.0	44 44.17N	103 51.54W
BELLEVILLE	BL	NDB	362.0	38 27.81N	89 45.39W
BELLGRADE	BDD	NDB	254.0	37 8.74N	88 40.22W
BELLGROVE	BZJ	NDB	328.0	40 26.16N	76 33.18W
BELLINGHAM	BLI	VOR	113.0	48 56.73N	122 34.75W
BEMIDJI	BJI	VOR	108.6	47 34.56N	95 1.48W
BENFI (LOM)	BENF	NDB	353.0	40 44.54N	84 4.87W
BENJE	BHU	NDB	382.0	40 22.54N	79 16.30W
BENNETTSVILLE	BES	NDB	230.0	34 37.22N	79 43.99W
BENSON	BBB	NDB	239.0	45 19.64N	95 39.02W
BENTON	BEE	NDB	414.0	38 0.39N	88 55.92W
BENTON	BEZ	NDB	347.0	34 5.34N	78 51.98W
BENTON RIDGE	BNR	NDB	209.0	41 1.01N	83 40.00W
BENZA (LOM)	BENZ	NDB	338.0	48 53.96N	122 32.09W
BERENS RIVER	YBV	NDB	370.0	52 21.26N	97 1.47W
BERLIN	BML	VOR	110.4	44 38.01N	71 11.17W
BERMUDA	BDA	VOR	113.9	32 21.73N	64 41.39W
BERZ	UIZ	NDB	215.0	42 39.69N	82 57.93W
BESSEMER	BEQ	NDB	368.0	33 18.72N	86 55.39W
BETHEL	BET	VOR	114.1	60 47.10N	161 49.46W
BETHEL (LMM)	ET	NDB	344.0	60 47.81N	161 49.28W
BETHPAGE	BPA	NDB	248.0	40 45.77N	73 26.72W
BETTE (LMM/NDB)	BETT	NDB	308.0	39 45.24N	104 52.96W
BETTLES	BTT	VOR	116.0	66 54.31N	151 32.15W
BIAK	BIK	VOR	112.5	1 10.90S	136 5.10E
BIBLE GROVE	BIB	VOR	109.0	38 55.23N	88 28.91W
BIG BLUE	BJU	NDB	248.0	40 21.83N	96 48.78W
BIG DELTA	BIG	VOR	114.9	64 0.28N	145 43.03W
BIG DOCTOR	BXR	NDB	203.0	45 49.21N	92 22.00W
BIG LAKE	BGQ	VOR	112.5	61 34.18N	149 58.03W
BIG PINEY	BPI	VOR	116.5	42 34.78N	110 6.55W
BIG SPRING	BGS	VOR	114.3	32 23.14N	101 29.02W
BIG SUR	BSR	VOR	114.0	36 10.89N	121 38.53W
BIGBEE	IGB	VOR	116.2	33 29.14N	88 30.82W
BILLINGS	BIL	VOR	114.5	45 48.52N	108 37.47W
BILMART	AOV	NDB	341.0	36 58.19N	92 40.64W
BILOY (LOM/NDB)	BILO	NDB	521.0	39 7.23N	95 41.23W
BIMINI	ZBB	NDB	396.0	25 42.54N	79 16.33W
BIMINI	ZBV	VOR	116.7	25 42.26N	79 17.67W
BINGHAMTON	BGM	VOR	112.2	42 9.46N	76 8.19W
BIORKA ISLAND	BKA	VOR	113.8	56 51.58N	135 33.08W
BISCAYNE BAY	BSY	VOR	117.1	25 40.32N	80 10.65W
BISHOP	BIH	VOR	109.6	37 22.62N	118 21.99W
BISHOP	BZP	NDB	371.0	64 44.26N	156 48.53W
BISMARCK	BIS	VOR	116.5	46 45.72N	100 39.92W
BLACK HILLS	SPF	NDB	300.0	44 29.07N	103 47.07W
BLACK RIVER FALLS	BCK	NDB	362.0	44 15.29N	90 50.94W
BLACKSTONE	BKT	NDB	326.0	37 7.68N	78 2.48W
BLANDING	BDG	NDB	340.0	37 31.05N	109 29.57W
BLAYD (LOM/NDB)	BLAY	NDB	242.0	37 59.22N	84 39.61W
BLOCK ISLAND	BID	NDB	216.0	41 10.01N	71 34.77W
BLOOD (LOM/NDB)	BLOO	NDB	365.0	31 49.83N	86 6.32W
BLOOMFIELD	BEX	NDB	269.0	40 44.71N	92 25.83W

Name	Ident.	Type	Freq.	Latitude	Longitude
BLOOMINGTON	BMI	VOR	108.2	40 28.86N	88 55.88W
BLUE EARTH	SBU	NDB	332.0	43 35.83N	94 5.81W
BLUE MESA	HBU	VOR	114.9	38 27.13N	107 2.38W
BLUE RIDGE	BUJ	VOR	114.9	33 17.00N	96 21.90W
BLUEFIELD	BLF	VOR	110.0	37 18.39N	81 11.65W
BLUIE (LOM)	BLUI	NDB	219.0	29 28.48N	98 31.12W
BLYTHE	BLH	VOR	117.4	33 35.77N	114 45.67W
BOBTOWN	BBO	NDB	269.0	39 43.61N	79 56.37W
BOCAS DEL TORO	BDT	VOR	114.9	9 20.29N	82 15.05W
BODEY (LOM/NDB)	BODE	NDB	411.0	44 18.49N	121 1.14W
BOGEY (LOM)	BOGE	NDB	342.0	41 42.98N	70 12.18W
BOGGA (LOM)	BOGG	NDB	211.0	33 32.07N	85 55.88W
BOILER	BVT	VOR	115.1	40 33.38N	87 4.16W
BOILING FORK	BGF	NDB	263.0	35 10.69N	86 4.09W
BOING (LMM)	BOIN	NDB	245.0	32 44.40N	117 12.95W
BOISE	BOI	VOR	113.3	43 33.18N	116 11.53W
BOLES	BWS	VOR	109.6	32 49.28N	106 0.79W
BOLL WEEVIL	BVG	NDB	308.0	31 20.22N	85 59.00W
BONG	SUW	NDB	260.0	46 41.47N	92 6.21W
BONHAM	HJM	NDB	415.0	33 36.85N	96 10.56W
BONNEVILLE	BVL	VOR	112.3	40 43.58N	113 45.45W
BOOIE (LOM/NDB)	BOOI	NDB	221.0	36 23.92N	82 29.77W
BOONE	BNW	NDB	407.0	42 3.27N	93 51.18W
BORGER	BGD	VOR	108.6	35 48.43N	101 22.93W
BORINQUEN	BQN	VOR	113.5	18 29.88N	67 6.49W
BORLAND	HBT	NDB	390.0	55 18.95N	160 31.10W
BORTEX	BPX	VOR	224.0	35 37.93N	101 23.87W
BOSTON	BOS	VOR	112.7	42 21.46N	70 59.37W
BOULDER CITY	BLD	VOR	116.7	35 59.75N	114 51.82W
BOULDER JUNCTION	BDJ	VOR	206.0	46 8.04N	89 39.34W
BOURSONNE	BSN	VOR	112.5	49 11.31N	3 3.40E
BOUTN (LOM/NDB)	BOUT	NDB	230.0	39 49.16N	83 12.29W
BOWLING GREEN	BWG	VOR	117.9	36 55.73N	86 26.61W
BOWMAN	BOD	NDB	374.0	46 11.11N	103 25.73W
BOWMAN	BQM	VOR	112.2	38 13.82N	85 39.89W
BOYNE FALLS	BFA	NDB	263.0	45 10.01N	84 55.32W
BOYSEN RESERVOIR	BOY	VOR	117.8	43 27.80N	108 17.98W
BOZEMAN	BZN	VOR	112.2	45 47.04N	111 9.33W
BRACY (LOM/NDB)	BRAC	NDB	399.0	44 27.62N	69 44.09W
BRADFORD	BDF	VOR	114.7	41 9.59N	89 35.27W
BRADFORD	BFD	VOR	116.6	41 47.19N	78 37.16W
BRADLEY	BDL	VOR	109.0	41 56.46N	72 41.32W
BRADSHAW	BSF	NDB	339.0	19 45.64N	155 35.68W
BRADY	BBD	NDB	380.0	31 10.69N	99 19.36W
BRAFO (LOM/NDB)	BRAF	NDB	224.0	41 45.27N	78 34.42W
BRAINERD	BRD	VOR	116.9	46 20.91N	94 1.56W
BRANDON	BR	NDB	233.0	49 54.48N	100 4.41W
BRANDON	YBR	VOR	113.8	49 54.61N	99 56.74W
BRANTFORD	FD	NDB	207.0	43 4.41N	80 24.97W
BRANTLEY	XBR	NDB	410.0	31 33.72N	86 17.58W
BRASHEAR	BHG	NDB	338.0	33 9.51N	95 37.10W
BRAY	BRY	VOR	114.1	48 24.41N	3 17.70E
BRAY	BRY	NDB	277.0	48 24.41N	3 17.70E
BRAZOS RIVER	GZV	NDB	280.0	32 57.10N	98 24.79W
BRECKENRIDGE	BKD	NDB	245.0	32 44.85N	98 53.47W
BRECKENRIDGE-WAHP	BWP	NDB	233.0	46 14.71N	96 36.22W
BREIT (LOM)	BREI	NDB	400.0	43 7.60N	77 33.23W
BRENHAM	BNH	NDB	362.0	30 13.35N	96 22.38W
BRENNER	FNB	NDB	404.0	40 4.59N	95 35.21W
BRENZ (LOM/NDB)	BREN	NDB	260.0	32 24.79N	90 15.68W
BREWSTER COUNTY	BWR	NDB	201.0	30 27.60N	103 38.78W
BRIDGE	BDQ	NDB	208.0	35 8.36N	92 42.74W
BRIDGE	OGY	NDB	414.0	40 34.10N	73 52.98W
BRIDGEPORT	BDR	VOR	108.8	41 9.65N	73 7.47W
BRIDGEPORT	BPR	VOR	116.5	33 14.27N	97 45.98W
BRIDGEWATER	VBW	NDB	241.0	38 21.94N	78 57.67W
BRIEL (LOM)	BRIE	NDB	395.0	44 28.62N	74 7.45W
BRIGGS	BSV	VOR	112.4	40 44.45N	81 25.93W
BRIGHAM CITY	BMC	NDB	294.0	41 30.97N	112 4.68W
BRIJJ (LOM)	BRIJ	NDB	379.0	37 34.34N	122 15.59W
BRINKLEY	BKZ	NDB	242.0	34 52.90N	91 10.67W
BRINN (LOM)	BRIN	NDB	219.0	39 37.04N	86 24.47W
BRISTOW	TZO	NDB	251.0	35 46.20N	96 25.48W
BRITTON	BTN	NDB	386.0	45 48.84N	97 44.64W
BROAD RIVER	BRA	NDB	379.0	35 16.37N	82 28.26W
BROADUS	BDX	NDB	335.0	45 26.16N	105 24.67W
BROADVIEW	YDR	VOR	117.5	50 21.79N	102 32.41W
BROADWAY	BWZ	VOR	114.2	40 47.92N	74 49.31W
BROCKVILLE	3B	NDB	300.0	44 42.10N	75 42.00W
BROKEN BOW	BBW	NDB	290.0	41 26.05N	99 38.15W
BROMONT	6R	NDB	343.0	45 14.45N	72 47.67W
BRONS (LOM)	BRON	NDB	407.0	33 2.68N	96 52.23W
BROOKE	BRV	VOR	114.5	38 20.19N	77 21.17W
BROOKFIELD	BZK	NDB	383.0	39 45.86N	93 6.55W
BROOKHAVEN	BVV	NDB	407.0	31 36.49N	90 24.62W
BROOKINGS	BKX	VOR	108.8	44 18.20N	96 48.91W
BROOKLEY	BFM	VOR	112.8	30 36.77N	88 3.33W
BROOKS COUNTY	BKS	NDB	353.0	27 12.43N	98 7.28W
BROOKSVILLE	BKV	NDB	278.0	28 28.44N	82 26.99W
BROOKWOOD	OKW	VOR	111.0	33 14.38N	87 15.00W
BROWERVILLE	VIR	NDB	281.0	71 16.97N	156 47.08W
BROWNE	HYX	NDB	385.0	43 25.90N	83 51.49W
BROWNFIELD	BFE	NDB	311.0	33 10.76N	102 11.53W
BROWNSVILLE	BRO	VOR	116.3	25 55.45N	97 22.53W
BROWNWOOD	BWD	VOR	108.6	31 53.56N	98 57.45W
BRUCK (LOM)	BRUC	NDB	387.0	61 10.07N	150 10.62W
BRUNSWICK	SSI	VOR	109.8	31 3.04N	81 26.76W
BRUNSWICK (NAVY)	NHZ	VOR	115.2	43 54.15N	69 56.71W
BRUNY (LOM)	BRUN	NDB	315.0	39 50.50N	84 20.95W
BRYAN	BYN	NDB	260.0	41 28.80N	84 27.96W
BRYAN	STF	NDB	281.0	33 25.93N	88 51.02W
BRYCE CANYON	BCE	VOR	112.8	37 41.36N	112 18.23W
BUCHOLZ	NDJ	NDB	359.0	8 43.25N	167 43.65E
BUCKEYE	BUD	VOR	109.8	40 37.00N	83 3.81W
BUCKEYE	BXK	VOR	110.6	33 27.21N	112 49.48W
BUCKHORN	BHN	NDB	391.0	37 41.86N	92 6.23W
BUCKLAND	BVK	NDB	325.0	65 58.80N	161 8.96W
BUFFALO	BFK	NDB	215.0	36 51.86N	99 37.21W
BUFFALO	BUA	VOR	109.4	45 32.76N	103 28.58W
BUFFALO	BUF	VOR	116.4	42 55.75N	78 38.78W
BUKA	BUK	NDB	269.0	5 26.50S	154 40.10E
BULLDOG	BJT	NDB	221.0	33 57.10N	83 13.18W
BULLION	BQU	VOR	114.5	40 45.59N	115 45.68W
BULLOCK COUNTY	IBU	NDB	407.0	32 24.93N	81 39.84W
BUNAN (LOM)	BUNA	NDB	371.0	47 26.71N	94 50.10W
BURBUN	BUU	VOR	114.5	42 41.37N	88 18.11W
BURKE COUNTY	BXG	NDB	356.0	33 2.56N	82 0.29W
BURKE LAKEFRONT	BKL	NDB	416.0	41 31.74N	81 39.79W
BURLEY	BYI	VOR	114.1	42 34.82N	113 51.95W
BURLINGTON	BRL	VOR	111.4	40 43.41N	90 55.55W
BURLINGTON	BTV	VOR	117.5	44 23.84N	73 10.96W
BURLINGTON	BUY	NDB	329.0	36 3.00N	79 28.80W
BURLN (LOM/NDB)	BURL	NDB	321.0	39 2.76N	84 46.39W
BURNET	BMQ	NDB	341.0	30 44.35N	98 14.24W
BURNHAM	BUP	NDB	348.0	44 41.85N	69 21.47W
BURNS (LOM)	BURN	NDB	390.0	40 39.26N	91 7.38W
BURNS FLAT	BFV	VOR	110.0	35 14.22N	99 12.37W
BURWASH	DB	NDB	341.0	61 20.43N	138 59.01W
BURWELL	BUB	VOR	112.8	41 46.59N	99 8.86W
BURWI	ULH	NDB	332.0	35 27.70N	86 14.50W
BUSHE (LOM)	BUSH	NDB	233.0	33 17.22N	81 56.81W
BUSHI (LOM/NDB)	BUSH	NDB	346.0	37 46.94N	80 28.11W
BUTLER	BUM	VOR	115.9	38 16.33N	94 29.29W
BUTTONVILLE	KZ	NDB	248.0	43 56.03N	79 19.75W
BUTTS	FCS	NDB	408.0	38 40.85N	104 45.41W
CABBI (LOM)	CABB	NDB	388.0	37 52.21N	89 14.73W
CABO ROJO	CRO	VOR	114.3	17 56.00N	71 39.00W
CADDO MILLS	MII	NDB	316.0	33 2.43N	96 14.91W
CADILLAC	CAD	NDB	269.0	44 16.51N	85 24.85W
CADIZ	CFX	NDB	239.0	40 14.21N	81 0.79W

Name	Ident.	Type	Freq.	Latitude	Longitude
CAGUR (LOM)	CAGU	NDB	347.0	42 50.63N	97 18.12W
CAHABA	CAQ	VOR	114.9	32 20.70N	86 59.49W
CAHOKIA	CPS	VOR	375.0	38 34.65N	90 9.96W
CAIDY	CYR	NDB	338.0	30 53.30N	84 9.56W
CAIRN MOUNTAIN	CRN	NDB	281.0	61 5.97N	155 33.14W
CAIRNS	OZR	VOR	111.2	31 16.15N	85 43.58W
CAIRO	CIR	NDB	397.0	37 3.71N	89 13.41W
CALAB (LOM)	CALA	NDB	267.0	33 53.12N	78 37.80W
CALEDONIA	CBM	VOR	115.2	33 38.50N	88 26.31W
CALEDONIA	CHU	NDB	209.0	43 35.22N	91 29.42W
CALERA	AOA	NDB	215.0	33 7.11N	86 46.03W
CALGARY	YC	NDB	344.0	51 4.86N	113 54.53W
CALGARY	YYC	VOR	116.7	51 6.91N	113 52.93W
CALHOUN	OUK	NDB	323.0	34 24.10N	84 55.59W
CALIN (LOM)	CALI	NDB	266.0	44 34.16N	90 9.06W
CALLAHAN	CNQ	NDB	379.0	37 15.69N	80 9.48W
CALLOWAY	CEY	NDB	348.0	36 39.80N	88 22.08W
CALOO (LOM)	CALO	NDB	341.0	26 30.97N	81 57.00W
CALVERTON	CCC	VOR	117.2	40 55.79N	72 47.93W
CAMARILLO	CMA	VOR	115.8	34 12.76N	119 5.66W
CAMBRIDGE	CAM	VOR	115.0	42 59.67N	73 20.64W
CAMBRIDGE	CBG	NDB	350.0	45 33.46N	93 15.73W
CAMBRIDGE	CDI	NDB	223.0	39 57.85N	81 35.29W
CAMBRIDGE	CGE	NDB	257.0	38 32.30N	76 1.91W
CAMBRIDGE BAY	YCB	VOR	112.7	69 7.07N	105 10.36W
CAMDEN	CDH	NDB	335.0	33 36.82N	92 46.05W
CAMDEN	CDN	NDB	263.0	34 17.05N	80 33.70W
CAMERON	EZZ	NDB	394.0	39 43.76N	94 16.33W
CAMILLA	CXU	NDB	369.0	31 12.88N	84 14.21W
CAMOR (LOM/NDB)	CAMO	NDB	299.0	39 52.98N	79 44.68W
CAMP	CPC	NDB	227.0	34 16.32N	78 42.83W
CAMPBELL LAKE	CMQ	NDB	338.0	61 10.27N	150 2.86W
CAMPBELL RIVER	YBL	NDB	203.0	50 0.39N	125 21.45W
CAMPI (LOM/NDB)	CAMP	NDB	407.0	31 39.45N	93 4.66W
CANARSIE	CRI	VOR	112.3	40 36.76N	73 53.67W
CANTON	CTK	NDB	236.0	40 33.96N	90 4.62W
CANTON	DJD	NDB	415.0	34 15.15N	84 29.26W
CAP HAITIEN	HCN	VOR	113.9	19 43.64N	72 11.83W
CAP HAITIEN	HTN	NDB	288.0	19 44.05N	72 12.00W
CAPE CHARLES	CCV	VOR	112.2	37 20.91N	75 59.97W
CAPE GIRARDEAU	CGI	VOR	112.9	37 13.66N	89 34.34W
CAPE LISBURNE	LUR	NDB	385.0	68 51.97N	166 4.18W
CAPE NEWENHAM	EHM	NDB	385.0	58 39.36N	162 4.55W
CAPE ROMANZOF	CZF	NDB	275.0	61 47.45N	165 58.17W
CAPE SCOTT	ZES	NDB	353.0	50 46.95N	128 25.61W
CAPITAL	CAP	VOR	112.7	39 53.54N	89 37.53W
CAPITAN	CEP	NDB	260.0	33 29.42N	105 24.27W
CAPITOL	CVP	NDB	317.0	46 36.41N	111 56.23W
CAPOK (LOM)	CAPO	NDB	360.0	27 59.72N	82 42.19W
CAPPY (LOM)	CAPP	NDB	410.0	42 50.39N	87 54.77W
CAPSHAW	CWH	NDB	350.0	34 46.43N	86 46.74W
CAPTAIN	EQZ	NDB	308.0	38 52.05N	85 58.38W
CARBON	LQX	NDB	339.0	40 48.73N	75 45.54W
CARBON	PUC	VOR	115.5	39 36.20N	110 45.21W
CARBONDALE	CQL	NDB	344.0	39 24.71N	107 9.57W
CARGL (LOM/NDB)	CARG	NDB	230.0	42 21.38N	82 57.26W
CARLETON	CRL	VOR	115.7	42 2.89N	83 27.46W
CARLSBAD	CNM	VOR	116.3	32 15.40N	104 13.56W
CARLZ (LOM)	CARL	NDB	402.0	32 16.01N	104 20.31W
CARMA (LOM/NDB)	CARM	NDB	353.0	30 52.91N	89 51.73W
CARMEL	CMK	VOR	116.6	41 16.81N	73 34.88W
CARMI	CUL	NDB	332.0	38 5.65N	88 7.19W
CARMI	YXO	NDB	335.0	49 29.72N	119 5.35W
CARNEY	CAN	NDB	274.0	47 24.64N	122 50.33W
CAROLINA BEACH	CLB	NDB	216.0	34 6.38N	77 57.68W
CARROLL	CIN	NDB	397.0	42 2.52N	94 47.26W
CARROLLTON	GPQ	NDB	239.0	33 33.95N	85 7.85W
CARTER	CJD	NDB	263.0	36 27.68N	94 4.17W
CARTERSVILLE	EVZ	NDB	308.0	34 12.00N	84 50.61W
CARTHAGE	RPF	NDB	332.0	32 10.82N	94 17.78W
CASANOVA	CSN	VOR	116.3	38 38.48N	77 51.93W
CASCADE	CQD	NDB	372.0	42 7.16N	80 6.27W
CASER (LOM)	CASE	NDB	338.0	39 44.94N	82 32.12W
CASEY	CZB	NDB	359.0	39 18.32N	88 0.12W
CASSE (LOM/NDB)	CASS	NDB	260.0	39 27.12N	104 50.75W
CASTLE	UCP	NDB	272.0	41 1.43N	80 24.89W
CASTLEGAR	CG	NDB	227.0	49 26.84N	117 34.50W
CASTROVILLE	CVB	NDB	338.0	29 20.77N	98 50.95W
CATTA (LOM)	CATT	NDB	375.0	33 38.81N	84 32.53W
CAVALRY	CVY	NDB	314.0	39 1.57N	96 47.67W
CAVERNS	LUA	NDB	245.0	38 41.98N	78 28.30W
CAYMAN BRAC	CBC	NDB	217.0	19 41.39N	79 51.42W
CECIL	VQQ	VOR	117.9	30 12.79N	81 53.45W
CEDAR CITY	CDC	VOR	108.6	37 47.25N	113 4.09W
CEDAR LAKE	VCN	VOR	115.2	39 32.27N	74 58.03W
CEDAR RAPIDS	CID	VOR	117.6	41 53.26N	91 47.14W
CENTER POINT	CSI	VOR	117.5	29 55.35N	99 12.85W
CENTERVILLE	TVK	NDB	290.0	40 41.24N	92 54.00W
CENTRAL	CEM	NDB	373.0	65 34.41N	144 47.65W
CENTRAL	SFZ	NDB	241.0	41 55.15N	71 29.31W
CENTRAL CITY	CCT	VOR	109.8	37 22.95N	87 15.82W
CENTRAL WISCONSIN	HWS	NDB	377.0	44 46.62N	89 40.73W
CENTRALIA	ENL	VOR	115.0	38 25.21N	89 9.54W
CHADRON	CDR	VOR	113.4	42 33.54N	103 18.73W
CHALLIS	LLJ	NDB	397.0	44 31.17N	114 12.94W
CHAMPAIGN	CMI	VOR	110.0	40 2.08N	88 16.56W
CHAMPLAIN	BV	NDB	336.0	46 52.28N	71 16.89W
CHANDALAR LAKE	CQR	NDB	263.0	67 30.16N	148 28.16W
CHANDLER	FCH	NDB	344.0	36 43.44N	119 50.02W
CHANNEL HEAD	CM	NDB	379.0	47 34.03N	59 9.56W
CHANUTE	CNU	VOR	109.2	37 37.58N	95 35.61W
CHAPARROSA RANCH	CPZ	NDB	385.0	28 54.60N	100 0.34W
CHAPLEAU	YLD	NDB	335.0	47 45.36N	83 24.76W
CHAPPELL	CNP	NDB	383.0	41 4.61N	102 27.53W
CHARDON	CXR	VOR	112.7	41 31.02N	81 9.79W
CHARITON	CNC	NDB	209.0	41 1.01N	93 21.72W
CHARLES CITY	CCY	NDB	375.0	43 4.12N	92 36.49W
CHARLES-DE-GAULLE (PARIS)	CGO	NDB	343.0	48 59.31N	2 24.10E
CHARLES-DE-GAULLE (PARIS)	CGZ	NDB	370.0	49 0.41N	2 44.50E
CHARLES-DE-GAULLE (PARIS)	RSO	NDB	364.0	49 0.71N	2 21.70E
CHARLES-DE-GAULLE (PARIS)	CGN	VOR	115.4	49 1.21N	2 30.10E
CHARLES-DE-GAULLE (PARIS)	RSY	NDB	356.0	49 1.91N	2 42.40E
CHARLESTON	CHQ	NDB	208.0	36 50.71N	89 21.40W
CHARLESTON	CHS	VOR	113.5	32 53.67N	80 2.27W
CHARLESTON	HVQ	VOR	117.4	38 20.99N	81 46.19W
CHARLEVOIX	CVX	NDB	222.0	45 18.19N	85 15.89W
CHARLEVOIX	ML	NDB	392.0	47 37.41N	70 19.49W
CHARLO	CL	NDB	207.0	48 0.55N	66 26.21W
CHARLOTTE	CLT	VOR	115.0	35 11.42N	80 57.11W
CHARLOTTETOWN	YG	NDB	347.0	46 11.55N	63 8.89W
CHARLOTTETOWN	YYG	VOR	114.1	46 12.45N	62 58.73W
CHARTRES	CHW	VOR	115.2	48 28.81N	0 59.30E
CHASE CITY	CXE	NDB	342.0	36 47.50N	78 30.05W
CHATEAUDUN	CDN	VOR	116.1	48 3.51N	1 22.70E
CHATEAUDUN	CDN	NDB	359.5	48 3.81N	1 21.80E
CHATHAM	4L	NDB	236.0	42 18.75N	82 4.66W
CHATHAM	CAT	NDB	254.0	40 44.47N	74 25.79W
CHATHAM	F9	NDB	530.0	47 0.51N	65 25.60W
CHATILLON	CTL	VOR	117.6	49 8.31N	3 34.70E
CHENA	CUN	NDB	257.0	64 50.31N	147 29.39W
CHERAW	CQW	NDB	409.0	34 44.52N	79 51.94W
CHERN (LOM/NDB)	CHER	NDB	359.0	42 49.41N	71 36.13W
CHEROKEE	CKW	VOR	115.0	41 45.35N	107 34.92W
CHEROKEE COUNTY	JSO	NDB	263.0	31 52.22N	95 12.93W
CHERRY POINT MCAS	NKT	NDB	245.0	34 50.05N	76 48.15W

Name	Ident.	Type	Freq.	Latitude	Longitude
CHESA (LOM)	CHES	NDB	241.0	40 35.63N	74 13.80W
CHESAPEAKE	CPK	NDB	261.0	36 39.99N	76 19.47W
CHESTER	CTR	VOR	115.1	42 17.49N	72 56.96W
CHESTERFIELD	CTF	VOR	108.2	34 39.04N	80 16.49W
CHETWYND	F6	NDB	210.0	55 41.68N	121 32.26W
CHEYENNE	CYS	VOR	113.1	41 12.67N	104 46.38W
CHIBOO	MT	NDB	209.0	49 47.98N	74 29.72W
CHICAGO HEIGHTS	CGT	VOR	114.2	41 30.61N	87 34.29W
CHICAGO O'HARE INTL	I-FJ	VOR	110.1	41 58.27N	87 52.71W
CHICAGO O'HARE INTL	I-HN	VOR	111.3	41 59.95N	87 53.69W
CHICAGO O'HARE INTL	I-IA	VOR	110.5	41 59.04N	87 55.30W
CHICAGO O'HARE INTL	I-ID	VOR	110.8	42 0.29N	87 55.08W
CHICAGO O'HARE INTL	I-JA	VOR	110.5	41 59.04N	87 53.17W
CHICAGO O'HARE INTL	I-LQ	VOR	110.1	41 57.10N	87 54.09W
CHICAGO O'HARE INTL	I-ME	VOR	111.1	41 58.15N	87 52.68W
CHICAGO O'HARE INTL	I-OH	VOR	110.9	41 58.80N	87 53.39W
CHICAGO O'HARE INTL	I-OR	VOR	109.8	41 57.67N	87 54.00W
CHICAGO O'HARE INTL	I-RV	VOR	109.0	41 59.52N	87 56.08W
CHICAGO O'HARE INTL	I-RX	VOR	111.3	41 58.27N	87 55.54W
CHICAGO O'HARE INTL	I-TS	VOR	111.1	41 58.15N	87 55.54W
CHICAGO O'HARE INTL	ORD	VOR	113.9	41 59.27N	87 54.29W
CHICKASHA	OLR	NDB	290.0	35 6.28N	97 58.30W
CHICO	CIC	VOR	109.8	39 47.40N	121 50.83W
CHIHUAHUA	CUU	VOR	114.1	28 48.51N	105 57.50W
CHILDRESS	CDS	VOR	117.6	34 22.15N	100 17.34W
CHILLICOTHE	CHT	NDB	375.0	39 46.64N	93 29.65W
CHINA LAKE (NAVY)	NID	NDB	348.0	35 41.18N	117 41.49W
CHINEN	TIC	VOR	114.2	26 9.61N	127 47.80E
CHOCOWINITY	RNW	NDB	388.0	35 30.58N	77 6.40W
CHOCTAW	BCZ	NDB	228.0	32 6.86N	88 7.29W
CHOO CHOO	GQO	VOR	115.8	34 57.68N	85 9.20W
CHOTEAU	CHX	NDB	269.0	47 49.36N	112 10.26W
CHUALAR	UAD	NDB	263.0	36 29.46N	121 28.49W
CHUKK	IY	NDB	417.0	43 8.04N	92 43.69W
CHUPP (LOM)	CHUP	NDB	388.0	41 52.65N	72 45.98W
CHURCHILL	YYQ	VOR	114.1	58 44.52N	94 8.12W
CHUTE-DES-PASSES	DG	NDB	244.0	49 53.88N	71 15.24W
CIMARRON	CIM	VOR	116.4	36 29.49N	104 52.32W
CINCINNATI	CVG	VOR	117.3	39 0.97N	84 42.21W
CINCINNATI	LUK	NDB	335.0	39 9.56N	84 20.53W
CINDY (LOM)	CIND	NDB	326.0	41 53.15N	91 48.15W
CIRCLE	CRR	NDB	245.0	47 25.11N	105 33.53W
CIRCLEVILLE	CYO	NDB	366.0	39 31.19N	82 58.78W
CITY LAKE	CQJ	NDB	266.0	35 42.98N	79 51.92W
CIUDAD JUAREZ	CJS	VOR	116.7	31 38.17N	106 25.58W
CIVIC MEMORIAL	CVM	NDB	263.0	38 53.55N	90 3.38W
CLAM COVE	CMJ	NDB	396.0	55 20.74N	131 41.79W
CLAM LAKE	CXK	NDB	251.0	44 53.97N	85 14.38W
CLARENDON	CNZ	NDB	281.0	34 54.63N	100 52.08W
CLARINDA	ICL	NDB	353.0	40 43.61N	95 1.65W
CLARION	CAV	NDB	387.0	42 44.76N	93 45.53W
CLARION	CIP	VOR	112.9	41 8.78N	79 27.48W
CLARK COUNTY	CCJ	NDB	341.0	39 52.43N	83 46.77W
CLARKSBURG	CKB	VOR	112.6	39 15.20N	80 16.07W
CLARKSDALE	CKM	NDB	341.0	34 17.59N	90 30.95W
CLARKSVILLE	CKV	VOR	110.6	36 37.33N	87 24.76W
CLARKSVILLE	CZE	NDB	201.0	35 28.16N	93 25.41W
CLAWW (LOM/NDB)	CLAW	NDB	229.0	38 5.23N	85 45.45W
CLAY	CJY	NDB	275.0	43 3.18N	75 15.87W
CLAY CENTER	CYW	NDB	362.0	39 22.85N	97 9.67W
CLAYE (LOM/NDB)	CLAY	NDB	382.0	39 3.39N	86 35.95W
CLEMSON	CEU	NDB	257.0	34 40.44N	82 53.21W
CLERA (LOM)	CLER	NDB	362.0	41 24.16N	73 7.19W
CLIFS (LOM/NDB)	CLIF	NDB	410.0	39 19.33N	85 49.11W
CLINTON	CLK	NDB	320.0	35 32.36N	98 56.10W
CLINTON	CTZ	NDB	412.0	34 58.53N	78 21.78W
CLINTON	CWI	NDB	377.0	41 49.73N	90 19.66W
CLINTONVILLE	CLI	NDB	209.0	44 37.14N	88 43.99W
CLOQUET	COQ	NDB	335.0	46 41.84N	92 30.20W
CLOVIS	CZQ	VOR	112.9	36 53.07N	119 48.91W

Name	Ident.	Type	Freq.	Latitude	Longitude
COALDALE	OAL	VOR	117.7	38 0.21N	117 46.23W
COCHISE	CIE	VOR	115.8	32 2.01N	109 45.49W
CODEE (LOM)	CODE	NDB	389.0	42 33.63N	88 1.73W
CODY	COD	VOR	111.8	44 37.23N	108 57.88W
COEHILL	VIE	VOR	115.1	44 39.66N	77 53.29W
COEUR D ALENE	COE	VOR	108.8	47 46.43N	116 49.24W
COFFEE CO	OWC	NDB	390.0	31 24.30N	82 55.43W
COFFEYVILLE	CFV	NDB	212.0	37 5.76N	95 34.43W
COFFI (LOM)	COFF	NDB	242.0	31 41.64N	97 12.23W
COFIELD	CVI	VOR	114.6	36 22.38N	76 52.29W
COGAN	TZ	NDB	364.0	39 5.20N	78 4.12W
COGHLAN ISLAND	CGL	NDB	212.0	58 21.57N	134 41.96W
COLBE (LOM)	COLB	NDB	278.0	38 16.73N	75 24.35W
COLBY	CBK	NDB	400.0	39 25.67N	101 3.19W
COLD BAY	CDB	VOR	112.6	55 16.06N	162 46.46W
COLE SPRING	CPP	NDB	230.0	34 22.08N	86 49.43W
COLEMAN	COM	NDB	385.0	31 50.48N	99 24.32W
COLFA (LOM)	COLF	NDB	232.0	39 39.42N	86 11.13W
COLIJ (LOM/NDB)	COLI	NDB	230.0	46 41.90N	100 38.87W
COLLEGE STATION	CLL	VOR	113.3	30 36.31N	96 25.24W
COLLIER COUNTY	CCE	VOR	108.6	26 9.21N	81 46.69W
COLLIERS	IRQ	VOR	113.9	33 42.45N	82 9.72W
COLLN (LOM)	COLL	NDB	400.0	40 21.80N	104 58.28W
COLORADO SPRINGS	COS	VOR	112.5	38 56.68N	104 38.01W
COLTS NECK	COL	VOR	115.4	40 18.71N	74 9.59W
COLUMBIA	CAE	VOR	114.7	33 51.44N	81 3.23W
COLUMBIA	COU	VOR	110.2	38 48.66N	92 13.10W
COLUMBIA	CUF	NDB	404.0	38 1.87N	120 24.83W
COLUMBUS	CSG	VOR	117.1	32 36.92N	85 1.06W
COLUMBUS	CUS	VOR	111.2	31 49.15N	107 34.47W
COLUMBUS	OLU	VOR	112.2	41 27.01N	97 20.45W
COMMERCE	DDA	NDB	244.0	34 3.74N	83 31.26W
COMOX	QQ	NDB	400.0	49 45.25N	124 57.49W
COMPIEGNE	CO	NDB	553.5	49 26.11N	2 48.40E
COMPTON	CPM	NDB	378.0	33 53.34N	118 14.84W
CONCORD	CCR	VOR	117.0	38 2.70N	122 2.71W
CONCORD	CON	VOR	112.9	43 13.20N	71 34.53W
CONCORDIA	CNK	NDB	335.0	39 33.21N	97 39.07W
CONDA (LOM/NDB)	COND	NDB	373.0	40 35.22N	73 47.97W
CONES	ETL	VOR	110.2	38 2.42N	108 15.52W
CONEY	OHY	NDB	400.0	31 59.83N	83 51.76W
CONIS (LOM)	CONI	NDB	275.0	32 46.49N	96 46.51W
CONNERSVILLE	CEV	NDB	275.0	39 41.86N	85 8.06W
CONOR (LOM/NDB)	CONO	NDB	382.0	27 50.08N	97 34.59W
CONRAD	CRD	NDB	293.0	48 11.15N	111 54.85W
CONWAY	CWS	NDB	302.0	35 5.05N	92 25.61W
COOK	CKK	NDB	365.0	25 47.90N	80 20.92W
COOK	CQM	NDB	233.0	47 49.27N	92 41.48W
COOKEVILLE	CJE	NDB	326.0	36 11.58N	85 29.07W
COOLE (LOM)	COOL	NDB	404.0	37 10.82N	93 25.02W
COPPERTOWN	CPN	VOR	111.6	46 1.98N	112 44.83W
CORINTH	CRX	VOR	338.0	34 54.75N	88 36.02W
CORNING	CRZ	NDB	296.0	40 59.79N	94 45.41W
CORO	CRO	VOR	117.3	11 25.00N	69 42.00W
CORONA	CNX	VOR	115.5	34 22.03N	105 40.68W
CORONACA	GIW	NDB	239.0	34 15.23N	82 5.17W
CORPUS CHRISTI	CRP	VOR	115.5	27 54.23N	97 26.70W
CORRY	ORJ	NDB	258.0	41 54.76N	79 38.90W
CORSICANA	CRS	NDB	396.0	32 1.67N	96 23.71W
CORTEZ	CEZ	VOR	108.4	37 23.40N	108 33.70W
CORVALLIS	CVO	VOR	115.4	44 29.98N	123 17.62W
COSME (LOM)	COSM	NDB	368.0	28 5.12N	82 31.51W
COTULLA	COT	VOR	115.8	28 27.72N	99 7.11W
COULOMMIERS	CLM	VOR	112.9	48 50.71N	3 0.90E
COUNCIL	CQI	NDB	274.0	44 45.10N	116 26.57W
COURT HOUSE	CSS	NDB	414.0	39 35.98N	83 23.53W
COVINGTON	COO	NDB	326.0	35 35.39N	89 35.24W
COWETA CO	EQQ	NDB	234.0	33 15.41N	84 42.76W
COWLEY	HCY	NDB	257.0	44 54.86N	108 26.59W
COYLE	CYN	VOR	113.4	39 49.05N	74 25.90W

Name	Ident.	Type	Freq.	Latitude	Longitude
COZEY (LOM)	COZE	NDB	251.0	32 37.93N	108 3.80W
COZUMEL	CZM	VOR	112.6	20 29.00N	86 57.00W
COZUMEL	CZM	NDB	330.0	20 30.60N	86 56.55W
CRAIG	CRG	VOR	114.5	30 20.34N	81 30.60W
CRAKK (LOM/NDB)	CRAK	NDB	230.0	32 30.11N	93 52.69W
CRANBROOK	XC	NDB	242.0	49 40.98N	115 46.98W
CRANBROOK	YXC	VOR	112.1	49 33.31N	116 5.26W
CRAWFORDSVILLE	CFJ	NDB	388.0	39 58.87N	86 54.94W
CRAZY WOMAN	CZI	VOR	117.3	43 59.99N	106 26.14W
CREIL	CRL	VOR	109.2	49 15.31N	2 31.00E
CRESAP	RYP	NDB	339.0	39 30.15N	78 46.35W
CRESCENT CITY	CEC	VOR	109.0	41 46.78N	124 14.45W
CRESCO	CJJ	NDB	293.0	43 21.97N	92 7.86W
CRESTVIEW	CEW	VOR	115.9	30 49.58N	86 40.75W
CRETE	CEK	NDB	420.0	40 37.46N	96 55.66W
CROOKSTON	CKN	NDB	400.0	47 50.37N	96 36.95W
CROSBYTON	CZX	NDB	332.0	33 37.43N	101 14.31W
CROSS CITY	CTY	VOR	112.0	29 35.95N	83 2.92W
CROSSETT	CRT	NDB	396.0	33 10.51N	91 52.76W
CROSSROADS	CSZ	NDB	215.0	32 3.82N	95 57.46W
CROW HILL	CLY	NDB	392.0	42 15.81N	71 46.71W
CRYSTAL LAKE	CYE	NDB	410.0	41 12.63N	75 49.91W
CUBA	UBX	NDB	380.0	38 3.93N	91 25.64W
CUBLA (LOM/NDB)	CUBL	NDB	299.0	39 21.21N	83 52.54W
CULPEPER	CJR	NDB	252.0	38 31.87N	77 51.48W
CULTUS	LU	NDB	241.0	49 1.28N	122 2.98W
CULVER	CPB	NDB	391.0	41 13.01N	86 23.08W
CULVR	ML	NDB	380.0	33 9.12N	83 9.57W
CUMBERLAND	CBE	NDB	317.0	39 38.90N	78 44.84W
CUMBERLAND	UBE	NDB	375.0	45 30.56N	91 58.60W
CUMBERLAND RIVER	CDX	NDB	388.0	36 59.78N	84 40.87W
CUNNINGHAM	CNG	VOR	113.1	37 0.53N	88 50.21W
CURACAO	PJG	VOR	116.7	12 12.02N	69 0.60W
CUSHING	CUH	NDB	242.0	35 53.41N	96 46.52W
CUSTER COUNTY	CUZ	VOR	108.2	41 29.05N	99 41.34W
CUT BANK	CTB	VOR	114.4	48 33.91N	112 20.60W
DAFOE	VX	NDB	368.0	51 52.40N	104 34.18W
DAGGETT	DAG	VOR	113.2	34 57.75N	116 34.69W
DAISETTA	DAS	VOR	116.9	30 11.39N	94 38.70W
DAISY	CQN	NDB	341.0	35 10.00N	85 9.44W
DALHART	DHT	VOR	112.0	36 5.49N	102 32.68W
DALLAS-FT WORTH	DFW	VOR	117.0	32 51.96N	97 1.68W
DALTON	DXT	NDB	370.0	42 28.27N	73 10.21W
DANVILLE	DAN	VOR	113.1	36 34.14N	79 20.20W
DANVILLE	DNV	VOR	111.0	40 17.64N	87 33.43W
DARLINGTON	UDG	NDB	245.0	34 26.60N	79 53.24W
DARR	RRX	NDB	326.0	40 50.68N	99 51.37W
DARWIN	DN	VOR	112.4	12 24.20S	130 51.80E
DARWIN	DWN	VOR	109.0	45 5.26N	94 27.23W
DAUPHIN	YDN	VOR	116.1	51 6.31N	100 3.16W
DAVEE (LOM)	DAVE	NDB	223.0	38 39.70N	77 6.62W
DAVENPORT	CVA	VOR	113.8	42 42.51N	90 29.01W
DAVID	DAV	VOR	114.3	8 23.08N	82 26.27W
DAVID HOOKS	DWH	NDB	521.0	30 7.54N	95 33.96W
DAVIE	DVZ	NDB	354.0	35 54.82N	80 27.37W
DAVIS	MEE	VOR	108.6	35 39.80N	95 22.06W
DAWES (LOM)	DAWE	NDB	362.0	42 45.28N	103 10.51W
DAWSON	DA	NDB	214.0	64 1.75N	139 10.08W
DAWSON CREEK	DQ	NDB	394.0	55 43.67N	120 4.10W
DAWSON-MADISON	DXX	NDB	227.0	44 59.06N	96 10.75W
DAYTON	DQN	VOR	114.5	40 0.99N	84 23.81W
DE LANCEY	DNY	VOR	112.1	42 10.71N	74 57.42W
DE QUEEN	DEQ	NDB	281.0	34 2.76N	94 23.96W
DE QUINCY	DQU	NDB	410.0	30 26.13N	93 28.01W
DEADHORSE	SCC	VOR	113.9	70 11.97N	148 24.97W
DEANA (LOM/NDB)	DEAN	NDB	350.0	41 58.08N	88 1.59W
DEASE LAKE	YDL	NDB	200.0	58 27.23N	129 59.77W
DEAUVILLE	DVL	VOR	110.2	49 18.61N	0 18.80E
DEBERT	8F	NDB	239.0	45 25.33N	63 27.58W
DECATUR	DCU	VOR	112.8	34 38.91N	86 56.37W
DECATUR	DEC	VOR	117.2	39 44.26N	88 51.38W
DECKERVILLE	DQV	NDB	378.0	43 34.59N	82 39.16W
DECORAH	DEH	NDB	347.0	43 16.55N	91 44.19W
DEER PARK	DPK	VOR	117.7	40 47.51N	73 18.22W
DEERPARK	DPY	NDB	216.0	47 58.07N	117 25.59W
DEFIANCE	DFI	NDB	246.0	41 20.08N	84 25.61W
DEKALB	DKB	NDB	209.0	41 55.94N	88 42.45W
DEL NORTE	ADN	VOR	115.4	25 51.91N	100 14.32W
DELAND	DED	NDB	201.0	29 4.06N	81 16.46W
DELAWARE	DLZ	NDB	215.0	40 16.69N	83 6.54W
DELICIAS	DEL	VOR	113.5	28 13.01N	105 27.00W
DELLS	DLL	VOR	117.0	43 33.06N	89 45.81W
DELTA	DTA	VOR	116.1	39 18.15N	112 30.33W
DELTA	UDE	NDB	269.0	50 10.00N	98 18.44W
DELTA	DJN	NDB	347.0	64 1.42N	145 41.21W
DELTA JUNCTION	DMN	VOR	108.6	32 16.56N	107 36.34W
DEMING	DNI	NDB	341.0	33 49.45N	96 40.18W
DENISON	DNS	NDB	350.0	41 59.05N	95 22.76W
DENISON	DEN	VOR	117.0	39 48.04N	104 53.24W
DENVER	DEOR	NDB	210.0	32 46.80N	117 2.69W
DEORO (LOM)	DEPO	NDB	393.0	25 59.02N	97 30.54W
DEPOO (LOM)	DEPR	NDB	332.0	44 23.92N	88 7.97W
DEPRE (LOM/NDB)	DRY	NDB	338.0	42 52.21N	71 23.83W
DERRY	DERY	NDB	380.0	44 16.25N	105 31.33W
DERYK (LOM/NDB)	DSM	VOR	114.1	41 26.26N	93 38.91W
DES MOINES	DSD	VOR	117.6	44 15.18N	121 18.21W
DESCHUTES	DXO	VOR	113.4	42 12.80N	83 22.00W
DETROIT	DTL	VOR	111.2	46 49.54N	95 52.92W
DETROIT LAKES	DVL	VOR	111.0	48 6.80N	98 54.49W
DEVILS LAKE	HHH	NDB	359.0	29 8.14N	98 56.49W
DEVINE	DEWI	NDB	201.0	36 50.38N	96 0.84W
DEWIE (LOM)	DXE	NDB	423.0	36 47.29N	89 56.45W
DEXTER	DIK	VOR	112.9	46 51.61N	102 46.41W
DICKINSON	DKO	NDB	352.0	42 38.77N	71 43.61W
DICKINSON	DMZ	NDB	203.0	36 7.65N	87 25.94W
DICKSON	DPE	VOR	115.8	49 55.61N	1 10.30E
DIEPPE	Y9	NDB	220.0	44 32.86N	65 47.35W
DIGBY	DLG	VOR	116.4	58 59.67N	158 33.13W
DILLINGHAM	DLC	NDB	274.0	34 27.02N	79 22.13W
DILLON	DLN	NDB	113.0	45 14.92N	112 32.83W
DILLON	DMD	NDB	343.0	28 31.44N	99 49.52W
DIMMIT COUNTY	DINN	NDB	344.0	30 27.92N	81 48.08W
DINNS (LOM/NDB)	DIW	NDB	198.0	34 34.12N	77 27.18W
DIXON	DOBB	NDB	304.0	36 1.85N	86 43.34W
DOBBS (LOM)	DDC	VOR	108.2	37 51.04N	100 0.34W
DODGE CITY	DGD	VOR	109.4	37 1.42N	92 52.61W
DOGWOOD	DOMA	NDB	341.0	35 33.32N	106 8.40W
DOMAN (LOM)	DKG	NDB	348.0	40 4.83N	83 4.73W
DON SCOTT	ONG	NDB	352.0	31 0.64N	84 52.53W
DONALDSONILLE	DOND	NDB	224.0	47 21.85N	122 18.54W
DONDO (LOM/NDB)	DNJ	VOR	116.2	44 46.04N	116 12.38W
DONNELLY	DONN	NDB	371.0	46 31.55N	120 22.33W
DONNY (LOM)	DOON	NDB	367.0	34 54.76N	76 52.38W
DOONE (LOM)	DDP	NDB	391.0	18 28.10N	66 24.74W
DORADO	DORC	NDB	212.0	40 6.59N	80 41.33W
DORCH (LOM)	DYB	NDB	365.0	33 3.68N	80 16.64W
DORCHESTER CO	DOTT	NDB	359.0	39 13.26N	94 44.99W
DOTTE (LOM/NDB)	DGW	VOR	108.6	42 40.57N	105 13.57W
DOUGLAS	DUG	VOR	108.8	31 28.37N	109 36.12W
DOUGLAS	DVC	VOR	114.6	37 48.53N	108 55.88W
DOVE CREEK	YZD	NDB	356.0	43 45.26N	79 28.69W
DOWNSVIEW	DTN	VOR	108.6	32 32.40N	93 44.48W
DOWNTOWN	DYL	NDB	237.0	40 20.15N	75 7.33W
DOYLE	DAO	NDB	410.0	31 35.15N	110 20.66W
DOYLESTOWN	DAK	VOR	108.8	36 2.58N	94 11.85W
DRAGOO	DRK	VOR	114.1	34 42.16N	112 28.82W
DRAKE	DRF	NDB	368.0	60 35.65N	152 8.55W
DRAKE	GTB	NDB	257.0	44 4.12N	75 44.16W
DRIFT RIVER	DRU	VOR	117.1	46 38.18N	113 11.19W
DRUM	DRM	NDB	218.0	46 0.45N	83 44.53W
DRUMMOND					
DRUMMOND ISLAND					

Name	Ident.	Type	Freq.	Latitude	Longitude
DRUMMONDVILLE	Y8	NDB	401.0	45 50.84N	72 23.94W
DRYDEN	YHD	NDB	413.0	49 51.88N	92 50.94W
DRYER	DJB	VOR	113.6	41 21.49N	82 9.72W
DUBLIN	DBN	VOR	113.1	32 33.65N	82 49.99W
DUBOIS	DBS	VOR	116.9	44 5.34N	112 12.56W
DUBUQUE	DBQ	VOR	115.8	42 24.10N	90 42.55W
DUDLE (LOM)	DUDL	NDB	308.0	35 13.05N	106 42.77W
DUGWAY	DPG	NDB	284.0	40 10.96N	112 56.25W
DULANEY	DYQ	NDB	263.0	36 8.16N	82 53.42W
DULUTH	DLH	VOR	112.6	46 48.14N	92 12.17W
DUMAS	DZM	NDB	305.0	33 53.07N	91 31.89W
DUNCA (LOM)	DUNC	NDB	279.0	42 16.64N	72 1.20W
DUNCAN	DUC	VOR	111.0	34 23.08N	97 55.01W
DUNEZ (LOM)	DUNE	NDB	331.0	46 20.30N	119 0.75W
DUNKIRK	DKK	VOR	116.2	42 29.44N	79 16.45W
DUNNS (LOM)	DUNN	NDB	366.0	44 24.66N	69 51.64W
DUNOIR	DNW	VOR	113.4	43 49.71N	110 20.13W
DUPAGE	DPA	VOR	108.4	41 53.43N	88 21.01W
DUPAGE	GVK	NDB	111.7	41 54.58N	88 14.90W
DUPONT	DQO	VOR	114.0	39 40.70N	75 36.42W
DUPREE	DPR	VOR	116.8	45 4.70N	101 42.90W
DURAN (LOM)	DURA	NDB	400.0	37 59.20N	79 45.57W
DURANGO	DRO	VOR	108.2	37 9.20N	107 44.98W
DURANT	DUA	NDB	359.0	33 56.55N	96 23.92W
DURRETT	DUX	NDB	414.0	35 51.80N	102 0.77W
DUSTT (LOM)	DUST	NDB	368.0	38 44.33N	94 53.52W
DUTCH (LOM)	DUTC	NDB	248.0	37 15.21N	89 42.04W
DUTCH HARBOR	DUT	NDB	283.0	53 54.32N	166 32.95W
DWIGHT	DTG	NDB	344.0	41 8.01N	88 26.09W
DYANA (LOM/NDB)	DYAN	NDB	338.0	34 41.47N	82 26.62W
DYER	DYO	NDB	239.0	43 35.04N	72 57.69W
DYERSBURG	DYR	VOR	116.8	36 1.13N	89 19.06W
EAGLE	EAA	NDB	519.0	64 46.68N	141 8.44W
EAGLE	EGE	NDB	357.0	39 38.80N	106 54.86W
EAGLE GROVE	EAG	NDB	302.0	42 42.52N	93 54.63W
EAGLE LAKE	ELA	VOR	116.4	29 39.77N	96 19.01W
EAGLE RIVER	EGV	NDB	341.0	45 56.01N	89 15.77W
EARLE (LOM)	EARL	NDB	401.0	40 25.60N	87 3.11W
EARLI (LOM/NDB)	EARL	NDB	278.0	36 40.11N	90 19.62W
EARLTON	YXR	NDB	257.0	47 42.77N	79 47.42W
EAST KUPURA	ACU	NDB	268.0	68 50.42N	153 18.96W
EAST LIVERPOOL	EVO	NDB	385.0	40 40.60N	80 38.31W
EAST TEXAS	ETX	VOR	110.2	40 34.87N	75 41.04W
EASTEX	ETO	NDB	201.0	30 20.90N	94 5.33W
EASTMAIN	ZEM	NDB	338.0	52 13.85N	78 31.05W
EASTMAN	EZM	NDB	270.0	32 12.85N	83 7.52W
EASTON	ESN	NDB	212.0	38 48.30N	76 4.17W
EASTPORT	EYA	NDB	357.0	30 25.41N	81 36.57W
EATON	LBY	VOR	110.6	31 25.12N	89 20.26W
EAU CLAIRE	EAU	VOR	112.9	44 53.87N	91 28.71W
EAVES (LOM/NDB)	EAVE	NDB	227.0	38 40.65N	90 32.82W
EDENTON	EDE	NDB	265.0	36 1.54N	76 33.99W
EDISTO	EDS	VOR	111.4	33 27.35N	80 51.50W
EDMONTON	YEG	VOR	117.6	53 11.14N	113 52.01W
EDWARDS	EDW	VOR	116.4	34 58.95N	117 43.95W
EGG ISLAND	UEM	NDB	207.0	51 14.97N	127 50.05W
EIELSON	EAF	VOR	117.0	64 34.17N	147 0.96W
EL DORADO	ELD	VOR	115.5	33 15.38N	92 44.64W
EL DORADO	EQA	NDB	383.0	37 46.78N	96 48.98W
EL MONTE	EMT	NDB	359.0	34 5.31N	118 1.87W
EL NIDO	HYP	VOR	114.2	37 13.17N	120 24.02W
EL PASO	ELP	VOR	115.2	31 48.96N	106 16.91W
EL RENO	RQO	NDB	335.0	35 28.73N	98 0.54W
EL TORO	NZJ	VOR	117.2	33 40.57N	117 43.86W
EL TORO	NZJ	NDB	410.0	33 40.89N	117 43.86W
ELECTRIC CITY	ELW	VOR	108.6	34 25.16N	82 47.08W
ELEPHANT	EEF	NDB	391.0	58 10.27N	135 15.48W
ELEUTHERA	ZGV	VOR	112.5	25 15.46N	76 18.52W
ELFEE (LOM/NDB)	ELFE	NDB	341.0	55 17.78N	162 47.34W
ELIZABETH CITY	ECG	VOR	112.5	36 15.46N	76 10.54W

Name	Ident.	Type	Freq.	Latitude	Longitude
ELIZABETHTON	EZT	NDB	275.0	36 18.97N	82 16.22W
ELIZABETHTOWN	TGQ	NDB	398.0	34 31.72N	78 30.95W
ELK CITY	EZY	NDB	241.0	35 25.56N	99 23.89W
ELK SPRING	EKQ	NDB	290.0	36 51.38N	84 51.18W
ELKHART	EHA	NDB	377.0	37 0.08N	101 53.08W
ELKINS	EKN	VOR	114.2	38 54.88N	80 5.96W
ELLAS (LOM)	ELLA	NDB	261.0	34 45.04N	77 42.27W
ELLENSBURG	ELN	VOR	117.9	47 1.47N	120 27.51W
ELLICOTT	FND	NDB	371.0	39 17.25N	76 46.62W
ELLINGTON	EFD	VOR	109.4	29 36.38N	95 9.60W
ELLIOT LAKE	YEL	NDB	276.0	46 22.31N	82 37.70W
ELLWOOD CITY	EWC	VOR	115.8	40 49.52N	80 12.69W
ELM GROVE	EMG	VOR	111.2	32 24.02N	93 35.71W
ELM RIVER	FOA	NDB	353.0	38 40.15N	88 27.19W
ELMIRA	ELM	VOR	109.7	42 5.67N	77 1.49W
ELMWOOD	EMD	VOR	111.0	42 6.67N	92 54.61W
ELVIS (LOM/NDB)	ELVI	NDB	371.0	34 57.22N	89 58.43W
ELWHA (LOM/NDB)	ELWH	NDB	515.0	48 9.02N	123 40.21W
ELWIN (LOM)	ELWI	NDB	275.0	39 46.69N	88 58.88W
ELY	ELO	VOR	109.6	47 49.32N	91 49.81W
ELY	ELY	VOR	110.6	39 17.90N	114 50.90W
EMANUEL COUNTY	EEX	VOR	109.0	32 40.02N	82 27.14W
EMIRE (LOM/NDB)	EMIR	NDB	378.0	43 23.69N	124 18.61W
EMMETSBURG	EGQ	NDB	410.0	43 6.07N	94 42.43W
EMMONAK	ENM	VOR	117.8	62 47.02N	164 29.26W
EMORY	EMR	NDB	385.0	33 27.78N	81 59.81W
EMPORIA	EMP	VOR	112.8	38 17.48N	96 8.28W
EMPORIA	EMV	NDB	346.0	36 40.97N	77 28.93W
EMPRESS	YEA	VOR	115.9	50 55.60N	109 59.35W
EMVILLE	EVU	NDB	317.0	40 20.91N	94 54.93W
ENDERBY	NY	NDB	350.0	50 39.01N	118 55.52W
ENDERBY	YNY	VOR	115.2	50 40.69N	118 56.32W
ENGEL	EZE	NDB	226.0	41 29.34N	81 43.37W
ENGLISH BAY	EGY	NDB	374.0	57 7.45N	170 16.34W
ENOLA (LOM)	ENOL	NDB	204.0	34 14.79N	76 54.03W
ENOREE	EOE	NDB	278.0	34 18.70N	81 38.16W
ENTERPRISE	EDN	VOR	116.6	31 17.77N	85 54.20W
EPERNON	EPR	VOR	115.7	48 37.51N	1 39.30E
EPHRATA	EPH	VOR	112.6	47 22.69N	119 25.44W
EPSOM (LOM/NDB)	EPSO	NDB	216.0	43 7.14N	71 27.15W
ERABU	ONC	VOR	113.1	27 26.01N	128 42.00E
ERDING	ERD	VOR	113.6	48 19.61N	11 57.30E
ERIE	ERI	VOR	109.4	42 1.05N	80 17.56W
ERMIN (LOM/NDB)	ERMI	NDB	332.0	41 43.15N	87 50.19W
ESCANABA	ESC	VOR	110.8	45 43.37N	87 5.38W
ESCONDIDO	EKG	NDB	374.0	33 9.37N	117 5.14W
ESLER	ESF	VOR	117.9	31 26.86N	92 19.32W
ESMER (LOM)	ESME	NDB	349.0	42 2.33N	80 15.32W
ESTEVAN	L7	NDB	395.0	49 12.60N	102 51.60W
ESTEVAN POINT	EP	NDB	373.0	49 23.05N	126 32.64W
ESTHERVILLE	EST	VOR	110.4	43 24.56N	94 44.67W
ETAMPES	EM	NDB	295.5	48 22.61N	2 4.90E
EUFAULA	EUF	VOR	109.2	31 57.02N	85 7.83W
EUGENE	EUG	VOR	112.9	44 7.26N	123 13.37W
EURACH	EUR	VOR	115.2	47 44.21N	11 15.00E
EUREKA	EUR	NDB	392.0	48 57.84N	115 5.53W
EVADALE	EVA	NDB	219.0	30 24.28N	94 7.63W
EVANS	CFY	VOR	420.0	33 51.37N	79 45.95W
EVANSTON	EVW	VOR	110.0	41 16.51N	111 1.55W
EVANSVILLE	EAV	NDB	391.0	66 53.61N	151 33.83W
EVANSVILLE	PDW	NDB	284.0	38 2.42N	87 31.86W
EVELETH	EVM	VOR	108.2	47 25.47N	92 30.11W
EVINGTON	EVI	NDB	385.0	37 12.74N	79 16.64W
EVREUX	EVX	VOR	112.4	49 1.91N	1 13.30E
EWABE (LOM/NDB)	EWAB	NDB	242.0	21 19.50N	158 2.93W
EXCAL (LOM)	EXCA	NDB	278.0	46 36.63N	68 1.13W
EXECC (LOM)	EXEC	NDB	356.0	38 27.00N	121 32.78W
FAIRBANKS	FAI	VOR	108.2	64 48.02N	148 0.72W
FAIRBURY	FBY	NDB	293.0	40 10.61N	97 9.95W
FAIRFIELD	FFL	NDB	332.0	41 0.68N	91 59.31W

Name	Ident.	Type	Freq.	Latitude	Longitude
FAIRFIELD	FFU	VOR	116.6	40 16.50N	111 56.43W
FAIRMONT	FRM	VOR	110.2	43 38.77N	94 25.35W
FAIRMONT	FRT	NDB	248.0	34 54.15N	81 59.08W
FAIRMONT HOT SPRN	D6	NDB	261.0	50 19.63N	115 52.59W
FAIRVIEW	FAU	NDB	246.0	36 17.12N	98 28.68W
FALCON	FQF	VOR	116.3	39 41.42N	104 37.29W
FALFURRIAS	FFR	NDB	230.0	27 28.02N	98 24.18W
FALL RIVER	FLR	NDB	406.0	41 45.34N	71 6.73W
FALLS	FAH	VOR	110.0	43 46.14N	87 50.92W
FALMOUTH	FLM	VOR	117.0	38 38.98N	84 18.64W
FAMIS (LOM)	FAMI	NDB	356.0	44 26.44N	88 14.38W
FAREWELL LAKE	FXW	NDB	412.0	62 32.60N	153 37.19W
FARGO	FAR	VOR	116.2	46 45.21N	96 51.08W
FARLY (LOM/NDB)	FARL	NDB	326.0	31 59.29N	102 19.50W
FARMINGTON	FAM	VOR	115.7	37 40.41N	90 14.04W
FARMINGTON	FGT	VOR	115.7	44 37.87N	93 10.93W
FARMINGTON	FMN	VOR	115.3	36 44.91N	108 5.94W
FARMVILLE	FVX	NDB	367.0	37 21.18N	78 26.28W
FARO	ZFA	NDB	378.0	62 12.73N	133 23.22W
FARRINGTON	FIO	NDB	263.0	36 58.21N	88 34.04W
FAYETTE	FDF	NDB	204.0	33 42.88N	87 48.82W
FAYETTEVILLE	FAY	VOR	108.8	34 59.14N	78 52.50W
FELKER	FAF	NDB	226.0	37 8.33N	76 37.11W
FELLOWS	FLW	VOR	117.5	35 5.59N	119 51.93W
FELPS (LOM)	FELP	NDB	206.0	44 57.65N	83 33.60W
FELTS	SFF	NDB	365.0	47 41.18N	117 18.71W
FENIX (LOM)	FENI	NDB	355.0	32 27.12N	85 2.51W
FERDINAND	FNZ	NDB	239.0	38 14.93N	86 50.27W
FERGUS FALLS	FFM	VOR	110.4	46 17.37N	96 9.40W
FERNI (LOM/NDB)	FERN	NDB	413.0	31 15.28N	90 30.63W
FESTUS	FES	NDB	269.0	38 11.76N	90 23.26W
FETCH (LOM)	FETC	NDB	338.0	41 12.03N	80 55.77W
FICHY (LOM)	FICH	NDB	224.0	44 45.34N	87 27.05W
FIDDLERS	FIQ	NDB	391.0	35 42.62N	81 40.28W
FILLMORE	FIM	VOR	112.5	34 21.41N	118 52.88W
FIN CREEK	FNK	NDB	320.0	69 29.91N	147 35.59W
FINDLAY	FDY	VOR	108.2	40 57.33N	83 45.36W
FIRST RIVER	SLP	NDB	368.0	35 15.29N	81 35.85W
FISH HOOK	FIS	NDB	332.0	24 32.91N	81 47.18W
FITCHBURG	FIT	NDB	365.0	42 33.06N	71 45.43W
FITZGERALD	SUR	NDB	362.0	31 36.79N	83 17.44W
FIVE MILE	FVM	NDB	312.0	65 55.04N	149 49.84W
FLAGSTAFF	FLG	VOR	108.2	35 8.84N	111 40.45W
FLANC (LOM/NDB)	FLAN	NDB	344.0	33 45.75N	84 38.34W
FLAT ROCK	FAK	VOR	113.3	37 31.72N	77 49.69W
FLEMINGSBURG	FGX	NDB	400.0	38 32.30N	83 44.81W
FLICK (LOM)	FLIC	NDB	513.0	41 24.11N	95 53.60W
FLINT	FNT	VOR	116.9	42 57.97N	83 44.46W
FLIPPIN	FLP	VOR	112.8	36 17.99N	92 27.50W
FLORENCE	FLO	VOR	115.2	34 13.98N	79 39.43W
FLORENVILLE	FNA	NDB	371.0	34 49.55N	89 49.20W
FLORIDA	FIA	NDB	329.0	34 6.03N	106 54.03W
FLORY (LOM)	FLOR	NDB	344.0	38 40.90N	97 38.70W
FLOWERY BRAN	FKV	NDB	365.0	34 12.21N	83 54.38W
FLOYD	OYD	NDB	388.0	34 17.93N	85 9.85W
FLUFY (LOM)	FLUF	NDB	350.0	31 13.14N	94 49.50W
FLYING CLOUD	FCM	VOR	111.8	44 49.55N	93 27.40W
FLYING T	FTA	NDB	388.0	43 23.42N	103 26.23W
FOLEY	FPY	NDB	254.0	29 59.78N	83 35.18W
FOLLETT	FTE	NDB	407.0	36 26.14N	100 7.30W
FOND DU LAC	FLD	NDB	248.0	43 46.18N	88 29.08W
FOOTHILLS	ODF	VOR	113.4	34 41.76N	83 17.86W
FOREM (LOM)	FORE	NDB	344.0	41 28.94N	93 34.85W
FOREST CITY	FXY	NDB	359.0	43 14.12N	93 37.26W
FORESTVILLE	FE	NDB	239.0	48 44.73N	69 6.05W
FORIS (LOM/NDB)	FORI	NDB	230.0	45 41.75N	118 43.84W
FORISTELL	FTZ	NDB	110.8	38 41.68N	90 58.28W
FORNEY	TBN	VOR	110.0	37 44.55N	92 8.34W
FORREST CITY	FCY	NDB	332.0	34 56.48N	90 46.41W
FORSYTH	FOR	NDB	236.0	46 16.18N	106 31.05W

Name	Ident.	Type	Freq.	Latitude	Longitude
FORT A.P. HILL	APH	NDB	396.0	38 5.27N	77 19.49W
FORT BRAGG	FGP	NDB	393.0	35 8.34N	78 48.75W
FORT BRIDGER	FBR	VOR	108.6	41 22.72N	110 25.44W
FORT DAVIS	FDV	NDB	529.0	64 29.69N	165 18.84W
FORT DE FRANCE	FOF	VOR	117.5	14 35.00N	60 60.00W
FORT DE FRANCE	FXF	NDB	314.0	14 35.97N	61 5.72W
FORT DODGE	FOD	VOR	113.5	42 36.68N	94 17.69W
FORT FRANCES	YAG	NDB	376.0	48 41.39N	93 32.34W
FORT GOOD HOPE	YGH	VOR	112.3	66 14.18N	128 37.37W
FORT JONES	FJS	VOR	109.6	41 26.99N	122 48.39W
FORT KNOX	FTK	VOR	109.6	37 54.45N	85 58.37W
FORT LAUDERDALE	FLL	VOR	114.4	26 4.49N	80 9.15W
FORT LIARD	YJF	NDB	368.0	60 14.32N	123 27.94W
FORT MCPHERSON	ZFM	NDB	373.0	67 24.61N	134 52.31W
FORT MEADE	FME	NDB	353.0	39 5.08N	76 45.60W
FORT MILL	FML	VOR	112.4	34 59.35N	80 57.29W
FORT NELSON	YE	NDB	382.0	58 47.75N	122 43.36W
FORT NELSON	YYE	VOR	112.9	58 53.52N	123 0.96W
FORT ORD	OAR	NDB	236.0	36 38.39N	121 40.86W
FORT PAYNE	FTP	NDB	426.0	34 31.28N	85 40.40W
FORT PIERCE	FPR	VOR	275.0	27 29.21N	80 22.40W
FORT RICHARDSON	FRN	NDB	196.0	61 16.60N	149 38.94W
FORT RILEY	FRI	VOR	109.4	38 58.22N	96 51.66W
FORT SAINT JOHN	YXJ	VOR	114.2	56 17.06N	120 53.74W
FORT SCOTT	FSK	NDB	379.0	37 47.68N	94 45.92W
FORT SIMPSON	YFS	VOR	117.9	61 46.45N	121 17.92W
FORT SMITH	FSM	VOR	110.4	35 23.31N	94 16.29W
FORT ST. JOHN	XJ	NDB	326.0	56 17.08N	120 50.69W
FORT STOCKTON	FST	VOR	112.8	30 57.13N	102 58.54W
FORT WAYNE	FWA	VOR	117.8	40 58.75N	85 11.28W
FORT YUKON	FYU	VOR	114.4	66 34.47N	145 16.60W
FORTUNA	FOT	VOR	114.0	40 40.29N	124 14.07W
FOSSI (LOM/NDB)	FOSS	NDB	393.0	35 27.05N	99 12.09W
FOSSTON	FSE	NDB	224.0	47 35.39N	95 46.19W
FOSTORIA	FZI	NDB	379.0	41 11.35N	83 23.78W
FOSTR (LOM)	FOST	NDB	226.0	28 54.92N	97 0.03W
FOX	FOX	NDB	356.0	64 58.16N	147 34.80W
FOX VALLEY	FXV	NDB	407.0	44 15.48N	88 31.56W
FOXTROT	F	NDB	304.0	46 2.31N	64 47.00W
FOXWORTH	FOH	NDB	331.0	31 17.77N	89 49.12W
FRAKK (LOM)	FRAK	NDB	260.0	44 12.78N	123 13.23W
FRANCE	FTD	VOR	109.0	9 21.67N	79 51.95W
FRANKFORT	FFT	VOR	109.4	38 10.95N	84 54.52W
FRANKFORT	FKR	NDB	278.0	40 16.24N	86 33.77W
FRANKLIN	FKL	VOR	109.6	41 26.33N	79 51.41W
FRANKLIN	FKN	VOR	110.6	36 42.86N	77 0.74W
FRANKSTON	FZT	VOR	111.4	32 4.48N	95 31.85W
FREDERICK	FDK	VOR	109.0	39 24.74N	77 22.51W
FREDERICK	FDR	NDB	222.0	34 21.24N	98 59.19W
FREDERICKS POINT	FPN	NDB	372.0	56 47.55N	132 49.25W
FREDERICKSBURG	FKB	NDB	388.0	30 14.93N	98 54.62W
FREDERICTON	FC	NDB	326.0	45 55.05N	66 35.98W
FREDERICTON	YFC	VOR	113.0	45 53.70N	66 25.13W
FREEP (LOM)	FREE	NDB	263.0	29 11.67N	95 27.80W
FREEPORT	FEP	NDB	335.0	42 14.74N	89 35.16W
FREEPORT	ZFP	VOR	113.2	26 33.32N	78 41.90W
FREEPORT	ZFP	VOR	209.0	26 31.11N	78 46.50W
FREEPORT/GRAND BA	BHF	NDB	326.0	26 34.44N	78 39.83W
FREMONT	FET	NDB	311.0	41 27.03N	96 31.09W
FRENCHVILLE	FVE	NDB	257.0	47 16.10N	68 15.40W
FRIANT	FRA	VOR	115.6	37 6.27N	119 35.73W
FRIDAY HARBOR	FHR	NDB	284.0	48 31.62N	123 1.67W
FRIKK (LOM)	FRIK	NDB	407.0	40 46.60N	73 28.95W
FRUITA	RHU	VOR	109.0	39 11.04N	108 38.32W
FT. SIMPSON	FS	NDB	375.0	61 47.17N	121 15.64W
FULER (LOM/NDB)	FULE	NDB	515.0	40 4.42N	83 11.88W
FULTON	USE	NDB	375.0	41 36.56N	84 7.96W
FUROR (LOM)	FURO	NDB	526.0	38 56.12N	94 44.26W
GADSDEN	GAD	VOR	112.3	33 58.59N	86 5.01W
GAGE	GAG	VOR	115.6	36 20.63N	99 52.81W

Name	Ident.	Type	Freq.	Latitude	Longitude
GAINES CO	GNC	NDB	344.0	32 40.33N	102 38.75W
GAINESVILLE	GLE	NDB	330.0	33 42.21N	97 11.85W
GAINESVILLE	GNV	VOR	116.2	29 34.34N	82 21.76W
GAITHERSBURG	GAI	NDB	385.0	39 10.08N	77 9.82W
GALBRAITH LAKE	GBH	NDB	417.0	68 28.76N	149 29.91W
GALENA	GAL	VOR	114.8	64 44.30N	156 46.63W
GALESBURG	GBG	VOR	109.8	40 56.25N	90 26.07W
GALEX (LOM)	GALE	NDB	272.0	47 7.83N	93 28.89W
GALEY (LOM/NDB)	GALE	NDB	275.0	47 6.95N	88 24.07W
GALLATIN	GYN	VOR	214.0	36 22.78N	86 24.70W
GALLIPOLIS	GAS	NDB	362.0	38 50.01N	82 9.69W
GALLUP	GUP	VOR	115.1	35 28.57N	108 52.36W
GALLY (LOM/NDB)	GALL	NDB	350.0	35 17.71N	97 35.32W
GALVESTON	GLS	NDB	206.0	29 20.04N	94 45.37W
GAMBELL	GAM	NDB	369.0	63 46.94N	171 44.20W
GAMIE (LOM)	GAMI	NDB	230.0	44 9.75N	88 35.10W
GANSE (LOM)	GANS	NDB	209.0	43 15.31N	73 36.35W
GARDEN CITY	GCK	VOR	113.3	37 55.15N	100 43.50W
GARDNER	GDM	VOR	110.6	42 32.77N	72 3.49W
GARFY (LOM)	GARF	NDB	341.0	36 16.51N	97 47.44W
GARIE (LOM)	GARI	NDB	236.0	41 34.35N	87 19.62W
GARRISON	VTI	NDB	338.0	42 13.31N	92 1.21W
GARYS (LOM)	GARY	NDB	272.0	29 57.55N	97 56.94W
GASPE	GP	NDB	232.0	48 46.10N	64 23.11W
GASPE	YGP	VOR	115.4	48 45.80N	64 24.27W
GATOR	GUV	NDB	359.0	31 1.70N	93 11.09W
GAVIOTA	GVO	VOR	113.8	34 31.89N	120 5.46W
GAYLORD	GLR	VOR	109.2	45 0.77N	84 42.24W
GEIGER LAKE	GGL	NDB	375.0	28 35.59N	80 48.98W
GEN WILLIAM J FO	GWF	NDB	282.0	34 44.32N	118 13.01W
GENESEO	GEE	VOR	108.2	42 50.07N	77 43.97W
GENEVA	GVA	NDB	224.0	37 48.23N	87 46.24W
GEORGETOWN	GEO	NDB	219.0	38 52.93N	83 53.11W
GEORGETOWN	GGE	NDB	242.0	33 18.93N	79 19.47W
GEORGETOWN	GGT	VOR	117.8	42 47.35N	75 49.61W
GEORGETOWN	GTN	NDB	323.0	38 55.79N	77 7.45W
GEORGETOWN	GUO	NDB	332.0	30 41.07N	97 40.79W
GERALDTON	YGQ	VOR	114.2	49 46.20N	86 59.07W
GERFI (LOM/NDB)	GERF	NDB	320.0	41 22.02N	95 57.38W
GERING	GIG	NDB	341.0	41 56.67N	103 40.98W
GERMANY - MUNICH	IMNE	VOR	110.3	48 22.13N	11 49.60E
GERMANY - MUNICH	IMNW	VOR	108.7	48 21.81N	11 45.90E
GERMANY - MUNICH	IMSE	VOR	110.3	48 20.78N	11 48.60E
GERMANY - MUNICH	IMSW	VOR	108.3	48 20.48N	11 44.90E
GERONA	UNG	NDB	412.0	21 45.20N	82 52.88W
GIBRALTAR POINT	TZ	NDB	257.0	43 36.78N	79 23.14W
GIBSON	TGC	NDB	378.0	35 56.06N	88 51.05W
GILA BEND	GBN	VOR	116.6	32 57.38N	112 40.46W
GILES	GZS	NDB	375.0	35 9.10N	87 3.48W
GILL	GLL	VOR	114.2	40 30.24N	104 33.18W
GILLETTE	GCC	VOR	114.6	44 20.87N	105 32.61W
GILMORE	GQE	VOR	113.0	35 20.83N	90 28.69W
GILMY (LOM)	GILM	NDB	275.0	42 6.88N	89 5.92W
GIPER	GIJ	VOR	115.4	41 46.13N	86 19.10W
GLACIER RIVER	GCR	NDB	404.0	60 29.94N	145 28.47W
GLADE SPRING	GZG	VOR	110.2	36 49.52N	82 4.74W
GLASGOW	GGW	VOR	113.9	48 12.93N	106 37.53W
GLENDIVE	GDV	NDB	410.0	47 8.01N	104 48.28W
GLENNALLEN	GLA	NDB	248.0	62 11.74N	145 28.08W
GLENPOOL	GNP	VOR	110.6	35 55.26N	95 58.12W
GLENS FALLS	GFL	VOR	110.2	43 20.51N	73 36.70W
GLOBE	GAZ	NDB	255.0	33 21.28N	110 39.99W
GODERICH	GD	NDB	286.0	43 44.79N	81 43.85W
GODMAN	GOI	NDB	396.0	37 57.53N	85 58.60W
GOFFS	GFS	VOR	114.4	35 7.88N	115 10.59W
GOLD	OYN	NDB	208.0	64 30.78N	165 26.09W
GOLD BEACH	GOL	NDB	396.0	42 25.08N	124 25.41W
GOLDEN EAGLE	OEG	NDB	413.0	32 51.33N	114 26.46W
GOLDEN VALLEY	GLY	NDB	388.0	38 21.54N	93 41.08W
GOLF	G	NDB	398.0	42 14.65N	83 2.84W
GOLF	G	NDB	364.0	44 48.15N	63 35.38W
GOLF	G 1	NDB	400.0	46 21.00N	63 6.73W
GOODALL	DVK	NDB	311.0	37 34.59N	84 45.84W
GOODHUE	GDE	NDB	368.0	30 4.19N	94 12.15W
GOODLAND	GLD	VOR	115.1	39 23.28N	101 41.54W
GOODWIN LAKE	GDX	VOR	227.0	38 57.25N	77 49.87W
GOOGL (LOM)	GOOG	NDB	264.0	40 14.90N	75 26.82W
GOOSE	GOS	NDB	278.0	42 9.19N	120 24.31W
GOPHER	GEP	VOR	117.3	45 8.75N	93 22.39W
GORDON	GRN	NDB	414.0	42 48.08N	102 10.76W
GORDONSVILLE	GVE	VOR	115.6	38 0.82N	78 9.18W
GORE BAY	YZE	NDB	245.0	45 55.71N	82 36.91W
GORMAN	GMN	VOR	116.1	34 48.25N	118 51.68W
GOSHEN	GSH	VOR	113.7	41 31.52N	86 1.68W
GOSNELL	GOJ	VOR	111.8	35 57.07N	89 56.43W
GRAGG-WADE	GGY	NDB	338.0	32 51.20N	86 36.66W
GRAHAM	GHM	VOR	111.6	35 50.05N	87 27.11W
GRAHAM	GHX	NDB	371.0	33 9.96N	98 29.80W
GRAIN	GVV	VOR	280.0	45 56.39N	116 13.29W
GRAN ROQUE	LRS	VOR	113.1	11 57.00N	66 40.00W
GRAND CANYON	GCN	VOR	113.1	35 57.63N	112 8.76W
GRAND CAYMAN	GCM	VOR	115.6	19 17.40N	81 22.30W
GRAND CAYMAN	ZIY	NDB	344.0	19 17.00N	81 23.00W
GRAND FORKS	GFK	VOR	114.3	47 57.30N	97 11.12W
GRAND ISLAND	GRI	VOR	112.0	40 59.05N	98 18.88W
GRAND ISLE	GNI	NDB	236.0	29 11.52N	90 4.50W
GRAND JUNCTION	JNC	VOR	112.4	39 3.58N	108 47.56W
GRAND MARAIS	GRM	NDB	391.0	47 49.65N	90 22.54W
GRAND PRAIRIE	GPM	NDB	227.0	32 41.63N	97 2.80W
GRAND RAPIDS	GPZ	VOR	111.4	47 9.83N	93 29.31W
GRAND RAPIDS	GRR	VOR	110.2	42 47.21N	85 29.83W
GRAND STRAND	CRE	VOR	117.6	33 48.84N	78 43.47W
GRAND TURK	GT	NDB	232.0	21 26.20N	71 8.78W
GRAND TURK	GTK	VOR	114.2	21 26.42N	71 8.08W
GRANDE PRAIRIE	YQU	VOR	113.1	55 10.47N	119 1.81W
GRANITE POINT	GRP	NDB	356.0	60 57.70N	151 20.04W
GRANT	GGF	NDB	359.0	40 52.27N	101 43.83W
GRANTS PASS	GNA	NDB	219.0	42 30.87N	123 22.60W
GRANTSVILLE	GRV	VOR	112.3	39 38.11N	79 3.03W
GRAY	GRK	VOR	111.8	31 1.98N	97 48.83W
GRAYE (LOM/NDB)	GRAY	NDB	216.0	47 9.03N	122 36.29W
GRAYLING	CGG	VOR	109.8	44 40.91N	84 43.74W
GRAYLING	GYG	NDB	359.0	44 45.01N	84 49.70W
GREAT BARRINGTON	GBR	NDB	395.0	42 10.99N	73 24.24W
GREAT FALLS	GTF	VOR	115.1	47 27.01N	111 24.73W
GREAT INAGUA	ZIN	NDB	376.0	20 57.59N	73 40.65W
GREEN BAY	GRB	VOR	115.5	44 33.32N	88 11.69W
GREENCASTLE	TVX	NDB	521.0	39 42.85N	86 48.37W
GREENE COUNTY	GCV	VOR	115.7	31 5.88N	89 29.17W
GREENFIELD	GFZ	NDB	338.0	41 19.54N	94 26.67W
GREENSBORO	EJK	VOR	397.0	33 35.70N	83 8.44W
GREENSBORO	EOG	NDB	417.0	32 36.15N	87 39.78W
GREENSBORO	GSO	VOR	116.2	36 2.75N	79 58.58W
GREENVILLE	GEF	VOR	109.0	30 33.09N	83 46.99W
GREENVILLE	GLH	VOR	110.2	33 31.42N	90 58.98W
GREENVILLE	GRE	NDB	233.0	38 50.06N	89 22.34W
GREENWOOD	GRD	VOR	115.5	34 15.10N	82 9.25W
GREENWOOD	GRW	VOR	114.7	33 27.84N	90 16.64W
GREENWOOD	HFY	NDB	318.0	39 37.97N	86 5.44W
GREENWOOD	YZX	NDB	0.0	44 55.38N	65 6.11W
GREER (LOM)	GREE	NDB	287.0	34 48.93N	82 16.81W
GREEY (LOM)	GREE	NDB	348.0	40 27.40N	104 40.16W
GREGG COUNTY	GGG	VOR	112.4	32 25.07N	94 45.19W
GRENS (LOM)	GREN	NDB	272.0	40 0.62N	83 1.74W
GREON (LOM)	GREO	NDB	382.0	35 47.82N	78 52.96W
GREYBULL	GEY	NDB	275.0	44 30.70N	108 4.98W
GRIMM (LOM)	GRIM	NDB	268.0	40 35.85N	73 39.44W
GRINDSTONE	GR	NDB	370.0	47 22.46N	61 54.41W
GRINDSTONE	YGR	VOR	112.0	47 25.83N	61 46.44W
GRINDSTONE MTN	GMZ	NDB	356.0	33 36.33N	97 46.40W

Name	Ident.	Type	Freq.	Latitude	Longitude
GRINNELL	GGI	NDB	248.0	41 42.59N	92 43.78W
GRISSOM	GUS	VOR	116.5	40 38.70N	86 9.10W
GROS CAP	A	NDB	286.0	46 30.74N	84 36.90W
GROSSE ILE	RYS	NDB	419.0	42 6.08N	83 9.18W
GROTON	TMU	VOR	111.8	41 19.83N	72 3.12W
GUADALUPE	GLJ	VOR	111.0	34 57.15N	120 31.29W
GUATEMALA	TGE	NDB	375.0	14 35.00N	90 32.00W
GULFPORT	GPT	VOR	109.0	30 24.42N	89 4.61W
GULKANA	GKN	VOR	115.6	62 9.16N	145 27.02W
GUSTAVUS	GAV	NDB	219.0	58 25.33N	135 42.28W
GUTHRIE	FTT	NDB	317.0	38 50.58N	92 0.28W
GUTHRIE	GTH	VOR	114.5	33 46.70N	100 20.17W
GUTHRIE CENTER	GCT	NDB	518.0	41 40.93N	94 26.00W
GUYMON	GUY	NDB	275.0	36 42.33N	101 30.31W
GWENN (LOM/NDB)	GWEN	NDB	365.0	44 44.08N	85 25.76W
GWINNER	GWR	NDB	278.0	46 13.41N	97 38.60W
GWNET (LOM/NDB)	GWNE	NDB	419.0	33 58.41N	83 58.45W
HABERSHAM	AJR	NDB	347.0	34 30.10N	83 32.99W
HADIN (LOM)	HADI	NDB	248.0	39 34.87N	75 36.84W
HAGERSTOWN	HGR	VOR	109.8	39 41.87N	77 51.34W
HAGET (LOM)	HAGE	NDB	402.0	42 38.66N	71 11.83W
HAILEY	HLE	NDB	220.0	43 19.75N	114 14.55W
HAINES	HNS	NDB	245.0	59 12.74N	135 25.85W
HALFWAY	FOW	VOR	111.2	44 12.27N	93 22.23W
HALIFAX	YHZ	VOR	115.1	44 55.40N	63 24.11W
HALL BEACH	YUX	VOR	117.3	68 46.71N	81 14.37W
HALLSVILLE	HLV	VOR	114.2	39 6.82N	92 7.69W
HALOS (LOM/NDB)	HALO	NDB	269.0	42 6.63N	77 54.91W
HALOW (LOM/NDB)	HALO	NDB	222.0	39 10.17N	121 36.59W
HAMBURG	B2	NDB	352.0	57 22.33N	119 47.34W
HAMILTON	HAB	VOR	110.4	34 11.71N	88 0.75W
HAMILTON	HAO	NDB	260.0	39 22.36N	84 34.35W
HAMILTON	HM	NDB	221.0	43 7.28N	80 0.41W
HAMILTON	HMM	NDB	410.0	46 15.42N	114 8.06W
HAMILTON	MNZ	NDB	251.0	31 37.22N	98 8.85W
HAMMOND	HMU	VOR	109.6	30 31.17N	90 25.05W
HAMPTON	HPT	NDB	230.0	42 43.54N	93 13.49W
HAMPTON	HTO	VOR	113.6	40 55.15N	72 19.00W
HANCHEY	HEY	VOR	110.6	31 22.46N	85 39.17W
HANCHEY	HYE	NDB	221.0	31 22.02N	85 39.00W
HANCO	AYI	NDB	221.0	30 27.07N	89 27.32W
HANCOCK	HNK	VOR	116.8	42 3.79N	75 18.98W
HAND	MKA	NDB	371.0	44 31.31N	98 57.54W
HANGTOWN	HNW	VOR	115.5	38 43.51N	120 44.93W
HANKSVILLE	HVE	VOR	115.9	38 25.02N	110 41.98W
HANNIBAL	HAE	NDB	411.0	39 43.65N	91 26.91W
HANOVER	LAH	NDB	276.0	43 42.15N	72 10.65W
HANOVER	S7	NDB	268.0	44 9.75N	81 3.62W
HAPPS (LOM)	HAPP	NDB	331.0	38 28.44N	76 42.68W
HARCUM	HCM	VOR	108.8	37 26.93N	76 42.68W
HARDEMAN	BAV	NDB	404.0	35 12.87N	89 2.53W
HARDIN COUNTY	HRD	NDB	524.0	30 20.25N	94 15.61W
HARDWICK	HDI	NDB	369.0	35 9.23N	84 54.35W
HARDWOOD	BHW	NDB	236.0	44 14.93N	84 5.03W
HARLAN	HNR	NDB	272.0	41 34.75N	95 20.44W
HARLINGEN	HRL	VOR	108.8	26 17.48N	97 47.60W
HARLOWTON	HWQ	NDB	242.0	46 26.11N	109 49.95W
HARNETT	HQT	NDB	417.0	35 26.00N	78 40.50W
HARRI (LOM/NDB)	HARR	NDB	344.0	41 20.33N	81 57.87W
HARRIS	HRS	VOR	109.8	34 56.59N	83 54.94W
HARRISBURG	HAR	VOR	112.5	40 18.14N	77 4.17W
HARRISBURG/RALEIG	HSB	NDB	230.0	37 48.70N	88 32.72W
HARRISON	HRO	VOR	112.5	36 19.11N	93 12.79W
HARRY STRUNK	CSB	NDB	389.0	40 18.26N	100 9.46W
HARTFORD	HFD	VOR	114.9	41 38.47N	72 32.86W
HARTFORD	HXF	NDB	200.0	43 20.89N	88 23.79W
HARTSVILLE	HVS	NDB	341.0	34 24.43N	80 6.92W
HARVEY	HRV	VOR	112.4	29 51.02N	90 0.17W
HARVI (LOM)	HARV	NDB	260.0	48 0.41N	96 5.75W
HARVS (LOM)	HARV	NDB	395.0	38 8.70N	97 16.57W

Name	Ident.	Type	Freq.	Latitude	Longitude
HASKELL	AKL	NDB	407.0	33 11.46N	99 43.21W
HASTINGS	HSI	VOR	108.8	40 36.28N	98 25.78W
HAUSER	HAU	NDB	386.0	46 34.15N	111 45.48W
HAVRE	HVR	VOR	111.8	48 32.44N	109 46.20W
HAVRE ST-PIERRE	YGV	NDB	344.0	50 15.90N	63 39.91W
HAWKEYE	UOC	NDB	524.0	41 37.93N	91 32.57W
HAWKY (LOM)	HAWK	NDB	219.0	42 49.05N	73 48.51W
HAYDEN	CHE	VOR	115.6	40 31.21N	107 18.29W
HAYES CENTER	HCT	VOR	117.7	40 27.25N	100 55.42W
HAYS	HYS	VOR	110.4	38 50.87N	99 16.61W
HAYWARD	HYR	VOR	113.4	46 1.12N	91 26.78W
HAZARD	AZQ	VOR	111.2	37 23.40N	83 15.98W
HAZEN	HZN	VOR	114.1	39 30.99N	118 59.86W
HAZER (LOM/NDB)	HAZE	NDB	356.0	30 38.00N	91 29.37W
HAZLEHURST	AZE	NDB	414.0	31 52.82N	82 38.84W
HAZLETON	HZL	VOR	109.4	40 58.51N	76 7.55W
HEATH POINT	HP	NDB	335.0	49 5.12N	61 42.04W
HEBBRONVILLE	HBV	NDB	266.0	27 21.24N	98 44.65W
HEBER SPRINGS	HBZ	NDB	296.0	35 30.87N	92 0.66W
HEBRON	HJH	NDB	323.0	40 9.03N	97 35.27W
HECTOR	HEC	VOR	112.7	34 47.83N	116 27.77W
HEGINBOTHAM	HEQ	NDB	404.0	40 34.89N	102 16.88W
HELENA	HLN	VOR	117.7	46 36.42N	111 57.21W
HELMUT	7X	NDB	216.0	59 22.01N	120 48.09W
HEMLOCK	BAR	NDB	320.0	36 9.22N	81 52.79W
HEMPHILL COUNTY	HHF	NDB	400.0	35 53.48N	100 24.33W
HENDERSON	HNN	VOR	115.9	38 45.26N	82 1.57W
HENDERSON	HNO	NDB	371.0	32 11.28N	94 51.66W
HENGCHUN	HCN	VOR	113.7	21 56.00N	120 50.00E
HENRY	PJS	NDB	375.0	37 7.98N	76 29.59W
HENRYETTA	HET	NDB	267.0	35 24.28N	96 0.83W
HEREFORD	HRX	NDB	341.0	34 51.39N	102 19.51W
HERINGTON	HRU	NDB	407.0	38 41.58N	96 48.67W
HERLONG	HEG	NDB	332.0	30 16.61N	81 48.54W
HERMOSILLO	HMO	VOR	112.8	29 5.72N	111 2.93W
HERNY (LOM)	HERN	NDB	221.0	28 30.42N	81 26.04W
HERRO (LOM)	HERR	NDB	219.0	44 31.95N	73 14.97W
HESTR (LOM)	HEST	NDB	281.0	41 8.73N	73 45.98W
HETTINGER	HEI	NDB	392.0	46 1.03N	102 38.94W
HIBBING	HIB	VOR	110.8	47 18.10N	92 42.24W
HICKS	IUI	NDB	299.0	35 56.27N	89 50.03W
HIG	HIG	VOR	110.6	39 4.38N	93 40.70W
HIGGINSVILLE	YOJ	VOR	113.3	58 33.23N	117 5.63W
HIGH LEVEL	HIGU	NDB	341.0	37 38.15N	87 9.74W
HIGUY (LOM)	HILA	NDB	266.0	36 43.81N	119 38.15W
HILAN (LOM)	HLC	VOR	113.7	39 15.53N	100 13.55W
HILL CITY	HOC	NDB	278.0	39 11.10N	83 32.55W
HILLSBORO	HLX	NDB	269.0	36 45.74N	80 49.32W
HILLSVILLE	HILL	NDB	517.0	41 45.11N	90 23.43W
HILLZ (LOM)	ITO	VOR	116.9	19 43.29N	155 0.66W
HILO	HIL	NDB	308.0	38 21.55N	98 54.18W
HILYN	HCH	VOR	117.6	35 46.87N	84 58.71W
HINCH MOUNTAIN	HBK	NDB	362.0	60 23.66N	146 5.42W
HINCHINBROOK	HISA	NDB	335.0	34 21.05N	103 10.46W
HISAN (LOM)	HOAG	NDB	251.0	40 55.84N	85 7.18W
HOAGY (LOM)	HBR	VOR	111.8	34 52.00N	99 3.80W
HOBART	HOB	VOR	111.0	32 38.30N	103 16.16W
HOBBS	HUB	VOR	117.6	29 39.02N	95 16.74W
HOBBY	JBL	NDB	256.0	32 12.08N	92 43.56W
HODGE	HOGA	NDB	521.0	41 34.46N	81 28.27W
HOGAF (LMM)	HDL	NDB	411.0	35 5.13N	96 24.80W
HOLDENVILLE	HDE	NDB	396.0	40 26.89N	99 20.43W
HOLDREGE	HLM	NDB	233.0	42 47.81N	86 9.47W
HOLLAND	HLI	VOR	112.4	34 46.22N	89 29.79W
HOLLY SPRINGS	HMV	VOR	114.6	36 26.23N	82 7.78W
HOLSTON MOUNTAIN	HDF	VOR	113.4	33 46.59N	117 11.12W
HOMELAND	HMJ	NDB	281.0	40 1.59N	87 57.19W
HOMER	HMQ	NDB	212.0	32 47.42N	93 0.04W
HOMER	HOM	VOR	114.6	59 42.58N	151 27.40W
HOMERVILLE	HOE	NDB	209.0	31 3.34N	82 46.33W

Name	Ident.	Type	Freq.	Latitude	Longitude
HONDO	HMA	NDB	329.0	29 22.41N	99 10.32W
HONEY GROVE	HIX	NDB	356.0	36 52.85N	87 20.25W
HONIARA	HN	VOR	112.6	9 25.90S	160 1.00E
HONOLULU	HNL	VOR	114.8	21 18.50N	157 55.83W
HOOD	HLR	NDB	347.0	31 7.75N	97 42.68W
HOOK FIELD	HKF	NDB	239.0	39 29.93N	84 26.85W
HOOPER BAY	HPB	VOR	115.2	61 30.89N	166 8.07W
HOOSIER	OOM	VOR	110.2	39 8.64N	86 36.78W
HOPE	HE	NDB	245.0	49 23.25N	121 25.43W
HOPE	HPC	NDB	362.0	33 43.08N	93 38.92W
HOPEWELL	HPW	VOR	112.0	37 19.74N	77 6.96W
HOPEY	PPI	NDB	400.0	44 52.40N	92 56.54W
HOPKINS	HPL	NDB	375.0	38 14.58N	108 34.00W
HOQUIAM	HQM	VOR	117.7	46 56.83N	124 8.96W
HORLICK	HRK	VOR	117.7	42 45.48N	87 48.86W
HORNEBROOK	HXK	NDB	281.0	44 34.63N	71 10.75W
HORRY	HYW	NDB	370.0	33 49.78N	79 7.44W
HORSE (LOM)	HORS	NDB	353.0	41 8.81N	104 40.73W
HORTON	HTN	NDB	320.0	46 24.74N	105 56.30W
HOSSY (LOM/NDB)	HOSS	NDB	385.0	34 25.37N	93 11.38W
HOT SPRINGS	HOT	VOR	110.0	34 28.72N	93 5.44W
HOTEL	H	NDB	407.0	45 33.86N	73 20.81W
HOTHAM	HHM	NDB	356.0	66 54.09N	162 33.86W
HOUGHTON	CMX	VOR	112.8	47 10.04N	88 28.91W
HOUGHTON LAKE	HTL	VOR	111.6	44 21.54N	84 39.94W
HOULTON	HUL	VOR	116.1	46 2.38N	67 50.05W
HOUMA (LOM)	HOUM	NDB	219.0	29 39.81N	90 39.58W
HOUSTON	YYD	VOR	114.7	54 27.15N	126 39.05W
HOWELL	OZW	NDB	242.0	42 38.04N	83 59.26W
HUBBARD	HBD	NDB	408.0	41 9.18N	80 31.84W
HUDSPETH	HUP	VOR	115.0	31 34.13N	105 22.58W
HUGGY (LOM)	HUGG	NDB	242.0	39 18.13N	94 51.07W
HUGO	HGO	VOR	112.1	38 48.91N	103 37.56W
HUGO	HHW	NDB	323.0	34 2.39N	95 32.36W
HUGOTON	HQG	NDB	365.0	37 9.82N	101 22.48W
HUGUENOT	HUO	VOR	116.1	41 24.59N	74 35.50W
HULL	SGR	NDB	388.0	29 37.96N	95 39.36W
HULLZ (LOM)	HULL	NDB	346.0	42 18.20N	70 55.32W
HUMBLE	IAH	VOR	116.6	29 57.42N	95 20.74W
HUMBOLDT	HML	VOR	112.4	48 52.16N	97 7.02W
HUMBOLT	HXM	NDB	366.0	40 59.32N	75 59.82W
HUMPHREY	HPY	NDB	275.0	29 47.46N	94 57.32W
HUMPHREYS	HVU	VOR	109.8	34 31.18N	99 16.50W
HUNTER	HEU	NDB	356.0	42 51.19N	73 56.06W
HUNTER	SVN	VOR	111.6	32 0.72N	81 8.44W
HUNTER LIGGETT	HGT	NDB	209.0	35 56.34N	121 9.73W
HUNTINGBURG	HNB	VOR	109.2	38 15.03N	86 57.38W
HUNTINGDON	HZD	NDB	217.0	36 5.30N	88 27.98W
HUNTINGTON	HHG	NDB	417.0	40 51.35N	85 27.86W
HUNTSBORO	HXO	NDB	271.0	36 18.03N	78 37.12W
HUNTSVILLE	UTS	NDB	308.0	30 44.45N	95 35.46W
HUNTT (LOM)	HUNT	NDB	226.0	38 23.95N	82 39.24W
HURON	HON	VOR	117.6	44 26.41N	98 18.66W
HURRICANE	SKN	NDB	256.0	35 59.05N	85 48.49W
HUSKK (LOM/NDB)	HUSK	NDB	382.0	39 46.40N	89 45.59W
HUSLIA	HSL	VOR	117.4	65 42.38N	156 22.24W
HUSSK (LOM)	HUSS	NDB	342.0	45 28.74N	93 58.15W
HUTCHINS	HEM	NDB	233.0	35 59.28N	85 35.17W
HUTCHINSON	HCD	NDB	209.0	44 51.42N	94 23.00W
HUTCHINSON	HUT	VOR	116.8	37 59.82N	97 56.05W
HYANNIS	HYA	VOR	114.7	41 42.70N	70 12.92W
ICE POOL	ICW	NDB	525.0	64 32.76N	149 4.61W
IDA GROVE	IDG	NDB	281.0	42 19.96N	95 26.85W
IDABEL	IBO	NDB	271.0	33 54.37N	94 50.58W
IDAHO FALLS	IDA	VOR	109.0	43 31.15N	112 3.83W
IDDER (LOM/NDB)	IDDE	NDB	385.0	30 45.13N	93 20.08W
IGNEK	CNR	NDB	209.0	69 35.70N	146 29.72W
ILIAMNA	ILI	NDB	328.0	59 44.89N	154 54.58W
ILOPANGO	YSV	VOR	114.7	13 42.00N	89 7.00W
IMPERIAL	IML	NDB	283.0	40 30.70N	101 37.65W
IMPERIAL	IPL	VOR	115.9	32 44.94N	115 30.51W
INDDY (LOM)	INDD	NDB	385.0	41 54.29N	87 48.37W
INDEPENDENCE	IDP	NDB	400.0	37 9.61N	95 46.33W
INDEPENDENCE CO	INY	NDB	317.0	41 51.86N	91 47.12W
INDIAN HEAD	IHD	VOR	108.2	39 58.46N	79 21.50W
INDIANA	INP	NDB	242.0	40 37.92N	79 3.96W
INDIANAPOLIS	VHP	VOR	116.3	39 48.89N	86 22.05W
INDIANOLA	IDL	NDB	284.0	33 28.82N	90 40.54W
INDUSTRY	IDU	VOR	110.2	29 57.37N	96 33.73W
INGLE (LOM)	INGL	NDB	329.0	36 50.43N	76 15.08W
INGOLSTADT	IGL	NDB	345.0	48 44.41N	11 38.80E
INNSBRUCK	INN	NDB	420.0	47 13.91N	11 24.20E
INSTITUTE	IUB	NDB	404.0	39 17.23N	76 37.51W
INTL FALLS	INL	VOR	111.0	48 33.96N	93 24.34W
INUVIK	EV	NDB	254.0	68 19.58N	133 35.57W
INUVIK	YEV	VOR	112.5	68 18.49N	133 32.90W
IONE	ION	NDB	379.0	48 42.62N	117 24.82W
IOWA CITY	IOW	VOR	116.2	41 31.15N	91 36.80W
IOWA FALLS	IFA	NDB	368.0	42 28.61N	93 15.93W
IRA	IRA	NDB	398.0	43 41.53N	72 59.15W
IRESH (LOM/NDB)	IRES	NDB	278.0	31 1.45N	97 42.48W
IRON MOUNTAIN	IMT	VOR	111.2	45 48.97N	88 6.73W
IRONHORSE	IHS	NDB	335.0	38 40.71N	104 45.20W
IRONWOOD	IWD	VOR	108.8	46 31.94N	90 7.55W
ISLE MADAME	W	NDB	304.0	45 33.60N	60 55.92W
ISLETA	ILT	NDB	247.0	34 59.23N	106 37.22W
ISSUE (LOM)	ISSU	NDB	233.0	32 47.60N	97 1.83W
ITHACA	ITH	VOR	111.8	42 29.71N	76 27.58W
IVISHAK	IVH	NDB	379.0	69 24.15N	148 16.19W
IWO JIMA	OX	NDB	360.0	24 46.91N	141 18.30E
JACKS CREEK	JKS	VOR	109.4	35 35.95N	88 21.53W
JACKSBORO	JAU	NDB	204.0	36 20.28N	84 9.66W
JACKSON	JAC	VOR	108.4	43 36.51N	110 44.08W
JACKSON	JAN	VOR	112.6	32 30.46N	90 10.06W
JACKSON	JXN	VOR	109.6	42 15.56N	84 27.51W
JACKSON COUNTY	MJQ	NDB	353.0	43 38.84N	94 59.17W
JACKSONVILLE	EDX	NDB	201.0	29 0.10N	96 35.08W
JAKSO (LOM)	IJX	VOR	108.6	39 46.60N	90 14.32W
JAMBE (LOM/NDB)	JAKS	NDB	212.0	42 19.08N	84 21.93W
JAMESTOWN	JAMB	NDB	235.0	35 46.07N	77 57.88W
JAMESTOWN	JHW	VOR	114.7	42 11.33N	79 7.28W
JANESVILLE	JMS	VOR	114.5	46 55.98N	98 40.73W
JANESVILLE	JVL	VOR	114.3	42 33.49N	89 6.32W
JASPER	JVL	NDB	375.0	42 36.92N	89 2.48W
JASPER	APT	NDB	382.0	35 3.61N	85 35.01W
JEANS (LOM)	JAS	NDB	344.0	30 57.28N	94 2.01W
JECCA	JEAN	NDB	219.0	39 10.77N	76 46.15W
JEFFERSON	JUG	NDB	388.0	32 40.15N	96 31.93W
JEFFERSON	EFW	NDB	391.0	42 0.86N	94 20.27W
JEFFERSON	JFN	VOR	115.2	41 45.62N	80 44.88W
JEFFI (LOM)	JXT	NDB	346.0	36 6.64N	83 28.53W
JENKINS (LOM)	JEFF	NDB	275.0	31 13.71N	81 32.56W
JETT	MX	NDB	232.0	38 55.19N	76 52.29W
JHON F KENNEDY INTL	JET	NDB	365.0	38 12.92N	84 49.53W
JIFFY (LOM)	JFK	VOR	115.9	40 37.98N	73 46.28W
JIGEL	JIFF	NDB	219.0	32 59.75N	97 1.77W
JNALL	JB	NDB	384.0	34 32.77N	79 8.30W
JOCKY (LOM)	EUU	NDB	251.0	35 36.42N	78 21.27W
JOHNO (LOM)	JOCK	NDB	257.0	41 53.68N	87 49.58W
JOHNS ISLAND	JOHN	NDB	375.0	42 54.44N	106 34.20W
JOHNSON COUNTY	JZI	NDB	283.0	32 42.08N	80 0.34W
JOHNSTONE POINT	OJC	VOR	113.0	38 50.19N	94 44.21W
JOHNSTOWN	JOH	VOR	116.7	60 28.87N	146 35.96W
JOHNSTOWN	JJH	NDB	523.0	42 59.97N	74 19.95W
JOLIET	JST	VOR	113.0	40 19.01N	78 50.05W
JONESBORO	JOT	VOR	112.3	41 32.79N	88 19.11W
JONNY (LOM)	JBR	VOR	108.6	35 52.50N	90 35.31W
JORDAN	JONN	NDB	382.0	37 50.36N	88 58.24W
JORGE (LMM)	JDN	NDB	263.0	47 20.01N	106 56.29W
	JORG	NDB	249.0	37 20.94N	121 54.90W

Name	Ident.	Type	Freq.	Latitude	Longitude
JOTLY (LOM)	JOTL	NDB	271.0	37 49.92N	121 8.13W
JUDD	JUY	NDB	264.0	31 18.27N	86 23.45W
JUDKY (LOM)	JUDK	NDB	521.0	34 46.81N	82 20.99W
JULIAN	JLI	VOR	114.0	33 8.44N	116 35.16W
JULIET	J	NDB	236.0	43 36.98N	79 41.30W
JULIET	J	NDB	397.0	45 13.68N	65 57.48W
JULIET	J	NDB	385.0	44 58.01N	63 25.63W
JUMPI (LOM)	JUMP	NDB	423.0	29 3.39N	82 13.39W
JUMPR (LOM)	JUMP	NDB	219.0	32 15.82N	84 55.83W
JUNCTION	JCT	VOR	116.0	30 35.89N	99 49.05W
JUNEAU	UNU	NDB	344.0	43 25.83N	88 42.04W
K I SAWYER	SAW	VOR	116.3	46 21.92N	87 23.39W
KACHEMAK	ACE	NDB	277.0	59 38.49N	151 30.01W
KAISER	AIZ	NDB	272.0	38 5.81N	92 33.18W
KALAMAZOO	AZO	VOR	109.0	42 14.23N	85 33.19W
KALISPELL	FCA	VOR	108.4	48 12.86N	114 10.55W
KAMUELA	MUE	VOR	113.3	19 59.89N	155 40.19W
KANAN (LOM)	KANA	NDB	335.0	38 2.79N	122 2.01W
KANEOHE BAY(MARIN	NGF	NDB	265.0	21 27.11N	157 45.20W
KANKAKEE	IKK	VOR	111.6	41 4.47N	87 50.99W
KANSAS CITY	MKC	VOR	112.6	39 16.77N	94 35.48W
KAOLIN	OKZ	NDB	212.0	32 57.88N	82 50.29W
KARPEN	PEN	NDB	201.0	46 8.38N	123 35.24W
KASING	YYU	NDB	341.0	49 27.90N	82 30.34W
KATFI (LOM)	KATF	NDB	362.0	35 1.29N	77 4.77W
KATHI (LOM)	KATH	NDB	329.0	43 6.56N	78 50.30W
KAVIENG	KAU	VOR	116.3	2 35.40S	150 48.90E
KAZOO (LOM)	KAZO	NDB	257.0	29 59.78N	94 6.38W
KEANS (LOM)	KEAN	NDB	357.0	35 31.98N	82 35.24W
KEARN (LOM)	KEAR	NDB	371.0	39 16.56N	123 14.43W
KEARNEY	EAR	VOR	111.2	40 43.54N	99 0.31W
KEATING	ETG	VOR	116.0	41 12.91N	78 8.56W
KEDZI (LOM/NDB)	KEDZ	NDB	248.0	41 44.50N	87 41.38W
KEELER	ELX	VOR	116.6	42 8.67N	86 7.36W
KEENE	EEN	VOR	109.4	42 47.67N	72 17.51W
KEHOE (LOM)	KEHO	NDB	380.0	40 52.38N	98 18.88W
KELLYVILLE	EPX	NDB	233.0	43 19.38N	72 22.67W
KELOWNA	LW	NDB	257.0	50 3.65N	119 24.99W
KELSO	LSO	NDB	256.0	46 9.23N	122 54.74W
KELSO	TNY	NDB	358.0	35 8.05N	86 32.52W
KEMMERER	EMM	NDB	407.0	41 49.35N	110 33.30W
KEMPTEN	KPT	VOR	109.6	47 44.81N	10 21.10E
KENAI	ENA	VOR	117.6	60 36.90N	151 11.71W
KENAN	DPL	NDB	344.0	35 2.87N	77 56.73W
KENIE (LOM/NDB)	KENI	NDB	365.0	47 0.57N	96 48.91W
KENNEBUNK	ENE	VOR	117.1	43 25.55N	70 36.81W
KENNEDY	ENY	NDB	254.0	46 33.19N	90 54.87W
KENNETT	TKX	NDB	358.0	36 13.74N	90 2.17W
KENORA	YQK	NDB	326.0	49 47.56N	94 25.46W
KENOSHA	ENW	VOR	109.2	42 35.95N	87 56.00W
KENZY (LOM)	KENZ	NDB	344.0	39 13.26N	94 33.85W
KEOKUK	EOK	NDB	366.0	40 27.76N	91 26.01W
KEOTE (LOM)	KEOT	NDB	338.0	29 25.90N	98 52.97W
KERNN (LOM)	KERN	NDB	338.0	40 40.88N	111 57.78W
KESSEL	ESL	VOR	110.8	39 13.54N	78 59.37W
KETTLE MORAINE	LLE	NDB	329.0	43 25.54N	88 7.79W
KEWANEE	EWA	VOR	113.8	32 22.02N	88 27.50W
KEWANEE	EZI	NDB	245.0	41 12.08N	89 57.56W
KEY WEST	EYW	VOR	113.5	24 35.15N	81 48.03W
KEYES (LOM)	KEYE	NDB	248.0	25 47.45N	80 11.66W
KEYLI (LOM)	KEYL	NDB	353.0	30 11.59N	93 15.79W
KICKAPOO	HBW	NDB	251.0	43 39.32N	90 19.99W
KILLALOE	YXI	VOR	115.6	45 39.80N	77 36.17W
KIMBALL	IBM	NDB	317.0	41 11.49N	103 40.19W
KIMBERLY	IMB	VOR	115.6	44 38.91N	119 42.70W
KINCARDINE	D7	NDB	350.0	44 12.21N	81 36.19W
KING SALMON	AKN	VOR	112.8	58 43.39N	156 45.13W
KINGFISHER	IFI	VOR	114.7	35 48.32N	98 0.24W
KINGMAN	IGM	VOR	108.8	35 15.64N	113 56.04W
KINGSTON	IGN	VOR	117.6	41 39.94N	73 49.34W

Name	Ident.	Type	Freq.	Latitude	Longitude
KINGSTON	KIN	VOR	115.9	17 58.42N	76 53.63W
KINGSTON	KIN	NDB	360.0	17 57.80N	76 52.55W
KINGSTON	YGK	NDB	263.0	44 17.81N	76 36.33W
KINGSTREE	CKI	NDB	404.0	33 43.07N	79 51.30W
KINSTON	ISO	VOR	109.6	35 22.26N	77 33.50W
KINTE (LOM/NDB)	KINT	NDB	338.0	30 1.52N	90 23.99W
KIOWA	IOC	VOR	117.5	39 26.16N	104 20.26W
KIPNUK	IIK	VOR	115.9	59 56.58N	164 2.06W
KIRBY (LOM)	KIRB	NDB	360.0	38 42.05N	76 52.21W
KIRIWINA	KWA	NDB	287.0	8 30.30S	151 5.40E
KIRKI (LOM)	KIRK	NDB	242.0	43 6.74N	76 0.16W
KIRKLAND/LAKE ON	YKX	NDB	201.0	48 13.63N	79 52.19W
KIRKSVILLE	IRK	VOR	114.6	40 8.11N	92 35.50W
KISSIMMEE	ISM	NDB	329.0	28 17.37N	81 26.06W
KIT CARSON	ITR	NDB	209.0	39 14.78N	102 17.03W
KITIMAT	ZKI	NDB	203.0	54 3.25N	128 40.20W
KITSAP	PWT	NDB	206.0	47 29.87N	122 45.62W
KLAMATH FALLS	LMT	VOR	115.9	42 9.20N	121 43.65W
KLEBERG COUNTY	TKB	NDB	347.0	27 36.36N	98 5.38W
KLICKITAT	LTJ	VOR	112.3	45 42.82N	121 6.05W
KLINT (LOM)	KLIN	NDB	217.0	43 0.86N	108 18.31W
KLUMP (LOM)	KLUM	NDB	231.0	43 0.02N	78 39.05W
KNIGHT	TPF	VOR	270.0	27 54.51N	82 27.26W
KNOBS (LOM)	KNOB	NDB	263.0	42 53.75N	85 22.71W
KNOX	OXI	VOR	115.6	41 19.33N	86 38.96W
KNOXVILLE	OXV	NDB	284.0	41 17.78N	93 6.74W
KOBRA (LOM)	KOBR	NDB	201.0	30 51.19N	86 32.19W
KODIAK	ODK	VOR	117.1	57 46.51N	152 20.39W
KOKO HEAD	CKH	VOR	113.9	21 15.91N	157 42.18W
KOKOMO	OKK	VOR	109.8	40 31.68N	86 3.48W
KOLOE (LOM/NDB)	KOLO	NDB	400.0	46 19.96N	84 32.54W
KOMAKK	AJ	NDB	239.0	69 35.70N	140 11.01W
KONA	IAI	VOR	115.7	19 39.27N	156 1.49W
KONA	INE	NDB	521.0	47 5.67N	114 23.81W
KOROR	ROR	NDB	371.0	7 21.65N	134 32.41E
KOSCIUSKO	OSX	NDB	269.0	33 5.46N	89 32.42W
KOSRAE	UKS	NDB	393.0	5 21.88N	162 58.38E
KOTTI (LOM)	KOTT	NDB	335.0	29 26.75N	100 59.32W
KOTZEBUE	OTZ	VOR	115.7	66 53.15N	162 32.40W
KOYUK	KKA	NDB	299.0	64 55.93N	161 8.87W
KREMMLING	RLG	VOR	113.8	40 0.17N	106 26.55W
KRING (LOM)	KRIN	NDB	279.0	42 35.09N	74 59.18W
KUKULIAK	ULL	VOR	117.3	63 41.55N	170 28.20W
KULIK LAKE	HCP	NDB	334.0	59 1.08N	155 36.02W
KUPARUK	UUK	NDB	218.0	70 17.06N	149 8.35W
KUSHIMOTO	KEC	VOR	112.9	33 26.81N	135 47.70E
LA BELLE	LBV	VOR	110.4	26 49.70N	81 23.49W
LA CROSSE	LSE	VOR	108.4	43 52.58N	91 15.36W
LA FONDA RANCH	BRX	NDB	269.0	29 12.52N	100 37.44W
LA GRANDE	LGD	NDB	296.0	45 22.35N	117 59.61W
LA GRANGE	LGC	VOR	115.6	33 2.95N	85 12.37W
LA GUARDIA	LGA	VOR	113.1	40 47.04N	73 52.11W
LA JUNTA	LHX	NDB	239.0	38 2.90N	103 37.27W
LA PRYOR	LKX	NDB	223.0	28 55.80N	99 51.29W
LA TONTOUTA	LTO	VOR	112.9	22 0.50S	166 12.50E
LA TUQUE	YLQ	NDB	289.0	47 24.93N	72 47.14W
LAANG (LOM)	LAAN	NDB	414.0	38 8.70N	85 38.00W
LABERGE	JB	NDB	236.0	60 56.95N	135 8.26W
LAC LA MARTRE	Z3	NDB	304.0	63 8.64N	117 15.99W
LACOMAS	LAC	NDB	328.0	47 0.49N	122 33.39W
LADOS (LOM)	LADO	NDB	418.0	33 17.17N	92 43.69W
LAFAYETTE	LFB	NDB	245.0	36 30.91N	86 3.66W
LAFAYETTE	LFT	VOR	109.8	30 11.63N	91 59.55W
LAFFS (LOM)	LAFF	NDB	375.0	30 17.37N	91 54.47W
LAKE CHARLES	LCH	VOR	113.4	30 11.13N	93 6.33W
LAKE CITY	LCQ	NDB	204.0	30 11.13N	82 34.72W
LAKE HAVASU	HII	NDB	364.0	34 34.51N	114 21.85W
LAKE HENRY	LHY	VOR	110.8	41 28.56N	75 28.96W
LAKE HUGHES	LHS	VOR	108.4	34 40.99N	118 34.62W
LAKE KEOWEE	LQK	NDB	408.0	34 48.57N	82 42.07W

Name	Ident.	Type	Freq.	Latitude	Longitude
LAKE LAWN	LVV	NDB	404.0	42 42.48N	88 35.59W
LAKE PROVIDENCE	BLE	NDB	278.0	32 49.85N	91 11.41W
LAKEFIELD	CQA	NDB	205.0	40 28.93N	84 33.86W
LAKEHURST (NAVY)	NEL	NDB	396.0	40 2.69N	74 20.14W
LAKELAND	LAL	VOR	116.0	27 59.18N	82 0.83W
LAKELAND	LQL	NDB	263.0	41 40.95N	81 22.74W
LAKER (LOM/NDB)	LAKE	NDB	332.0	45 32.48N	122 27.74W
LAKESHORE	XG	NDB	338.0	60 6.78N	128 47.97W
LAKESIDE	LYD	NDB	249.0	29 48.99N	95 40.66W
LAKEVIEW	LKV	VOR	112.0	42 29.58N	120 30.43W
LAMAR	LAA	VOR	116.9	38 11.83N	102 41.25W
LAMESA	LSA	NDB	338.0	32 45.43N	101 54.93W
LAMONI	LMN	VOR	116.7	40 35.81N	93 58.06W
LAMPASAS	LZZ	VOR	112.5	31 11.14N	98 8.51W
LAMPSON	LOP	NDB	217.0	38 59.72N	122 53.02W
LANAI	LLD	NDB	353.0	20 46.70N	156 57.98W
LANAI	LNY	VOR	117.7	20 45.87N	156 58.13W
LANCASTER	LKR	NDB	400.0	34 43.43N	80 51.49W
LANCASTER	LNC	NDB	239.0	32 34.67N	96 43.30W
LANCASTER	LRP	VOR	117.3	40 7.21N	76 17.48W
LAND O LAKES	LNL	NDB	396.0	46 9.26N	89 12.68W
LANDSBERG	LQ	NDB	448.0	48 5.61N	11 2.20E
LANDY (LOM/NDB)	LAND	NDB	407.0	38 21.76N	75 11.98W
LANEE (LOM)	LANE	NDB	400.0	38 37.02N	121 36.20W
LANGRUTH	VLR	VOR	112.2	50 25.34N	98 43.42W
LANSING	LAN	VOR	110.8	42 43.05N	84 41.86W
LAPORTE	LQP	NDB	387.0	40 34.94N	105 2.08W
LARAMIE	LAR	VOR	117.6	41 20.28N	105 43.26W
LAREDO	LRD	VOR	117.4	27 28.73N	99 25.06W
LAREW (LOM)	LARE	NDB	251.0	46 27.41N	94 1.36W
LAREZ (LOM)	LARE	NDB	349.0	39 47.20N	86 11.77W
LARNED	LQR	NDB	296.0	38 12.28N	99 5.26W
LAS CRUCES	LCR	NDB	299.0	32 16.94N	106 55.41W
LAS VEGAS	LAS	VOR	116.9	36 4.79N	115 9.59W
LAS VEGAS	LVS	VOR	117.3	35 39.46N	105 8.13W
LASCASSAS	MBT	NDB	317.0	35 52.36N	86 22.77W
LASKY (LOM/NDB)	LASK	NDB	353.0	34 40.14N	92 18.33W
LASSN (LOM)	LASS	NDB	367.0	40 23.58N	122 17.68W
LATLE (LOM)	LATL	NDB	219.0	40 10.70N	77 0.34W
LAUGHLIN	DLF	VOR	114.4	29 21.66N	100 46.30W
LAURENS	LUX	NDB	307.0	34 30.50N	81 56.99W
LAWRENCE	LWC	NDB	284.0	39 0.43N	95 13.28W
LAWRENCE	LWM	VOR	112.5	42 44.43N	71 5.69W
LAWRENCE CO	TNZ	NDB	227.0	36 12.34N	90 55.39W
LAWRENCEBURG	LRT	NDB	269.0	35 14.14N	87 15.64W
LAWRENCEVILLE	LVL	VOR	112.9	36 49.09N	77 54.18W
LAWRENCEVILLE	LWV	VOR	113.5	38 46.18N	87 35.95W
LAWSON	AWS	NDB	335.0	32 17.60N	85 1.40W
LAWSON	LSF	VOR	111.4	32 19.95N	84 59.60W
LAWTON	LAW	VOR	109.4	34 29.78N	98 24.78W
LE BOURGET (PARIS)	BGW	NDB	334.0	48 56.31N	2 16.80E
LE BOURGET (PARIS)	BT	VOR	108.8	48 58.51N	2 27.40E
LE HAVRE	LHO	NDB	346.0	49 35.81N	0 11.00E
LE MARS	LRJ	NDB	382.0	42 46.48N	96 11.55W
LEAMA (LOM)	LEAM	NDB	368.0	42 4.16N	87 59.45W
LEBANON	IEB	NDB	414.0	37 34.30N	92 39.49W
LEBANON	LDQ	NDB	414.0	36 11.21N	86 18.85W
LEBANON	LEB	VOR	113.7	43 40.74N	72 12.96W
LEE BIRD	LED	NDB	375.0	41 6.73N	100 40.54W
LEE COUNTY	EEJ	NDB	428.0	35 22.40N	79 13.38W
LEE COUNTY	GYB	NDB	385.0	30 10.14N	96 58.79W
LEE COUNTY	RSW	VOR	111.8	26 31.80N	81 46.55W
LEEDS	LDS	NDB	389.0	48 32.74N	109 41.42W
LEEHI (LOM)	LEEH	NDB	400.0	40 35.16N	75 32.97W
LEENY (LOM)	LEEN	NDB	347.0	47 44.58N	116 57.66W
LEEVILLE	LEV	VOR	113.5	29 10.52N	90 6.24W
LEEVY (LOM/NDB)	LEEV	NDB	350.0	35 55.64N	78 43.32W
LEMMON	LEM	VOR	111.4	45 55.20N	102 6.22W
LEONA	LOA	VOR	110.8	31 7.45N	95 58.08W
LEROI (LOM)	LERO	NDB	283.0	31 44.46N	97 4.68W

Name	Ident.	Type	Freq.	Latitude	Longitude
LETHBRIDGE	QL	NDB	248.0	49 36.33N	112 53.64W
LETHBRIDGE	YQL	VOR	115.7	49 38.08N	112 40.07W
LEVEL ISLAND	LVD	VOR	116.5	56 28.08N	133 4.99W
LEVELLAND	LLN	NDB	266.0	33 33.35N	102 22.51W
LEWIE (LOM)	LEWI	NDB	240.0	43 57.84N	70 20.14W
LEWISBURG	LWG	NDB	225.0	44 36.82N	123 16.24W
LEWISTOWN	LWT	VOR	112.0	47 3.19N	109 36.37W
LEWISTOWN	LWT	NDB	353.0	47 4.06N	109 32.12W
LEXINGTON	HYK	VOR	112.6	37 58.00N	84 28.35W
LG-4	YFM	NDB	332.0	53 42.70N	73 42.18W
LIARD RIVER	ZL	NDB	263.0	59 28.12N	126 8.61W
LIBBY	FHU	VOR	111.6	31 35.44N	110 20.57W
LIBERAL	LBL	VOR	112.3	37 2.67N	100 58.27W
LIBERTY	LIB	VOR	113.0	35 48.71N	79 36.76W
LICAN (LOM)	LICA	NDB	215.0	44 48.21N	97 9.01W
LIHUE	LIH	VOR	113.5	21 57.92N	159 20.29W
LIMA	L	NDB	368.0	43 37.18N	79 32.87W
LIMA	L	NDB	284.0	45 32.56N	73 39.41W
LIMA	L	NDB	281.0	47 58.41N	66 13.41W
LIMA	LYL	NDB	362.0	40 42.28N	84 1.39W
LIMON	LIO	NDB	380.0	9 58.60N	83 1.97W
LINCOLN	LNK	VOR	116.1	40 55.44N	96 44.52W
LINCOLN	LRG	NDB	216.0	45 21.40N	68 32.22W
LINCOLN PARISH	LPZ	NDB	308.0	32 30.95N	92 37.64W
LINCOLNTON	IZN	NDB	432.0	35 32.27N	81 5.19W
LINDBERGH	LKG	NDB	242.0	32 10.47N	84 6.49W
LINDEN	LDN	VOR	114.3	38 51.27N	78 12.33W
LINDEN	LIN	VOR	114.8	38 4.48N	121 0.23W
LITCHFIELD	LFD	VOR	111.2	42 3.76N	84 45.91W
LITCHFIELD	LTD	NDB	371.0	39 9.98N	89 40.14W
LITTLE FALLS	LXL	NDB	359.0	45 57.01N	94 20.50W
LITTLE ROCK	LIT	VOR	113.9	34 40.67N	92 10.83W
LITTLE SIOUX	LTU	NDB	326.0	43 7.63N	95 7.96W
LITTLEFIELD	LIU	NDB	212.0	33 55.17N	102 23.20W
LIVERPOOL	A9	NDB	330.0	44 13.63N	64 51.51W
LIVINGSTON	LVM	VOR	116.1	45 42.16N	110 26.55W
LIVINGSTON	LVT	VOR	108.4	36 35.08N	85 10.00W
LIZAH (LOM)	LIZA	NDB	204.0	40 36.45N	74 13.08W
LLANO	LLO	VOR	108.2	30 47.79N	98 47.24W
LOCHRIDGE RANCH	LIQ	NDB	335.0	32 0.65N	95 57.16W
LOGAN	LGU	VOR	109.8	41 50.66N	111 51.92W
LOGAN COUNTY	LCY	NDB	326.0	35 50.74N	97 25.00W
LOGANSPORT	GGP	NDB	263.0	40 42.56N	86 22.42W
LOGOTALA HILL	LOG	NDB	242.0	14 21.53S	170 44.86W
LOKKS (LOM)	LOKK	NDB	366.0	40 43.75N	73 11.41W
LOMIS (LOM/NDB)	LOMI	NDB	244.0	41 38.14N	72 37.54W
LOMPOC	LPC	NDB	223.0	34 39.89N	120 27.78W
LONDON	LOZ	VOR	116.1	37 2.00N	84 6.61W
LONDON	U	NDB	201.0	42 58.95N	81 5.31W
LONDON	UYF	NDB	284.0	39 56.06N	83 27.98W
LONDON	XU	NDB	383.0	43 5.50N	81 13.11W
LONDON	YXU	VOR	117.2	43 2.30N	81 8.91W
LONE ROCK	LNR	VOR	112.8	43 17.67N	90 7.99W
LONE STAR	LST	NDB	305.0	32 55.68N	94 44.59W
LONG HOLLOW	LQV	NDB	252.0	36 42.43N	83 4.44W
LOOSAHATCHEE	LHC	NDB	265.0	35 17.09N	89 40.28W
LORRS (LOM)	LORR	NDB	226.0	40 43.53N	73 41.59W
LOS ANGELES	LAX	VOR	113.6	33 56.00N	118 25.92W
LOST NATION	LNN	VOR	110.2	41 41.04N	81 23.73W
LOUISA	IQK	NDB	382.0	38 1.23N	77 51.55W
LOUISVILLE	IIU	VOR	114.8	38 22.36N	85 34.45W
LOUISVILLE	LMS	NDB	212.0	33 8.63N	89 3.65W
LOUVALE	XLE	NDB	407.0	32 9.58N	84 50.49W
LOVELOCK	LLC	VOR	116.5	40 7.50N	118 34.66W
LOVINGTON	LGX	NDB	396.0	32 56.83N	103 24.60W
LOWE	LOR	NDB	269.0	31 21.62N	85 44.61W
LUBBI (LOM)	LUBB	NDB	272.0	33 39.77N	101 43.39W
LUBBOCK	LBB	VOR	109.2	33 42.31N	101 54.85W
LUCIN	LCU	VOR	113.6	41 21.79N	113 50.44W
LUDINGTON	LDM	NDB	341.0	43 57.80N	86 24.57W

Name	Ident.	Type	Freq.	Latitude	Longitude
LUFKIN	LFK	VOR	112.1	31 9.75N	94 43.02W
LUMBERTON	LBT	VOR	110.0	34 36.65N	79 3.28W
LUMSDEN	VLN	VOR	114.2	50 40.03N	104 53.42W
LUNNS (LOM)	LUNN	NDB	344.0	37 12.19N	94 33.51W
LYNCHBURG	LYH	VOR	109.2	37 15.29N	79 14.19W
LYNDONVILLE	LLX	NDB	353.0	44 30.26N	72 1.75W
LYNDY (LOM/NDB)	LYND	NDB	382.0	42 27.13N	70 57.80W
LYNN LAKE	YYL	VOR	112.6	56 51.87N	101 4.52W
LYNNE (LOM)	LYNN	NDB	278.0	30 19.60N	85 46.94W
LYONS	LYO	NDB	386.0	38 20.84N	98 13.62W
MAAGG (LMM)	MAAG	NDB	337.0	33 41.34N	117 51.64W
MACHIAS	MVM	NDB	251.0	44 42.28N	67 28.70W
MACKALL	HFF	NDB	278.0	35 1.68N	79 29.14W
MACKENZIE	2U	NDB	284.0	55 18.31N	123 8.24W
MACOMB	JZY	NDB	251.0	40 31.11N	90 33.62W
MACON	MCM	VOR	112.9	39 39.25N	92 28.93W
MACON	MCN	VOR	114.2	32 41.48N	83 38.83W
MADDS (LOM)	MADD	NDB	338.0	42 29.70N	83 5.60W
MADEIRA	MDE	NDB	379.0	39 13.36N	84 21.33W
MADISON	IMS	NDB	404.0	38 45.66N	85 27.63W
MADISON	MAD	VOR	110.4	41 18.84N	72 41.53W
MADISON	MSN	VOR	108.6	43 8.70N	89 20.38W
MADISONVILLE	MNV	NDB	361.0	35 32.71N	84 22.98W
MAGGS (LOM)	MAGG	NDB	239.0	44 56.69N	91 22.42W
MAGNOLIA	AGO	NDB	266.0	33 13.63N	93 12.91W
MAHN	GMA	NDB	386.0	44 21.75N	71 41.16W
MAIQUETIA	MIQ	VOR	114.8	10 37.00N	67 1.00W
MAIQUETIA	MIQ	NDB	292.0	10 37.00N	67 1.00W
MAISACH	MAH	VOR	108.4	48 15.91N	11 18.80E
MAJOR (LOM)	MAJO	NDB	201.0	33 9.38N	96 3.81W
MAJURO	MAJ	NDB	316.0	7 4.03N	171 16.73E
MALAD CITY	MLD	VOR	117.4	42 12.00N	112 27.07W
MALDEN	MAW	VOR	111.2	36 33.31N	89 54.69W
MALLY (LOM)	MALL	NDB	397.0	42 7.62N	86 18.80W
MALTA	MLK	NDB	272.0	48 21.11N	107 53.64W
MALVERN	MVQ	NDB	215.0	34 20.01N	92 45.74W
MANCHESTER	MHT	VOR	114.4	42 52.12N	71 22.17W
MANHATTAN	MHK	VOR	110.2	39 8.73N	96 40.12W
MANISTEE	MBL	VOR	111.4	44 16.33N	86 13.77W
MANITOUWADGE	YMG	NDB	219.0	49 2.98N	85 54.03W
MANITOWOC	MTW	VOR	111.0	44 7.72N	87 40.79W
MANIWAKI	YMW	NDB	366.0	46 12.48N	75 57.40W
MANKATO	MKT	VOR	110.8	44 13.20N	93 54.74W
MANKATO	TKO	VOR	109.8	39 48.39N	98 15.60W
MANNI (LOM)	MANN	NDB	266.0	45 52.32N	111 17.14W
MANNING	MNI	NDB	381.0	33 35.30N	80 12.37W
MANNS (LOM/NDB)	MANN	NDB	372.0	40 45.97N	82 26.70W
MANS	YMS	VOR	114.5	44 8.60N	80 8.77W
MANSFIELD	IHM	NDB	220.0	42 0.18N	71 11.83W
MANSFIELD	MFD	VOR	108.8	40 52.13N	82 35.46W
MANSFIELD	MSD	NDB	414.0	32 3.87N	93 45.87W
MANTECA	ECA	VOR	116.0	37 50.02N	121 10.28W
MANTEO	MQI	NDB	370.0	35 54.93N	75 41.70W
MANY	MMY	NDB	272.0	31 34.28N	93 32.49W
MANZANILLO	UMZ	VOR	116.0	20 18.20N	77 6.03W
MANZANILLO	UMZ	NDB	232.0	20 16.14N	77 10.08W
MAPLES	MAP	VOR	113.4	37 35.45N	91 47.31W
MAPLETON	MEY	NDB	335.0	42 10.84N	95 47.68W
MAQUOKETA	OQW	NDB	386.0	42 3.09N	90 44.46W
MARACAIBO	MAR	VOR	115.7	10 35.15N	71 42.75W
MARATHON	IMP	NDB	388.0	30 15.85N	103 14.23W
MARATHON	MAH	VOR	114.9	41 0.91N	83 39.88W
MARATHON	MTH	NDB	260.0	24 42.72N	81 5.72W
MARATHON	YSP	VOR	115.9	48 44.61N	86 19.65W
MARBE (LOM)	MARB	NDB	379.0	30 4.49N	95 24.77W
MARBLE FALLS	MFS	NDB	403.0	30 31.40N	98 21.47W
MARCO	MKY	NDB	375.0	25 59.95N	81 40.52W
MARENGO	RZO	NDB	391.0	32 24.87N	88 0.92W
MARFA	MRF	VOR	115.9	30 17.91N	103 57.28W
MARGARITA	MTA	VOR	114.1	10 55.42N	63 57.67W

Name	Ident.	Type	Freq.	Latitude	Longitude
MARGARITA	MTA	NDB	206.0	10 55.20N	63 57.40W
MARIANNA	MAI	VOR	114.0	30 47.18N	85 7.47W
MARION	MAO	NDB	388.0	34 11.12N	79 19.99W
MARION	MNN	NDB	201.0	40 37.03N	83 4.15W
MARION	MWA	VOR	110.4	37 45.26N	89 0.70W
MARION	MZZ	VOR	108.6	40 29.61N	85 40.75W
MARK ANTON	DTE	NDB	394.0	35 28.92N	84 55.86W
MARKS	MMS	NDB	391.0	34 13.99N	90 17.39W
MARKSVILLE	MKV	NDB	347.0	31 5.74N	92 4.36W
MARKY (LOM)	MARK	NDB	254.0	36 10.03N	80 2.14W
MARQUETTE	MQT	VOR	116.8	46 31.74N	87 35.13W
MARRA (LOM)	MARR	NDB	245.0	32 18.70N	86 30.63W
MARS	URX	NDB	269.0	48 0.91N	70 49.14W
MARSH HARBOUR	ZMH	NDB	361.0	26 30.67N	77 4.62W
MARSHALL	MHL	NDB	329.0	39 5.96N	93 12.19W
MARSHALL	MML	VOR	111.0	44 26.92N	95 49.49W
MARSHALLTOWN	MIW	NDB	239.0	42 6.61N	92 55.02W
MARSHFIELD	IMR	NDB	368.0	42 5.88N	70 40.52W
MARSHFIELD	MFI	NDB	391.0	44 38.46N	90 11.26W
MARTHAS VINEYARD	I-MV	VOR	108.7	41 23.11N	70 37.27W
MARTHAS VINEYARD	MVY	VOR	114.5	41 23.78N	70 36.76W
MARTIN	MTN	NDB	342.0	39 17.99N	76 22.81W
MARTINSBURG	MRB	VOR	112.1	39 23.14N	77 50.90W
MARYSVILLE	MRT	NDB	263.0	40 13.61N	83 20.88W
MARYSVILLE	MYV	VOR	110.8	39 5.93N	121 34.38W
MARYSVILLE	MYZ	NDB	341.0	39 51.18N	96 38.00W
MASON CITY	MCW	VOR	114.9	43 5.69N	93 19.79W
MASON CO	MNC	NDB	348.0	47 14.91N	123 5.19W
MASSENA	MSS	VOR	114.1	44 54.87N	74 43.36W
MASSET	1U	NDB	278.0	54 1.91N	132 7.63W
MATAGAMI	NM	NDB	218.0	49 43.45N	77 44.50W
MATAMOROS	MAM	VOR	114.3	25 46.26N	97 31.43W
MATANE	ME	NDB	216.0	48 50.01N	67 32.97W
MATTOON	MTO	VOR	109.4	39 28.69N	88 17.16W
MAUI	OGG	VOR	114.3	20 53.93N	156 25.91W
MAURY COUNTY	PBC	NDB	365.0	35 36.50N	87 5.48W
MAVIS (LOM)	MAVI	NDB	368.0	32 7.80N	81 19.89W
MAXTN	ME	NDB	257.0	34 44.05N	79 26.66W
MAXWELL	MXR	NDB	284.0	36 42.04N	104 32.38W
MAXWELL	MXW	VOR	110.0	39 19.06N	122 13.29W
MAYAGUEZ	MAZ	VOR	110.6	18 15.39N	67 9.06W
MAYAGUEZ	MAZ	NDB	254.0	18 15.23N	67 9.15W
MAYFIELD	GGK	NDB	401.0	36 41.47N	88 35.54W
MAYO	MA	NDB	365.0	63 37.74N	135 53.59W
MC ALESTER	MLC	VOR	112.0	34 50.97N	95 46.94W
MC ALLEN	MFE	VOR	117.2	26 10.44N	98 14.45W
MC CALL	IOM	NDB	363.0	44 48.35N	116 6.14W
MC CLELLAN	MCC	VOR	109.2	38 40.05N	121 24.26W
MC COMB	MCB	VOR	116.7	31 18.27N	90 15.49W
MC COOK	MCK	VOR	116.5	40 12.24N	100 35.66W
MC COY	CMY	NDB	412.0	43 56.28N	90 38.51W
MC DEN (LOM/NDB)	BH	NDB	224.0	33 30.68N	86 50.74W
MC DERMITT STATE	RMD	NDB	204.0	42 0.70N	117 43.26W
MC DOWELL CREEK	MQD	NDB	391.0	39 7.06N	96 37.76W
MC DUFFIE	THG	NDB	341.0	33 31.68N	82 26.31W
MC ENTIRE	MMT	NDB	427.0	33 56.15N	80 47.94W
MC GRATH	MCG	VOR	115.5	62 57.07N	155 36.68W
MC GUIRE	GXU	VOR	110.6	40 0.58N	74 35.78W
MC INTOSH	MOQ	NDB	263.0	31 49.84N	81 30.59W
MC KEESPORT	MKP	NDB	287.0	40 21.32N	79 46.86W
MC KELLAR	MKL	VOR	112.0	35 36.22N	88 54.63W
MC KINNON	JUK	NDB	353.0	31 9.22N	81 23.37W
MC MINN CO	MMI	NDB	242.0	35 23.26N	84 33.70W
MC PHERSON	MPR	NDB	227.0	38 20.91N	97 41.24W
MC RAE	MQW	NDB	280.0	32 5.68N	82 53.03W
MCCHORD	TCM	VOR	109.6	47 8.87N	122 28.50W
MCINNES ISLAND	MS	NDB	388.0	52 15.70N	128 43.40W
MEADE	MEJ	NDB	389.0	37 17.06N	100 21.51W
MECKLENBURG	MBV	NDB	356.0	36 41.55N	78 3.38W
MEDFORD	MDZ	NDB	335.0	45 6.31N	90 18.49W

Name	Ident.	Type	Freq.	Latitude	Longitude
MEDFORD	XED	NDB	371.0	36 47.59N	97 44.79W
MEDICINE BOW	MBW	VOR	111.6	41 50.74N	106 0.26W
MEDICINE HAT	XH	NDB	332.0	50 0.80N	110 47.95W
MEDICINE HAT	YXH	VOR	116.5	49 57.90N	110 48.87W
MEEKER	EKR	VOR	115.2	40 4.06N	107 55.49W
MEGGI (LOM)	MEGG	NDB	217.0	37 47.48N	113 1.29W
MEIER (LOM/NDB)	MEIE	NDB	403.0	41 34.56N	73 57.92W
MELBOURNE	MLB	VOR	110.0	28 6.32N	80 38.12W
MELFA	MFV	NDB	388.0	37 39.37N	75 45.49W
MELLON RANCH	MNO	NDB	375.0	28 16.81N	97 12.35W
MELUN	MEL	VOR	109.8	48 27.41N	2 48.80E
MELUN	MV	NDB	434.0	48 33.21N	2 58.70E
MELVILLE HALL	DOM	NDB	273.0	15 33.00N	61 18.00W
MEMORIAL	MEO	NDB	397.0	38 33.24N	92 4.68W
MEMPHIS	MEM	VOR	117.5	35 3.77N	89 58.90W
MENA	MEZ	NDB	242.0	34 32.93N	94 12.59W
MENDENHALL	MND	NDB	332.0	58 21.54N	134 38.02W
MENDOCINO	ENI	VOR	112.3	39 3.20N	123 16.45W
MENOMINEE	MNM	VOR	109.6	45 10.82N	87 38.83W
MERCURY	MCY	NDB	326.0	36 37.65N	116 1.65W
MERIDA	MID	VOR	117.7	20 55.00N	89 39.00W
MERIDEN	MMK	NDB	238.0	41 30.64N	72 49.70W
MERIDIAN	MEI	VOR	117.0	32 22.71N	88 48.26W
MERIDIAN	MPA	NDB	238.0	43 35.74N	116 34.73W
MERLE (LOM)	MERL	NDB	362.0	41 54.18N	93 39.55W
MERRILL	LFA	NDB	347.0	41 59.12N	121 38.57W
MERRILL	RRL	NDB	257.0	45 11.94N	89 42.24W
MERSY (LOM)	MERS	NDB	394.0	35 30.94N	88 57.41W
MERTZ (LOM)	MERT	NDB	302.0	38 17.04N	104 38.82W
MESQUITE	PQF	NDB	248.0	32 48.55N	96 31.73W
METCALF	MTQ	NDB	359.0	33 25.53N	90 58.93W
METRE (LOM)	METR	NDB	230.0	38 47.70N	121 35.98W
METROPOLIS	MIX	NDB	281.0	37 11.10N	88 45.67W
METROPOLITAN	UMP	NDB	338.0	39 56.27N	86 3.01W
METROPOLITAN OAKLAND INT	I-AA	VOR	111.9	37 42.05N	122 12.78W
METROPOLITAN OAKLAND INT	I-IN	VOR	108.7	37 43.51N	122 14.97W
METROPOLITAN OAKLAND INT	I-OA	VOR	109.9	37 43.91N	122 13.57W
METTER	MHP	NDB	432.0	32 22.35N	82 5.04W
MEXIA	LXY	NDB	329.0	31 38.38N	96 30.73W
MIAMI	MIA	VOR	115.9	25 57.81N	80 27.63W
MIAMI	MMW	NDB	317.0	36 54.50N	94 53.45W
MICHIGAN CITY	MGC	NDB	203.0	41 42.44N	86 49.00W
MIDDLETON ISLAND	MDO	VOR	115.3	59 25.32N	146 21.00W
MIDLAND	MAF	VOR	114.8	32 0.56N	102 11.43W
MIDLAND	YEE	VOR	112.8	44 34.91N	79 47.59W
MIDLAND (LMM)	AF	NDB	201.0	31 57.07N	102 13.53W
MIDWAY	XGB	VOR	112.9	41 47.32N	87 45.25W
MIDWEST	MXQ	VOR	112.9	39 25.79N	83 48.07W
MIKE	M	NDB	348.0	45 31.44N	73 39.26W
MIKE	M	NDB	366.0	46 6.26N	64 47.51W
MIKE	MIQ	NDB	426.5	48 34.31N	11 36.00E
MILE HIGH	DVV	VOR	114.7	39 53.69N	104 37.49W
MILES CITY	MLS	VOR	112.1	46 22.94N	105 57.21W
MILFORD	MLF	VOR	112.1	38 21.63N	113 0.79W
MILK RIVER	MKR	NDB	339.0	48 12.48N	106 37.57W
MILL BAY	MB	NDB	293.0	48 40.27N	123 32.21W
MILLARD	MLE	NDB	371.0	41 11.70N	96 6.84W
MILLDORF	MDF	VOR	117.0	48 14.11N	12 20.30E
MILLERSBURG	MLR	NDB	382.0	40 32.51N	81 52.36W
MILLINGTON	MIG	NDB	232.0	35 16.74N	89 55.99W
MILLINOCKET	MLT	VOR	117.9	45 35.21N	68 30.93W
MILLSAP	MQP	VOR	117.7	32 43.58N	97 59.84W
MILNOT	LNT	NDB	344.0	45 38.92N	68 33.01W
MILTON	MIP	NDB	109.2	41 14.11N	76 39.92W
MILTT (LOM)	MILT	NDB	375.0	42 16.43N	71 2.95W
MINA	MVA	VOR	115.1	38 33.93N	118 1.97W
MINAMI DAITO	MD	NDB	405.0	25 50.61N	131 14.50E

Name	Ident.	Type	Freq.	Latitude	Longitude
MINCHUMINA	MHM	NDB	227.0	63 53.05N	152 18.99W
MINDEN	MNE	NDB	201.0	32 38.48N	93 18.11W
MINDI (LOM)	MIND	NDB	272.0	44 0.25N	91 15.65W
MINERAL CREEK	MNL	NDB	524.0	61 7.47N	146 21.13W
MINERAL POINT	MRJ	NDB	365.0	42 53.29N	90 13.59W
MINERAL WELLS	MWL	NDB	266.0	32 47.12N	98 3.44W
MINGO (LOM)	MING	NDB	329.0	43 51.31N	92 24.65W
MINNE (LOM)	MINN	NDB	383.0	45 14.78N	123 1.78W
MINNEAPOLIS	MSP	VOR	115.3	44 52.92N	93 13.99W
MINOT	MOT	VOR	117.1	48 15.63N	101 17.22W
MIRABEL	YMX	VOR	116.7	45 53.31N	74 22.54W
MISHA (LOM)	MISH	NDB	341.0	41 42.35N	86 13.14W
MISSE (LOM)	MISS	NDB	278.0	44 51.26N	74 54.95W
MISSI (LOM)	MISS	NDB	388.0	26 15.24N	98 18.62W
MISSION BAY	MZB	VOR	117.8	32 46.94N	117 13.52W
MISSOULA	MSO	VOR	112.8	46 54.49N	114 5.02W
MITCHELL	MHE	VOR	109.2	43 46.63N	98 2.25W
MIYAKE JIMA	MJE	VOR	117.8	34 7.11N	139 29.90E
MIYAKO JIMA	MYC	VOR	117.5	24 47.21N	125 18.00E
MOAB	OAB	VOR	109.8	38 45.38N	109 44.96W
MOBERLY	MBY	NDB	302.0	39 27.89N	92 25.90W
MOBRIDGE	MBG	VOR	108.8	45 33.13N	100 21.96W
MOCCA (LOM)	MOCC	NDB	299.0	36 33.34N	82 19.08W
MODENA	MXE	VOR	113.2	39 55.09N	75 40.25W
MODESTO	MOD	VOR	114.6	37 37.65N	120 57.47W
MOHALL	HBC	NDB	350.0	48 45.85N	101 32.16W
MOLINE	MZV	VOR	114.4	41 19.27N	90 38.29W
MOLLI (LOM)	MOLL	NDB	215.0	41 26.95N	90 37.11W
MOLLY RIDGE	MRK	NDB	338.0	32 24.42N	91 46.36W
MOLOKAI	MKK	VOR	116.1	21 8.29N	157 10.04W
MONAH (LOM/NDB)	MONA	NDB	400.0	43 3.77N	89 20.75W
MONAHANS	OHE	NDB	214.0	31 34.70N	102 54.34W
MONARCH	MSB	NDB	410.0	37 47.49N	95 24.90W
MONCKS CORNER	MKS	NDB	354.0	33 11.47N	80 2.01W
MONCTON	QM	NDB	224.0	46 6.65N	64 34.91W
MONCTON	YQM	VOR	117.3	46 11.35N	64 34.24W
MONGA (LOM/NDB)	MONG	NDB	359.0	41 46.01N	74 51.65W
MONROE	JNM	NDB	429.0	33 44.26N	83 43.61W
MONROE	MLU	VOR	117.2	32 31.02N	92 2.16W
MONROEVILLE	MVC	VOR	116.8	31 27.63N	87 21.16W
MONRY (LOM)	MONR	NDB	227.0	25 51.72N	81 0.66W
MONT JOLI	YYY	VOR	115.9	48 36.75N	68 12.54W
MONT-JOLI	YY	NDB	340.0	48 34.01N	68 15.52W
MONTAGUE	MOG	NDB	382.0	41 43.64N	122 28.91W
MONTDIDIER	MTD	VOR	113.7	49 33.21N	2 29.40E
MONTE VISTA	MVI	NDB	311.0	37 31.69N	106 2.70W
MONTEBELLO	MOL	VOR	115.3	37 54.04N	79 6.41W
MONTEGO BAY	MBJ	VOR	115.7	18 29.85N	77 55.52W
MONTEGO BAY	MBJ	NDB	248.0	18 30.05N	77 55.17W
MONTERREY	MTY	VOR	114.7	25 46.41N	100 6.10W
MONTEVIDEO	MVE	VOR	111.6	44 58.37N	95 42.72W
MONTEZUMA	IZS	NDB	426.0	32 22.05N	84 0.44W
MONTGOMERY	MGM	VOR	112.1	32 13.35N	86 19.18W
MONTICELLO	MON	VOR	111.6	33 33.73N	91 42.94W
MONTICELLO	MXO	NDB	397.0	42 12.04N	91 8.23W
MONTOUR	MMJ	VOR	112.0	40 29.30N	80 11.63W
MONTPELIER	MPV	VOR	110.8	44 5.14N	72 26.96W
MONTREAL	UL	NDB	248.0	45 27.63N	73 50.84W
MONTREAL	YUL	VOR	116.3	45 36.95N	73 58.26W
MONTROSE	MTJ	VOR	108.6	38 30.22N	107 53.72W
MOORELAND	MDF	NDB	284.0	36 29.19N	99 11.57W
MOOSBURG	MBG	VOR	117.2	48 34.51N	12 15.80E
MOOSE JAW	YMJ	NDB	375.0	50 17.51N	105 26.37W
MOOSENEE	YMO	VOR	112.9	51 17.50N	80 36.44W
MOOSONEE	MO	NDB	224.0	51 16.95N	80 37.67W
MORA	JMR	NDB	327.0	45 53.43N	93 16.08W
MOREE (LOM)	MORE	NDB	392.0	40 52.80N	74 20.06W
MOREHEAD	MRH	NDB	269.0	34 43.83N	76 39.25W
MORGANTOWN	MGW	VOR	111.6	39 33.41N	79 51.62W
MORMON MESA	MMM	VOR	114.3	36 46.16N	114 16.65W

Name	Ident.	Type	Freq.	Latitude	Longitude
MORRILTON	MPJ	NDB	410.0	35 7.13N	92 55.51W
MORRIS	MOX	VOR	109.6	45 33.96N	95 58.15W
MORRISON	DBX	NDB	212.0	39 45.71N	97 2.54W
MORRISVILLE-STOWE	JRV	NDB	375.0	44 34.73N	72 35.24W
MORRO BAY	MQO	VOR	112.4	35 15.14N	120 45.57W
MOSES LAKE	MWH	VOR	115.0	47 12.66N	119 19.01W
MOSES POINT	MOS	VOR	116.3	64 41.81N	162 4.27W
MOSSY (LOM)	MOSS	NDB	418.0	30 18.41N	93 11.77W
MOULTRIE	MGR	VOR	108.8	31 4.94N	83 48.25W
MOUNT AIRY	AXI	NDB	284.0	36 27.80N	80 33.10W
MOUNT CARMEL	AJG	NDB	524.0	38 36.73N	87 43.57W
MOUNT MANSFIELD	VKN	NDB	268.0	44 23.21N	72 41.61W
MOUNT PLEASANT	MOP	VOR	110.6	43 37.41N	84 44.70W
MOUNT PLEASANT	MPZ	NDB	212.0	40 56.58N	91 30.56W
MOUNT PLEASANT	MSA	NDB	381.0	33 7.71N	94 58.45W
MOUNT SNOW	VWD	NDB	224.0	42 55.66N	72 51.84W
MOUNTAIN CITY	JJO	NDB	396.0	36 25.00N	81 49.46W
MOUNTAIN HOME	MUO	VOR	114.9	42 58.97N	115 46.45W
MOUNTAIN VIEW	MNF	NDB	365.0	36 59.64N	91 42.76W
MT EDGECUMBE	IME	NDB	414.0	57 2.87N	135 22.02W
MT MACAJNA	AJA	NDB	385.0	13 27.14N	144 44.07E
MT VERNON	VNN	VOR	113.8	38 21.73N	88 48.44W
MUDDY MOUNTAIN	DDY	VOR	116.2	43 5.46N	106 16.62W
MUFFE (LOM)	MUFF	NDB	336.0	26 29.03N	81 50.07W
MUFIN (LOM/NDB)	MUFI	NDB	365.0	32 53.59N	97 22.41W
MUHLENBERG	GMH	NDB	362.0	37 13.63N	87 9.55W
MULLAN PASS	MLP	VOR	117.8	47 27.43N	115 38.76W
MUNCIE	MIE	VOR	114.4	40 14.25N	85 23.64W
MUNICH	MNE	NDB	358.0	48 21.41N	11 40.60E
MUNICH	MNW	NDB	338.0	48 22.51N	11 54.90E
MUNICH	MSE	NDB	385.0	48 20.11N	11 39.30E
MUNICH	MSW	NDB	400.0	48 21.21N	11 54.30E
MUNICH	MUN	VOR	112.3	48 10.91N	11 49.10E
MUNSO (LOM)	MUNS	NDB	385.0	36 37.25N	121 56.32W
MURRY (LOM)	MURR	NDB	362.0	33 58.04N	81 14.69W
MUSCATINE	MUT	NDB	272.0	41 21.74N	91 8.77W
MUSCLE SHOALS	MSL	VOR	116.5	34 42.42N	87 29.49W
MUSKEGON	MKG	VOR	115.2	43 10.16N	86 2.36W
MUSKO (LOM)	MUSK	NDB	219.0	43 7.28N	86 10.11W
MUSKOGEE	MKO	NDB	306.0	35 35.70N	95 17.23W
MUSKOKA	YQA	NDB	272.0	45 2.36N	79 16.97W
MUSTANG	FMG	VOR	117.9	39 31.88N	119 39.37W
MYSTIC	MYS	VOR	108.2	37 53.65N	86 14.67W
MYTON	MTU	VOR	112.7	40 8.71N	110 7.66W
NAADA (LOM)	NAAD	NDB	336.0	39 29.90N	74 40.34W
NABB	ABB	VOR	112.4	38 35.34N	85 38.16W
NABESNA	AES	NDB	390.0	62 57.96N	141 53.30W
NACOGDOCHES	OCH	NDB	391.0	31 38.03N	94 44.03W
NADI	NN	VOR	112.5	17 39.20S	177 24.00E
NADOS	OC	NDB	253.0	31 29.12N	94 43.18W
NADZAB	NZ	VOR	113.6	6 34.30S	146 43.90E
NAKINA	QN	NDB	233.0	50 10.81N	86 37.75W
NALLY DUNSTON	DNT	NDB	343.0	35 59.71N	89 24.35W
NANAIMO	YCD	NDB	251.0	49 7.68N	123 52.30W
NANTUCKET	ACK	VOR	116.2	41 16.92N	70 1.60W
NANTUCKET	TUK	NDB	194.0	41 16.13N	70 10.80W
NANUMEA	NM	NDB	358.0	5 40.30S	176 8.20E
NANWAK	AIX	NDB	323.0	60 23.11N	166 12.89W
NAPLES	APF	NDB	201.0	26 9.35N	81 46.46W
NAPOLEON	ANX	VOR	114.0	39 5.73N	94 7.73W
NARAMATA	UNT	NDB	312.0	49 35.84N	119 36.15W
NARCO (LOM/NDB)	NARC	NDB	266.0	44 49.55N	93 5.48W
NASHVILLE	BNA	VOR	114.1	36 8.23N	86 41.09W
NASSAU	ZQA	VOR	112.7	25 1.69N	77 27.00W
NASSAU	ZQA	NDB	251.0	25 2.42N	77 28.22W
NATCHEZ	HEZ	VOR	110.0	31 37.10N	91 17.98W
NAURU	NI	NDB	355.0	0 32.70S	166 55.00E
NAUSET	CQX	NDB	279.0	41 41.52N	69 59.39W
NAUSORI	NA	VOR	112.2	18 2.50S	178 33.90E
NAUTLA	NAU	VOR	112.3	20 11.90N	96 44.90W
NAUTLA	NAU	NDB	392.0	20 12.00N	96 45.00W
NAVASOTA	TNV	VOR	115.9	30 17.35N	96 3.51W
NAVY WHIDBEY ISL	NUW	NDB	407.0	48 21.32N	122 39.94W
NEAH BAY	EBY	NDB	391.0	48 21.47N	124 33.38W
NEEDLES	EED	VOR	115.2	34 45.97N	114 28.45W
NEEDMORE	PED	NDB	221.0	36 32.19N	86 55.05W
NEELY (LOM/NDB)	NEEL	NDB	335.0	41 29.16N	74 13.68W
NEFOR (LOM)	NEFO	NDB	274.0	41 37.31N	71 1.06W
NEILLSVILLE	VIQ	NDB	368.0	44 33.44N	90 30.91W
NEMISCAU	K8	NDB	214.0	51 41.35N	76 8.06W
NENANA	ENN	VOR	115.8	64 35.41N	149 4.37W
NEOSHO	EOS	VOR	116.6	36 50.55N	94 26.14W
NEPCO (LOM)	NEPC	NDB	326.0	44 15.60N	89 53.27W
NETTE (LOM)	NETT	NDB	374.0	44 16.10N	99 15.08W
NEVADA	EAD	NDB	209.0	37 51.54N	94 18.16W
NEW BERN	EWN	VOR	113.6	35 4.40N	77 2.70W
NEW BRAUNFELS	BAZ	NDB	212.0	29 42.47N	98 2.08W
NEW CASTLE	UWL	NDB	385.0	39 52.81N	85 19.13W
NEW HAVEN	HVN	VOR	109.8	41 15.75N	72 53.11W
NEW HOPE	EWO	VOR	110.8	37 37.92N	85 40.55W
NEW MADRID	EIW	NDB	314.0	36 32.19N	89 36.10W
NEW ORLEANS	MSY	VOR	113.2	30 1.80N	90 10.33W
NEW ORLEANS (NAVY	NBG	NDB	366.0	29 49.08N	90 2.21W
NEW RICHMOND	RNH	NDB	257.0	45 8.56N	92 32.06W
NEW RIVER (MARINE	NCA	NDB	356.0	34 43.31N	77 25.78W
NEW SMYRNA BEACH	EVB	NDB	417.0	29 3.27N	80 56.46W
NEW ULM	ULM	NDB	272.0	44 19.42N	94 30.05W
NEWARK	HEH	NDB	524.0	40 1.56N	82 27.81W
NEWBERG	UBG	VOR	117.4	45 21.20N	122 58.69W
NEWBERRY	ERY	VOR	108.2	46 18.78N	85 27.86W
NEWCASTLE	ECS	VOR	108.2	43 52.88N	104 18.47W
NEWCOMBE	ECB	VOR	110.4	38 9.51N	82 54.60W
NEWCOMERSTOWN	CTW	VOR	111.8	40 13.76N	81 28.59W
NEWMAN	EWM	VOR	112.4	31 57.11N	106 16.34W
NEWPORT	EFK	NDB	242.0	44 57.18N	72 10.64W
NEWPORT	EWP	NDB	400.0	35 38.53N	91 10.84W
NEWPORT	ONP	VOR	117.1	44 34.53N	124 3.64W
NEWTON	EWK	NDB	281.0	38 3.85N	97 16.41W
NEWTON	TNU	VOR	112.5	41 47.04N	93 6.54W
NEZ PERCE	MQG	VOR	108.2	46 22.90N	116 52.17W
NICHOLAS	IJZ	NDB	272.0	38 10.51N	80 55.20W
NICHOLS	ICK	NDB	266.0	55 4.26N	131 36.30W
NICHOLSON	UC	NDB	329.0	69 55.65N	128 58.38W
NILEY (LOM)	NILE	NDB	385.0	35 22.35N	118 58.89W
NIMITZ	UNZ	VOR	115.3	13 27.19N	144 43.86E
NIMMONS	IMZ	NDB	332.0	42 6.30N	75 53.48W
NIUE	NU	VOR	345.0	19 4.10S	169 54.60W
NIXIN (LOM)	NIXI	NDB	326.0	29 59.60N	95 12.90W
NOAH	ONH	NDB	515.0	38 38.24N	92 14.69W
NOATAK	OQK	NDB	414.0	67 34.33N	162 58.43W
NODINE	ODI	VOR	117.9	43 54.75N	91 28.06W
NOGALES	ENZ	NDB	394.0	31 25.29N	110 50.79W
NOGALES	OLS	VOR	108.2	31 24.90N	110 50.93W
NOLIN (LOM)	NOLI	NDB	278.0	39 43.65N	77 35.45W
NOLLA (LOM)	NOLL	NDB	362.0	47 37.96N	122 23.37W
NOME	OME	VOR	115.0	64 29.12N	165 15.19W
NORDE (LOM)	NORD	NDB	327.0	39 53.22N	121 55.99W
NORDLINGEN	NDG	NDB	375.0	48 49.81N	10 25.20E
NORFOLK	OFK	VOR	109.6	41 59.28N	97 26.08W
NORFOLK	ORF	VOR	116.9	36 53.52N	76 12.02W
NORGE (LOM)	NORG	NDB	517.0	39 3.68N	94 39.35W
NORMAN	OUN	NDB	260.0	35 14.25N	97 28.87W
NORMAN WELLS	VQ	NDB	326.0	65 15.19N	126 40.18W
NORMAN WELLS	YVQ	VOR	112.7	65 15.87N	126 43.51W
NORTH BAY	YB	NDB	394.0	46 23.08N	79 28.12W
NORTH BAY	YYB	VOR	115.4	46 21.85N	79 26.19W
NORTH BEND	OTH	VOR	112.1	43 24.94N	124 10.11W
NORTH PHILADELPHI	PNE	VOR	112.0	40 4.93N	75 0.57W
NORTH PLATTE	LBF	VOR	117.4	41 2.93N	100 44.83W
NORTH RIVER	JNR	NDB	382.0	63 54.48N	160 48.72W

Name	Ident.	Type	Freq.	Latitude	Longitude
NORTH VERNON	OVO	NDB	374.0	39 3.00N	85 36.07W
NORTHBROOK	OBK	VOR	113.0	42 13.44N	87 57.10W
NORTHWAY	ORT	VOR	116.3	62 56.84N	141 54.77W
NORTON	NRN	NDB	230.0	39 51.33N	99 53.34W
NORTON BAY	OAY	NDB	263.0	64 41.78N	162 3.77W
NORWICH	OIC	NDB	233.0	42 30.41N	75 29.46W
NORWICH	ORW	VOR	110.0	41 33.39N	71 59.96W
NOTTINGHAM	OTT	VOR	113.7	38 42.36N	76 44.69W
NOVEMBER	N	NDB	347.0	43 43.91N	79 31.25W
NUEVAS	UNV	VOR	116.3	21 23.84N	77 13.72W
NUEVAS	UNV	NDB	256.0	21 24.11N	77 13.80W
NUEVO LAREDO	NLD	VOR	112.6	27 26.01N	99 34.00W
O NEILL	ONL	VOR	113.9	42 28.24N	98 41.22W
OAKLAND	OAK	VOR	116.8	37 43.56N	122 13.42W
OAKLEY	OEL	NDB	380.0	39 6.76N	100 48.93W
OAKTOWN	OTN	NDB	260.0	38 50.76N	87 30.42W
OBERLIN	OIN	NDB	341.0	39 49.79N	100 32.26W
OBERPFAFFENHOFEN	OBI	NDB	429.0	48 4.91N	11 17.20E
OBION	OQZ	NDB	212.0	36 17.86N	88 59.69W
OBLEON	OBN	VOR	113.2	18 26.24N	72 16.48W
OBLIO (LOM/NDB)	OBLI	NDB	338.0	38 48.03N	90 28.49W
OCALA	OCF	VOR	113.7	29 10.65N	82 13.58W
OCEAN CAPE	OCC	NDB	385.0	59 32.63N	139 43.69W
OCEANSIDE	OCN	VOR	115.3	33 14.45N	117 25.06W
OCONTO	OCQ	NDB	388.0	44 52.63N	87 54.74W
OELWEIN	OLZ	NDB	260.0	42 41.06N	91 58.58W
OGDEN	OGD	VOR	115.7	41 13.45N	112 5.89W
OGIVE (LOM)	OGIV	NDB	358.0	44 42.10N	75 21.18W
OILLR (LOM)	OILL	NDB	338.0	36 5.85N	95 53.33W
OKANAGAN	ON	NDB	356.0	49 20.57N	119 34.10W
OKINAWA	OK	NDB	308.0	26 6.11N	127 39.90E
OKMULGEE	OKM	VOR	112.2	35 41.59N	95 51.96W
OLD CROW	YOC	NDB	284.0	67 34.28N	139 50.78W
OLD RIP	OIP	NDB	410.0	32 23.92N	98 48.62W
OLD TOWN	OLD	NDB	272.0	45 0.41N	68 38.00W
OLDFIELD POINT	OP	NDB	316.0	40 58.62N	73 7.11W
OLEAN	LYS	NDB	360.0	42 17.03N	78 20.10W
OLIKTOK	OLI	NDB	329.0	70 29.82N	149 53.39W
OLIVE BRANCH	OLV	NDB	275.0	34 58.78N	89 47.40W
OLNEY	OLY	NDB	272.0	38 43.10N	88 10.37W
OLNEY	ONY	NDB	272.0	33 21.08N	98 48.97W
OLSTE (LOM)	OLST	NDB	257.0	43 27.70N	84 10.78W
OLYMPIA	OLM	VOR	113.4	46 58.31N	122 54.11W
OMAHA	OMA	VOR	116.3	41 10.05N	95 44.20W
OMAK	OMK	NDB	396.0	48 27.22N	119 31.00W
ONIDA (LOM)	ONID	NDB	223.0	39 34.70N	84 19.42W
ONTARIO	ONO	NDB	305.0	44 1.19N	117 0.50W
ONTONAGON	OGM	NDB	375.0	46 51.02N	89 21.91W
ONYUN	UQN	NDB	372.0	32 13.40N	82 17.89W
OPERY (LOM/NDB)	OPER	NDB	344.0	36 12.24N	86 39.17W
OPOLE (LOM)	OPOL	NDB	423.0	32 30.56N	85 26.23W
ORANGE	COG	NDB	428.0	38 13.15N	78 8.50W
ORANGE	ORE	NDB	205.0	42 33.65N	72 12.07W
ORANGE	ORG	NDB	211.0	30 4.22N	93 47.70W
ORANGE CITY	ORC	NDB	521.0	42 59.49N	96 3.64W
ORANGEBURG	OGB	NDB	209.0	33 25.83N	80 53.58W
ORANJ	RRJ	NDB	368.0	38 31.68N	86 31.67W
ORCHY (LOM)	ORCH	NDB	385.0	40 52.00N	73 48.21W
ORD	ODX	NDB	356.0	41 37.43N	98 56.88W
ORHAM (LOM)	ORHA	NDB	394.0	43 39.16N	70 26.46W
ORLANDO	ORL	VOR	112.2	28 32.57N	81 20.10W
ORLEANS	OAN	NDB	385.0	48 0.11N	1 46.20E
ORLY (PARIS)	OL	VOR	111.2	48 43.91N	2 23.30E
ORLY (PARIS)	OLS	NDB	328.0	48 38.81N	2 20.80E
ORLY (PARIS)	ORW	NDB	402.0	48 40.41N	2 11.00E
ORLY (PARIS)	OYE	NDB	349.0	48 45.21N	2 32.40E
ORMOND BEACH	OMN	VOR	112.6	29 18.20N	81 6.76W
OROVILLE	OVE	NDB	212.0	39 29.69N	121 37.33W
ORR	ORB	NDB	341.0	48 1.14N	92 51.69W
ORTONVILLE	VVV	NDB	332.0	45 18.11N	96 25.29W
OSCAR	O	NDB	344.0	45 16.68N	75 45.00W
OSCARVILLE	OSE	NDB	251.0	60 47.49N	161 52.36W
OSCEOLA	OEO	NDB	233.0	45 18.76N	92 41.16W
OSHAWA	OO	NDB	391.0	43 52.91N	78 55.25W
OSHKOSH	OKS	NDB	233.0	41 24.02N	102 20.91W
OSHKOSH	OSH	VOR	111.8	43 59.43N	88 33.36W
OSKALOOSA	OOA	NDB	414.0	41 13.54N	92 29.24W
OSWEGO	OSW	VOR	117.6	37 9.46N	95 12.22W
OTIMS (LOM)	OTIM	NDB	353.0	41 26.72N	74 17.46W
OTIS (LOM)	OTIS	NDB	362.0	41 43.97N	70 26.45W
OTTAWA	OIX	VOR	266.0	41 21.76N	88 51.25W
OTTAWA	OW	NDB	236.0	45 21.61N	75 33.46W
OTTAWA	OWI	NDB	251.0	38 32.56N	95 15.27W
OTTAWA	PDR	NDB	233.0	41 1.88N	83 58.51W
OTTAWA	YOW	VOR	114.6	45 26.51N	75 53.81W
OTTO	OTO	VOR	114.0	35 4.34N	105 56.16W
OTTUMWA	OTM	VOR	111.6	41 1.76N	92 19.56W
OWASO (LOM/NDB)	OWAS	NDB	375.0	36 18.45N	95 52.52W
OWENSBORO	OWB	VOR	108.6	37 44.62N	87 9.96W
OXFORD	OXD	NDB	282.0	39 30.45N	84 46.93W
OXONN (LOM/NDB)	OXON	NDB	332.0	38 45.97N	77 1.60W
OZARK	OZZ	NDB	329.0	35 30.46N	93 50.45W
PACOIMA	PAI	NDB	370.0	34 15.59N	118 24.80W
PAGE	PGA	VOR	117.6	36 55.69N	111 27.04W
PAGELAND	PYG	NDB	270.0	34 44.71N	80 20.28W
PAGO PAGO	TUT	VOR	112.5	14 20.26S	170 42.42W
PAGO PAGO	TUT	NDB	403.0	14 20.22S	170 43.08W
PAHOA	POA	NDB	332.0	19 32.47N	154 58.33W
PAHOKEE	PHK	VOR	115.4	26 46.97N	80 41.49W
PAINE	PAE	VOR	110.6	47 55.20N	122 16.67W
PAJAR (LOM/NDB)	PAJA	NDB	327.0	36 54.82N	121 48.48W
PALACIOS	PSX	VOR	117.3	28 45.87N	96 18.37W
PALATKA	IAK	NDB	243.0	29 39.17N	81 48.70W
PALESTINE	PLX	NDB	391.0	39 0.81N	87 38.45W
PALESTINE	PSN	NDB	375.0	31 46.82N	95 42.06W
PALISADES PARK	PPK	NDB	233.0	40 49.77N	73 58.47W
PALM BEACH	PBI	VOR	115.7	26 40.81N	80 5.19W
PALM SPRINGS	PSP	VOR	115.5	33 52.21N	116 25.79W
PALMDALE	PMD	VOR	114.5	34 37.89N	118 3.83W
PALMER	PMX	NDB	212.0	42 13.58N	72 18.69W
PAMLICO	OUC	NDB	404.0	35 7.00N	75 59.24W
PAMPA	PPA	NDB	368.0	35 36.68N	100 59.77W
PANAMA CITY	PFN	VOR	114.3	30 12.98N	85 40.85W
PANBE (LOM/NDB)	PANB	NDB	416.0	41 4.11N	100 34.35W
PANCK (LOM)	PANC	NDB	383.0	36 57.88N	100 57.38W
PANDE (LOM/NDB)	PAND	NDB	251.0	35 8.79N	101 48.34W
PANOCHE	PXN	VOR	112.6	36 42.93N	120 46.92W
PAPA	P	NDB	350.0	54 18.33N	130 27.75W
PARADISE	PDZ	VOR	112.2	33 55.11N	117 31.80W
PARIS	PRG	NDB	341.0	39 41.91N	87 40.45W
PARIS	PRX	VOR	113.6	33 32.55N	95 26.90W
PARIS - CHARLES DE GAULL	CGE	VOR	110.1	49 1.39N	2 34.00E
PARIS - CHARLES DE GAULL	CGW	VOR	110.7	49 1.24N	2 30.55E
PARIS - CHARLES DE GAULL	GAU	VOR	109.1	48 59.76N	2 32.97E
PARIS - CHARLES DE GAULL	GLE	VOR	108.7	48 59.94N	2 36.42E
PARIS - ORLY	OLN	VOR	110.3	48 44.51N	2 23.38E
PARIS - ORLY	OLO	VOR	110.9	48 43.21N	2 18.82E
PARIS - ORLY	OLW	VOR	109.5	48 43.18N	2 21.19E
PARIS - ORLY	ORE	VOR	108.5	48 44.31N	2 21.97E
PARK RAPIDS	PKD	VOR	110.6	46 53.90N	95 4.25W
PARKER	PKE	VOR	117.9	34 6.13N	114 40.92W
PARKERSBURG	JPU	VOR	108.6	39 26.48N	81 22.49W
PARKK (LOM)	PARK	NDB	281.0	47 31.95N	122 18.42W
PARSHALL	PSH	NDB	379.0	47 56.18N	102 8.23W
PARSONS	PPF	NDB	293.0	37 20.30N	95 30.52W
PASCO	PSC	VOR	108.4	46 15.79N	119 6.94W

Name	Ident.	Type	Freq.	Latitude	Longitude
PASER (LOM/NDB)	PASE	NDB	206.0	42 40.96N	87 53.97W
PASO ROBLES	PRB	VOR	114.3	35 40.36N	120 37.63W
PATERSON	PNJ	NDB	347.0	40 56.80N	74 9.05W
PATTEN	GTP	NDB	245.0	30 57.46N	83 49.60W
PATTERSON	FFO	VOR	115.2	39 49.10N	84 3.28W
PATTERSON	PTN	NDB	245.0	29 42.88N	91 20.20W
PATTY (LOM/NDB)	PATT	NDB	330.0	18 24.53N	66 5.35W
PATUXENT	PXT	VOR	117.6	38 17.28N	76 24.01W
PATUXENT RIVER	NHK	NDB	400.0	38 17.16N	76 24.18W
PAULS VALLEY	PVJ	NDB	384.0	34 42.93N	97 13.76W
PAWLING	PWL	VOR	114.3	41 46.19N	73 36.03W
PAWNEE CITY	PWE	VOR	112.4	40 12.03N	96 12.38W
PEABODY	PBY	NDB	259.0	36 28.49N	110 24.71W
PEACE RIVER	YPE	VOR	117.2	56 12.43N	117 30.71W
PEACH SPRINGS	PGS	VOR	112.0	35 37.49N	113 32.67W
PEACHTREE	PDK	VOR	116.6	33 52.55N	84 17.93W
PEASE	PSM	VOR	116.5	43 5.08N	70 49.92W
PECAN	PZD	VOR	116.1	31 39.32N	84 17.59W
PECAT (LOM/NDB)	PECA	NDB	316.0	33 18.05N	84 29.18W
PECK	ECK	VOR	114.0	43 15.36N	82 43.07W
PECONIC	PIC	NDB	339.0	40 48.59N	72 54.37W
PECOS	PEQ	VOR	111.8	31 28.17N	103 34.48W
PEEBLES	PZO	NDB	329.0	38 55.28N	83 19.61W
PEKKS (LOM)	PEKK	NDB	405.0	27 38.55N	99 27.49W
PELEE ISLAND	PT	NDB	283.0	41 46.78N	82 40.19W
PELLA	PEA	NDB	257.0	41 24.33N	92 56.59W
PELLSTON	PLN	VOR	111.8	45 37.85N	84 39.84W
PELLY (LOM/NDB)	PELL	NDB	408.0	47 6.94N	119 16.49W
PEMBROKE	YTA	NDB	409.0	45 48.18N	77 13.15W
PENDLETON	PDT	VOR	114.7	45 41.91N	118 56.32W
PENDY	ACZ	NDB	379.0	34 42.98N	78 0.21W
PENN YAN	PYA	NDB	260.0	42 38.65N	77 3.35W
PENNRIDGE	CKZ	VOR	108.9	40 23.46N	75 17.32W
PENO BOTTOMS	AFT	NDB	311.0	35 19.37N	94 28.45W
PENTICTON	YYF	NDB	290.0	49 29.27N	119 36.17W
PENUE (LOM)	PENU	NDB	388.0	40 54.63N	77 44.50W
PEORIA	PIA	VOR	115.2	40 40.81N	89 47.57W
PEOTONE	EON	VOR	113.2	41 16.19N	87 47.46W
PERONNE-ST. QUENTIN	PM	NDB	382.0	49 52.11N	3 8.20E
PERRINE	PRI	NDB	367.0	37 45.91N	90 25.76W
PERRY	PRO	NDB	251.0	41 49.84N	94 9.63W
PERRYTON	PYX	NDB	266.0	36 24.78N	100 44.31W
PERSIMMON	PRN	NDB	359.0	31 51.07N	86 36.86W
PERSON (LOM/NDB)	HUR	NDB	220.0	36 14.01N	79 3.95W
PESTE (LOM)	PEST	NDB	241.0	17 41.52N	64 53.08W
PETAWAWA	YWA	NDB	516.0	45 53.70N	77 16.30W
PETERBOROUGH	YPQ	NDB	379.0	44 12.80N	78 27.49W
PETERS CREEK	PEE	NDB	305.0	62 19.88N	150 5.78W
PETERSBURG	PTB	NDB	284.0	37 7.82N	77 34.48W
PETEY (LOM/NDB)	PETE	NDB	407.0	38 41.67N	104 42.98W
PETHS (LOM)	PETH	NDB	332.0	40 42.88N	73 55.76W
PETIS (LOM)	PETI	NDB	397.0	34 3.39N	117 21.96W
PETLI (LOM)	PETL	NDB	269.0	42 58.10N	83 53.41W
PHILADELPHIA	MPE	NDB	219.0	32 47.92N	89 7.48W
PHILIP	PHP	VOR	108.4	44 3.51N	101 39.85W
PHILIPSBURG	PSB	VOR	115.5	40 54.98N	77 59.56W
PHILLIPS	PBH	NDB	263.0	45 42.19N	90 24.77W
PHILLIPS	PPM	VOR	108.4	39 28.01N	76 10.27W
PHILLIPSBURG	PHG	NDB	368.0	39 42.38N	99 17.31W
PHILMONT	PFH	NDB	272.0	42 15.18N	73 43.39W
PHOENIX	PXR	VOR	115.6	33 25.99N	111 58.21W
PHORT (LOM)	PHOR	NDB	388.0	42 47.93N	117 27.01W
PHURN (OM)	PHUR	NDB	322.0	42 50.58N	82 35.80W
PIARCO	POS	VOR	116.9	10 27.87N	61 23.62W
PIARCO	POS	NDB	382.0	10 35.65N	61 25.58W
PICAYUNE	PCU	VOR	112.2	30 33.68N	89 43.83W
PICHE (LOM/NDB)	PICH	NDB	332.0	37 34.70N	97 27.35W
PICKENS	PKZ	NDB	326.0	30 26.23N	87 10.70W
PICKENS CO	JZP	NDB	285.0	34 27.28N	84 27.58W
PICKLE LAKE	YPL	NDB	382.0	51 26.53N	90 13.34W
PICKNEYVILLE	PJY	NDB	215.0	37 58.51N	89 21.79W
PICNY (LOM/NDB)	PICN	NDB	388.0	27 51.68N	82 32.76W
PICTURE ROCKS	PIX	NDB	344.0	41 16.62N	76 42.61W
PIERRE	PIR	VOR	112.5	44 23.68N	100 9.77W
PIEVE (LOM/NDB)	PIEV	NDB	347.0	37 49.75N	100 43.46W
PILOT ROCK	CKP	NDB	423.0	42 43.94N	95 33.18W
PINCK (LOM)	PINC	NDB	257.0	33 16.99N	97 11.78W
PINE BLUFF	PBF	VOR	116.0	34 14.81N	91 55.57W
PINE MOUNTAIN	PIM	NDB	272.0	32 50.58N	84 52.35W
PINEY GROVE	BPO	NDB	403.0	36 32.38N	84 28.56W
PINHOOK	HHY	NDB	242.0	35 13.55N	88 12.33W
PINON	PIO	VOR	110.4	32 31.76N	105 18.31W
PIONEER	PER	VOR	113.2	36 44.80N	97 9.61W
PIPESTONE	PQN	NDB	284.0	43 59.17N	96 17.78W
PITHIVIERS	PTV	VOR	116.5	48 9.31N	2 15.90E
PITSAND	PYC	NDB	290.0	70 19.70N	149 38.12W
PITT MEADOWS	PK	NDB	227.0	49 12.70N	122 42.86W
PITTSBURG	PTS	NDB	365.0	37 26.55N	94 43.60W
PITTSFIELD	PPQ	NDB	344.0	39 38.46N	90 46.81W
PLAINVIEW	PVW	VOR	112.9	34 5.18N	101 47.41W
PLANT CITY	PCM	NDB	346.0	28 0.16N	82 9.41W
PLANTATION	PJN	NDB	242.0	26 7.94N	80 13.13W
PLATTE CENTER	PLT	NDB	407.0	41 29.80N	97 22.90W
PLATTEVILLE	PVB	VOR	203.0	42 41.29N	90 26.19W
PLATTSBURGH	PLB	VOR	116.9	44 41.11N	73 31.36W
PLATTSMOUTH	PMV	NDB	329.0	40 57.09N	95 54.95W
PLAZZ (LOM)	PLAZ	NDB	204.0	42 52.44N	78 48.99W
PLEASANT LAKE	AC	NDB	230.0	43 51.66N	66 2.62W
PLEASANTON	PEZ	NDB	275.0	28 57.30N	98 31.12W
PLEIN (LOM/NDB)	PLEI	NDB	329.0	43 13.36N	75 28.95W
PLENTYWOOD	PWD	NDB	251.0	48 47.41N	104 31.63W
PLYMOUTH	FFF	NDB	257.0	41 50.86N	70 48.16W
PLYMOUTH	PMZ	NDB	221.0	35 48.60N	76 45.76W
POBER (LOM)	POBE	NDB	395.0	43 52.44N	88 33.46W
POCAHONTAS	POH	NDB	314.0	42 44.82N	94 38.88W
POCATELLO	PIH	VOR	112.6	42 52.23N	112 39.13W
POCKET CITY	PXV	VOR	113.3	37 55.71N	87 45.74W
POGGI	PGY	VOR	109.8	32 36.63N	116 58.74W
POHNPEI	PNI	NDB	366.0	6 58.97N	158 12.53E
POINT HOPE	PHO	NDB	221.0	68 20.71N	166 47.85W
POINT LAY	PIZ	NDB	347.0	69 44.08N	163 0.81W
POINT LOOKOUT	PLK	NDB	326.0	36 37.66N	93 13.79W
POINT REYES	PYE	VOR	113.7	38 4.79N	122 52.07W
POINTE A PITRE	AR	NDB	402.0	16 16.27N	61 37.50W
POINTE A PITRE	PPR	VOR	115.1	16 16.00N	61 31.00W
POINTE A PITRE	PPR	NDB	300.0	16 15.67N	61 31.00W
POINTE-DES-MONTS	TG	NDB	300.0	49 19.01N	67 22.83W
POKEMOUCHE	2T	NDB	227.0	47 43.08N	64 53.38W
POLK	FXU	VOR	108.4	31 6.71N	93 13.08W
POLK	POJ	NDB	344.0	32 16.19N	86 55.65W
POLLO (LOM)	POLL	NDB	219.0	33 44.27N	101 49.75W
POLO	PLL	VOR	111.2	41 57.95N	89 31.45W
POLSON	PLS	NDB	275.0	47 41.76N	114 11.27W
POMONA	POM	VOR	110.4	34 4.71N	117 47.22W
POMONA	UNO	NDB	335.0	36 52.70N	91 54.04W
POMPANO BEACH	PMP	VOR	108.8	26 14.89N	80 6.51W
PONCA (LOM/NDB)	PONC	NDB	275.0	36 49.51N	97 6.03W
PONCE	PSE	VOR	109.0	17 59.55N	66 31.15W
PONTIAC	PNT	VOR	109.6	40 49.28N	88 44.01W
PONTIAC	PSI	VOR	111.0	42 42.02N	83 31.96W
PONTOISE	PON	VOR	111.6	49 5.81N	2 2.20E
POPE (LOM/NDB)	POB	NDB	338.0	35 13.62N	78 57.26W
PORT AU PRINCE	HHP	NDB	270.0	18 34.59N	72 17.22W
PORT AU PRINCE	PAP	VOR	115.3	18 34.59N	72 18.27W
PORT CITY	RTY	VOR	108.8	41 22.18N	91 8.60W
PORT CLINTON	PCW	NDB	414.0	41 31.12N	82 52.12W
PORT HARDY	YZT	VOR	112.0	50 41.07N	127 21.91W
PORT HARDY	Z	NDB	394.0	50 42.88N	127 25.56W
PORT HARDY	ZT	NDB	242.0	50 41.97N	127 25.63W
PORT HAWKESBURY	PD	NDB	229.0	45 39.33N	61 16.17W

Name	Ident.	Type	Freq.	Latitude	Longitude
PORT HEIDEN	PDN	NDB	371.0	56 57.25N	158 38.93W
PORT LAVACA	PKV	NDB	515.0	28 39.04N	96 40.88W
PORT MENIER	PN	NDB	360.0	49 50.26N	64 23.18W
PORT MORESBY	PY	VOR	117.0	9 27.10S	147 13.00E
PORTAGE	PG	NDB	353.0	49 50.34N	98 10.85W
PORTALES	PRZ	NDB	407.0	34 9.08N	103 24.38W
PORTERVILLE	PTV	VOR	109.2	35 54.79N	119 1.25W
PORTLAND	PDX	VOR	111.8	45 35.63N	122 36.37W
PORTLAND	PLD	NDB	257.0	40 27.23N	84 59.01W
PORTS (LOM)	PORT	NDB	275.0	40 59.18N	78 8.55W
PORTSMOUTH	PMH	NDB	373.0	38 46.91N	82 50.69W
PORTSMOUTH	PVG	NDB	241.0	36 46.82N	76 26.73W
POST	PFL	NDB	308.0	34 36.54N	98 24.23W
POTSDAM	PTD	NDB	400.0	44 43.41N	74 52.96W
POTTS (LOM/NDB)	POTT	NDB	385.0	40 44.84N	96 45.75W
POTTSTOWN	PTW	VOR	116.5	40 13.35N	75 33.62W
POWELL	CGQ	NDB	344.0	32 3.85N	96 25.68W
POWELL	POY	NDB	344.0	44 52.02N	108 47.18W
POWELL RIVER	YPW	NDB	382.0	49 50.22N	124 30.09W
POZA RICA	PAZ	VOR	111.5	20 36.44N	97 28.05W
PRAGUE	GGU	NDB	314.0	35 31.01N	96 43.12W
PRAHL	PLV	NDB	366.0	45 17.01N	122 46.25W
PRAIZ (LOM/NDB)	PRAI	NDB	221.0	26 11.54N	80 17.90W
PRATT	PTT	NDB	356.0	37 43.44N	98 44.82W
PRENTISS	PJR	NDB	252.0	31 35.78N	89 54.31W
PRESO (LOM)	PRES	NDB	388.0	35 45.32N	95 56.92W
PRESQUE ISLE	PQI	VOR	116.4	46 46.46N	68 5.67W
PRICE (LOM)	PRIC	NDB	382.0	42 37.34N	92 30.57W
PRIEST	ROM	VOR	110.0	36 8.43N	120 39.90W
PRINCE ALBERT	YPA	VOR	113.0	53 12.99N	105 39.99W
PRINCE GEORGE	XS	NDB	272.0	53 49.71N	122 39.24W
PRINCE GEORGE	YXS	VOR	112.3	53 53.66N	122 27.34W
PRINCE RUPERT	PR	NDB	218.0	54 15.81N	130 25.43W
PRINCETON	DC	NDB	326.0	38 28.19N	120 31.01W
PRINCETON	PNN	VOR	114.3	45 19.76N	67 42.25W
PRINCETON	YDC	VOR	113.9	49 22.90N	120 22.42W
PRISON	RVJ	NDB	424.0	32 3.47N	82 9.14W
PROBERTA	PBT	NDB	338.0	40 6.84N	122 14.25W
PROSPECT CREEK	PPC	NDB	340.0	66 49.07N	150 38.04W
PROSSER	PSS	NDB	338.0	46 41.18N	98 28.65W
PROVIDENCE	PVD	VOR	115.6	41 43.47N	71 25.78W
PROVIDENCIALES	PV	NDB	387.0	21 46.64N	72 15.65W
PROVIDENIYA	BC	NDB	320.0	64 17.51N	173 19.00W
PROVO	PVU	VOR	108.4	40 12.90N	111 43.28W
PRUDHOE BAY	PUO	NDB	368.0	70 14.92N	148 23.65W
PUBBS (LOM/NDB)	PUBB	NDB	392.0	37 20.01N	77 27.21W
PUEBLO	PUB	VOR	116.7	38 17.66N	104 25.77W
PUERTO PLATA	PTA	VOR	115.1	19 45.51N	70 34.29W
PUFF	PUF	NDB	345.0	43 21.07N	94 44.26W
PULASKI	PSK	VOR	116.8	37 5.27N	80 42.77W
PULLIAM	PUU	NDB	379.0	35 8.52N	111 40.24W
PULLMAN	PMM	VOR	112.1	42 27.94N	86 6.35W
PULLMAN	PUW	VOR	109.0	46 40.47N	117 13.41W
PULLY (LOM/NDB)	PULL	NDB	266.0	39 38.70N	86 23.38W
PUMIE (LOM)	PUMI	NDB	373.0	42 27.06N	122 54.80W
PUNTA CAUCEDO	CDO	VOR	114.7	18 25.99N	69 40.03W
PUNTA GORDA	PGD	VOR	110.2	26 55.01N	81 59.47W
PUNTILLA LAKE	PTI	NDB	397.0	62 4.41N	152 43.99W
PUT RIVER	PVQ	NDB	234.0	70 13.40N	148 25.03W
PUTNAM	PUT	VOR	117.4	41 57.34N	71 50.65W
PUTNY (LOM/NDB)	PUTN	NDB	227.0	31 27.38N	84 16.57W
PYKLA (LOM/NDB)	PYKL	NDB	379.0	46 50.75N	92 21.30W
PYRAMID	PYF	NDB	418.0	31 51.77N	96 11.85W
QEEZY (LOM)	QEEZ	NDB	266.0	25 38.51N	80 30.29W
QUAKERTOWN	UKT	NDB	208.0	40 25.50N	75 17.84W
QUEBEC	QB	NDB	230.0	46 45.00N	71 27.76W
QUEBEC	YQB	VOR	112.8	46 42.33N	71 37.59W
QUESNEL	YQZ	NDB	359.0	52 57.64N	122 29.19W
QUINCY	UIN	VOR	113.6	39 50.89N	91 16.74W
QUINCY (LOM/NDB)	UI	NDB	293.0	39 53.23N	91 15.22W

Name	Ident.	Type	Freq.	Latitude	Longitude
QUINHAGAK	AQH	VOR	114.7	59 45.10N	161 53.42W
QUITMAN	UIM	VOR	114.0	32 52.83N	95 22.01W
RACEPOINT	RZP	NDB	232.0	42 3.78N	70 14.55W
RAINBOW	RNB	NDB	363.0	39 25.11N	75 8.11W
RAINBOW LAKE	YOP	NDB	344.0	58 27.42N	119 15.10W
RAINELLE	RNL	VOR	116.6	37 58.53N	80 48.39W
RAIZE (LOM/NDB)	RAIZ	NDB	353.0	48 28.89N	93 16.68W
RALEIGH/DURHAM	RDU	VOR	117.2	35 52.36N	78 47.00W
RALLY	UZ	NDB	227.0	34 53.42N	81 4.86W
RAMBOUILLET	RBT	VOR	114.7	48 39.21N	1 59.70E
RANCH (LOM/NDB)	RANC	NDB	254.0	43 57.90N	102 59.93W
RANDOLPH	RND	VOR	112.3	29 31.15N	98 17.10W
RANDOLPH COUNTY	RQY	NDB	284.0	38 53.12N	79 51.27W
RANGELEY	RQM	NDB	221.0	44 56.08N	70 45.07W
RANGIROA	RAN	VOR	112.3	14 56.90S	147 41.00W
RAPID CITY	RAP	VOR	112.3	43 58.57N	103 0.74W
RAPIDS	RZZ	NDB	407.0	36 26.47N	77 42.50W
RAROTONGA	RG	VOR	113.5	21 11.80S	159 48.90W
RATTENBERG	RTT	NDB	303.0	47 25.91N	11 56.40E
RAVINE	RAV	VOR	114.6	40 33.21N	76 35.96W
RAWLINS	RWL	VOR	109.4	41 48.30N	107 12.26W
RAYMOND	RYB	NDB	375.0	32 18.10N	90 24.69W
RAZER (LMM/NDB)	RAZE	NDB	215.0	58 41.43N	156 40.69W
RAZORBACK	RZC	VOR	116.4	36 14.79N	94 7.28W
REAGAN CO	LUJ	NDB	341.0	31 11.57N	101 28.12W
RED BLUFF	RBL	VOR	115.7	40 5.94N	122 14.18W
RED LAKE	RL	NDB	218.0	51 3.67N	93 47.09W
RED LAKE	YRL	VOR	114.0	51 4.30N	93 45.72W
RED LODGE	RED	NDB	203.0	45 14.41N	109 15.86W
RED OAK	RDK	NDB	230.0	41 9.98N	95 15.20W
RED TABLE	DBL	VOR	113.0	39 26.37N	106 53.68W
RED WING	RGK	NDB	248.0	44 35.34N	92 29.53W
REDAN (LOM/NDB)	REDA	NDB	266.0	33 38.73N	84 18.67W
REDBIRD	RBD	NDB	287.0	32 40.62N	96 52.27W
REDDING	RDD	VOR	108.4	40 30.28N	122 17.50W
REDSTONE	HUA	NDB	287.0	34 41.92N	86 41.28W
REDWOOD FALLS	RWF	VOR	113.3	44 28.04N	95 7.70W
REENO (LOM)	REEN	NDB	317.0	36 4.26N	80 10.01W
REESE	RVO	VOR	114.9	33 35.81N	102 2.64W
REEVE	SNP	NDB	362.0	57 9.11N	170 13.52W
REGINA	QR	NDB	290.0	50 22.20N	104 34.38W
REGINALD GRANT	RGD	NDB	302.0	32 56.23N	84 20.42W
REIGA (LOM/NDB)	REIG	NDB	374.0	32 53.18N	121 41.04W
REIMS	REM	VOR	112.3	49 18.71N	4 2.80E
RENCH (LOM)	RENC	NDB	335.0	41 38.52N	71 29.68W
RENEY (LOM)	RENE	NDB	203.0	45 23.16N	98 19.69W
RENO (LMM)	NO	NDB	351.0	39 31.18N	119 46.15W
RENOVA	RNV	NDB	272.0	33 48.43N	90 45.76W
RENSSELAER	RZL	NDB	362.0	40 56.83N	87 11.02W
RENTON	RNT	VOR	353.0	47 29.74N	122 12.88W
REPUBLICAN	RPB	NDB	414.0	39 48.80N	97 39.49W
REVLOC	REC	VOR	110.6	40 32.80N	78 44.82W
REVUP (LOM)	REVU	NDB	388.0	42 7.21N	83 25.91W
REYNOSA	REX	VOR	112.4	26 0.71N	98 14.00W
RHINELANDER	RHI	VOR	109.2	45 38.03N	89 27.47W
RIBOO (LOM)	RIBO	NDB	260.0	46 22.24N	119 15.55W
RICE LAKE	IKE	VOR	110.0	45 28.56N	91 43.51W
RICE LAKE	RIE	NDB	407.0	45 28.79N	91 43.28W
RICH MOUNTAIN	PGO	VOR	113.5	34 40.84N	94 36.54W
RICHMOND	RIC	VOR	114.1	37 30.15N	77 19.22W
RICHMOND	RID	VOR	110.6	39 45.31N	84 50.33W
RIKKY (LOM)	RIKK	NDB	426.0	41 13.19N	95 49.07W
RIMOUSKI	YXK	NDB	373.0	48 28.68N	68 33.48W
RINGY (LOM)	RING	NDB	245.0	27 19.70N	82 28.70W
RIO SALADO	RSZ	NDB	281.0	33 26.30N	111 55.65W
RIPLEY	XCR	NDB	404.0	46 4.72N	94 20.60W
RIPLY (LOM)	RIPL	NDB	326.0	38 53.10N	95 34.89W
RITTS (LOM)	RITT	NDB	396.0	48 3.18N	122 17.33W
RIVERBEND	RVB	NDB	407.0	45 33.01N	100 24.61W
RIVERSIDE	RAL	VOR	112.4	33 57.13N	117 26.95W

Name	Ident.	Type	Freq.	Latitude	Longitude	Name	Ident.	Type	Freq.	Latitude	Longitude
RIVERSIDE	RIS	VOR	111.4	39 7.23N	94 35.79W	RUSSELLVILLE	RUE	NDB	379.0	35 15.43N	93 5.66W
RIVERTON	RIW	VOR	108.8	43 3.95N	108 27.33W	RUTHERFORD	RFE	NDB	344.0	35 20.95N	81 57.17W
RIVIERE DU LOUP	YRI	VOR	113.9	47 45.46N	69 35.39W	RYAN	RYN	NDB	338.0	32 8.31N	111 9.69W
RIVIERE OUELLE	Z8	NDB	347.0	47 26.51N	69 58.90W	SABAR (LOM)	SABA	NDB	219.0	32 27.25N	92 6.25W
RIVIERE-DU-LOUP	RI	NDB	201.0	47 45.83N	69 34.69W	SABINE PASS	SBI	VOR	115.4	29 41.21N	94 2.28W
ROAMY (LOM)	ROAM	NDB	394.0	42 3.37N	88 0.47W	SABLE ISLAND	SA	NDB	374.0	43 55.85N	60 1.37W
ROANOKE	ROA	VOR	109.4	37 20.61N	80 4.23W	SABON (LOM)	SABO	NDB	395.0	46 51.78N	98 34.84W
ROBBINSVILLE	RBV	VOR	113.8	40 12.15N	74 29.70W	SAC CITY	SKI	NDB	356.0	42 22.56N	94 58.87W
ROBERTS	RBS	VOR	116.8	40 34.91N	88 9.86W	SACRAMENTO	SAC	VOR	115.2	38 26.63N	121 33.10W
ROBERVAL	RJ	NDB	378.0	48 32.70N	72 17.67W	SAGINAW	MBS	VOR	112.9	43 31.91N	84 4.64W
ROBESON	RSY	NDB	359.0	34 36.82N	79 3.58W	SAGUENAY	VBS	VOR	114.2	48 1.04N	71 16.15W
ROBINSON	PJ	NDB	329.0	60 26.38N	134 51.68W	SAIGE (LOM)	SAIG	NDB	251.0	45 51.14N	108 41.66W
ROBINSON	ROB	NDB	400.0	31 30.24N	97 4.17W	SAINT FRANCIS	SYF	NDB	386.0	39 43.63N	101 45.89W
ROBINSON	RSV	NDB	108.4	39 1.09N	87 38.92W	SAINT GEORGE	OZN	VOR	109.8	37 5.29N	113 35.51W
ROBLES	RBJ	NDB	220.0	32 4.45N	111 21.62W	SAINT JOHN	SJ	NDB	212.0	45 23.51N	65 49.13W
ROCHESTER	RCR	NDB	216.0	41 3.91N	86 11.42W	SAINT JOHN	YSJ	VOR	113.5	45 24.45N	65 52.21W
ROCHESTER	ROC	VOR	110.0	43 7.25N	77 40.41W	SAINT LANDRY	OPL	NDB	335.0	30 39.34N	92 5.91W
ROCHESTER	RST	VOR	112.0	43 46.98N	92 35.81W	SAIPAN	SN	NDB	312.0	15 6.77N	145 42.70E
ROCK COUNTY	RBE	NDB	341.0	42 34.42N	99 34.67W	SALDO (LOM/NDB)	SALD	NDB	400.0	58 44.26N	156 46.67W
ROCK RAPIDS	RRQ	NDB	515.0	43 27.07N	96 10.69W	SALEM	SLO	NDB	400.0	38 38.65N	88 58.04W
ROCK RIVER	RYV	NDB	371.0	43 10.26N	88 43.34W	SALEM	SVM	VOR	114.3	42 24.54N	83 35.65W
ROCK SOUND	RSD	NDB	353.0	24 53.59N	76 10.20W	SALINA	SLN	VOR	117.1	38 55.59N	97 37.27W
ROCK SPRINGS	OCS	VOR	116.0	41 35.42N	109 0.92W	SALINAS	SNS	VOR	117.3	36 39.84N	121 36.19W
ROCKDALE	RCK	NDB	221.0	30 17.02N	96 59.02W	SALISBURY	SBY	VOR	111.2	38 20.71N	75 30.63W
ROCKDALE	RKA	VOR	112.6	42 27.99N	75 14.35W	SALISBURY	SRW	NDB	233.0	35 40.69N	80 30.36W
ROCKET	RQZ	VOR	112.2	34 47.83N	86 38.03W	SALIX (LOM/NDB)	SALI	NDB	414.0	42 19.66N	96 17.42W
ROCKFORD	RFD	VOR	110.8	42 13.54N	89 11.96W	SALLISAW	IQS	NDB	520.0	35 23.93N	94 47.66W
ROCKHAMPTON	RK	VOR	116.9	23 23.00S	150 28.30E	SALMON	LKT	VOR	113.5	45 1.29N	114 5.05W
ROCKPORT	RKP	NDB	391.0	28 5.44N	97 2.73W	SALT FLAT	SFL	VOR	113.0	31 44.89N	105 5.21W
ROCKSPRINGS	RSG	VOR	111.2	30 0.88N	100 17.99W	SALT LAKE CITY	SLC	VOR	116.8	40 51.02N	111 58.92W
ROCKY MOUNTAIN	YRM	VOR	114.3	52 30.14N	115 19.42W	SALTT (LOM)	SALT	NDB	404.0	38 7.42N	97 55.61W
RODING	RDG	VOR	114.7	49 2.51N	12 31.70E	SALYER FARMS	COR	NDB	205.0	36 5.09N	119 32.72W
ROEBY (LOM)	ROEB	NDB	394.0	33 36.46N	86 40.73W	SALZBURG	SBG	VOR	113.8	48 0.21N	12 53.60E
ROGERS CITY	PZQ	NDB	215.0	45 24.29N	83 49.22W	SALZBURG	SBG	NDB	382.0	47 58.11N	12 53.70E
ROGERSVILLE	RVN	NDB	329.0	36 27.36N	82 53.06W	SALZBURG	SI	NDB	410.0	47 49.21N	12 59.30E
ROGUE VALLEY	OED	VOR	113.6	42 28.78N	122 54.78W	SALZBURG	SU	NDB	356.0	42 52.81N	12 57.10E
ROKKY (LOM/NDB)	ROKK	VOR	245.0	43 29.66N	96 49.73W	SAMSVILLE	SAM	VOR	116.6	38 29.12N	88 5.15W
ROLLA	RLL	NDB	263.0	48 52.89N	99 36.89W	SAN ANDRES	SPP	NDB	387.0	12 35.00N	81 42.00W
ROLLINS	ESG	NDB	260.0	43 13.22N	70 49.70W	SAN ANGELO	SJT	VOR	115.1	31 22.51N	100 27.29W
ROME	REO	VOR	112.5	42 35.44N	117 52.09W	SAN ANTONIO	SAT	VOR	116.8	29 38.65N	98 27.68W
ROME	RMG	VOR	115.4	34 9.76N	85 7.16W	SAN CLEMENTE	NUC	NDB	350.0	33 1.64N	118 34.29W
ROMEN (LOM)	ROME	NDB	278.0	33 57.90N	118 16.68W	SAN FRANCISCO	SFO	VOR	115.8	37 37.18N	122 22.43W
ROMEO	R	NDB	403.0	43 44.31N	79 42.19W	SAN FRANCISCO INTL	I-GW	VOR	111.7	37 37.82N	122 23.82W
ROMEO	R	NDB	317.0	44 3.18N	77 37.60W	SAN FRANCISCO INTL	I-SF	VOR	109.6	37 37.61N	122 23.63W
ROMEO	R	NDB	377.0	45 16.11N	75 34.41W	SAN FRANCISCO INTL	I-SI	VOR	108.9	37 36.28N	122 22.93W
ROMULUS	RYK	VOR	108.4	42 42.79N	76 52.93W	SAN JACINTO	SJY	VOR	227.0	33 47.70N	116 59.96W
RORAY (LMM)	RORA	NDB	341.0	37 43.29N	122 11.65W	SAN JOSE	SJC	VOR	114.1	37 22.49N	121 56.68W
ROSANKY	RYU	NDB	266.0	29 53.75N	97 20.27W	SAN JUAN	SJU	VOR	114.0	18 26.78N	65 59.37W
ROSCOE	RCZ	NDB	375.0	34 51.17N	79 41.62W	SAN MARCUS	RZS	VOR	114.9	34 30.58N	119 46.26W
ROSEAU	ROX	NDB	108.8	48 51.29N	95 41.70W	SAN NICOLAS NAVY	NSI	NDB	203.0	33 14.16N	119 26.96W
ROSEBURG	RBG	VOR	108.2	43 10.95N	123 21.14W	SAN SIMON	SSO	VOR	115.4	32 16.16N	109 15.79W
ROSEBURG	RBG	NDB	400.0	43 14.12N	123 21.48W	SANDHILLS	SDZ	VOR	111.8	35 12.93N	79 35.28W
ROSEWOOD	ROD	VOR	117.5	40 17.28N	84 2.59W	SANDPOE	SZT	NDB	264.0	48 17.46N	116 33.81W
ROSS COUNTY	RZT	NDB	236.0	39 26.38N	83 1.64W	SANDSPIT	YZP	VOR	114.1	53 15.15N	131 48.42W
ROSS RIVER	YDM	NDB	218.0	61 58.42N	132 25.62W	SANDSPIT	Z	NDB	248.0	53 21.01N	131 56.49W
ROSWELL	ROW	VOR	116.1	33 20.26N	104 37.28W	SANDSPIT	ZP	NDB	368.0	53 11.80N	131 46.65W
ROTA	GRO	NDB	332.0	14 10.22N	145 14.25E	SANDUSKY	SKY	VOR	109.2	41 26.08N	82 39.29W
ROUEN	ROU	VOR	116.8	49 27.91N	1 16.90E	SANDY POINT	SEY	VOR	117.8	41 10.06N	71 34.56W
ROUNDUP	RPX	NDB	362.0	46 28.84N	108 34.04W	SANDY POINT	SYG	VOR	338.0	29 30.17N	95 28.10W
ROWAN	RUQ	VOR	111.0	35 38.63N	80 31.35W	SANFD (LOM)	SANF	NDB	349.0	43 20.08N	70 50.06W
ROWDY (LOM)	ROWD	NDB	260.0	30 29.61N	96 20.27W	SANFORD	SFB	NDB	408.0	28 47.10N	81 14.60W
RUBIN (LOM/NDB)	RUBI	NDB	356.0	26 41.27N	80 12.61W	SANJAC	JPA	NDB	347.0	29 40.12N	95 4.19W
RUCKR (LOM/NDB)	RUCK	NDB	212.0	31 13.54N	85 48.96W	SANTA CATALINA	SXC	VOR	111.4	33 22.51N	118 25.19W
RUGBY	RUG	NDB	212.0	48 23.28N	100 1.62W	SANTA ELENA	SNE	NDB	260.0	26 43.14N	98 34.64W
RUMML (LOM)	RUMM	NDB	400.0	40 13.03N	78 44.64W	SANTA FE	SAF	VOR	110.6	35 32.44N	106 3.90W
RUNDI (LOM)	RUND	NDB	284.0	30 34.98N	91 12.66W	SANTA MONICA	SMO	VOR	110.8	34 0.62N	118 27.40W
RUOYN	YUY	NDB	218.0	48 10.38N	78 56.31W	SANTA ROSA	STS	VOR	113.0	38 30.50N	122 48.64W
RUSHSYLVANIA	RUV	NDB	326.0	40 27.54N	83 40.08W	SANTA YNEZ	IZA	NDB	394.0	34 36.36N	120 4.57W
RUSK COUNTY	RCX	NDB	356.0	45 30.11N	91 0.08W	SANTIAGO	STG	VOR	114.5	8 5.25N	80 56.38W
RUSKIN	RNQ	NDB	404.0	31 14.92N	82 24.09W	SARANAC LAKE	SLK	VOR	109.2	44 23.08N	74 12.27W

Name	Ident.	Type	Freq.	Latitude	Longitude
SARASOTA	SRQ	VOR	115.2	27 23.87N	82 33.26W
SARATOGA	ARF	NDB	296.0	34 15.18N	86 13.41W
SARNIA	ZR	NDB	404.0	42 56.45N	82 14.01W
SASKATOON	XE	NDB	257.0	52 11.40N	106 48.84W
SASKATOON	YXE	VOR	116.2	52 10.88N	106 43.19W
SATELLITE	SQT	NDB	257.0	28 5.97N	80 42.06W
SAUFLEY	NUN	VOR	108.8	30 28.34N	87 20.16W
SAULT STE MARIE	SSM	VOR	112.2	46 24.73N	84 18.89W
SAUSALITO	SAU	VOR	116.2	37 51.33N	122 31.36W
SAVANNAH	SAV	VOR	112.7	32 9.64N	81 6.75W
SAVOY (LOM/NDB)	SAVO	NDB	356.0	32 14.84N	88 46.30W
SAWCY (LOM)	SAWC	NDB	353.0	37 5.39N	97 2.18W
SAYRE	SYO	VOR	115.2	35 20.72N	99 38.12W
SCAGGS ISLAND	SGD	VOR	112.1	38 10.77N	122 22.39W
SCHOLES	VUH	VOR	113.0	29 16.17N	94 52.06W
SCHOOLCRAFT CO	ISQ	VOR	110.4	45 58.61N	86 10.44W
SCOBEY	SBQ	NDB	245.0	33 53.48N	89 52.47W
SCOBEY	SCO	NDB	283.0	48 48.53N	105 26.17W
SCOTLAND	SKB	NDB	344.0	33 47.41N	98 29.19W
SCOTT	SCG	NDB	385.0	48 15.61N	92 28.48W
SCOTTSBLUFF	BFF	VOR	112.6	41 53.66N	103 28.92W
SCOTTSDALE	SDL	NDB	224.0	33 37.75N	111 54.47W
SCURRY	SCY	VOR	112.9	32 27.88N	96 20.25W
SEA ISLE	SIE	VOR	114.8	39 5.74N	74 48.02W
SEAL BEACH	SLI	VOR	115.7	33 47.01N	118 3.28W
SEARCY	SRC	NDB	323.0	35 12.73N	91 43.96W
SEARLE	SAE	VOR	110.2	41 7.16N	101 46.58W
SEATTLE	SEA	VOR	116.8	47 26.13N	122 18.58W
SEBAGO	SZO	NDB	227.0	43 54.26N	70 46.94W
SEBAS (LOM/NDB)	SEBA	NDB	338.0	26 18.32N	97 39.43W
SEBRING	SEF	NDB	382.0	27 27.64N	81 20.99W
SECO	XYC	NDB	393.0	37 45.49N	84 1.81W
SEDALIA	DMO	NDB	281.0	38 42.27N	93 10.60W
SEDLY (LOM/NDB)	SEDL	NDB	212.0	41 27.08N	86 52.65W
SEDONA	SEZ	NDB	334.0	34 49.73N	111 48.86W
SEELEY	SLY	NDB	344.0	46 6.62N	91 23.03W
SELAWIK	WLK	VOR	114.2	66 36.01N	159 59.49W
SELINSGROVE	SEG	VOR	110.4	40 47.46N	76 53.04W
SEMINOLE	SRE	NDB	278.0	35 16.31N	96 40.49W
SEMMES	SJI	VOR	115.3	30 43.57N	88 21.56W
SENECA	SSN	NDB	208.0	42 44.68N	76 54.28W
SEPT-ILES	YZV	VOR	114.5	50 13.93N	66 16.41W
SEPT-ILES	ZV	NDB	273.0	50 12.20N	66 9.13W
SEWANEE	UOS	NDB	275.0	35 12.26N	85 53.75W
SEWARD	SWT	NDB	269.0	40 51.90N	97 6.36W
SEWART	SWZ	NDB	391.0	35 57.42N	86 27.84W
SHAFTER	EHF	VOR	115.4	35 29.08N	119 5.84W
SHAKER HILL	SKR	NDB	251.0	42 27.35N	71 10.71W
SHANGRI-LA	AGB	NDB	272.0	36 34.66N	94 51.61W
SHANNON	EZF	NDB	237.0	38 15.93N	77 26.92W
SHAPP (LOM)	SHAP	NDB	356.0	40 18.40N	75 56.98W
SHARPE	LRO	NDB	282.0	37 49.67N	121 16.26W
SHAW	HWB	NDB	263.0	40 15.91N	96 45.43W
SHAWN (LOM/NDB)	SHAW	NDB	296.0	33 54.65N	98 27.27W
SHAWNEE	SNL	NDB	227.0	35 21.31N	96 56.74W
SHEARWATER	YAW	NDB	353.0	44 36.15N	63 26.83W
SHEBB (LOM)	SHEB	NDB	338.0	43 50.92N	87 46.47W
SHEEP MOUNTAIN	SMU	NDB	221.0	61 47.25N	147 40.70W
SHEIN (LOM/NDB)	SHEI	NDB	263.0	29 54.91N	99 0.49W
SHELBY	SBX	NDB	347.0	48 32.48N	111 51.93W
SHELBYVILLE	SHB	VOR	112.0	39 37.96N	85 49.46W
SHELBYVILLE	SYI	VOR	109.0	35 33.73N	86 26.35W
SHELBYVILLE	SYZ	NDB	365.0	39 24.41N	88 50.62W
SHELDON	DDL	VOR	108.6	43 12.74N	95 50.03W
SHELDON	SHL	NDB	338.0	43 12.86N	95 50.03W
SHELL LAKE	SSQ	NDB	212.0	45 43.67N	91 55.17W
SHEMYA	SYA	VOR	109.0	52 43.11N	174 3.73E
SHEMYA	SYA	NDB	221.0	52 43.33N	174 3.62E
SHENANDOAH	SDA	NDB	411.0	40 45.43N	95 24.95W
SHERBROOKE	SC	NDB	362.0	45 28.48N	71 47.27W

Name	Ident.	Type	Freq.	Latitude	Longitude
SHERBROOKE	YSC	VOR	113.2	45 19.00N	71 47.29W
SHERIDAN	SHR	VOR	115.3	44 50.55N	107 3.67W
SHINGE POINT	UA	NDB	226.0	68 55.39N	137 15.75W
SHISHMAREF	SHH	NDB	365.0	66 15.50N	166 3.15W
SHOW LOW	SOW	NDB	206.0	34 16.04N	110 0.49W
SHREVEPORT	SHV	VOR	117.4	32 46.29N	93 48.60W
SHUGR (LOM/NDB)	SHUG	NDB	414.0	39 17.64N	101 36.02W
SIBLEY	ISB	NDB	269.0	43 22.09N	95 45.15W
SIBLEY	SZY	NDB	386.0	35 14.22N	88 30.96W
SIDNEY	SDY	NDB	359.0	47 42.70N	104 10.91W
SIDNEY	SNY	VOR	115.9	41 5.81N	102 58.98W
SIERRA	S	NDB	344.0	46 41.01N	80 44.96W
SIKESTON	SIK	NDB	272.0	36 53.28N	89 33.89W
SILER CITY	TOX	NDB	371.0	35 45.70N	79 27.73W
SILOAM SPRINGS	SLG	NDB	284.0	36 11.36N	94 29.31W
SILVER CITY	SVC	VOR	111.8	32 38.27N	108 9.67W
SIMMONS	FBG	VOR	109.8	35 8.00N	78 55.00W
SIMONES	USR	NDB	315.0	21 44.75N	78 48.72W
SINCLAIR	SIR	NDB	368.0	41 48.13N	107 5.53W
SIOUX CENTER	SOY	NDB	368.0	43 7.99N	96 11.38W
SIOUX CITY	SUX	VOR	116.5	42 20.68N	96 19.42W
SIOUX FALLS	FSD	VOR	115.0	43 38.98N	96 46.87W
SIOUX LOOKOUT	YXL	NDB	405.0	50 7.10N	91 53.87W
SIOUX NARROWS	VBI	VOR	115.2	49 28.64N	94 2.83W
SIREN	RZN	VOR	109.4	45 49.24N	92 22.47W
SISTERS ISLAND	SSR	VOR	114.0	58 10.67N	135 15.53W
SITKA	SIT	NDB	358.0	56 51.29N	135 32.06W
SKAGIT/BAY VIEW	BVS	NDB	240.0	48 28.13N	122 25.12W
SKEENA	TB	NDB	254.0	54 28.97N	128 35.49W
SKI	SKX	NDB	414.0	36 27.48N	105 40.58W
SKIPI (LOM)	SKIP	NDB	321.0	39 47.52N	104 26.06W
SKOOKUM	SX	NDB	368.0	49 57.29N	115 47.56W
SKWENTNA	SKW	NDB	269.0	61 57.98N	151 12.09W
SLAMMER	SIF	NDB	423.0	36 22.94N	79 45.80W
SLATE CREEK	SLX	NDB	280.0	64 33.74N	142 30.97W
SLATE RUN	SLT	VOR	113.9	41 30.77N	77 58.21W
SLEETMUTE	SLQ	NDB	406.0	61 41.98N	157 9.78W
SLOVER	JES	NDB	323.0	31 33.15N	81 53.24W
SMITH FALLS	YSH	NDB	334.0	44 54.06N	76 0.63W
SMITH LAKE	SAK	NDB	515.0	48 6.51N	114 27.68W
SMITHERS	YD	NDB	230.0	54 44.86N	127 6.47W
SMITHVILLE	SLW	NDB	400.0	40 52.51N	81 49.99W
SMYRNA	ENO	VOR	111.4	39 13.91N	75 30.96W
SNOHOMISH COUNTY (PAINE	I-PA	VOR	109.3	47 53.71N	122 17.12W
SNOOP (LOM)	SNOO	NDB	326.0	38 38.37N	90 46.03W
SNOW	SXW	VOR	109.2	39 37.78N	106 59.47W
SNOW HILL	SWL	VOR	112.4	38 3.40N	75 27.83W
SNOWBIRD	SOT	VOR	108.8	35 47.41N	83 3.14W
SNUFF (LOM)	SNUF	NDB	335.0	36 31.63N	87 23.19W
SNYDER	SDR	NDB	359.0	32 42.08N	100 56.84W
SOCORRO	ONM	VOR	116.8	34 20.34N	106 49.23W
SOD HOUSE	SDO	VOR	114.3	41 24.64N	118 1.99W
SOFKE (LOM)	SOFK	NDB	290.0	32 38.72N	83 42.79W
SOLBERG	SBJ	VOR	112.9	40 34.99N	74 44.50W
SOLDOTNA	OLT	NDB	346.0	60 28.51N	150 52.73W
SOLON SPRINGS	OLG	NDB	388.0	46 19.02N	91 48.84W
SONORA	SOA	NDB	371.0	30 34.92N	100 38.82W
SOUTH BOSTON	SBV	VOR	110.4	36 40.51N	79 0.87W
SOUTH KAUAI	SOK	VOR	115.4	21 54.03N	159 31.73W
SOYYA	SMY	NDB	329.0	30 52.30N	85 13.50W
SPAIN	SPQ	NDB	414.0	35 12.10N	90 3.09W
SPARKS	SPK	NDB	254.0	39 41.83N	119 46.12W
SPARREVOHN	SQA	VOR	117.2	61 5.92N	155 38.07W
SPARTA	SAR	NDB	239.0	38 8.73N	89 42.14W
SPARTA	SAX	VOR	115.7	41 4.06N	74 32.30W
SPARTANBURG	SPA	VOR	115.7	35 2.03N	81 55.62W
SPEEZ (LOM)	SPEE	NDB	222.0	39 54.09N	75 5.68W
SPENC (LOM)	SPEN	NDB	223.0	42 13.20N	83 12.20W
SPENCER	SPW	VOR	110.0	43 9.74N	95 12.06W

Name	Ident.	Type	Freq.	Latitude	Longitude
SPIDA (LOM/NDB)	SPID	NDB	269.0	46 50.06N	94 58.51W
SPOFFORD	PFO	NDB	356.0	29 8.72N	100 25.66W
SPOKANE	GEG	VOR	115.5	47 33.91N	117 37.61W
SPORTYS	PWF	NDB	245.0	39 4.61N	84 12.93W
SPRING HILL	XNE	NDB	281.0	31 41.07N	85 58.46W
SPRING RIVER	LLU	NDB	356.0	37 29.23N	94 18.61W
SPRINGFIELD	IKY	NDB	429.0	37 38.08N	85 14.20W
SPRINGFIELD	SGF	VOR	116.9	37 21.37N	93 20.04W
SPRINGFIELD	SGH	VOR	113.2	39 50.20N	83 50.70W
SPRINGFIELD	SXD	NDB	265.0	43 16.21N	72 35.18W
SPRINGHILL	SPH	NDB	375.0	32 59.00N	93 24.44W
SPRUCEHEAD	SUH	NDB	356.0	43 59.87N	69 7.05W
SQUAW	XQA	NDB	236.0	45 31.31N	69 40.47W
SQUAW VALLEY	SWR	VOR	113.2	39 10.83N	120 16.18W
SQUIR (LOM)	SQUI	NDB	400.0	40 54.28N	72 33.39W
ST AUGUSTINE	SGJ	VOR	109.4	29 57.49N	81 20.29W
ST CATHERINES	SN	NDB	408.0	43 8.83N	79 15.29W
ST CLOUD	STC	VOR	112.1	45 32.47N	94 3.45W
ST CROIX	COY	VOR	108.2	17 44.07N	64 42.04W
ST GEORGE	SGG	NDB	201.0	56 36.29N	169 32.51W
ST JAMES	SJX	NDB	382.0	45 41.51N	85 34.01W
ST JEAN	YJN	VOR	115.8	45 15.36N	73 19.28W
ST JOHNS	SJN	VOR	112.3	34 25.45N	109 8.61W
ST JOSEPH	STJ	VOR	115.5	39 57.64N	94 55.51W
ST LEONARD	YSL	NDB	404.0	47 12.48N	67 52.19W
ST LOUIS	STL	VOR	117.4	38 51.65N	90 28.94W
ST MAARTEN	PJD	NDB	284.0	18 2.30N	63 7.10W
ST MAARTEN	PJM	VOR	113.0	18 2.30N	63 7.13W
ST MAARTEN	PJM	NDB	308.0	18 2.17N	63 7.05W
ST MARYS	SMA	NDB	230.0	62 3.52N	163 17.50W
ST PETERSBURG	PIE	VOR	116.4	27 54.47N	82 41.06W
ST THOMAS	STT	VOR	108.6	18 21.35N	65 1.47W
ST THOMAS	THS	VOR	115.0	39 56.00N	77 57.06W
ST VINCENT	SV	VOR	403.0	13 8.00N	61 12.00W
ST-FELIX-DE-VALOI	UFX	NDB	260.0	46 11.54N	73 25.14W
ST-HONORE	YRC	NDB	213.0	48 32.18N	71 9.51W
ST. THOMAS	7B	NDB	375.0	42 46.26N	81 6.34W
STALS (LOM)	STAL	NDB	401.0	35 14.64N	77 41.90W
STAMFORD	TMV	NDB	290.0	32 52.13N	99 43.98W
STANFIELD	TFD	VOR	114.8	32 53.16N	111 54.52W
STANLEY	VFU	NDB	411.0	40 51.76N	84 36.83W
STANLY COUNTY	SWY	NDB	362.0	35 24.72N	80 9.37W
STANWYCK	SKU	NDB	261.0	41 31.69N	74 2.70W
STAPLES	SAZ	NDB	257.0	46 22.95N	94 48.30W
STARN (LOM/NDB)	STAR	NDB	323.0	31 10.08N	97 52.69W
STATESVILLE	SVH	NDB	404.0	35 50.95N	80 55.59W
STAUT (LOM)	STAU	NDB	375.0	38 12.11N	78 57.44W
STE-FOY	OU	NDB	329.0	46 46.68N	71 17.39W
STEELHEAD	HDG	NDB	211.0	42 54.98N	114 40.46W
STELLA MARIS	ZLS	NDB	526.0	23 34.84N	75 15.83W
STEPHENVILLE	JT	NDB	390.0	48 32.64N	58 45.29W
STEPHENVILLE	SEP	NDB	223.0	32 13.08N	98 11.00W
STEPHENVILLE	YJT	VOR	113.1	48 34.96N	58 40.15W
STEVENS POINT	STE	VOR	110.6	44 32.60N	89 31.83W
STILLWATER	STW	VOR	109.6	40 59.76N	74 52.14W
STILLWATER	SWO	VOR	108.4	36 13.46N	97 4.87W
STINSON	SSF	VOR	108.4	29 15.51N	98 26.61W
STIRLING	VQC	VOR	113.5	44 23.18N	77 43.05W
STOGE (LOM)	STOG	NDB	397.0	42 7.19N	71 7.70W
STONEWALL	STV	VOR	113.1	30 12.41N	98 42.34W
STONEYFORK	SFK	VOR	108.6	41 41.73N	77 25.19W
STONIA	GHJ	NDB	293.0	35 11.48N	81 9.43W
STORM LAKE	SLB	NDB	227.0	42 36.04N	95 14.66W
STOYSTOWN	SYS	NDB	209.0	40 5.15N	78 54.99W
STRIK (LOM)	STRI	NDB	389.0	42 28.73N	114 21.26W
STRINGTOWN	SWN	NDB	326.0	39 9.21N	106 19.60W
STROH (LOM/NDB)	STRO	NDB	407.0	40 36.89N	77 43.08W
STROTHER	SOR	VOR	109.6	37 10.26N	97 2.40W
STUCKEY	HEK	NDB	236.0	33 43.72N	79 31.50W
STURGEON	STI	NDB	333.0	43 6.83N	115 40.14W
STURGEON BAY	SUE	NDB	414.0	44 50.08N	87 25.37W
STURGIS	IRS	NDB	382.0	41 48.80N	85 26.03W
STUTTGART	SGT	NDB	269.0	34 39.88N	91 35.51W
SUDBURY	SB	NDB	362.0	46 38.90N	80 55.29W
SUDBURY	YSB	VOR	112.3	46 37.76N	80 47.89W
SUFFOLK	SFQ	NDB	203.0	36 40.83N	76 36.50W
SUGARLOAF MOUNTAI	SUG	VOR	112.2	35 24.40N	82 16.12W
SULLIVAN	SIV	NDB	326.0	39 6.82N	87 26.81W
SULPHUR SPRINGS	SLR	VOR	109.0	33 11.93N	95 32.55W
SUMIE (LOM/NDB)	SUMI	NDB	391.0	39 59.18N	82 45.27W
SUMMERDALE	ESU	NDB	204.0	30 29.97N	87 43.55W
SUMMERSIDE	YSU	NDB	254.0	46 23.83N	63 52.90W
SUMMIT	UMM	NDB	326.0	63 19.70N	149 7.84W
SUMNER STRAIT	SQM	NDB	529.0	56 27.89N	133 5.84W
SUMTER	SMS	NDB	252.0	33 59.45N	80 21.64W
SUNSHINE	SHY	VOR	108.4	38 2.44N	92 36.14W
SURFF (LOM)	SURF	NDB	308.0	43 3.16N	93 19.66W
SURRY (LOM/NDB)	SURR	NDB	330.0	44 32.34N	68 18.42W
SUZZE (LOM/NDB)	SUZZ	NDB	335.0	36 55.26N	81 14.54W
SWAN LAKE (LOM/ND	LKA	NDB	257.0	33 58.49N	117 33.13W
SWEARING	SEN	NDB	260.0	35 46.82N	80 17.90W
SWEDEN	SWU	NDB	350.0	43 25.94N	112 9.75W
SWEETWATER	SWW	NDB	275.0	32 27.70N	100 27.96W
SWIFT CURRENT	YYN	VOR	117.4	50 17.83N	107 41.46W
SYDNEY	QY	NDB	263.0	46 12.70N	59 58.54W
SYDNEY	YQY	VOR	114.9	46 9.21N	60 3.35W
SYLACAUGA	SCD	VOR	284.0	33 10.46N	86 19.09W
SYLVANIA	JYL	NDB	245.0	32 38.95N	81 35.62W
SYRACUSE	SYR	VOR	117.0	43 9.64N	76 12.27W
TABEY (LOM)	TABE	NDB	248.0	41 34.15N	81 34.42W
TABOGA ISLAND	TBG	VOR	110.0	8 47.14N	79 33.62W
TABOGA ISLAND	TBG	NDB	311.0	8 47.00N	79 34.00W
TACLOBAN	TAC	VOR	115.5	11 13.10N	125 1.70E
TAFFS (LOM)	TAFF	NDB	414.0	41 59.07N	87 47.34W
TAHITI	TAF	VOR	112.9	17 32.90S	149 36.10W
TAHLEQUAH	TQH	NDB	215.0	35 55.60N	95 0.35W
TAKOTNA RIVER	VTR	NDB	350.0	62 56.83N	155 33.44W
TALKEETNA	TKA	VOR	116.2	62 17.93N	150 6.33W
TALLADEGA	TDG	VOR	108.8	33 34.52N	86 2.56W
TALLAHALA	THJ	NDB	346.0	31 41.26N	89 11.39W
TALLAHASSEE	TLH	VOR	117.5	30 33.38N	84 22.44W
TALLULAH	TTT	NDB	344.0	32 24.76N	91 9.02W
TAMPICO	TAM	VOR	117.5	22 17.36N	97 51.77W
TANANA	TAL	VOR	116.6	65 10.64N	152 10.65W
TANGO	T	NDB	341.0	43 37.68N	79 43.87W
TANGO	T	NDB	263.0	43 23.76N	89 13.44W
TAOS	TAS	VOR	117.6	36 36.53N	105 54.38W
TAR RIVER	TYI	VOR	117.8	35 58.61N	77 42.22W
TARGY (LOM/NDB)	TARG	NDB	415.0	44 34.53N	111 11.85W
TARIO (LOM)	TARI	NDB	260.0	39 40.55N	94 54.42W
TATOOSH	TOU	VOR	112.2	48 18.00N	124 37.62W
TAUNTON	TAN	NDB	227.0	41 52.60N	71 1.02W
TAWBA (LOM/NDB)	TAWB	NDB	332.0	35 47.20N	81 18.34W
TAYLOR	TAY	VOR	112.9	30 30.29N	82 33.18W
TAYLOR COUNTY	TYC	NDB	272.0	37 24.12N	85 14.62W
TAYLORVILLE	TAZ	NDB	395.0	39 32.18N	89 19.42W
TECCO (LOM)	TECC	NDB	247.0	33 31.45N	93 54.36W
TECH	TEC	NDB	257.0	37 12.48N	80 24.72W
TECUMSEH	TCU	NDB	239.0	42 2.18N	83 52.83W
TEELS (LOM/NDB)	TEEL	NDB	242.0	42 54.55N	88 2.46W
TEGUCIGALPA	TGU	NDB	355.0	13 56.79N	87 14.87W
TEKAMAH	TQE	VOR	108.4	41 45.59N	96 10.72W
TELKWA	TK	NDB	391.0	54 40.19N	126 59.54W
TELL CITY	TEL	NDB	206.0	38 0.86N	86 41.41W
TEMPLE	TPL	VOR	110.4	31 12.57N	97 25.50W
TEOCK (LOM)	TEOC	NDB	349.0	33 35.52N	90 5.06W
TERRACE	XT	NDB	332.0	54 22.45N	128 34.99W
TERRACE BAY	YTJ	NDB	250.0	48 47.71N	87 9.70W
TERRE HAUTE	TTH	VOR	115.3	39 29.35N	87 14.94W
TESLIN	ZW	NDB	269.0	60 10.68N	132 44.21W

Name	Ident.	Type	Freq.	Latitude	Longitude
TETERBORO	TEB	VOR	108.4	40 50.93N	74 3.73W
TEXARKANA	TXK	VOR	116.3	33 30.84N	94 4.39W
TEXICO	TXO	VOR	112.2	34 29.72N	102 50.38W
THE PAS	YQD	VOR	113.6	53 58.43N	101 6.01W
THEDFORD	TDD	VOR	108.6	41 58.91N	100 43.14W
THERMAL	TRM	VOR	116.2	33 37.70N	116 9.61W
THETFORD MINES	R1	NDB	275.0	46 2.75N	71 16.07W
THIEF RIVER FALLS	TVF	VOR	108.4	48 4.17N	96 11.19W
THOMPSON-ROBBINS	HEE	NDB	251.0	34 34.28N	90 40.56W
THORNTON	TOT	NDB	281.0	39 53.60N	104 52.29W
THORP	BCY	VOR	212.0	36 45.33N	102 32.09W
THREE RIVERS	HAI	NDB	407.0	41 57.51N	85 35.50W
THREE RIVERS	THX	VOR	111.4	28 30.32N	98 9.07W
THUNDER BAY	QT	NDB	332.0	48 20.81N	89 26.02W
THUNDER BAY	YQT	VOR	114.1	48 15.24N	89 26.24W
THURMAN	TXC	VOR	112.9	39 41.91N	103 12.90W
THURSDAY ISLAND	HID	NDB	356.0	10 35.50S	142 17.60E
TIBBY	TBD	VOR	112.0	29 39.87N	90 49.74W
TIDIOUTE	TDT	VOR	117.6	41 42.79N	79 25.04W
TIFFIN	TII	NDB	269.0	41 5.90N	83 12.46W
TIFT MYERS	IFM	VOR	112.5	31 25.73N	83 29.33W
TIFTO	TM	NDB	409.0	31 21.80N	83 26.64W
TIGER PASS	VTP	NDB	253.0	29 16.31N	89 21.46W
TIJUANA	TIJ	VOR	116.5	32 32.07N	116 57.03W
TILGHMAN	CQB	NDB	396.0	35 43.34N	96 49.12W
TILLE (LOM)	TILL	NDB	346.0	38 50.84N	77 26.27W
TIMBER	BKU	NDB	344.0	46 21.76N	104 14.78W
TIMMERMAN	LJT	VOR	112.5	43 6.59N	88 2.24W
TIMMINS	TS	NDB	212.0	48 33.98N	81 27.18W
TIMMINS	YTS	NDB	113.0	48 34.33N	81 22.20W
TIN CITY	TNC	NDB	347.0	65 33.93N	167 54.53W
TINKER	TIK	VOR	115.8	35 26.19N	97 22.77W
TIVERTON	TVT	VOR	116.5	40 27.49N	82 7.61W
TIZAYUCA	TIZ	NDB	341.0	19 52.00N	98 59.00W
TOBE	TBE	VOR	115.8	37 15.53N	103 36.00W
TOCUMEN	TUM	VOR	117.1	9 3.00N	79 24.02W
TOFINO	YAZ	NDB	359.0	49 2.90N	125 42.35W
TOGIAK	TOG	NDB	393.0	59 3.85N	160 22.45W
TOLEDO	TDO	NDB	219.0	46 28.65N	122 48.54W
TOLSON	TSO	NDB	395.0	40 33.76N	81 4.86W
TOMBALL	TMZ	NDB	408.0	30 4.42N	95 33.34W
TOMHI (LOM)	TOMH	NDB	353.0	32 17.94N	99 40.45W
TOMMI (LOM/NDB)	TOMM	NDB	305.0	42 27.63N	96 27.73W
TOMOK (LOM)	TOMO	NDB	263.0	29 8.66N	81 8.86W
TOMOLTA	TTQ	NDB	335.0	35 7.00N	83 57.39W
TONCONTIN	TNT	NDB	405.0	14 3.57N	87 13.40W
TONEYVILLE	TYV	NDB	290.0	34 57.15N	92 1.16W
TONGA	TN	NDB	285.0	21 11.10S	175 13.10W
TONOPAH	TPH	VOR	117.2	38 1.85N	117 2.01W
TOOELE	TVY	NDB	371.0	40 36.46N	112 20.91W
TOPAN (LOM/NDB)	TOPA	NDB	305.0	33 21.93N	104 26.53W
TOPEKA	TOP	VOR	117.8	39 8.23N	95 32.95W
TOPHR (LOM)	TOPH	NDB	219.0	41 33.22N	83 55.27W
TOPSFIELD	TOF	NDB	269.0	42 37.17N	70 57.41W
TORBAY	YT	NDB	260.0	47 40.19N	52 48.51W
TORBAY	YYT	VOR	113.5	47 29.14N	52 51.14W
TORBY (LOM)	TORB	NDB	214.0	40 48.28N	74 7.95W
TORONTO	YYZ	VOR	113.3	43 40.95N	79 38.55W
TORRINGTON	TOR	NDB	293.0	42 3.97N	104 9.20W
TOTTE (LOM)	TOTT	NDB	227.0	44 43.66N	68 42.77W
TOWNSVILLE	TL	VOR	114.1	19 14.70S	146 45.50E
TRADEWATER	TWT	NDB	276.0	37 27.91N	87 56.92W
TRAIL	OFZ	NDB	388.0	34 46.89N	98 24.14W
TRAINER	TIQ	NDB	410.0	36 14.98N	88 24.92W
TRAVERSE CITY	TVC	VOR	114.6	44 40.08N	85 33.00W
TRAVIS	AVZ	NDB	299.0	32 45.62N	96 14.95W
TRAVIS	TZZ	VOR	116.4	38 20.66N	121 48.64W
TREASURE CAY	ZTC	VOR	112.9	26 44.09N	77 22.75W
TREASURE CAY	ZTC	NDB	233.0	26 44.09N	77 18.00W
TRENN (LOM)	TREN	NDB	369.0	40 12.77N	74 53.91W

Name	Ident.	Type	Freq.	Latitude	Longitude
TRENTON	5Y	NDB	338.0	45 36.72N	62 37.51W
TRENTON	TRX	NDB	400.0	40 4.83N	93 35.58W
TRENTON	YTR	NDB	215.0	44 11.63N	77 24.20W
TRI COUNTY	BKK	NDB	275.0	30 51.10N	85 36.08W
TRIBE (LOM)	TRIB	NDB	239.0	45 3.70N	87 41.76W
TRINA (LOM)	TRIN	NDB	353.0	46 10.54N	118 11.77W
TRINIDAD	TAD	NDB	329.0	37 18.37N	104 20.00W
TRINITY	MHF	VOR	113.6	29 32.79N	94 44.85W
TROIS-RIVIERES	YRQ	NDB	205.0	46 22.16N	72 39.91W
TROUT LAKE	7I	NDB	258.0	60 26.43N	121 14.51W
TROY	TOI	VOR	110.0	31 51.81N	86 0.66W
TROY	TOY	VOR	116.0	38 44.36N	89 55.12W
TROYES	TRO	VOR	116.0	48 15.11N	3 57.80E
TROYES	TY	NDB	320.5	48 24.01N	4 0.30E
TRUAX	NGP	VOR	114.0	27 41.18N	97 17.69W
TRUK	TKK	NDB	375.0	7 27.32N	151 50.24E
TRULY	ITU	NDB	371.0	47 21.96N	111 22.37W
TRUTH OR CONSEQ	TCS	VOR	112.7	33 16.96N	107 16.83W
TRYON (LOM)	TRYO	NDB	242.0	35 9.48N	81 1.21W
TUBA CITY	TBC	VOR	113.5	36 7.29N	111 16.17W
TUCSON	TUS	VOR	116.0	32 5.72N	110 54.89W
TUCUMCARI	TCC	VOR	113.6	35 10.94N	103 35.91W
TUKTOYAKTUK	UB	NDB	380.0	69 26.08N	133 1.03W
TULANCINGO	TCG	NDB	308.0	20 5.00N	98 22.00W
TULOO (LOM/NDB)	TULO	NDB	406.0	35 28.29N	97 36.33W
TULSA	TUL	VOR	114.4	36 11.78N	95 47.28W
TUNGG (LOM)	TUNG	NDB	356.0	40 36.35N	89 35.59W
TUNNG (LOM)	TUNN	NDB	426.0	34 23.10N	89 37.56W
TUPELO	TUP	VOR	109.8	34 13.44N	88 47.84W
TURKEY CREEK	UPK	NDB	251.0	32 29.04N	83 0.65W
TURNO (LOM)	TURN	NDB	266.0	44 50.86N	122 56.99W
TUSCALOOSA	TCL	VOR	117.8	33 15.54N	87 32.21W
TUSCOLA	TQA	VOR	111.6	32 14.15N	99 49.01W
TUSKE (LOM)	TUSK	NDB	362.0	33 9.50N	87 40.22W
TUSKEGEE	TGE	VOR	117.3	32 29.10N	85 40.16W
TUTTE (LOM)	TUTT	NDB	395.0	29 35.36N	95 20.42W
TWENTYNINE PALMS	TNP	VOR	114.2	34 6.74N	115 46.19W
TWIN FALLS	TWF	VOR	115.8	42 28.80N	114 29.37W
TWO HARBORS	TWM	NDB	243.0	47 3.14N	91 44.68W
TYHEE (LOM)	TYHE	NDB	383.0	42 57.83N	112 30.98W
TYLER	TYR	VOR	114.2	32 21.36N	95 24.21W
TYLER (LOM/NDB)	TYLE	NDB	320.0	32 24.95N	95 28.18W
TYRONE	TON	VOR	114.9	40 44.12N	78 19.88W
UCONN (LOM)	UCON	NDB	324.0	43 35.87N	111 58.86W
ULYSSES	ULS	NDB	395.0	37 35.86N	101 22.03W
UMIAT	UMT	NDB	360.0	69 22.19N	152 8.30W
UNALAKLEET	UNK	VOR	116.9	63 53.53N	160 41.06W
UNIFORM	U	NDB	201.0	45 27.26N	73 46.43W
UNION COUNTY	UNE	NDB	422.0	40 57.43N	94 20.76W
UNION COUNTY	UOT	NDB	326.0	34 41.05N	81 38.54W
UNITED	UTX	NDB	405.0	26 54.54N	98 24.00W
UNIVERSITY	UGS	NDB	250.0	39 15.44N	82 7.56W
UNIVERSITY OF ILLINOIS-W	I-CM	VOR	109.1	40 2.99N	88 17.32W
UPLANDS	YUP	NDB	352.0	45 13.76N	75 29.58W
UPOLU POINT	UPP	VOR	112.3	20 12.04N	155 50.60W
USTIK (LOM/NDB)	USTI	NDB	359.0	43 35.82N	116 18.93W
UTICA	UCA	VOR	111.2	43 1.60N	75 9.87W
UTOPIA CREEK	UTO	NDB	272.0	65 59.53N	153 43.27W
UVALDE	UVA	NDB	281.0	29 10.69N	99 43.54W
V C BIRD	ANU	VOR	114.5	17 7.60N	61 47.88W
V C BIRD	ANU	NDB	351.0	17 7.50N	61 48.60W
V C BIRD	ZDX	NDB	369.0	17 9.00N	61 47.00W
VAGEY (LOM)	VAGE	NDB	338.0	44 49.46N	93 18.36W
VAL-D'OR	VO	NDB	239.0	48 3.42N	77 47.60W
VAL-D'OR	YVO	VOR	113.7	48 10.53N	77 49.22W
VALDOSTA	OTK	VOR	114.8	30 46.83N	83 16.78W
VALENTINE	VTN	NDB	314.0	42 51.71N	100 32.98W
VALLEY	VYS	NDB	230.0	41 21.29N	89 8.89W
VALLEY CITY	VCY	NDB	382.0	46 52.66N	97 54.84W

Name	Ident.	Type	Freq.	Latitude	Longitude
VALLEY ISLAND	VYI	NDB	327.0	20 52.85N	156 26.56W
VALTR (LOM/NDB)	VALT	NDB	242.0	31 51.63N	106 19.06W
VAN HORN	VHN	NDB	233.0	31 3.72N	104 47.18W
VAN NUYS	I-VN	VOR	111.3	34 11.68N	118 29.34W
VAN NUYS	VNY	VOR	113.1	34 13.41N	118 29.50W
VANCE	END	VOR	115.4	36 20.74N	97 55.13W
VANCE	VAN	VOR	110.4	33 28.50N	80 26.92W
VANCOUVER	VR	NDB	266.0	49 10.38N	123 3.43W
VANCOUVER	YVR	VOR	115.9	49 4.65N	123 8.95W
VANDALIA	VLA	VOR	114.3	39 5.63N	89 9.75W
VARDER	UVR	NDB	272.0	23 5.40N	81 22.03W
VARNA (LOM)	VARN	NDB	266.0	42 25.81N	76 22.08W
VEALS (LOM)	VEAL	NDB	407.0	39 57.98N	88 10.95W
VEELS (LOM)	VEEL	NDB	410.0	32 27.34N	94 47.86W
VENICE	VEC	NDB	263.0	29 7.12N	89 12.34W
VENICE	VNC	NDB	206.0	27 3.69N	82 25.83W
VENTURA	VTU	VOR	108.2	34 6.91N	119 2.97W
VERMILLION	VMR	VOR	375.0	42 45.81N	96 56.07W
VERNAL	VEL	VOR	108.2	40 22.74N	109 29.60W
VERO BEACH	VEP	NDB	392.0	27 39.86N	80 25.17W
VERO BEACH	VRB	VOR	117.3	27 40.71N	80 29.38W
VERON (LOM)	VERO	NDB	420.0	34 10.82N	88 46.13W
VERONA	LUG	NDB	251.0	35 30.05N	86 48.62W
VERSAILLES	VES	NDB	356.0	40 12.38N	84 31.36W
VERSI (LOM)	VERS	NDB	388.0	39 15.26N	81 29.09W
VICCI (LOM)	VICC	NDB	219.0	38 7.61N	87 26.45W
VICHY	VIH	VOR	117.7	38 9.25N	91 42.41W
VICKSBURG	VKS	NDB	382.0	32 13.98N	90 55.59W
VICTOR	V	NDB	368.0	49 11.50N	123 13.18W
VICTORIA	VCT	VOR	109.0	28 54.03N	96 58.73W
VICTORIA	YJ	VOR	200.0	48 38.65N	123 23.97W
VICTORIA	YYJ	VOR	113.7	48 43.63N	123 29.06W
VICTORIAVILLE	F8	NDB	384.0	46 6.64N	71 55.62W
VIDFO (LOM/NDB)	VIDE	NDB	371.0	40 4.19N	85 30.65W
VIENNA	VNA	VOR	116.5	32 12.81N	83 29.84W
VIERTEL	VER	NDB	347.0	38 57.06N	92 41.38W
VILIA (LOM)	VILI	NDB	220.0	36 15.29N	119 18.88W
VILLACOUBLAY	HOL	NDB	315.0	48 43.91N	1 49.30E
VILLACOUBLAY	TA	NDB	286.5	48 46.31N	2 5.40E
VILLACOUBLAY	TH	NDB	302.0	48 46.71N	2 22.90E
VINCENNES	OEA	NDB	251.0	38 41.50N	87 33.32W
VINEE (LMM)	VINE	NDB	253.0	34 11.91N	118 22.67W
VINTON	VIT	NDB	277.0	37 12.25N	79 52.89W
VIOLE (LMM)	VIOL	NDB	356.0	42 23.36N	122 52.84W
VISALIA	VIS	VOR	109.4	36 22.05N	119 28.93W
VIVIAN	VIV	NDB	284.0	32 51.58N	94 0.61W
VOLUNTEER	VXV	VOR	116.4	35 54.30N	83 53.68W
VULCAN	VUZ	VOR	114.4	33 40.22N	86 53.99W
VULCAN	Z5	NDB	274.0	50 24.01N	113 16.92W
WABASH	IWH	NDB	329.0	40 45.83N	85 47.86W
WACO	ACT	VOR	115.3	31 39.75N	97 16.14W
WAGNER	AGZ	NDB	392.0	43 3.76N	98 17.54W
WAHOO	AHQ	NDB	400.0	41 14.36N	96 35.90W
WAIVS (LOM)	WAIV	NDB	248.0	41 18.68N	69 59.21W
WAKE ISLAND	AWK	VOR	113.5	19 17.95N	166 36.07E
WAKEFIELD	AKQ	NDB	274.0	36 59.00N	77 0.07W
WAKI	G8	NDB	327.0	46 16.11N	75 59.73W
WAKUL (LOM/NDB)	WAKU	NDB	379.0	30 19.58N	84 21.50W
WALCOTT	PZX	NDB	221.0	36 1.82N	90 35.82W
WALDA	WLD	VOR	112.8	48 34.81N	11 7.90E
WALLA WALLA	ALW	VOR	116.4	46 5.23N	118 17.55W
WALNUT RIDGE	ARG	VOR	114.5	36 6.61N	90 57.22W
WALTERBORO	RBW	NDB	221.0	32 55.56N	80 38.41W
WAMPA (LOM)	WAMP	NDB	344.0	34 47.87N	95 49.24W
WAPISK	YAT	NDB	260.0	52 55.83N	82 26.00W
WAPSIE	IIB	NDB	206.0	42 27.14N	91 57.06W
WARREN	REN	NDB	226.0	33 32.83N	92 5.76W
WARRI (LOM/NDB)	WARR	NDB	209.0	35 45.15N	85 45.85W
WARROAD	RAD	NDB	397.0	48 55.90N	95 20.42W
WASECA	ACQ	NDB	371.0	44 4.22N	93 33.15W
WASHINGTON	AWG	NDB	219.0	41 16.80N	91 40.37W
WASHINGTON	DCA	VOR	111.0	38 51.58N	77 2.18W
WASHINGTON	DCY	NDB	212.0	38 41.78N	87 7.95W
WASHINGTON CO	PNU	NDB	255.0	40 8.68N	80 9.75W
WASHINGTON-WILKE	IIY	NDB	435.0	33 46.50N	82 48.79W
WASKAGANISH	YKQ	NDB	351.0	51 29.23N	78 44.68W
WASSA (LOM)	WASS	NDB	335.0	32 0.25N	80 59.16W
WATERBURY	TBY	NDB	257.0	41 31.76N	73 8.63W
WATERLOO	ALO	VOR	112.2	42 33.40N	92 23.94W
WATERLOO	ATR	VOR	112.6	38 48.60N	75 12.68W
WATERLOO	YWT	VOR	115.0	43 27.53N	80 22.76W
WATERLOO-GUELPH R	K	NDB	335.0	43 29.56N	80 17.22W
WATERSMEET	RXW	NDB	407.0	46 17.31N	89 16.72W
WATERTOWN	ART	VOR	109.8	43 57.13N	76 3.88W
WATERTOWN	ATY	VOR	116.6	44 58.79N	97 8.51W
WATERVILLE	VWV	VOR	113.1	41 27.10N	83 38.32W
WATFORD CITY	AFD	NDB	400.0	47 47.90N	103 15.18W
WATON (LOM)	WATO	NDB	382.0	48 4.57N	122 9.24W
WATONGA	JWG	NDB	299.0	35 51.73N	98 25.52W
WATSON LAKE	QH	NDB	248.0	60 10.63N	128 50.75W
WATSON LAKE	YQH	VOR	114.9	60 5.20N	128 51.47W
WAUKE (LOM)	WAUK	NDB	379.0	42 27.85N	87 48.09W
WAUKESHA	UES	NDB	359.0	43 2.69N	88 14.11W
WAUKON	UKN	VOR	116.6	43 16.80N	91 32.24W
WAUPACA	PCZ	NDB	382.0	44 19.94N	89 0.99W
WAUSAU	AUW	VOR	111.6	44 50.82N	89 35.19W
WAVERLY	AEY	NDB	329.0	36 6.98N	87 44.48W
WAWA	XZ	NDB	205.0	48 1.31N	84 44.83W
WAWA	YXZ	VOR	112.7	47 57.05N	84 49.38W
WAYCROSS	AYS	VOR	110.2	31 16.17N	82 33.39W
WAYNE	LCG	NDB	389.0	42 14.16N	96 59.15W
WAYNE (LOM/NDB)	JYN	NDB	208.0	35 31.57N	77 54.07W
WAYNE COUNTY	FWC	NDB	257.0	38 22.81N	88 24.59W
WEARR (LOM)	WEAR	NDB	230.0	64 54.00N	147 42.43W
WEATHERFORD	OJA	NDB	272.0	35 31.81N	98 40.24W
WEBSTER CITY	EBS	NDB	323.0	42 26.49N	93 52.15W
WEISER	EYQ	NDB	286.0	29 56.04N	95 38.46W
WELLINGTON	EGT	NDB	414.0	37 19.44N	97 23.37W
WELLS	LWL	VOR	114.2	41 8.70N	114 58.65W
WELLSVILLE	ELZ	VOR	111.4	42 5.39N	77 59.97W
WENATCHEE	EAT	VOR	111.0	47 23.99N	120 12.65W
WENTWORTH	MDS	NDB	400.0	44 0.84N	97 5.30W
WENZ	PNA	VOR	392.0	42 47.83N	109 48.21W
WESIE (LOM)	WESI	NDB	230.0	42 14.91N	72 41.78W
WESLEY	TWL	NDB	204.0	34 57.18N	80 42.31W
WESSELS	ESS	NDB	260.0	59 25.61N	146 20.59W
WEST BEND	BJB	VOR	109.8	43 25.33N	88 7.52W
WEST BRANCH	BXZ	VOR	113.2	44 14.57N	84 11.01W
WEST END	ZWE	NDB	317.0	26 41.01N	78 59.00W
WEST MEMPHIS	AWM	NDB	362.0	35 8.45N	90 13.97W
WEST UNION	AMT	VOR	359.0	38 51.36N	83 33.83W
WEST UNION	XWY	NDB	278.0	42 56.64N	91 46.94W
WEST WOODWARD	OWU	NDB	329.0	36 20.07N	99 31.45W
WESTERLY	RLS	NDB	264.0	41 20.68N	71 48.86W
WESTMINSTER	EMI	VOR	117.9	39 29.71N	76 58.71W
WESTOVER	CEF	VOR	114.0	42 11.86N	72 31.58W
WHARTON	ARM	NDB	245.0	29 15.24N	96 9.30W
WHEATON	ETH	NDB	326.0	45 47.01N	96 32.81W
WHEELER	HHI	NDB	373.0	21 28.49N	158 1.85W
WHEELING	HLG	VOR	112.2	40 15.60N	80 34.12W
WHINE	VJ	NDB	236.0	36 44.05N	81 56.96W
WHITE CLOUD	HIC	VOR	117.6	43 34.50N	85 42.97W
WHITE COUNTY	MCX	NDB	377.0	40 42.63N	86 45.73W
WHITE LAKE	LLA	VOR	111.4	29 39.80N	92 22.42W
WHITE RIVER	IVV	NDB	379.0	43 33.62N	72 27.93W
WHITE ROCK	WC	NDB	332.0	49 0.22N	122 45.01W
WHITEHALL	HIA	VOR	113.7	45 51.72N	112 10.18W
WHITEHORSE	XY	NDB	302.0	60 46.38N	135 6.31W
WHITEHORSE	YXY	VOR	116.6	60 37.14N	135 8.35W
WHITESIDE	BOZ	NDB	254.0	41 42.68N	89 47.13W

Name	Ident.	Type	Freq.	Latitude	Longitude
WHITFIELD	UWI	NDB	400.0	34 47.38N	84 56.76W
WHITNEY	HIN	NDB	275.0	42 49.74N	103 5.63W
WHT SULPHUR SPRNG	SSU	VOR	108.4	37 45.84N	80 18.10W
WIARTON	VV	NDB	326.0	44 41.89N	81 10.78W
WIARTON	YVV	VOR	117.7	44 44.70N	81 6.32W
WICHITA	ICT	VOR	113.8	37 44.72N	97 35.03W
WICHITA FALLS	SPS	VOR	112.7	33 59.24N	98 35.61W
WIGGINS	GDW	NDB	209.0	43 58.21N	84 28.50W
WILBARGER	VRT	NDB	230.0	34 13.56N	99 16.75W
WILCOX	VLX	NDB	348.0	35 52.06N	92 5.68W
WILCOX CO	IWE	NDB	350.0	31 58.83N	87 20.22W
WILDHORSE	ILR	VOR	113.8	43 35.60N	118 57.30W
WILDWOOD	IWW	NDB	379.0	60 35.94N	151 12.67W
WILEY	IEY	NDB	248.0	71 17.14N	156 48.51W
WILEY POST	PWA	VOR	113.4	35 31.98N	97 38.83W
WILKES BARRE	AVP	VOR	111.6	41 16.38N	75 41.37W
WILKI (LOM/NDB)	WILK	NDB	209.0	36 6.78N	81 5.00W
WILL ROGERS	IRW	VOR	114.1	35 21.52N	97 36.55W
WILLARD	ILJ	NDB	254.0	37 17.97N	93 26.45W
WILLIAM POGUE	OWP	NDB	362.0	36 10.01N	96 9.02W
WILLIAMS	ILA	VOR	114.4	39 4.28N	122 1.63W
WILLIAMS	MWX	NDB	257.0	44 7.24N	72 31.10W
WILLIAMS LAKE	YWL	VOR	113.6	52 14.24N	122 10.13W
WILLIAMSPORT	IPT	VOR	114.4	41 20.32N	76 46.49W
WILLIAMSTON	MCZ	NDB	336.0	35 51.55N	77 10.68W
WILLIE	IWA	VOR	113.3	33 18.20N	111 39.09W
WILLISTON	ISN	VOR	116.3	48 15.22N	103 45.04W
WILLISTON	ISN	NDB	275.0	48 8.76N	103 35.03W
WILLMAR	ILL	VOR	113.7	45 7.06N	95 5.45W
WILLOW	DWL	NDB	353.0	40 52.38N	100 4.36W
WILLOW GROVE(NAV)	NXX	NDB	388.0	40 11.36N	75 8.72W
WILMINGTON	ILM	VOR	117.0	34 21.10N	77 52.46W
WILSON	TKW	NDB	271.0	45 29.10N	123 51.38W
WILSON CREEK	ILC	VOR	116.3	38 15.02N	114 23.65W
WINAMAC	RWN	NDB	335.0	41 5.64N	86 36.27W
WINCHESTER	AWW	NDB	212.0	40 10.10N	84 55.31W
WINDOM	MWM	NDB	203.0	43 54.57N	95 6.55W
WINDOW ROCK	AWR	NDB	254.0	35 39.88N	109 4.09W
WINDSOR	QG	NDB	353.0	42 18.78N	82 52.11W
WINDSOR	YQG	VOR	113.8	42 15.00N	82 49.73W
WINK	INK	VOR	112.1	31 52.49N	103 14.62W
WINNEMUCCA	EMC	NDB	375.0	40 57.80N	117 50.49W
WINNEMUCCA	INA	VOR	108.2	40 53.97N	117 48.74W
WINNER	ISD	VOR	112.8	43 29.28N	99 45.68W
WINNFIELD	IFJ	NDB	402.0	31 57.78N	92 39.42W
WINNIPEG	WG	NDB	248.0	49 53.96N	97 20.95W
WINNIPEG	YWG	VOR	115.5	49 55.68N	97 14.35W
WINNSBORO	FDW	NDB	414.0	34 18.87N	81 6.76W
WINONA	ONA	VOR	111.4	44 4.58N	91 42.34W
WINSLOW	INW	VOR	112.6	35 3.70N	110 47.70W
WINTERS	IEW	NDB	396.0	31 57.22N	99 59.02W
WIREGRASS	RRS	VOR	111.6	31 17.07N	85 25.88W
WIREY (LOM)	WIRE	NDB	227.0	27 56.13N	82 4.55W
WISCASSET	ISS	NDB	407.0	43 58.96N	69 38.42W
WISCONSIN RAPIDS	ISW	NDB	215.0	44 21.85N	89 50.39W
WISLE (LOM/NDB)	WISL	NDB	248.0	30 45.65N	88 18.17W
WIZER (LOM/NDB)	WIZE	NDB	223.0	35 21.26N	94 13.03W
WOLBACH	OBH	VOR	114.8	41 22.55N	98 21.21W
WOLF LAKE	OLK	VOR	110.4	41 14.82N	85 29.84W
WOLF POINT	OLF	NDB	404.0	48 6.28N	105 36.11W
WOOD RIVER	BTS	NDB	429.0	58 59.99N	158 32.90W
WOODRING	ODG	VOR	109.0	36 22.43N	97 47.29W
WOODRUFF	RUF	NDB	236.0	45 50.08N	89 43.83W
WOODRUM	ODR	VOR	114.9	37 19.46N	79 58.74W
WOODSIDE	OSI	VOR	113.9	37 23.56N	122 16.88W
WOODSTOWN	OOD	VOR	112.8	39 38.17N	75 18.18W
WOODVILLE	LLW	NDB	254.0	36 15.79N	76 17.87W
WOODY ISLAND	RWO	NDB	394.0	57 46.48N	152 19.39W
WOOLE (LOM)	WOOL	NDB	356.0	31 16.79N	100 34.57W
WORLAND	RLY	VOR	114.8	43 57.86N	107 57.05W

Name	Ident.	Type	Freq.	Latitude	Longitude
WORTHINGTON	OTG	VOR	110.6	43 38.82N	95 34.92W
WOWAR (LOM)	WOWA	NDB	367.0	37 34.39N	120 51.31W
WRANGELL	RGL	NDB	206.0	56 29.23N	132 23.26W
WRIGHT BROTHERS	RBX	VOR	111.6	35 55.24N	75 41.81W
WRIGLEY	WY	NDB	222.0	63 12.79N	123 25.77W
WRIGLEY	YWY	VOR	113.1	63 11.05N	123 21.73W
WYNDS (LOM/NDB)	WYND	NDB	269.0	29 40.22N	82 10.34W
XENIA	XEN	NDB	395.0	39 42.91N	83 55.80W
XRAY	X	NDB	385.0	43 44.30N	79 34.29W
XRAY	X	NDB	353.0	60 38.18N	135 0.65W
YAKATAGA	CYT	NDB	209.0	60 5.18N	142 29.32W
YAKIMA	YKM	VOR	116.0	46 34.23N	120 26.68W
YAKUTAT	YAK	VOR	113.3	59 30.66N	139 38.88W
YANKEE	Y	NDB	404.0	46 19.83N	79 31.49W
YANKS (LOM/NDB)	YANK	NDB	260.0	43 3.61N	87 52.60W
YANKTON	YKN	VOR	111.4	42 55.11N	97 23.10W
YAP	YP	NDB	317.0	9 29.82N	138 5.78E
YARDLEY	ARD	VOR	108.2	40 15.21N	74 54.45W
YARMOUTH	QI	NDB	206.0	43 47.61N	66 7.57W
YARMOUTH	YQI	VOR	113.3	43 49.51N	66 4.95W
YAUPON	SUT	NDB	233.0	33 55.67N	78 4.50W
YELLOW BUD	XUB	VOR	112.5	39 31.61N	82 58.67W
YELLOWKNIFE	YZF	VOR	115.5	62 27.87N	114 26.20W
YELLOWSTONE	ESY	NDB	338.0	44 41.39N	111 7.27W
YINNO (LOM/NDB)	YINN	NDB	245.0	39 23.28N	87 23.86W
YIPPS (LOM)	YIPP	NDB	359.0	42 10.46N	83 37.29W
YOAKUM	OKT	NDB	350.0	29 18.77N	97 8.32W
YORK	EUD	NDB	285.0	39 55.21N	76 52.65W
YORK	JYR	NDB	257.0	40 53.86N	97 37.02W
YORK	YRK	VOR	112.8	38 38.66N	82 58.70W
YORKTON	QV	NDB	385.0	51 12.98N	102 32.51W
YORKTON	YQV	VOR	115.8	51 15.86N	102 28.13W
YOUNGSTOWN	YNG	VOR	109.0	41 19.87N	80 40.48W
YUKON RIVER	FTO	NDB	242.0	66 34.82N	145 12.77W
YUSON (LOM)	YUSO	NDB	275.0	48 7.10N	103 30.69W
ZANESVILLE	ZZV	VOR	111.4	39 56.46N	81 53.56W
ZANESVILLE	ZZV	NDB	204.0	39 54.39N	81 55.16W
ZEBRE (LOM/NDB)	ZEBR	NDB	347.0	39 26.49N	88 10.39W
ZEPHYR	ZEF	NDB	326.0	36 18.80N	80 43.40W
ZEPHYRHILLS	RHZ	NDB	253.0	28 13.42N	82 9.69W
ZILOM (LOM)	ZILO	NDB	341.0	42 19.39N	90 35.94W
ZIONSVILLE	HZP	NDB	248.0	39 56.39N	86 14.98W
ZODIA (LOM)	ZODI	NDB	407.0	38 43.00N	92 16.11W
ZUMAY (LOM)	ZUMA	NDB	404.0	38 47.29N	90 16.73W
ZUNI	ZUN	VOR	113.4	34 57.95N	109 9.27W

VOR/NDBs for the Western Pacific, Including Alaska, Parts of Canada, Hawaii, and Pacific Islands From 130°W to 180°W.

Name	Ident.	Type	Freq.	Latitude	Longitude
ADAK, Alaska	NUD	NDB	347.0	51 55.03N	176 34.01W
AITUTAKI, Cook Islands, New Zealand	AI	NDB	320.0		
18 49.40S	159 46.60W				
AKLAVIK, Canada	YKD	NDB	0.0	68 13.64N	135 0.59W
AMBLER, Alaska	AMF	NDB	403.0	67 6.42N	157 51.48W
ANADYR, Russia	KB	NDB	790.0	64 44.01N	177 45.00W
ANCHORAGE, Alaska	ANC	VOR	114.3	61 9.06N	150 12.39W
ANIAK, Alaska	ANI	NDB	359.0	61 35.42N	159 35.87W
ANNETTE ISLAND, Alaska	ANN	VOR	117.1	55 3.64N	131 34.70W

Name	Ident.	Type	Freq.	Latitude	Longitude
ANVIK, Alaska	ANV	NDB	365.0	62 38.50N	160 11.40W
APOLLO, Johnston Atoll	APO	NDB	388.0	16 43.60N	169 32.80W
ATLIN, Alaska	YSQ	NDB	260.0	59 37.85N	133 40.52W
BARROW, Alaska	BRW	VOR	116.2	71 16.42N	156 47.28W
BARTER ISLAND, Alaska	BTI	NDB	308.0	70 7.86N	143 38.63W
BEAR CREEK, Alaska	BCC	NDB	212.0	65 10.45N	152 12.36W
BEAVER CREEK, Alaska	YXQ	NDB	239.0	62 24.54N	140 51.70W
BETHEL, Alaska	BET	VOR	114.1	60 47.10N	161 49.46W
BETHEL (LMM), Alaska	ET	NDB	344.0	60 47.81N	161 49.28W
BETTLES, Alaska	BTT	VOR	116.0	66 54.31N	151 32.15W
BIG DELTA, Alaska	BIG	VOR	114.9	64 0.28N	145 43.03W
BIG LAKE, Alaska	BGQ	VOR	112.5	61 34.18N	149 58.03W
BIORKA ISLAND, Alaska	BKA	VOR	113.8	56 51.58N	135 33.08W
BISHOP, Alaska	BZP	NDB	371.0	64 44.26N	156 48.53W
BORLAND, Alaska	HBT	NDB	390.0	55 18.95N	160 31.10W
BRADSHAW, Hawaii	BSF	NDB	339.0	19 45.64N	155 35.68W
BROWERVILLE, Alaska	VIR	NDB	281.0	71 16.97N	156 47.08W
BRUCK (LOM), Alaska	BRUC	NDB	387.0	61 10.07N	150 10.62W
BUCKLAND, Alaska	BVK	NDB	325.0	65 58.80N	161 8.96W
BURWASH, Alaska	DB	NDB	341.0	61 20.43N	138 59.01W
CAIRN MOUNTAIN, Alaska	CRN	NDB	281.0	61 5.97N	155 33.14W
CAMPBELL LAKE, Alaska	CMQ	NDB	338.0	61 10.27N	150 2.86W
CAPE LISBURNE, Alaska	LUR	NDB	385.0	68 51.97N	166 4.18W
CAPE NEWENHAM, Alaska	EHM	NDB	385.0	58 39.36N	162 4.55W
CAPE ROMANZOF, Alaska	CZF	NDB	275.0	61 47.45N	165 58.17W
CENTRAL, Alaska	CEM	NDB	373.0	65 34.41N	144 47.65W
CHANDALAR LAKE, Alaska	CQR	NDB	263.0	67 30.16N	148 28.16W
CHENA, Alaska	CUN	NDB	257.0	64 50.31N	147 29.39W
CLAM COVE, Alaska	CMJ	NDB	396.0	55 20.74N	131 41.79W
COGHLAN ISLAND	CGL	NDB	212.0	58 21.57N	134 41.96W
COLD BAY, Alaska	CDB	VOR	112.6	55 16.06N	162 46.46W
DAWSON, Canada	DA	NDB	214.0	64 1.75N	139 10.08W
DEADHORSE, Alaska	SCC	VOR	113.9	70 11.97N	148 24.97W
DELTA JUNCTION, Alaska	DJN	NDB	347.0	64 1.42N	145 41.21W
DILLINGHAM, Alaska	DLG	VOR	116.4	58 59.67N	158 33.13W
DRIFT RIVER, Alaska	DRF	NDB	368.0	60 35.65N	152 8.55W
DUTCH HARBOR, Alaska	DUT	NDB	283.0	53 54.32N	166 32.95W
EAGLE, Alaska	EAA	NDB	519.0	64 46.68N	141 8.44W
EAST KUPURA, Alaska	ACU	NDB	268.0	68 50.42N	153 18.96W
EIELSON, Alaska	EAF	VOR	117.0	64 34.17N	147 0.96W
ELEPHANT	EEF	NDB	391.0	58 10.27N	135 15.48W
ELFEE (LOM/NDB), Alaska	ELFE	NDB	341.0	55 17.78N	162 47.34W
EMMONAK, Alaska	ENM	VOR	117.8	62 47.02N	164 29.26W
ENGLISH BAY, Alaska	EGY	NDB	374.0	57 7.45N	170 16.34W
EVANSVILLE, Alaska	EAV	NDB	391.0	66 53.61N	151 33.83W
EWABE (LOM/NDB), Hawaii	EWAB	NDB	242.0	21 19.50N	158 2.93W
FAIRBANKS, Alaska	FAI	VOR	108.2	64 48.02N	148 0.72W
FAREWELL LAKE, Alaska	FXW	NDB	412.0	62 32.60N	153 37.19W
FARO, Canada	ZFA	NDB	378.0	62 12.73N	133 23.22W
FIN CREEK, Alaska	FNK	NDB	320.0	69 29.91N	147 35.59W
FIVE MILE, Alaska	FVM	NDB	312.0	65 55.04N	149 49.84W
FORT DAVIS, Alaska	FDV	NDB	529.0	64 29.69N	165 18.84W
FORT MCPHERSON, Canada	ZFM	NDB	373.0	67 24.61N	134 52.31W
FORT RICHARDSON, Alaska	FRN	NDB	196.0	61 16.60N	149 38.94W
FORT YUKON, Alaska	FYU	VOR	114.4	66 34.47N	145 16.60W
FOX, Alaska	FOX	NDB	356.0	64 58.16N	147 34.80W
FREDERICKS POINT	FPN	NDB	372.0	56 47.55N	132 49.25W
GALBRAITH LAKE, Alaska	GBH	NDB	417.0	68 28.76N	149 29.91W

Name	Ident.	Type	Freq.	Latitude	Longitude
GALENA, Alaska	GAL	VOR	114.8	64 44.30N	156 46.63W
GAMBELL, Alaska	GAM	NDB	369.0	63 46.94N	171 44.20W
GLACIER RIVER, Alaska	GCR	NDB	404.0	60 29.94N	145 28.47W
GLENNALLEN, Alaska	GLA	NDB	248.0	62 11.74N	145 28.08W
GOLD, Alaska	OYN	NDB	208.0	64 30.78N	165 26.00W
GRANITE POINT, Alaska	GRP	NDB	356.0	60 57.70N	151 20.04W
GULKANA, Alaska	GKN	VOR	115.6	62 9.16N	145 27.02W
GUSTAVUS, Alaska	GAV	NDB	219.0	58 25.33N	135 42.28W
HAINES, Alaska	HNS	NDB	245.0	59 12.74N	135 25.85W
HILO, Hawaii	ITO	VOR	116.9	19 43.29N	155 0.66W
HINCHINBROOK, Alaska	HBK	NDB	362.0	60 23.66N	146 5.42W
HOMER, Alaska	HOM	VOR	114.6	59 42.58N	151 28.40W
HONOLULU, Hawaii	HNL	VOR	114.8	21 18.50N	157 55.83W
HOOPER BAY, Alaska	HPB	VOR	115.2	61 30.89N	166 8.07W
HOTHAM, Alaska	HHM	NDB	356.0	66 54.09N	162 33.86W
HUSLIA, Alaska	HSL	VOR	117.4	65 42.38N	156 22.24W
ICE POOL, Alaska	ICW	NDB	525.0	64 32.76N	149 4.61W
IGNEK, Alaska	CNR	NDB	209.0	69 35.70N	146 29.72W
ILIAMNA, Alaska	ILI	NDB	328.0	59 44.89N	154 54.58W
INUVIK, Canada	YEV	VOR	112.5	68 18.49N	133 32.90W
INUVIK, Canada	EV	NDB	254.0	68 19.58N	133 35.57W
IVISHAK, Alaska	IVH	NDB	379.0	69 24.15N	148 16.19W
JOHNSTONE POINT, Alaska	JOH	VOR	116.7	60 28.87N	146 35.96W
KACHEMAK, Alaska	ACE	NDB	277.0	59 38.49N	151 30.01W
KAMUELA, Hawaii	MUE	VOR	113.3	19 59.89N	155 40.19W
KANEOHE BAY, Hawaii	NGF	NDB	265.0	21 27.11N	157 45.20W
KENAI, Alaska	ENA	VOR	117.6	60 36.90N	151 11.71W
KING SALMON, Alaska	AKN	VOR	112.8	58 43.49N	156 45.13W
KIPNUK, Alaska	IIK	VOR	115.9	59 56.58N	164 2.06W
KODIAK, Alaska	ODK	VOR	117.1	57 46.51N	152 20.39W
KOKO HEAD, Hawaii	CKH	VOR	113.9	21 15.91N	157 42.18W
KOMAKK	AJ	NDB	239.0	69 35.70N	140 11.01W
KONA, Hawaii	IAI	VOR	115.7	19 39.27N	156 1.49W
KOTZEBUE, Alaska	OTZ	VOR	115.7	66 53.15N	162 32.40W
KOYUK, Alaska	KKA	NDB	299.0	64 55.93N	161 8.87W
KUKULIAK, Alaska	ULL	VOR	117.3	63 41.55N	170 28.20W
KULIK LAKE, Alaska	HCP	NDB	334.0	59 1.08N	155 36.02W
KUPARUK, Alaska	UUK	NDB	218.0	70 17.06N	149 8.35W
LABERGE, Canada	JB	NDB	236.0	60 56.95N	135 8.26W
LANAI, Hawaii	LNY	NDB	117.7	20 45.87N	156 58.13W
LANAI, Hawaii	LLD	NDB	353.0	20 46.70N	156 57.98W
LEVEL ISLAND, Alaska	LVD	VOR	116.5	56 28.08N	133 4.99W
LIHUE, Hawaii	LIH	VOR	113.5	21 57.92N	159 20.29W
LOGOTALA HILL, American Samoa	LOG	NDB	242.0	14 21.53S	170 44.86W
MASSET	1U	NDB	278.0	54 1.91N	132 7.63W
MAUI, Hawaii	OGG	VOR	114.3	20 53.93N	156 25.91W
MAYO, Canada	MA	NDB	365.0	63 37.74N	135 53.59W
MC GRATH, Alaska	MCG	VOR	115.5	62 57.07N	155 36.68W
MENDENHALL, Canada	MND	NDB	332.0	58 21.54N	134 38.02W
MIDDLETON ISLAND, Alaska	MDO	VOR	115.3	59 25.32N	146 21.00W
MINCHUMINA, Alaska	MHM	NDB	227.0	63 53.05N	152 18.99W
MINERAL CREEK, Alaska	MNL	NDB	524.0	61 7.47N	146 21.13W
MOLOKAI, Hawaii	MKK	VOR	116.1	21 8.29N	157 10.04W
MOSES POINT, Alaska	MOS	VOR	116.3	64 41.81N	162 4.27W
MT EDGECUMBE, Alaska	IME	NDB	414.0	57 2.87N	135 22.02W
NABESNA, Alaska	AES	NDB	390.0	62 57.96N	141 53.30W
NANWAK, Alaska	AIX	NDB	323.0	60 23.11N	166 12.89W
NENANA, Alaska	ENN	VOR	115.8	64 35.41N	149 4.37W
NICHOLS, Canada	ICK	NDB	266.0	55 4.26N	131 36.30W
NIUE, Tonga, Samoa Islands	NU	NDB	345.0	19 4.10S	169 54.60W
NOATAK, Alaska	OQK	NDB	414.0	67 34.33N	162 58.43W
NOME, Alaska	OME	VOR	115.0	64 29.12N	165 15.19W
NORTH RIVER, Alaska	JNR	NDB	382.0	63 54.48N	160 48.72W
NORTHWAY, Alaska	ORT	VOR	116.3	62 56.84N	141 54.77W
NORTON BAY, Alaska	OAY	NDB	263.0	64 41.78N	162 3.77W
OCEAN CAPE, Alaska	OCC	NDB	385.0	59 32.63N	139 43.69W

Name	Ident.	Type	Freq.	Latitude	Longitude
OLD CROW, Canada	YOC	NDB	284.0	67 34.28N	139 50.78W
OLIKTOK, Alaska	OLI	NDB	329.0	70 29.82N	149 53.39W
OSCARVILLE, Alaska	OSE	NDB	251.0	60 47.49N	161 52.36W
PAGO PAGO, West Samoa	TUT	VOR	112.5	14 20.26S	170 42.42W
PAGO PAGO, American Samoa	TUT	NDB	403.0	14 20.22S	170 43.08W
PAHOA, Hawaii	POA	NDB	332.0	19 32.47N	154 58.33W
PAPA, Canada	P	NDB	350.0	54 18.33N	130 27.75W
PETERS CREEK, Alaska	PEE	NDB	305.0	62 19.88N	150 5.78W
PITSAND, Alaska	PYC	NDB	290.0	70 19.70N	149 38.12W
POINT HOPE, Alaska	PHO	NDB	221.0	68 20.71N	166 47.85W
POINT LAY, Alaska	PIZ	NDB	347.0	69 44.08N	163 0.81W
PORT HEIDEN, Alaska	PDN	NDB	371.0	56 57.25N	158 38.93W
PRINCE RUPERT, Canada	PR	NDB	218.0	54 15.81N	130 25.43W
PROSPECT CREEK, Alaska	PPC	NDB	340.0	66 49.07N	150 38.04W
PROVIDENIYA, Russia	BC	NDB	320.0	64 17.51N	173 19.00W
PRUDHOE BAY, Alaska	PUO	NDB	368.0	70 14.92N	148 23.65W
PUNTILLA LAKE, Alaska	PTI	NDB	397.0	62 4.41N	152 43.99W
PUT RIVER, Alaska	PVQ	NDB	234.0	70 13.40N	148 25.03W
QUINHAGAK, Alaska	AQH	VOR	114.7	59 45.10N	161 53.42W
RANGIROA, Tahiti	RAN	VOR	112.3	14 56.90S	147 41.00W
RAROTONGA, Cook Islands	RG	VOR	113.5	21 11.80S	159 48.90W
RAZER (LMM/NDB), Alaska	RAZE	NDB	215.0	58 41.43N	156 40.69W
REEVE, Alaska	SNP	NDB	362.0	57 9.11N	170 13.52W
ROBINSON, Canada	PJ	NDB	329.0	60 26.38N	134 51.68W
ROSS RIVER, Canada	YDM	NDB	218.0	61 58.42N	132 25.62W
SALDO (LOM/NDB), Alaska	SALD	NDB	400.0	58 44.26N	156 46.67W
SANDSPIT, Canada	YZP	VOR	114.1	53 15.15N	131 48.42W
SANDSPIT, Canada	Z	NDB	248.0	53 21.01N	131 56.49W
SANDSPIT, Canada	ZP	NDB	368.0	53 11.80N	131 46.65W
SELAWIK, Alaska	WLK	VOR	114.2	66 36.01N	159 59.49W
SHEEP MOUNTAIN, Alaska	SMU	NDB	221.0	61 47.25N	147 40.70W
SHINGE POINT, Canada	UA	NDB	226.0	68 55.39N	137 15.75W
SHISHMAREF, Alaska	SHH	NDB	365.0	66 15.50N	166 3.15W
SISTERS ISLAND, Alaska	SSR	VOR	114.0	58 10.67N	135 15.53W
SITKA, Alaska	SIT	NDB	358.0	56 51.29N	135 32.06W
SKWENTNA, Alaska	SKW	NDB	269.0	61 57.98N	151 12.09W
SLATE CREEK, Alaska	SLX	NDB	280.0	64 33.74N	142 30.97W
SLEETMUTE, Alaska	SLQ	NDB	406.0	61 41.98N	157 9.78W
SOLDOTNA, Alaska	OLT	NDB	346.0	60 28.51N	150 52.73W
SOUTH KAUAI, Hawaii	SOK	VOR	115.4	21 54.03N	159 31.73W
SPARREVOHN, Alaska	SQA	VOR	117.2	61 5.92N	155 38.07W
ST GEORGE, Alaska	SGG	NDB	201.0	56 36.29N	169 32.51W
ST MARYS, Alaska	SMA	NDB	230.0	62 3.52N	163 17.50W
SUMMIT, Alaska	UMM	NDB	326.0	63 19.70N	149 7.84W
SUMNER STRAIT, Alaska	SQM	NDB	529.0	56 27.89N	133 5.84W
TAHITI, French Polynesia	TAF	VOR	112.9	17 32.90S	149 36.10W
TAKOTNA RIVER, Alaska	VTR	NDB	350.0	62 56.83N	155 33.44W
TALKEETNA, Alaska	TKA	VOR	116.2	62 17.93N	150 6.33W
TANANA, Alaska	TAL	NDB	116.6	65 10.64N	152 10.65W
TESLIN, Canada	ZW	NDB	269.0	60 10.68N	132 44.21W
TIN CITY, Alaska	TNC	NDB	347.0	65 33.93N	167 54.53W
TOGIAK, Alaska	TOG	NDB	393.0	59 3.85N	160 22.45W
TONGA, Samoa Islands	TN	NDB	285.0	21 11.10S	175 13.10W
TUKTOYAKTUK, Canada	UB	NDB	380.0	69 26.08N	133 1.03W
UMIAT, Alaska	UMT	NDB	360.0	69 22.19N	152 8.30W
UNALAKLEET, Alaska	UNK	VOR	116.9	63 53.53N	160 41.06W
UPOLU POINT, Hawaii	UPP	VOR	112.3	20 12.04N	155 50.60W
UTOPIA CREEK, Alaska	UTO	NDB	272.0	65 59.53N	153 43.27W
VALLEY ISLAND, Hawaii	VYI	NDB	327.0	20 52.85N	156 26.56W
WEARR (LOM), Alaska	WEAR	NDB	230.0	64 54.00N	147 42.43W
WESSELS, Alaska	ESS	NDB	260.0	59 25.61N	146 20.59W

Name	Ident.	Type	Freq.	Latitude	Longitude
WHEELER, Hawaii	HHI	NDB	373.0	21 28.49N	158 1.85W
WHITEHORSE, Canada	YXY	VOR	116.6	60 37.14N	135 8.35W
WHITEHORSE, Canada	XY	NDB	302.0	60 46.38N	135 6.31W
WILDWOOD, Alaska	IWW	NDB	379.0	60 35.94N	151 12.67W
WILEY, Alaska	IEY	NDB	248.0	71 17.14N	156 48.51W
WOOD RIVER, Alaska	BTS	NDB	429.0	58 59.99N	158 32.90W
WOODY ISLAND, Alaska	RWO	NDB	394.0	57 46.48N	152 19.39W
WRANGELL, Alaska	RGL	NDB	206.0	56 29.23N	132 23.26W
XRAY, Canada	X	NDB	353.0	60 38.18N	135 0.65W
YAKATAGA, Alaska	CYT	NDB	209.0	60 5.18N	142 29.32W
YAKUTAT, Alaska	YAK	VOR	113.3	59 30.66N	139 38.88W
YUKON RIVER, Alaska	FTO	NDB	242.0	66 34.82N	145 12.77W

VOR/NDBs for the Eastern Pacific Including Parts of Japan, Australia, and Pacific Islands From 122°E to 180°E.

Name	Ident.	Type	Freq.	Latitude	Longitude
AMCHITKA , Alaska	NIA	VOR	113.2	51 22.54N	179 16.45E
ATTU, Alaska	ATU	NDB	375.0	52 49.75N	173 10.82E
BALESIN, Phillipines	BAL	VOR	116.9	14 26.70N	122 2.50E
BIAK, New Guinea	BIK	VOR	112.5	1 10.90S	136 5.10E
BUCHOLZ, Marshall Islands	NDJ	NDB	359.0	8 43.25N	167 43.65E
BUKA, Soloman Islands	BUK	NDB	269.0	5 26.50S	154 40.10E
CHINEN, Japan	TIC	VOR	114.2	26 9.61N	127 47.80E
DARWIN, Australia	DN	VOR	112.4	12 24.20S	130 51.80E
ERABU, Japan	ONC	VOR	113.1	27 26.01N	128 42.00E
HENGCHUN, Taiwan	HCN	VOR	113.7	21 56.00N	120 50.00E
HONIARA, Soloman Islands	HN	VOR	112.6	9 25.90S	160 1.00E
IWO JIMA, Japan	OX	NDB	360.0	24 46.91N	141 18.30E
KAVIENG, Admiralty Islands	KAU	VOR	116.3	2 35.40S	150 48.90E
KIRIWINA, Papua New Guinea	KWA	NDB	287.0	8 30.30S	151 5.40E
KOROR, Palau	ROR	NDB	371.0	7 21.65N	134 32.41E
KOSRAE, Caroline Islands	UKS	NDB	393.0	5 21.88N	162 58.38E
KUSHIMOTO, Japan	KEC	VOR	112.9	33 26.81N	135 47.70E
LA TONTOUTA, Vanuatu, New Hebrides Islands	LTO	VOR	112.9	22 0.50S	166 12.50E
MAJURO, Marshall Islands	MAJ	NDB	316.0	7 4.03N	171 16.73E
MINAMI DAITO, Japan	MD	VOR	405.0	25 50.61N	131 14.50E
MIYAKE JIMA, Japan	MJE	VOR	117.8	34 7.11N	139 29.90E
MIYAKO JIMA, Japan	MYC	VOR	117.5	24 47.21N	125 18.00E
MT MACAJNA, Guam	AJA	NDB	385.0	13 27.14N	144 44.07E
NADI, Fiji	NN	VOR	112.5	17 39.20S	177 24.00E
NADZAB, Papua New Guinea	NZ	VOR	113.6	6 34.30S	146 43.90E
NANUMEA, Tuvalu, Ellice Islands	NM	NDB	358.0	5 40.30S	176 8.20E
NAURU, Kiribati, Gilbert Islands	NI	NDB	355.0	0 32.70S	166 55.00E
NAUSORI, Fiji	NA	VOR	112.2	18 2.50S	178 33.90E
NIMITZ, Guam	UNZ	VOR	115.3	13 27.19N	144 43.86E
OKINAWA, Japan	OK	NDB	308.0	26 6.11N	127 39.90E
POHNPEI, Caroline Islands	PNI	NDB	366.0	6 58.97N	158 12.53E
PORT MORESBY, Papua New Guinea	PY	VOR	117.0	9 27.10S	147 13.00E

Name	Ident.	Type	Freq.	Latitude	Longitude
ROCKHAMPTON, Australia	RK	VOR	116.9	23 23.00S	150 28.30E
ROTA, Mariana Islands	GRO	NDB	332.0	14 10.22N	145 14.25E
SAIPAN, Near Guam	SN	NDB	312.0	15 6.77N	145 42.70E
SHEMYA, Alaska	SYA	VOR	109.0	52 43.11N	174 3.73E
SHEMYA, Alaska	SYA	NDB	221.0	52 43.33N	174 3.62E
TACLOBAN, Phillipines	TAC	VOR	115.5	11 13.10N	125 1.70E
THURSDAY ISLAND, Australia	HID	NDB	356.0	10 35.50S	142 17.60E
TOWNSVILLE, Australia	TL	VOR	114.1	19 14.70S	146 45.50E
TRUK ISLAND, Caroline Islands	TKK	NDB	375.0	7 27.32N	151 50.24E
WAKE ISLAND	AWK	VOR	113.5	19 17.95N	166 36.07E
YAP ISLAND, Caroline Islands	YP	NDB	317.0	9 29.82N	138 5.78E

Name	Ident.	Type	Freq.	Latitude	Longitude
STEPHENVILLE, Newfoundland, Canada	YJT	VOR	113.1	48 34.96N	58 40.15W
STEPHENVILLE, Newfoundland, Canada	JT	NDB	390.0	48 32.64N	58 45.29W
SYDNEY, Cape Breton Island, Nova Scotia, Canada	YQY	VOR	114.9	46 9.21N	60 3.35W
SYDNEY, Cape Breton Island, Nova Scotia, Canada	QY	NDB	263.0	46 12.70N	59 58.54W
TORBAY, St. Johns, Newfoundland, Canada	YYT	VOR	113.5	47 29.14N	52 51.14W
TORBAY, St. Johns, Newfoundland, Canada	YT	NDB	260.0	47 40.19N	52 48.51W
TRENTON, Nova Scotia, Canada	5Y	NDB	338.0	45 36.72N	62 37.51W
V C BIRD, West Indies	ANU	VOR	114.5	17 7.60N	61 47.88W
V C BIRD, West Indies	ANU	NDB	351.0	17 7.50N	61 48.60W
V C BIRD, West Indies	ZDX	NDB	369.0	17 9.00N	61 47.00W

VOR/NDBs for the North Atlantic Region From 0°W to 62°W

Name	Ident.	Type	Freq.	Latitude	Longitude
ADAMS, West Indies	BGI	VOR	112.7	13 4.35N	59 29.13W
ADAMS, West Indies	BGI	NDB	345.0	13 4.12N	59 29.53W
ALENCON, France	AL	NDB	380.0	48 27.01N	0 6.80E
CHANNEL HEAD, Canada	CM	NDB	379.0	47 34.03N	59 9.56W
CHARLOTTETOWN, Prince Edward Island, Canada	YYG	VOR	114.1	46 12.45N	62 58.73W
CHARTRES, France	CHW	VOR	115.2	48 28.81N	0 59.30E
DEAUVILLE, France	DVL	VOR	110.2	49 18.61N	0 18.80E
FORT DE FRANCE, Lesser Antilles	FOF	VOR	117.5	14 35.00N	60 60.00W
FORT DE FRANCE, Lesser Antilles	FXF	NDB	314.0	14 35.97N	61 5.72W
GRINDSTONE, Cape Breton Island, Nova Scotia, Canada	YGR	VOR	112.0	47 25.83N	61 46.44W
GRINDSTONE, Cape Breton Island, Nova Scotia, Canada	GR	NDB	370.0	47 22.46N	61 54.41W
HEATH POINT, Anticosti, Quebec, Canada	HP	NDB	335.0	49 5.12N	61 42.04W
ISLE MADAME, Sable Island, Nova Scotia, Canada	W	NDB	304.0	45 33.60N	60 55.92W
LE HAVRE, France	LHO	NDB	346.0	49 35.81N	0 11.00E
MELVILLE HALL, Lesser Antilles	DOM	NDB	273.0	15 33.00N	61 18.00W
PIARCO, Trinidad	POS	VOR	116.9	10 27.87N	61 23.62W
PIARCO, Trinidad	POS	NDB	382.0	10 35.65N	61 25.58W
POINTE A PITRE, West Indies	PPR	VOR	115.1	16 16.00N	61 31.00W
POINTE A PITRE, West Indies	AR	NDB	402.0	16 16.27N	61 37.50W
POINTE A PITRE, West Indies	PPR	NDB	300.0	16 15.67N	61 31.67W
PORT HAWKESBURY, Nova Scotia, Canada	PD	NDB	229.0	45 39.33N	61 16.17W
SABLE ISLAND, Nova Scotia, Canada	SA	NDB	374.0	43 55.85N	60 1.37W
ST VINCENT, Lesser Antilles	SV	NDB	403.0	13 8.00N	61 12.00W

VOR/NDBs for Mexico, Portions of the Southern USA, and Caribbean Ocean Region. (Covers Area From 60 °W to 120 °W, and 0 °N to 33 °N)

Name	Ident.	Tupe	Freq.	Latitude	Longitude
ABILENE	ABI	VOR	113.7	32 28.89N	99 51.81W
ACADI (LOM/NDB)	ACAD	NDB	269	29 57.38N	91 51.80W
ACTON	AQN	VOR	110.6	32 26.08N	97 39.83W
ALAMO (LOM/NDB)	ALAM	NDB	368	29 36.46N	98 34.18W
ALAMOGORDO	ALM	NDB	341	32 51.03N	105 58.88W
ALEGRE	UPA	NDB	382	22 22.42N	78 46.38W
ALEXANDER CITY	DER	NDB	382	32 52.76N	85 57.68W
ALEXANDRIA	AEX	VOR	116.1	31 15.41N	92 30.04W
ALIBI (LOM/NDB)	ALIB	NDB	281	30 25.93N	95 28.58W
ALICE	ALI	VOR	114.5	27 44.39N	98 1.28W
ALLEN (LOM)	ALLE	NDB	365	32 24.76N	90 7.17W
ALLENTOWN (NAVY)	NVK	NDB	368	30 46.13N	87 4.36W
ALMA	AMG	VOR	115.1	31 32.20N	82 30.48W
AMASON	CZJ	NDB	341	31 50.18N	94 8.99W
AMBASSADOR	ABG	NDB	404	32 35.13N	95 6.78W
ANAHUAC	CBC	NDB	413	29 46.40N	94 39.79W
ANDALUSIA	UIA	VOR	110.2	31 18.58N	86 23.53W
ANDRA (LOM)	ANDR	NDB	223	31 23.53N	92 10.92W
ANDRAU	AAP	NDB	269	29 44.15N	95 35.41W
ANDREW	AEW	NDB	20.4	25 44.13N	80 9.80W
ANDREWS	ANR	NDB	245	32 20.95N	102 32.19W
ANGER (LOM)	ANGE	NDB	212	30 36.39N	90 25.27W
ARTESIA	ATS	NDB	414	32 51.16N	104 27.70W
ARUBA	PJH	VOR	112.5	12 30.54N	69 56.47W
ASHLY (LOM/NDB)	ASHL	NDB	329	32 58.58N	80 5.86W
ATHENS	AHX	NDB	269	32 9.57N	95 49.81W
AUSTI (LOM/NDB)	AUST	NDB	353	30 14.15N	97 37.54W
AUSTIN	AUS	VOR	117.1	30 17.86N	97 42.20W
AYR HILL	AYR	VOR	115.5	18 13.49N	77 30.50W
BALLINGER	UBC	NDB	239	31 40.83N	99 58.49W
BARD	BZA	VOR	116.8	32 46.10N	114 36.17W
BARRANQUILLA	BAQ	VOR	113.7	10 48.04N	74 51.75W
BARRANQUILLA	BA	NDB	244	10 48.00N	74 52.00W
BASTROP	BQP	NDB	329	32 45.31N	91 53.01W
BATON ROUGE	BTR	VOR	116.5	30 29.11N	91 17.65W
BAY CITY	BYY	NDB	344	28 58.35N	95 51.60W
BAY CREEK	BEP	NDB	350	32 27.82N	83 45.95W
BAYOU (LOM)	BAYO	NDB	360	30 29.13N	89 9.72W
BEAUMONT	BPT	VOR	114.5	29 56.77N	94 0.97W
BEEVILLE	BEA	NDB	284	28 22.07N	97 47.67W

Name	Ident.	Type	Freq.	Latitude	Longitude
BELIZE	BZE	NDB	392	17 32.00N	88 18.00W
BERMUDA	BDA	VOR	113.9	32 21.73N	64 41.39W
BIG SPRING	BGS	VOR	114.3	32 23.14N	101 29.02W
BIMINI	ZBV	VOR	116.7	25 42.26N	79 17.67W
BIMINI	ZBB	NDB	396	25 42.54N	79 16.33W
BISCAYNE BAY	BSY	VOR	117.1	25 40.32N	80 10.65W
BLOOD (LOM/NDB)	BLOO	NDB	365	31 49.83N	86 6.32W
BLUIE (LOM)	BLUI	NDB	219	29 28.48N	98 31.12W
BOCAS DEL TORO	BDT	VOR	114.9	9 20.29N	82 15.05W
BOING (LMM)	BOIN	NDB	245	32 44.40N	117 12.95W
BOLES	BWS	VOR	109.6	32 49.28N	106 0.79W
BOLL WEEVIL	BVG	NDB	308	31 20.22N	85 59.00W
BORINQUEN	BQN	VOR	113.5	18 29.88N	67 6.49W
BRADY	BBD	NDB	380	31 10.69N	99 19.36W
BRANTLEY	XBR	NDB	410	31 33.72N	86 17.58W
BRAZOS RIVER	GZV	NDB	280	32 57.10N	98 24.79W
BRECKENRIDGE	BKD	NDB	245	32 44.85N	98 53.47W
BRENHAM	BNH	NDB	362	30 13.35N	96 22.38W
BRENZ (LOM/NDB)	BREN	NDB	260	32 24.79N	90 15.68W
BREWSTER COUNTY	BWR	NDB	201	30 27.60N	103 38.78W
BROOKHAVEN	BVV	NDB	407	31 36.49N	90 24.62W
BROOKLEY	BFM	VOR	112.8	30 36.77N	88 3.33W
BROOKS COUNTY	BKS	NDB	353	27 12.43N	98 7.28W
BROOKSVILLE	BKV	NDB	278	28 28.44N	82 26.99W
BROWNSVILLE	BRO	VOR	116.3	25 55.45N	97 22.53W
BROWNWOOD	BWD	VOR	108.6	31 53.56N	98 57.45W
BRUNSWICK	SSI	VOR	109.8	31 3.04N	81 26.76W
BULLOCK COUNTY	IBU	NDB	407	32 24.93N	81 39.84W
BURNET	BMQ	NDB	341	30 44.35N	98 14.24W
CABO ROJO	CRO	VOR	114.3	17 56.00N	71 39.00W
CAHABA	CAQ	VOR	114.9	32 20.70N	86 59.49W
CAIDY	CYR	NDB	338	30 53.30N	84 9.56W
CAIRNS	OZR	VOR	111.2	31 16.15N	85 43.58W
CALOO (LOM)	CALO	NDB	341	26 30.97N	81 57.00W
CAMILLA	CXU	NDB	369	31 12.88N	84 14.21W
CAMPI (LOM/NDB)	CAMP	NDB	407	31 39.45N	93 4.66W
CAP HAITIEN	HCN	VOR	113.9	19 43.64N	72 11.83W
CAP HAITIEN	HTN	NDB	288	19 44.05N	72 12.00W
CAPOK (LOM)	CAPO	NDB	360	27 59.72N	82 42.19W
CARLSBAD	CNM	VOR	116.3	32 15.40N	104 13.56W
CARLZ (LOM)	CARL	NDB	402	32 16.01N	104 20.31W
CARMA (LOM/NDB)	CARM	NDB	353	30 52.91N	89 51.73W
CARTHAGE	RPF	NDB	332	32 10.82N	94 17.78W
CASTROVILLE	CVB	NDB	338	29 20.77N	98 50.95W
CAYMAN BRAC	CBC	NDB	217	19 41.39N	79 51.42W
CECIL	VQQ	VOR	117.9	30 12.79N	81 53.45W
CENTER POINT	CSI	VOR	117.5	29 55.35N	99 12.85W
CHAPARROSA RANCH	CPZ	NDB	385	28 56.60N	100 0.34W
CHARLESTON	CHS	VOR	113.5	32 53.67N	80 2.27W
CHEROKEE COUNTY	JSO	NDB	263	31 52.22N	95 12.93W
CHIHUAHUA	CUU	VOR	114.1	28 42.80N	105 57.50W
CHOCTAW	BCZ	NDB	228	32 6.86N	88 7.29W
CIUDAD JUAREZ	CJS	VOR	116.7	31 38.17N	106 25.58W
COCHISE	CIE	VOR	115.8	32 2.01N	109 45.49W
COFFEE CO	OWC	NDB	390	31 24.30N	82 55.43W
COFFI (LOM)	COFF	NDB	242	31 41.64N	97 12.23W
COLEMAN	COM	NDB	385	31 50.08N	99 24.37W
COLLEGE STATION	CLL	VOR	113.3	30 36.31N	96 25.24W
COLLIER COUNTY	CCE	VOR	108.6	26 9.21N	81 46.69W
COLUMBUS	CUS	VOR	111.2	31 49.15N	107 34.47W
COLUMBUS	CSG	VOR	117.1	32 36.92N	85 1.06W
CONEY	OHY	NDB	400	31 59.83N	83 51.76W
CONIS (LOM)	CONI	NDB	275	32 46.49N	96 46.51W
CONOR (LOM/NDB)	CONO	NDB	382	27 50.08N	97 34.59W
COOK	CKK	NDB	365	25 47.90N	80 20.92W
CORO	CRO	VOR	117.3	11 25.00N	69 42.00W
CORPUS CHRISTI	CRP	VOR	115.5	27 54.23N	97 26.70W
CORSICANA	CRS	NDB	396	32 1.67N	96 23.71W
COSME (LOM)	COSM	NDB	368	28 5.12N	82 31.51W
COTULLA	COT	VOR	115.8	28 27.72N	99 7.11W
COZEY (LOM)	COZE	NDB	251	32 37.93N	108 3.80W
COZUMEL	CZM	VOR	112.6	20 29.00N	86 57.00W
COZUMEL	CZM	NDB	330	20 30.60N	86 56.55W
CRAIG	CRG	VOR	114.5	30 20.34N	81 30.60W
CRAKK (LOM/NDB)	CRAK	NDB	230	32 30.11N	93 52.69W
CRESTVIEW	CEW	VOR	115.9	30 49.58N	86 40.75W
CROSS CITY	CTY	VOR	112	29 35.95N	83 2.92W
CROSSROADS	CSZ	NDB	215	32 3.82N	95 57.46W
CURACAO	PJG	VOR	116.7	12 12.02N	69 0.60W
DAISETTA	DAS	VOR	116.9	30 11.39N	94 38.70W
DALLAS-FT WORTH	DFW	VOR	117	32 51.96N	97 1.68W
DAVID	DAV	VOR	114.3	8 23.08N	82 26.27W
DAVID HOOKS	DWH	NDB	521	30 7.54N	95 33.96W
DE QUINCY	DQU	NDB	410	30 26.13N	93 28.01W
DEL NORTE	ADN	VOR	115.4	25 51.91N	100 14.32W
DELAND	DED	NDB	201	29 4.06N	81 16.46W
DELICIAS	DEL	VOR	113.5	28 13.01N	105 27.00W
DEMING	DMN	VOR	108.6	32 16.56N	107 36.34W
DEORO (LOM)	DEOR	NDB	210	32 46.80N	117 2.69W
DEPOO (LOM)	DEPO	NDB	393	25 59.02N	97 30.54W
DEVINE	HHH	NDB	359	29 8.14N	98 56.49W
DIMMIT COUNTY	DMD	NDB	343	28 31.44N	99 49.52W
DINNS (LOM/NDB)	DINN	NDB	344	30 27.92N	81 48.08W
DONALDSONILLE	ONG	NDB	352	31 0.64N	84 52.53W
DORADO	DDP	NDB	391	18 28.10N	66 24.74W
DOUGLAS	DUG	VOR	108.8	31 28.37N	109 36.12W
DOWNTOWN	DTN	VOR	108.6	32 32.40N	93 44.48W
DRAGOO	DAO	NDB	410	31 35.15N	110 20.66W
DUBLIN	DBN	VOR	113.1	32 33.65N	82 49.99W
EAGLE LAKE	ELA	VOR	116.4	29 39.77N	96 19.01W
EASTEX	ETO	NDB	201	30 20.90N	94 5.33W
EASTMAN	EZM	NDB	270	32 12.85N	83 7.52W
EASTPORT	EYA	NDB	357	30 25.41N	81 36.57W
EATON	LBY	VOR	110.6	31 25.12N	89 20.26W
EL PASO	ELP	VOR	115.2	31 48.96N	106 16.91W
ELEUTHERA	ZGV	VOR	112.5	25 15.46N	76 18.52W
ELLINGTON	EFD	VOR	109.4	29 36.38N	95 9.60W
ELM GROVE	EMG	VOR	111.2	32 24.02N	93 35.71W
EMANUEL COUNTY	EEX	NDB	309	32 40.02N	82 27.14W
ENTERPRISE	EDN	VOR	116.6	31 17.77N	85 54.20W
ESLER	ESF	VOR	117.9	31 26.86N	92 19.32W
EUFAULA	EUF	VOR	109.2	31 57.02N	85 7.83W
EVADALE	EVA	NDB	219	30 24.28N	94 7.63W
FALFURRIAS	FFR	NDB	230	27 28.02N	98 24.18W
FARLY (LOM/NDB)	FARL	NDB	326	31 59.29N	102 19.50W
FENIX (LOM)	FENI	NDB	355	32 27.12N	85 2.51W
FERNI (LOM/NDB)	FERN	NDB	413	31 15.28N	90 30.63W
FISH HOOK	FIS	NDB	332	24 32.91N	81 47.18W
FITZGERALD	SUR	NDB	362	31 36.79N	83 17.44W
FLORENVILLE	FNA	NDB	371	30 24.94N	89 49.20W
FLUFY (LOM)	FLUF	NDB	350	31 13.14N	94 49.50W
FOLEY	FPY	NDB	254	29 59.78N	83 35.18W
FORT DE FRANCE	FOF	VOR	117.5	14 35.00N	60 60.00W
FORT DE FRANCE	FXF	NDB	314	14 35.97N	61 5.72W
FORT LAUDERDALE	FLL	VOR	114.4	26 4.49N	80 9.15W
FORT PIERCE	FPR	NDB	275	27 29.21N	80 22.40W
FORT STOCKTON	FST	VOR	112.8	30 57.13N	102 58.54W
FOSTR (LOM)	FOST	NDB	226	28 54.92N	97 0.03W
FOXWORTH	FOH	NDB	331	31 17.77N	89 49.12W
FRANCE	FTD	VOR	109	9 21.67N	79 51.95W
FRANKSTON	FZT	VOR	111.4	32 4.48N	95 31.85W
FREDERICKSBURG	FKB	NDB	388	30 14.93N	98 54.62W
FREEP (LOM)	FREE	NDB	263	29 11.67N	95 27.80W
FREEPORT	ZFP	VOR	113.2	26 33.32N	78 41.90W
FREEPORT	ZFP	NDB	209	26 31.11N	78 46.50W
FREEPORT/GRAND BA	BHF	NDB	326	26 34.44N	78 39.83W
GAINES CO	GNC	NDB	344	32 40.33N	102 38.75W
GAINESVILLE	GNV	VOR	116.2	29 34.34N	82 21.76W
GALVESTON	GLS	NDB	206	29 20.04N	94 45.37W
GARYS (LOM)	GARY	NDB	272	29 57.55N	97 56.94W

Name	Ident.	Type	Freq.	Latitude	Longitude
GATOR	GUV	NDB	359	31 1.70N	93 11.09W
GEIGER LAKE	GGL	NDB	375	28 35.59N	80 48.98W
GEORGETOWN	GUO	NDB	332	30 41.07N	97 40.79W
GERONA	UNG	NDB	412	21 45.20N	82 52.88W
GILA BEND	GBN	VOR	116.6	32 57.38N	112 40.46W
GOLDEN EAGLE	OEG	NDB	413	32 51.33N	114 26.46W
GOODHUE	GDE	NDB	368	30 4.19N	94 12.15W
GRAGG-WADE	GGY	NDB	338	32 51.20N	86 36.66W
GRAN ROQUE	LRS	VOR	113.1	11 57.00N	66 40.00W
GRAND CAYMAN	GCM	VOR	115.6	19 17.40N	81 22.30W
GRAND CAYMAN	ZIY	NDB	344	19 17.00N	81 23.00W
GRAND ISLE	GNI	NDB	236	29 11.52N	90 4.50W
GRAND PRAIRIE	GPM	NDB	227	32 41.63N	97 2.80W
GRAND TURK	GTK	VOR	114.2	21 26.42N	71 8.08W
GRAND TURK	GT	NDB	232	21 26.20N	71 8.78W
GRAY	GRK	VOR	111.8	31 1.98N	97 48.83W
GREAT INAGUA	ZIN	NDB	376	20 57.59N	73 40.65W
GREENE COUNTY	GCV	VOR	115.7	31 5.88N	88 29.17W
GREENSBORO	EOG	NDB	417	32 36.15N	87 39.78W
GREENVILLE	GEF	VOR	109	30 33.09N	83 46.99W
GREGG COUNTY	GGG	VOR	112.4	32 25.07N	94 45.19W
GUATEMALA	TGE	NDB	375	14 35.00N	90 32.00W
GULFPORT	GPT	VOR	109	30 24.42N	89 4.61W
HAMILTON	MNZ	NDB	251	31 37.22N	98 8.85W
HAMMOND	HMU	VOR	109.6	30 31.17N	90 25.05W
HANCHEY	HEY	VOR	110.6	31 22.46N	85 39.17W
HANCHEY	HYE	NDB	221	31 22.02N	85 39.00W
HANCO	AYI	NDB	221	30 27.07N	89 27.32W
HARDIN COUNTY	HRD	NDB	524	30 20.25N	94 15.61W
HARLINGEN	HRL	VOR	108.8	26 17.48N	97 47.60W
HARVEY	HRV	VOR	112.4	29 51.02N	90 0.17W
HAZER (LOM/NDB)	HAZE	NDB	356	30 38.00N	91 29.37W
HAZLEHURST	AZE	NDB	414	31 52.82N	82 38.84W
HEBBRONVILLE	HBV	NDB	266	27 21.24N	98 44.65W
HENDERSON	HNO	NDB	371	32 11.28N	94 51.66W
HERLONG	HEG	NDB	332	30 16.61N	81 48.54W
HERMOSILLO	HMO	VOR	112.8	29 5.72N	111 2.93W
HERNY (LOM)	HERN	NDB	221	28 30.42N	81 26.04W
HOBBS	HOB	VOR	111	32 38.30N	103 16.16W
HOBBY	HUB	VOR	117.6	29 39.02N	95 16.74W
HODGE	JBL	NDB	256	32 12.08N	92 43.56W
HOMER	HMQ	NDB	212	32 47.42N	93 0.04W
HOMERVILLE	HOE	NDB	209	31 3.34N	82 46.33W
HONDO	HMA	NDB	329	29 22.41N	99 10.32W
HOOD	HLR	NDB	347	31 7.75N	97 42.68W
HOUMA (LOM)	HOUM	NDB	219	29 39.81N	90 39.58W
HUDSPETH	HUP	VOR	115	31 34.13N	105 22.58W
HULL	SGR	NDB	388	29 37.96N	95 39.36W
HUMBLE	IAH	VOR	116.6	29 57.42N	95 20.74W
HUMPHREY	HPY	NDB	275	29 47.46N	94 57.32W
HUNTER	SVN	VOR	111.6	32 0.72N	81 8.44W
HUNTSVILLE	UTS	NDB	308	30 44.45N	95 35.46W
IDDER (LOM/NDB)	IDDE	NDB	385	30 45.13N	93 20.08W
ILOPANGO	YSV	VOR	114.7	13 42.00N	89 7.00W
IMPERIAL	IPL	VOR	115.9	32 44.94N	115 30.51W
INDUSTRY	IDU	VOR	110.2	29 57.37N	96 33.73W
IRESH (LOM/NDB)	IRES	NDB	278	31 1.45N	97 42.48W
ISSUE (LOM)	ISSU	NDB	233	32 47.60N	97 1.83W
JACKSON	JAN	VOR	112.6	32 30.46N	90 10.06W
JACKSON COUNTY	EDX	NDB	201	29 0.10N	96 35.08W
JASPER	JAS	NDB	344	30 57.28N	94 2.01W
JECCA	JUG	NDB	388	32 40.15N	96 31.93W
JEFFI (LOM)	JEFF	NDB	275	31 13.71N	81 32.56W
JIFFY (LOM)	JIFF	NDB	219	32 59.75N	97 1.77W
JOHNS ISLAND	JZI	NDB	283	32 42.08N	80 0.34W
JUDD	JUY	NDB	264	31 18.27N	86 23.45W
JUMPI (LOM)	JUMP	NDB	423	29 3.39N	82 13.39W
JUMPR (LOM)	JUMP	NDB	219	32 15.82N	84 55.83W
JUNCTION	JCT	VOR	116	30 35.89N	99 49.05W
KAOLIN	OKZ	NDB	212	32 57.88N	82 50.29W

Name	Ident.	Type	Freq.	Latitude	Longitude
KAZOO (LOM)	KAZO	NDB	257	29 59.78N	94 6.38W
KEOTE (LOM)	KEOT	NDB	338	29 25.90N	98 52.97W
KEWANEE	EWA	VOR	113.8	32 22.02N	88 27.50W
KEY WEST	EYW	VOR	113.5	24 35.15N	81 48.03W
KEYES (LOM)	KEYE	NDB	248	25 47.45N	80 11.66W
KEYLI (LOM)	KEYL	NDB	353	30 11.59N	93 15.79W
KINGSTON	KIN	VOR	115.9	17 58.42N	76 53.63W
KINGSTON	KIN	NDB	360	17 57.80N	76 52.55W
KINTE (LOM/NDB)	KINT	NDB	338	30 1.52N	90 23.99W
KISSIMMEE	ISM	NDB	329	28 17.37N	81 26.06W
KLEBERG COUNTY	TKB	NDB	347	27 36.36N	98 5.38W
KNIGHT	TPF	NDB	270	27 54.51N	82 27.26W
KOBRA (LOM)	KOBR	NDB	201	30 51.19N	86 32.19W
KOTTI (LOM)	KOTT	NDB	335	29 26.75N	100 59.32W
LA BELLE	LBV	VOR	110.4	26 49.70N	81 23.49W
LA FONDA RANCH	BRX	NDB	269	29 12.52N	100 37.44W
LA PRYOR	LKX	NDB	223	28 55.80N	99 51.29W
LAFAYETTE	LFT	VOR	109.8	30 11.63N	91 59.55W
LAFFS (LOM)	LAFF	NDB	375	30 17.37N	91 54.47W
LAKE CHARLES	LCH	VOR	113.4	30 8.50N	93 6.33W
LAKE CITY	LCQ	NDB	204	30 11.13N	82 34.72W
LAKE PROVIDENCE	BLE	NDB	278	32 49.85N	91 11.41W
LAKELAND	LAL	VOR	116	27 59.18N	82 0.83W
LAKESIDE	LYD	NDB	249	29 48.99N	95 40.66W
LAMESA	LSA	NDB	338	32 45.43N	101 54.93W
LAMPASAS	LZZ	VOR	112.5	31 11.14N	98 8.51W
LANCASTER	LNC	NDB	239	32 34.67N	96 43.30W
LAREDO	LRD	VOR	117.4	27 28.73N	99 25.06W
LAS CRUCES	LCR	NDB	299	32 16.94N	106 55.41W
LAUGHLIN	DLF	VOR	114.4	29 21.66N	100 46.30W
LAWSON	LSF	VOR	111.4	32 19.95N	84 59.60W
LAWSON	AWS	NDB	335	32 17.60N	85 1.40W
LEE COUNTY	RSW	VOR	111.8	26 31.80N	81 46.55W
LEE COUNTY	GYB	NDB	385	30 10.14N	96 58.79W
LEEVILLE	LEV	VOR	113.5	29 10.52N	90 6.24W
LEONA	LOA	VOR	110.8	31 7.45N	95 58.08W
LEROI (LOM)	LERO	NDB	283	31 44.46N	97 4.68W
LIBBY	FHU	VOR	111.6	31 35.44N	110 20.57W
LIMON	LIO	NDB	380	9 58.60N	83 1.97W
LINCOLN PARISH	LPZ	NDB	308	32 30.95N	92 37.64W
LINDBERGH	LKG	NDB	242	32 10.47N	84 6.49W
LLANO	LLO	VOR	108.2	30 47.79N	98 47.24W
LOCHRIDGE RANCH	LIQ	NDB	335	32 0.65N	95 57.16W
LONE STAR	LST	NDB	305	32 55.68N	94 44.59W
LOUVALE	XLE	NDB	407	32 9.58N	84 50.49W
LOVINGTON	LGX	NDB	396	32 56.83N	103 24.60W
LOWE	LOR	NDB	269	31 21.62N	85 44.61W
LUFKIN	LFK	VOR	112.1	31 9.75N	94 43.02W
LYNNE (LOM)	LYNN	NDB	278	30 19.60N	85 46.94W
MACON	MCN	VOR	114.2	32 41.48N	83 38.83W
MAIQUETIA	MIQ	VOR	114.8	10 37.00N	67 1.00W
MAIQUETIA	MIQ	NDB	292	10 37.00N	67 1.00W
MANSFIELD	MSD	NDB	414	32 3.87N	93 45.87W
MANY	MMY	NDB	272	31 34.28N	93 32.49W
MANZANILLO	UMZ	VOR	116	20 18.20N	77 6.03W
MANZANILLO	UMZ	NDB	232	20 16.14N	77 10.08W
MARACAIBO	MAR	VOR	115.7	10 35.15N	71 42.75W
MARATHON	MTH	NDB	260	24 42.72N	81 5.72W
MARATHON	IMP	NDB	388	30 15.85N	103 14.23W
MARBE (LOM)	MARB	NDB	379	30 4.49N	95 24.77W
MARBLE FALLS	MFS	NDB	403	30 31.40N	98 21.47W
MARCO	MKY	NDB	375	25 59.95N	81 40.52W
MARENGO	RZO	NDB	391	32 24.87N	88 0.92W
MARFA	MRF	VOR	115.9	30 17.91N	103 57.28W
MARGARITA	MTA	VOR	114.1	10 55.42N	63 57.67W
MARGARITA	MTA	NDB	206	10 55.20N	63 57.40W
MARIANNA	MAI	VOR	114	30 47.18N	85 7.47W
MARKSVILLE	MKV	NDB	347	31 5.74N	92 4.36W
MARRA (LOM)	MARR	NDB	245	32 18.70N	86 30.63W
MARSH HARBOUR	ZMH	NDB	361	26 30.67N	77 4.62W

Name	Ident.	Type	Freq.	Latitude	Longitude
MATAMOROS	MAM	VOR	114.3	25 46.26N	97 31.43W
MAVIS (LOM)	MAVI	NDB	368	32 7.80N	81 19.89W
MAYAGUEZ	MAZ	VOR	110.6	18 15.39N	67 9.06W
MAYAGUEZ	MAZ	NDB	254	18 15.23N	67 9.15W
MC ALLEN	MFE	VOR	117.2	26 10.44N	98 14.45W
MC COMB	MCB	VOR	116.7	31 18.27N	90 15.49W
MC INTOSH	MOQ	NDB	263	31 49.84N	81 30.59W
MC KINNON	JUK	NDB	353	31 9.22N	81 23.37W
MC RAE	MQW	NDB	280	32 5.68N	82 53.03W
MELBOURNE	MLB	VOR	110	28 6.32N	80 38.12W
MELLON RANCH	MNO	NDB	375	28 16.81N	97 12.35W
MELVILLE HALL	DOM	NDB	273	15 33.00N	61 18.00W
MERIDA	MID	VOR	117.7	20 55.00N	89 39.00W
MERIDIAN	MEI	VOR	117	32 22.71N	88 48.26W
MESQUITE	PQF	NDB	248	32 48.55N	96 31.73W
METTER	MHP	NDB	432	32 22.35N	82 5.04W
MEXIA	LXY	NDB	329	31 38.38N	96 30.73W
MIAMI	MIA	VOR	115.9	25 57.81N	80 27.63W
MIDLAND	MAF	VOR	114.8	32 0.56N	102 11.43W
MIDLAND (LMM)	AF	NDB	201	31 57.07N	102 13.53W
MILLSAP	MQP	VOR	117.7	32 43.58N	97 59.84W
MINDEN	MNE	NDB	201	32 38.48N	93 18.11W
MINERAL WELLS	MWL	NDB	266	32 47.12N	98 3.44W
MISSI (LOM)	MISS	NDB	388	26 15.24N	98 18.62W
MISSION BAY	MZB	VOR	117.8	32 46.94N	117 13.52W
MOLLY RIDGE	MRK	NDB	338	32 24.42N	91 46.36W
MONAHANS	OHE	NDB	214	31 34.70N	102 54.34W
MONROE	MLU	VOR	117.2	32 31.02N	92 2.16W
MONROEVILLE	MVC	VOR	116.8	31 27.63N	87 21.16W
MONRY (LOM)	MONR	NDB	227	25 51.72N	81 0.66W
MONTEGO BAY	MBJ	VOR	115.7	18 29.85N	77 55.52W
MONTEGO BAY	MBJ	NDB	248	18 30.05N	77 55.17W
MONTERREY	MTY	VOR	114.7	25 46.41N	100 6.10W
MONTEZUMA	IZS	NDB	426	32 22.05N	84 0.44W
MONTGOMERY	MGM	VOR	112.1	32 13.35N	86 19.18W
MOSSY (LOM)	MOSS	NDB	418	30 18.41N	93 11.77W
MOULTRIE	MGR	VOR	108.8	31 4.94N	83 48.25W
MUFFE (LOM)	MUFF	NDB	336	26 29.03N	81 50.07W
MUFIN (LOM/NDB)	MUFI	NDB	365	32 53.59N	97 22.41W
NACOGDOCHES	OCH	NDB	391	31 38.03N	94 44.03W
NADOS	OC	NDB	253	31 29.12N	94 43.18W
NAPLES	APF	NDB	201	26 9.35N	81 46.46W
NASSAU	ZQA	VOR	112.7	25 1.69N	77 27.00W
NASSAU	ZQA	NDB	251	25 2.42N	77 28.22W
NATCHEZ	HEZ	VOR	110	31 37.10N	91 17.98W
NAUTLA	NAU	VOR	112.3	20 11.90N	96 44.90W
NAUTLA	NAU	NDB	392	20 12.00N	96 45.00W
NAVASOTA	TNV	VOR	115.9	30 17.35N	96 3.51W
NEW BRAUNFELS	BAZ	NDB	212	29 42.47N	98 2.08W
NEW ORLEANS	MSY	VOR	113.2	30 1.80N	90 10.33W
NEW ORLEANS (NAVY)	NBG	NDB	366	29 49.08N	90 2.21W
NEW SMYRNA BEACH	EVB	NDB	417	29 3.27N	80 56.46W
NEWMAN	EWM	VOR	112.4	31 57.11N	106 16.34W
NIXIN (LOM)	NIXI	NDB	326	29 59.60N	95 12.90W
NOGALES	OLS	VOR	108.2	31 24.90N	110 50.93W
NOGALES	ENZ	NDB	394	31 25.29N	110 50.79W
NUEVAS	UNV	VOR	116.3	21 23.84N	77 13.72W
NUEVAS	UNV	NDB	256	21 24.11N	77 13.80W
NUEVO LAREDO	NLD	VOR	112.6	27 26.01N	99 34.00W
OBLEON	OBN	VOR	113.2	18 26.24N	72 16.48W
OCALA	OCF	VOR	113.7	29 10.65N	82 13.58W
OLD RIP	OIP	NDB	410	32 23.92N	98 48.62W
ONYUN	UQN	NDB	372	32 13.40N	82 17.89W
OPOLE (LOM)	OPOL	NDB	423	32 30.56N	85 26.23W
ORANGE	ORG	NDB	211	30 4.22N	93 47.70W
ORLANDO	ORL	VOR	112.2	28 32.57N	81 20.10W
ORMOND BEACH	OMN	VOR	112.6	29 18.20N	81 6.76W
PAHOKEE	PHK	VOR	115.4	26 46.97N	80 41.49W
PALACIOS	PSX	VOR	117.3	28 45.87N	96 18.37W
PALATKA	IAK	NDB	243	29 39.17N	81 48.70W
PALESTINE	PSN	NDB	375	31 46.82N	95 42.06W
PALM BEACH	PBI	VOR	115.7	26 40.81N	80 5.19W
PANAMA CITY	PFN	VOR	114.3	30 12.98N	85 40.85W
PATTEN	GTP	NDB	245	30 57.46N	83 49.60W
PATTERSON	PTN	NDB	245	29 42.88N	91 20.20W
PATTY (LOM/NDB)	PATT	NDB	330	18 24.53N	66 5.35W
PECAN	PZD	VOR	116.1	31 39.32N	84 17.59W
PECOS	PEQ	VOR	111.8	31 28.17N	103 34.48W
PEKKS (LOM)	PEKK	NDB	405	27 38.55N	99 27.49W
PERSIMMON	PRN	NDB	359	31 51.07N	86 36.86W
PESTE (LOM)	PEST	NDB	241	17 41.52N	64 53.08W
PHILADELPHIA	MPE	NDB	219	32 47.92N	89 7.48W
PIARCO	POS	VOR	116.9	10 27.87N	61 23.62W
PIARCO	POS	NDB	382	10 35.65N	61 25.58W
PICAYUNE	PCU	NDB	112.2	30 33.68N	89 43.83W
PICKENS	PKZ	NDB	326	30 26.23N	87 10.70W
PICNY (LOM/NDB)	PICN	NDB	388	27 51.68N	82 32.76W
PINE MOUNTAIN	PIM	NDB	272	32 50.58N	84 52.35W
PINON	PIO	VOR	110.4	32 31.76N	105 18.31W
PLANT CITY	PCM	NDB	346	28 0.16N	82 9.41W
PLANTATION	PJN	NDB	242	26 7.94N	80 13.13W
PLEASANTON	PEZ	NDB	275	28 57.30N	98 31.12W
POGGI	PGY	VOR	109.8	32 36.63N	116 58.74W
POINTE A PITRE	PPR	VOR	115.1	16 16.00N	61 31.00W
POINTE A PITRE	AR	NDB	402	16 16.27N	61 37.50W
POINTE A PITRE	PPR	NDB	300	16 15.67N	61 31.67W
POLK	FXU	VOR	108.4	31 6.71N	93 13.08W
POLK	POJ	NDB	344	32 16.19N	86 55.65W
POMPANO BEACH	PMP	VOR	108.8	26 14.89N	80 6.51W
PONCE	PSE	VOR	109	17 59.55N	66 31.15W
PORT AU PRINCE	PAP	VOR	115.3	18 34.59N	72 18.27W
PORT AU PRINCE	HHP	NDB	270	18 34.59N	72 17.22W
PORT LAVACA	PKV	NDB	515	28 39.04N	96 40.88W
POWELL	CGQ	NDB	344	32 3.85N	96 25.68W
POZA RICA	PAZ	VOR	111.5	20 36.44N	97 28.05W
PRAIZ (LOM/NDB)	PRAI	NDB	221	26 11.54N	80 17.90W
PRENTISS	PJR	NDB	252	31 35.78N	89 54.31W
PRISON	RVJ	NDB	424	32 3.47N	82 9.14W
PROVIDENCIALES	PV	NDB	387	21 46.64N	72 15.65W
PUERTO PLATA	PTA	VOR	115.1	19 45.51N	70 34.29W
PUNTA CAUCEDO	CDO	VOR	114.7	18 25.99N	69 40.03W
PUNTA GORDA	PGD	VOR	110.2	26 55.01N	81 59.47W
PUTNY (LOM/NDB)	PUTN	NDB	227	31 27.38N	84 16.57W
PYRAMID	PYF	NDB	418	31 51.77N	96 11.85W
QEEZY (LOM)	QEEZ	NDB	266	25 38.51N	80 30.29W
QUITMAN	UIM	VOR	114	32 52.83N	95 22.01W
RANDOLPH	RND	VOR	112.3	29 31.15N	98 17.10W
RAYMOND	RYB	NDB	375	32 18.10N	90 24.69W
REAGAN CO	LUJ	NDB	341	31 11.57N	101 28.12W
REDBIRD	RBD	NDB	287	32 40.62N	96 52.27W
REGINALD GRANT	RGD	NDB	302	32 56.23N	84 20.42W
REYNOSA	REX	VOR	112.4	26 0.71N	98 14.00W
RINGY (LOM)	RING	NDB	245	27 19.70N	82 28.70W
ROBINSON	ROB	NDB	400	31 30.24N	97 4.17W
ROBLES	RBJ	NDB	220	32 4.45N	111 21.62W
ROCK SOUND	RSD	NDB	353	24 53.59N	76 10.20W
ROCKDALE	RCK	NDB	221	30 17.02N	96 59.02W
ROCKPORT	RKP	NDB	391	28 5.44N	97 2.73W
ROCKSPRINGS	RSG	VOR	111.2	30 0.88N	100 17.99W
ROSANKY	RYU	NDB	266	29 53.75N	97 20.27W
ROWDY (LOM)	ROWD	NDB	260	30 29.61N	96 20.27W
RUBIN (LOM/NDB)	RUBI	NDB	356	26 41.27N	80 12.61W
RUCKR (LOM/NDB)	RUCK	NDB	212	31 13.54N	85 48.96W
RUNDI (LOM)	RUND	NDB	284	32 47.98N	91 12.66W
RUSKIN	RNQ	NDB	404	31 14.92N	82 24.09W
RYAN	RYN	NDB	338	32 8.31N	111 9.69W
SABAR (LOM)	SABA	NDB	219	32 27.25N	92 6.25W
SABINE PASS	SBI	VOR	115.4	29 41.21N	94 2.28W
SAINT LANDRY	OPL	NDB	335	30 39.34N	92 5.91W
SALT FLAT	SFL	VOR	113	31 44.89N	105 5.21W

Name	Ident.	Type	Freq.	Latitude	Longitude
SAN ANDRES	SPP	NDB	387	12 35.00N	81 42.00W
SAN ANGELO	SJT	VOR	115.1	31 22.51N	100 27.29W
SAN ANTONIO	SAT	VOR	116.8	29 38.65N	98 27.68W
SAN JUAN	SJU	VOR	114	18 26.78N	65 59.37W
SAN SIMON	SSO	VOR	115.4	32 16.16N	109 15.79W
SANDY POINT	SYG	NDB	338	29 30.17N	95 28.10W
SANFORD	SFB	NDB	408	28 47.10N	81 14.60W
SANJAC	JPA	NDB	347	29 40.12N	95 4.19W
SANTA ELENA	SNE	NDB	260	26 43.14N	98 34.64W
SANTIAGO	STG	VOR	114.5	8 5.25N	80 56.38W
SARASOTA	SRQ	VOR	115.2	27 23.87N	82 33.26W
SATELLITE	SQT	NDB	257	28 5.97N	80 42.06W
SAUFLEY	NUN	VOR	108.8	30 28.34N	87 20.16W
SAVANNAH	SAV	VOR	112.7	32 9.64N	81 6.75W
SAVOY (LOM/NDB)	SAVO	NDB	356	32 14.84N	88 46.30W
SCHOLES	VUH	VOR	113	29 16.17N	94 52.06W
SCURRY	SCY	VOR	112.9	32 27.88N	96 20.25W
SEBAS (LOM/NDB)	SEBA	NDB	338	26 18.32N	97 39.43W
SEBRING	SEF	NDB	382	27 27.64N	81 20.99W
SEMMES	SJI	VOR	115.3	30 43.57N	88 21.56W
SHEIN (LOM/NDB)	SHEI	NDB	263	29 54.91N	99 0.49W
SHREVEPORT	SHV	VOR	117.4	32 46.29N	93 48.60W
SILVER CITY	SVC	VOR	111.8	32 38.27N	108 9.67W
SIMONES	USR	NDB	315	21 44.75N	78 48.72W
SLOVER	JES	NDB	323	31 33.15N	81 53.24W
SNYDER	SDR	NDB	359	32 42.08N	100 56.84W
SOFKE (LOM)	SOFK	NDB	290	32 38.72N	83 42.79W
SONORA	SOA	NDB	371	30 34.92N	100 38.82W
SOYYA	SMY	NDB	329	30 52.30N	85 13.50W
SPOFFORD	PFO	NDB	356	29 8.72N	100 25.66W
SPRING HILL	XNE	NDB	281	31 41.07N	85 58.46W
SPRINGHILL	SPH	NDB	375	32 59.00N	93 24.44W
ST AUGUSTINE	SGJ	VOR	109.4	29 57.49N	81 20.29W
ST CROIX	COY	VOR	108.2	17 44.07N	64 42.04W
ST MAARTEN	PJM	VOR	113	18 2.30N	63 7.13W
ST MAARTEN	PJD	NDB	284	18 2.30N	63 7.10W
ST MAARTEN	PJM	NDB	308	18 2.17N	63 7.05W
ST PETERSBURG	PIE	VOR	116.4	27 54.47N	82 41.06W
ST THOMAS	STT	VOR	108.6	18 21.35N	65 1.47W
ST VINCENT	SV	NDB	403	13 8.00N	61 12.00W
STAMFORD	TMV	NDB	290	32 52.13N	99 43.98W
STANFIELD	TFD	VOR	114.8	32 53.16N	111 54.52W
STARN (LOM/NDB)	STAR	NDB	323	31 10.08N	97 52.69W
STELLA MARIS	ZLS	NDB	526	23 34.84N	75 15.83W
STEPHENVILLE	SEP	NDB	223	32 13.08N	98 11.00W
STINSON	SSF	VOR	108.4	29 15.51N	98 26.61W
STONEWALL	STV	VOR	113.1	30 12.41N	98 42.34W
SUMMERDALE	ESU	NDB	204	30 29.97N	87 43.55W
SWEETWATER	SWW	NDB	275	32 27.70N	100 27.96W
SYLVANIA	JYL	NDB	245	32 38.95N	81 35.62W
TABOGA ISLAND	TBG	VOR	110	8 47.14N	79 33.62W
TABOGA ISLAND	TBG	NDB	311	8 47.00N	79 34.00W
TALLAHALA	THJ	NDB	346	31 41.26N	89 11.30W
TALLAHASSEE	TLH	VOR	117.5	30 33.38N	84 22.44W
TALLULAH	TTT	NDB	344	32 24.76N	91 9.02W
TAMPICO	TAM	VOR	117.5	22 17.36N	97 51.77W
TAYLOR	TAY	VOR	112.9	30 30.29N	82 33.18W
TEGUCIGALPA	TGU	NDB	355	13 56.79N	87 14.87W
TEMPLE	TPL	VOR	110.4	31 12.57N	97 25.50W
THREE RIVERS	THX	VOR	111.4	28 30.32N	98 9.07W
TIBBY	TBD	VOR	112	29 39.87N	90 49.74W
TIFT MYERS	IFM	VOR	112.5	31 25.73N	83 29.33W
TIFTO	TM	NDB	409	31 21.80N	83 26.64W
TIGER PASS	VTP	NDB	253	29 16.31N	89 21.46W
TIJUANA	TIJ	VOR	116.5	32 32.07N	116 57.03W
TIZAYUCA	TIZ	NDB	341	19 52.00N	98 59.00W
TOCUMEN	TUM	VOR	117.1	9 3.00N	79 24.02W
TOMBALL	TMZ	NDB	408	30 4.42N	95 33.34W
TOMHI (LOM)	TOMH	NDB	353	32 17.94N	99 40.45W
TOMOK (LOM)	TOMO	NDB	263	29 8.66N	81 8.86W

Name	Ident.	Type	Freq.	Latitude	Longitude
TONCONTIN	TNT	NDB	405	14 3.57N	87 13.40W
TRAVIS	AVZ	NDB	299	32 45.62N	96 14.95W
TREASURE CAY	ZTC	VOR	112.9	26 44.09N	77 22.75W
TREASURE CAY	ZTC	NDB	233	26 44.09N	77 18.00W
TRI COUNTY	BKK	NDB	275	30 51.10N	85 36.08W
TRINITY	MHF	VOR	113.6	29 32.79N	94 44.85W
TROY	TOI	VOR	110	31 51.81N	86 0.66W
TRUAX	NGP	VOR	114	27 41.18N	97 17.69W
TUCSON	TUS	VOR	116	32 5.72N	110 54.89W
TULANCINGO	TCG	NDB	308	20 5.00N	98 22.00W
TURKEY CREEK	UPK	NDB	251	32 29.04N	83 0.65W
TUSCOLA	TQA	VOR	111.6	32 14.15N	99 49.01W
TUSKEGEE	TGE	VOR	117.3	32 29.10N	85 40.16W
TUTTE (LOM)	TUTT	NDB	395	29 35.36N	95 20.42W
TYLER	TYR	VOR	114.2	32 21.36N	95 24.21W
TYLER (LOM/NDB)	TYLE	NDB	320	32 24.95N	95 28.18W
UNITED	UTX	NDB	405	26 54.54N	80 20.10W
UVALDE	UVA	NDB	281	29 10.69N	99 43.54W
V C BIRD	ANU	VOR	114.5	17 7.60N	61 47.88W
V C BIRD	ANU	NDB	351	17 7.50N	61 48.60W
V C BIRD	ZDX	NDB	369	17 9.00N	61 47.60W
VALDOSTA	OTK	VOR	114.8	30 46.83N	83 16.78W
VALTR (LOM/NDB)	VALT	NDB	242	31 51.63N	106 19.06W
VAN HORN	VHN	NDB	233	31 3.72N	104 47.18W
VARDER	UVR	NDB	272	23 5.40N	81 22.03W
VEELS (LOM)	VEEL	NDB	410	32 27.34N	94 47.86W
VENICE	VNC	NDB	206	27 3.69N	82 25.83W
VENICE	VEC	NDB	263	29 7.12N	89 12.34W
VERO BEACH	VRB	VOR	117.3	27 40.71N	80 29.38W
VERO BEACH	VEP	NDB	392	27 39.86N	80 25.17W
VICKSBURG	VKS	NDB	382	32 13.98N	90 55.59W
VICTORIA	VCT	VOR	109	28 54.03N	96 58.73W
VIENNA	VNA	VOR	116.5	32 12.81N	83 29.84W
VIVIAN	VIV	NDB	284	32 51.58N	94 0.61W
WACO	ACT	VOR	115.3	31 39.75N	97 16.14W
WAKUL (LOM/NDB)	WAKU	NDB	379	30 19.58N	84 21.50W
WALTERBORO	RBW	NDB	221	32 55.56N	80 38.41W
WASSA (LOM)	WASS	NDB	335	32 0.25N	80 59.16W
WAYCROSS	AYS	VOR	110.2	31 16.17N	82 33.39W
WEISER	EYQ	NDB	286	29 56.04N	95 38.46W
WEST END	ZWE	NDB	317	26 41.01N	78 59.00W
WHARTON	ARM	NDB	245	29 15.24N	96 9.30W
WHITE LAKE	LLA	VOR	111.4	29 39.80N	92 22.42W
WILCOX CO	IWE	NDB	350	31 58.83N	87 20.22W
WINK	INK	VOR	112.1	31 52.49N	103 14.62W
WINNFIELD	IFJ	NDB	402	31 57.78N	92 39.42W
WINTERS	IEW	NDB	396	31 57.22N	99 59.02W
WIREGRASS	RRS	VOR	111.6	31 17.07N	85 25.88W
WIREY (LOM)	WIRE	NDB	227	27 56.13N	82 4.55W
WISLE (LOM/NDB)	WISL	NDB	248	30 45.65N	88 18.17W
WOOLE (LOM)	WOOL	NDB	356	31 16.79N	100 34.57W
WYNDS (LOM/NDB)	WYND	NDB	269	29 40.22N	82 10.34W
YOAKUM	OKT	NDB	350	29 18.77N	97 8.32W
ZEPHYRHILLS	RHZ	NDB	253	28 13.42N	82 9.69W

VOR/NDBs for Europe

Name	Ident.	Type	Freq.	Latitude	Longitude
ABSAM	AB	NDB	313	47 17.41N	11 30.10E
ALENCON	AL	NDB	380	48 27.01N	0 6.80E
AMIENS	GI	NDB	339	49 50.51N	2 29.00E
AUGSBURG	AGB	NDB	318	48 25.51N	10 56.00E
BEAUVAIS	BVS	VOR	115.9	49 26.31N	2 9.30E

Name	Ident.	Type	Freq.	Latitude	Longitude
BEAUVAIS	BV	NDB	391	49 29.51N	2 1.80E
BOURSONNE	BSN	VOR	112.5	49 11.31N	3 3.40E
BRAY	BRY	VOR	114.1	48 24.41N	3 17.70E
BRAY	BRY	NDB	277	48 24.41N	3 17.70E
CHARLES-DE-GAULLE (PARIS)	RSO	NDB	364	49 0.71N	2 21.70E
CHARLES-DE-GAULLE (PARIS)	CGO	NDB	343	48 59.31N	2 24.10E
CHARLES-DE-GAULLE (PARIS)	RSY	NDB	356	49 1.91N	2 42.40E
CHARLES-DE-GAULLE (PARIS)	CGZ	NDB	370	49 0.41N	2 44.50E
CHARLES-DE-GAULLE (PARIS)	CGN	VOR	115.35	49 1.21N	2 30.10E
CHARTRES	CHW	VOR	115.2	48 28.81N	0 59.30E
CHATEAUDUN	CDN	VOR	116.1	48 3.51N	1 22.70E
CHATEAUDUN	CDN	NDB	359.5	48 3.81N	1 21.80E
CHATILLON	CTL	VOR	117.6	49 8.31N	3 34.70E
COMPIEGNE	CO	NDB	553.5	49 26.11N	2 48.40E
COULOMMIERS	CLM	VOR	112.9	48 50.71N	3 0.90E
CREIL	CRL	VOR	109.2	49 15.31N	2 31.00E
DEAUVILLE	DVL	VOR	110.2	49 18.61N	0 18.80E
DIEPPE	DPE	VOR	115.8	49 55.61N	1 10.30E
EPERNON	EPR	VOR	115.65	48 37.51N	1 39.30E
ERDING	ERD	VOR	113.6	48 19.61N	11 57.30E
ETAMPES	EM	NDB	295.5	48 22.61N	2 4.90E
EURACH	EUR	VOR	115.2	47 44.21N	11 15.00E
EVREUX	EVX	VOR	112.4	49 1.91N	1 13.30E
GERMANY - MUNICH	IMSW	VOR	108.3	48 20.48N	11 44.90E
GERMANY - MUNICH	IMNW	VOR	108.7	48 21.81N	11 45.90E
GERMANY - MUNICH	IMNE	VOR	110.3	48 22.13N	11 49.60E
GERMANY - MUNICH	IMSE	VOR	110.9	48 20.78N	11 48.60E
INGOLSTADT	IGL	NDB	345	48 44.41N	11 38.80E
INNSBRUCK	INN	NDB	420	47 13.91N	11 24.20E
KEMPTEN	KPT	VOR	109.6	47 44.81N	10 21.10E
LANDSBERG	LQ	NDB	448	48 5.61N	11 2.20E
LE BOURGET (PARIS)	BT	VOR	108.8	48 58.51N	2 27.40E
LE BOURGET (PARIS)	BGW	NDB	334	48 56.31N	2 16.80E
LE HAVRE	LHO	NDB	346	49 35.81N	0 11.00E
MAISACH	MAH	VOR	108.4	48 15.91N	11 18.80E
MELUN	MEL	VOR	109.8	48 27.41N	2 48.80E
MELUN	MV	NDB	434	48 33.21N	2 58.70E
MIKE	MIQ	NDB	426.5	48 34.31N	11 36.00E
MILLDORF	MDF	VOR	117	48 14.11N	12 20.30E

Name	Ident.	Type	Freq.	Latitude	Longitude
MONTDIDIER	MTD	VOR	113.65	49 33.21N	2 29.40E
MOOSBURG	MBG	VOR	117.15	48 34.51N	12 15.80E
MUNICH	MUN	VOR	112.3	48 10.91N	11 49.10E
MUNICH	MSE	NDB	385	48 20.11N	11 39.30E
MUNICH	MNE	NDB	358	48 21.41N	11 40.60E
MUNICH	MSW	NDB	400	48 21.21N	11 54.30E
MUNICH	MNW	NDB	338	48 22.51N	11 54.90E
NORDLINGEN	NDG	NDB	375	48 49.81N	10 25.20E
OBERPFAFFENHOFEN	OBI	NDB	429	48 4.91N	11 17.20E
ORLEANS	OAN	NDB	385	48 0.11N	1 46.20E
ORLY (PARIS)	OL	VOR	111.2	48 43.91N	2 23.30E
ORLY (PARIS)	ORW	NDB	402	48 40.41N	2 11.00E
ORLY (PARIS)	OLS	NDB	328	48 38.81N	2 20.80E
ORLY (PARIS)	OYE	NDB	349	48 45.21N	2 32.40E
PARIS - CHARLES DE GAULLE	GLE	VOR	108.7	48 59.94N	2 36.42E
PARIS - CHARLES DE GAULLE	GAU	VOR	109.1	48 59.76N	2 32.97E
PARIS - CHARLES DE GAULLE	CGE	VOR	110.1	49 1.39N	2 34.00E
PARIS - CHARLES DE GAULLE	CGW	VOR	110.7	49 1.24N	2 30.55E
PARIS - ORLY	ORE	VOR	108.5	48 44.31N	2 21.97E
PARIS - ORLY	OLW	VOR	109.5	48 43.18N	2 21.19E
PARIS - ORLY	OLN	VOR	110.3	48 44.51N	2 23.38E
PARIS - ORLY	OLO	VOR	110.9	48 43.21N	2 18.82E
PERONNE-ST. QUENTIN	PM	NDB	382	49 52.11N	3 8.20E
PITHIVIERS	PTV	VOR	116.5	48 9.31N	2 15.90E
PONTOISE	PON	VOR	111.6	49 5.81N	2 2.20E
RAMBOUILLET	RBT	VOR	114.7	48 39.21N	1 59.70E
RATTENBERG	RTT	NDB	303	47 25.91N	11 56.40E
REIMS	REM	VOR	112.3	49 18.71N	4 2.80E
RODING	RDG	VOR	114.7	49 2.51N	12 31.70E
ROUEN	ROU	VOR	116.8	49 27.91N	1 16.90E
SALZBURG	SBG	VOR	113.8	48 0.21N	12 53.60E
SALZBURG	SBG	NDB	382	47 58.11N	12 53.70E
SALZBURG	SU	NDB	356	47 52.81N	12 57.10E
SALZBURG	SI	NDB	410	47 49.21N	12 59.30E
TROYES	TRO	VOR	116	48 15.11N	3 57.80E
TROYES	TY	NDB	320.5	48 24.01N	4 0.30E
VILLACOUBLAY	HOL	NDB	315	48 43.91N	1 49.30E
VILLACOUBLAY	TA	NDB	286.5	48 46.31N	2 5.40E
VILLACOUBLAY	TH	NDB	302	48 46.71N	2 22.90E
WALDA	WLD	VOR	112.8	48 34.81N	11 7.90E

AIRPORT DIRECTORY LIST

Chicago Airport Directory

City	Airport	North	West	Elevation	Fuel	ILS	ATIS
Chicago/Aurora	Chicago/Aurora Municipal	41°46'	88°28'	707		32R/110.7	
Bloomington/ Normal	Bloomington/Normal	40°29'	88°55'	875			
Champaign-Urbana	Champaign-Urbana/ Univ. of Ill. Willard	40°02'	88°17'	754	*	32L/109.1	124.8
Chicago	Chicago-Midway	41°47'	87°45'	619	*		132.75
Chicago	Chicago-O'Hare Intl.	41°59'	87°54'	667	*	4L/111.3	135.4
						4R/110.1	
						9L/110.5	
						9R/111.1	
						14L/110.9	
						14R/109.7	
						22L/110.1	
						22R/111.3	
						27L/111.1	
						27R/110.5	
						32L/109.1	
						32R/110.7	
Chicago	Chicago/Lansing Mun.	41°32'	87°32'	616			
Chicago	Chicago/ Merrill C. Meiga	41°52'	87°36'	592			121.3
Chicago/ Schaumburg Air	Schaumburg Air Park	41°56'	88°06'	797			
Chicago (West Chicago)	Chicago/DuPage	41°54'	88°15'	758			
Danville	Danville/Vermillion Co.	40°2'	87°36'	696			
Dwight	Dwight	41°08'	88°26'	632			
Frankfort	Frankfort	41°29'	87°51'	778			
Gibson City	Gibson City Mun.	40°29'	88°16'	758			
Joliet	Joliet Park Dist.	41°31'	88°11'	581			
Kankakee	Kankakee/ Greater Kankakee	41°04'	87°51'	629			
Monee	Monee/Sanger	41°32'	87°41'	790			
Morris	Morris Mun.	41°26'	88°25'	588			
New Lenox	New Lenox-Howell	41°29'	87°55'	753			
Paxton	Paxton	40°27'	88°08'	779			
Plainfield	Plainfield/Clow Intl.	41°42'	88°08'	670			

City	Airport	North	West	Elevation	Fuel	ILS	ATIS
Chicago	Chicago/Lewis Univ.	41°36'	88°05'	668			
Urbana	Urbana/Frasca Field	40°39'	88°12'	735			

Munich Airport Directory

City	Airport	North	East	Elevation	Fuel	ILS	ATIS
Aalen-Heidenheim	Aalen-Heidenheim Elchingen	48°47'	10°16'	1916			
Arnbruck	Arnbruck	49°08'	12°59'	1716			
Augsburg	Augsburg	48°26'	10°56'	1515			118.22
Deggendorf	Deggendorf	48°50'	12°53'	1030			
Donauwörth	Donauwörth	48°42'	10°51'	1312			
Eggenfelden	Eggenfelden	48°24'	12°44'	1342			
Furstenzell	Furstenzell	48°31'	13°21'	1345			
Heidenheim an der Brenz	Giengen/Brenz	48°38'	10°13'	1695			
Gunzenhausen	Gunzenhausen-Reutberg	49°07'	10°47'	1591			
Innsbruck, Austria	Innsbruck	47°16'	11°21'	1906			126.02
Jesenwang	Jesenwang	48°11'	11°08'	1861			122.42
Landshut	Landshut	48°31'	12°02'	1312			
Leutkirch	Leutkirch-Unterzeil	47°52'	10°01'	2099			
Mindelheim	Mindelheim-Mattsies	48°07'	10°32'	1857			
Muhldorf	Muhldorf	48°17'	12°30'	1325			
Munich	Munich	48°21'	11°47'	1486	*	08L/110.3 08R/110.9 26L/108.3 26R/108.7	118.37
Nördlingen	Nördlingen	48°52'	10°30'	1384			
Oberpfaffenhofen	Oberpfaffenhofen	48°05'	11°17'	1947			
Regensburg	Regensburg-Oberhub	49°09'	12°05'	1298			
Salzburg, Austria	Salzburg	47°48'	13°00'	1411			
Schärding, Austria	Schärding/Suben	48°24'	13°27'	1070			
St. Johann in Tirol, Austria	St. Johann/Tirol	47°31'	12°27'	2198			
Straubing	Straubing-Wallmuhle	48°54'	12°31'	1046			
Vilshofen	Vilshofen	48°38'	13°12'	991			
Halfing	Vogtareuth	47°57'	12°12'	1535			
Zell Am See, Austria	Zell Am See	47°18'	12°47'	2470			

New York Airport Directory

City	Airport	North	West	Elevation	Fuel	ILS	ATIS
Block Island	Block Island State	41°10'	71°35'	109	*		
Boston	Boston/Gen. Edward Lawrence Logan Intl.	42°22'	71°00'	20	*		135.0
Bridgeport	Bridgeport/Igor L. Sikorsky Mem.	41°10'	73°08'	10	*		119.15
Chester	Chester	41°32'	72°30'	416			
Danbury	Danbury Mun.	41°22'	73°29'	457			
Danielson	Danielson	41°49'	71°54'	238			
Farmingdale	Farmingdale/Rep.	40°44'	73°25'	81			
Hartford	Harford-Brainard	41°44'	72°39'	19			
Islip	Islip/Long Island	40°48'	73°06'	99			
Martha's Vineyard	Martha's Vineyard	41°24'	70°37'	68	*	24/108.7	126.25
Meriden	Meriden Markham Municipal	41°31'	72°50'	103			
New Haven	New Haven/ Tweed New Haven	41°16'	72°53'	14			
New York	New York/ John F.Kennedy Intl.	40°38'	73°46'	13	*		128.73
New York	New York/LaGuardia	40°47'	73°52'	22			
Oxford	Oxford/ Waterbury Oxford	41°29'	73°08'	727			
Southbridge	Southbridge Mun.	42°06'	72°02'	697			
White Plains	White Plains/ Westchester Co.	41°04'	73°43'	439			
Willimantic	Willimantic/Windham	41°45'	72°11'	247			
Windsor	Windsor Locks/ Bradley Intl.	41°56'	72°41'	174			

Seattle Airport Directory

City	Airport	North	West	Elevation	Fuel	ILS	ATIS
Alderwood Manor	Martha Lake	47°52'	122°14'	500			
Arlington	Arlington Mun.	48°10'	122°09'	137			
Auburn	Auburn Mun.	47°20'	122°14'	57		·	
Bremarton	Bremarton Natl.	47°30'	122°46'	439			
Everett	Everett/ Snohornish Co. (Paine Field)	47°54'	122°17'	606	*		
Monroe	First Air Field	47°52'	122°00'	50			
Olympia	Olympia	46°58'	122°54'	206	*		124.4

City	Airport	North	West	Elevation	Fuel	ILS	ATIS
Puyallup	Pierce Co. Trun Fld.	47°06'	122°17'	530			
Port Angeles	William R. Fairchild Intl.	48°07'	123°30'	288			134.15
Port Orchard	Port Orchard	47°27'	122°40'	370			
Renton	Renton Mun.	47°30'	122°13'	29			
Seattle	Seattle/Boeing Fld./ King Co. Intl.	47°32'	122°18'	18	*		127.75
Seattle	Seattle-Tacoma	47°27'	122°18'	429	*		118.0
Shelton	Shelton/Sanderson Fld.	47°14'	123°09'	278			
Snohomish	Harvey Fl.d	47°54'	122°06'	16			
Spanaway	Shady Acres	47°04'	122°22'	445			
Spanaway	Spanaway	47°05'	122°26'	373			
Tacoma	Tacoma Narrows	47°16'	122°35'	292			

San Francisco Airport Directory

City	Airport	North	West	Elevation	Fuel	ILS	ATIS
Chico	Chico Municipal	39°48'	121°51'	238			
Colombia	Colombia	38°02'	120°25'	2118			
Concord	Buchanan Fld.	37°59'	122°03'	23			
Crows Landing	NALF Crows Landing	37°25'	121°06'	166			
Fresno	Chandler Downtown	36°44'	119°49'	278			
Fresno	Fresno Air Terminal	36°47'	119°43'	333			
Garberville	Garberville	40°05'	123°49'	546			
Half Moon Bay	Half Moon Bay	37°31'	122°30'	67			
Hayward	Hayward Air Terminal	37°40'	122°07'	47			
Little River	Mendocino Co.	39°15'	123°45'	572			
Livermore	Livermore Muni.	37°42'	121°49'	397			
Lodi	Kingdon	38°06'	121°22'	15			
Lodi	Lodi	38°12'	121°16'	58			
Marysville	Yuba Co.	39°06'	121°34'	62			
Merced	Merced Municipal-Macready Fld.	37°17'	120°31'	153			
Minden	Douglas Co.	39°00'	119°45'	4718			
Modesto	Modesto City	37°38'	120°57'	97			
Monterey	Monterey Peninsula	36°35'	121°51'	254			
Mountain View	NAS Moffett	37°19'	122°09'	34			
Novato	Hamilton	38°04'	122°31'	3			
Oakland	Metro Oakland Intl.	37°43'	122°13'	6	*	11/111.9 27R/109.9 29/108.7	128.5

Oakland	NAS Alameda	37°47'	122°19'	16			
Oroville	Oroville Muni.	39°29'	121°37'	190			
Palo Alto	Palo Alto	37°28'	122°07'	5			
Placerville	Placerville	38°43'	120°45'	2583			
Red Bluff	Red Bluff Muni.	40°09'	122°15'	349			
Reno	Reno Cannon Intl.	39°30'	119°46'	4412			
Reno	Reno/Stead	39°40'	119°52'	5046			
Sacramento	Sacramento Metro	38°42'	121°35'	24			
Sacramento	Sacramento Exec.	38°31'	121°30'	21			
Salinas	Salinas Muni.	36°40'	121°36'	84			
San Carlos	San Carlos	37°31'	122°15'	2			
San Francisco	San Francisco Intl.	37°37'	122°22'	11	*		118.85
San Jose	Reid-Hillview	37°20'	121°49'	133			
San Jose	San Jose Intl.	37°22'	121°56'	56			
Santa Rosa	Santa Rosa/Sonoma Co.	38°31'	122°49'	125			
South Lake Tahoe	South Lake Tahoe/ Lake Tahoe	38°54'	120°00'	6264			
Stockton	Stockton Metro	37°54'	121°14'	30			
Truckee	Truckee-Tahoe	39°19'	120°08'	5900			
Visalia	Visalia Muni.	36°19'	119°24'	292			
Watsonville	Watsonville Muni.	36°56'	121°47'	160			
Willows	Willows-Glenn Co.	39°31'	122°13'	139			

Los Angeles Airport Directory

City	Airport	North	West	Elevation	Fuel	ILS	ATIS
Avalon	Catalina (PVT)	33°24'	118°25'	1602	*		
Carlsbad	McClennan-Palomar	33°08'	117°17'	328			
Chino	Chino	33°58'	117°38'	650			
Compton	Compton	33°53'	118°15'	97			
Corona	Corona Mun.	33°54'	117°36'	533			
El Monte	El Monte	34°05'	118°02'	296			
Fallbrook	Fallbrook Comm. Airpark	33°21'	117°15'	708			
Hawthorne	Hawthorne Municipal	33°55'	118°20'	63			
La Verne	Brackett Field	34°05'	117°47'	1011			
Los Angeles	Los Angeles International	33°57'	118°24'	126	*		133.8
Oceanside	Oceanside Municipal	33°13'	117°21'	28			
Ontario	Ontario Intl.	34°03'	117°36'	943			
Riverside	Riverside Municipal	33°57'	117°27'	816			

City	Airport	North	West	Elevation	Fuel	ILS	ATIS
San Diego	San Diego Int. Lindbergh Field	32°44'	117°11'	15	*		134.8
Santa Ana	John Wayne Airport/Orange	33°41'	117°52'	54	*		126.0
Santa Monica	Santa Monica Municipal	34°01'	118°27'	175	*		119.15
Torrance	Torrance Mun.	33°48'	118°20'	101			
Van Nuys	Van Nuys	34°13'	118°29'	799	*	16R/111.3	118.45

Paris Airport Directory

City	Airport	North	West	Elevation	Fuel	ILS	ATIS
Amiens	Amiens	49°52'	02°23'	797			
Beauvais	Beauvais	49°27'	02°07'	358			
Chateaudun	Chateaudun	48°04'	01°23'	433			
Deauville	Deauville	49°22'	00°10'	479			
Paris	I. Ch. de Gaulle	49°01'	02°33'	387	*	09/110.1 10/108.7 27/110.7 28/109.1	128.0
Joigny	Joigny	47°60'	03°24'	728			
Paris	P. Le Bourget	48°59'	02°27'	217	*		120.0
Le Havre	Octeville	49°32'	00°05'	312	*		119.5
Le Mans	Le Mans	47°57'	00°12'	194			
Cambrai	C. Niergnies	50°09'	03°16'	361			
Paris	P.Orly	48°44'	02°23'	292	*	02L/110.3 07/108.5 25/110.9 26/109.5	126.5
St. Quentin	Peronne	49°52'	03°02'	292			
Persan	Persan	49°10'	02°19'	148			
Boissy	Pontoise	49°06'	02°03'	325			
Reims	Prunay	49°13'	04°09'	312			
Rouen	Boos	49°24'	01°11'	515			
St. Andre	St. Andre	48°54'	01°15'	489			
Toussus-le-Noble	Toussus	48°45'	02°07'	538			
Troyes	Barberey	48°19'	04°01'	394			

LIST OF AIRPORTS AROUND THE WORLD

ID	City	Elev	VOR Frequency	RWY-ILS	NDB Frequency	COM Frequency	ATIS
	Afr:ALGIER	1518		09/27 118.70			
	Afr: ALGIER	1518		05/23			
CAI	Afr: CAIRO, Egypt						
CMM	Afr: CASABLANCA, Moracco						
TIP	Afr: TRIPOLI, Libya						
TUN	Afr: TUNIS, Tunisia						
BGW	Asia: BAGHDAD, Iraq						
BEY	Asia: BEIRUT, Lebanon						
HKG	Asia: HONG KONG						
IST	Asia: ISTANBUL, Turkey						
SVO	Asia: MOSCOW, Russia						
	Asia: NEW TOKYO, Japan	139	110.10	110.10			
TLV	Asia: TEL AVIV, Israel						
	Asia: TOKYO INT, Japan						
LPA	Canary: LAS PALMAS						
YBC	Can: BAIE-COMEAU, QU	72		10/28			
	Can: BRANTFORD, ON	813	115.00				
	Can: BUTTONVILLE, ON	649	113.30				
TTC	Can: CALGARY, AL						
YYG	Can: CHARL'TOWN, PEI	160	114.10	03 - 110.90	347	126.20	120.10
YCH	Can: CHATHAM, NB	111		09/27			
YCC	Can: CORNWALL, ON	174		10/28			
	Can: DEBERT, NS	142	115.10	10/21		126.20	122.80
	Can: DEBERT, NS	142	115.10	16/24		126.20	112.880
YYG	Can: DIGBY, NS	98	113.30	06/24		126.20	
	Can: DOWNSVIEW, ON	649	113.30				
YEG	Can: EDMONTON, AL						
CN3	Can: EDMUNSTON, NB	488		18/36			
YFC	Can: FREDERICTON, NB	65	113.00	00/27	326		
YFC	Can: FREDERICTON, NB	65	113.00	15/33	326		
YQX	Can: GANDER, NFLD	496	112.70	13/31 109.50		126.20	119.10
YQX	Can: GANDER, NFLD	496	112.70	22/04 109.90		126.20	119.10
YND	Can: GATINEAU, QU	209		09/27			
YYR	Can: GOOSE BAY, NS	160	117.30	26 - 110.30			

Note: Many of these airports are not included as part of FS 5.0's built-in Airport/NAVAID database. Future scenery disks for the world may include these airports.

Warning: Use only with *Flight Simulator*. Not to be used for real navigational purposes.

ID	City	Elev	VOR Frequency	RWY-ILS	NDB Frequency	COM Frequency	ATIS
YHZ	Can: HALIFAX, NS	482	115.10	24 - 109.90	353	126.20	118.40
YHZ	Can: HALIFAX, NS	482	115.10	15 - 109.10	353	126.20	118.40
	Can: HAMILTON, ON	781	115.00				
YGR	Can: IS, DE LA M'LAINE, Qu	32	112.00	08/26	370		
	Can: LONDON, ON	912	117.20				
YQM	Can: MONCTON, NB	232	117.30	02/20	224		
YQM	Can: MONCTON, NB	232	117.30	11/29	224		
YQM	Can: MONCTON, NB	232	117.30	06/24	224		
YUL	Can: MONTREAL Mir, QU	118	116.30	06L-109.30	248		
YMX	Can: MONTREAL Mir, QU	260	116.70	06/24	248		
YMX	Can: MONTREAL Mir, QU	260	116.70	11/29	248		
	Can: NORTH BAY, ON	1214	115.40				
	Can: OSHAWA, ON	49	114.50				
YOW	Can: OTTAWA, ON	373	114.40	14/32	236		
YOW	Can: OTTAWA, On	373	114.60	07/25	236		
YPD	Can: PT HAWK'BURY, NS	380	114.90	11/29		126.20	
YQB	Can: QUEBEC, QU	242	112.80	12/30	230		
YQB	Can: QUEBEC, QU	242	112.80	06/24	230		
YRI	Can: RIV DU LOUP, QU	426		05/23			
YXE	Can: SASKATOON, SA						
	Can: SAULT S MARIE, ON	1689	111.80				
YZV	Can: SEPT-ILES, QU	180		09/27			
YAW	Can: SHEARWATER, NS	167	110.10	16/34	353		
YAW	Can: SHEARWATER,NS	167	110.10	11/29	353		
	Can: ST CATHARIN, ON	321	116.40				
YSJ	Can: ST JOHN, NB	357	113.50	14/32	212		
YSJ	Can: ST JOHN, NB	357	113.50	05/23 113.50	212		
YYT	Can: ST JOHN'S, NFLD	461	113.50	16 - 109.50		126.20	119.30
YYT	Can: ST JOHN'S, NFLD	461	113.50	29 - 110.30		126.20	119.30
	Can: ST PIERRE (Fr)	16	113.50	15 - 110.30		126.20	119.10
	Can: SUDBURY, ON						
YSU	Can: SUMMERSIDE, PEI	65	112.60	12.30	254	126.20	120.20
YSU	Can: SUMMERSIDE, PEI	65	112.60	06/24 117.05	254	126.20	120.20
YQY	Can: SYDNEY, NS	203	114.90	25 - 110.30		126.20	118.10
YQY	Can: SYDNEY, NS	203	114.90	07 - 109.50		126.20	118.10
YAZ	Can: TOFINO, BC	79	112.30		359		
	Can: TORONTO, ON		113.30				
	Can: TORONTO ISLD, ON	253	113.30				
YTR	Can: TRENTON, ON	288	109.70	13/31			
YTR	Can: TRENTON, ON	288	109.70	06/24			

ID	City	Elev	VOR Frequency	RWY-ILS	NDB Frequency	COM Frequency	ATIS
YRQ	Can: TROIS RIVIERE, QU	203		05/23			
	Can: VAL D'OR, QU	1105	113.70				
YVR	Can: VANCOUVER, BC						
	Can: WATERLOO, ON	1040	115.00				
YQG	Can: WINDSOR, ON	622		24 - 111.60			134.50
YWG	Can: WINNEPEG, MAN						
YQI	Can: YARMOUTH, NS	141	113.30	06/24 109.70	206	126.20	122.20
BDA	Carib: BERMUDA						
	Carib: FREEPORT, Bahamas	7	113.20				
HAV	Carib: HAVANA, Cuba						
KIN	Carib: KINGSTON, Jamaica						
	Carib: NASSAU, Bahamas	10	112.70				
POS	Carib: PORT OF SPAIN, Trin						
SJU	Carib: SAN JUAN, PR						
AMR	Eur: ALMERIA, Spain	50	114.10	26 - 109.90	284		
ATH	Eur: ATHENS, Greece						
	Eur: BARCELL El Prat, Spain		114.30	25 - 109.50			
	Eur: BARCELL El Prat, Spain		114.30	07 - 110.30			
	Eur: BARI, Italy	170	115.35	07 - 109.30			
	Eur: BELFAST, Aldergr, Ir		117.20	17 - 110.90			
	Eur: BELFAST, Aldergr, Ir		117.20	25 - 109.70			
	Eur: BERGAMO, Italy	779	112.60	29 - 108.70			
	Eur: BOLOGNA, Italy	125	112.20	12 - 108.90			
	Eur: BRISTOL, UK	620	117.45				
BRU	Eur: BRUSSELS Nat'l, Belgium		114.65	07L - 110.00		118.25	123.45
BRU	Eur: BRUSSELS Nat'l, Belgium		114.65	25R - 111.25		118.25	123.45
	Eur: CAGLIARI, Sard (It)	12	112.00	32/14 109.50			
	Eur: CARDIFF, UK220	117.45					
	Eur: CATANIA Sicily, Italy	43	112.10	08/26 109.90			
COR	Eur: CORDOBA, Spain	295		04/22	366		
	Eur: DUSSELDORF, Germany		115.15				
	Eur: EELDE, Holland		112.40	06/24		113.85	
	Eur: EELDE, Holland		112.40	01/19		113.86	
	Eur: FIRENZE, Italy	137	112.50				
FRA	Eur: FRANKFURT Rh. Mair	364	114.20	07R - 111.10			
FRA	Eur: FRANKFURT Rh. Mair	364	114.20	25R - 109.50			
FRA	Eur: FRANKFURT Rh. Mair	364	114.20	07L - 110.10			
FRA	Eur: FRANKFURT Rh. Mair	364	114.20	25L - 110.70			
	Eur: GENOVA, Italy	13		29 - 109.30			
	Eur: GENOVA, Italy	1518		05/23 119.90		127.30	127.55

ID	City	Elev	VOR Frequency	RWY-ILS	NDB Frequency	COM Frequency	ATIS
GBR	Eur: GIBRALTAR	15		09 - 117.25			
	Eur: GLASGOW Int'l, UK	26	115.40	05 - 110.10			
	Eur: GLASGOW Int'l, UK	26	115.40	23 - 109.30			123.45
PIK	Eur: GLASGOW Prestwick	66	117.50	13 - 109.50			123.45
PIK	Eur: GLASGOW, Prestwick	66	117.50	31 - 110.30			127.15
GDA	Eur: GRANADA, Spain	1860	113.40	09 - 109.30	285		127.15
	Eur: ISLE OF MAN, UK		112.20	27 - 110.90	359		
	Eur: ISLE OF MAN, UK		112.20	09 - 111.75	366		
JRZ	Eur: JEREZ, Spain	91	113.80	21 - 108.90	274		
	Eur: KOLN, Germany		112.15	34L - 110.90			
	Eur: KOLN, Germany		112.15	32R - 109.70			
	Eur: LAMPEDUSA Isl, (It)	72	108.20	08/26			
	Eur: LE HAVRE, France	312	110.20				
	Eur: LE MANS, France	194	115.20				
	Eur: LE TOUQUET, France	36	113.80				
	Eur: LILLE, France	159	112.60				
LIS	Eur: LISBON, Portugal						
LGW	Eur: LONDON Gatwick, UK	203	115.30				
LHR	Eur: LONDON Heathrow, UK	79	113.60				
MAD	Eur: MADRID, Spain						
MGA	Eur: MALAGA, Spain	52	112.80	32 - 109.90	330		
MGA	Eur: MALAGA, Spain52	112.80	14 - 109.50	350			
MLA	Eur: MALTA, Luqa						
MAN	Eur: MANCHESTER, UK		113.55	06 - 109.50			
MAN	Eur: MANCHESTER, UK		113.55	24 - 110.50			
	Eur: MANNHEIM, Germany	308	115.95				
MRS	Eur: MARSEILLES, France						
MIL	Eur: MILANO Linate, Italy	353	116.00	36R - 116.00			
	Eur: MILANO Malpensa, Italy	768	111.20	35R - 109.90			
MRN	Eur: MORON (AFB), Spain	287	115.30	21	280		
MUC	Eur: MUNICH, Germany	1738	112.30				
	Eur: NAPOLI, Italy	296	115.80	24 - 109.50			
NCE	Eur: NICE, France	1518		05/23R 110.25		127.90	129.60
NCE	Eur: NICE, France	1518		5R/23L 110.85		127.90	129.60
	Eur: NURENBERG, Germany	1486	121.90	08R - 110.90			118.35
	Eur: NURENBERG, Germany	1486	121.90	26R - 108.70			118.35
	Eur: NURENBERG, Germany	1486	121.90	08L - 110.30			118.35
	Eur: NURENBERG, Germany	1486	121.90	26L - 108.30			118.35
	Eur: PALERMO Sicily, Italy	64	113.00	02/20 109.90			

ID	City	Elev	VOR Frequency	RWY-ILS	NDB Frequency	COM Frequency	ATIS
	Eur: PALERMO Sicily, Italy	64	113.00	07/25 109.50			
	Eur: PALMA Mallorca, Spain	1518		6R/24L			119.25
	Eur: PALMA Mallorca, Spain	1518		6L/24R 119.40			119.25
	Eur: PANTELLERIA Isl., (It)	633	116.10	08/26			
	Eur: PANTELLERIA Isl., (It)	633	116.10	03/21			
CDG	Eur: PARIS De Gaulle, France	387	112.90	09/27 121.15		131.35	128.00
CDG	Eur: PARIS De Gaulle, France	387	112.90	10/28 119.85		131.35	128.00
ORY	Eur: PARIS Orly, France	292	111.20				
	Eur: REGGIO CALABRIA	84	110.00	23 - 109.30			
	Eur: ROMA Ciampino, Italy	426		15 - 109.90			
FCO	Eur: ROMA Fiumicino, Italy	14	114.90	34R - 109.30			
FCO	Eur: ROMA Fiumicino, Italy	14	114.90	16L - 108.10			
FCO	Eur: ROMA Fiumicino, Italy	14	114.90	16R - 110.30			
FCO	Eur: ROMA Fiumicino, Italy	14	114.90	25 - 109.70			
AOG	Eur: ROTA (Navy), Spain	86		28 - 108.60	265		
	Eur: ROTTERDAM, Holland			22 - 116.90		127.55	
	Eur: ROTTERDAM, Holland		10.00	04 - 116.80		127.55	
	Eur: SCHIPOL Amsterdam	-39	117.35	09 - 114.10			
	Eur: SCHIPOL Amsterdam	-39	117.35	27 - 114.20			
	Eur: SCHIPOL Amsterdam	-39	117.35	01 - 114.30			
	Eur: SCHIPOL Amsterdam	-39	117.35	19R - 114.40			
SVQ	Eur: SEVILLE, Spain	112	113.70	28 - 110.10	260		
SNN	Eur: SHANNON, Ireland						
	Eur: SHOREHAM, UK	7	117.00				
	Eur: STRASBOURG, Germany	502	115.60				
	Eur: TEUGE, Holland		111.10	08/26		124.10	
	Eur: TORINO, Italy	89	109.50	36 - 109.50			
	Eur: TRIESTE, Italy	39	114.20	09 - 109.70			
VCE	Eur: VENEZIA, Italy	7		04 - 110.30			
	Eur: VERONA, Italy		115.80	05 - 110.10			
HNL	Haw:HONOLULU						
ACA	Mex: ACAPULCO						
MEX	Mex: MEXICO CITY						
ALB	USA: ALBANY, NY	285		01/19 - 109.5			
ANC	USA: ANCHORAGE, AL	144	114.30	62 - 111.30			
	USA: ANDREWS AFB, DC	281	113.10	01L - 111.50			
	USA: ANDREWS AFB, DC	281	113.10	19R - 110.50			
ATL	USA: ATLANTA, GA						
PIY	USA: ATLANTIC CITY, NJ	76	108.60	31 - 108.00			

ID	City	Elev	VOR Frequency	RWY-ILS	NDB Frequency	COM Frequency	ATIS
PIY	USA: ATLANTIC CITY, NJ	76	108.60	04 - 108.20			
PIY	USA: ATLANTIC CITY, NJ	76	108.60	13 - 108.10			
BWI	USA: BALTIMORE, MA	146	111.70	09/27 109.90			
BGR	USA: BANGOR, ME	193	114.80	33 - 110.30	272	114.80	
BGR	USA: BANGOR, ME	193	114.80	15 - 109.50	272	114.80	
MPV	USA: BARRE/MONT, VT	1161		17 - 108.70			
BED	USA: BEDFORD	131		11 - 109.50			
BID	USA: BLOCK ISLAND, RI	104	117.20	10/28			
BOS	USA: BOSTON, MA	19	112.70	04/22 110.30		120.30	
BOS	USA: BOSTON, MA	19	112.70	27 - 111.30		120.30	
BOS	USA: BOSTON, MA	19	112.70	15R/33 110.70		120.30	
BDR	USA: BRIDGEPORT, CT	9		06/24 110.70			
BUF	USA: BUFFALO, NY	725	116.40				
BTV	USA: BURLINGTON, VT	334	117.50	15 - 110.30	257		
	USA: CHAMPAIGN, IL	754	110.00				
	USA: CHARLESTON, SC	20	114.50				
	USA: CHARLESTON, SC	20	114.50				
ORD	USA: CHICAGO O'Hare, IL	662	113.90				
ORD	USA: CHICAGO O'Hare, IL	662	113.90				
ORD	USA: CHICAGO O'Hare, IL	662	113.90				
ORD	USA: CHICAGO O'Hare, IL	662	113.90				
ORD	USA: CHICAGO O'Hare, IL	663	113.90				
	USA: CLEARWATER, FL	11	116.40				
	USA: CLEVELAND Hopkin	797		28 - 110.70			
	USA: CLEVELAND Hopkin	797		23L - 109.90			
	USA: CLEVELAND Hopkin	797		05R - 111.90			
	USA: DALLAS, TX		117.00	18L - 111.30			
	USA: DAYTONA BEACH, FL	35	112.60				
DEN	USA: DENVER, CO	5871	117.00				
DTW	USA: DETROIT Metro Wyr	639		03L 0 110.70		124.55	
DTW	USA: DETROIT Metro Wyr	639		21R - 110.75		124.55	
DTW	USA: DETROIT Metro Wyr	639		03R - 111.50		124.55	
DTW	USA: DETROIT Metro Wyr	639		21L - 111.55		124.55	
DTW	USA: DETROIT Metro Wyr	639		03L - 110.70		124.55	
	USA: EUGENE, OR	364	112.90				
	USA: EVERETT, WA	604					
FLL	USA: TF LAUDERDALE, FL	14	111.40				135.00
CXY	USA: HARRISBURG, PA	344		12/30			
CXY	USA: HARRISBURG, PA	344		08/26			

ID	City	Elev	VOR Frequency	RWY-ILS	NDB Frequency	COM Frequency	ATIS
HFD	USA: HARTFORD, CT	19		02/20			
HFD	USA: HARTFORD, CT	19		11/29			
IAH	USA: HOUSTON, TX						
IHT	USA: ITHICA, NY	1095		14/32			
	USA: JACKSONVILLE, FL	30	108.90				
	USA: KEYWEST, FL	4	113.50				
YGK	USA: KINGSTON, OR	311		01/19			
LAS	USA: LAS VEGAS, NV	2175					
LAX	USA LOS ANGELES, CA	126	113.60				
MHT	USA: MANCHESTER, NH	232		35 - 109.10			
	USA: MARTHA'S VINEYARD	75	108.20	06/24 108.70			
	USA: MARYLAND	171		17/35 123.00			
OED	USA: MEDFORD, OR	1332	113.60				
	USA: MEIGS, IL	592	114.20				
	USA: MEIGS FIELD, IL	590	113.90				
MIA	USA: MIAMI, FL	10	109.10	27L - 109.50			135.00
MIA	USA: MIAMI, FL	10	109.10				135.00
ACK	USA: NANTUCKET, MA			24 - 109.10			
NSY	USA: NEW ORLEANS, LO						
JFK	USA: NEW YORK Kennedy	13	115.90	22L - 110.90			
JFK	USA: NEW YORK Kennedy	13	115.90	31R - 111.50			
JFK	USA: NEW YORK Kennedy	13	115.90	04R - 109.50			
JFK	USA: NEW YORK Kennedy	13	115.90	04L - 110.90			
JFK	USA: NEW YORK Kennedy	13	115.90	13L - 111.50			
JFK	USA: NEW YORK Kennedy	13	115.90	22R - 109.50			
LGA	USA: NEW YORK La Guardia	22	113.10	13 - 108.50			
LGA	USA: NEW YORK La Guardia	22	113.10	22 - 110.50			
LGA	USA: NEW YORK La Guardia	22	113.10	04 - 110.50			
EWR	USA: NEWARK, NJ	16		04/22			
EWR	USA: NEWARD, NJ			04R - 108.70			
EWR	USA: NEWARK, NJ	16		11/09			
OAK	USA: OAKLAND, CA		116.80				
OLM	USA: OLYMPIA, WA	207	113.40	35			
OLM	USA: OLYMPIA, WA	207	113.40	08			
MCO	USA: ORLANDO, FL	96	112.20				
PBI	USA: PALM BEACH, FL		115.70	09L - 109.30			123.75
PHL	USA: PHILLY INT, PA	19	109.30	32L - 109.30			
PHL	USA: PHILLY INT, PA	19	109.30	34 - 111.50			
PHL	USA: PHILLY INT, PA	19	109.30	05 - 109.30			

ID	City	Elev	VOR Frequency	RWY-ILS	NDB Frequency	COM Frequency	ATIS
PHX	USA: PHOENIX, AZ						
	USA: PORT ANGELES, WA	288	112.20				
PDX	USA: PORTLAND INT, OR	26	116.60				
SPD	USA: PORTLAND INT, OR	25	116.60	28R - 111.30		119.80	128.35
SPD	USA: PORTLAND INT, OR	25	116.60	20 - 108.90		119.80	128.35
SPD	USA: PORTLAND INT, OR	25	116.60	10R - 109.90		119.80	128.35
PQI	USA: PRESQUE ISLE, ME	531	116.40	01/19			
PQI	USA: PRESQUE ISLE, ME	531	116.40	10/28			
PVD	USA: PROVIDENCE, RI	44		05r - 109.30			
PVU	USA: PROVO, UT	4600	108.40	36			
PVU	USA: PROVO, UT	4600	108.40	6			
PVU	USA: PROVO, UT	4600	108.40	13			
SMF	USA: SACRAMENTO, CA	24		34L - 111.10	400		
SMF	USA: SACRAMENTO, CA	24		16R - 111.15	230		
SLC2	USA: SALT LAKE CITY, UT	4608	116.80	16R			
SLC2	USA: SALT LAKE CITY, UT	4608	116.80	14			
SLC2	USA: SALT LAKE CITY, UT	4608	116.80	16			
SAT	USA: SAN ANTONIO, TX	810	116.80				
SAN	USA: SAN DIEGO, CA						
SFO	USA: SAN FRANCISCO, CA		115.80	28L - 109.50			

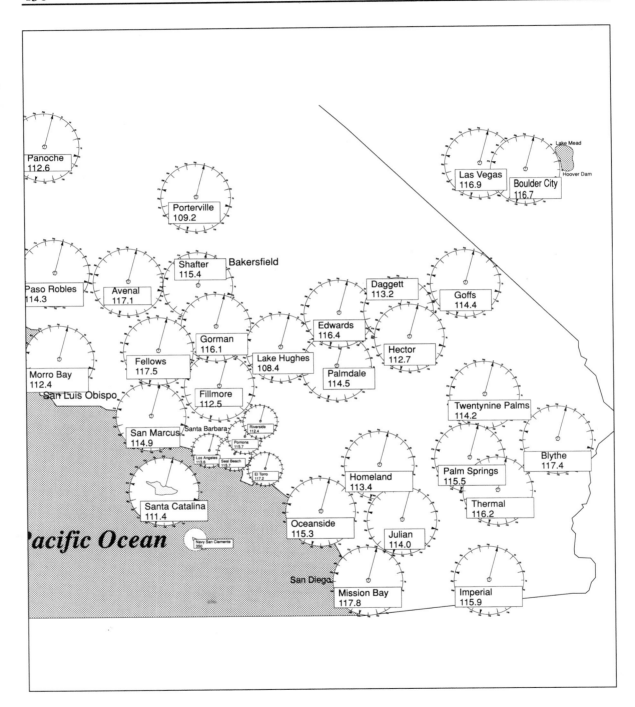

Los Angeles Sectional Map

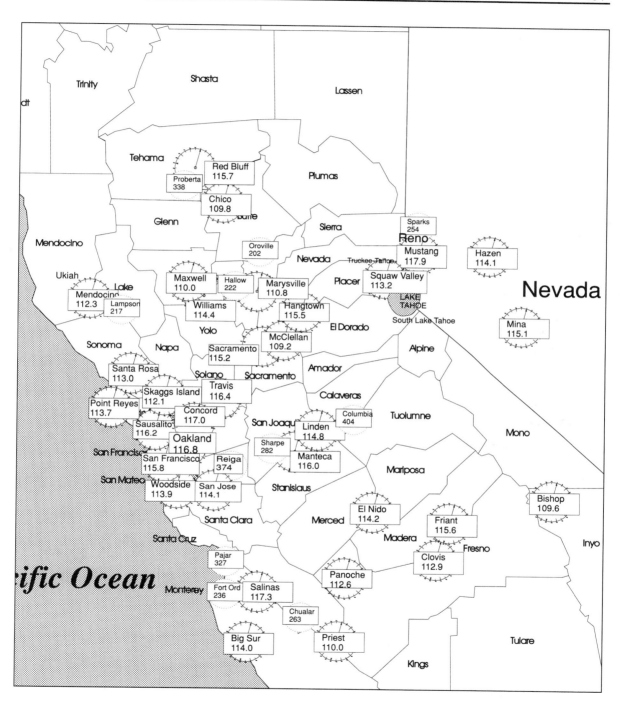

San Francisco Sectional Map

Pacific Ocean

Vancouver Island

Bellingham
113.0

Canada

British Columbia

Washington

Victoria
113.7

Tatoosh
112.2

Paine
110.6

Wenatchee
111.0

Spokane
115.5

Ephrata
112.6

McChord AFB
109.6

Ellensburg
117.9

Moses Lake
115.0

Pullman
109.0

Hoquiam
117.7

Yakima
116.0

Pasco
108.4

Nez Perce
108.2

Astoria
114.0

Battleground
116.6

Klickitat
112.3

Walla Walla
116.4

Pendleton
114.7

Portland
111.8

Newberg
117.4

Baker
115.3

Newport
117.1

Corvallis
115.4

Kimberly
115.6

Eugene
112.9

Oregon

Medford
Rogue Valley
113.6

Klamath Falls
115.9

Seattle Sectional Map

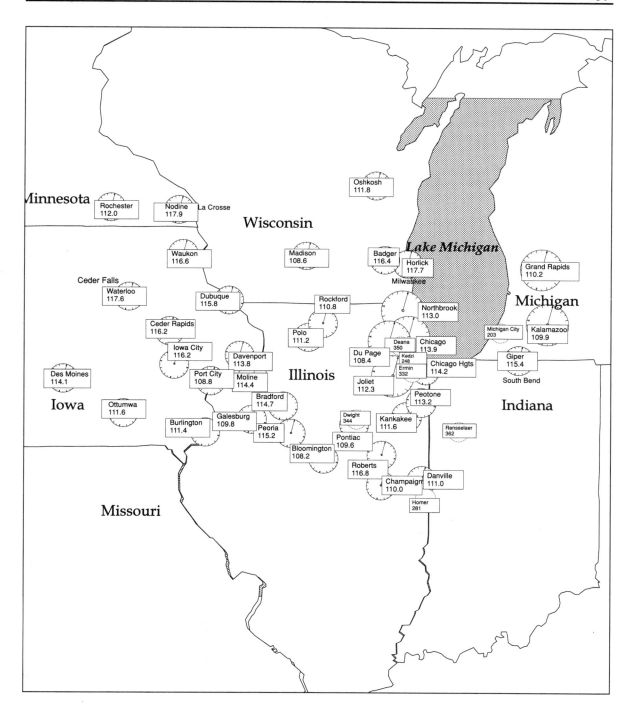

Chicago Sectional Map

New York Sectional Map

A P P E N D I X

C

Keyboard Summary

This appendix summarizes all the keyboard functions in *Flight Simulator 5.0*. In many cases, some program functions can be accessed only by multiple keystrokes. In those instances, you will see two key identifiers presented side by side. For example, to shift your view direction from the front to the rear, you would see the following keystrokes: [Shift] [8]. This would mean that you must press and hold the [Shift] key down and then press [8] on the numeric keypad. Whenever you see a number key identified, it is always assumed to be a *numeric keypad number, not one of the numbers on the main keyboard*. For some functions, the number keys on the main keyboard are used; for example, if you wanted to increase a single engine throttle on the Learjet you would press [E] [1] (on the main keyboard) or [E] [2] (on the main keyboard) followed by [9] on the numeric keypad. To avoid confusion, always press the number keys on the numeric keypad, unless otherwise told.

On the other hand, whenever you see [+] or [−], it is assumed that you must press the keys that are located on the main keyboard, not the numeric keypad.

FUNCTION KEYS ON THE MAIN KEYBOARD

Key	Function
[A]	Set ADF Radio Press [A] for First Digit, [A] [A] for Second Digit, [A] [A] [A] for third Digit, followed by [+] or [−].
[B]	Calibrate Altimeter
[C]	Set COM Radio Frequency. Press [C] followed by [+] or [−] for integer portion; Press [C] [C] followed by [+] or [−] for fractional portion.

KEY	FUNCTION
D	Calibrate Directional Gyro
E	Engine Control. Press E 1 (on the main keyboard) for Left Engine 1; Press E 2 for Right Engine 2; or Press E 1 2 for Both Engines followed by 9 (numeric keypad) to increase throttle, or 3 (numeric keypad) to decrease throttle.
F	DME Radio Control. Press F 1 (on the main keyboard) for DME 1, or F 2 for DME 2, followed by + to toggle between readout of speed toward station in knots (KTS) or distance in nautical miles (NM)
G	Landing Gear Up/Down
H	Carburetor Heat On/Off
I	Smoke/Spray On/Off
J	Jet Starter Switch On/Off. Press J 1 (on the main keyboard) for Left Engine 1, or J 2 for Right Engine 2, followed by + or -.
K	Calibrate Joystick
L	All Lights On/Off. For Instrument Lights only, press Shift L . For Landing Lights, press Ctrl L .
M	Magnetos On/Off. Press M followed by + or -.
N	NAV Radio Control. Set NAV Radio Frequency. For NAV 1 Radio, press N 1 (on the main keyboard) followed by + or - for integer portion; Press N N followed by + or - for fractional portion. For NAV 2 Radio, press N 2.
O	Strobe On/Off
P	Pause/Resume Flight
Q	Sound On/Off
R	Rate of Simulation. Press R followed by + or -.
S	Cycle through Cockpit, Tower, and Spot View
T	Transponder. Press T (first digit), T T (second digit), T T T (third digit), T T T T (fourth digit), followed by + or -.
U	Move EGT Bug Needle. Press U + to increase or U - to decrease.
V	VOR OBI Course Selector. Press V 1 (on the main keyboard) for OBI 1, or V 2 for OBI 2, followed by + or -. Shift + or Shift - adjusts in 10° increments.

KEY	FUNCTION
⬚W⬚	Enlarge active window to full screen (toggle key).
⬚X⬚	Land Me
⬚Y⬚	Enter Slew Mode (toggle key)
⬚Z⬚	Autopilot On/Off
⬚Shift⬚ ⬚Z⬚	Display Latitude/Longitude Coordinates
⬚Ctrl⬚ ⬚Z⬚	Autopilot Altitude Lock On
⬚Backspace⬚	Normal 1X Magnification
⬚Tab⬚	Switch Between Instrument Sub Panels.
⬚Shift⬚ ⬚Tab⬚	On Cessna, switches between VOR 2 and the ADF Indicator. On the Learjet, switches between VOR 1, VOR 2, and ADF Indicator.
⬚Esc⬚	Turn Menu Bar On/Off
⬚Num Lock⬚	Map View. Press ⬚Num Lock⬚ Twice to Close
⬚Ctrl⬚ ⬚Print Screen⬚	Reset Situation
⬚Ctrl⬚ ⬚C⬚	Exit Flight Simulator
⬚Ctrl⬚ ⬚Break⬚	Go to MS-DOS Prompt
⬚.⬚	Brakes On/Off and Release Parking Brakes
⬚Ctrl⬚ ⬚.⬚	Parking Brake On
⬚;⬚	Save Situation
⬚"⬚	Bring Selected or Active Window to Top
⬚?⬚	Spoilers (Learjet)/Dive Brake(Sailplane) On/Off
⬚+⬚	Zoom In. For fine zoom in, press ⬚Shift⬚ ⬚+⬚
⬚-⬚	Zoom Out. For fine zoom out, press ⬚Shift⬚ ⬚-⬚
⬚[⬚	View 3-D View Window 1. Press⬚[⬚ ⬚[⬚ to Close
⬚]⬚	View 3-D View Window 2. Press ⬚]⬚ ⬚]⬚ to Close
⬚\⬚	Stop Recording a Video, or Stop Maneuver Analysis
⬚Spacebar⬚	Close Open Menu. Also, Formation Flying Catch Up.
⬚Ctrl⬚ ⬚Spacebar⬚	Catch Up With Flying Companion while in Dual Player Mode (First make sure you are both on the ground, or both in the air, otherwise the simulation crashes).
⬚0⬚ (on main keyboard)	Send Message to Flying Companion while in Dual Player Mode (For the first message, click on the Send Message button in Dual-Player Dialog Box; thereafter use ⬚0⬚).

The Following Keys are on the Numeric Keypad:

KEYPAD	FUNCTION
[1]	Elevator Trim Up (Nose Up)
[2]	Elevator Up (Nose Up)
[3]	Decrease Throttle
[4]	Bank Left (Left Ailerons)
[5]	Center Ailerons & Rudder
[6]	Bank Right (Right Ailerons)
[7]	Elevator Trim Down (Nose Down)
[8]	Elevator Down (Nose Down)
[9]	Increase Throttle
[0]	Left Rudder (only in uncoordinated flight mode) or Steer Left while Taxiing
[Enter] (on numeric keypad)	Right Rudder (only in uncoordinated flight mode) or Steer Right while Taxiing

FUNCTION KEYS ON THE ENHANCED KEYBOARD (FUNCTION KEYS ON TOP)

If you are using an enhanced 101 keyboard with the function keys on the top row, use the following keys to perform the operations listed:

FUNCTION KEY	FUNCTION

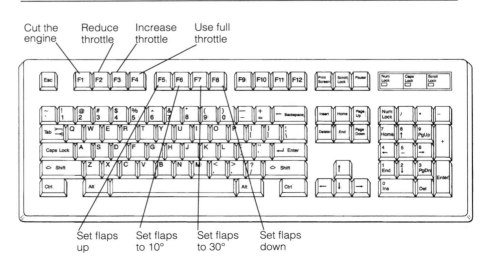

Figure C.1
Function keys on the top row of the keyboard

Key	Function
F1	Cut Throttle
F2	Decrease Throttle One Step
F3	Increase Throttle One Step
F4	Full Throttle
F5	Flaps Fully Retracted (0°)
F6	Flaps 10°
F7	Flaps 30°
F8	Flaps 40°
F11	Left Differential Brake
F12	Right Differential Brake

FUNCTION KEYS ON THE STANDARD KEYBOARD (FUNCTION KEYS ON SIDE)

If you are using a standard keyboard, with the function keys on the left side of the keyboard, use the following keys to perform the operations listed:

FUNCTION KEY	FUNCTION
F1	Flaps Fully Retracted (0°)
F2	
F3	Flaps 10°
F4	Full Throttle
F5	Flaps 20°
F6	Increase Throttle One Step
F7	Flaps 30°
F8	Decrease Throttle One Step
F9	Flaps 40°
F10	Cut Throttle
F11	Left Differential Brake
F12	Right Differential Brake

FLIGHT CONTROLS ON THE NUMERIC KEYPAD

The following keyboard functions for the numeric keypad allow you to set your flight controls:

CONTROL		KEY
Ailerons		
	Left	4
	Center	5
	Right	6
Elevator		
	Nose up	2
	Nose down	8
Elevator trim		
	Nose up	1
	Nose down	7
Rudder		
	Left	0
	Center	5
	Right	Enter
		(on numeric keypad)
Flap Controls	Key (Function Keys on Top)	Key (Function Keys on Left)
Flaps Retracted		
0°	F5	F1
10°	F6	F3
20°		F5
30°	F7	F7
40°	F8	F9

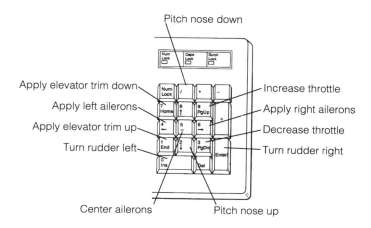

Figure C.2
Flight controls on the numeric keypad

ENGINE CONTROLS

The following keys and key combinations control your engines:

CONTROL	KEY (FUNCTION KEYS ON TOP)	KEY (FUNCTION KEYS ON LEFT)
Throttle		
Increase a step	9	9
Decrease a step	3	3
Cut	F1	F10
Decrease a step	F2	F8
Increase a step	F3	F6
Full	F4	F4
Propeller Control		
Increase	Ctrl 9	Ctrl 9
Decrease	Ctrl 3	Ctrl 3
Cut	Ctrl F1	Ctrl F10
Decrease	Ctrl F2	Ctrl F8
Increase	Ctrl F3	Ctrl F6
Full	Ctrl F4	Ctrl F2

CONTROL	KEY (FUNCTION KEYS ON TOP)	KEY (FUNCTION KEYS ON LEFT)
Mixture Control		
Increase	[Ctrl] [Shift] [9]	[Ctrl] [Shift] [9]
Decrease	[Ctrl] [Shift] [3]	[Ctrl] [Shift] [3]
Cut	[Ctrl] [Shift] [F1]	[Ctrl] [Shift] [F10]
Decrease	[Ctrl] [Shift] [F2]	[Ctrl] [Shift] [F8]
Increase	[Ctrl] [Shift] [F3]	[Ctrl] [Shift] [F6]
Full	[Ctrl] [Shift] [F4]	[Ctrl] [Shift] [F2]
EGT Bug Needle		
Move Needle Forward	[U] [+]	[U] [+]
Move Needle Back	[U] [−]	[U] [−]
Jet Engine Shutdown		[Ctrl] [Shift] [F1]
Jet Starter	[J] [+] or [J] [−]	[J] [+] or [J] [−]

NAVIGATION COMMUNICATION KEYS

Certain keys or key combinations control navigation and communication functions, as is shown in the following list:

KEY COMBINATION	FUNCTION
[A] [+]	Set first digit of ADF Radio (ADF Radio must be activated first)
[A] [A] [+]	Set second digit of ADF radio
[A] [A] [A] [+]	Set third digit of ADF radio
[C] [+]	Set integer portion of COM Radio frequency
[C] [C] [+]	Set fractional portion of COM Radio frequency
[F1] (on main keyboard) [+]	DME 1 Radio control toggle between readout of speed toward station in knots (KTS) or distance in nautical miles (NM)
[F2] (on main keyboard) [+]	DME 2 Radio control toggle between readout of speed toward station in knots (KTS) or distance in nautical miles (NM)
[N] [1] [+]	Set integer portion of NAV 1 Radio frequency

KEY COMBINATION	FUNCTION
[N] [N] [1] [+]	Set fractional portion of NAV 2 Radio frequency
[N] [2] [+]	Set integer portion of NAV 1 Radio frequency
[N] [N] [2] [+]	Set fractional portion of NAV 2 Radio frequency
[T] [+]	Set first digit of Transponder Squawk Code
[T] [T] [+]	Set second digit of Transponder Squawk Code
[T] [T] [T] [+]	Set third digit of Transponder Squawk Code
[T] [T] [T] [T] [+]	Set fourth digit of Transponder Squawk Code

For the above list of keyboard combinations, you can substitute [−] for the [+] to reduce the frequency setting.

VIEW KEYS

Certain keys or key combinations control viewing functions (from the numeric keypad), as is shown by the following:

VIEW DIRECTION	FUNCTION
Front	[Shift] [8]
Rear	[Shift] [2]
Left	[Shift] [4]
Right	[Shift] [6]
Left front	[Shift] [7]
Right front	[Shift] [9]
Left rear	[Shift] [1]
Right rear	[Shift] [3]
Down	[Shift] [5]
Pan up	[Shift] [Backspace]
Pan down	[Shift] [Enter]
Pan left	[Shift] [Ctrl] [Backspace]
Pan right	[Shift] [Ctrl] [Enter]
Straight and Level (No Pan)	[Scroll Lock]

Other Viewing Keys

KEY COMBINATION	FUNCTION
S	Cycle through Cockpit, Tower, and Spot View
Shift S	Reverse cycle through Cockpit, Tower, and Spot View
W	Maximize currently active window to full screen
+	Zoom in
Shift +	Fine Zoom in
−	Zoom out
Shift −	Fine Zoom out
Backspace	1X Normal Magnification
[	Open 3-D View Window 1. Press [[to Close.
]	Open 3-D View Window 2. Press]] to Close.
Num Lock	Bring up Map Window. Press Num Lock twice to Close.

SLEWING CONTROLS

Slewing is a special nonflight mode that allows you to quickly move from point to point in the *Flight Simulator* world. In addition actually moving the aircraft in three dimensions (called translation), you can also reorient the plane to any attitude (called rotation).

The slewing controls will work only when you enter slew mode. To enter and exit slew mode, press Y.

Slewing Translation

The following keys allow you to move the aircraft in three dimensions:

SLEW TRANSLATION	KEY (FUNCTION KEYS ON TOP)	KEY (FUNCTION KEYS ON LEFT)
Up or Down in Altitude		
Up Slowly	Q	Q
Up Quickly	F4	F2
Down Slowly	A	A
Down Quickly	F1	F10
Freeze	5	5

Forward & Backward
 Forward 8 8
 Backward 2 2
 Freeze 5 5
Sideways
 Left 4 4
 Right 6 6
 Freeze 5 5

Slewing Rotation

The following keys allow you to reorient the aircraft's pitch, bank (roll), and heading:

SLEW ROTATION	KEY (FUNCTION KEYS ON TOP)	KEY (FUNCTION KEYS ON LEFT)
Up or Down in Altitude		
Up Slowly	Q	Q
Pitch		
Nose up slowly	9 (on main keyboard)	9 (on main keyboard)
Nose up fast	$F5$	$F1$
Freeze	$F6$	$F5$
Nose down fast	$F8$	$F9$
Nose down slowly	0 (on main keyboard)	$F7$
Bank (Roll)		
Left	7	7
Right	9	9
Freeze	5	5
Heading (Yaw)		
Left	1	1
Right	3	3
Freeze	5	5

Other Slewing Functions

Other slewing functions include the following:

[Z]	Toggle Position Display Between On/Off/Latitude-Longitude/North-East Coordinate Systems
[Spacebar]	Reset Aircraft Orientation so that it is level:

Heading: North
Pitch: 0°
Bank: 0°

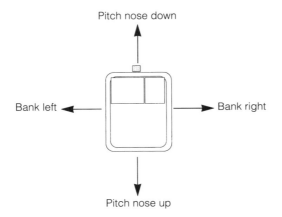

Figure C.3
Mouse movements affect flight controls (first press right mouse button so cursor disappears)

MOUSE CONTROLS

The mouse can act as a flight control in *Flight Simulator*. By pressing the right mouse button, the cursor will disappear and the mouse can be rolled left or right, backwards or forwards, to affect the yoke controls. To exit mouse yoke control, simply press the right mouse button once again.

MOUSE MOVEMENT (FIRST PRESS RIGHT MOUSE BUTTON SO CURSOR DISAPPEARS)	FUNCTION
Forward	Pitch Nose Down (Elevator Down)
Backward	Pitch Nose Up (Elevator Up)
Left	Bank Left (Set Left Aileron & Rudder)
Right	Bank Right (Set Right Aileron & Rudder)

In addition, if you hold down the left mouse button while moving the mouse, you can control the throttle and brakes.

MOUSE MOVEMENT WHILE HOLDING LEFT MOUSE BUTTON DOWN	FUNCTION
Forward	Increase Throttle
Backward	Decrease Throttle
Left	Apply Brakes
Right	Release Brakes

Using the Mouse in Slew Mode

While in slew mode, the mouse can also be used to move the plane. First enter slew mode by pressing Y. Then, to activate the mouse, press the right mouse button so that the mouse pointer disappears. To move forward, move the mouse forward; to move backward, move the mouse backward. To rotate the plane left or right, roll the mouse left or right, but notice that the plane is merely rotating in place and not moving from its present position. To stop all motion, click the left mouse button. To make the mouse pointer reappear, click the right mouse button.

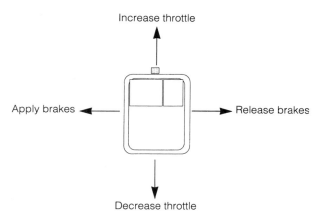

Figure C.4
Mouse functions for controlling engine and brakes

USING THE VIDEO RECORDER

The following keystrokes will work only when you are recording videos by using the Video Recorder command under the Options menu.

KEY	FUNCTION
\	Stop Recording a Video
6 (on main keyboard)	Record at a 1 Second Interval
7 (on main keyboard)	Record at a 5 Second Interval
,	Insert Messages During Playback
Esc	Stop Playback

Bibliography

How to Order These Books and Publications.

Many of the aviation books and publications listed in this bibliography can be ordered directly from:

> The Aviator Store
> 7201 Perimeter Road South
> Seattle, WA 98108
> Their toll-free U.S. telephone number is 1-800-635-2007

Books

Broadbent, Stephen. *Jane's Avionics 1987-88*. New York: Jane's Publishing Inc., 1988.

Cessna 1986 Turbo Skylane RG Information Manual. Wichita, Kansas: Cessna Aircraft Company, 1985.

Conns, Keith. *The LORAN, GPS & NAV/COM Guide*. Templeton, CA: Butterfield Press, 1992.

Conway, Carle. *The Joy of Soaring: A Training Manual*. Hobbs, New Mexico: The Soaring Society of America, 1989.

Federal Aviation Regulations/Airman's Information Manual FAR/AIM 1993. ASA-93-FR-AM-BK. Renton, Washington: Aviation Supplies & Academics, Inc., 1993.

Federal RadioNavigation Plan 1992. DOT-VNTSC-RSPA-92-2/DOD-4650.5. Washington D.C.: U.S. Department of Transportation and Department of Defense, 1992.

Flight Training Handbook. AC-61-21A. Washington D.C.: U.S. Department of Transportation, Federal Aviation Administration, 1980.

Hobbs, Richard R. *Marine Navigation 2: Celestial and Electronic.* Second Edition. Annapolis, Maryland: Naval Institute Press, 1981.

Instrument Flying Handbook. AC-61-27C. Washington D.C.: U.S. Department of Transportation, Federal Aviation Administration, 1980.

Lambert, Mark. *Jane's All the World's Aircraft 1991-92.* Alexandria, VA: Jane's Information Group, 1992.

Microsoft Flight Simulator Pilot's Handbook. Bellingham, Washington: Microsoft Press, 1993.

Porter, Donald J. *Learjets.* Blue Ridge Summit, PA: Tab Books, 1987.

Serway, Raymond A. *Physics For Scientists & Engineers with Modern Physics.* Third Edition. San Francisco: Saunders College Publishing, 1990.

Pamphlets

Aeronautical Charts and Related Products, U.S. Department of Commerce, National Oceanic and Atmospheric Administration, National Ocean Service. Riverdale, Maryland. 1993.

Cost of Operation: Learjet 35A. Wichita, Kansas: Learjet Inc.

Learjet 35A. Wichita, Kansas: Learjet Inc.

Mission Planning Guide: Learjet 35A. Wichita, Kansas: Learjet Inc.

Optional Equipment Description & Pricing: Learjet 35A. Wichita, Kansas: Learjet Inc.

The Schweizer 2-32 Sailplane Flight-Erection-Maintenance Manual. Elmira, New York: Schweizer Aircraft Corp.

Specification & Description: Learjet 35A. Wichita, Kansas: Learjet Inc.

Magazines

Collins, Richard L. "Skylane Round Robin." *Flying Magazine,* November 1979, pp. 77-83.

MacKay, Robert. "Microsoft's Flight Simulator 5.0." *MicroWINGS Magazine,* August 1993, Vol. 1, No. 3, pg 12-15.

Navin, Patrick. "GPS Update." InFlight *Aviation News Monthly,* June 1993, pp. 54-55.

North, David M. "Learjet 60 Stakes Claim in Corporate Market." *Aviation Week & Space Technology*, June 28, 1993, pp.38-43.

Schiff, Barry. "Skyregs Review: Controlled Airspace." *AOPA Pilot Magazine*, February 1985, pp. 44-47.

How to order maps and aeronautical sectionals from the NOAA in Maryland.

Flight Simulator is best enjoyed if you have the real navigational maps that pilots use. The Federal Government's National Oceanic and Atmospheric Administration agency publishes all the maps you might need to use. They have a free catalog, called the Aeronautical Charts and Related Products, which lists all the maps they publish and their prices. To order the NOAA map catalog, or to place an order, contact the NOAA at:

NOAA Distribution Branch, N/CG33
National Ocean Service
Riverdale, Maryland 20737-1199
Telephone and FAX orders are also accepted by the NOAA Distribution Branch:

General Information and Individual Orders   301-436-6990

FAX Orders   301-436-6829

Maps and Sectionals

There are several different kinds of maps that the NOAA publishes. They are listed as follows:

- VFR (Visual Flying Rules) Terminal Area Charts
- Sectional Aeronautical Charts
- Enroute Low Altitude Victor Airway Maps
- IFR (Instrument Flying Rules) Enroute High Altitude Jet Airway Maps
- Global Route Maps

Visual Flying Rules (VFR) terminal area charts are maps that show the the area immediately surrounding the city's major airports. They include landmarks, airspace obstruction information, lakes, dams, rivers, roads, large buildings, as well as VOR/NDB stations. The terminal area charts also show the runway orientations so that you know where to head your airplane when landing. Basically, you use the terminal area chart to plan your final approach to the airport. The terminal area charts that are most useful for Flight Simulator include the following:

- Los Angeles Terminal Area Chart
- San Francisco Terminal Area Chart
- Seattle Terminal Area Chart
- Chicago Terminal Area Chart
- New York Terminal Area Chart

Sectional aeronautical charts show terrain and topographical features as well as VOR/NDB stations. However, they cover a much larger region than the terminal area charts. Here is a listing of the charts used for Flight Simulator's main U.S. scenery areas:

- Los Angeles Sectional
- San Francisco Sectional
- Seattle Sectional
- Chicago Sectional
- New York Sectional

The low altitude victor airway charts show only VOR/NDB stations and the air routes for flights that take place below 18,000 feet. No geographical or topographical information is included. Some of the more popular of these charts are listed as follows:

- L-1/L-2: Covers the West Coast of the U.S.,except for Santa Barbara down to Los Angeles.
- L-3: Covers Santa Barbara to San Diego, California eastward to Arizona
- L-19: Covers east coast of Florida.
- L-27/L-28: Covers East Coast of U.S. from Georgia to New York.
- L-11/L-23: Covers the area around Chicago, Illinois.
- L-13: Covers the area around Dallas, Ft. Worth.

As with the victor airway maps, the high altitude jet airway charts do not include geographical or topographical map features. They include only the air routes and the VOR/NDB stations and are to be used for flights above 18,000 feet. If you get all three of the following H charts, you will have a navigational map of the entire U.S.:

- Northwest H-1/Northeast H-3 IFR Enroute High Altitude U.S. Chart: Covers the northern U.S. west from the Northern California coast to the New York coast.

- Southwest H-2/Southeast H-4 IFR Enroute High Altitude U.S. Chart: Covers the southern U.S. west from Southern California to Northern Florida coast.
- H-5 IFR Enroute High Altitude U.S. Chart: Covers Southern Texas to Southern Florida.

For transoceanic flights you will need these charts:

- North Pacific Route Chart Composite: Covers the entire North Pacific from California/Alaska to Japan, and includes Taiwan, Indonesia, Northern Australia, the Hawaiian Islands, the Phillipines, Tahiti, Wake Island, and many other South Pacific islands. Includes VOR/NDB stations and latitude/longitude waypoints for the principal air corridors of the Pacific Ocean region.
- North Atlantic Route Chart: Covers the U.S. and Canadian Eastern Seaboard, the Caribbean region, Bermuda, Cuba, Venezuela, Greenland, Iceland, England, Ireland, Azores, Spain, Morroco, and Western Sahara, down to Dakar, Africa. Includes VOR/NDB stations and latitude/longitude waypoints for the principal air corridors for the North and mid-Atlantic Ocean regions.

Index

COMPUTER GAME BOOKS

SimEarth: The Official Strategy Guide	$19.95
Harpoon Battlebook: The Official Strategies and Tactics Guide	$19.95
Wing Commander I and II: The Ultimate Strategy Guide	$19.95
Chuck Yeager's Air Combat Handbook	$19.95
The Official Lucasfilm Games Air Combat Strategies Book	$19.95
Sid Meier's Civilization, or Rome on 640K a Day	$19.95
Ultima: The Avatar Adventures	$19.95
Ultima VII and Underworld: More Avatar Adventures	$19.95
JetFighter II: The Official Strategy Guide	$19.95
A-Train: The Official Strategy Guide	$19.95
PowerMonger: The Official Strategy Guide	$19.95
Global Conquest: The Official Strategy Guide (w/disk)	$24.95
Gunship 2000: The Authorized Strategy Guide	$19.95
Falcon 3: The Official Combat Strategy Book (w/disk)	$27.95
Dynamix Great War Planes: The Ultimate Strategy Guide	$19.95
SimLife: The Official Strategy Guide	$19.95
Stunt Island: The Official Strategy Guide	$19.95
Populous: The Official Strategy Guide	$19.95
Prince of Persia: The Official Strategy Guide	$19.95
X-Wing: The Official Strategy Guide	$19.95
Empire Deluxe: The Official Strategy Guide	$19.95
F-15 Strike Eagle III: The Official Strategy Guide	$19.95
Lemmings: The Official Companion	$19.95
Secret of Mana: Official Game Secrets	$19.95
The 7th Guest: Official Strategy Guide	$19.95
Myst: The Official Strategy Guide	$19.95

NOW AVAILABLE

VIDEO GAME BOOKS

Nintendo Games Secrets, Volumes 1, 2, 3, and 4	$12.95	each
Nintendo Game Boy Secrets, Volumes 1 and 2	$12.95	each
Sega Genesis Secrets, Volumes 1, 2, 3, 4, and 5	$12.95	each
Official Sega Genesis Power Tips Book, 2nd Edition (in full color!)	$14.95	
TurboGrafx-16 and TurboExpress Secrets, Volumes 1 and 2	$11.95	each
Super NES Games Secrets, Volumes 1, 2, 3, and 4	$12.95	each
GamePro Presents: Nintendo Games Secrets Greatest Tips	$11.95	
GamePro Presents: Sega Genesis Games Secrets Greatest Tips	$11.95	
Game Pro Presents: Super NES Games Secrets Greatest Tips	$11.95	
Super Mario World Game Secrets	$12.95	
The Legend of Zelda: A Link to the Past Game Secrets	$12.95	
Super Star Wars: The Official Strategy Guide	$12.95	
Super Empire Strikes Back Official Game Secrets	$12.95	
Battletoads: The Official Battlebook	$12.95	

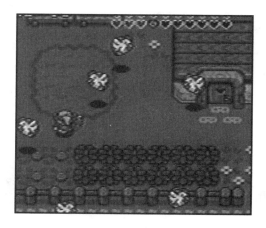

TO ORDER BOOKS

Please send me the following items:

Quantity	Title	Unit Price	Total
_____	_____	$_____	$_____
_____	_____	$_____	$_____
_____	_____	$_____	$_____
_____	_____	$_____	$_____
_____	_____	$_____	$_____
_____	_____	$_____	$_____
	Subtotal		$_____
	7.25% SALES TAX (CALIFORNIA ONLY)		$_____
	SHIPPING AND HANDLING*		$_____
	TOTAL ORDER		$_____

By telephone: With Visa or MC, call 1-800-255-8989 x504. Mon.–Fri. 9–4 PST. By mail: Just fill out the information below and send with your remittance to:

PRIMA PUBLISHING
P.O. Box 1260BK
Rocklin, CA 95677

Satisfaction unconditionally guaranteed

My name is_____

I live at_____

City_____ State_____ Zip_____

Visa / MC#_____Exp._____

Signature_____

*$4.00 shipping and handling charge for the first book, and $0.50 for each additional book.